Why Do You Need This New Edition?

If you're wondering why you should buy this new edition of *Breaking Through: College Reading*, here are 5 good reasons!

1. **Eleven brand new reading selections** include such topics as the ins and outs of recycling plastic; the costs of drinking and driving; a personal history about a World War II holocaust hero; the methods used to make commercial foods irresistible; an unusual explanation of the basics of mathematics, and more.

2. A new casebook that explores *"What Makes Work Satisfying?"* will get you thinking about your career goals.

3. **Student Learning Objectives** have been included to give you clear chapter goals. These open every chapter, are repeated throughout the chapter at key sections, and are restated at the end of the chapter in a listing of Summary Points.

4. A new feature entitled *Brain Booster* is inserted in key locations throughout the book to help you understand how the brain learns and how you can use the knowledge to improve achievement.

5. The *Reading Workshop segments* have been summarized in each chapter and listed together in their entirety in Appendix 5, so you will more readily be able to incorporate pleasure reading into your classroom experience.

PEARSON

Breaking Through

COLLEGE READING

TENTH EDITION

Brenda D. Smith

Professor Emerita, Georgia State University

LeeAnn Morris

San Jacinto College

PEARSON

Boston   Columbus   Indianapolis   New York   San Francisco   Upper Saddle River
Amsterdam   Cape Town   Dubai   London   Madrid   Milan   Munich   Paris   Montreal   Toronto
Delhi   Mexico City   São Paulo   Sydney   Hong Kong   Seoul   Singapore   Taipei   Tokyo

To my Mother and in Memory of my Father
                                        —B.D.S.

To the students whose dreams rest on college success
                                        —L.M.

Senior Acquisitions Editor: Nancy Blaine
Development Editor: Janice Wiggins-Clarke
Marketing Manager: Kurt Massey
Senior Supplements Editor: Donna Campion
Executive Digital Producer: Stefanie A. Snajder
Digital Project Manager: Janell Lantana
Digital Editor: Rob St. Laurent
Production Manager: Ellen MacElree
Project Coordination, Text Design, and Electronic Page Makeup:
   Cenveo Publisher Services
Cover Design Manager: Wendy Ann Fredericks
Cover Designer: Bernadette Skok
Cover Images: © Comstock Images/Fotosearch
Senior Manufacturing Buyer: Dennis J. Para
Printer/Binder: Courier/Kendallville
Cover Printer: Courier/Kendallville

This title is restricted to sales and distribution in North America only.

Credits and acknowledgments borrowed from other sources, and reproduced,
with permission, in this textbook, appear on pages 586–588.

10 9 8 7 6 5 4 3—V011—15 14

Student ISBN-13: 978-0-205-19324-0
Student ISBN-10: 0-205-19324-2
AIE ISBN-13: 978-0-205-24458-4
AIE ISBN-10: 0-205-24458-0

www.pearsonhighered.com

CONTENTS

Preface xiv

Chapter 1 — Student Success 1

Think Success 2

Set Goals 2 • Create a Positive Attitude 2 • Seek Excellence 3

READING 1 • RUN THE RACE . . . IT'S YOURS TO RUN
Perseverance As a Key To Success, by Calvin Mackie 4
"When I graduated from high school with an 800 Scholastic Aptitude Test (SAT) score and began Morehouse College in remedial reading, there were not too many people betting that four years later I would graduate number one in mathematics . . ."

Plan for Success and Manage Your Time 5

READING 2 • MAKING THE MOST OF PRIORITIES
from *How to Get Control of Your Time and Your Life,* by Alan Lakein 5
"People at the top and people at the bottom both know about To Do Lists, but one difference between them is that the people at the top use a To Do List every single day. . . ."

Plan Your Week 8 • Use a Calendar to Decode a Syllabus 8

Act Successful 11

College Professor "Takes" American History 11 • The Sweet 17 Successful Academic Behaviors 12

READING 3 • BOUNCING BACK FROM FAILURE
5 Tips For Overcoming Failure, by Marelisa Fábrega 20
"How do you get back up when you've fallen flat on your face? . . . 5 tips to help you gather the pieces and pull yourself back together after you've failed."

SUMMARY POINTS 23 • MYREADINGLAB 24 • THE READING WORKSHOP 24

Everyday Reading Skills Researching Online 25

Chapter 2 — Stages of Reading 31

What Is the Reading Process? 32

Stages of Reading 32

Stage One: Previewing 32 • Stage Two: Integrating Knowledge 36 • Stage Three: Recall 42

Assess Your Progress as a Learner 45

Levels of Reading Comprehension 45

SUMMARY POINTS 47 • MYREADINGLAB 47 • THE READING WORKSHOP 47

SELECTION 1 • ENVIRONMENTAL SCIENCE 48
"PLASTICS" 49
from *Engines of Our Ingenuity,* by Andrew Boyd
"Recycling plastic isn't as simple as just melting it down and forming it into something new . . ."

SELECTION 2 • SCIENCE   56

"THE GALVESTON DISASTER"   56
from Oceanography, Fifth Edition, by Tom Garrison
"At first light residents flocked to the shore to gawk at the monstrous waves crashing on the beaches."

SELECTION 3 • CRIMINAL JUSTICE   62

"WAS ERIC CLARK INSANE OR JUST TROUBLED?"   62
from Pauline Arrillaga, The Associated Press
"Should Clark be imprisoned, treated for his mental illness, or both?"

VOCABULARY LESSON: Not, Not, and Not   70

Everyday Reading Skills   Reading News and Feature Stories in the Newspaper   73

Chapter 3   Vocabulary   77

Learning New Words   78

Remembering New Words   78
Use Association   78 • Use Concept Cards   79 • Practice Your New Words   80

Unlocking the Meaning of New Words   80
Use Context Clues   80 • Use Knowledge of Word Parts   81 •
Use the Glossary and the Dictionary   81

Types of Context Clues   81
Definition   82 • Elaborating Details   83 • Elaborating Examples   84 •
Comparison   85 • Contrast   86 • Multiple Meanings of a Word   87

Word Parts   88
Roots   89 • Prefixes   90 • Suffixes   91

The Dictionary   92
Guide Words   93 • Pronunciation   93 • Spelling   93 •
Word Meaning   93 • Parts of Speech   93 • Word History   95

Word Origins   95

Textbook Glossary   97

Thesaurus   99

Analogies   101

Easily Confused Words   103

Enriching Your Vocabulary   104

SUMMARY POINTS   105 • **MYREADINGLAB**   106 •
THE READING WORKSHOP   106 • **VOCABULARY LESSON:** For or Against?   107

Everyday Reading Skills   Getting News and Other Information from Websites and Forums   110

Chapter 4   Main Idea   113

What Is a Topic? What Is a Main Idea?   114

What Are Major and Minor Supporting Details?   114

Identifying Topics   115
Recognize General and Specific Words   115 • Recognize General and Specific Phrases   116 • Recognize the General Topic for Sentences   117

Identifying Topics and Main Ideas   120
Recognize General and Supporting Sentences   120 • Differentiate Topic, Main Idea, and Supporting Details   124

Answering Topic and Main Idea Test Questions   126
Differentiate Distractors In Test Questions About the Topic   126

Questioning for the Main Idea   128
1. Establish the Topic   128 • 2. Identify the Key Supporting Details   128 • 3. Focus on the Message of the Topic   128 • Stated Main Ideas   128 • Unstated Main Ideas   133 • Getting the Main Idea of Longer Selections   139
SUMMARY POINTS   140 • MYREADINGLAB   142 • THE READING WORKSHOP   142

SELECTION 1 • PSYCHOLOGY   143
"SLEEPING AND DREAMING"   143
from *Psychology: What It Is/How to Use It,* by David Watson
"Everyone dreams about 20 percent of the time they are sleeping—that is, they show REM sleep about that much."

SELECTION 2 • LITERATURE: SHORT STORY   151
"SHATTER PROOF"   151
from *Manhunt Magazine,* by Jack Ritchie
"I know the enemies I've made and you are a stranger."

SELECTION 3 • HISTORY   161
"THE DREAM OF NONVIOLENT REFORM"   162
from From *These Beginnings,* Sixth Edition, Vol. 2, by Roderick Nash and Gregory Graves
"King's eloquence dramatized the anguish of black history."

VOCABULARY LESSON: Before and After   170

Everyday Reading Skills   Selecting a Book   173

Chapter 5   Supporting Details and Organizational Patterns   177

What Is a Detail?   178
Recognize Levels of Importance   178 • The Roles of Major and Minor Details   181 • Follow Detailed Directions   187

Patterns of Organization   191

Simple Listing   191 • Classification   195 • Definitions with Examples   197 •
Description   199 • Time Order, Sequence, or Narration   202 • Comparison and
Contrast   206 • Cause and Effect   210 • Clues to the Organizational Pattern   213

SUMMARY POINTS   215 • MYREADINGLAB   216 • THE READING WORKSHOP   216

SELECTION 1 • PSYCHOLOGY   218

"BECOMING HEALTHY"   218

from *Psychology: An Introduction to Human Behavior,* Second Edition,
by Morris Holland

*"To learn about yourself and others, to love and to be loved, and to live actively
and productively—all are growth-producing."*

SELECTION 2 • CRIMINAL JUSTICE   227

"DRINKING, DRIVING, AND PAYING"   227

from *The New York Times,* by David Updike

*"And while all this is happening, you find yourself thinking more and more about something
else that could have happened: you could have crashed and killed someone including yourself."*

SELECTION 3 • HISTORY   235

"THE HISTORY OF CANCER"   236

from American Cancer Society, Inc., www.cancer.org

*"Our oldest description of cancer . . . was discovered in Egypt and dates back to
approximately 1600 BCE."*

VOCABULARY LESSON: One Too Many   245

(Everyday Reading Skills) Selecting Magazines   248

(Reading Casebook) What Makes Work Satisfying?   250

What Is Most Important to Me in a Career?   251

SELECTION 1 • POETRY   252

"I HEAR AMERICA SINGING"   252
by Walt Whitman

"Each singing what belongs to him or her and to none else"

"WHAT WORK IS"   252
by Philip Levine

"You know what work is—if you're old enough to read this you know what work is . . ."

SELECTION 2 • NEWSPAPER FEATURE ARTICLE   255

"JOB SATISFACTION VS A BIG PAYCHECK"   255
by Phyllis Korkki, in *The New York Times*

"Does earning a higher salary make you happier?"

SELECTION 3 • BUSINESS   259

"EIGHT STEPS TO FINDING FULFILLMENT IN THE WORK PLACE"   259

from *The Career Key*

*"According to a 2010 survey of U.S. households by The Conference Board, job
dissatisfaction is widespread among workers of all ages across all income brackets."*

Chapter 6 Textbook Learning 263

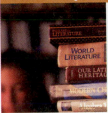

Expect To Learn From Reading 264

Annotating 264

When to Annotate 264 • How to Annotate 264

Notetaking 267

When to Take Notes 267 • The Cornell Method of Notetaking 267
Summarizing 270 • Outlining 275 • Mapping 283

Take Organized Lecture Notes 287

SUMMARY POINTS 287 • MYREADINGLAB 289 • THE READING WORKSHOP 289

SELECTION 1 • HEALTH 290

"Behavior Change" 291
from *Health: The Basics,* Fifth Edition, by Rebecca J. Donatelle
*"On any given day, countless numbers of us get out of bed and resolve to begin
to change a given behavior 'today'."*

SELECTION 2 • HISTORY 300

"Finding a Hero Amid Fading Memories" 301
by Kim Masters, from *Weekend Edition Saturday,* National Public Radio
*"The three girls left home on June 29, 1939, on a special train—a kindertransport—
arranged to protect children from the advancing Nazis."*

SELECTION 3 • COMMUNICATION 310

"Eye Communication" 311
from *The Interpersonal Communication Book,* Twelfth Edition, by Joseph A. DeVito
*"In much of the United States direct eye contact is considered an expression of honesty
and forthrightness. But the Japanese often view this as a lack of respect."*

VOCABULARY LESSON: See, Hear, and Voice Your Concerns 320

Everyday Reading Skills Reading and Organizing Research
Materials 323

Chapter 7 Test-Taking Strategies 327

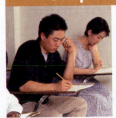

Achieve Your Highest Potential 328

Be Prepared 328

Stay Alert 329

Seek Feedback 330

Standardized Reading Tests 331

Read to Comprehend 332 • Interact 332 • Anticipate 332 • Relax 332 •
Read to Learn 332 • Recall 332

Understand Major Question Types   333

Main Idea Questions   334 • Detail Questions   335 • Inference Questions   337 • Purpose Questions   338 • Vocabulary Questions   340

Hints for Taking Multiple-Choice and True-False Tests   341

Read All Options   341 • Predict the Correct Answer   341 • Avoid Answers with "100 Percent" Words   342 • Consider Answers with Qualifying Words   342 • Do Not Overanalyze   342 • True Statements Must Be True Without Exception   342 • If Two Options Are Synonymous, Eliminate Both   343 • Figure Out the Difference Between Similar Options   343 • Use Logical Reasoning When Two Answers Are Correct   343 • Look Suspiciously at Directly Quoted Pompous Phrases   344 • Simplify Double Negatives by Canceling Out Both   344 • Certain Responses Are Neither True nor False   344 • Validate True Responses   344 • Recognize Flaws in Test Making   344

Hints for Taking Essay Exams   346

Predict and Practice   346 • Reword the Statement or Question   346 • Notice Key Words   346 • Answer the Question   347 • Organize Your Answer   347 • Use a Formal Writing Style   348 • Be Aware of Appearance   348 • Write to Earn Points   348 • Read an "A" Paper for Feedback   349

SUMMARY POINTS   350 • **MYREADINGLAB**   351 • **THE READING WORKSHOP**   351 •

VOCABULARY LESSON: Call Out and Remember to Send   352

Everyday Reading Skills   Using Mnemonics   355

Chapter 8   Efficient Reading   357

What Is Your Reading Rate?   358

What Is an Average Reading Rate?   359

How Can You Increase Your Reading Speed?   360

Be Aggressive—Attack!   360 • Concentrate   361 • Stop Regressions   363 • Avoid Vocalization   363 • Expand Fixations   364 • Use a Pen as a Pacer   366 • Preview Before Reading   370 • Set a Time Goal for an Assignment   370 • Be Flexible   370 • Practice   370

SUMMARY POINTS   371 • **MYREADINGLAB**   371 • **THE READING WORKSHOP**   371

TIMED READING 1 • BUSINESS   372

"WHEN INTERVIEW QUESTIONS TURN ILLEGAL"   372
from *Interviewing for Success,* by Arthur H. Bell and Dayle M. Smith
"You're probably aware that interviewers are not supposed to ask you certain questions. There are five areas of special sensitivity in selection interviewing."

TIMED READING 2 • HEALTH   377

"THE DARK SIDE OF FOOD SCIENCE"   377
by Catherine Guthrie, from *Experience Life Magazine*
"Commercial foods like chicken nuggets, French fries, chips, crackers, cookies and pastries are designed to be virtually irresistible. And, for a lot of reasons most of us don't fully understand, they are."

TIMED READING 3 • MATHEMATICS 382

"FROM FISH TO INFINITY" 382
by Steven Strogatz, from *The New York Times*
"I have a friend who gets a tremendous kick out of science, even though he's an artist. . . . But when it comes to math, he feels at sea, and it saddens him. The strange symbols keep him out."

Everyday Reading Skills Managing Workplace Reading 386

Chapter 9   Analytical Reasoning   389

Identify Analytical Thinking 390
An Unsuccessful Student   390 • A Successful Student   390 • Engage in Problem Solving   391

Analytical Reasoning in Textbooks 394

SUMMARY POINTS   405 • MYREADINGLAB   406 • THE READING WORKSHOP   406

SELECTION 1 • SCIENCE 407

"PROFILE OF A HURRICANE" 408
from *The Atmosphere*, Seventh Edition, by Frederick Lutgens and Edward Tarbuck
"Hurricanes develop most often in the late summer when ocean waters have reached temperatures of 27°C or higher and are thus able to provide the necessary heat and moisture to the air."

SELECTION 2 • SOCIOLOGY 414

"GENDER AND SOCIAL INSTITUTIONS" 415
from *Social Problems*, Third Edition, by John J. Macionis
"Gender biases in advertising can be subtle."

SELECTION 3 • BUSINESS 423

"MOTIVATING YOURSELF" 423
from *Your Attitude Is Showing*, Ninth Edition, by Elwood N. Chapman and Sharon Lund O'Neil
"How can you motivate yourself to live close to your potential despite a negative environment?"

VOCABULARY LESSON: Turn and Throw   433

Everyday Reading Skills Reading Direct Mail Advertisements   436

Chapter 10   Inference   439

What Is an Inference? 440
Inference from Cartoons   440 • Recognizing Suggested Meaning   442 • Connecting with Prior Knowledge   442 • Recognizing Slanted Language   444 • Drawing Conclusions   447

SUMMARY POINTS   453 • MYREADINGLAB   454 • THE READING WORKSHOP   454

SELECTION 1 • **LITERATURE: SHORT STORY**   455

"THE BEST PLACE"   456
by A. F. Oreshnik
"I wonder what makes a man decide to be a criminal?"

SELECTION 2 • **LITERATURE: SHORT STORY**   464

"THE ALCHEMIST'S SECRET"   464
by Arthur Gordon
"She died, I believe, poor woman. Quite suddenly."

SELECTION 3 • **LITERATURE: SHORT STORY**   469

"A DEAL IN DIAMONDS"   469
by Edward D. Hoch, from *Ellery Queen's Mystery Magazine*
"It was seeing a girl toss a penny into the plaza fountain that gave Pete Hopkins the idea."

VOCABULARY LESSON: Come Together, Hold Together, and Shut   478

Everyday Reading Skills   Reading Newspaper Editorials   481

Chapter 11   Critical Reading   483

What Do Critical Readers Do?   484

Recognize the Author's Purpose or Intent   484 • Recognize the Author's Point of View or Bias   487 • Recognize the Author's Tone   491 • Distinguish Fact from Opinion   498 • Recognize Valid and Invalid Support for Arguments   501

SUMMARY POINTS   509 • **MYREADINGLAB**   510 • **THE READING WORKSHOP**   510

SELECTION 1 • **LITERATURE: SHORT STORY**   511

"THE DINNER PARTY"   512
by Mona Gardner, from *Saturday Review of Literature*
"'A woman's unfailing reaction in any crisis,' the colonel says, 'is to scream.'"

SELECTION 2 • **ESSAY**   519

"SHEDDING THE WEIGHT OF MY DAD'S OBSESSION"   520
by Linda Lee Andujar, from *Newsweek*
"I heard the garage door rumble shut, and I knew that Daddy was home. He came in the back door, kissed Mother, and asked what my weight was for the day."

SELECTION 3 • **ESSAY**   528

"WE'LL GO FORWARD FROM THIS MOMENT"   528
by Leonard Pitts, *Miami Herald*
"As Americans we will weep, as Americans we will mourn, and as Americans, we will rise in defense of all that we cherish."

VOCABULARY LESSON: Bend, Born, and Body   535

Everyday Reading Skills   Evaluating Internet Information   538

Appendix 1 Spelling Confusing Words 540

Appendix 2 Sample Textbook Chapter 541
Chapter 14, from *Introduction to Hospitality*, Fifth Edition,
by John R. Walker

Appendix 3 Word Parts: Prefixes, Roots, and Suffixes 565

Appendix 4 ESL: Making Sense of Figurative Language and Idioms 569

Appendix 5 The Reading Workshop: Thinking, Talking,
and Writing About Books 576

Glossary 582
Acknowledgments 586
Index 589

PREFACE

The tenth edition of *Breaking Through* upholds the philosophy and purpose that undergirded previous editions—to guide students to be independent readers who can understand, digest, and retain the material in college level texts. Like its predecessors, the tenth edition aims to motivate and equip students to achieve their academic and career goals while building background knowledge. The instructional methods emphasize strategic learning in individual and collaborative contexts. The tenth edition teaches effective reading techniques; provides extensive practice; provides independent, partner, and group activities; and engages students with reading selections on a variety of topics pertinent to the college community.

NEW AND SPECIAL FEATURES IN THE TENTH EDITION

- **Eleven new reading selections** represent a broad spectrum of academic disciplines including mathematics, environmental and food science, history, literature, and business. They are from college texts, newspapers, electronic media; they are set in a variety of modes—expository, narrative, persuasive, poetry.
- A **brand new casebook** explores a topic of immediate interest to students who are preparing for careers, "What Makes Work Satisfying?" Students begin by identifying the characteristics that are most important to them in a career. They continue to examine the topic through the perspectives of poets, a columnist reporting on research, and experts on career development. Activities throughout the casebook encourage students to use what they are reading to think critically about their career goals.
- **Student Learning Objectives** have been included to give you clear chapter goals. The opening page of every chapter introduces the objectives that readers will find clearly identified by a distinctive logo as they progress through the text. The end-of-chapter summary points complete the link by tying directly to the objectives.
- A new feature entitled **Brain Boosters** brings results of neuroscientific research on the physiological aspects of learning to practical use. These brief inserts, written in an accessible, student friendly tone, are placed throughout the text to help readers understand and assist the biological process of change in the human brain that we call learning. Information in the Brain Boosters was drawn from several sources, including *Brain Rules: 12 Principles for Surviving and Thriving at Work, Home, and School* by John Medina; *Brain-Based Learning: The New Paradigm of Teaching*, Second Edition, by Eric Jensen; and *The Art of Changing the Brain* by James E. Zull.
- **Extended Writing** topics have been added to the already numerous opportunities in this book to exploit the learning potential of linking reading and writing. At the conclusion of each end-of-chapter reading, this new feature provides writing prompts in a variety of rhetorical modes that cause students to reflect or expand on ideas in the reading.
- **QR codes** for selected readings will lead students to a link where they can hear an audio version of the reading.

Two features in the ninth edition have been enhanced to better meet the needs of students and instructors. The **MyReadingLab** icons at the end of Chapters 1 through 11 alert students to revised material in this electronic supplement to the text. Brief notes direct students to the area of the MyReadingLab website that offers practice related to the topic of that chapter. The website provides extensive skill development activities in reading, vocabulary, and study skills, as well as useful research tools. Also at the end of each chapter, **The Reading Workshop** segments guide students and instructors who want to include supplementary reading in the course to Appendix 5. The suggestions for thinking and writing about pleasure reading that were introduced in the ninth edition are now collected in the Appendix 5 for easy access. The Reading Workshop is a flexible tool that professors may use in conjunction with a book read in common by the whole class, a few titles shared in reading circles, or with individual, self-selected books. The workshop activities make use of the powerful connection between reading and writing by prompting students to maintain a Reading Workshop journal. The underlying purposes of The Reading Workshop are to develop background knowledge, fluency, enjoyment, and, ultimately, lifelong readers.

The Instructor's Annotated Edition of *Breaking Through*, Tenth Edition, notes the **grade-level equivalencies (GLEs)** for the longer readings. The GLEs are included to help instructors match readings with students' skill levels. GLEs are based on style features such as sentence and word length, but other factors such as readers' interest, background knowledge, and depth of the concepts are also critical comprehension factors. GLEs were determined using the Raygor Readability Estimate.

ORGANIZATION OF THE TEXT

The text opens with an introductory chapter on student success and a chapter offering perspective on the reading process. From there the chapter topics progress from the literal levels of reading to the inferential and critical levels expected of mature readers. Each chapter begins with a list of Student Learning Objectives and ends with the Summary Points feature. Nine of the eleven chapters conclude with three, longer reading selections and accompanying exercises.

Chapter 1 focuses on motivation, attitude, and academic success. It offers inspirational readings and a collection of student success strategies. Chapter 2 moves to theories of reading and the strategies used by successful readers. It emphasizes control of the reading process through three stages—before, during, and after reading—which are reinforced throughout the text. Chapter 3 is devoted to vocabulary. Context clues and word structure are introduced and practiced as strategies for attacking unknown words. Instruction and exercises on analogies and the use of the dictionary, thesaurus, and glossary are included.

Understanding the main idea—the most important reading comprehension skill—begins with models and practice exercises in Chapter 4 and extends into Chapter 5 with attention to supporting details, organizational patterns, and the beginning stages of notetaking. Chapter 6 explains annotating, and three specific forms of notetaking—the Cornell System, outlining, and mapping.

Chapter 7 offers advice on multiple-choice and true-false test-taking, as well as essay responses. Heightened awareness can give students a winning edge and help improve test scores. The efficient reading discussion in Chapter 8 presents techniques for reading rate improvement and provides exercises to assess students' rates.

Chapter 9 recognizes college students as analytical thinkers and problem solvers with exercises to develop and refine analytical reasoning skills. Chapter 10, on implied meaning, and Chapter 11, on critical reading, focus on unstated attitudes and assumptions. These chapters are designed to help students develop critical reading skills necessary for college work.

The reading casebook, "What Makes Work Satisfying?", follows a different organizational plan. It contains several readings on the same topic but has fewer exercises than other chapters. The focus of the casebook is on a single topic to foster personal discovery and growth. The casebook follows Chapter 5.

BOOK-SPECIFIC ANCILLARY MATERIALS

For Instructors

Annotated Instructor's Edition (AIE) (0-205-24458-0)
An exact replica of the student text, with answers provided on the write-in lines in the text.

Instructor's Manual (ISBN 0-205-25234-6)
The instructor's manual features lecture hints, in-class activities, and handouts to accompany each chapter, as well as sample course outlines and other helpful resources for structuring and managing a developmental reading course. Available both in print and for download from the Instructor Resource Center.

Test Bank (ISBN 0-205-24457-2)
The test bank includes two tests per chapter, with a variety of questions in the multiple-choice, true-false, essay, and short answer formats.

MyTest Test Bank (ISBN 0-205-25093-9)
Pearson MyTest is a powerful assessment generation program that helps instructors easily create and print quizzes, study guides, and exams. Select questions from the test bank to accompany *Breaking Through* or from other developmental reading test banks; supplement them with your own questions. Save the finished test as a Word document or PDF or export it to WebCT or Blackboard. Available at *www.pearsonmytest.com*.

PowerPoint Presentation (ISBN 0-205-25094-7)
PowerPoint presentations to accompany each chapter consist of classroom-ready lectures outline slides, lecture tips and classroom activities, and review questions. Available for download from the Instructor Resource Center.

Answer Key (ISBN 0-205-87425-8)
The Answer Key contains the solutions to the exercises in the student edition of the text. Available for download from the Instructor Resource Center.

ACKNOWLEDGMENTS

We want to thank Nancy Blaine, senior acquisitions editor, for her support during the current revision of this book. She arrived on the job with a wealth of experience in publishing but new to *Breaking Through* and developmental reading. She was a remarkably quick study and a helpful resource. Likewise, we very much appreciate the expertise and gentle, practiced guidance of our development editor Janice Wiggins-Clarke. Janice's skill and creativity ensured that the excellent quality inherent in the previous editions of this book continued in this tenth edition. Finally, we would like to acknowledge the reviewers of the ninth edition whose suggestions were critical to this revision:

Jane Anderson, Northland Community and Technical College; Jacci Barry, Bristol Community College; Angela Blankenship, Arkansas Northeastern College; Fran Boffo, St. Philip's College; Karen Cheney, College of the Desert; Carol Francia, Miami Dade College, Homestead; Elizabeth Hall, Riverside Community College; Elsie McAvoy, Glendale Community College; Gwendalina McClain-Digby, Prince George's Community College; Shirley Melcher, Austin Community College; Candice Meyer, Central Piedmont Community College; Betty Payne, Montgomery College; Donna L. Taylor, Arizona Western College; Ann Thomas, DeKalb Technical College; and Dr. Brenda Tuberville, Rogers State University.

Brenda D. Smith
LeeAnn Morris

1 Student Success

Learning Objectives

From this chapter, readers will learn:

1 To prepare mentally for college success
2 To manage time effectively
3 To adopt the behaviors of successful students

Everyday Reading Skills: Researching Online

THINK SUCCESS

Learning Objective 1

Prepare mentally for college success

Are you mentally ready to go to college? Do you have a desire to achieve? Have you set goals for yourself, and are you ready to plan for achieving those goals? College life and college work are fun, but they require extra effort. Begin by cultivating an attitude for success.

Most of this book focuses on strategies for reading college texts. Before you concentrate on the books, however, take a look at yourself and your dreams. You are now shaping your future. To become a winner and reap the rewards, you must first think like a winner. Studies show that not only do college graduates enjoy more social and self-esteem benefits, but they also earn more than those with only high school diplomas. In 2010, the median weekly earnings for a person with a high school diploma and no college were $444. The figure increased to $626 per week for workers with an associate's degree and to $1038 for workers with a bachelor's degree.[1]

This chapter will help you shape your thinking and behaviors by presenting the thoughts and describing the actions of successful people. Working on yourself can be as important as working on the books.

Set Goals

Entering college is a major turning point in life. College offers freedom, variety, and increased responsibility. Success in college requires a commitment of time, money, and energy. College is an investment in the future that requires a sacrifice in the present.

Build a team of caring people to support you as you go after your goals. Begin with your instructor. Respond thoughtfully to the Personal Feedback sections that appear throughout this text and hand them in to your instructor. Share your dreams, enthusiasm, and anxieties in order to build a learning partnership and strengthen your determination. This partnership will be only as strong as each of you allows it to be. Your instructor is not a mind reader, so reveal who you really are. Move beyond the academic and respond to questions regarding your habits, responsibilities, joys, and stresses. Your instructor wants to know you as a person and wants to help you be successful.

For the first Personal Feedback section, think about your feelings as you begin your college career, and then respond to the questions.

Create a Positive Attitude

Your dreams are your goals. Hold them in a corner of your mind as you go through college. You might even write them on a banner over your desk or on the cover of a notebook. On rough days, think of the dreams and picture the excitement of achieving your goals. Imagine your graduation celebration and think about those who will join in the fun. Allow your dreams to renew your enthusiasm and keep you focused on your goals. Let motivation overshadow your anxieties. Program your mind to think of success. Don't worry about why something *cannot* be done. Instead, think about how it *can* be accomplished. What you think of yourself determines what you will become.

---

[1]Bureau of Labor Statistics, U.S. Department of Labor. *Usual Weekly Earnings of Wage and Salary Workers, Fourth Quarter 2010,* January 20, 2011, Table 9 Quartiles and selected deciles of usual weekly earnings of full-time wage and salary workers by selected characteristics, 2010 annual averages. www.bls.gov/news.release/pdf/wkyeng.pdf

BRAIN BOOSTER

Now that medical technology makes it possible to see inside the human brain while it is working, scientists can tell us a lot about how we learn. Throughout this book you will notice a feature called Brain Boosters. In these short pieces, you will find practical ways to keep your brain working at its best—all thanks to research in the neurosciences.

Curiosity

Think about how babies learn that they can make a toy squeak or that a kitten might bite. Is there a quiz or a flashcard involved? Human brains are wired to explore and learn from the results. As you pursue this adventure called a college education, remember that curiosity about new ideas can be one of your best assets. In every class, find something that you want to know more about, and go for it! The spark that ignites your interest might lie waiting in a textbook, in a lecture, or in an assignment. Fan that spark by going to the Internet, asking your professor, reading a book, doing an experiment, or talking to other students. Your natural curiosity might lead to a college major, a career, a lifelong hobby, or an A in the class.

PERSONAL FEEDBACK   **1**   **Name** _____

1. What three dreams and/or influences motivated you to come to college?

(a) _____

(b) _____

(c) _____

2. In five years what do you hope to be doing both professionally and personally?

(a) Professionally: _____

_____

(b) Personally: _____

_____

3. Explain three anxieties that you have as you begin college.

(a) _____

(b) _____

(c) _____

Tear out and submit to your instructor.

Seek Excellence

All of us would like to do well. Some people, however, set higher goals and eventually achieve more than others. What explains the differences? In the following article, Dr. Calvin Mackie remembers that his college years were tough, and there were many obstacles in his way. He cites perseverance as the key to success and the example set by his father as his inspiration.

Reading 1

RUN THE RACE ... IT'S YOURS TO RUN

Dr. Calvin Mackie is a motivational speaker, author, inventor, and former professor of mechanical engineering at Tulane University. He began college in developmental reading because of weak test scores and went on to earn two bachelor's degrees, a master's degree, and a doctorate in mechanical engineering.

While working on my doctoral degree, I learned many different aspects of fluid dynamics, material processing, and hydrodynamic stability, but more importantly I learned a lot about myself and about life. The myopic view which accompanies our youth presents us with a Superman-type attitude of invincibility that is assisting in our daily defeat academically, socially, and psychologically. Education is a lifelong process that does not end with the presentation of a sheepskin after a finite time of instruction and examinations. After 10 years of college and four technical degrees, I had the virtues of sacrifice and perseverance instilled in me. Matriculation at two institutions has taught me that life is a race; not a 100-yard dash, but a marathon with hills and hurdles that challenge you physically and mentally. To run and win a marathon, one must continue to train, because the course is never the same, and the challenges are forever increasing.

In any race, inspiration, endurance and models are needed. I am not speaking of a role model but a real model, someone who has run the race and fought the battles and won! Presently, we live in an information age where corporate takeovers and downsizing are staples of Corporate America's culture. Advances in computers, communications, and transportation are transforming national markets into global markets, and the number of employees necessary to perform identical tasks of 10 years ago is continuously decreasing. At the end of the day, at the end of the race, who will be the last one standing? Real models of perseverance, strength, and character are needed not only to demonstrate how to run the race of life, but also to present us with functional, honest reasons why we should run this race.

Today many of our youth are choosing not to run in any race. Many of us are questioning the necessity or validity of a college degree or post-baccalaureate studies. When I graduated from high school with an 800 Scholastic Aptitude Test (SAT) score and began Morehouse College in remedial reading, there were not too many people betting that four years later I would graduate number one in mathematics, number five in the graduating class, magna cum laude, and a member of Phi Beta Kappa National Honor Society. Well, as a little "happy-headed boy" growing up in the inner city of New Orleans, I spent endless hours searching for someone, a real model, that I could emulate, model myself after, and call my hero. After years of searching, I found a person whom I could hold responsible for the successful course that my life has taken. This man took me, unformed and shapeless, and molded me into a young man who is physically and psychologically prepared to take on the trials and tribulations that life has in store for me. This remarkable person, this remarkable man, is my father. Through his life experiences, he transformed my line of thinking, value system, and motivation.

The son of a sharecropper and one of 14 children, he could not attend school regularly because he had to pick cotton from sun up to sun down to help support his family in St. Francisville, Louisiana. Although he only completed junior high school, he is the co-owner of a successful business. He often tells me how each day on his way to the fields he would cry and pray that tomorrow he would be able to attend school. We often laugh together when he tells me that the only time he made an "A" or a "B" in school was when he received an "A" for absent or a "B" for boy. Therefore, when I think of his accomplishments and all of the adversity he had to overcome, I realize that the seemingly impossible is actually possible. He has made me realize that an education is something that everyone does not have the opportunity to obtain. It is an opportunity that all of us should cherish! Over the years, people often wondered why I study so hard and so long. The reason is that a long time ago I realized that I am not attending school just for Calvin Mackie; I am attending school for my mother, my father, and everyone else who did not have that opportunity.

Every Sunday, I anxiously wait for his call to inspire me to take on the world and all of its challenges. No, during our conversations his subjects and verbs do not always agree. No, he does not have a M.D., Ph.D., J.D. or D.D.S., but he is the greatest man that I know and love. So, this is one man's story, proof that the race of life is not won by the swiftest or the strongest, the smartest or the slickest, but by those who endure to the end. So straight from the heart, brothers and sisters, run the race and shun not the struggle, for you have been the lucky ones chosen to run. Run the race of life—for it's yours to run!

—From *The Black Collegian* by Calvin Mackie, PhD.

EXERCISE 1   **Think and Write**. Answer the following questions.

1. Explain what is meant by the sentence "… life is a race; not a 100-yard dash, but a marathon with hills and hurdles …" _____

_____

2. Dr. Mackie closes this essay by urging readers "shun not the struggle." Why should we embrace difficulties rather than resent or try to ignore them?

_____

_____

PLAN FOR SUCCESS AND MANAGE YOUR TIME

Learning Objective 2
Manage time effectively

A business maxim known as Parkinson's Law states that work expands to fill the time available for its completion. Have you ever had all Saturday to finish an assignment and found that it did in fact take all day, whereas if you had planned to finish it in four hours, you probably could have done so?

Time is limited, and everyone has only twenty-four hours in a day, even the president of the United States. Does the president get more done than you do? The key to success is to plan and use the minutes and hours wisely. Establish a routine and stick to it. Plan for both work and play.

Reading 2

MAKING THE MOST OF PRIORITIES

Alan Lakein, the Harvard graduate who invented time management consulting, works with businesspeople all over the country. His book, How to Get Control of Your Time and Your Life, *has sold over 3 million copies and is used as a textbook in business courses. He offers the following daily method of planning for achievement.*

The main secret of getting more done every day took me several months of research to discover. When I first started delving into better time use, I asked successful people what the secret of their success was. I recall an early discussion with a vice-president of Standard Oil Company of California who said, "Oh, I just keep a To Do List." I passed over that quickly, little suspecting at the time the importance of what he said. I happened to travel the next day to a large city to give a time management seminar. While I was there I had lunch with a businessman who practically owned the town. He was chairman of the gas and light company, president of five manufacturing companies, and had his hand in a dozen other enterprises. By all standards he was a business success. I asked him the same question of how he managed to get more done and he said, "Oh, that's easy—I keep a To Do List."

ONLY A DAILY LIST WILL DO

People at the top and people at the bottom both know about To Do Lists, but one difference between them is that the people at the top use a To Do List every single day to make better use of their time; people at the bottom know about this tool but don't use it effectively. One of the real secrets of getting more done is to make a To Do List every day, keep it visible, and use it as a guide to action as you go through the day.

Because the To Do List is such a fundamental time-planning tool, let's take a closer look at it. The basics of the list itself are simple: Head a piece of paper "To Do," then list those items on which you want to work; cross off items as they are completed and add others as they occur to you; rewrite the list at the end of the day or when it becomes hard to read.

Some people try to keep To Do Lists in their heads, but in my experience this is rarely as effective. Why clutter your mind with things that can be written down? It's much better to leave your mind free for creative pursuits.

WHAT BELONGS ON THE LIST

Are you going to write down everything you have to do, including routine activities? Are you only going to write down exceptional events? Are you going to put down everything you *might* do today or only whatever you decided you *will* do today? There are many alternatives, and different people have different solutions. I recommend that you do not list routine items but do list everything that has high priority today and might not get done without special attention.

Don't forget to put the A-activities for your long-term goals on your To Do List. Although it may appear strange to see "begin learning French" or "find new friends" in the same list with "bring home a quart of milk" or "buy birthday card," you want to do them in the same day. If you use your To Do List as a guide when deciding what to work on next, then you need the long-term projects represented, too, so you won't forget them at decision time and consequently not do them.

Depending on your responsibilities, you might, if you try hard enough, get all the items on your To Do List completed by the end of each day. If so, by all means try. But probably you can predict in advance that there is no way to do them all. When there are too many things to do, conscious choice as to what (and what not) to do is better than letting the decision be determined by chance.

I cannot emphasize strongly enough: You must *set priorities*. Some people do as many items as possible on their lists. They get a very high percentage of tasks done, but their effectiveness is low because the tasks they've done are mostly of C-priority. Others like to start at the top of the list and go right down it, again with little regard to what's important. The best way is to take your list and label each item according to ABC priority, delegate as much as you can, and then polish off the list accordingly.

—From *How to Get Control of Your Time and Your Life*
by Alan Lakein

EXERCISE 2   Answer the following questions and make a To Do List.

1. What does the author believe is the difference between the To Do Lists of people at the top and those of people at the bottom? _____

_____

_____

2. Prior to reading this passage, what method have you used to keep up with things you need to remember to do? _____

_____

3. What kinds of things does the author say belong on a To Do List?

_____

4. How can you indicate levels of priority on your To Do List? _____

_____

5. Why do you think a student would feel that it is not necessary to keep a daily To Do List? _____

_____

6. Make your own To Do List today. In the left margin, indicate priorities with an A, B, or C. Keep your list in a notepad, your assignment book, or an electronic device, so that it is always handy. Remember to cross off each item as you complete it.

Example

A   (1) Pay rent
B   (2) Change oil in car
A   (3) Call Maria
C   (4) Buy dictionary
B   (5) Get breakfast foods

To Do List

_____ (1) _____

_____ (2) _____

_____ (3) _____

_____ (4) _____

_____ (5) _____

_____ (6) _____

_____ (7) _____

Think and Write
What did Ben Franklin mean by "Employ thy time well if thou meanest to gain leisure"?

_____

_____

PERSONAL FEEDBACK 2

Name _____

1. Identify three people on your personal support team.

   (a) _____

   (b) _____

   (c) _____

2. What are three things you want to learn from this reading course?

   (a) _____

   (b) _____

   (c) _____

3. List three responsibilities you have as a college student who wants to be a high achiever with excellent grades.

   (a) _____

   (b) _____

   (c) _____

4. What do you expect from a college instructor? List four responsibilities of a good instructor.

   (a) _____

   (b) _____

   (c) _____

Tear out and submit to your instructor.

Plan Your Week

Organize yourself every week. Project your schedule for next week and put it on the following time chart. Be specific about each item and note what you anticipate studying when listing a study time. Most experts recommend two hours of study outside of class for every hour spent in class. Be realistic about your activities and plan recreation and work time.

The majority of your activities will remain routine. For example, your class hours are probably the same each week. Put them on the chart first. If you have a job, plug in your work hours. If you work while attending college, you will have even fewer minutes to waste, and thus you must become a superefficient time manager. Put in your mealtimes and your bedtime. If you can't live without a favorite television show, plug that in as well. Be honest with yourself and never pretend that you are going to be studying and then not live up to your expectations.

Lay out your life the way you would like to live it for the week, then stick to the plan. At the beginning of each week, adjust your plan for any changes that you foresee. Use your weekly schedule as a goal.

Reader's TIP   Making a Learning Schedule

Use your assignment calendar to devise a learning schedule. Mark important dates for this class.

- Enter all test dates and due dates for papers and projects.
- Divide large textbook reading assignments into manageable units and record as daily and weekly goals. Leave several days for study and review before tests.
- Record dates for completing extra library and Internet readings.
- Analyze assigned projects and create daily or weekly goals. Record start dates and interim small-step goals.
- Designate dates for completing the first draft of written reports.
- Use your calendar of expected achievements to stay on schedule in each of your classes.

Use a Calendar to Decode a Syllabus

Students who just glance at the course syllabus might think there is no immediate assignment because the first test is four weeks away. Wrong! These students will find themselves falling behind by the second class session because of their "slow start" or "no start" strategy. Avoid this pitfall. As soon as the course begins, use your calendar along with the syllabus to divide your work according to the days and weeks of the course.

Be cautious of unlimited freedom; it could become the freedom to fail. Some professors make short-term goal setting entirely the student's responsibility. For example, some courses have only a midterm and a final. No interim goals are provided. Thus students must take control and design their own detailed learning plans.

BRAIN BOOSTER

Sleep

As you work out a weekly schedule that allots specific times for studying, remember that sleep is very important to learning, too. Scientists cannot say how much sleep is right for you, but for most people it is about 7 or 8 hours. Research studies show that getting less or more sleep than your brain needs causes difficulty paying attention, thinking logically, and performing physical tasks. Schedule bed and wake-up times at about the same times each day to get the most from your brain.

—Adapted from John J. Medina, *Brain Rules*.
© 2008 John J. Medina. Pear Press: Seattle, WA

WEEKLY TIME CHART

Time	Sunday	Monday	Tuesday	Wednesday	Thursday	Friday	Saturday
8–9							
9–10							
10–11							
11–12							
12–1							
1–2							
2–3							
3–4							
4–5							
5–6							
6–7							
7–8							
8–9							
9–10							
10–11							
11–12							

Tear out and submit to your instructor.

Reader's TIP   Time Savers

Using time wisely becomes a habit. Analyze your current activities according to the following principles of time management to gain greater control of yourself and your environment.

1. Plan. Keep an appointment book by the day and hour. Write a daily To Do List. Use a notepad or an electronic device.
2. Start with the most critical activity of the day and work your way down to the least important one.
3. Ask yourself, "What is the best use of my time right now?"
4. Don't do what doesn't need doing.
5. Concentrate completely on one thing at a time.
6. Block out big chunks of time for large projects.
7. Make use of five-, ten-, and fifteen-minute segments of time.
8. Keep phone calls and texts short or avoid them.
9. Listen well for clear instructions.
10. Learn to say No! to yourself and others.
11. Limit your online, TV, video game, and text messaging time.
12. Strive for excellence, but realize that perfection may not be worth the cost.

ACT SUCCESSFUL

Learning Objective 3

Adopt the behaviors of successful students

Brenda Smith

Successful people share certain observable characteristics. Study those characteristics and adopt the accompanying successful behaviors. Watching other students reveals behaviors that lead to success—or failure.

College Professor "Takes" American History

In order to prepare for a course to assist students in learning history, I "took" American History 113. I put the word *took* in quotation marks because I skipped the hard part; I did not study or take the exams. I did, however, attend class, take notes, observe, and learn.

Since the university operated on the quarter system at that time, classes met for ten weeks with an extra week for exams. My particular class met on Tuesdays and Thursdays from 10:50 to 1:05, which meant the class lasted for two hours and fifteen minutes. I attended all but one class.

I had an excellent professor who seemed concerned that students learn and make good grades. In fact, after the first class, I would have been astonished if any student could fail. To my amazement, the professor distributed a list of ten questions from which he would choose the two essay questions on the first exam. After talking with students in other classes, I learned that this was not unusual; many professors distributed lists of possible exam questions.

As the course progressed, I noticed that some students were their own worst enemies. I could see opportunities for learning that students were ignoring. I began taking notes on student behaviors, as well as my regular notes on the history lectures. From my observations of the entire course, I formed opinions about why some students make A's and others barely pass or even fail. For example, I observed that many students skipped class or came late; some took very sketchy lecture notes; students rarely talked to each other; and many students did not seem to have grasped clearly defined expectations. Although my observations were made only in a history course, after talking to other students and professors, I believe that the behaviors necessary for success apply to most college courses. I wanted to say to some individuals, "You are shooting yourself in the foot." Some of the suggestions outlined below are simple and obvious, yet many students ignored them.

The Sweet 17 Successful Academic Behaviors

Notice the other students in your classes. Can you predict which ones are most likely to do well? Give yourself the best chance by doing what professors and experienced students agree are behaviors that create success.

1 Study the Syllabus

The Syllabus Is Like a Contract for the Course. On the first day of class almost every professor distributes a syllabus that outlines the goals, objectives, and assignments for the entire course. The syllabus includes examination dates and an explanation of the grading system. Depending on the professor, the syllabus may be a general overview or a more detailed schedule of each class session. Keep your syllabus for quick reference; it is your guide to the professor's plan for your learning. Sophisticated students do not use class time to ask questions about test dates or details that they could find by looking at the syllabus.

EXERCISE 3 Review the following history syllabus and answer the questions.

United States History Syllabus

Class: 9–10 daily   10-Week Quarter: 1/4–3/12
Dr. J. A. Johnson   Office Hrs.: 10–12 daily
Office: 422G   Phone: 562-3367
                           E-mail: jaj@gsu.edu

Required Texts
(1) *A People and a Nation* by Norton et al.
(2) One book on immigration selected from the list for a report.

Course Content
This course is a survey of United States history from the early explorations to the present. The purpose is to give you an understanding of the major forces and events that have interacted to make modern America.

Method of Training
Thematic lectures will be presented in class. You are expected to read and master the factual material in the text as well as take careful notes in class. Tests will cover both class lectures and textbook readings.

Grading
Grades will be determined in the following manner:

> Tests (3 tests at 20% each)
> Final Exam (20%)
> Written Report (20%)

Each test will include multiple-choice and identification items and two essay questions.

Important Dates
> Test 1: 1/22   Final Exam: 3/18
> Test 2: 2/11   Written Report: 3/10
> Test 3: 3/3   Makeup Test (with permission): 3/16

Written Report

Your written report on immigration should answer one of the three designated questions and reflect your reading of a book from the list. Each book is approximately 200 pages long. Your report should be at least six typed pages. More information to follow.

Assignments

Week 1: Ch. 1 (pp. 1–27), Ch. 2 (pp. 28–49), Ch. 3 (pp. 50–68)
Week 2: Ch. 4 (pp. 69–86), Ch. 5 (pp. 87–103), Ch. 6 (pp. 104–122)
Week 3: Ch. 7 (pp. 123–139), Ch. 8 (pp. 140–159), Ch. 9 (pp. 160–176), Ch. 10 (pp. 177–194)

Test 1: Chaps. 1–10

Week 4: Ch. 11 (pp. 195–216), Ch. 12 (pp. 217–236), Ch. 13 (pp. 237–253)
Week 5: Ch. 14 (pp. 254–272), Ch. 15 (pp. 273–288), Ch. 16 (pp. 289–304), Ch. 17 (pp. 305–320)
Week 6: Ch. 18 (pp. 321–344), Ch. 19 (pp. 345–358), Ch. 20 (pp. 359–375)

Test 2: Chaps. 11–20

Week 7: Ch. 21 (pp. 376–391), Ch. 22 (pp. 392–410), Ch. 23 (pp. 411–428)
Week 8: Ch. 24 (pp. 429–450), Ch. 25 (pp. 451–466), Ch. 26 (pp. 467–484), Ch. 27 (pp. 486–504)
Week 9: Ch. 28 (pp. 505–520), Ch. 29 (pp. 521–533), Ch. 30 (pp. 534–553)

Test 3: Chaps. 21–28

Week 10: Ch. 31 (pp. 554–569), Ch. 32 (pp. 570–586), Ch. 33 (pp. 587–599)

Final Exam: Chaps. 1–33

1. What is the stated purpose of this history course? _____
   _____

2. How will your grade be determined? _____

3. How many pages do you have to read during the first week? _____ Second week? _____ Third week? _____

4. On average, how many pages should you read each day for the first week?
   _____

5. Will you have any pop quizzes? _____

6. Does the final exam count more than the individual tests? _____

7. What questions might you ask about the tests? _____
   _____

8. Do you have questions that are not answered by this syllabus?

_____

9. Have you saved your professor's and two classmates' numbers in your cell phone? _____

PERSONAL FEEDBACK **3**   **Name** _____

1. When did you receive the syllabus for this reading course? Where is it now?

_____

2. When is your next test, and how much does it count toward your final grade?

_____

3. What material does your next major exam cover? Will the questions be multiple choice or essay?

_____

_____

4. Is there a penalty for turning work in late?

_____

5. What is the purpose of this course?

_____

6. What questions do you have about how your final grade will be determined?

_____

_____

7. What questions do you have about the syllabus or the course?

_____

_____

Tear out and submit to your instructor.

---

2 Attend Class

"I Missed the Last Class. Did We Do Anything?"   Does this sound familiar? Although the class lasted almost two and a half hours and covered too much to repeat, some students seem unconvinced that an absence puts them at a disadvantage. In my history class, the professor used the exam questions as a guide in organizing his lectures. I was astounded at how many students skipped classes. Even though 40 students were registered for the course, no more than 33 ever showed up at any one session. At the session following the midterm exam, only 17 students were present. I asked myself, "Why would a student pay for a course, yet not take advantage of the instruction?" Professors cannot teach students who are not there.

Assume Some of the Responsibility for Your Class Sessions.   If your interest is not sufficiently stimulated, move beyond blaming it all on the professor. Ask questions and participate in class discussions. Arrive prepared so class sessions will be more meaningful. Talk with other students. Suggest ideas to the professor. Every class period can be significant if you, the professor, and other class members participate in making it meaningful.

3 Be on Time for Class

Be in Your Seat for the "Business Announcements."   Professors usually begin with important reminders about test questions, assignments, or papers, and then give an overview of what will be discussed in class that day. If you come late, you arrive for the details and miss the "big picture." You put yourself at a disadvantage and must scramble to catch up. In my history class, sometimes as many as seven students arrived late, strolling into class with sodas and snacks, suggesting they did not make a prompt arrival their first priority.

4 Be Aware of Essential Class Sessions

Class Sessions Vary from Vital to Crucial.   Always strive for a solid beginning, a "fast start" rather than a shaky one. At the first class meeting students usually ask questions to clarify the syllabus, and the professor responds with important, unwritten details that can help you improve your grades. For example, does your history professor expect you to memorize dates, to understand the causes and effects of social change, or to critique historical interpretations? Goals such as these will be explained on the first day.

Students who do not attend the last class before an exam put themselves at an extreme disadvantage. By this time, the professor has usually written the exam and feels pressured to cover anything that he or she will ask on the test that has not been previously discussed in class. Student questions usually prompt a brief but extremely helpful review, pinpointing essential areas of study. Hearing the professor comment, "That's not really important," helps you eliminate study areas and save time. In addition, be sure you have studied enough before this session so that you know which things you need to clarify.

Never miss an exam unless you are on your death bed! The exam makeup may be in a noisy study area or scheduled two weeks later. This could mean you receive academic feedback too late to use it to improve. "Makeup" is just what the word implies, trying to move from behind to regain a position. Unfortunately, I observed that some students did not start studying or take the course seriously until after the first exam. Be sure to be in class when exams are returned. Listen to the professor's description of a good answer. Learn from the professor's responses to other students. Find out what you did right, what you did wrong, and exactly what is expected. Also, find out who made the best grades and ask those students how they studied. The exam and subsequent discussions help you understand expectations and set your future learning goals.

5 Be Equipped for Success

Be Prepared, Organized, and Ready to Learn.   Some students arrive on the first day of class without paper and end up writing lecture notes on the back of the syllabus. Every college student should always have at hand the equipment listed in Exercise 4.

EXERCISE 4   Put a check mark next to each item of equipment that you have with you.

_____ Assignment calendar with large daily spaces *or* personal digital assistant

_____ Spiral notebook or laptop for lecture notes

_____ Three-ring binder for organizing papers

_____ Three-ring hole punch for putting handouts in binder

_____ Notebook paper

_____ Notebook dividers (at least five) or flags for organizing by topic

_____ Some sort of container in which to keep the following:

_____ pencil   _____ regular pen

_____ erasable pen   _____ highlighter

_____ correction fluid or tape   _____ small pencil sharpener

_____ small stapler   _____ small Post-it notes

_____ small paper clips

6 Preview Your Textbook

Understand How Your Textbook Is Organized So You Can Use It to Your Best Advantage.   Quickly flip through the book to absorb some of its features. Do you see pictures, graphs, text boxes, exercises or other special features? Now glance at the title page. Who is the author, and what are the author's credentials? Examine the table of contents. Do you see any features that are repeated in most or all chapters? Get an idea of the topics that are covered. Look at the end of the table of contents. Are there special sections that may be of use to you? Is there an answer key? An index? A glossary? Do this with every textbook you have.

EXERCISE 5   Read the table of contents of this text and glance through the chapters. Notice the format of the chapters and selectively scan the subheadings. Preview the text to answer the following questions:

1. How many major chapters are in this book? _____

2. Other than the obvious differences of topics covered, how does the

   organizational format of Chapter 3 differ from the format of Chapter 4?

   _____

   _____

   _____

3. What is My Reading Lab? _____

   _____

4. What is the Reading Workshop in Appendix 5? _____

   _____

5. What is the purpose of Summary Points? _____

   _____

6. In which chapter would you find information on making inferences?

_____

7. In Chapter 4, Main Idea, what other words are sometimes used to mean the same as *main idea*? _____

_____

8. Name five college subjects represented in the longer selections at the end of the chapters. _____

9. In which chapter would you learn more about patterns of organization?

_____

10. What is the purpose of Appendix 1? _____

11. In which chapter would you find hints on time management? _____

7 Mark Your Textbooks

Get the Most from Your Books and Use Them as Learning Tools.   Read your textbooks with a pen or highlighter in hand and mark information that you will most likely need to know later. A well-marked textbook is a treasure that you may want to keep as a reference for later courses.

Don't miss an opportunity to learn by being reluctant to mark in your text. Marking your text actively involves you in reading and studying. The small amount of money that you receive in a textbook resale may not be worth what you have lost in active involvement. Some books, such as this one, are workbooks. Use this book to practice, to give and get feedback, and to keep a record of your progress.

8 Communicate with Your Instructor

Don't Be an Anonymous Student.   Let your professor know who you are. Get your money's worth and more. Make a special effort to speak to your professor about assignments you found interesting or something you did not understand. Overcome your fear and seek help when you need it. Contrary to popular opinion, good students are more likely to seek help than weak ones. Visit during office hours, call, or send an e-mail when you have a question or concern. Professors want their students to be successful.

9 Review Your Lecture Notes

Review Your Lecture Notes Within Twenty-Four Hours after Each Class Session.   Recite to yourself what the professor said. Identify gaps of knowledge and seek clarification. This kind of review reinforces your learning and reminds you of what the professor thinks is important. Unfortunately, most students wait until test time to review notes, thus missing these easy opportunities to solidify learning. Your notebook is a valuable resource; use it.

10 Network with Other Students

Use the Other Students in the Classroom as Learning Resources.   For the first four weeks of my history class, almost none of the students spoke to each other. I was amazed. Even when I arrived five or ten minutes early to observe behavior, no one spoke. Most stared straight ahead, some read the history text, and some read the newspaper. After the first exam, however, students started to compare scores and to talk about correct answers.

Put fellow students on your learning team. Research shows that students who are part of a study group are less likely to drop out of school. Study groups teach students to collaborate and to form academic bonds. Networking is important for all students, including older, returning students who may initially feel out of the mainstream.

Begin your team building on the first day of class. In each course, ask for the name, telephone number, and e-mail address of at least two other students. Write this information in your text or lecture notebook so you won't lose it. Better yet, enter it into your cell phone right away. These names and numbers are insurance policies. If you are absent or unclear about an assignment, call a classmate for clarification, homework, and lecture notes. Students *can* help other students. Begin your network right now with two people. Don't be bashful.

Classmate _____   Phone _____   E-mail _____

Classmate _____   Phone _____   E-mail _____

11 Collaborate to Make the Best Use of Time

Find a "Study Buddy" to Share the Work.   In my history class, only two essay questions would be chosen for the exam from the list of ten distributed on the first day. The professor expected answers to include information from the lectures as well as details from the history text. To be thoroughly prepared for the exam, each student should have a written study outline answering each of the ten questions. Such an assignment presents an obvious opportunity to cut work in half. Why not get a study buddy and each prepare five possible essay answers and share? Seize every opportunity to collaborate and divide work efficiently. Of course, it is then each person's responsibility to study and learn the information.

However, beware of academic dishonesty! Although working with your study buddies to help each other understand the material is an excellent strategy for learning, the work you turn in must be entirely your own. Brainstorm together but write your own papers. Never copy someone else's work or allow anyone to copy yours. This is a serious breach of academic honesty policies that can result in a zero on the assignment, an F in the class, or even dismissal from the college.

12 Review an "A" Paper

When Exams Are Returned, Always Find Out the Correct Answers.   For essay responses, always ask to see an "A" paper. Ask the professor or a top-scoring student to allow you "an opportunity to read an excellent paper." Who would deny such a request? Analyze the "A" paper to determine how you can improve. Ask yourself, "What is this student doing that I'm not doing?" Even if you made an "A," read another paper. Maybe your next exam response will earn an "A+." In my history class, I noticed that the good students sought examples, but the weak students slipped out of the room without seeking any help or insight from others.

13 Use Technology to Communicate

Communicate Without Wasting Time.   Do you really need to meet face to face to study together? Conflicting class and work schedules make getting study groups together difficult. Cell phones, fax machines, e-mail, electronic discussion boards, and chat rooms can eliminate some of those barriers. Outlines, lecture notes, and math problems can be discussed and sent back and forth rapidly.

14 Consider an Audio Recording

If You Need Audio Reinforcement, Try Using an Electronic Recording Device. Do not use the recording as an excuse to postpone the organizing and setting of priorities involved in notetaking. Instead, use the audio replay as another sensory tool for learning. One history student said she listened to the replays while driving her car or fixing dinner.

15 Pass the First Test

Always Overprepare for the First Exam. Success on the first exam builds confidence, allays fears, and saves you from desperately trying to come from behind.

16 Use DVDs, Podcasts, and Online Resources

Visual Learning Is Powerful. Find DVDs at the college or public library, go online for podcasts (which can also be downloaded to a smart phone), or visit YouTube for videos on a wide variety of subject areas. Also check out the websites of well-known museums such as the American Museum of Natural History or the Museum of Modern Art, as they offer videos and podcasts related to museum exhibitions. Watch movies, old or new, that will help you visualize a place, event, topic, or time period you are studying.

17 Predict Exam Questions

Predict Both Essay Questions and Multiple-Choice Items for Exams. Not all professors provide possible essay questions and study guides. On your own you can review your textbook's table of contents and turn major headings and chapter titles into possible essay questions. Consider subheadings and boldface print a ripe source of multiple-choice items. Review lecture notes for any indication the professor has given about areas of special importance. Ask previous students about the professor's exams. The format and questions of a major exam should not come as a total shock to you. Predict and be prepared.

PERSONAL FEEDBACK 4

Name _____

1. What procrastination tactics do you use to delay homework?
_____

2. Describe a personal intention that you regret not putting in action.
_____

3. What specific activities do you think academic winners do that academic losers do
not want to do? _____
_____

4. Why might speaking up in class be considered risk taking? _____
_____

5. What are the rewards for speaking up in class? _____
_____

6. Describe a situation in which you have sought help individually from a college
instructor. _____
_____

Tear out and submit to your instructor.

Reading 3

BOUNCING BACK FROM FAILURE

It is a very rare person who achieves a dream without meeting problems and disappointments along the way. Even the people we consider the most successful have made mistakes, suffered setbacks, and felt discouraged. What makes some people keep going after a failure? In this article you will find five good suggestions and the inspirational story of a person who overcame many obstacles on the way to success. What suggestions can you use in your life?

There's an old Japanese proverb that counsels: "Fall seven times, stand up eight." But how do you get back up when you've fallen flat on your face? Below you'll find 5 tips to help you gather the pieces and pull yourself back together after you've failed.

1. Always expect success. However, you need to get rid of the notion of the "overnight success" or the "get-rich-quick-scheme." People who appear to be overnight successes have actually spent a lot of time before-hand honing their skill. Success requires a lot of preparation and a prolonged effort. Unfortunately, there are a lot of people who feel like failures when something doesn't work immediately and they just give up. If you don't succeed right away this doesn't mean that you've failed. Recognize that setbacks are simply part of the process, and that hard work and perseverance are two of the most important ingredients of success. If you've failed in the short run it simply means you need to take a longer term view of success.

2. Do not identify yourself with your failures. You are not your actions. To say that you have failed many times is not the same thing as saying that you are a failure. Whatever happens, keep referring to yourself, in your conversations with others and in your self-talk, as someone who has the full capacity to succeed.

3. Create a "fame wall." Hang your diplomas or certificates on this wall. You can also add framed photographs of yourself with your friends and family having fun or sharing a close moment. Anything that gives you a sense of accomplishment can go up on the wall. In times of failure, refer to your wall. It will serve to remind you that you have succeeded in the past and that you will succeed again in the future

4. Collect stories of failure about people who have gone on to become successful so that you can use them as inspiration when you're down. For example, consider the following life story.

This person:

At age 22—Failed in business;
At age 23—Was defeated for the State Legislature;
At age 24—Again failed in business;
At age 25—Was elected to the State Legislature;
At age 26—His sweetheart died;
At age 27—He suffered a nervous breakdown;
At age 29—Was defeated for the office of speaker;
At age 31—Was defeated for elector;
At age 34—Was defeated for Congress;
At age 37—Was elected to Congress;
At age 39—Was defeated for Congress;
At age 46—Was defeated for the Senate;
At age 47—Was defeated for Vice-President;
At age 49—Was defeated for the Senate;
At age 51—Was elected President of the United States.
This person was Abraham Lincoln.

PERSONAL FEEDBACK 5

Name _____

1. Consider the obstacles that might get in the way of your success in college. Write them in the chart below. (Lack of motivation or interest, the distraction of friends, lack of transportation, family responsibilities, illness, unhealthy habits, a difficult class, procrastination are some common examples.)

2. Share at least part of your list with a classmate and listen as he or she suggests possible solutions. Write them in the chart below.

3. Switch roles and offer suggestions to your partner.

Obstacles I might face	Possible solutions
_____	_____
	_____
	_____
	_____
_____	_____
	_____
_____	_____
	_____

4. Now, make a plan. What will you do if the obstacle comes your way? Be specific. How will you get to class if the car breaks down? How will you keep up in class if you are ill? What will you say when your friends want to go out and you have an exam the next day? Who might help you if your child is sick? Where can you get help with a tough class?

Obstacle	The plan
_____	_____
_____	_____
_____	_____

Tear out and submit to your instructor.

5. Keep things in perspective; do not over-generalize. The fact that you've failed at something does not mean that your life is over. It does not mean that your reputation is forever ruined and that you'll never get another chance. Don't make the situation bigger or more pervasive than it really is. Instead, remember the famous line: "And this too shall pass . . ."

—5 Tips for Overcoming Failure by Marelisa Fábrega

EXERCISE 6   **Think and Write.** Answer the following questions.

1. How have you responded to past failures and disappointments?

   _____

   _____

2. Select two of the tips in this article and explain how you might apply them to your life. _____

   _____

   _____

SUMMARY POINTS

1 How can you mentally prepare for college success? (page 2)

Think like a winner. Set goals and build a support team. Develop a positive attitude and believe you can succeed. Aim high and expect excellence from yourself.

2 How can you manage your time effectively? (page 5)

Use To Do Lists to set daily goals and priorities. Check off your accomplishments, and relist items that were not achieved.
Use the due dates listed in the syllabus to plan ahead to complete major assignments.
Make a weekly plan that includes specific blocks of time for studying.
Aim for two hours of study outside of class for every hour in class.

3 Adopt the "Sweet 17" behaviors of successful students. (page 11)

Study the syllabus	Network with other students
Attend class	Collaborate to make the best use of time
Be on time for class	
Be aware of essential class sessions	Review an "A" paper
Be equipped for success	Use technology to communicate
Preview your textbooks	Consider an audio recording
Mark your textbooks	Pass the first test
Communicate with your instructors	Use DVDs, podcasts, and online resources
Review your lecture notes	Predict exam questions

Form a five-member group and select one of the following activities. Brainstorm and then outline your major points on a transparency. Choose a member to present the group findings to the class.

➤ Make a list of the top ten ways college students waste time.

➤ Make a list of the top ten lifestyle (nutritional and fitness) errors made by college students.

➤ Make a list of the top ten ways to overcome procrastination.

➤ Write instructions for getting an e-mail address on your campus.

MyReadingLab

MyReadingLab (MRL) www.myreadinglab.com

➤ The MyReadingLab website contains many materials to help you advance your reading and study skills. MRL offers an excellent opportunity to improve your reading skills by building on your current strengths and working on weaknesses. In addition to the reading sections, you will find links to the Longman Vocabulary website, Longman Study Skills website and the Research Navigator.

Your professor will tell you if you will be using MRL as part of this course and, if so, provide instructions for creating an account.

If you will not be using MRL in the course, you can still purchase an access code and use the materials to practice your reading skills. Open your Web browser and go to **www.myreadinglab.com.** The instructions for purchasing an access code and setting up an account are available there.

When you have created an account and login, it is a good idea to take the diagnostic tests first. The program will create a personalized study plan based on the results. In the Skills section you will find practice exercises within modules that relate to each chapter in this book. In the Levels section, you will read interesting selections, answer questions about them, and see your reading level (Lexile) change. Your professor will tell you which parts you should use.

Take some time to explore the site and see what is available for you there.

For support in meeting this chapter's objectives, log in to **www.myreadinglab.com** and select "Memorization and Concentration."

THE READING WORKSHOP

If reading a novel, biography, or other book is part of your course experience, refer to The Reading Workshop: Thinking, Talking, and Writing about Books in Appendix 5 for suggestions.

Researching Online

The Internet has become as much a part of everyday life for people all over the world as televisions and automobiles. We use it for social networking, business communication, entertainment, driving directions, and to locate the nearest coffee shop or fast-food restaurant. Many college students are experts at navigating the Internet for these purposes, but very few come to college knowing how to use it for academic research. Academic research on the Internet, such as you will be required to do in college, requires some specialized knowledge and skills.

Definitions

Let's start with a few definitions and the parts that make up a typical Web address, or URL (uniform resource locator). This is the URL for the United States Library of Congress: http://www.loc.gov. Add "topics" to the end, and the address takes you directly to the "browse by topic" part of the site.

The following is a key to the numbered components of the sample URL.

1. **Protocol** This is standard for Web addresses and indicates *hypertext transfer protocol,* the type of language computers on the Internet use to communicate with each other. Secure sites are indicated with the "https" protocol.
2. **Server name** This indicates the computer network over which you will "travel" to reach the desired location. In most cases this will be the World Wide Web.
3. **Domain name** This is a name registered by the website owner.
4. **Domain type** This indicates the category to which the site owner belongs.
    "gov" indicates an official government site.
    "edu" indicates a school or educational institution's site.
    "org" indicates an organization or group such as the American Cancer Society.
    "com" indicates a commercial site whose main purpose is to promote or sell a product.
5. **Directory path** This indicates a particular location within the website's host computer.

Navigating a Website

After you have entered the URL and reached the desired website, get an overview of what the site has to offer by scanning headlines, graphics, buttons, animation, category headings, site maps, and tables of contents. Many sites have a "Search" option near the top of the page that will help you find a specific topic.

Library of Congress; www.loc.gov

Notice the section tabs and search box at the top of the page. Many of the photos and topics on this page are hypertext links, or simply links. A click of the mouse moves you to another page with more information about that topic. Usually, clicking the "Back" arrow returns you to the original page.

 **EXERCISE** **1**

Research the following information about the National Aeronautics and Space Administration (NASA), First, go to the website (**www.nasa.gov**), click on the home page, and examine the different headings. When you rest the cursor on the major headings, subtopics will appear. Use this navigational tool to answer the following questions.

1. What does NASA do? _____

    _____

2. Name two ways that NASA's work impacts earth _____

    _____

    _____

    _____

    _____

3. What types of careers are available at NASA? _____

_____

_____

4. Check the latest NASA news items. List two. Write the categories under which

you found them. _____

_____

_____

5. Use the "Search" feature to learn what significant event took place on July 20,

1969 _____

_____

Academic Research

College professors often require students to learn about specific topics through scholarly research. The assignment might result in a term paper, project, or an oral presentation. Your professor will tell you the kinds of information sources that are acceptable, but most professors insist on scholarly sources that reflect the results of solid, reliable research. These materials can be found within the walls of your college library, or they may be accessed through the Internet. In fact, the materials in the most respected libraries in the world can be viewed from your computer or any Internet-capable device. The vast collection in the United States Library of Congress is a good example.

Getting Started

Although Wikipedia and Google are not usually acceptable sources of information for an academic research assignment, they are good places to get a quick overview of a topic. Wikipedia is an online encyclopedia to which users can add and revise entries. The site is monitored, but it does not promise unbiased, factual information. It can, though, provide ideas for narrowing your research topic and search terms. A Google search of your topic is likely to yield a list of many possible sources of information. Scan the list of "hits" for one or two that have promise, and skim them. Again, look for general information and for related topics that might help focus your research.

Scholarly Databases

When you have gained a general knowledge of your topic and have narrowed it to something that can be reasonably covered in the scope of your assignment, begin searching for scholarly, research-based sources of information. Libraries buy subscriptions to databases that contain many publications. Your college library probably offers online access to many such sources either from computers in the library building or through the college website. The snapshot below shows the first few databases in a very long list at one college library site. Notice that many of the databases are related to a field of study. When you have decided on a college major and have taken several courses in that field, you will become familiar with the best sources of information in that subject area.

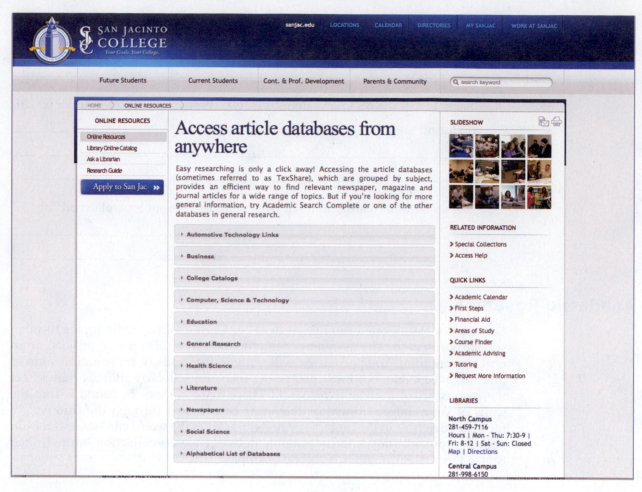

San Jacinto College, www.sanjac.edu

 **EXERCISE 2** Explore your college library's website or find the site for another college library that is available to visitors. Locate the scholarly databases, and list three that might be useful to you.

URL of the library website _____

1. _____

2. _____

3. _____

Tracking and Recording Your Search

Keep track of all useful sources so you can find them again easily. There are several ways to do this:

- *Write down* the URL or the steps in the path you took to find a database or article.
- *Print* the material. If you do this, use both sides of the page if possible to reduce paper usage. Be sure that you also record the URL so you can find the material again and cite the source in your research report.

- *Save* the material to your computer's hard drive or a portable thumb drive. Be sure to name and organize the various sources so you can find and identify them later.
- *Bookmark* or save the site to "Favorites" if you are using your own computer. If you are using a public machine, emailing a document or a link to yourself is sometimes an option.

No matter how you keep track of your searches, it is extremely important that you have all the source information for any publication whose information you will use. You must cite the sources when you write your research report so that a reader can find the material you used. Ask your instructor if a particular citation style is required.

Evaluating Sources

Not every article or book you find will be of equal value, so read selectively. Look for titles that contain the focus of your topic. Articles in scholarly journals usually begin with an abstract, a brief summary of the article. Read the abstracts quickly to determine the value of the article for your purpose. Don't waste time on materials that are too general or that focus on a different aspect of your subject.

When you find an article that has information you need, read carefully and take notes in your own words. Use what you are learning in your reading course to critically evaluate the material. Pay attention to the tone of the language for clues to the author's purpose in writing. Consider the title, the author, the date it was written, the references cited in it, and the source itself. Scholarly journals are respected for publishing the best research and reporting only factual information. Other sources, however, may seek to persuade readers to accept a particular point of view. For example, an article in the National Rifle Association's magazine can be expected to take a certain position on gun control legislation. Gather information from many sources and draw your own conclusions based on the facts.

Academic Honesty

Colleges and college professors are very serious about academic honesty. Purchasing a paper, cutting and pasting from work that isn't yours, paraphrasing someone else's work, or in any way using someone else's words or ideas as if they were your own constitutes **plagiarism**. The consequences of plagiarism range from a zero grade on the assignment to expulsion from the college.

Sometimes students are unaware that they have plagiarized. Avoid this by "translating" the wording of the original source into your own words when you make notes. Then, when you compose the sentences of your paper, you will not accidentally use the author's phrasing. Remember that your goal is learning. Protect your honorable standing at your institution.

EXERCISE 3 Search a scholarly database for information on distance learning, and record your search results here.

1. Name of the database _____

2. For each of three publications that look interesting, list the title, author, and

   source:

- _____
  _____
- _____
  _____
- _____
  _____

3. Open one of the publications. Read the abstract, if there is one, or survey the entire article. Briefly describe the focus of the information.

   _____
   _____
   _____

4. If you were researching information for a paper or project, you would need a more narrow, focused topic than "distance learning." Write an idea for a narrowed search topic. (Hint: Glance through the list of titles from your search to find focused topics.)

   _____

Reader's TIP   Limiting Your Search

- Enter *AND* or a plus (+) sign between each word of your search. For example, using the words *Apple Computer* for your search will turn up thousands of hits that include not only sites about the company, but also sites related to apple (the fruit) and sites about computers in general. Using *AND* in your key phrase (*Apple AND Computer*) will return sites that only contain both words in the phrase.
- Enter *OR* to broaden a search. *Apple OR Computer* will return sites that contain information about either apples or computers.
- Enter *NOT* to exclude items. *Apple AND Computer NOT fruit* will exclude sites that mention fruit.
- Use quotation marks when you want only hits that contain the exact phrase, such as "Apple Computer Financial Report for 2011."

2 Stages of Reading

Learning Objectives
From this chapter, readers will learn:

1 To use the three stages of good reading
2 To preview before reading
3 The meaning and importance of a *schema*
4 The meaning and importance of *metacognition*
5 To use six thinking strategies during reading to integrate existing and new knowledge
6 To apply active recall methods after reading

Everyday Reading Skills: Reading News and Feature Stories in the Newspaper

WHAT IS THE READING PROCESS?

In the past, experts thought of reading comprehension as a *product*. They assumed that if you could pronounce the words fluently, you would automatically be able to comprehend. Instruction focused on practicing and checking for the correct answers rather than on explaining comprehension skills. Newer approaches, by contrast, teach reading comprehension as a *process* in which you use your understanding of different skills and stages to achieve an understanding of the whole. Students are now taught how to predict upcoming ideas, activate existing knowledge, relate old information with new, form a main idea, and make inferences.

STAGES OF READING

Learning Objective 1

Use the three stages of good reading

Good reading is divided into three thinking stages:

1. **Before reading:** *Preview* to find out what the material is about, what you already know about the topic, and what you need to find out while reading.
2. **During reading:** *Integrate* old and new knowledge, anticipate upcoming information, visualize, mark the text, and assess your own understanding in order to make adjustments.
3. **After reading:** *Recall* and react to what you have learned.

Many experts have devised study skills strategies that break these three thinking stages into small steps. A historical example is SQ3R, which was devised by Francis P. Robinson at Ohio State University. The letters stand for *Survey, Question, Read, Recite,* and *Review.* Any such system can be successful, but all are designed to systematically engage the reader in thought *before, during,* and *after* reading.

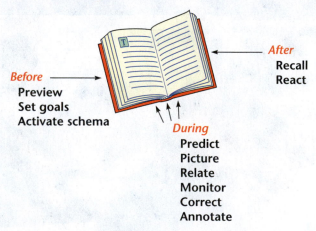

Before
Preview
Set goals
Activate schema

During
Predict
Picture
Relate
Monitor
Correct
Annotate

After
Recall
React

Stage One: Previewing

Previewing is a method of assessing the material, your knowledge of the subject, and your goals for reading. Try to connect with the topic and get an overview of the assignment before starting on the first paragraph. At the beginning of each new course, preview the table of contents of your new textbook to get an overview of the scope of the material. Before reading a chapter, use the signposts such as subheadings, boldface or italic type, and summaries to anticipate what you will be learning.

Reader's **TIP**   **Questions for Previewing**

Use the following questions as guides to energize your reading and help you become an active learner.

1. What is the topic of the material?
2. What do I already know about the subject?
3. What is my purpose for reading?
4. How is the material organized?
5. What will be my plan of attack?

Learning Objective 2

Preview before reading

Signposts for Previewing.   Notice the following typical features of college textbooks when previewing. These are the parts to read when previewing a textbook chapter:

Introductory Material.   A textbook chapter usually begins with an introduction. This section prepares the reader for the major ideas that will be covered. Pay close attention to it!

Learning Questions.   Many textbook chapters start with questions designed to heighten your interest and stimulate your thinking. Such questions directly relate to what the material covers and thus help you set goals.

Title.   The title of a book, chapter, or article is the first clue to its meaning. Some titles are designed to be clever to attract attention, but most try to communicate the important thought in the text. Identify the *who, what,* or *why* of the title to anticipate the content of the material and its importance to you.

Headings and Subheadings.   These are the titles of the sections and subsections within chapters that, like the major titles, describe the content. Usually headings and subheadings appear in bold or italic type and outline the author's message. Turn them into questions to anticipate what you will need to know from the reading. For example, the heading "Estimating Revenue Potential" in a marketing text could be changed to "How Do You Estimate Revenue Potential?".

Italics, Boldface, and Numbers.   Italic and bold type highlight words that merit special emphasis. These words are usually terms that you will need to define and remember. Numbers are also used to list important details that you may need to learn.

Visual Aids or Marginal Notations.   A biology professor at a major university tells his students to at least look at the illustrations and read the captions in the assigned material before coming to class, even if they don't read the assignment. He wants his students to have a visual overview. Authors use photos, charts, and graphs to enhance meaning, heighten interest, and help readers visualize information. Additional notations and definitions may be added in the page margins to further simplify the material for the reader.

Concluding Summary or Review.   Most textbook chapters end with a summary of the most important points, which may be several paragraphs or a list of the important ideas. Regardless of its form, the summary helps you recall the material and reflect on its importance.

EXERCISE 1

To get an overview of this chapter, look at the learning questions at the opening of the chapter on page 31. Read the Summary Points on page 47 and scan to understand the headings, subheadings, and the boldfaced and italicized words. Spend a few moments reviewing the contents of the Reader's Tip boxes. Preview the chapter to answer the following questions:

1. What is the purpose of previewing? _____

2. List the six thinking strategies good readers use during the reading process:
   _____
   _____

3. What is meant by *recall*? _____
   _____
   _____
   _____

4. How do good readers reflect? _____
   _____
   _____

5. Why would good readers keep records of their own learning progress?
   _____

The Power of Prior Knowledge. Experts say that prior knowledge is the most important factor in reading comprehension. Thus, if you know very little about a subject, the initial reading in that area will be difficult. The good news, however, is that the more you know, the easier it is for you to read and learn. Every new idea added to your framework of knowledge about a subject makes the next reading assignment on the topic a little bit easier.

Students who already know a lot about history may think that American history assignments are easy. But students who perhaps excel in science and know little history might disagree. Because of prior knowledge, most students would probably agree that senior-level college courses are much easier than freshman survey courses.

> **BRAIN BOOSTER**
>
> **The ever-growing brain!**
> Did you know that every time you learn something, visible growth occurs in your brain? Picture a thin tree trunk with a few branches. That is very much what a *dendrite* looks like. A dendrite growing from a brain cell (a *neuron*) is the physical evidence of a *schema* or piece of knowledge on a very specific subject. When you learn something new about that subject, its dendrite sprouts new branches. If the new learning also relates to another subject, then the dendrites connect to each other with a synapse to form a neural network. Before you know it, your brain is a mass of billions of intertwined dendrites, sparking their synapses with electrical current. This is why relating what we already know to new information is so powerful.

Learning Objective 3

The meaning and importance of a *schema*

Previewing to Activate Schemata. Your prior knowledge on a subject is a schema. According to theory, a **schema** (plural, *schemata*) is the skeleton of knowledge in your mind on a particular subject. As you expand your knowledge, the skeleton grows. Here's another way to think about a schema: A schema is like a computer chip in your brain that holds everything you know on a particular subject. You pull it out when the need arises, add to it, and then return it to storage.

Your preview of the material will help you know which "computer chips" to activate. Call on what you already know and blend it with the new ideas. If you embellish the new thoughts with your past experience, your reading will become more meaningful.

Students tend to know more than they think they know. No matter how unfamiliar the topic may seem, you can probably provide some small link from your own experience. Pick up the signals from the written material and use them to retrieve prior knowledge and form a link of understanding with the next text.

PERSONAL FEEDBACK   **1**   **Name** _____

1. What was your favorite subject in high school, and why? _____
   _____

2. What magazines do you like to read? _____
   _____

3. What sections do you like to read in the newspaper? _____
   _____

4. What is the best book you have read? _____
   _____

5. What television programs do you watch regularly? _____
   _____

6. How does prior knowledge seem to relate to your areas of greatest interest?
   _____

Tear out and submit to your instructor.

EXAMPLE   Read the following sentence and activate your schema. Identify a knowledge link. Briefly describe an idea or image that comes to mind.

> Cuba became an obsession of American policy makers in 1959, when Fidel Castro and rebels of his 26th of July Movement ousted America's longtime ally Fulgencio Batista.
>
> —*A People and a Nation* by Mary Beth Norton et al.

EXPLANATION   You may know little Cuban history, but you probably know that Miami, Florida, has a large and flourishing Hispanic population, begun by people who left Cuba. Do you know why they left Cuba? Link this knowledge of Cubans in Florida to the new information.

Stage Two: Integrating Knowledge

If you watch two students reading silently, can you tell which student comprehends better? Probably not. The behaviors of good silent readers are thinking behaviors that cannot be observed or learned by watching others. These behaviors, however, need not be mysterious to college students.

Learning Objective 4

The meaning and importance of *metacognition*

Knowing About Knowing.   A myth in reading, probably inspired by the speed reading craze, is that good readers begin an assignment, race through it, and never stop until the last period. In fact, however, *good readers work hard* to assimilate the information they read. If they do not understand or if they get confused, they go back and reread to resolve the confusion. Good readers also understand the processes involved in reading and consciously control them. This awareness and control of the reading processes is called **metacognition,** which one expert defines as "knowing about knowing."[1]

Some students don't know when they don't know. They continue to read even though they are not comprehending. Poor readers tolerate such confusion because they either don't realize that it exists or don't know what to do about it. Poor readers focus on facts, whereas good readers try to assimilate details into a larger cognitive pattern. Good readers monitor their own comprehension. In other words, they supervise their own understanding of the material. They recognize inadequate comprehension and interrupt their reading to seek solutions.

Learning Objective 5

Use six thinking strategies during reading to integrate knowledge

Six Thinking Strategies of Good Readers.   In order to find out what good readers do, Beth Davey studied the research on good and poor readers. She discovered that good readers, both consciously and subconsciously, use the five thinking strategies below.[2] In addition a sixth strategy—annotating—will help you recall material you read.

1. Predict: Make Educated Guesses.   Good readers make predictions about thoughts, events, outcomes, and conclusions. With the appearance of each new character in a James Patterson mystery novel, the reader makes a guess about who the culprit might be. Textbook predictions, although a little less dramatic, are equally important. While reading the facts in a science text, for example, you may be anticipating the concluding theory.

As you read, your predictions are confirmed or denied. If they prove invalid, you make new predictions. For example, in reading an economics text, you might predict that inflation hurts everyone. But after further reading, you discover that real estate investors make money by selling at the inflated prices. Thus your initial prediction proved invalid, and you readjusted your thinking on inflation. Your predictions involved you with the author's thinking and helped you learn.

EXAMPLE

What are your predictions for the rest of the section based on these beginning sentences?

---

[1] Ann L. Brown, "The Development of Memory: Knowing, Knowing About Knowing, and Knowing How to Know," in *Advances in Child Development and Behavior* (vol. 2), ed. H. W. Reese (New York: Academic Press, 1975).

[2] Adapted from Beth Davey, "Think Aloud—Modeling the Cognitive Processes of Reading Comprehension," *Journal of Reading*, 27 (Oct. 1983): 44–47.

At least one bank recognized opportunity in this situation. Instead of classifying low-to-moderate-income Hispanics as credit risks to be avoided at all costs, Puerto Rico–based Banco Popular saw them as an untapped market for personal and business banking services. Having witnessed Banco Popular's success, mainstream banks such as Chase Manhattan and Citibank are . . .

—*Business*, Sixth Edition, by Ricky W. Griffin
and Ronald J. Ebert

EXPLANATION   The rest of this section explains how traditional banks are moving aggressively into the Hispanic market to offer banking services and win customers.

2. Picture: Form Images.   For good readers, the words and the ideas on the page trigger mental images that relate directly or indirectly to the material. Because these mental images depend on the reader's experience, visualization is a highly individualistic process. One learner might read about Maine and picture the countryside and the rockbound coast, whereas another, with no experience in the area, might visualize the shape and location of the state on a map. Images are like movies in your head. You form a visualization to enhance the message in the text. Fiction quickly moves you into a new world of enjoyment or terror through visualization. Expository or textbook writing may require more imagination than fiction, but the images created also strengthen the message.

EXAMPLE   Describe your visualizations for the following passage.

A dress so loud it hurts my eyes. There are yellows and oranges enough to throw back the light of the sun. I feel my whole face warming from the heat waves it throws out. Earrings gold, too, and hanging down to her shoulders. Bracelets dangling and making noises when she moves her arm . . .

—"Everyday Use" from *In Love & Trouble:
Stories of Black Women* by Alice Walker

EXPLANATION   Imagine a woman dressed in yellows and oranges that are perhaps too bright with long earrings and dangling bracelets. Depending on prior knowledge, you may visualize someone you know.

3. Relate: Draw Comparisons.   When you relate your existing knowledge to the new information in the text, you are embellishing the material and making it part of your framework of ideas. A phrase or a situation may remind you of a personal experience that relates to the text. For example, a description of ocean currents may remind you of a strong undertow you once fought while swimming. Such related experiences help you digest the new experience as part of something you already know.

EXAMPLE   Are these methods of coping with stress helpful to you?

A third effective buffer between stressors and illness is exercise. People who are physically fit have fewer health problems than people who are less fit even when they are under the same pressures. They also show lower physiological arousal to stressors (Vita et al., 1998). These activities, along with any others that calm your body and focus your mind—prayer, music, dancing, baking bread—are all good for health.

—*Psychology*, Tenth Edition, by Carole Wade and Carol Tavris

EXPLANATION   What do you do to relieve stress? Which of the methods mentioned seem most useful? Name two other activities that "calm your body and focus your mind."

4. Monitor: Check Understanding.   Monitor your ongoing comprehension to test your understanding of the material. Keep an internal summary of the information as it is presented and how it relates to the overall message. Your summary will build with each new detail as long as the author's message is consistent. If, however, certain information seems confusing or erroneous, stop and seek a solution to the problem. Monitor and supervise your own comprehension. Remember that poor readers continue to read even when confused, but good readers seek to resolve the difficulty. Good readers demand complete understanding and know whether it has been achieved.

EXAMPLE   What is confusing about the following sentence?

> "Another such victory like that on July 1," wrote Richard Harding Davis, "and our troops must retreat."

> —*America and Its People*, Third Edition,
> by James Martin et al.

EXPLANATION   The words *retreat* and *victory* refer to opposite ideas. Usually the defeated army retreats. Davis must mean that the victory was too costly, and thus was hardly a victory at all. Davis must be speaking sarcastically, but a second reading might be necessary to figure this out.

5. Resolve Gaps in Understanding.   Do not accept gaps in your reading comprehension. They may signal a failure to understand a word or a sentence. Stop and resolve the problem so you can continue to synthesize and build your internal summary. Seek solutions to confusion. Usually, this means rereading a sentence or looking back at a previous page for clarification. If an unknown word is causing confusion, the definition may emerge through further reading. Changing predictions is also a corrective strategy. For example, while reading a geography textbook you may be predicting that heavy rains saved a country from famine, but, as the conclusion emerges, it seems that fertilizers and irrigation were the saviors. If you cannot fill the gaps yourself, seek help from the instructor or another student.

EXAMPLE   How could you seek to understand the scope of time mentioned in this textbook excerpt?

> . . . [T]hose who study Earth science must routinely deal with vast time periods—millions or billions (thousands of millions) of years. When viewed in the context of Earth's 4.6-billion-year history, an event that occurred 100 million years ago may be characterized as "recent" by a geologist, and a rock sample that has been dated at 10 million years may be called "young."

> —*Earth Science*, Thirteenth Edition, by Edward J. Tarbuck
> and Frederick K. Lutgens

EXPLANATION   First, are there any words whose definitions are unclear to you? Do you know the meaning of *vast* or *context*, for instance? If not, using the clues in the paragraph or consulting a dictionary will help. If you're not sure what a geologist does, check the glossary in the back of the textbook. Next, is there a time line or other visual aid on the nearby pages that helps to put the huge periods of time into perspective?

6. Annotate the Text as You Read.   By circling, underlining, and writing brief notes in the margin, you will be reacting to the material and highlighting the important information. This is a critical thinking process, that will help you understand and remember the material. Keeping your brain and your pen active while you read will help you stay focused and prevent your mind from wandering. An added bonus is that you will create a record of your thinking that you can return to when preparing for a test.

EXAMPLE   Notice how marking the text makes the major details stand out.

1990s rap

In the 1990s one of the elements of rap music shifted toward the DJs or turntablists who created sounds by manipulating the turntables on which LPs were played. The most commonly used technique involves moving the record rapidly back and forth while it is being played. DJs battle each other in displays of virtuosity. They work with two turntables simultaneously, cutting in and out of the sound made by scratching, while the other LP is playing . . .

(2 common techniques)

Sampling involves the use of a short extract of a previous recording as a musical element in a new recording. The most commonly used samples are those of a recognizable riff or a catchy instrumental introduction from a song. Sung or spoken extracts can also be sampled . . .

—From *Understanding Music,* Fifth Edition, by Jeremy Yudkin

EXPLANATION   As you read, did you notice that the passage describes a term, *turntablists*, and two characteristics of rap music? By circling the term and underlining its meaning, they are made visually clear. Similarly, circling the two characteristics and underlining the most important parts of their descriptions make the information stand out from the minor details. The marginal notes serve as labels for the marking. This process keeps the reader active and thinking. Plus, the annotations serve as a great aid to recall in the after reading stage. Whether you circle, underline, make marginal notes, or use some combination of these methods depends on the material itself and your purpose for reading.

Applying All Six Thinking Strategies.   The following passage illustrates the use of the six thinking strategies. Some of the reader's thoughts appear as handwritten comments in the margins. Keep in mind that each person reacts differently. This example merely represents one reader's attempt to integrate knowledge.

EXAMPLE   Which of the six thinking strategies do the handwritten, marginal notes represent?

PREVENTING FLOODS: FOR BETTER OR WORSE?

Attempts to prevent floods might cause them? What is a levee? Like the flooding in New Orleans during Hurricane Katrina? I can see this in my mind.

Human interference with the stream system can worsen or even cause floods. A prime example is the failure of a dam or an artificial levee. These structures are built for flood protection. They are designed to contain floods of a certain magnitude. If a larger flood occurs, the dam or levee is overtopped. If the dam or levee fails or is washed out, the water behind it is released to become a flash flood. The bursting of a dam in 1889 on the Little Conemaugh River caused the devastating Johnstown, Pennsylvania, flood that took some 3,000 lives. A second dam failure occurred there again in 1977 and caused 77 fatalities.

—*Earth Science*, Thirteenth Edition, by Edward J. Tarbuck
and Frederick K. Lutgens

EXPLANATION   The handwritten comments demonstrate the reader's use of several thinking strategies: Predicting, monitoring, and recognizing the need to correct, relating, and picturing. Using these strategies improves comprehension and demonstrates *metacognition*—awareness and control of the reading process.

EXERCISE 2   For the following passages, answer the questions and make a conscious effort to use the six strategies as you read:

1. Predict (develop hypotheses)
2. Picture (develop images)
3. Relate (link prior knowledge with new ideas)
4. Monitor (notice ongoing comprehension)
5. Use corrective strategies (fix comprehension problems)
6. Annotate (mark the text)

Passage 1

ONCE UPON A SEPTEMBER DAY

Another meeting! One after another without coming up with a proposal that would fly.

This one took place in early September and (not surprisingly) only a few people showed up—12, to be precise. And so they talked for some days and finally came up with a plan for still another meeting, eight months hence. It was hoped this would offer sufficient time to generate interest in the matter.

They also moved the location. It was not that the September site had been unpleasant—on the contrary, the facilities were quite good—but variety in meeting places might induce more individuals to attend.

They were a relatively young group; the average age was 42. The youngest was 30 and the oldest 82 and prone to nod during long meetings. Although some were lackluster in ability, most were able and would later move to high executive positions.

They were together for 116 days, taking off only Sundays and 12 other days. And you might have guessed it: During a very hot summer they were without air conditioning. In addition to the formal sessions of the entire group, much of their work was done in committee and after hours.

There was still criticism of the final proposal. It was much too short, some argued—only 4,000 words. Four months of work and only 4,000 words! It was scarcely enough to fill a few sheets of paper. But 39 of them felt it was the best they could come up with. It was good enough to sign, which they did on the 17th day of September, 1787.

And they called their proposal the Constitution of the United States.

—From "Once Upon a September Day" by Thomas V. DiBacco,
The Los Angeles Times, September 28, 1983

1. What did you predict to be the purpose of the meeting? _____

2. Who did you picture as the attendees of the meeting? _____

3. The passage mentions that the site of the meeting place had been changed with the hope that more individuals would attend. Have you experienced this same problem (a meeting at which not too many people showed up)? What sort of incentives are used to induce people to attend meetings?

_____

_____

_____

4. Why do you suppose the meeting was continued so many times?

_____

_____

_____

5. Underline any part of the passage you found confusing or needed to reread.

6. Did you annotate as you read? Now that you know the topic, go back and circle the clues.

Passage 2

REAL LIFE CRIME SCENE INVESTIGATION

The popular television show CSI (Crime Scene Investigation) has brought the role of the crime scene investigator to the public, creating considerable interest in forensic science. Of course, crime scene investigators require very specific training with regard to crime scene protection and the identification and preservation of evidence, and not every law enforcement agency is able to support a dedicated CSI unit. A description of the crime scene unit (CSU) is provided by Michael Weisberg:

> The CSU provides support services in the form of crime processing, fingerprint identification, and forensic photography. The CSU responds to major crime scenes to detect, preserve, document, impound and collect physical evidence. The unit assists in the identification of unknown subjects, witnesses and victims involved in criminal investigations.... The CSU will work closely in conjunction with the Detective Bureau in providing assistance in follow-up investigations, as well as subject apprehension and arrest. Members of the CSU may be either sworn or non-sworn.

—*Criminal Investigation: The Art and the Science,* Sixth Edition
by Michael D. Lyman

1. Have you seen television shows that feature crime scene investigation situations? Explain how your experience or lack of it affected you as you read this passage. _____

_____

_____

_____

_____

2. What is the meaning of *forensic*? _____

_____

In what way did knowing the definition affect your understanding of this passage? _____

3. Where do you think crime scene investigators receive training?

_____

_____

4. Does the crime scene unit help to catch offenders? _____

Underline anything in the passage that supports your answer.

5. Was there anything in the passage you did not understand? Write it here:

_____

6. Did you annotate to emphasize the important details?

_____

Stage Three: Recall

Recall is your review of what you have read. Recall is self-testing and can be a silent, oral, or written recitation. When you recall, you take an additional few minutes to tell yourself what you have learned before you close the book. Poor readers tend to finish the last paragraph of an assignment, sigh with relief, and close the book without another thought. Study strategies developed by experts, however, stress the importance of a final recall or review stage. The experts emphasize that this final step improves both comprehension and memory.

As a part of monitoring your comprehension, maintain a running summary as you read. The end of an assignment is the time to give voice to this internal summary and review the material for gaps of knowledge. You can do the recall step in your head, aloud or on paper. To recall, talk to yourself and test your understanding. Pull the material together under one central idea or generalization, and then review the relevant details and commit them to memory.

BRAIN BOOSTER

Use it or lose it!

The dendrites created in our brains when we learn need tending. Although experts think they never go away completely, the synapses that connect our dendrites in neural networks have to be fired electrically to flourish. Dendrites that are not used shrink to make room and energy for others, but those we use often grow stronger. How does this apply to learning in college? Fire those synapses to keep the knowledge you've acquired. Think about what you've read, talk about it, write about it, read more, and REPEAT!

Do not neglect this last stage. From a metacognitive point of view, you are adding related ideas to existing schemata and creating new knowledge networks or "computer chips" for storage. Recall makes a significant difference in what you retain from your reading.

Learning Objective 6

Apply active recall methods after reading

How to Recall.   The recall stage of reading can be silent or voiced, organized conversation with yourself or others, or a written reorganization. What method you choose depends on the difficulty of the material or your purpose for learning. Keep in mind that the goal is self-testing. Rather than wait for the professor's inquiry, answer your own question, "What did I get from this material?"

Think About It.   What was the main point? What did you learn from each section? Do you have opinions or experiences related to this topic?

Talk About It.   Say out loud, to yourself or to someone else, what you learned from the selection. Voice your opinions, questions, and experiences.

Write About It.   If your purpose is to remember the information for the long term, for a test, perhaps, make notes on a separate sheet of paper. Use your text annotations as the basis for the notes. If your purpose is shorter term or general recall, so you can join a discussion with friends, for example, write a one- or two-sentence summary. You might also write any questions you want to discuss about the topic.

Feel free to accept or reject ideas according to your prior knowledge and the logic of the presentation. Your response is subjective, but as a critical thinker, you should base it on what you already know and what you have just found out.

EXAMPLE   Read the following passage and decide what it is about and whether you agree or disagree with the author.

> Access is a very important resource for an interest group. As we have noted, a person who makes a campaign contribution will often say something like this: "I don't want any special promise from you; all I want is the right to come and talk to you when I need to." This seemingly modest request may in fact be significant. Access is power.
>
> —Fred Harris, *America's Democracy: The Ideal and the Reality,*
> 3rd edition. Glenview, IL: Scott Foresman, 1986.

EXPLANATION What is your position on the issue of access and power? You may agree with the author's position. The message is that if you can manage to talk to a powerful political figure, you have an excellent chance of influencing decisions. Because face-to-face contact can be convincing, access probably does give power.

EXERCISE 3 Read the following passages and decide whether you agree or disagree with their messages. You are giving your *reactions* to the ideas, so there are no right or wrong answers. Think and react.

Passage 1

GENDER DIFFERENCES

Men and women differ with respect to gossip, according to Deborah Tannen in *You Just Don't Understand: Women and Men in Conversation*. It isn't that one group gossips and the other does not. It is the subjects of their talks. "When most men talk to their friends or on the phone," Tannen says, "they may discuss what's happening in business, the stock market, the soccer match, or politics. For most women, getting together and talking about their feelings and what is happening in their lives is at the heart of friendship."

Men and women differ when it comes to lecturing and listening. Experimental studies support Tannen in finding that "men are more comfortable than women in giving information and opinions and speaking in an authoritative way to a group, whereas women are more comfortable than men in supporting others."

—*You Just Don't Understand: Women and Men in Conversation*
by Deborah Tannen

1. What is the message? _____

_____

2. Why do you agree or disagree with these assertions of gender differences on

gossip, lecturing, and listening?

(a) Gossip? _____

(b) Lecturing? _____

(c) Listening? _____

Passage 2

SEATBELT VIOLATION ARREST

By an unusual 5–4 split, with Justice David Souter writing the majority opinion, the Supreme Court said Fourth Amendment protection against unreasonable seizures does not cover Gail Atwater, who was ordered out of her pickup in 1997 for not using seatbelts for herself and her young children.

Atwater said she had let her daughter, 5, and son, 3, out of their belts as they were driving in Lago Vista so that they could better look for a toy that had dropped outside of the truck.

Bart Turek, the arresting officer, said Atwater told him she also did not have her license and insurance information, as required by Texas law, because her purse had been stolen the day before.

Turek cuffed Atwater, put her in a squad car and took her to jail, where she was forced to remove her shoes and empty her pockets and a "mug shot" was taken. Souter acknowledged that the officer engaged in "gratuitous humiliations." However, he said the law has long allowed police to arrest people if they believe a crime is being committed, no matter how small.

—From Joan Biskupic, "High Court Upholds Mom's Arrest in Seatbelt Violation: Cuffs, Jail Allowed in Minor Offenses," *USA Today*, April 25, 2001, p. A.01. Reprinted with permission.

1. What is the message? _____

    _____

    _____

2. Do you agree with the ruling? Why or why not? _____

3. Do you think that the manner in which the arresting officer treated the

    mother was appropriate? Explain your answer. _____

    _____

    _____

    _____

ASSESS YOUR PROGRESS AS A LEARNER

This textbook creates an artificial environment for you to learn about your own reading. Normally after reading, you do not answer ten comprehension questions and ten vocabulary questions. You read, reflect, and move on. In this book, however, the questions are provided to help you monitor your thinking. To improve your skills, reflect seriously on what you are getting right and what you are getting wrong. Making a good homework or classwork grade is part of the process, but it is not the real purpose. Understanding and improving are the goals, and they require your active participation as a learner. Assume responsibility for your own improvement.

Levels of Reading Comprehension

In order to give you more insight into your strengths and weaknesses, the comprehension questions at the end of each long reading selection in this text are labeled *main idea, detail,* and *inference.* These question types represent different levels of sophistication in reading that can be ranked and defined as follows.

   1. Literal—What did the author say? These are detail questions about the facts, and the answers are clearly stated within the material. This is the beginning level of reading comprehension, the least sophisticated level. You might be able to answer detail questions and still not understand the overall meaning of the passage.

   Example: Captain Thomas Hunt came to Plymouth Bay to capture Indians for the slave market. (True or False)

PERSONAL FEEDBACK 2

Name _____

1. Why do you think students are reluctant to recall (Stage 3) what they have read?

   _____

2. What have you learned in this chapter that is positive about your reading habits?

   _____

   _____

3. What three immediate changes would you suggest for your own reading improvement?

   (a) _____

   (b) _____

   (c) _____

   Tear out and submit to your instructor.

2. Interpretive—*What did the author mean by what was said?* These are main idea and inference questions. In order to answer, you must interpret the facts along with the author's attitude, using implied meaning to make assumptions and draw conclusions. At this level, you are considering both what is stated and what is unstated in order to figure out what the author is trying to say.

Example: The author suggests that Squanto's Pawtuxet Indian tribe valued all of the following except (a) bravery, (b) endurance, (c) wealth, or (d) strength.

3. Applied—*How does the author's message apply to other situations?* These are questions that call for reaction, reflection, and critical thinking. This is the highest level of sophistication and involves analyzing, synthesizing, and evaluating. You are putting together what was said with what was meant and applying it to new situations and experiences. You are attempting to make wider use of what you have just learned.

Example: Explain how the cultural values, goals, and ethics of the Native Americans as illustrated by Squanto in his youth differed from those of the European settlers and thus caused conflict.

Use the questions in this book as diagnostic information. What do your responses tell you about yourself? What kinds of questions do you always answer correctly? What do your errors tell you about your reading? Learn from your mistakes and begin to categorize your own reading strengths and weaknesses. Throughout the course, refer back to previous work as a reference for your own development. Keeping records and reflecting on your own learning are essential parts of your improvement plan.

SUMMARY POINTS

1 What are the three stages of good reading? (page 32)

Stage 1: Before reading, preview to find out what the material is about.
Stage 2: During reading, integrate existing knowledge with the new information.
Stage 3: After reading, actively recall what you have learned.

2 What should I read during a preview? (page 33)

Read the introductory material, learning questions, title, headings and sub-headings, special print, visual aids, and concluding summary or review.

3 What is a schema and why is it important? (page 34)

A schema is the skeleton of knowledge in your mind on a particular subject. Usually, readers have several schemata surrounding a topic. They are important because what we already know allows us to relate and link to the new material, thus understanding and remembering it better.

4 What is *metacognition* and why is it important? (page 36)

Metacognition is the awareness and control of the reading and thinking process. It is important because of the control it provides. Awareness of comprehension problems enables the reader to do something about them, and awareness of good comprehension causes readers to repeat successful methods.

5 How can I integrate existing knowledge with the new information? (page 36)

Apply the six thinking strategies that good readers use: predict, picture, relate, monitor your understanding, correct gaps in understanding, and annotate the text.

6 What active recall methods will help me remember the material? (page 43)

Think about it. Talk about it. Write about it.

COLLABORATIVE   PROBLEM SOLVING

Form a five-member group and select one of the following activities. Brainstorm and then outline your major points. Choose a member to present the group findings to the class.

➤ Make a list of five questions about your college at the literal level.

➤ Make a list of five questions about your college at the interpretive level.

➤ Make a list of five questions about your college at the applied level.

➤ Explain how recalling, connecting, and reacting help you remember what you have read.

MyReadingLab

MyReadingLab (MRL) www.myreadinglab.com

➤ For support in meeting this chapter's objectives, log in to **www.myreadinglab.com** and select "Active Reading Strategies" and "Reading Textbooks."

THE READING WORKSHOP

If reading a novel, biography, or other book is part of your course experience, refer to The Reading Workshop: Thinking, Talking, and Writing about Books in Appendix 5 for suggestions.

SELECTION 1 Environmental Science

"Our choices at all levels—individual, community, corporate and government—affect nature. And they affect us."

—David Suzuki

According to the New York State Department of Environmental Conservation, nearly 2.5 billion bottles of water a year are sold in that state. That's enough to reach the moon if they were stacked end to end. The petroleum used to make these bottles equals enough gasoline to fuel 120,000 automobiles for a year. Nationally, only 10% of plastic water bottles are recycled. Of course, we use many other plastic products every day, too—car bodies, shoes, disposable cups, fast-food containers, grocery bags—to name just a few. What happens to these items when we're through with them? What might be done to reduce plastic waste?

THINKING BEFORE READING

Preview the selection for clues to content. What do you already know about recycling plastic items? Activate your prior knowledge. Anticipate the author's ideas and your purpose for reading. Think!

What plastic items do you use regularly?

Do you recycle any of the plastic materials you use? Why or why not?

What are the benefits of recycling plastic?

I'll read this to find out _____

_____

VOCABULARY PREVIEW

Are you familiar with these words?

memorable	disposable	recycling	identification	surrounded
voluntary	economical	density	manufacturers	consumers

Does *recycling* always mean melting and making something new?

Is something *economical* if it is inexpensive?

Are you a *consumer* of plastic?

Your instructor may choose to give a true-false vocabulary review before or after reading.

THINKING DURING READING

As you read, use the six thinking strategies of a good reader: predict, picture, relate, monitor, correct, and annotate.

Reader's TIP — Reading and Studying Science

- Master a concept by explaining it in your own words.
- Draw your own scientific models and diagram the processes to reinforce learning them.
- Use illustrations as a reading and review tool before exams.
- Use chapter summaries as study checklists to be sure you have reviewed all the chapter material.
- Think like a scientist at the textbook website by participating in virtual research activities.
- Use mnemonics to memorize. For example—**M**any **P**eople **F**ind **P**arachuting **A**larming—to remember the five kingdoms, which are Monera, Protista, Fungi, Plantae, and Animalia.
- Know the theories you are applying in the lab and their significance.
- Blend lecture, lab, and textbook notes.

PLASTICS

The 1967 film *The Graduate* was filled with unforgettable lines. One of the most memorable was advice offered to a young Dustin Hoffman, who was trying to decide what to do with his life.

Why would someone advise plastics as a future career in 1967?

Adult offering advice: I just want to say one word to you—just one word—

5 Hoffman: Yes sir.

Adult offering advice: Are you listening?

Hoffman: Yes sir, I am.

Adult offering advice: Plastics.

Today we're surrounded by plastics. We couldn't live without them. And they're so cheap
10 we use them to make disposable products—water bottles, picnic cups, grocery bags, milk jugs—the list goes on and on. We throw away so much plastic that many cities have recycling programs. But recycling plastic isn't as simple as just melting it down and forming it into something new. There are many *types* of plastics. You can't simply mix one with another and expect to get something usable.

15 That's why the Society of the Plastics Industry developed plastic identification codes. Most plastic containers fall into one of six categories. Each category has a name and a number. It's the number that shows up on containers, surrounded by three arrows forming a triangle. In most cases you'll find it near the bottom center of a container. Using identification codes was voluntary when they were first introduced. But today most states
20 require it. The codes make it *much* easier to sort plastics.

Does my state require it?

01 PET   02 PE-HD   03 PVC   04 PE-LD   05 PP   06 PS   07 O

The seven different identification codes for plastics. Code seven is used when nothing else fits.

But just because plastics are sorted properly doesn't mean they can be recycled. Some types are economical to recycle. Others aren't. Plastic number one—polyethylene terephthalate—is easy to recycle. Water and soda bottles are commonly made from it. Plastic number two—high density polyethylene—is also pretty good. It's found in milk and
25   laundry detergent jugs, and it's often recycled into plastic lumber and made into decks or park benches.

Which types can I recycle?

Plastic number five—polypropylene—isn't so easy to recycle. It's used for yogurt and margarine tubs because it handles grease and chemicals so well. Disposable dishes are made of plastic number six—polystyrene. It's also used to make Styrofoam products like
30   packing peanuts and insulated cups. Some cities recycle number one and two plastics, but they ask residents to sort out and throw away the other numbers because there's no recycler the city can sell them to. They go to the landfill with all the other waste. Plastic manufacturers and consumers are aware that some plastics are harder to recycle than others, but solving the problem's not as easy as using only recyclable plastics. Different
35   plastics have different properties. The plastic used to make a soda bottle may not be good for making forks and knives.

Is this a promising field for today's college graduates?

So engineers keep looking for improved plastics—plastics that do their job and aren't bad for the environment. Today, we might want to give not one, but two words of advice to the graduate: *better* plastics.

(490 words)

—"Plastics" from Houston Public Radio's *Engines of Our Ingenuity*
by E. Andrew Boyd. Reprinted with the permission of E. Andrew Boyd.

The Product Identification Code was introduced by the Society of the Plastics Industry, Inc. which provides a uniform system for the identification of different polymer types and helps recycling companies to separate different plastics for reprocessing. Manufacturers of plastic products are required to use PIC labels in some countries/regions and can voluntarily mark their products with the PIC where there are no requirements. Consumers can identify the plastic types based on the codes usually found at the base or at the side of the plastic products, including food/chemical packaging and containers. The PIC is usually not present on packaging films, as it is not practical to collect and recycle most of this type of waste.

Plastic Identification Code	Type of Plastic Polymer	Properties	Common Packaging Applications
♳ 01 PET	Polyethylene terephthalate (PET, PETE)	Clarity, strength, toughness, barrier to gas and moisture	Soft drink, water, and salad dressing bottles; peanut butter and jam jars
♴ 02 PE-HD	High-density polyethylene (HDPE)	Stiffness, strength, toughness, resistance to moisture, permeability to gas	Water pipes, hula hoop rings, five-gallon buckets, milk, juice, and water bottles; the occasional shampoo/toiletry bottle
♵ 03 PVC	Polyvinyl chloride (PVC)	Versatility, ease of blending, strength, toughness	Blister packaging for non-food items; cling films for non-food use. Not used for food packaging as the plasticisers needed to make natively rigid PVC flexible are usually toxic. Non-packaging uses are electrical cable insulation, rigid piping, vinyl records.
♶ 04 PE-LD	Low-density polyethylene (LDPE)	Ease of processing, strength, toughness, flexibility, ease of sealing, barrier to moisture	Frozen food bags; squeezable bottles, e.g., honey, mustard; cling films; flexible container lids
♷ 05 PP	Polypropylene (PP)	Strength; toughness; resistance to heat, chemicals, grease, and oil; versatile; barrier to moisture	Reusable microwaveable ware, kitchenware, yogurt containers, margarine tubs, microwaveable disposable take-away containers, disposable cups, plates
♸ 06 PS	Polystyrene (PS)	Versatility, clarity, easily formed	Egg cartons; packing peanuts; disposable cups, plates, trays and cutlery; disposable take-away containers
♹ 07 O	Other (often polycarbonate or ABS)	Dependent on polymers or combination of polymers	Beverage bottles; baby milk bottles; non-packaging uses for polycarbonate: compact discs; "unbreakable" glazing; electronic apparatus housings

Based on resin identification codes developed by the Society of the plastics Industry, 1988.

THINKING AND WRITING AFTER READING

RECALL Self-test your understanding.

Your instructor may choose to give you a true-false comprehension review.

REACT Does this article convince me that recycling plastic items is good practice? Why or why not? _____

_____

REFLECT How do your habits contribute to helping or harming the environment?

_____

THINKING CRITICALLY There are costs involved in recycling efforts. Are you willing to pay extra for your city to recycle the plastic items you discard? Why or why not?

_____

THINK AND WRITE Now that you have read the article and the chart, examine the list of plastic items that you made before reading and add to it any materials you regularly use that you missed. Next, list the items you are willing to recycle or even do without. _____

_____

EXTENDED WRITING Using the lists you made above write an article that could be published in your college newspaper. First, describe the kinds of materials that you and other students use frequently. Next, suggest ways recycling could be encouraged on your campus or in your city.

Interpret THE QUOTE

Go back to the beginning of the selection and read the opening quote again. What choices do individuals, communities, corporations, and governments make that affect the environment?

SELECTION 1

Name —————————————————

Date —————————————————

COMPREHENSION QUESTIONS

Answer the following with *a, b, c,* or *d,* or fill in the blank. In order to help you analyze your strengths and weaknesses, the question types are indicated.

Main Idea ———— 1. The best statement of the main idea of this selection is

   a. A career in developing different plastics is a promising choice for a college graduate.
   b. People should recycle plastic waste to better protect the environment.
   c. There are seven identification codes for plastics.
   d. Plastic identification codes allow for more effective recycling efforts.

Detail ———— 2. Soft drink bottles are made of this type of plastic.

   a. Polyethylene terephthalate
   b. Polyvinyl chloride
   c. Low-density polyethylene
   d. Polystyrene

Detail ———— 3. According to the article and chart, which of the following items is most difficult to recycle?

   a. Milk jugs
   b. Salad dressing bottles
   c. Disposable dishes
   d. Water pipes

Inference ———— 4. We can infer from the article that there are fewer recyclers for some plastic items because ——————.

   a. the cost of recycling them is too high to be economical
   b. not enough people are interested in recycling those items
   c. citizens have not requested that their cities begin recycling those items
   d. people do not use many of those items

Main Idea ———— 5. Which of the following best describes the topic of this article?

   a. Plastics
   b. Plastic identification codes
   c. Reasons to recycle plastic items
   d. Plastic recycling programs

Detail ———— 6. The chart explains that this plastic is toxic.

   a. HDPE
   b. LDPE
   c. PET
   d. PVC

Inference _____ 7. We can infer from the selection that _____.

       a. only major cities can afford to have recycling programs
       b. some cities sponsor recycling programs
       c. all cities in the U.S. are required to have recycling programs
       d. cities should sponsor recycling programs

Answer the following with *T*, (true) or *F* (false).

Inference _____ 8. One should not store water in a container made of polyvinyl chloride.

Detail _____ 9. According to the article, most states now require the use of identification codes on plastic items.

Detail _____ 10. The plastic identification codes were developed by the U.S. government.

VOCABULARY

Answer the following with *a, b, c,* or *d* for the word or phrase that best defines the boldface word used in the selection. The number in parentheses indicates the line of the passage in which the word appears. In addition to the context clues, use a dictionary to more precisely define the technical terms.

_____ 1. "most **memorable** advice" (1–2)

    a. valuable
    b. unforgettable
    c. surprising
    d. often heard

_____ 2. "make **disposable** products" (10)

    a. throw-away
    b. unusable
    c. inexpensive
    d. practical

_____ 3. "**recycling** programs" (11–12)

    a. natural
    b. environmental
    c. cleaning
    d. treatment for further use

_____ 4. "**identification** codes" (15)

    a. legal
    b. pass
    c. labeling
    d. restricted

_____ 5. "**surrounded** by three arrows" (17)

    a. marked
    b. enclosed
    c. underlined
    d. defined

_____ 6. "using codes was **voluntary**" (19)

    a. permissible
    b. preferable
    c. impossible
    d. not required

_____ 7. "**economical** to recycle" (22)

    a. cost effective
    b. expensive
    c. easy
    d. frivolous

_____ 8. "high **density** polyethylene" (24)

    a. toxicity
    b. compact
    c. frequency
    d. power

_____ 9. "plastic **manufacturers**" (33)

    a. materials
    b. handlers
    c. makers
    d. engineers

_____ 10. "**consumers** are aware" (33)

    a. composers
    b. owners
    c. sellers
    d. users

Your instructor may choose to give a true-false vocabulary review.

ASSESS YOUR LEARNING

Review questions that you did not understand, found confusing, or answered incorrectly. Seek clarification. Indicate beside each item the source of your confusion and notice the question type. Make notes beside confusing vocabulary items to help you remember them. Use your textbook as a learning tool.

SELECTION 2 Science

Refer to the
Reader's **TIP**
for **Science** on
page 49.

"... We have very little control over external forces such as tornadoes, earthquakes, floods, disasters, illness, and pain. What really matters is the internal force. How do I respond to those disasters?"

—Leo Buscaglia

In 2005 Hurricane Katrina hit the Gulf Coast and New Orleans with devastating results. Damage grew into the billions of dollars. People lost family, homes, businesses, jobs, possessions, and security. Survivors were scattered around the nation, and some bravely returned to rebuild. Was Katrina the worst disaster to hit the Gulf? The answer is no. In 1900 Galveston suffered the destruction of a similar storm. As in the case of Katrina, several factors came together to intensify the horror of the storm's rage.

THINKING BEFORE READING

Preview the selection for clues to content. Activate your schema, and anticipate what you will learn.

Have you experienced a hurricane, tornado, flood, or other natural disaster?

When is hurricane season?

How does television help save lives in a natural disaster?

I'll read this to find out_____.

VOCABULARY PREVIEW

Are you familiar with these words?

fatalities	barrier island	amiss	flocked	gawk
imminent	plummeted	flotsam	dredged	sediment

Is it polite to *gawk* at another person?

Is there a difference between *imminent* and *impending*?

Your instructor may choose to give a true-false vocabulary review before or after reading.

THINKING DURING READING

As you read, use the six thinking strategies of a good reader: predict, picture, relate, monitor, correct, and annotate. Answer the questions in the margins.

THE GALVESTON DISASTER

Why was this storm considered the United States' greatest natural disaster?

5

The greatest natural disaster to strike the United States was the tropical cyclone that hit Galveston, Texas, on the night of 8 September 1900. The combination of high wind, great waves, and storm surge killed about 8,000 people—more than the Johnstown Flood, the San Francisco Earthquake, the 1938 New England Hurricane, and the Great Chicago Fire combined. Indeed this one event accounts for more than a third of all tropical storm- or hurricane-related fatalities ever recorded in the United States.

Describe the geography of Galveston Island.

10   In 1900 Galveston, home to about 37,000 people, was one of the most important cotton markets in America. The island city was (and is) located at the eastern end of Galveston Island, a low sand barrier island off the Texas coast about 48 kilometers (30 miles) long and 3.2 kilometers (2 miles) wide. When the hurricane struck, the highest point in Galveston was only 2.7 meters (8.7 feet) above sea level.

Why did Dr. Isaac Cline think something was wrong?

15   Unlike today, there were no geosynchronous satellites, ship-to-shore radios, or networks of weather forecasters to warn of the coming storm. Forecasting was done by experience and hunch, and few were better guessers than Dr. Isaac Cline, chief of the U.S. Weather Bureau's Galveston station. On the evening of 7 September, as many of Galveston's residents were settling down to dinner, Cline became increasingly concerned about the 26-kilometer- (16-mile-) per-hour northerly wind that had blown steadily all day. Something was amiss—the wind was from the wrong direction, and high clouds at sunset were moving in nearly the opposite way, from the southeast. By midnight the wind had

20   shifted toward the northeast and had grown to about 60 kilometers (50 miles) per hour. At first light residents flocked to the shore to gawk at the monstrous waves crashing on the beaches. Then the water began to rise. Cline sensed a hurricane was imminent and believed he knew what was going to happen next, but as he spread emergency warnings to evacuate the island, a steamship was torn from its moorings and smashed through the

25   three bridges connecting the island to the mainland. There would be no escape.

What is a storm surge?

The atmospheric pressure plummeted and the wind speed increased as the storm approached and intensified. The tropical cyclone's low pressure drew the ocean into a broad mound, and the winds drove this mound ashore—a phenomenon known as a storm surge. As misfortune would have it, the surge arrived at a time of high tide. Waters from the Gulf

30   of Mexico and Galveston Bay rose to meet each other. Residents scrambled to the second, third, or fourth stories of buildings to avoid the rising water. Winds that reached 200 kilometers (125 miles) per hour collapsed the structures, freeing masses of flotsam that hammered anyone outside. By the afternoon of 8 September, buildings crumbled and people were battered by debris and drowned. At 8:30 that evening, the water stood 3.4 meters (11 feet)

35   above Galveston Island's highest point. People died in the thousands, clinging to heaving rafts of wreckage and each other. Property damage was extraordinary.

Galveston was rebuilt. In 1902 residents began to construct a 5-meter- (16-foot-) thick, 5.2-meter- (17-foot-) high seawall covering 3 miles of oceanfront. (The seawall today extends for 16 kilometers, or 10 miles.) They also dredged enough sediment from

40   Galveston Bay to raise the island 2.5 meters (8 feet).

How was Galveston changed to protect itself from future hurricanes?

Between 80% and 90% of the residents of hurricane-prone areas have not experienced a major hurricane. The smaller storms they have seen often leave them with the false impression of a hurricane's true potential for damage. Galveston proves otherwise.

(591 words)

—From *Oceanography*, 5th ed. by Tim Garrison. © 2005 Brooks/Cole, part of Cengage Learning, Inc. Reproduced by permission. www.cengage.com/permissions

THINKING AND WRITING AFTER READING

RECALL   Self-test your understanding.

Your instructor may choose to give you a true-false comprehension review.

REACT   What factors combined to make the Galveston storm so deadly? _____
_____

REFLECT   How can the experiences of Galveston be applied today in hurricane-prone areas? _____
_____

THINKING CRITICALLY   Compare the disaster of Galveston to the effects of Katrina or another major hurricane. _____
_____

THINK AND WRITE   How would you respond to a natural disaster where you live in order to save your life and the lives of others? _____
_____

EXTENDED WRITING   In an essay, elaborate on the factors from the list you created above that contributed to the severity of this storm's damage. Then, speculate on how the effects of such a storm might be similar or different if it were to occur today. If you are familiar with Hurricane Ike, which struck Galveston in 2008, use your knowledge of that storm to further support your points.

Interpret THE QUOTE

Now that you have finished reading the selection "The Galveston Disaster," go back to the beginning of the selection and read the opening quote again. Do we have any control over disasters such as earthquakes and floods? On a separate sheet of paper, list five reasons why you believe we do or do not have control during major disasters, and list five ways that we can appropriately respond to one.

Name ——————————————————

Date ——————————————————

COMPREHENSION QUESTIONS

Answer the following with *a, b, c,* or *d,* or fill in the blank. In order to help you analyze your strengths and weaknesses, the question types are indicated.

Main Idea ——————— 1. The best statement of the main idea of this selection is:

    a. Galveston lacked an evacuation plan that could have saved thousands.

    b. A seawall could have saved the people of Galveston from the disaster of 1900.

    c. The residents of Galveston did not understand the potential force of a major hurricane.

    d. The Galveston storm was a huge disaster because of a combination of circumstances.

Detail ——————— 2. The percentage of Galveston's population killed in the tropical cyclone disaster of 1900 was approximately

    a. 100%.

    b. 50%.

    c. 20%.

    d. 10%.

Inference ——————— 3. The reader can conclude that some people survived the disaster by

    a. running to higher ground.

    b. staying on the first floor of their homes.

    c. floating.

    d. seeking government-provided shelter in small elementary schools.

Inference ——————— 4. The author implies that Dr. Isaac Cline feared an unusual disaster because

    a. the waves were high on September 7.

    b. the winds were 16 miles per hour.

    c. the clouds were higher than usual at sunset.

    d. the water level, wind direction, and cloud direction changed from the usual.

Detail ——————— 5. A storm surge is

    a. a violent wind.

    b. a wave of water.

    c. a mound of low pressure.

    d. the violent meeting of water from two sources.

Detail ——————— 6. In the 1902 rebuilding of Galveston, residents

    a. built a protective seawall between Galveston Island and the mainland.

    b. deepened Galveston Bay to manage the tides.

    c. raised the land level of Galveston.

    d. raised the sea level of Galveston Island.

Inference _____ 7. The reader can conclude that most people in the Galveston disaster were killed by

    a. water.
    b. wind.
    c. floating wreckage.
    d. low pressure.

Answer the following with *T* (true) or *F* (false).

Inference _____ 8. The reader can conclude that low tide would have decreased the height of the storm surge.

Detail _____ 9. The island evacuation routes were destroyed by a steamship.

Inference _____ 10. The reader can conclude that the highest point in Galveston is now 20.7 feet above sea level.

VOCABULARY

Answer the following with *a, b, c,* or *d* for the word or phrase that best defines the boldface word used in the selection. The number in parentheses indicates the line of the passage in which the word appears.

_____ 1. "hurricane-related **fatalities**" (6)

    a. injuries
    b. deaths
    c. property destruction
    d. warnings

_____ 2. "**barrier island**" (9)

    a. underwater
    b. surface
    c. barricade
    d. rocky

_____ 3. "Something was **amiss**" (18)

    a. right
    b. windy
    c. crazy
    d. wrong

_____ 4. "residents **flocked**" (21)

    a. flew
    b. gathered
    c. left
    d. boycotted

_____ 5. "**gawk** at the monstrous waves" (21)

    a. surf
    b. escape
    c. stop
    d. stare

_____ 6. "a hurricane was **imminent**" (22)

    a. almost over
    b. miles away
    c. about to happen
    d. gone

_____ 7. "atmospheric pressure **plummeted**" (26)

    a. increased gradually
    b. increased quickly
    c. decreased gradually
    d. decreased quickly

_____ 8. "masses of **flotsam**" (32)

    a. houses
    b. wreckage
    c. boats
    d. people

_____ 9. "They also **dredged**" (39)

    a. drained
    b. filled
    c. dried
    d. detoured

_____ 10. "enough **sediment**" (39)

    a. fishes
    b. bones
    c. deposits
    d. water

Your instructor may choose to give a true-false vocabulary review.

ASSESS YOUR LEARNING

Review confusing questions, seek clarification, and make notes in your text to help you remember new information and vocabulary.

SELECTION 3 ⚖ Criminal Justice

"The good of the people is the chief law."

—Cicero (106–43 BCE)

Psychological theories of criminal behavior focus on personality traits and behavior. Crime-control methods based on psychological views center on treating individuals with appropriate therapy to overcome their criminal tendencies. These methods rely on some measure of "dangerousness," or how likely the person is to do harm. Several important issues surround such psychological views. Should a mentally ill person be treated by the courts in the same way that a sane person is treated? What determines whether or not a person is insane? Can a mentally ill person who commits a crime be "cured" so that he or she can function safely in normal society?

THINKING BEFORE READING

Preview the selection for clues to content. Activate your schema, and anticipate what you will learn.

Have you heard news stories about people who have committed crimes and claimed that they were insane at the time?

What is the definition of *insanity*?

Why might society hesitate to punish mentally ill offenders in the same way that it punishes sane individuals?

This selection will probably tell me _____.

VOCABULARY PREVIEW

Are you familiar with these words and figures of speech?

abruptly	incarceration	took a dive	schizophrenia	severity
competent	acquittal	alluded	surmised	psychosis

Is there a difference between *surmised* and *inferred*?

Do you see a familiar word part in *psychosis* that might hint at the meaning?

Your instructor may choose to give a true-false vocabulary review before or after reading.

THINKING DURING READING

As you read, use the six thinking strategies of a good reader: predict, picture, relate, monitor, correct, and annotate. Answer the questions in the margins.

WAS ERIC CLARK INSANE OR JUST TROUBLED?

Have you had an experience so alarming that it seemed unreal?

The phone roused Terry Clark from sleep. She eyed the clock: 5 A.M. Who could be calling at this hour?

"Flagstaff Police Department," a voice announced abruptly. The next minutes and hours would pass like a slow-moving horror film where the evil emerges bit by bit.

Reader's TIP — Reading and Studying Criminal Justice

- Identify criminal acts in legal terms. Make lists to commit to memory.
- Distinguish between the types of crimes and categories of criminals. Use charts to form groups.
- Know the legal behaviors and responsibilities required for making an arrest and gathering evidence. Make timelines.
- Understand the processes of the courts and the sequencing of legal actions. Create a flowchart for a visual display.
- Relate possible legal decisions and police actions to the balance of police powers and democratic freedoms.

((•• Scan this QR code to hear this reading.

5   At first, investigators told her only that a policeman had been shot. She heard a name, Officer Jeff Moritz. He was called to the neighborhood after residents reported a pickup circling round and round, blaring loud music.

Her son Gentry's pickup sat abandoned—driver's-side door flung open, keys in the ignition, a Dr. Dre CD in the player—next to the sidewalk where the police officer had

10   died.

Her son was the prime suspect. Not Gentry, though, who had been at home in bed, safe. Her other son, Eric. The one who had been a star football player and a good student with dreams.

The one who just two months earlier had called his mother and father aliens.

SLAYING SHOCKED TOWN

15   What happened in those early morning hours of June 21, 2000, left an entire town in shock. The victim was the only police officer ever killed in the line of duty in this mountain community north of Phoenix.

Whose side would the town probably take?

He was a caring cop who cut firewood for the handicapped and bought burgers for hungry transients he arrested. He was a husband and father with one young son and a

20   second on the way.

The accused was a 17-year-old high school senior who had a history of marijuana use and had been arrested two months earlier for drunken driving and drug possession. Police had found two dozen hits of LSD in his car.

A portrait quickly emerged of a drug-crazed teen with no regard for life. But as the

25   facts slowly surfaced so did a different picture of Eric Michael Clark—that of a decent boy from a stable family who had descended into schizophrenia.

With this revelation came a question: How do you measure justice when a killer is a mentally ill kid?

What was the verdict?

It took three years for Eric Clark to be found competent to stand trial. His lawyers

30   pushed for a verdict of "guilty except insane," meaning incarceration in a psychiatric facility. Instead, a judge found him guilty of first-degree, intentional murder and sentenced him to life in prison, where treatment isn't assured.

What were the legal issues in the U.S. Supreme Court case?

On Wednesday, the U.S. Supreme Court is scheduled to take up the case of *Clark v. Arizona* and the issue of just how difficult states can make it for criminal defendants to

35   prove insanity.

It's the first time the court has dealt with a direct constitutional challenge to the insanity defense since lawmakers around the country imposed new restrictions following John Hinckley's acquittal by reason of insanity in the 1981 shooting of President Reagan.

Eric Clark leaving the Coconino County Courthouse in Arizona prior to sentencing.

"When is it just to punish, or not?" says Richard Bonnie, director of the Institute of
40   Law, Psychiatry and Public Policy at the University of Virginia. "There are some cases where
a person was so mentally disturbed at the time of the offense that it would be inhumane
and morally objectionable to convict and punish them."

SIGNPOSTS OF MENTAL ILLNESS

Looking back now, Terry Clark remembers things, little things, and wonders when it all
started.

What were the signs
of mental illness?

45   Eric was a gifted athlete who played soccer, baseball, basketball, football. As a running back at Flagstaff High, he was one of the young stars selected to play varsity and
dreamed of becoming a professional athlete. Then he lost interest in sports.

He had been popular—a homecoming court nominee—but his friends quit calling.
His grades, usually As and Bs, took a dive.

50   On June 21, 1999, Terry and her husband, Dave, had their son admitted to Aspen Hill,
a local mental health facility. He'd abandoned his car on a road.

At Aspen Hill, Eric tested positive for marijuana, and Terry wondered whether drugs
had triggered his behavior. But doctors alluded to something else—the possibility of schizophrenia. With no mental illness on either side of the family. Terry pushed that idea aside.

55   Eric seemed to improve and she had him discharged after only three days. "He's getting better," Terry convinced herself. He got worse.

That fall, Eric quit school. He became obsessed with Y2K, took his dad's debit card
and charged $1,700 worth of survival gear. He wore layers upon layers of clothing and
carried his possessions in a garbage bag.

60   When January 1, 2000, came and went, Eric's mood improved. He went back to high
school. "He's getting better," Terry thought again—until Eric started mentioning "them."

That April, Eric suddenly referred to her as an alien. Eric called his father an alien, too.
"If you'd go get some tools," he told them matter-of-factly, "I'd show you."

Terry now believed the doctors were right about schizophrenia. She was relieved
65   when, that same month, Eric was arrested on drunken driving and drug charges; she
thought that would lead to getting help. But authorities decided to postpone prosecution
until Eric turned 18 later in the year.

She and Dave searched for counselors, but Eric refused to go. Terry left messages at treatment facilities that were never returned.

70   On June 19, 2000, Eric called his mother an alien again. "How would you like to be me," he said, "and never know who your real mother is?"

Terry contacted her lawyer and begged him to convince the county to pursue the drug charges. Prosecutors still wanted to wait until Eric was an adult, so he'd face longer prison time if convicted.

INTENT OR INSANITY?

75   Investigators surmise that sometime after 1:30 A.M. on June 21, 2000, Eric made his way home, sneaked into his brother Gentry's bedroom, took his keys and left in Gentry's truck.

What happened after that, and why, no one can know for certain; Eric never talked about the events of that morning.

At the 2003 trial, prosecutors and defense attorneys agreed that Eric suffered from
80   paranoid schizophrenia and was mentally ill. But legal insanity is another matter; Arizona law spells out its limited use as a defense.

What are the arguments for the prosecution?

"A person may be found guilty except insane if, at the time of the commission of the criminal act, the person was afflicted with a mental disease or defect of such severity that the person did not know the criminal act was wrong," the law states.

85   The Prosecutor, Assistant Attorney General David Powell, argued Eric did know. "Officer Moritz walked into . . . an ice-cold ambush," he said at trial.

What are the arguments for the defense?

Defense lawyers insisted Eric's psychosis was so severe he was incapable of hatching such a plan.

They noted that two months after the shooting, Eric called his parents from jail and
90   told them Flagstaff was a "platinum city" inhabited by 50,000 aliens. Before hanging up, he added: "The only thing that will stop aliens are bullets."

In his appeal to the U.S. Supreme Court, lawyer David Goldberg asserts that Arizona law is so restrictive that it violates a mentally ill defendant's right to a fair trial.

For one, he says, Arizona law prohibited the trial court from considering Eric's mental
95   illness in weighing whether he intentionally killed the police officer. Testimony about his mental illness was not permitted until the second phase of the two-part trial.

Goldberg also argues that Arizona's right-wrong test is too narrow in determining legal insanity. Eric might have known that killing was wrong in the abstract, Goldberg says, but if he believed Moritz was an alien, "he didn't understand the nature of what he was doing."

100   The Supreme Court's decision, expected later this year, could also mean a retrial for Eric Clark, something the Moritz family would see as unjust.

"An angry young man who sets out to kill a cop, or anybody else, ought to be locked up for the rest of his life," says the victim's father, Dan Moritz, a psychologist who questions whether Clark actually is a paranoid schizophrenic.

105   For the Clarks, a new trial would mean a chance for their son to receive psychiatric care.

"Lock him up for his crime," Terry Clark says, "but treat him for his mental illness, please. Eric didn't choose to be mentally ill. It chose him."

(1,361 words)

—Pauline Arrillaga, "Was Eric Clark Insane or Just Troubled?" The Associated Press, April 15, 2006. Copyright © 2006 by The Associated Press. All rights reserved. Reprinted with permission.

Author's note: Eric Clark's conviction was upheld by the U.S. Supreme Court.

THINKING AND WRITING AFTER READING

RECALL   Self-test your understanding.

Your instructor may choose to give you a true-false comprehension review.

REACT Do you agree more strongly with Eric Clark's mother or with Officer Moritz's family? Why? _____

_____

_____

REFLECT Have you seen a movie or TV show about people who have a mental illness? Do you know anyone with a mental illness? What kind of therapy or treatment did they receive? Was it successful? _____

_____

_____

THINK CRITICALLY If you had been on the jury in Eric Clark's trial, how do you think you would have decided? _____

_____

_____

THINK AND WRITE Imagine that you are either the lawyer defending Eric Clark or the one prosecuting him. Write the main arguments you would present to support your case._____

_____

_____

EXTENDED WRITING Develop the main arguments you listed above into a persuasive essay. Your purpose is to convince a jury that Eric Clark is either guilty or not guilty of first-degree murder. Use the facts of this case as presented in the article as you present your case.

Interpret THE QUOTE

Now that you have finished reading the selection, "Was Eric Clark Insane or Just Troubled?" go back to the beginning of the selection and read the opening quote again. How is the "good of the people" best served? By giving harsh sentences that do not allow for treatment of mentally ill criminals or by giving sentences that do allow for treatment? Explain your answer on a separate sheet of paper.

Name —————————————————

Date —————————————————

COMPREHENSION QUESTIONS

Answer the following with *a*, *b*, *c*, or *d*, or fill in the blank. In order to help you analyze your strengths and weaknesses, the question types are indicated.

Main Idea ———— 1. The best statement of the main idea of this selection is
   a. Eric Clark's case involved Flagstaff's first death of a police officer in the line of duty.
   b. Eric Clark's case highlights the difficulty of determining how the law should be applied to a mentally ill person who commits a crime.
   c. Eric Clark stole a car and murdered a police officer.
   d. People who commit murder should be punished in the same way whether or not they are insane.

Detail ———— 2. Which of the following statements describes Eric Clark before signs of mental illness appeared?
   a. He had a difficult childhood and was often in trouble at school.
   b. He was a quiet, sweet child who was shy in social situations.
   c. He was a poor student who struggled in school.
   d. He was a well-liked athlete.

Inference ———— 3. At about what age did Eric Clark begin to show signs of mental illness?
   a. as an infant
   b. age 5
   c. age 16
   d. age 18

Detail ———— 4. When Eric Clark was tried in Arizona, the court
   a. found him not guilty by reason of insanity.
   b. sentenced him to treatment in a mental health facility.
   c. pronounced him guilty and sentenced him to death.
   d. found him guilty and sentenced him to life in prison.

Inference ———— 5. The information in this selection suggests that
   a. the laws in Eric Clark's state are more harsh toward mentally ill offenders than in other states.
   b. the laws determining punishment for mentally ill offenders are the same throughout the United States.
   c. the laws defining insanity are the same in all states.
   d. the legal definition of insanity is very clear.

Detail ———— 6. The early signs of Eric Clark's mental illness included
   a. a history of marijuana use.
   b. seeing visions of people and things that were not there.
   c. violent acts against his classmates.
   d. loss of interest in athletics, friends, and school.

Inference _____ 7. The author suggests that the shooting of President Reagan by John Hinckley

    a. raised questions about whether insanity is an acceptable defense.
    b. had no bearing on Eric Clark's case.
    c. resulted in an incorrect punishment for Hinckley.
    d. made it clear that it is inhumane to convict and punish someone who is mentally ill.

Answer the following with *T* (true) or *F* (false).

Detail _____ 8. Eric and his brother Gentry were both involved in the murder.

Inference _____ 9. Eric had been arrested before the murder of Officer Moritz.

Detail _____ 10. The U.S. Supreme Court ruled in favor of Eric Clark.

VOCABULARY

Answer the following with *a, b, c,* or *d* for the word or phrase that best defines the boldface word used in the selection. The number in parentheses indicates the line of the passage in which the word appears.

_____ 1. "a voice announced **abruptly**" (3)
    a. quietly
    b. bluntly
    c. easily
    d. prettily

_____ 2. "to be found **competent**" (29)
    a. dead
    b. sick
    c. capable
    d. unable

_____ 3. "meaning **incarceration**" (30)
    a. freedom
    b. therapy
    c. imprisonment
    d. hospitalization

_____ 4. "John Hinckley's **acquittal**" (38)
    a. judgment of not guilty
    b. terrible act
    c. personality
    d. youth

_____ 5. "As and Bs **took a dive**" (49)
    a. improved
    b. went swimming
    c. were earned
    d. got worse

_____ 6. "But doctors **alluded** to" (53)
    a. referred
    b. demanded
    c. allowed
    d. tried

_____ 7. "the possibility of **schizophrenia**" (53–54)
    a. a kind of cancer
    b. a mental illness
    c. drug addiction
    d. heart disease

_____ 8. "Investigators **surmise**" (75)
    a. are sure
    b. state
    c. testify
    d. infer

_____ 9. "defect of such **severity**" (83)
    a. lightness
    b. evil
    c. seriousness
    d. unimportance

_____ 10. "Eric's **psychosis** was so severe" (87)
    a. serious mental illness
    b. jail time
    c. punishment
    d. reaction

Your instructor may choose to give a true-false vocabulary review.

ASSESS YOUR LEARNING

Review confusing questions, seek clarification, and make notes in your text to help you remember new information and vocabulary.

ADDITIONAL VOCABULARY LESSONS

Use the vocabulary lessons in this textbook to expand your vocabulary. Each lesson follows a structural approach and links words through shared prefixes, roots, and suffixes. The words are organized into clusters or families to enhance memory, to organize your learning, and to emphasize that most new words are made up of familiar old parts. Strengthen your vocabulary by identifying your old friends in the new words. Then apply your knowledge of word parts to unlock and remember the meanings of the new words.

Your instructor may choose to introduce the words at the beginning of the week, assign review items for practice, and quiz your knowledge of the words at the end of the week. Learn over 200 words through this easy word-family approach.

VOCABULARY LESSON

Not, Not, and Not

Study the following prefixes, words, and sentences.

Prefixes	*in, im*: not	*dis*: not	*un*: not

Words with in or im = not

Can *invisible* fences restrain pets? Will the *inability* to type help you with the computer?

- inadequate: not enough

  Having *inadequate* health care causes many flu victims to go untreated.

- inaccessible: not able to be reached

  Some mountain areas are *inaccessible* except by foot.

- inclement: not mild

  Keep an umbrella handy for *inclement* weather.

- intolerable: not bearable

  Children learn by suffering consequences for *intolerable* behaviors.

- inhospitable: not welcoming

  The *inhospitable* island was cold, windy, and barren.

- insatiable: cannot be satisfied

  Young readers have an *insatiable* desire for more Harry Potter.

- improbable: not likely to occur

  Because of overbooking, a doctor's appointment today is *improbable*.

- immoral: not conforming to accepted standards of right and wrong.

  The politician's *immoral* actions were scorned by the voters.

- impassable: blocked

  With the bridge washed out from the flood, the road was *impassable*.

- immortal: cannot die

  An *immortal* flame burns to honor the assassinated president.

- immobilized: rendered not able to move

  The zookeepers had to *immobilize* the lion before treating its infected foot.

Words with dis = not

Do the tabloids *dishonor* celebrities? Can you *disclaim* a relative?

- disarm: take weapons away

  The troops were *disarmed* after the surrender.

- disadvantage: handicap

  The major *disadvantage* of the sofa is that its light-colored fabric easily shows dirt.

- discredit: cause disbelief in

  To *discredit* his character, the opposition circulated a rumor of drugs.

- disgrace: shame

  With an indictment pending, the mayor resigned in *disgrace*.

- disloyal: unfaithful

  The *disloyal* employee revealed company secrets.

- distrust: doubt

  If you *distrust* the management, don't invest your money in the company.

- disconcerted: upset

  The workers were *disconcerted* and even angry about the computer virus.

- disregard: not pay attention to

  If you have already paid, please *disregard* this bill.

- dissolved: melted away

  The sugar *dissolved* into the hot espresso.

- disinherit: to deny an inheritance

  Few parents will *disinherit* a child.

Words with un = not

Is an *unsaid* rule clearly stated? Is an *uneducated* guess mostly luck?

- unable: not having the ability

  Because of a shortage, the company was *unable* to ship the software.

- unabridged: not shortened

  For the derivation of words, use an *unabridged* dictionary.

- unaffected: not touched

  Although we saw the funnel, our house was *unaffected* by the tornado.

- unaltered: not changed

  With no additional work, the original plans remain *unaltered*.

- untouchable: cannot be touched

  The children were told that the food was *untouchable* until the guests arrived.

Review

Part I

Answer the following with *T* (true) or *F* (false).

_____ 1. An abridged dictionary contains more than an unabridged dictionary.

_____ 2. Counties seek inaccessible voting locations for citizens.

_____ 3. A disinherited relative receives no gift from the deceased.

_____ 4. An invisible correction can be easily detected.

_____ 5. To discredit a source is to cast doubt on its worth.

_____ 6. Renters usually desire intolerant landlords.

_____ 7. An immobilized elephant is unlikely to charge.

_____ 8. An unaltered proposal remains in its original format.

_____ 9. Disloyal fans boost the morale of a team.

_____10. Powdered milk will dissolve in water.

Part II

Choose the best word from the list to complete each of the following sentences.

inadequate	disregard	unaffected	immoral	disgrace
impassable	disarm	inclement	untouchable	disconcerting

11. The three-foot snow left the roads _____.

12. Humor can _____ the anger of a complaining customer.

13. The _____ weather did not stop the snow skiers from skiing.

14. The _____ actions of the spouse were grounds for the divorce.

15. In a museum, signs indicate that the paintings are _____.

16. By not traveling, they were _____ by the hotel shortage.

17. The _____ protesters rudely interrupted the speaker.

18. Spenders who _____ money may soon be in debt.

19. To get good grades, do not take tests with _____ preparation.

20. When convicted of the crime, the defendant hung her head in _____.

Reading News and Feature Stories in the Newspaper

Readership of daily newspapers is declining across the United States and elsewhere as more people rely on the Internet, television, and radio to learn the news. These media often provide a briefer, summary version of news events to satisfy a busy public, and then produce special segments or links for people who want greater depth. The next Everyday Reading Skills feature examines electronic news sources. Whether the news source is electronic or printed on paper, however, the formats are similar. Understanding how newspapers and news reports are organized will help you get the most from them. The following Everyday Reading Skills section explains.

What do you usually read first if you read a newspaper? You probably already have a pattern for reading your favorite parts. To help you locate different topics, newspapers are divided into *sections*: national and international news; local or regional news; sports; entertainment and the arts (including music, movies, and television); classified ads, plus any other categories the editors believe are appropriate for the local community. The front page always carries the most important stories from all the categories. Those articles are often continued in a section in which other articles related to the lead story appear. Some newspapers include an index on the front page to help you locate high-interest articles or regular sections.

Understand the Evolution of Newspaper Style

To appreciate the organization of newspaper stories, you must first understand that the journalistic style of newspaper writing developed as a response to the telegraph machine, a new technology that could break down at any time.

As protection against a communication breakdown or a deadline cutoff, as well as to ensure that readers received the most important parts of the news story, reporters got into the habit of including only the most important points in the first paragraphs. The major and minor details of the story were then placed in the following paragraphs in *descending* order of importance. Thus the **inverted pyramid** format of news writing was invented. Although technology has improved dramatically, this format has continued.

Reader's TIP — Reading a News Story

- Get an overview from the headline and photographs.
- Answer the 5 *W*'s and the *H*.

Who is the story about?
What happened?
When did it happen?
Where did the event or events take place?
Why did this event occur?
How did this happen?

- Continue to read according to the amount of detail desired.

News Stories

News stories are the front-page articles that objectively report facts in descending order of importance. The **lead** is the first paragraph, which catches the reader's attention, often summarizes the essential points of the story, and establishes a focus. Many leads contain the 5 *W*'s and one *H*: *Who, What, When, Where, Why,* and *How*? Think of the first paragraph as a condensed version of the event.

Subsequent paragraphs present details in a hierarchy of importance. A news story has no ending, but rather tapers down from major to minor details. As you read further, more complete information is given about the five basic questions. Your level of interest will determine how far you read for more details. The following excerpt is an example of the inverted pyramid format in a news story.

THE NATION

Sunday, April 17, 2011   ***   HOUSTON CHRONICLE **A3**

Storms leave death, debris, despair across South

Carolinas dig through rubble as Alabama mourns

By Tom Breen
ASSOCIATED PRESS

Most important points

RALEIGH, N.C. — A brutal spring storm raged across North Carolina on Saturday, flattening businesses, flipping cars and destroying homes, leaving an unknown number of casualties from a system already blamed for killing at least 21 people in five states.

Major details

North Carolina officials said there are at least four fatalities and they were working to confirm others. Search and rescue teams were in two counties looking for residents who might be trapped in damaged buildings.

Minor details

In South Carolina, a church with six people inside collapsed after it was hit by a tornado, but somehow no one was injured. And in Sanford, N.C., the manager of a Lowe's hardware store was credited with saving more than 100 workers and employees by ushering them to the back of the store, which acted as a makeshift shelter as the weather rolled in.

EXERCISE 1   Select a news story that you find interesting and clip it from a newspaper. Identify the who, what, when, where, why, and how on a separate sheet of paper. On the news clipping itself, draw an inverted pyramid over the most important points.

Feature Stories

Feature stories differ from news stories in their timeliness, style, and length. Whereas news stories cover breaking news, a feature story might discuss less time-sensitive issues, such as a profile of an actor or an important local businessperson, the reopening of a historical hotel, or a new lifestyle trend. In other words, articles such as these would have similar impact if you read them today or five days from now. Unlike the inverted pyramid style of news stories, the style of feature stories is characterized by a beginning, middle, and end, as well as a thesis. The feature may take up one or two complete pages of the newspaper. Other shorter articles related to the same primary topic often accompany feature stories.

Feature stories are usually found in the section appropriate to their subject. In the previous examples, an actor's profile would be found in *arts/entertainment*, the profile of a local businessperson would be in the *business section*, the refurbishing of a landmark hotel would be in *local news*, and new trends would be in the *lifestyle* or *living section*. They add a fresh angle to recent news by including overlooked or undisclosed information. *Exposés* are based on in-depth investigation to reveal or "expose" shocking or surprising information, such as abuses of power or the quality of public education in your area.

Reader's TIP — Reading a Feature Story

- How does the angle or focus of a feature story differ from that of a straight news story?
- How credible are the sources cited?
- Is it factual or sensationalized?
- Does the reporter show a bias?
- Does the reporter judge, or do you decide?

EXERCISE 2

Locate a feature story that interests you and clip it from a newspaper. If your college publishes a newspaper, look for a story in a recent edition. Discuss the factors that make this article a feature rather than a news story. In particular, think of timeliness (time-sensitivity), style, and length. What is the angle of the story, and why is it being printed now? Circle any credible sources that are cited, and underline sentences or phrases that show a positive or negative bias by the reporter.

3 Vocabulary

Learning Objectives

From this chapter, readers will learn:

1. To use a system for expanding vocabulary
2. To use strategies for unlocking the meaning of unfamiliar words
3. To use context clues to unlock unfamiliar words
4. To use common word parts to unlock meaning
5. To use the dictionary for rich information about words
6. To consult the glossary to define words used in the textbook
7. To find synonyms and antonyms in a thesaurus
8. To refine word knowledge by solving analogies
9. To spell easily confused words

Everyday Reading Skills: Reading News and Feature Stories in the Newspaper

LEARNING NEW WORDS

Recognizing the meaning of words is essential to understanding what you read. If you have a weak vocabulary and stumble over unknown words when you read, you will lose your train of thought and end up concentrating on words rather than on meaning. A poor vocabulary severely limits your reading comprehension and speed.

Research tells us that you are already phenomenally successful at vocabulary acquisition. On the average, you have learned 3,000 to 5,000 words each year from kindergarten through twelfth grade. Experts estimate that only 300 new words are systematically taught each year by a teacher, so congratulate yourself that independently you have learned approximately 2,700 words every year! Were you afraid of new words? Apparently not, because during each of those years, you encountered 15,000 to 30,000 unknown words and you survived. That makes you a very efficient vocabulary builder. Continue to expand your vocabulary knowledge using those skills that have already made you an expert.

To the college reader, being able to recognize a large number of words is more important than being able to use each one of them. Studies show that we use only about 20 percent of the words we know. The average high school graduate recognizes about 50,000 words and uses only 10,000, whereas the average college graduate recognizes around 70,000 words and uses approximately 15,000. This means that during your years in college you probably will learn about 20,000 new words.

The English language contains about one million words. This number includes technical words in all disciplines, many of which the average person would never use. As a college student, however, you are becoming an expert in a particular field and a mini-expert in several areas. Each time you take a course in a new discipline, you face a vocabulary unique to that subject. It takes a little time and a lot of effort to master these new words. After overcoming the initial shock of vocabulary adjustment for each new course, you will find that reading becomes easier and comprehension improves.

REMEMBERING NEW WORDS

Learning Objective 1

Use a system for expanding vocabulary

As you read this section on remembering new words you might notice that memorizing words and definitions is not included. Memorizing is seldom effective for the long term. Instead, focus on understanding the meaning and recognizing the spelling and sound of the word. Think about how the word is used and repeat your exposure to it until it becomes part of your growing vocabulary.

Use Association

Certain new words, especially college-level words, are hard to remember because you don't hear them every day and can't easily work them into casual conversation. To latch on to a new word, form an association with it. Try to remember the word in the context in which it was used. Visualize the word or a situation pertaining to the word. Always try to think of a new word in a phrase, rather than in isolation. For example, do you know the word *surrogate*? Perhaps you encountered the word in psychology class when studying Harlow's experiments on the need for love in infants. The surrogates were wire models substituted for real monkey mothers to test the infant monkey's attraction. To remember the word *surrogate*, think of it in the phrase *surrogate mother* and visualize the infant monkey cuddling up to a wire artificial mother for love and affection. This association creates an indelible picture in your mind.

Make Sense with the Senses!

All information enters your brain through your senses—vision, hearing, smell, touch, and taste. When it enters through more than one channel, the effect is stronger. How can college students apply this fact of brain life? Access multiple inputs when you are studying. Draw, use a computer keyboard, make and manipulate flashcards, write notes in an organized, clear visual form, say or sing the material aloud, watch related videos. Background music that has a regular rhythm and is not distracting can be helpful. When used judiciously, even fragrances and tastes can be associated with specific information and easily remembered. Which senses will be involved when you make concept cards to learn new vocabulary?

Use Concept Cards

You can also use concept cards to help you remember vocabulary. *Concept* means idea. On a concept card you expand the definition of a single word into a fully developed idea. You are creating an episode for the new word by providing a sentence, a picture, and a source reference.

Keep a concept card file of new words. Include more than the usual "mystery word" on the front of the card and the definition on the back. Use the technique of association, and on the front of the card write the word within a meaningful phrase or sentence, or both. Also on the front, note where you encountered the new word. On the back of the card, write the definition, and, to add a further memory link, draw a picture that illustrates the way you are using the word in your phrase or sentence. See the illustration on the next page for an example.

PERSONAL FEEDBACK **1**   Name _____

1. For the ten vocabulary items following the selection in Chapter 2 on the Galveston disaster (60), why do you think the line numbers are given for the words? _____
   _____

2. Why do instructors say that studying Latin is a useful way to increase your vocabulary?
   _____
   _____

3. What do you feel are the benefits of having a large vocabulary?
   _____
   _____

4. List ten adjectives that describe you. Stretch your vocabulary and go beyond simple one- and two-syllable words. _____
   _____

Tear out and submit to your instructor.

FRONT

BACK

surrogate mother

The baby monkey preferred
the terry cloth surrogate mother

Passage text on love

Def: substitute, as in the wire
mothers in experiments with
monkeys

When making concept cards, your limits depend only on your creativity and talent. For example, in *Vocabulary Cartoons*, a book by Sam, Max, and Bryan Burchers, the authors link the sounds within words to exaggerated visual images. The resulting cartoons, as shown on the next page, depict the links and suggest the definitions by using sound associations and visual images, along with humor, to improve memory.

> **BRAIN BOOSTER**
>
> **Meaning Matters!**
> Human brains are wired to remember meaningful information. Have you ever memorized a list of definitions and promptly forgotten them after the quiz? When learning new words, think of them as ideas that link to many other ideas with which you are already familiar. For example, *magma* is melted rock that is expelled from an erupting volcano. Magma > melted rock > lava > ash > fire > smoke > volcano > Mt. St. Helen's > Mt. Etna > Pompeii > eruption > death > destruction. Strive for meaning and association. Then use what you have learned, and use it often. REPEAT!

Practice Your New Words

Review your concept cards regularly. Look at the word on the front and quiz yourself on the definition. When you feel you have a clear understanding of the meaning, use your new word in writing or in conversation.

Notice the words around you. As you begin to pay attention to unfamiliar terms in print and in conversation, you will more than likely discover that you encounter many interesting new words.

UNLOCKING THE MEANING OF NEW WORDS

Learning Objective 2

Use strategies to unlock the meaning of unfamiliar words

Use Context Clues

To figure out the meaning of a new word, do not immediately charge off to the dictionary and record a definition as if it were one more addition to a giant list of words. Contrary to what you may have heard, the dictionary is a *last* resort when you aren't sure what a word means. Instead, first try to figure out the meaning from the **context clues** in the sentence or paragraph in which the word is used. What do the surrounding words—the context—tell you about the new word?

HOVEL
(HUV ul)
a small, miserable dwelling;
an open, low shed
Link: **SHOVEL**

"The mice's HOVEL was an old, rusted SHOVEL."

EDIFICE
(ED uh fis)
a building, especially one of imposing
appearance or size
Link: **ATE A FACE**

HE ONLY EATS THE FINEST BUILDINGS!

*"The Great Kong ATE the north FACE of
the EDIFICE."*

Use Knowledge of Word Parts

Another way to discover the meaning of a word is to examine its parts. Do you recognize any prefixes, suffixes, or roots, such as *pseudo* (meaning *false*) or *nym* (meaning *name*) in the word *pseudonym*? If you know these word parts, you can easily figure out that *pseudonym* means a false name rather than a real one. Samuel Clemens's use of the name Mark Twain is an example of a pseudonym.

Use the Glossary and the Dictionary

If a word is specific to a subject area, such as the marketing term *promotional mix*, refer to the glossary in the back of the textbook for a definition that pertains specifically to that field. If all of these strategies fail to unlock the meaning of a new word and you can't understand what you are reading without a definition of the word, then go to the dictionary. But if the word is not essential to your general comprehension, skip it entirely or come back to it later. Your purpose for reading is to get meaning, not to collect vocabulary words. As you read more and encounter more new words, your vocabulary will naturally expand. Make a habit of noticing new words, and try to remember them by association.

TYPES OF CONTEXT CLUES

Learning Objective 3
Use context clues to unlock meaning

The first line of attack on a new word is to try to figure out the meaning from its *context*, or the way it is used in the sentence or paragraph. There are several types of context clues. The following examples show how each type can be used to figure out word meaning.

Definition

The unknown word is defined within the sentence or paragraph.

EXAMPLE The explorers landed in an *alien* environment, a place both <u>foreign and strange</u> to their beloved homeland.

EXPLANATION The definition is set off by a comma following the phrase in which the word appears. *Alien* means *strange* or *foreign*.

EXERCISE 1 For each of the context clue exercises in this section, underline the context clue and mark *a*, *b*, *c*, or *d* for the meaning closest to that of the boldface word. Do not use a dictionary.

_____ 1. The CIA was engaged in **covert** activities in South America that were not made public.

  a. foreign
  b. dishonest
  c. dangerous
  d. hidden

FRONT

covert operations
in South America

CIA activities

BACK

hidden or secret

_____ 2. The meeting was brief, and the message was **concise** and to the point.

  a. laborious
  b. lengthy
  c. short
  d. important

_____ 3. If we have to have a pet around the house, get one that is **docile** and easy to manage.

  a. gentle
  b. short
  c. sick
  d. young

_____ 4. The professor gave an **ultimatum** about tardiness, saying today would be the last time anyone would be allowed to enter class late.
   a. final demand
   b. new proposal
   c. lecture
   d. choice

_____ 5. Checking the references in the bibliography for errors was **tedious** and uninteresting.
   a. educational
   b. necessary
   c. exhausting
   d. boring

Elaborating Details

Descriptive details suggest the meaning of the unknown word.

EXAMPLE   The natives were _hostile_ when the settlers approached their village. They lined up across the road and drew their weapons. The settlers were afraid to go farther.

EXPLANATION   As described in the sentences after the word, _hostile_ must mean _unfriendly_.

EXERCISE 2   _____ 1. **Wearily**, the young woman climbed into bed after a long night shift for a well-deserved nap.
   a. relieved
   b. bored
   c. tired
   d. sadly

_____ 2. The gaping wound bled **profusely**, needing several bandages to absorb its flow.
   a. lightly
   b. unnoticeably
   c. slowly
   d. greatly

_____ 3. The boy received a **superficial** cut, the cat's claw having barely grazed his skin.
   a. shallow
   b. visible
   c. deep
   d. lengthy

_____ 4. The instructions left for the babysitter were **delineated** in several sentences with great detail.
   a. ignored
   b. described
   c. discovered
   d. questioned

_____ 5. The politician went on and on with his **harangue** while his fellow senators were forced to keep listening.
   a. noisy laughter
   b. simple explanation
   c. prolonged speech
   d. short conversation

Elaborating Examples

An anecdote or example before or after the word suggests the meaning.

EXAMPLE   The bird's appetite is _voracious_. In one day he ate enough worms to equal three times his body weight.

> **EXPLANATION**   Because the bird ate an extraordinary amount, _voracious_ means extremely _hungry_ or _greedy_.

EXERCISE 3   _____ 1. The dancer's movements were not rehearsed but were a **spontaneous** response to the music.
   a. planned
   b. simple
   c. unplanned
   d. smooth

_____ 2. The embargo will **restrict** previously flourishing trade with the country and stop the goods from entering the seaport.
   a. promote
   b. enlist
   c. renew
   d. confine

_____ 3. The **affluent** members of the community live in big homes with swimming pools.
   a. powerful
   b. wealthy
   c. athletic
   d. political

FRONT

BACK

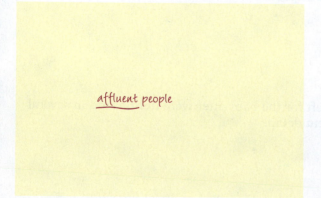

_____ 4. Because the employer had never heard of the three companies listed as references, she was **dubious** about the applicant's previous work history.
   a. relaxed
   b. unconcerned
   c. doubtful
   d. hopeful

_____ 5. The ophthalmologist gave a favorable **prognosis**, saying that in two weeks her vision would be clear, and she would no longer need the dark glasses.
   a. forecast
   b. prescription
   c. warning
   d. notification

Comparison

A similar situation suggests the meaning of the unknown word.

EXAMPLE   The smell of the flower was as *compelling* as a magnet's pull on a paper clip.

> **EXPLANATION**   Because a magnet will pull a paper clip to it, the comparison suggests that the smell of the flower had a strong attraction. *Compelling* means *forceful*.

EXERCISE 4   _____ 1. I am as **skeptical** about its chances of success as I am about my chances of winning the lottery.
   a. doubtful
   b. confident
   c. remorseful
   d. hopeful

_____ 2. Confirming an appointment before leaving the office is as **prudent** as never letting your gas tank go lower than one-quarter full.
   a. annoying
   b. reckless
   c. rewarding
   d. wise

_____ 3. With a great deal of feeling, Ellen made an **impassioned** plea for her family to adopt the stray puppy.
   a. illogical
   b. soft-spoken
   c. emotional
   d. short-lived

_____ 4. Because there is always a first time for everything, each of us is a **novice** at some point in our lives.
   a. fool
   b. master
   c. manager
   d. beginner

———— 5. If the climber is in fact a circus performer, it is **plausible** that he attempted such a dangerous feat on the tall building.
   a. doubtful
   b. impossible
   c. terrible
   d. believable

Contrast

An opposite situation suggests the meaning of the unknown word.

EXAMPLE   In America she is an *eminent* journalist, even though she is virtually unknown in England.

> **EXPLANATION**   The phrase *Even though* signals that an opposite is coming. Thus *eminent* means the opposite of *unknown*; it means *well-known* or *famous*.

EXERCISE 5   ———— 1. Unlike **introverted** people, very talkative folks love crowds and conversation.
   a. quiet
   b. loud
   c. friendly
   d. hostile

———— 2. His favorites were not the old stories of days gone by but the works of more **contemporary** authors.
   a. intelligent
   b. recent
   c. revolutionary
   d. meaningful

———— 3. He did not mean to cause the problem. While looking for his hat, the young man **inadvertently** knocked over the lamp.
   a. purposely
   b. knowingly
   c. unintentionally
   d. suddenly

———— 4. Now that she is an adult college student who is in control of her emotions, she no longer engages in the **infantile** outbursts that marked her behavior as a child.
   a. immature
   b. sudden
   c. angry
   d. short

———— 5. Although she had had a crush on him all fall, Maria's interest in Michael began to **wane** when he asked two other girls to the holiday party.
   a. grow
   b. lessen
   c. accelerate
   d. intensify

WANE
(wain)
to decrease gradually
Link: **RAIN**

"Snowmen WANE in the RAIN."

EXERCISE 6   Use context clues to determine the meanings of the boldface words, which appear frequently in health textbooks.

1. A condition such as arthritis can limit a person's **range of motion** in the shoulders, hips, wrists, and other joints. _____

2. Low **carbohydrate** diets are difficult to follow for lovers of sweets, baked goods, pasta, and potatoes. _____

3. Racehorses are sometimes given a **diuretic** to reduce body fluids before racing. _____

4. Exercise physiologists suggest that people who exercise at the appropriate level of **intensity** ought to be able to carry on a conversation at the same time. _____

5. Final exams would be excellent examples of **stressors** for most students.

_____

Multiple Meanings of a Word

Some words are confusing because they have several different meanings. For example, the dictionary lists more than thirty meanings for the word *run*. To determine the proper meaning, use the context of the sentence and paragraph in which the word occurs. Many of the multiple-meaning words are simple words that are used frequently. If you are puzzling over an unusual use of a common word, consider the context and be aware that the word may have another meaning.

EXERCISE 7   The boldface words in the following sentences have multiple meanings. For each word, write a second sentence in which the word is used differently.

1. The puppy snuggled in the **covers**. _____

   _____

2. The **pitch** was low and inside home plate. _____

   _____

   _____

3. Her neighbors objected to the dog **run** in her backyard. _____

   _____

   _____

4. I **suspect** it was your brother's mess. _____

   _____

   _____

5. Debbie had no **choice** in the matter, for it was already decided. _____

   _____

6. The orchestra members took a **bow** at the end of the performance. _____

   _____

7. Water spilled over the **stern** of the ship during the height of the storm.

   _____

   _____

8. Nicholas prefers four slices of cinnamon **toast** for breakfast. _____

   _____

9. The waves began to **break** along the beach. _____

   _____

10. You cannot **hide** from the truth. _____

    _____

WORD PARTS

Learning Objective 4

Use common word parts to unlock meaning

Many words that at first may seem totally foreign to you are actually made up of words that you already know. One authority claims that learning approximately thirty key word parts will help you unlock the meaning of about 14,000 words. Although this claim may be exaggerated, it emphasizes the importance of roots, prefixes, and suffixes. Word parts are clues to the meaning of new words.

    Look at the following family of words. Some may be familiar, and some may be new to you. You probably know the meaning of the first two words and thus can deduce that *ped* means *foot*. Try to figure out the meaning of the other *ped* words by applying your knowledge of closely related words.

Pedal: lever pressed by the foot

Pedestrian: person walking on foot

What do the following words mean? Use the clues to write the definitions.

quadruped: _____ (Hint: quadruplets?)

centipede: _____ (Hint: turn of the century?)

pedometer: _____ (Hint: speedometer?)

Roots

The **root** is the stem or basic part of the word. The roots that we use are derived primarily from Latin and Greek. For example, *port* is a root derived from Latin meaning *to carry*, as in the word *porter*. *Thermo* is a Greek word meaning *heat*, as in *thermometer*. In both cases, additional letters have been added to the word, but the meaning of the word has not changed. Knowing the definition of the root helps unlock the meaning of each word.

EXAMPLE   The root forms *duc*, *duct*, and *duce* mean *to lead*. This root branches out into a large word family. Use the root to supply appropriate words to complete the following three sentences.

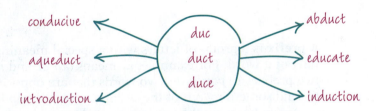

1. If the factory is ready, the new line of furniture will go into _____ in September.

2. The company is trying to cut down overhead in order to _____ expenses.

3. Legitimate business expenses can be _____ from your taxes if you keep the proper receipts.

EXPLANATION   The correct answers are *production*, *reduce*, and *deducted*.

EXERCISE 8   Complete the following sentences by using the given root to form an appropriate word.

grad, gred, gres: take steps, go, degree

1. The seniors will _____ from high school the first week in June.

2. The mountain trail began as a _____ climb and became steeper toward the top.

3. If we continue to work through lunch and all afternoon, we should make enough _____ on our project to finish by five o'clock.

port: carry

4. If we could _____ fewer goods into this country, our balance of payments would improve.

5. She wanted a _____ radio so she could listen to the game while riding in the boat on the lake.

6. Private contributions and volunteers _____ the efforts of the Salvation Army.

7. The organized _____ to and from the game will be by bus.

cred: believe

8. We could not believe what we saw; the feat was _____.

9. Some law schools in the country are not fully _____ by the state, and their courses do not transfer to other schools.

10. Derogatory remarks were made about his performance in an effort to _____ him.

Prefixes

A **prefix** is a group of letters with a special meaning that is added to the beginning of a word. For example, *ex* means *out of* and *im* means *into*. Adding these two prefixes to *port* gives two words that are opposite in meaning. *Export* means to send something out of the country, whereas *import* means to bring something in. Again, knowing the prefixes can help you identify the meaning.

EXAMPLE   The prefix *trans* means *across, over,* and *beyond*. Write a word beginning with *trans* to complete each of the following three sentences.

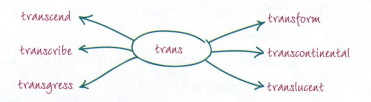

1. The radio station can now _____ programs to a wider audience.

2. Since she did not speak French, he acted as _____ while she conducted business in Paris.

3. When the business _____ was completed, the two executives shook hands.

EXPLANATION   The correct answers are *transmit, translator,* and *transaction.*

EXERCISE 9 Complete the following sentences by using the given prefix to form an appropriate word.

dis: take away, not, deprive of

1. When catching criminal suspects, the police carefully _____ them to remove any item that could be used as a weapon.

2. Because she missed the review in the last class before the final exam, the student was at a _____ in studying for the test.

3. Hospital employees are instructed to use special containers to _____ of used needles.

mis: wrong, bad

4. Because the child _____ in the restaurant, he was not allowed to go again.

5. The answer was not a lie, but it did _____ the truth.

6. Because of the lawyer's error, the judge declared a _____ and court was adjourned.

pre: before

7. Even a fortune-teller could not have _____ the fun we had scuba diving.

8. Police recommend alarm systems as a type of crime _____.

9. The student was so _____ with her mathematics assignment that she did not hear the doorbell ring.

10. If you order by phone, you will need a credit card to _____ for the concert tickets.

Suffixes

A **suffix** is a group of letters with a special meaning that is added to the end of a word. A suffix can alter the meaning of a word as well as the way the word is used in the sentence. For example, the *er* in *porter* means the *person who* and makes the word into the name of a person. But adding *able*, which means *capable of*, to *port* does not change the meaning as much as it changes the way the word can be used in the sentence. Some suffixes, therefore, have more meaning than others, but all alter the way the word can be used in a sentence.

EXAMPLE The suffix *ist* means *one who* or *that which*. Write a word ending with *ist* to complete each of the following three sentences.

1. If you have a toothache, go to your _____ immediately.
2. The _____ struck the keys of the instrument with such force that the floorboards shook.
3. The picture was painted by a well-known American _____.

EXPLANATION   The correct answers are *dentist, pianist,* and *artist.*

EXERCISE 10   Complete the following sentences by using the given suffix to form an appropriate word.

ion, sion, tion: act of, state of, result of

1. To honor his birthday, we invited his friends to a party and had a big _____.

2. If you don't clean out the wound and use a bandage, you are likely to get an _____.

3. The _____ bridge was held in the air by cables descending from two towers on either side of the river.

4. Use your _____ to visualize the festive atmosphere of music and outdoor dining.

ship: office, state, dignity, skill, quality, profession

5. After breaking her leg and missing two weeks of class, the student was advised to apply for a _____ withdrawal and make a fresh start the next semester.

6. The university also offered merit _____ that were not based on financial need.

7. The infantry soldier demonstrated excellent _____ by hitting the red mark with each shot.

less: without

8. Because the show was boring, I became _____ and could not sit still.

9. A baby lamb is _____ against fierce and determined predators.

10. Suffering from insomnia, she spent many _____ nights walking the halls.

THE DICTIONARY

Learning Objective 5

Use the dictionary for rich information about words

Use the dictionary as a last resort for finding the definition of a word while you are reading, unless the word is crucial to your understanding. Remember, stopping in the middle of a paragraph breaks your concentration and causes you to forget what you were reading. Mark unknown words with a dot in the margin, and then, when you have finished reading, look those words up in the dictionary.

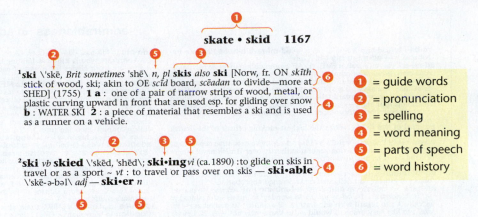

Dictionaries contain more than just the definition of a word. They contain the pronunciation, the spelling, the derivation or history, the parts of speech, and the many different meanings a word may have. An entry may also include an illustration or give context examples of the use of the word in a phrase. Consider the following entry.

Guide Words

The two words at the top of each dictionary page are called *guide words*. They represent the first and last words on the page. Because the words in the dictionary are in alphabetical order, you can use the guide words to quickly determine if the word you are looking for is on that particular page. The guide words for the sample entry are *skate* and *skid*.

Pronunciation

Each word is divided into sounds after the boldface main entry. Letters and symbols are used to indicate special sounds. A key to understanding the special sounds appears at the bottom of one of the two pages open to you.

Spelling

Spellings are given for the plural form of the word (if the spelling changes) and for any special endings. This is particularly helpful when letters are dropped or added to form the new word. In the sample entry, the plural of *ski* can be spelled correctly in two ways, either *skis* or *ski*. The first spelling is usually the preferred one.

Word Meaning

Frequently a word has many meanings. For example, *car* means automobile as well as the cargo part of an airship. In such a case, the dictionary uses a number to indicate each new meaning. In the sample entry, notice that a ski can be a narrow strip of wood or a piece of material that resembles a ski.

Parts of Speech

For each meaning of a word, the part of speech is given in abbreviated form. For example, *n* means *noun, adj* means *adjective, adv* means *adverb,* and *vi* or

admirableness • adrenocortical 17

ra·bil·i·ty \ˌad-m(ə-)rə-ˈbi-lə-tē\ *n* — **ad·mi·ra·ble·ness** \ˈad-m(ə-)rə-bəl-nəs\ *n* — **ad·mi·ra·bly** \-blē\ *adv*

ad·mi·ral \ˈad-m(ə-)rəl\ *n* [ME, fr. AF *amiral* commander & ML *admiralis* emir, *admirallus* admiral, fr. Ar *amīr-al-* commander of the (as in *amīr-al-baḥr* commander of the sea)] (15c) **1** *archaic* **:** the commander in chief of a navy **2 a :** FLAG OFFICER **b :** a commissioned officer in the navy or coast guard who ranks above a vice admiral and whose insignia is four stars — compare GENERAL **3** *archaic* **:** FLAGSHIP **4 :** any of several brightly colored nymphalid butterflies — compare RED ADMIRAL

admiral of the fleet (1660) **:** the highest-ranking officer of the British navy

ad·mi·ral·ty \ˈad-m(ə-)rəl-tē\ *n* (15c) **1** *cap* **:** the executive department or officers formerly having general authority over British naval affairs **2 :** the court having jurisdiction over questions of maritime law; *also* **:** the system of law administered by admiralty courts

ad·mi·ra·tion \ˌad-mə-ˈrā-shən\ *n* (15c) **1** *archaic* **:** WONDER **2 :** an object of esteem **3 :** delighted or astonished approbation

ad·mire \əd-ˈmī(-ə)r\ *vb* **ad·mired; ad·mir·ing** [MF *admirer,* to marvel at, fr. L *admirari,* fr. *ad-* + *mirari* to wonder, fr. *mirus* astonishing] *vt* (1560) **1 :** to regard with admiration **2** *archaic* **:** to marvel at ~ *vi, dial* **:** to like very much ⟨I would ~ to know why not —A. H. Lewis⟩ ***syn*** see REGARD — **ad·mir·er** *n* — **ad·mir·ing·ly** \-ˈmī-riŋ-lē\ *adv*

ad·mis·si·ble \əd-ˈmi-sə-bəl, ad-\ *adj* [F, fr. ML *admissibilis,* fr. L *admissus,* pp. of *admittere*] (1611) **1 :** capable of being allowed or conceded **:** PERMISSIBLE ⟨evidence legally ~ in court⟩ **2 :** capable or worthy of being admitted ⟨~ to the university⟩ — **ad·mis·si·bil·i·ty** \-ˌmi-sə-ˈbi-lə-tē\ *n*

ad·mis·sion \əd-ˈmi-shən, ad-\ *n* (15c) **1 a :** the act or process of admitting **b :** the state or privilege of being admitted **c :** a fee paid at or for admission **2 a :** the granting of an argument or position not fully proved **b :** acknowledgment that a fact or statement is true — **ad·mis·sive** \-ˈmi-siv\ *adj*

ad·mit \əd-ˈmit, ad-\ *vb* **ad·mit·ted; ad·mit·ting** [ME *admitten,* fr. L *admittere,* fr. *ad-* + *mittere* to send] *vt* (15c) **1 a :** to allow scope for **:** PERMIT ⟨~*s* no possibility of misunderstanding⟩ **b :** to concede as true or valid ⟨*admitted* making a mistake⟩ **2 a :** to allow entry (as to a place, fellowship, or privilege) ⟨an open window had *admitted* rain⟩ ⟨*admitted* to the club⟩ **b :** to accept into a hospital as an inpatient ⟨he was *admitted* last night for chest pains⟩ ~ *vi* **1 :** to give entrance or access **2 a :** ALLOW, PERMIT ⟨~*s* of two interpretations⟩ **b :** to make acknowledgment — used with *to* ***syn*** see ACKNOWLEDGE

ad·mit·tance \əd-ˈmi-tᵊn(t)s, ad-\ *n* (1536) **1 a :** the act or process of admitting **b :** permission to enter **2 :** the reciprocal of the impedance of a circuit

ad·mit·ted·ly \əd-ˈmi-təd-lē, ad-\ *adv* (1804) **1 :** as has been or must be admitted ⟨an ~ inadequate treatment⟩ **2 :** it must be admitted ⟨~, we took a chance⟩

ad·mix \ad-ˈmiks\ *vt* [back-formation fr. obs. *admixt* mingled (with), fr. ME, fr. L *admixtus*] (1533) **:** to mix in

ad·mix·ture \ad-ˈmiks-chər\ *n* [L *admixtus,* pp. of *admiscēre* to mix with, fr. *ad-* + *miscēre* to mix — more at MIX] (1605) **1 a :** the action of mixing **b :** the fact of being mixed **2 a :** something added by mixing **b :** a product of mixing **:** MIXTURE

ad·mon·ish \ad-ˈmä-nish\ *vt* [ME *admonesten,* fr. AF *amonester,* fr. VL **admonestare,* alter. of L *admonēre* to warn, fr. *ad-* + *monēre* to warn — more at MIND] (14c) **1 a :** to indicate duties or obligations to **b :** to express warning or disapproval to esp. in a gentle, earnest, or solicitous manner **2 :** to give friendly earnest advice or encouragement to ***syn*** see REPROVE — **ad·mon·ish·er** *n* — **ad·mon·ish·ing·ly** \-ni-shiŋ-lē\ *adv* — **ad·mon·ish·ment** \-mənt\ *n*

ad·mo·ni·tion \ˌad-mə-ˈni-shən\ *n* [ME *amonicioun,* fr. AF *amonicion,* fr. L *admonition-, admonitio,* fr. *admonēre*] (14c) **1 :** gentle or friendly reproof **2 :** counsel or warning against fault or oversight

ad·mon·i·to·ry \əd-ˈmä-nə-ˌtȯr-ē\ *adj* (1594) **:** expressing admonition **:** WARNING — **ad·mon·i·to·ri·ly** \-ˌmä-nə-ˈtȯr-ə-lē\ *adv*

ad·nate \ˈad-ˌnāt\ *adj* [L *adnatus, adgnatus,* pp. of *adgnasci* to be born in addition, grow later — more at AGNATE] (1661) **:** grown to a usu. unlike part esp. along a margin ⟨a calyx ~ to the ovary⟩ — **ad·na·tion** \ad-ˈnā-shən\ *n*

ad nau·se·am \ad-ˈnȯ-zē-əm *also* -ˌam\ *adv* [L] (1647) **:** to a sickening or excessive degree

ad·nexa \ad-ˈnek-sə\ *n pl* [NL, fr. L *annexa,* neut. pl. of *annexus,* pp. of *annectere* to bind to — more at ANNEX] (1899) **:** conjoined, subordinate, or associated anatomical parts — **ad·nex·al** \-səl\ *adj*

ado \ə-ˈdü\ *n* [ME, fr. *at do,* fr. *at* + *don, do* to do] (14c) **1 :** heightened fuss or concern **:** TO-DO **2 :** time-wasting bother over trivial details ⟨wrote the paper without further ~⟩ **3 :** TROUBLE, DIFFICULTY

ado·be \ə-ˈdō-bē\ *n* [Sp, fr. Ar *al-ṭūb* the brick, fr. Copt *tōbe* brick, fr. Egypt *ḏbt*] (1748) **1 :** a brick or building material of sun-dried earth and straw **2 :** a structure made of adobe bricks **3 :** a heavy clay used in making adobe bricks; *broadly* **:** alluvial or playa clay in desert or arid regions — **ado·be·like** \-ˌlīk\ *adj*

adobe 2

ado·bo \ə-ˈdō-bō, ä-ˈt͟hō-bō\ *n, pl* **-bos** [Sp] (ca. 1951) **:** a Philippine dish of fish or meat usu. marinated in a sauce containing vinegar and garlic, browned in fat, and simmered in the marinade

ad·o·les·cence \ˌa-də-ˈle-sᵊn(t)s\ *n* (15c) **1 :** the state or process of growing up **2 :** the period of life from puberty to maturity terminating legally at the age of majority **3 :** a stage of development (as of a language or culture) prior to maturity

[1]**ad·o·les·cent** \-sᵊnt\ *n* [F, fr. L *adolescent-, adolescens,* prp. of *adolescere* to grow up — more at ADULT] (15c) **:** one that is in the state of adolescence

[2]**adolescent** *adj* (1785) **1 :** of, relating to, or being in adolescence **2 :** emotionally or intellectually immature — **ad·o·les·cent·ly** *adv*

Ado·nai \ˌä-də-ˈnȯi, -ˈnī\ *n* [Heb *ʼădhōnāy*] (bef. 12c) — used in place of *YHWH* as a name of the God of the Hebrews during prayer recitation

Ado·nis \ə-ˈdä-nəs, -ˈdō-\ *n* [L, fr. Gk *Adōnis*] (1565) **1 :** a youth loved by Aphrodite who is killed at hunting by a wild boar and restored to Aphrodite from Hades for a part of each year **2 :** a very handsome young man

adopt \ə-ˈdäpt\ *vb* [ME, fr. MF or L; MF *adopter,* fr. L *adoptare,* fr. *ad-* + *optare* to choose] *vt* (1500) **1 :** to take by choice into a relationship; *esp* **:** to take voluntarily (a child of other parents) as one's own child **2 :** to take up and practice or use ⟨~*ed* a moderate tone⟩ **3 :** to accept formally and put into effect ⟨~ a constitutional amendment⟩ **4 :** to choose (a textbook) for required study in a course ~ *vi* **1 :** to adopt a child ⟨couples choosing to ~⟩ **2 :** to sponsor the care and maintenance of ⟨~ a highway⟩ — **adopt·abil·i·ty** \-ˌdäp-tə-ˈbi-lə-tē\ *n* — **adopt·able** \-ˈdäp-tə-bəl\ *adj* — **adopt·er** *n*

syn ADOPT, EMBRACE, ESPOUSE mean to take an opinion, policy, or practice as one's own. ADOPT implies accepting something created by another or foreign to one's nature ⟨forced to *adopt* new policies⟩. EMBRACE implies a ready or happy acceptance ⟨*embraced* the customs of their new homeland⟩. ESPOUSE adds an implication of close attachment to a cause and a sharing of its fortunes ⟨*espoused* the cause of women's rights⟩.

adopt·ee \ə-ˌdäp-ˈtē\ *n* (1892) **:** one who is adopted

adop·tion \ə-ˈdäp-shən\ *n* (14c) **:** the act of adopting **:** the state of being adopted

adop·tion·ism *or* **adop·tian·ism** \-shə-ˌni-zəm\ *n, often cap* (1874) **:** the doctrine that Jesus of Nazareth became the Son of God by adoption — **adop·tion·ist** \-sh(ə-)nist\ *n, often cap*

adop·tive \ə-ˈdäp-tiv\ *adj* (15c) **1 :** made or acquired by adoption ⟨the ~ father⟩ **2 :** of or relating to adoption — **adop·tive·ly** *adv*

ador·able \ə-ˈdȯr-ə-bəl\ *adj* (1611) **1 :** worthy of being adored **2 :** extremely charming ⟨an ~ child⟩ — **ador·abil·i·ty** \-ˌdȯr-ə-ˈbi-lə-tē\ *n* — **ador·able·ness** \-ˈdȯr-ə-bəl-nəs\ *n* — **ador·ably** \-blē\ *adv*

ad·o·ra·tion \ˌa-də-ˈrā-shən\ *n* (15c) **:** the act of adoring **:** the state of being adored

adore \ə-ˈdȯr\ *vt* **adored; ador·ing** [ME *adouren,* fr. AF *aurer, adourer,* fr. L *adorare,* fr. *ad-* + *orare* to speak, pray — more at ORATION] (14c) **1 :** to worship or honor as a deity or as divine **2 :** to regard with loving admiration and devotion ⟨*adored* his wife⟩ **3 :** to be very fond of ⟨~*s* pecan pie⟩ ***syn*** see REVERE — **ador·er** *n* — **ador·ing·ly** *adv*

adorn \ə-ˈdȯrn\ *vt* [ME, fr. L *adornare,* fr. *ad-* + *ornare* to furnish — more at ORNATE] (14c) **1 :** to enhance the appearance of esp. with beautiful objects **2 :** to enliven or decorate as if with ornaments ⟨people of fashion who ~*ed* the Court⟩

syn ADORN, DECORATE, ORNAMENT, EMBELLISH, BEAUTIFY, DECK, GARNISH mean to enhance the appearance of something by adding something unessential. ADORN implies an enhancing by something beautiful in itself ⟨a diamond necklace *adorned* her neck⟩. DECORATE suggests relieving plainness or monotony by adding beauty of color or design ⟨*decorate* a birthday cake⟩. ORNAMENT and EMBELLISH imply the adding of something extraneous, ORNAMENT stressing the heightening or setting off of the original ⟨a white house *ornamented* with green shutters⟩, EMBELLISH often stressing the adding of superfluous or adventitious ornament ⟨*embellish* a page with floral borders⟩. BEAUTIFY adds to EMBELLISH a suggestion of counterbalancing plainness or ugliness ⟨will *beautify* the grounds with flower beds⟩. DECK implies the addition of something that contributes to gaiety, splendor, or showiness ⟨a house all *decked* out for Christmas⟩. GARNISH suggests decorating with a small final touch and is used esp. in referring to the serving of food ⟨an entrée *garnished* with parsley⟩.

adorn·ment \-mənt\ *n* (14c) **1 :** the action of adorning **:** the state of being adorned **2 :** something that adorns

ADP \ˌā-(ˌ)dē-ˈpē\ *n* [*a*denosine *dip*hosphate] (1943) **:** a nucleotide $C_{10}H_{15}N_5O_{10}P_2$ composed of adenosine and two phosphate groups that is formed in living cells as an intermediate between ATP and AMP and that is reversibly converted to ATP for the storing of energy by the addition of a high-energy phosphate group — called also *adenosine diphosphate*

ad rem \(ˌ)ad-ˈrem\ *adv or adj* [L, to the thing] (1599) **:** to the point or purpose **:** RELEVANTLY

adren- *or* **adreno-** *comb form* [*adrenal*] **1 :** adrenal glands ⟨*adreno*cortical⟩ **2 :** adrenaline ⟨*adren*ergic⟩

[1]**ad·re·nal** \ə-ˈdrē-nᵊl\ *adj* [*ad-* + *renal*] (1875) **:** of, relating to, or derived from the adrenal glands or their secretions ⟨~ steroids⟩

[2]**adrenal** *n* (1882) **:** ADRENAL GLAND

ad·re·nal·ec·to·my \ə-ˌdrē-nə-ˈlek-tə-mē\ *n* (ca. 1910) **:** surgical removal of an adrenal gland — **ad·re·nal·ec·to·mized** \-ˌmīzd\ *adj*

adrenal gland *n* (1875) **:** either of a pair of complex endocrine organs near the anterior medial border of the kidney consisting of a mesodermal cortex that produces glucocorticoid, mineralocorticoid, and androgenic hormones and an ectodermal medulla that produces epinephrine and norepinephrine — called also *adrenal, suprarenal gland*

Adren·a·lin \ə-ˈdre-nə-lən\ *trademark* — used for a preparation of levorotatory epinephrine

adren·a·line \ə-ˈdre-nə-lən\ *n* (1901) **:** EPINEPHRINE — often used in nontechnical contexts ⟨the fans were jubilant, raucous, their ~ running high —W. P. Kinsella⟩

adren·al·ized \ə-ˈdre-nə-līzd\ *adj* (1973) **:** filled with a sudden rush of energy **:** EXCITED

ad·ren·er·gic \ˌa-drə-ˈnər-jik\ *adj* [*adren-* + *-ergic*] (1934) **1 :** liberating, activated by, or involving adrenaline or a substance like adrenaline ⟨an ~ nerve⟩ **2 :** resembling adrenaline esp. in physiological action ⟨~ drugs⟩ — **ad·ren·er·gi·cal·ly** \-ji-k(ə-)lē\ *adv*

ad·re·no·chrome \ə-ˈdrē-nō-ˌkrōm\ *n* (ca. 1913) **:** a red-colored mixture of quinones derived from epinephrine by oxidation

ad·re·no·cor·ti·cal \ə-ˌdrē-nō-ˈkȯr-ti-kəl\ *adj* (1936) **:** of, relating to, or derived from the cortex of the adrenal glands

\ə\ **abut** \ᵊ\ **kitten, F table** \ər\ **further** \a\ **ash** \ā\ **ace** \ä\ **mop, mar**
\au̇\ **out** \ch\ **chin** \e\ **bet** \ē\ **easy** \g\ **go** \i\ **hit** \ī\ **ice** \j\ **job**
\ŋ\ **sing** \ō\ **go** \ȯ\ **law** \ȯi\ **boy** \th\ **thin** \t͟h\ **the** \ü\ **loot** \u̇\ **foot**
\y\ **yet** \zh\ **vision, beige** \k̲, ⁿ, œ, ue, ʸ\ *see* Guide to Pronunciation

vt means *verb*. Other abbreviations are listed in the section in the front of your dictionary. In the example, *ski* is both a noun and a verb.

Word History

The language in which the word originally appeared is listed after the pronunciation or at the end of the entry. For example, *L* stands for Latin and *Gk* stands for Greek. Usually the original meaning is also listed. *Ski* is derived from the Norwegian (Norw) word *skith*, which means "stick of wood."

EXERCISE 11   Consult the dictionary page on page 94 to label the statements as either *T* (true) or *F* (false).

_____ 1. Garnish is a synonym for the word *adorn*.

_____ 2. To *adulate* is also to flatter or admire.

_____ 3. The word *Adonai* is taken from an ancient Greek myth.

_____ 4. An *admonition* is a severe form of punishment.

_____ 5. The word *adobe* can be used to refer to both a structure and a type of clay.

_____ 6. If a topic is discussed *ad nauseam*, most listeners are likely to be tired of hearing about it.

_____ 7. The word *Adonis* is used to refer to a young man of great intelligence.

_____ 8. To *admire* someone is to dislike them.

_____ 9. *Adolescent* is a term used for young people in high school.

_____ 10. Someone who dislikes raw vegetables would be unlikely to *adore* fresh salads.

WORD ORIGINS

Words have ancestors. Some of the ancestors are words that were borrowed from other languages. *Shampoo*, for example, comes from a Hindi word meaning *to press*, and *moccasin* comes from the Algonquian Indian word for *shoe*. Other word ancestors include mythology, literature, people, places, and customs. The origin of the word *sadist*, which refers to a person who enjoys inflicting pain on others, is attributed to the Marquis de Sade, an eighteenth-century French author who wrote with pleasure about such cruelty.

Etymology   The study of word origins is called **etymology**. An etymologist traces the development of a word back to its earliest recorded appearance. In dictionaries, the etymology of a word is usually given in brackets. The extent to which the word origin is explained varies from one dictionary to another. Compare the information on the etymology of the word *mentor* given in three dictionaries.

This entry is from the small paperback edition of the *American Heritage Dictionary*:

men•tor (měn′tôr′, -tər) *n.* A wise and trusted counselor or teacher. [< Gk. *Mentōr*,
counselor of Odysseus. See **men-**.]

Source: Copyright © 2001 by Houghton Mifflin
Harcourt Publishing Company. Reproduced
by permission from *The American Heritage
Dictionary*, Fourth Paperback Edition.

This entry is from the textbook-size edition of *Merriam-Webster's Collegiate®
Dictionary*:

¹men•tor \′men-ˌtȯr, -tər\ *n* [L, fr. Gk *Mentōr*] (1616)   **1** *cap* : a friend of
Odysseus entrusted with the education of Odysseus' son Telemachus
2 a : a trusted counselor or guide   **b** : TUTOR, COACH — **men•tor-
ship** \-ˌship\ *n*
²mentor *vt* (1976) : to serve as a mentor for : TUTOR

Source: By permission. From *Merriam-Webster's Collegiate®
Dictionary*, 11th Edition. © 2011 by Merriam-Webster
Incorporated (www.Merriam-Webster.com).

In both cases, the entries give information on the origin of the word, but the
second explains the mythological background more clearly. Both dictionaries are
abridged, which means that information has been condensed. An abridged dictionary is adequate for most college use. In special cases, however, you may desire
more information on the origin or the past use of a word. If so, an unabridged,
or unshortened, dictionary is necessary, but its large size dictates that you must
go to it rather than carry it around with you. Consider the entry for *mentor* in the
unabridged *Webster's Third New International® Dictionary*:

men•tor \′men-ˌtȯ(ə)r, -ȯ(ə), -ntə(r)\ *n* -s [after *Mentor*, tutor
of Telemachus in the Odyssey of Homer, fr. L, fr. Gk *Mentōr*]
1 : a close, trusted, and experienced counselor or guide ⟨every
one of us needs a ∼ who, because he is detached and dis-
interested, can hold up a mirror to us —P.W.Keve⟩ ⟨was much
more than a ∼; he supplied decisions —Hilaire Belloc⟩ ⟨has
been my ∼ since 1946 —Lalia P. Boone⟩ ⟨regarded by patrons
. . . as a personal friend as well as fashion ∼ —*N. Y. State
Legislative Committee on Problems of the Aging*⟩   **2** : TEA-
CHER, TUTOR, COACH ⟨a writer of monographs, and a ∼ of
seminars —*Atlantic*⟩ ⟨although he had never accepted a pupil
. . . she persuaded him to become her ∼ —*Current Biog.*⟩ ⟨one
of the game's most successful young ∼s —*Official Basketball
Guide*⟩

Source: By permission. From *Webster's Third
New International® Dictionary, Unabridged.*© 1993 by
Merriam-Webster Inc. (www.Merriam-Webster.com).

Your college library probably has several unabridged dictionaries in
the reference room. Other excellent choices for etymological research include
the *Random House Dictionary of the English Language* and the *American Heritage
Dictionary of the English Language*.

Why Study Etymology?   The more you know about a word, the easier it is to
remember. The etymology gives you the history of a word, which can help you
establish new relationships on your "computer chip," or schema, for that word.
"Meeting the ancestors" can also help you create a rich visual image of the word
by using the background information. For example, the word *trivial* means "of
little worth or importance." It comes from the Latin words *tri* for *three* and *via* for
way, which combine to mean "the crossing of three roads" in Latin. The Romans
knew that people would stand and talk at such an intersection. Because many
strangers would be listening to the conversations, it was advisable to talk only of
small, or trivial, matters. This history of *trivial* can increase your enjoyment of
the word while enhancing your ability to remember the definition.

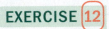

EXERCISE 12 Many English words have their roots in the names of characters in Greek mythology. The words represent a particular characteristic or predicament of the mythological person or creature. Read the entries here to discover their mythological origins, and answer the questions that follow.

> **at·las** \\'at-ləs\ *n* **1 a :** a book of maps often including descriptive text **b :** a book of tables, charts, or illustrations ⟨an *atlas* of anatomy⟩ **2 :** the first vertebra of the neck [*Atlas*, a Titan of Greek mythology]
>
> ***Word History*** Atlas was one of the Titans or giants of Greek mythology, whose rule of the world in an early age was overthrown by Zeus in a mighty battle. Atlas was believed to be responsible for holding up the sky, a task which he tried unsuccessfully to have Hercules assume. In his published collection of maps, the 16th century Flemish cartographer Gerhardus Mercator included on the title page a picture of Atlas supporting the heavens, and he gave the book the title *Atlas*. Other early collections of maps subsequently included similar pictures of Atlas, and such books came to be called *atlases*.
>
> By permission. From *Webster's New Explorer College Dictionary* © 2007 by Federal Street Press, a division of Merriam-Webster Inc.

1. *Atlas* means _____

2. Explain the myth. _____

_____

> **od·ys·sey** \\'äd-e-sē\ *n, pl* **-seys :** a long wandering usually marked by many changes of fortune [the *Odyssey*, epic poem attributed to Homer recounting the long wanderings of Odysseus]
>
> By permission. From *Webster's New Explorer College Dictionary* © 2007 by Federal Street Press, a division of Merriam-Webster Inc.

3. *Odyssey* means _____

_____

4. Explain the myth. _____

_____

TEXTBOOK GLOSSARY

Learning Objective 6

Consult the glossary to define words used in the textbook

Some technical terms located within a textbook glossary may not be found in an ordinary dictionary. An example might be the term *coupled reactions*. One might locate each word separately within a dictionary, but the words combined (having a particular scientific meaning) might be found only within the glossary of a science textbook. The textbook **glossary** defines words and phrases as they apply to particular fields of study. Consult it before using the dictionary for words that seem to be part of the terminology of the discipline.

EXERCISE 13 This exercise considers the types of words and the amount of information presented in a glossary. Notice that many of the words take on a special meaning within the particular field of study. Use the biology glossary on page 98 to answer the questions with *T* (true) or *F* (false).

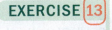

Cumulus   One of three basic cloud forms; also the name given one of the clouds of vertical development. Cumulus are billowy individual cloud masses that often have flat bases.

Cup anemometer   An instrument used to determine wind speed.

Curie point   The temperature above which a material loses its magnetization.

Cutoff   A short channel segment created when a river erodes through the narrow neck of land between meanders.

Cyclone   A low-pressure center characterized by a counterclockwise flow of air in the Northern Hemisphere.

Dark nebula   A cloud of interstellar dust that obscures the light of more distant stars and appears as an opaque curtain.

Deep-ocean basin   The portion of the seafloor that lies between the continental margin and the oceanic ridge. This region comprises almost 30 percent of Earth's surface.

Deep-ocean trench   A narrow, elongated depression on the floor of the ocean.

Deep-sea fan   A cone-shaped deposit at the base of the continental slope. The sediment is transported to the fan by turbidity currents that follow submarine canyons.

Deflation   The lifting and removal of loose material by wind.

Deformation   General term for the processes of folding, faulting, shearing, compression, or extension of rocks.

Degenerate matter   Incomprehensibly dense material formed when stars collapse and form a white dwarf.

Delta   An accumulation of sediment formed where a stream enters a lake or ocean.

Dendritic pattern   A stream system that resembles the pattern of a branching tree.

Density   The weight-per-unit volume of a particular material.

Deposition   The process by which water vapor is changed directly to a solid without passing through the liquid state.

Desalination   The removal of salts and other chemicals from seawater.

Desert   One of the two types of dry climate; the driest of the dry climates.

Desert pavement   A layer of coarse pebbles and gravel created when wind removed the finer material.

Detrital sedimentary rock   Rock formed from the accumulation of material that originated and was transported in the form of solid particles derived from both mechanical and chemical weathering.

Dew point   The temperature to which air has to be cooled in order to reach saturation.

Dike   A tabular-shaped intrusive igneous feature that cuts through the surrounding rock.

Dip-slip fault   A fault in which the movement is parallel to the dip of the fault.

Discharge   The quantity of water in a stream that passes a given point in a period of time.

Disconformity   A type of unconformity in which the beds above and below are parallel.

Discordant   A term used to describe plutons that cut across existing rock structures, such as bedding planes.

Dissolved load   That portion of a stream's load carried in solution.

Distributary   A section of a stream that leaves the main flow.

Diurnal tidal pattern   A tidal pattern exhibiting one high tide and one low tide during a tidal day; a daily tide.

Diurnal tide   Tides characterized by a single high and low water height each tidal day.

Divergence   The condition that exists when the distribution of winds within a given area results in a net horizontal outflow of air from the region. In divergence at lower levels the resulting deficit is compensated for by a downward movement of air from aloft; hence, areas of divergent winds are unfavorable to cloud formation and precipitation.

Divergent plate boundary   A region where the rigid plates are moving apart, typified by the mid-oceanic ridges.

Divide   An imaginary line that separates the drainage of two streams; often found along a ridge.

Dome   A roughly circular upfolded structure similar to an anticline.

Doppler effect   The apparent change in wavelength of radiation caused by the relative motions of the source and the observer.

Doppler radar   In addition to the tasks performed by conventional radar, this new generation of weather radar can detect motion directly and hence greatly improve tornado and severe storm warnings.

Drainage basin   The land area that contributes water to a stream.

Drawdown   The difference in height between the bottom of a cone of depression and the original height of the water table.

Drift   See *Glacial drift*.

Drumlin   A streamlined asymmetrical hill composed of glacial till. The steep side of the hill faces the direction from which the ice advanced.

Dry adiabatic rate   The rate of adiabatic cooling or warming in unsaturated air. The rate of temperature change is 1°C per 100 meters.

Ductile deformation   A type of solid-state flow that produces a change in the size and shape of a rock body without fracturing. Occurs at depths where temperatures and confining pressures are high.

Dune   A hill or ridge of wind-deposited sand.

Earthquake   The vibration of Earth produced by the rapid release of energy.

Echo sounder   An instrument used to determine the depth of water by measuring the time interval between emission of a sound signal and the return of its echo from the bottom.

Elastic rebound   The sudden release of stored strain in rocks that results in movement along a fault.

Electron   A negatively charged subatomic particle that has a negligible mass and is found outside an atom's nucleus.

Element   A substance that cannot be decomposed into simpler substances by ordinary chemical or physical means.

Elements of weather and climate   Those quantities or properties of the atmosphere that are measured regularly and that are used to express the nature of weather and climate.

Elliptical galaxy   A galaxy that is round or elliptical in outline. It contains little gas and dust, no disk or spiral arms, and few hot, bright stars.

Emergent coast   A coast where land that was formerly below sea level has been exposed either because of crustal uplift or a drop in sea level or both.

Emission nebula   A gaseous nebula that derives its visible light from the fluorescence of ultraviolet light from a star in or near the nebula.

End moraine   A ridge of till marking a former position on the front of a glacier.

Entrenched meander   A meander cut into bedrock when uplifting rejuvenated a meandering stream.

Environmental lapse rate   The rate of temperature decrease with increasing height in the troposphere.

Eon   The largest time unit on the geologic time scale, next in order of magnitude above era.

Ephemeral stream   A stream that is usually dry because it carries water only in response to specific episodes of rainfall. Most desert streams are of this type.

Epicenter   The location on Earth's surface that lies directly above the forces of an earthquake.

Epoch   A unit of the geologic calendar that is a subdivision of a period.

Equatorial low   A belt of low pressure lying near the equator and between the subtropical highs.

Equatorial system   A method of locating stellar objects much like the coordinate system used on Earth's surface.

Equinox (spring or autumnal)   The time when the vertical rays of the Sun are striking the equator. The length of daylight and darkness is equal at all latitudes at equinox.

_____ 1. A *cup anemometer* is used to measure rainfall.

_____ 2. A *dark nebula* consists of dust that masks views of more distant stars.

_____ 3. A *dendritic pattern* refers to the shape of a stream's path.

_____ 4. *Dew point* is the place at which dew collects on the ground.

_____ 5. A *divide* is a deep trench in the Earth's surface.

_____ 6. Information gained from *Doppler radar* is often used to warn of tornados and other severe storms.

_____ 7. A *drumlin* is a hill created by glacial ice.

_____ 8. A new country on a coastline that is created by treaty after a war is called an *emergent coast*.

_____ 9. The *epicenter* of an earthquake refers to the exact location of the fault under the Earth's surface.

_____ 10. An *equinox* occurs twice a year and marks the time when the hours of daylight are greater than hours of darkness.

THESAURUS

Learning Objective 7

Find synonyms and antonyms in a thesaurus

Dr. Peter Mark Roget, an English physician, collected lists of related words as a hobby, and in 1852 the lists were published in a **thesaurus**, or treasury of words. In the book he related words because they were synonyms, such as *illegal* and *unlawful*, as well as antonyms, such as *peaceful* and *warlike*. This book, still called *Roget's Thesaurus* because of the man who first had the idea, has been revised frequently through the addition of new words and the deletion of obsolete ones.

Roget's Thesaurus is not a dictionary, and you would probably not use it while reading. Instead, it is a valuable source for writers who are stuck on using a particular word again and again and want a substitute. For example, if you are writing a history term paper and have already used the noun *cause* twice in one paragraph and hesitate to use it again, consult *Roget's Thesaurus* for other options. You will find noun alternatives such as *origin, basis, foundation, genesis,* and *root*. If you need a verb for *cause,* you will find synonyms that include *originate, give rise to, bring about, produce, create, evoke,* and many others. Probably over a hundred words are listed as relating to *cause,* but not all of them are synonymous. Select the one that fits your need in the sentence, adds variety to your writing, and maintains the shade of meaning that you desire.

The words in a thesaurus are ordinarily listed in alphabetical order, and familiar dictionary abbreviations are used for parts of speech. The following example shows an entry for the word *influence*.

influence, *n. & v.* —*n.* influentialness; IMPORTANCE, POWER, mastery, sway, dominance, AUTHORITY, control, ascendancy, persuasiveness, ability to affect; reputation, weight; magnetism, spell; conduciveness; pressure. *Slang,* drag, pull. —*v.t.* affect; move, induce, persuade; sway, control, lead, actuate; modify; arouse, incite; prevail upon, impel; set the pace, pull the strings; tell, weigh. *Ant.,* see IMPOTENCE.

Source: From *The New American Roget's College Thesaurus* by Phillip D. Morehead and Andrew T. Morehead, copyright © 1958, 1962 by Albert H. Morehead. Copyright © 1978, 1985, renewed 1986 by Philip D. Morehead and Andrew T. Morehead. Used by permission of Dutton Signet, a division of Penguin Group (USA) Inc.

When a word is printed in small capitals, such as IMPORTANCE, POWER, and AUTHORITY, it means that you can find additional synonyms by looking that particular word up in its alphabetical order. Explanations sometimes appear in brackets, and not every word in the dictionary is listed.

Reader's TIP   Using an Electronic Thesaurus

Your word-processing program probably has a thesaurus. In many versions of Microsoft Word, for example, the thesaurus is found in the *Tools* pull-down menu, as one of the *Language* options. To use this, select the word for which you want alternatives by dragging the cursor over the word to highlight it and then clicking on the thesaurus. An array of words will appear, usually both in the *Meanings* box and in the *Replace with Synonyms* box, as indicated in the figure here displaying alternatives for the word *right*. Click and highlight a different word other than *just*, which is presently highlighted in the *Meanings* box, and you will get a different array of synonyms. For example, click on the word *sane* in the following illustration and your synonym options will be *normal, rational, sound, reasonable*, and *wise*.

This one word *right* has forty-nine synonym alternatives on this computer thesaurus in Microsoft Word. By moving the down arrow situated to the right of the word *claim*, you will uncover the word *Antonyms*, and the words *wrong, incorrect, erroneous*, and *lenient* will appear as options. Thus your computer thesaurus has many more words than appear at first glance. Search and choose an option that fits the context of your sentence. The procedure may vary depending on the version of Microsoft Word or other word-processing program you are using.

Thesaurus: English (United States)

Looked up:	Replace with Synonyms
right	just

Meanings:	just
just (adj.)	fair
suitable (adj.)	equitable
correct (adj.)	legitimate
sane (adj.)	upright
front (adj.)	honest
rightful (adj.)	good
claim (noun)	lawful

[Replace]   [Look Up]   [Previous]   [Cancel]

EXERCISE 14   Use the thesaurus entry for *right* to select an alternative word that fits the meaning of *right* in the sentences that follow.

1. The first amendment gives Americans the *right* of free speech. _____

2. It was not *right* for the government to force the Indians out of the Southeast in the Trail of Tears. _____

3. Can government payments help *right* some social wrongs of the past? _____

4. Do revolutionaries ignore the difference between *right* and wrong? _____

5. Employers want to make the *right* fit between employee skills and job demands.

_____

RIGHT, RIGHTNESS [922]

Nouns—**1,** rightness, right, what ought to be, what should be, fitness, propriety; JUSTICE, morality, PROBITY, honor, virtue, lawfulness.
2, privilege, prerogative, title, claim, grant, POWER, franchise, license.
3, rightness, correctness, accuracy, precision; exactness; TRUTH.
Verbs—**1,** be right, be just, stand to reason.
3, right, make right, correct, remedy, see justice done, play fair, do justice to, recompense, hold the scales even, give every one his due.
Adjectives—**1,** right, upright, good, just (see JUSTICE); reasonable, suitable, becoming.
2, right, correct, proper, precise, exact, accurate, true.
Adverbs—rightly, justly, fairly, correctly; in justice, in equity, in reason, without distinction of persons, on even terms.
Antonym, see WRONG.

Source: From *The New American Roget's College Thesaurus* by Phillip D. Morehead and Andrew T. Morehead, copyright © 1958, 1962 by Albert H. Morehead. Copyright © 1978, 1985, renewed 1986 by Philip D. Morehead and Andrew T. Morehead. Used by permission of Dutton Signet, a division of Penguin Group (USA) Inc.

ANALOGIES

An **analogy** is a comparison that mimics a previously stated relationship. Perhaps the best explanation is an example.

EXAMPLE *Apple* is to *fruit* as *potato* is to _____.

EXPLANATION The first step in solving an analogy is to pinpoint the initial relationship. What is the relationship between *apple* and *fruit?* Because an

---

Reader's **TIP**   Categories of Relationships for Analogies

Synonyms: Similar in meaning
   Start is to *begin* as *end* is to *finish.*

Antonyms: Opposite in meaning
   Retreat is to *advance* as *tall* is to *short.*

Function, use, or **purpose:** Identifies what something does. Watch for the object (noun) and then the action (verb).
   Car is to *drive* as *towel* is to *absorb.*

Classification: Identifies the larger group association
   Mosquito is to *insect* as *gasoline* is to *fuel.*

Characteristics and descriptions: Shows qualities or traits
   Sour is to *lemon* as *sweet* is to *sugar.*

Degree: Shows variations of intensity
   Walking is to *running* as *cool* is to *frozen.*

Part to whole: Shows the larger group
   Pupil is to *school* as *sailor* is to *navy.*

Cause and effect: Shows the reason (cause) and the result (effect)
   Work is to *success* as *virus* is to *illness.*

Learning Objective 8

Refine word knowledge by solving analogies

apple is a member of the fruit group, you might say that it is one part of a larger whole. To complete the analogy, you must establish a similar relationship for *potato*. In what larger group does a potato belong? *Vegetable* is the answer.

Analogies are challenging and can be very difficult. They test logical thinking as well as vocabulary. Working through analogies is an experience in problem solving.

The preceding Reader's Tip explains the many different relationships that can be expressed in an analogy. Study both the list and the examples.

EXERCISE 15   Study the following analogies to establish the relationship of the first two words. Record that relationship, using the categories just outlined. Then choose the word that duplicates that relationship to finish the analogy.

_____ 1. *Leg* is to *table* as *wheel* is to _____.

Relationship? _____
a. chair
b. car
c. motor
d. steer

_____ 2. *Soft* is to *firm* as *peaceful* is to _____.

Relationship? _____
a. pillow
b. kind
c. sleep
d. aggressive

_____ 3. *Turnip* is to *vegetable* as *oak* is to _____.

Relationship? _____
a. wood
b. fuel
c. house
d. glass

_____ 4. *Selling* is to *profit* as *germ* is to _____.

Relationship? _____
a. vaccination
b. carelessness
c. wealth
d. disease

_____ 5. *Kind* is to *considerate* as *courage* is to _____.

Relationship? _____
a. soldier
b. bravery
c. fear
d. fighting

_____ 6. *Towel* is to *absorb* as *oven* is to _____.

    Relationship? _____
    a. safety
    b. speed
    c. cook
    d. kitchen

_____ 7. *Tiny* is to *small* as *hot* is to _____.

    Relationship? _____
    a. summer
    b. warm
    c. cooking
    d. temperature

_____ 8. *Soft* is to *pillow* as *humid* is to _____.

    Relationship? _____
    a. swamp
    b. trip
    c. camp
    d. trees

_____ 9. *Work* is to *success* as *study* is to _____.

    Relationship? _____
    a. history
    b. knowledge
    c. professor
    d. college

_____ 10. *Needle* is to *sew* as *bulb* is to _____.

    Relationship? _____
    a. lamp
    b. illuminate
    c. electricity
    d. table

EASILY CONFUSED WORDS

Learning Objective 9

Spell commonly confused words

Many pairs of words cause confusion because they sound exactly alike or almost alike but are spelled and used differently. *Principal* and *principle* are examples of this confusion. A common error is to write, "The new school principle is Mrs. Thompson." Remember, the *al* word is the person, or "pal," and the *le* word is the rule. To keep most of these words straight, memorize and associate. Study the following words that sound similar and learn their differences.

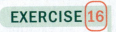 **EXERCISE 16**

Circle the correct boldface word to fit the context of each sentence.

1. She exercised on a (**stationary, stationery**) bicycle.
2. Her brother devoured the (**hole, whole**) pizza by himself.

Reader's TIP — Easily Confused Words

capital: city
capitol: building

to: in the direction of
too: also

their: belonging to them
there: opposite of here
they're: they are

accept: receive
except: all but

cite: quote
sight: vision
site: place

hole: a depression in the ground
whole: entire

stationary: fixed position
stationery: paper

its: belonging to it
it's: it is

your: belonging to you
you're: you are

threw: launched
through: in one side and out the other

3. The (**capital, capitol**) serves as a meeting place for both senators and representatives.

4. The line for the bookstore begins right (**their, they're, there**).

5. After such a late night, they were much (**to, too**) tired to wake up early.

6. In order to get (**threw, through**) college successfully, studying is necessary.

7. The overhead projector was placed directly in her (**cite, sight, site**) line for the speaker.

8. Sometimes it is difficult to (**accept, except**) the truth.

9. (**Your, you're**) first impression is often a lasting one.

10. (**Vain, vein**) students might spend extra time gazing at themselves in front of the mirror.

11. (**Its, It's**) not the best strategy to watch television while studying for a test.

ENRICHING YOUR VOCABULARY

Most reading selections in this text are followed by practice for vocabulary development called Vocabulary Enrichment (see p. 150 for an example). In addition, Vocabulary Lessons using a structural approach appear at the end of most chapters, including this one. In these lessons, prefixes, roots, and suffixes are linked to new words. Plan to make vocabulary enrichment an exciting, lifelong activity.

PERSONAL FEEDBACK **2**   Name _____

1. After reading this chapter, how will you change your system for remembering new words? _____

   _____

   _____

   _____

2. Why is it not recommended that you look up unknown words as you read? _____

   _____

   _____

   _____

3. List ten adjectives to describe characteristics that you would like in a spouse. Again, stretch your vocabulary beyond easy words. _____

   _____

   _____

   _____

   Tear out and submit to your instructor.

SUMMARY POINTS

1 What is a good system for learning expanding vocabulary? (page 78)
Use the power of association. Make concept cards that include the word, the definition, a sentence, a picture, and the source. Use the cards to quiz yourself repeatedly. Use the words!

2 What strategies are effective for unlocking the meaning of unfamiliar words? (page 80)
Use context clues, knowledge of word parts, the dictionary, and the glossary.

3 How can I use context clues to unlock unfamiliar words? (page 81)
Notice various types of clues surrounding the unfamiliar word: Definitions, elaborating details, elaborating examples, comparisons, contrasts. Also remember that some words have several meanings. Use the context to know which meaning is intended.

4 How can I use common word parts to unlock meaning? (page 88)
Use familiar prefixes, roots, and suffixes to predict the meaning of an unfamiliar word.

5 What information can a dictionary provide to enrich my word knowledge? (page 92)

Strengthen word knowledge by learning pronunciation, spelling, meaning, part of speech, word history, and word origin or etymology. All of these details can be found in the dictionary.

6 What information can I find in a glossary? (page 97)

Use the glossary at the back of the textbook to find the meanings of words as they are used in that text and in the discipline.

7 When is a thesaurus helpful? (page 99)

Use a thesaurus to find alternative words when writing.

8 What is the value of solving analogies? (page 102)

Analogies require precise thinking about the meanings and functions of words. The key to solving them is to first determine the relationship between the pair of words given and then select a word that repeats that relationship in the second pair.

9 What are some commonly confused words that I should learn to spell correctly? (page 103)

Practice using these words correctly: *stationary/stationery; hole/whole; capital/ capitol; their/they're/there; to/too; threw/through; cite/sight/site; accept/except; your/you're; vain/vein; its/it's.*

COLLABORATIVE   PROBLEM SOLVING

Form a five-member group and select one of the following activities. Brainstorm and then outline your major points. Choose a member to present the group findings to the class.

➤ Make a list of ten words that have multiple meanings.

➤ Create a list of ten words that begin with the prefix *pre.*

➤ Create five analogies, one for each of the following relationships: synonyms, antonyms, function, part to whole, and cause and effect.

➤ Create a list of ten words that end with the suffix *ous.*

MyReadingLab

MyReadingLab (MRL) www.myreadinglab.com

➤ For support in meeting this chapter's objectives, log in to **www.myreadinglab.com** and select "Vocabulary."

THE READING WORKSHOP

If reading a novel, biography, or other book is part of your course experience, refer to The Reading Workshop: Thinking, Talking, and Writing about Books in Appendix 5 for suggestions.

VOCABULARY LESSON

For or Against?

Study the prefixes, words, and sentences.

Prefixes   *pro*: for, forward, forth   *anti, ant*: against   *contra*: against

Words with *pro = for, forward, forth*

Do medical *procedures* require signed forms? Can you *proceed* inside with a ticket?

- Pro-choice: for abortion rights

  The *pro-choice* rally was held on the steps of the state capitol.

- Proponent: supporter

  Are you a *proponent* of building another oil pipeline in Alaska?

- Procure: to get or gain

  Campers need to *procure* supplies a week prior to departure.

- Profess: to openly admit

  I *profess* to enjoying double fudge chocolate brownie cake.

- Prolific: bringing forth young or fruit

  The *prolific* young couple had six small children.

- Proficient: showing skill

  To be *proficient* in Spanish requires a knowledge of grammar.

- Proliferate: to bring forth by rapid production

  Fast-food restaurants seem to *proliferate* near interstate highway exits.

Words with *anti* or *ant = against*

Do *antiabortionists* use signs? Will an *anticoagulant* stop bleeding?

- Antacid: a counteracting agent for acidity of the stomach

  Take an *antacid* tablet for a burning stomach.

- Antagonism: a strong feeling against a person or idea

  After they had shared several funny jokes, the *antagonism* between them evaporated.

- Antarctic: the opposite of the North Pole

  The *Antarctic* region is south of the Arctic.

- Anticlimax: a letdown from a greater event

  After the previous night's celebration, New Year's day was an *anticlimax*.

- Antipathy: a strong feeling of dislike

  The business partner's *antipathy* toward the accused swindler was evident.

- Antithesis: a contrast of ideas

  The son's liberal ideas are the *antithesis* of his father's conservative policies.

- Antibody: a substance in the body opposing diseases

  The scientists worked to create an *antibody* for the new flu strain.

- Antidote: a remedy for poison

  Jungle travelers carry an *antidote* for snake bites.

- Antifreeze: a substance to slow the freezing process

  Check your car for *antifreeze* before the first frost.

Words with *contra = against*

Does sex education stress *contraceptives*? Are *controversial* issues frequently argued?

- Contraband: illegal

  Contraband items can be seized by the police.

- Contradict: to speak against

  To *contradict* a speaker, you must be sure of your facts.

- Contrarian: person who takes contrary views

  Reasoning with a *contrarian* is not always possible.

Review

Part I

Answer the following with *T* (true) or *F* (false).

_____ 1. An antidote is an amusing story.

_____ 2. A prolific plant bears many fruits.

_____ 3. Supplies can be procured by illegal means.

_____ 4. A contrarian would be comfortable in a role involving questioning.

_____ 5. Pro-choice advocates demonstrate against abortion clinics.

_____ 6. If you contradict the evidence, you disagree with the facts.

_____ 7. An athlete must be proficient to play on a professional team.

_____ 8. A sick person usually welcomes an antibody.

_____ 9. A controversial news story seldom generates further discussion.

_____10. For a peaceful relationship, mutual antagonism should be resolved.

Part II

Choose the best word from the list as a synonym for the following.

profess	antacid	antithesis	proponent	antifreeze
procedure	controversy	anticlimax	contraband	antipathy

11. Liquid solution for machines _____

12. Feeling of dislike _____

13. Smuggled drugs _____

14. Admit _____

15. Medication _____

16. Plan _____

17. Opposite _____

18. Disagreement _____

19. Supporter _____

20. Disappointment _____

Getting News and Other Information from Websites and Forums

If you want up-to-the-minute news and other information, you can find it instantly on the Internet. A number of news sites headline current events and link in-depth stories with added details. Some sites, such as CNN.com, further link to blogs, which are personal Web blogs, journals, or newsletters from people with an observation or opinion.

For information on specific groups of interest to you, you can visit online communities called forums, which will pinpoint your interests. For example, you could log on to a cooking forum, or to be more specific, a salmon cooking forum. If you log on to a salmon forum, you may be reading about environmental issues concerning saving the salmon, not grilling them.

News-Related Websites

Searching for news stories is easy, using news-centered websites such as Google News <www.news.google.com> or CNN.com <www.CNN.com>. Both Google News and CNN offer home pages that list top news stories of the day and a search area where a topic or keywords can be typed in for related news stories. The sites also have separate sections for the United States and the world. You can get today's headline news in Rome, Mexico City, or Moscow. You can also search topics such as science/technology, sports, entertainment, and health.

You can also go to the websites of national newspapers, such as the *New York Times* <www.nytimes.com> and *USA Today* <www.usatoday.com>, to gather information. Your local newspaper probably has its own website. The newspaper sites require that you register with a password, but there is often no charge for this service.

 **EXERCISE 1**

Go to either Google.com or CNN.com and explore news stories that interest you. Record the Web address of two news stories and, on a separate piece of paper, explain what information you found about each.

Forums

Forums, also known as online communities, provide free, up-to-date information about specific subjects. Forums may be maintained by a company or an individual and are interactive in that a subscriber can post questions and receive timely answers. There are forums for almost every subject. Here are just a few forums found on the Internet.

- Music forums provide users with news, chats, and an online community.

  MusicBoards.com   www.musicboards.com

- Cooking forums offer experienced and inexperienced cooks information and tips on cooking.

  DiscussCooking.com   www.discusscooking.com

- Government forums are also informative.

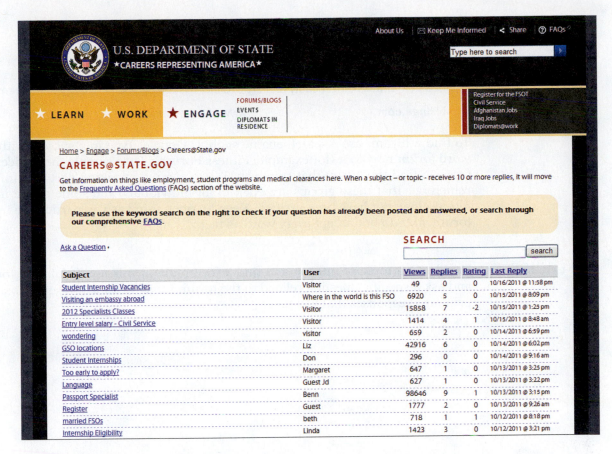

U.S. Department of State

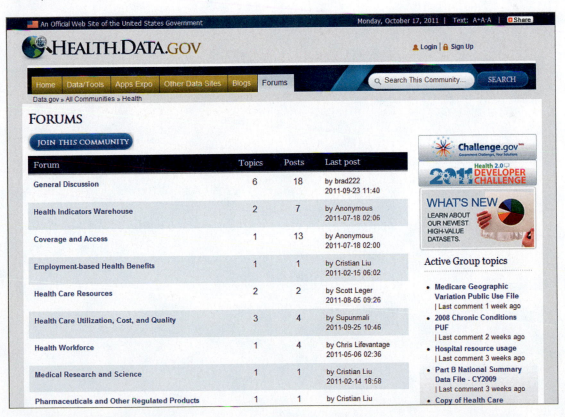

DATA.gov <http://DATA.gov>

- Forums on bicycling offer a wealth of information for bicycle enthusiasts.

  Cyclingforums.com   www.cyclingforums.com

- iVillage website features a variety of forums related to women's issues, such as health and well-being, beauty and style, diet and fitness, and pregnancy and parenting.

  ivillage.com   www.ivillage.com

To find a forum, use a search engine such as Google. Type in a subject with the word *forum* next to it (for example, Fitness Forum). Then sample the choices offered to find the forum that suits you. When visiting or taking part in a forum, remember that these groups are open to all individuals, and some of the information may not have been verified. Keep an open mind as you participate in the forum, and do not accept every word as fact.

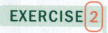 **EXERCISE 2**

Decide on a topic of interest and find a forum about this topic. Join the forum and ask a specific question related to the forum topic. Record your question and print any responses that you get.

4 Main Idea

Learning Objectives

From this chapter, readers will learn:

1 To define topic, main idea, and major and minor supporting details
2 To identify topics
3 To recognize stated main ideas
4 To identify supporting details
5 To master main idea and topic questions on tests
6 To use a three-question strategy for identifying the main idea
7 To identify unstated main ideas
8 To identify main ideas in longer selections

Everyday Reading Skills: Selecting a Book

WHAT IS A TOPIC? WHAT IS A MAIN IDEA?

The **topic** of a passage is its general subject. It is the answer to the question, "Who or what is this passage about?" The topic can be described in a single word or in a brief phrase. For example, "*mood disorders*" might be a topic featured in your psychology textbook.

The **main idea** of a passage is the core of the material, the particular point the author is trying to convey about the topic. The main idea of a passage can be stated in one sentence that condenses specific ideas or details in the passage into a general, all-inclusive statement of the author's message. For instance, if the topic is mood disorders, then the main idea might be, "*Mood disorders can take several forms.*" In classroom discussions, all of the following words are sometimes used to help students understand the meaning of the main idea.

thesis	gist
main point	controlling idea
central focus	central thought

Whether you read a single paragraph, a chapter, or an entire book, many experts agree that your most important single task is to understand the main idea of what you read.

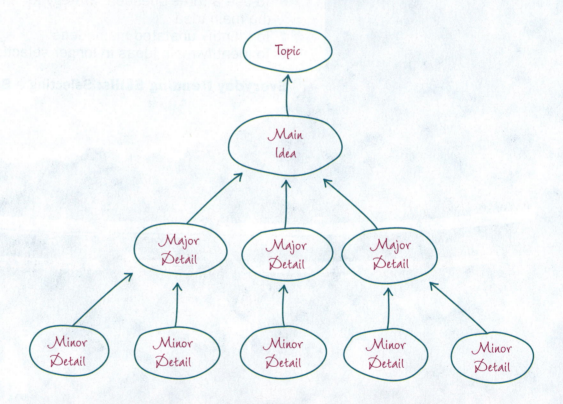

WHAT ARE MAJOR AND MINOR SUPPORTING DETAILS?

Major supporting details provide specific information that explains and elaborates on the main idea. For example, "*major depression*" and "*bipolar disorder*" might be major supporting details that explain the author's point that mood disorders can take several forms. **Minor supporting details** lend even more specific information that further explains the major details. Minor details might take the form of an example or interesting anecdote. They are often the link that helps us remember the more important details. For instance, *"the suicide of Nirvana's lead singer, Kurt Cobain,"* might be used to illustrate the effects of depression. Likewise, *"periods of abnormally high energy alternating with periods of extreme fatigue"* would describe bipolar disorder.

With the definitions of *topic*, *main idea*, and *major and minor supporting details* in mind, examine the diagram on the previous page. It illustrates the relationships among these elements of a written selection. Minor details illustrate and explain major details, which in turn support and explain the main idea, and the main idea makes a point about the topic.

IDENTIFYING TOPICS

Learning Objective 2
Identify topics

Recognize General and Specific Words

The first step in determining the main idea of a selection is to look at the specific ideas presented in the sentences and try to decide on a general topic or subject under which you can group these ideas. Before tackling sentences, begin with words. Pretend that the sentence ideas in a selection have been reduced to a short list of keywords. Pretend also that within the list is a general term that expresses an overall subject for the keywords. The general term encompasses or categorizes the key ideas and is considered the topic of the list.

EXAMPLE   The following list contains three specific ideas with a related general topic. Circle the general term that could be considered the subject of the list.

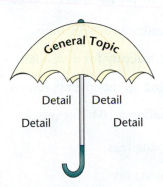

satin

wool

fabric

silk

EXPLANATION   Satin, wool, and silk are different types of fabric. Thus *fabric* is the general term or classification that could be considered the subject or topic.

EXERCISE 1   Circle the general term or subject for each of the following related groups of ideas.

1. chimpanzees	2. cirrus	3. oats	4. Alps	5. shrimp
orangutans	clouds	wheat	Appalachians	crustacean
apes	cumulus	corn	mountains	crab
gorillas	stratus	grain	Rockies	lobster

Recognize General and Specific Phrases

Topics of passages are more often stated as phrases rather than single words. The following list contains a phrase that is a general topic and three specific ideas related to that topic. Circle the general topic that could be the subject.

EXAMPLE   Turn on the ignition.

Press the accelerator.

Insert the key.

Start the car.

EXPLANATION   The first three details are involved in starting a car. The last phrase is the general subject or topic.

EXERCISE 2   Circle the phrase that could be the topic for each list.

1. totaling yearly income

   subtracting for dependents

   filing an income tax return

   mailing a 1040 form

2. paying fees

   buying books

   starting college

   going to class

3. picking up seashells

   vacationing at the beach

   walking in the surf

   riding the waves

4. pushing paper under sticks

   piling the logs

   building a fire

   striking a match

EXERCISE 3   Read the lists of specific details and write a general phrase that could be the subject or topic for each group.

1. separate the white and dark clothes

   add one cup of detergent

   insert quarters into the machine

   General topic? _____

2. dribble the ball

   pass the ball down court

   shoot a basket

   General topic? _____

3. pull up alongside car

   back into space

   straighten out

   General topic? _____

4. switch on power

   select a program

   open a file

   General topic? _____

5. boil water in a large pot

   add salt and oil

   pour noodles into water

   General topic? _____

Recognize the General Topic for Sentences

Paragraphs are composed of sentences that develop a single general topic. The next practice exercises contain groups in which the sentences of a paragraph are listed numerically. After reading the sentences, circle the phrase that best expresses the topic or general subject of the sentences.

EXAMPLE

1. The law of demand is illustrated in an experiment conducted by the makers of M&M candy.
2. For a twelve-month period, the price of M&Ms remained the same in 150 stores, but the number of M&Ms in a package increased, which dropped the price per ounce.
3. In those stores, sales immediately rose by 20 to 30 percent.

   Candy Maker's Experiment

   M&Ms Drop in Price

   M&Ms Prove the Law of Demand

EXPLANATION   The first phrase is too broad. The second relates a detail that is an important part of the experiment. The third links the candy with the purpose of the experiment and thus most accurately states the topic of the sentences.

EXERCISE 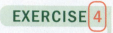 Circle the phrase that best describes the topic or subject for each group of sentences.

Group 1

1. To provide a favorable climate for growing grapes, the winter temperature should not go below 15° F, and the summers should be long.
2. During the growing season, rainfall should be light.
3. A gentle movement of air is required to dry the vines after rains, dispel fog, and protect the vines from fungus disease.

Protecting Grapes from Disease

Appropriate Temperatures for Growing Grapes

Appropriate Climate for Growing Grapes

Group 2

1. For example, addicted parents may neglect to properly care for their children.
2. Other individuals go from one job to another, never able to hold on to any position for very long.
3. For example, students who are addicted to drugs may repeatedly fail classes because they do not complete assignments.

Drug Abuse among College Students

Possible Symptoms of Drug Abuse and Addiction

Drug Abuse in Contemporary Society

Group 3

1. Aerobic fitness includes maintaining a strong heart, a healthy vascular system, and muscles that effectively use oxygen.
2. The goal of an aerobic workout is to achieve and maintain one's target heart rate for approximately 20–30 minutes.
3. One element of aerobic fitness is to engage in an aerobic workout three to five times a week.

Aerobic Fitness

Maintaining a Healthy Heart

The Proper Aerobic Workout

Group 4

1. Salsa, the popular blend of Latin American music, is also the word for *sauce*.
2. According to stories, the expression was contributed to the music world by a Cuban orchestra conductor.
3. While practicing a mambo that needed more life, the orchestra leader told his musicians to "echale salsita" or "throw in the sauce."

Latin American Salsa Music

The Naming of Salsa Music

Contribution of Salsa

Group 5

1. Simply drinking water is the best way to prevent dehydration from sweating.
2. Taking salt tablets before drinking water can dehydrate the body even more by extracting water from body tissue.
3. Plain water is better than beverages containing sugar or electrolytes because it is absorbed faster.

Salt Tablets versus Water

Value in Plain Water

Preventing Dehydration

BRAIN BOOSTER

Exercise and the Brain

Physical movement increases the amount of blood in the brain and thus the amount of oxygen and other nutrients the brain needs to function well. The greater blood supply also carries away waste materials more efficiently. If that isn't enough to convince us to get up and move, there's more. Exercise also produces BDNF, Brain Derived Neurotrophic Factor, a protein that helps to keep existing brain cells healthy and to generate new brain cells. How much exercise is enough? An aerobic workout 2 to 3 times a week plus strengthening exercises produces the best results, but just taking a walk helps boost thinking power.

—Adapted from John J. Medina, *Brain Rules*. © 2008
John J. Medina. Pear Press: Seattle, WA

EXERCISE 5   Read a group of three sentences, then write a phrase that best states the subject or general topic for the sentences.

Group 1

1. Psychologists conduct research with animals for several reasons.
2. Sometimes they simply want to know more about the behavior of a specific type of animal.
3. In other instances they want to see whether certain laws of behavior apply to both humans and animals.

General topic? _____

—*Psychology: Themes & Variations*, Sixth Edition,
by Wayne Weiten

Group 2

1. Scientists think that a more reasonably defined danger level would mean that only 50,000 homes have radon concentrations that pose a danger to occupants.
2. Scientists outside the EPA have concluded that the standards the EPA is using are too stringent.
3. The United States Environmental Protection Agency (EPA) regards 5 million American homes as having unacceptable radon levels in the air.

General topic? _____

_____

—*Physical Geology: Earth Revealed*, Fifth Edition,
by David McGeary, et al.

Group 3

1. They resist accepting a warm pink body as a corpse from which organs can be "harvested."
2. The Japanese do not incorporate a mind–body split into their models of themselves; they locate personhood throughout the body rather than in the brain.
3. In Japan the concept of brain death is hotly contested, and organ transplants are rarely performed.

General topic? _____

—*Cultural Anthropology*, Eleventh Edition,
by William A. Haviland, et al.

BRAIN BOOSTER

Water on the Brain

Our brains are made up of about 80 percent water, and brain function depends on maintaining adequate hydration. Only water will do! The sugars in coffee, tea, and soft drinks bind to the water in them, the body processes them as foods, and the benefits of the water are lost. In fact, these drinks actually act as diuretics and dehydrate the body rather then hydrate it. If you feel listless, sleepy, or cannot concentrate, you might just need a drink of water.

—Adapted from *Brain-Based Learning:*
The New Paradigm of Teaching, 2nd ed.,
by Eric Jensen, Corwin Press, 2008.

IDENTIFYING TOPICS AND MAIN IDEAS

Recognize General and Supporting Sentences

Read the sentences in each of the following groups. The sentences are related to a single subject, with two of the sentences expressing specific support and one sentence expressing the main idea. Circle the number of the sentence that best expresses the main idea. Then read the three phrases and circle the one that best describes the topic of the sentences.

EXAMPLE

1. An accountant who prefers to work alone rather than as a team member may be an important part of the organization but will not become a leader.
2. A CEO who steers a company into increased profits but exhibits poor people skills by yelling at employees and refusing to listen will not keep her job.
3. Companies now demand of their top employees a high level of emotional intelligence (EI), which refers to skills in adaptability, self-control, conflict management, and teamwork.

IQ No Longer Matters

The Importance of Emotional Intelligence

Polite Changes in the Workplace

Learning Objective 3

Recognize stated main ideas (*See also page 128.*)

EXPLANATION The third sentence best expresses the general subject. The other two sentences offer specific supporting ideas. The second phrase, "The Importance of Emotional Intelligence," best describes the general subject of the material. The first phrase is not really suggested, and the last phrase is one of the details mentioned.

EXERCISE  Circle the number of the sentence that best expresses the main idea. Then read the three topic phrases and circle the phrase that best describes the subject of the sentences.

Group 1

1. African American and Hispanic teens are not as likely to use tobacco as Caucasian adolescents.
2. Each day approximately three thousand teens start smoking, and eventually one third of them will die from smoking.
3. Despite the proven danger, in the past decade tobacco usage among teens has increased.

Tobacco Usage Among Teens

Dangers Teens Face

Harms of Smoking

Group 2

1. Berry Gordy, an ex-boxer and Ford auto worker, borrowed $700 from his family and began to manufacture and sell his own records on the Hitsville USA (later called Motown, for "motor town") label.
2. The next year Smokey Robinson and the Miracles recorded "Shop Around," which was Gordy's first million-copy hit.
3. Gordy signed an 11-year-old boy to record for him under the name of Stevie Wonder.

Gordy's Success

Stevie Wonder at Motown

The Recording Artists at Motown

Group 3

1. The czar's wife believed that the devious and politically corrupt Rasputin, known as the "mad monk," was the only one who could save her son.
2. The son of Nicholas II was afflicted with hemophilia, a condition in which the blood does not clot properly.
3. In Russia during the reign of Nicholas II, hemophilia played an important historical role.

Rasputin's Charm

Hemophilia

Influence of Hemophilia on Russia

Group 4

1. In the 1990s, however, doctors began advising parents to position babies for sleep on their backs, and now many babies never crawl but still learn to walk at about the same age.
2. What is considered normal infant development can change quickly when new recommendations in infant care are introduced.

3. For example, crawling at 6–8 months of age was once an expected milestone when babies were traditionally put to sleep lying on their stomachs.

Developmental Effects of Changes in Infant Care

The Importance of Proper Infant Care

Infant Sleeping Positions

Group 5

1. The success of Norman Rockwell's illustrations is based on his simple formula of drawing ordinary people doing ordinary things that make us laugh at ourselves.

2. Rockwell used humor to poke fun at situations but never at people.
3. Rockwell painted the people and children of the neighborhood, first from real life, then, in later years, from photographs.

Rockwell's Neighborhood

The Subjects of Rockwell's Paintings

Art from Photographs

EXERCISE 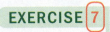 **7**   For each group of sentences, write a phrase that states the topic; then circle the number of the sentence that best expresses the main idea.

Group 1

1. Four hundred Navajos were recruited as marine radio operators, and the codes based on the Navajo language were never broken by the enemy.
2. During World War II, over 25,000 Native Americans served in the armed forces and made amazing contributions toward the war effort.
3. The most famous Indian GI was a Pima Indian, the marine Ira Hayes, who helped plant the American flag on Iwo Jima.

General Topic? _____

Group 2

1. Germans view health as having several components.
2. Hard work, cleanliness, and staying warm aid in health maintenance.
3. Stress and germs as well as drafts, unhappiness, and a sedentary lifestyle are believed to cause illness.

General topic? _____

—*Culture in Rehabilitation*,
edited by Matin Royeen
and Jeffrey L. Crabtree

Group 3

1. Logically, the probability of having a "good Samaritan" on the scene would seem to increase as group size increases.
2. When it comes to helping behavior, many studies have uncovered a puzzling situation called the bystander effect: People are less likely to provide needed help when they are in groups than when they are alone.
3. Evidence that your probability of getting help *declines* as group size increases was first described by John Darley and Bibb Latane, who were conducting research on helping behavior.

General topic? _____

—*Psychology: Themes & Variations*, Sixth Edition,
by Wayne Weiten

EXERCISE **8**   Each of the following sentence groups contains three specific supporting sentences. Write a general sentence that states the *main idea* for each group. In addition, write a phrase that briefly states the general *topic* of that sentence.

Group 1

1. The battered woman does not want to believe the man she loves is violent.
2. She doesn't want to face the possibility that he may be violent for the rest of their lives together.
3. She wants to hold on to the hope that someday he will quit drinking and the relationship will change.

—*Marriage and Families in a Diverse Society*,
by Robin Wolf

General sentence stating the main idea? _____

_____

General topic? _____

Group 2

1. Decades before Jamestown was hailed as the first permanent settlement in America, Pedro Menendez de Aviles founded St. Augustine in Florida.
2. Menendez brought 800 soldiers and colonists to establish this first European settlement in America and to protect the land for Spain.
3. St. Augustine, so named because the landing occurred in the month of August, became a permanent and prosperous Spanish settlement.

General sentence stating the main idea? _____

_____

General topic? _____

Group 3

1. According to a recent report, the average U.S. wedding in 2010 included 200 or more guests and cost $30,166.
2. In 2005, the average wedding hosted fewer than 200 guests and cost $24,168.
3. Among the many expenses included in the overall cost of a wedding are the reception, rings, wedding attire, and photography.

General sentence stating the main idea? _____

_____

General topic? _____

—*Business Mathematics*, Twelfth Edition,
by Gary Clendenen, et al.

Differentiate Topic, Main Idea, and Supporting Details

Learning Objective 4

Identify supporting details

We have said that a topic is a word or phrase that describes the subject or general category of a group of specific ideas. Frequently, the topic is stated as the title of a passage. The main idea, in contrast, is a complete sentence that states the topic and *adds the writer's position or focus on the topic*. The supporting details are the specifics that develop the topic and main idea.

Read the following example from a textbook paragraph and label the topic, the main idea, and a supporting detail.

EXAMPLE

_____ The Body Signaling Feeling

_____ Some signals of body language, like some facial expressions, seem to be "spoken" universally.

_____ When people are depressed, it shows in their walk, stance, and head position.

—*Psychology*, by Carole Wade and Carol Tavris

EXPLANATION   The first item is general enough to be the topic. The second item is a sentence that expresses the writer's point about the topic, and so it is the main idea. The third item is a specific example, so it is a detail.

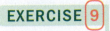 **EXERCISE 9**   Compare the items within each group and indicate which is the topic (T), the main idea (MI), and the specific supporting detail (D).

Group 1

_____ 1. Much in this American document comes from England's Magna Carta, which was signed in 1215.

_____ 2. British Roots in American Government

_____ 3. The American Constitution has its roots in the power of past documents.

Group 2

_____ 1. Children are highly valued in African American families.

_____ 2. Valuing Children

_____ 3. Like Latinos, African Americans view "children as wealth," believing that children are important in adding enjoyment and fulfillment to life.

—*Marriage and Families in a Diverse Society*,
by Robin Wolf

Group 3

_____ 1. The Fate of Mexican Americans

_____ 2. Some conquered Mexicans welcomed the Americans; many others, recognizing the futility of resistance, responded to the American conquest with ambivalence.

_____ 3. The 80,000 Mexicans who lived in the Southwest did not respond to the Mexican War with a single voice.

—*America and Its People*, Third Edition,
by James Martin, et al.

Group 4

_____ 1. Her early research led to an understanding of how viruses infect the plant and destroy its tissues.

_____ 2. Esau's Early Career with Beets

_____ 3. Sugar beets played a major role in the career of Dr. Katherine Esau, one of this century's most productive plant scientists.

—From *Biology*, Fourth Edition,
by Neil Campbell, et al.

Group 5

_____ 1. Discrimination Against Women in Higher Education

_____ 2. Harvard, for example, was one of the last to give up sex discrimination and began admitting women to its graduate business program only in 1963.

_____ 3. In general, the more prestigious the educational institutions, the more strongly they discriminated against women.

—From *Sociology: A Brief Introduction*,
Third Edition, by Alex Thio

ANSWERING TOPIC AND MAIN IDEA TEST QUESTIONS

Learning Objective 5

Master main idea and topic questions on tests

To gain insight into recognizing a correctly stated topic or main idea, categorizing incorrect responses to test questions can be helpful. First, remember that the topic is a brief phrase stating who or what the passage is about. The main idea is the point being made about the topic, and it is always in the form of a sentence. When stating the topic or main idea of a passage, it is easy to make the mistake of creating a phrase or a sentence that is either too broad or too narrow. The same mistakes occur when students answer topic and main idea questions on standardized tests. A phrase or sentence that is too broad suggests the inclusion of much more than is stated in the passage. A phrase or sentence that is too narrow is a detail within the passage. It may be an interesting and eye-catching detail, but it is not the subject or point of the passage.

Differentiate Distractors in Test Questions About the Topic

Test questions that require selecting the best title for a passage are really asking you to identify the topic.

EXAMPLE   After reading the following passage, decide which of the suggested titles is correct (C), too broad (TB), or a detail (D).

> One interesting research finding shows that listeners can accurately judge the socioeconomic status (whether high, middle, or low) of speakers from 60-second voice samples. In fact, many listeners reported that they made their judgments in fewer than 15 seconds. Speakers judged to be of high status were also rated as being of higher credibility than speakers rated middle and low in status. Listeners can also judge with considerable accuracy the emotional states of speakers from vocal expressions.

—*Human Communication*, Sixth Edition,
by Joseph DeVito

_____ 1. Importance of Voice

_____ 2. Speaking

_____ 3. Making Judgments by Voice

_____ 4. Emotional States of Speakers

EXPLANATION   The third response most accurately describes the topic of the passage. The first two are too broad and would include much more than is in the paragraph. The last response is a detail that is part of one of the experiments with listeners.

EXERCISE 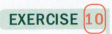 Read the passage and label the suggested titles for the passage as correct (C), too broad (TB), or a detail (D).

Passage 1

In California, Mexican Americans were outnumbered and vulnerable to discrimination. During the early years of the Gold Rush, Mexican Americans were robbed, beaten, and lynched with impunity. The 1850 Foreign Miners' Tax imposed a $20 a month tax on Mexican American miners, even though the Treaty of Guadalupe Hidalgo had granted them citizenship. Many Mexicans were forced to sell land to pay onerous taxes that fell heaviest on the Spanish speakers.

—*America and Its People*, Third Edition,
by James Martin, et al.

_____ 1. Treaty of Guadalupe Hidalgo

_____ 2. Discrimination

_____ 3. Foreign Miners' Tax During the Gold Rush

_____ 4. Discrimination Against Mexican Americans in California

Passage 2

Humpback whales strain their food from seawater. Instead of teeth, these giants have an array of brushlike plates called baleen on each side of their upper jaw. The baleen is used to sift food from the ocean. To start feeding, a humpback whale opens its mouth, expands its throat, and takes a huge gulp of seawater. When its mouth closes, the water squeezes out through spaces in the baleen, and a mass of food is trapped in the mouth. The food is then swallowed whole, passing into the stomach, where digestion begins. The humpback's stomach can hold about half a ton of food at a time, and in a typical day, the animal's digestive system will process as much as 2 tons of krill and fish.

—From *Biology*, Fourth Edition,
by Neil Campbell, et al.

_____ 1. Humpback Whales

_____ 2. Baleen for Teeth

_____ 3. The Digestive System of the Humpback Whale

_____ 4. How Whales Filter Food

Passage 3

Tar and nicotine are not the only harmful chemicals in cigarettes. In fact, tars account for only 8 percent of tobacco smoke. The remaining 92 percent consists of various gases, the most dangerous of which is carbon monoxide. In tobacco smoke, the concentration of carbon monoxide is 800 times higher than the level considered safe by the U.S. Environmental Protection Agency (EPA). In the human body, carbon monoxide reduces the oxygen-carrying capacity of the red blood cells by binding with the receptor sites for oxygen. This causes oxygen deprivation in many body tissues.

—*Health: the Basics*, Fifth Edition,
by Rebecca J. Donatelle

_____ 1. Carbon Monoxide

_____ 2. Harmful Tars and Nicotine

_____ 3. Carbon Monoxide Dangers from Smoking

_____ 4. Tobacco and Smoking

QUESTIONING FOR THE MAIN IDEA

Learning Objective 6

Use a three-question strategy for identifying the main idea

To determine the main idea of a body of material, ask questions in the following three basic areas. (The order may vary according to how much you already know about the subject.) Usually, you decide on the general topic first, sometimes from the title and sometimes by considering the details. If you are familiar with the material, constructing a main idea may seem almost automatic. If the material is unfamiliar, however, you may need to connect the key thoughts to formulate a topic and then create your main idea statement.

1. Establish the Topic

Question: Who or what is this about?   What general word or phrase identifies the subject? The topic should be broad enough to include all the ideas, but narrow enough to focus on the direction of the details. For example, identifying the topic of an article, such as "College Costs," "Change in College," or "Changing to Cut College Costs," might all be correct, but the last may be the most pointed and descriptive for the article.

2. Identify the Key Supporting Details

Question: What are the important details?   Look at the details that seem significant to see if they point in a particular direction. What aspect of the subject do they address? What seems to be the common message? In a passage on college costs, the details might describe benefits of larger classes, telecommunication networks, and video instruction. A common thread is that each idea relates to changes targeted at cutting the costs of college instruction.

3. Focus on the Message of the Topic

Question: What main idea is the author trying to convey about the topic? This statement should be:

- A complete sentence
- Broad enough to include the important details, and
- Focused enough to describe the author's slant

In the example about cutting college costs, the main idea might be "Several colleges experiment with ways to cut costs."

Learning Objective 3

Recognize stated main ideas (*See also page 120.*)

Stated Main Ideas

Research shows that readers comprehend better when the main idea is directly stated, particularly when it is stated at the beginning of a passage. Such an initial main idea statement, **thesis statement**, or **topic sentence** is a signpost for readers, briefing them on what to expect. This thesis or main idea statement provides an overview of the author's message and connects the supporting details. Read the following example and use the three-step method to determine the main idea.

EXAMPLE   Polygraph tests have been viewed as an invasion of privacy and criticized on ethical, legal, and scientific grounds. The physiological changes thought to reveal deception could result from anxiety about being interrogated, anger at being asked to take the test, or fear from pondering the consequences of "failing" the test. You might react in any of these ways if you were "hooked up" to a polygraph.

—*Psychology*, by Stephen F. Davis
and Joseph J. Palladino

1. Who or what is the topic of this passage? _____

2. Underline the key details.

3. What point is the author trying to make? _____

_____

EXPLANATION   The topic of this passage is "Polygraph Tests." The details give specifics about how physiological changes caused by anxiety, anger, or fear can show up the same way on a polygraph test as a lie response. The author states the main idea in the first sentence.

Textbook authors do not always state the main idea in the first sentence. Stated main ideas may be the beginning, middle, or concluding sentence of a passage. Therefore, do not think of stating the main idea only as a search for a particular sentence. Instead, rely on your own skill in answering the three questions about topic, details, and focus. Connect the details to form your own concept of the main idea, and, if a specific sentence in the paragraph restates it, you will recognize it as the main idea.

EXERCISE    Apply the three-question technique to identify the topic, key details, and main idea of the following passages, all of which have stated main ideas.

Passage 1

To gain a better idea of what *social structure* is, think of college football. You probably know the various positions on the team: center, guards, tackles, ends, quarterback, running backs, and the like. These positions provide a good example of a social structure. Each is a *status*; that is, each is a social position. For each of these statuses, there is a *role*; that is, each of these positions has certain expectations attached to it. The center is expected to snap the ball, the quarterback to pass it, the guards to block, the tackles to tackle or block, the ends to receive passes, and so on.

Those role expectations guide each player's actions; that is, the players try to do what their particular role requires.

—From James M. Henslin,
Sociology: A Down-to-Earth Approach, 7th ed.
© 2007 (excerpt from page 96). Reproduced by
permission of Pearson Education, Inc.

1. Who or what is the topic of this passage? _____
_____

2. Underline the key details.

3. What point is the author trying to make? _____
_____

Passage 2

Many of the techniques used by today's police differ quite a bit from those employed in days gone by. Listen to how a policeman, writing in the mid-1800s, describes the way pickpockets were caught in London 200 years ago: "I walked forth the day after my arrival, rigged out as the very model of a gentleman farmer, and with eyes, mouth, and pockets wide open, and a stout gold-headed cane in my hand, strolled leisurely through the fashionable thoroughfares, the pump-rooms, and the assembly rooms, like a fat goose waiting to be plucked. I wore a pair of yellow gloves well wadded, to save me from falling, through a moment's inadvertency, into my own snare, which consisted of about fifty fish-hooks, large black hackles, firmly sewn barb downward, into each of the pockets of my brand new leather breeches. The most blundering 'prig' alive might have easily got his hand to the bottom of my pockets, but to get it out again, without tearing every particle of flesh from the bones, was a sheer impossibility. . . . I took care never to see any of my old customers until the convulsive tug at one or other of the pockets announced the capture of a thief. I then coolly linked my arm in that of the prisoner, [and] told him in a confidential whisper who I was."

—From *Criminal Justice Today: An Introductory Text for the
Twenty-First Century,* Tenth Edition, by Frank J. Schmalleger

1. Who or what is the topic of this passage? _____
_____
_____

2. Underline the key details.

3. What point is the author trying to make? _____
_____

Passage 3

Today, many prosecutors, judges, and even mental health experts believe in the need for a verdict of "guilty but insane." Under this provision, if a person uses the insanity defense but a judge or jury finds the evidence insufficient for legal insanity, they can return a verdict of guilty but mentally ill. This indicates that the defendant is suffering from an emotional disorder severe enough to influence behavior but insufficient to render him or her insane. After such a finding, the court can impose any sentence it could have used on the crime charge. The convicted defendant is sent to prison, where the correctional authorities are required to provide therapeutic treatment. If the mental illness is cured, the offender is returned to the regular prison population to serve out the remainder of the sentence.

—*Introduction to Criminal Justice,* Ninth Edition,
by Joseph J. Senna and Larry J. Siegel

1. Who or what is the topic of this passage? _____
2. Underline the key details.
3. What point is the author trying to make? _____

_____

Passage 4

Different job roles in nursing require different educational preparation from on-the-job training to graduate level degrees. Entry level would be the Nursing Assistant. Most facilities offer on-the-job training for this position through their staff education departments. The Licensed Practical Nurse role requires one year of formal education and board certification. The Registered Nurse will need the minimum of a two-year associate degree or up to a four-year baccalaureate degree. Successful completion of board certification would also be required for practice. Registered Nurses with graduate level degrees such as a master's degree in nursing can practice at a higher level as a nurse practitioner diagnosing, treating, and supporting the patient with simple medical problems or promoting higher standards of care for a specific population of patients, such as the geriatric client.

—Adapted from *Health Science Fundamentals:
Exploring Career Pathways* by Shirley A. Badasch
and Doreen S. Chesebro

1. Who or what is the topic of this passage? _____

_____

2. Underline the key details.
3. What point is the author trying to make? _____

_____

Passage 5

Six Flags is a world-renowned theme park. The company owns and operates thirty-eight different parks spread out over North America, Latin America, and Europe. Locations include Mexico City, Belgium, France, Spain, Germany, and most major metropolitan areas in the United States. In fact, having a park in forty of the fifty major metropolitan areas in the United States has earned Six Flags the title of world's largest regional theme park company. Annually, more than 50 million visitors are reported to entertain themselves at Six Flags theme parks worldwide. The company prides itself in claiming that 98 percent of the U.S. population is within an 8-hour drive to any one of the numerous Six Flags theme parks.

—*Introduction to Hospitality,* Fourth Edition,
by John R. Walker

1. Who or what is the topic of this passage? _____

2. Underline the key details.

3. What point is the author trying to make? _____

_____

Passage 6

Colleges and universities are denying access to third party credit card marketers in increasing numbers. There were 22 campuses that disallowed the practice in 1988. That number has increased dramatically and is expected to cross 400 in the next couple of years. Private sources that monitor college credit card marketing (*College Marketing Intelligence*) contend that the number is much higher, estimating that 750 to 1000 college campuses have already banned on-campus credit card marketing.

—Taking Sides: Clashing Views on Controversial
Issues in Marketing, edited by Barton Macchiette
and Abhijit Roy

1. Who or what is the topic of this passage? _____

   _____

2. Underline the key details.

3. What point is the author trying to make? _____

   _____

Unstated Main Ideas

Research shows that only about half of the paragraphs in textbooks have directly stated main ideas. This should not be a problem if you understand the three-question technique for locating the main idea. The questions guide you in forming your own statement so that you are not dependent on finding a line in the text.

When the main idea is not directly stated, it is said to be *implied,* which means it is suggested in the thoughts that are revealed. In this case, the author has presented a complete idea, but for reasons of style and impact has chosen not to express it concisely in one sentence. As a reader, it is your job to systematically connect the details and focus the message.

In the following passage the main idea is not stated, but it may be determined by answering the three questions that follow.

EXAMPLE   In Australia and Belgium, nonvoters are subject to fines; not only the fine itself but the clear expectation that everyone is legally required to vote helps generate 90+ percent turnout rates. In Italy, nonvoters are not fined, but "Did Not Vote" is stamped on their identification papers, threatening nonvoters with the prospect of unsympathetic treatment at the hands of public officials should they get into trouble or need help with a problem.

—The New American Democracy, Election Update Edition,
by Morris Fiorina and Paul Peterson

1. Who or what is the topic of this passage? _____

   (This gives you the general topic or heading.)

2. What are the key terms or details? _____

   _____

3. What idea is the author trying to convey about nonvoting? _____

   _____

   (This is the main idea the author is trying to communicate.)

EXPLANATION   The sentence stating the main idea might very well have been the first, middle, or last sentence of the paragraph. Having it stated, however, was not necessary for understanding the passage. In many cases, readers spend time searching for a single sentence that encapsulates the meaning rather than digesting the information and forming ideas. Instead, answer these three questions: "Who or what is this about?" "What are the key terms?" and "What point is the author trying to make?" This passage is about penalties for not voting. The key terms are *"giving fines in Australia and Belgium, and stamping 'Did Not Vote' on identification papers in Italy."* The author's main idea is that in *"some countries nonvoters are penalized to encourage voting."* Apply the three-question technique to determine the main idea.

EXERCISE 12

Passage 1

Marilyn, a Southwest Airlines flight attendant, takes the mike as her plane backs away from the Houston terminal. "Could y'all lean in a little toward the center aisle please?" she chirps in an irresistible Southern drawl. "Just a bit, please. That's it. No, the other way, sir. Thanks."

Baffled passengers comply even though they have no idea why.

"You see," says Marilyn at last, "the pilot has to pull out of this space here, and he needs to be able to check the rearview mirrors."

Only when the laughter subsides does Marilyn launch into the standard aircraft safety speech that many passengers usually ignore.

—*Business Essentials,* Third Edition,
by Ronald Ebert and Ricky Griffin

1. Who or what is the topic of this passage? _____
2. Underline the key details.
3. What point is the author trying to make? _____

_____

Passage 2

Children have more taste buds than adults do, which may explain why they are often so picky about eating "grown-up" foods. Even among adults, individuals differ in their sensitivity to taste. Indeed, recent studies have shown that people can be divided into one of three groups: nontasters, medium tasters, and supertasters. Compared to most, supertasters use only half as much sugar or saccharin in their coffee or tea. They also suffer more oral burn from eating the active ingredient in chili peppers. Using videomicroscopy to count the number of taste buds on the tongue, researchers have found that nontasters have an average of 96 taste buds per square centimeter, medium tasters have 184, and supertasters have 425.

—*Psychology,* Second Edition, by Saul Kassin

1. Who or what is the topic of this passage? _____
2. Underline the key details.
3. What point is the author trying to make? _____

_____

Passage 3

If the person is extremely important, you had better be there early just in case he or she is able to see you ahead of schedule. As the individual's status decreases, it is less important for you to be on time. Students, for example, must be on time for conferences with teachers, but it is more important to be on time for deans and still more important to be on time for the president of the college. Teachers, on the other hand, may be late for conferences with students but not for conferences with deans or the president. Deans, in turn, may be late for teachers but not for the president. Business organizations and other hierarchies have similar rules.

—*Human Communication,* Sixth Edition,
by Joseph DeVito

1. Who or what is the topic of this passage? _____

_____

2. Underline the key details.
3. What point is the author trying to make? _____

_____

Passage 4

In his book *Bridges, Not Walls*, John Stewart dramatically illustrates the case of the famous "Wild Boy of Aveyron," who spent his early childhood without any apparent human contact. The boy was discovered in January 1800 while digging for vegetables in a French village garden. He showed no behaviors one would expect in a social human. The boy could not speak but uttered only unrecognizable cries. More significant than this absence of social skills was his lack of any identity as a human being. As author Roger Shattuck put it, "The boy had no human sense of being in the world. He had no sense of himself as a person related to other persons." Only after the influence of a loving "mother" did the boy begin to behave—and, we can imagine, think of himself as a human.

In 1970, authorities discovered a twelve-year-old girl (whom they called "Genie") who had spent virtually all her life in an otherwise empty, darkened bedroom with almost no human contact. The child could not speak and had no sense of herself as a person until she was removed from her family and "nourished" by a team of caregivers.

—*Understanding Human Communication,* Eighth Edition,
by Ronald Adler and George Rodman

1. Who or what is the topic of this passage? _____

_____

2. Underline the key details.
3. What point is the author trying to make? _____

_____

Passage 5

A mother had a son who threw temper tantrums: lying on the floor, pounding his fists, kicking his legs, and whining for whatever he wanted. One day while in a supermarket he threw one of his temper tantrums. In a moment of desperation, the mother dropped to the floor, pounded her fists, kicked her feet, and whined, "I wish you'd stop throwing temper tantrums! I can't stand it when you throw temper tantrums!" By this time, the son had stood up. He said in a hushed tone, "Mom, there are people watching! You're embarrassing me!" The mother calmly stood up, brushed off the dust, and said in a clear, calm voice, "That's what you look like when you're throwing a temper tantrum." Sometimes, traditional approaches such as bribing, threatening, ignoring, or giving in seem so natural that we overlook the possibility that something different, such as embarrassment, might work too.

—From *The Creative Problem Solver's Toolbox,*
by Richard Fobes

1. Who or what is the topic of this passage? _____

_____

2. Underline the key details.
3. What point is the author trying to make? _____

_____

EXERCISE 13   In some of the following passages the main ideas are stated. In others they are implied. Avoid simply searching for a sentence that states the main idea. Instead, apply the three-step technique that you have learned and practiced throughout this chapter to determine the author's main point.

Passage 1

God's message to Muhammad in the form of the Qur'an (a "reciting") was clear: The Prophet is to warn his people against worship of false gods and all immorality, especially injustice to the poor, orphans, widows and women in general. At the end of time, on Judgment Day, every person will be bodily resurrected to face eternal punishment in hellfire or eternal joy in paradise, according to how he or she has lived. The way to paradise lies in gratitude to God for the bounties of creation, his prophetic and revelatory guidance, and his readiness to forgive the penitent. Social justice and obedient worship of the one Lord are required of every person. Each is to recognize his or her creatureliness and God's transcendence. The proper response is "submission" (*islam*) to God's will, becoming *muslim* ("submissive" or surrendering") in one's worship and morality.

—The Heritage of World Civilizations Combined Edition,
Sixth Edition, by Albert M. Craig, William A. Graham,
Donald Kagan, Steven Ozment, and Frank M. Turner

1. Who or what is the topic of this paragraph? _____

_____

2. Underline the key details.

_____ 3. Select the best statement of the main idea of the passage.

    a. The word "Qur'an" means a reciting, and "islam" means submission.

    b. God warned people against worship of false gods.

    c. Muhammad was a prophet who received a message from God that became known as the Qur'an.

    d. God's message to Muhammad was that he must tell people that the way to paradise is to live with concern for justice and submission to God.

Passage 2

The two most prominent centers of civilization—and the focus of this chapter—were Mesoamerica, in what is today Mexico and Central America, and the Andean region of South America. Both regions have a long, rich history of civilization that reaches back thousands of years. At the time of the European conquest of the Americas in the sixteenth century both regions were dominated by powerful expansionist empires—the Aztecs, or Mexica, in Mesoamerica, and the Inca in the Andes. In both regions Spanish conquerors obliterated the native empires and nearly succeeded in obliterating native culture. But in both, Native American traditions have endured overlaid and combined in complex ways with Hispanic culture, to provide clues to the pre-Hispanic past.

—The Heritage of World Civilizations Combined Edition,
Sixth Edition, by Albert M. Craig, William A. Graham,
Donald Kagan, Steven Ozment, and Frank M. Turner

1. Who or what is the topic of this paragraph? _____

_____

2. Underline the key details.

_____ 3. Select the best statement of the main idea of the passage.
   a. The important, ancient cultures centered in Mesoamerica and the Andean region of south America produced recognizable traditions that are still visible today.
   b. The European conquest destroyed the Aztec and Inca civilizations.
   c. Mesoamerica was what is known as Mexico and Central America today.
   d. The Aztecs lived in Mesoamerica.

Passage 3

One hallmark of Chinese history is its striking continuity of culture, language, and geography. The Shang and Chou dynasties were centered in north China along the Yellow River or its tributary, the Wei. The capitals of China's first empire were in exactly the same areas, and north China would remain China's political center through history to the present. If Western civilization had experienced similar continuity, it would have progressed from Thebes in the valley of the Nile to Athens on the Nile; Rome on the Nile; and then, in time, to Paris, London, and Berlin on the Nile; and each of these centers of civilization would have spoken Egyptian and written in Egyptian hieroglyphics.

—*The Heritage of World Civilizations Combined Edition,*
Sixth Edition, by Albert M. Craig, William A. Graham,
Donald Kagan, Steven Ozment, and Frank M. Turner

1. Who or what is the topic of this paragraph? _____

   _____

2. Underline the key details.

_____ 3. Select the best statement of the main idea of the passage.

   a. Western civilization began in Thebes in the valley of the Nile.
   b. China's first imperial capitals were in North China along the Yellow River and the Wei River.
   c. Chinese history has been amazingly consistent in its geography.
   d. Chinese and Western civilizations have developed in much the same way.

Passage 4

One of the most important things to realize about the restaurant industry is that you can't do it alone. Each person in your operation has to work together for you to be successful. The most important ingredient in managing people is to respect them. Many words can be used to describe a manager (coach, supervisor, boss, mentor), but whatever term is used, you have to be in the game to be effective. Managing a kitchen is like coaching a football team—everyone must work together to be effective. The difference between a football team and a kitchen is that chefs/managers cannot supervise from the sidelines; they have to be in the game. One of my favorite examples of excellent people management skills is that of the general manager of a hotel who had the ware-washing team report directly to him. When asked why, he indicated that they are the people who know what is being thrown in the garbage, they are the people who know what the customers are not eating, and they are the people most responsible for the sanitation and safety of an operation. There are many components to managing people—training, evaluating, nurturing, delegating, and so on—but the most important is respect.

—*Introduction to Hospitality,* Fifth Edition,
by John R. Walker

1. Who or what is the topic of this paragraph? _____

_____

2. Underline the key details.

_____ 3. Select the best statement of the main idea of the passage.

    a. Managing a kitchen is like coaching a football team.
    b. To be successful a restaurant manager must develop a team in which respect is the key ingredient.
    c. The people with the least-skilled jobs often know what the customers like and don't like.
    d. One hotel manager had the ware-washing team report directly to him.

Passage 5

Employability traits are those skills that focus on attitude, passion, initiative, dedication, sense of urgency, and dependability. These traits are not always traits that can be taught, but a good chef can demonstrate them by example. Most of the employers with job opportunities for students consider these skills to be more important than technical skills. The belief is that if you have strong employability traits, your technical skills will be strong.

—*Introduction to Hospitality*, Fifth Edition,
by John R. Walker

1. Who or what is the topic of this paragraph? _____
2. Underline the key details.

_____ 3. Select the best statement of the main idea of the passage.

    a. Attitude is an important employability trait.
    b. Employability traits are often more important than technical skills.
    c. A good chef can teach by example.
    d. Employers like to employ students.

Getting the Main Idea of Longer Selections

Learning Objective 8

Identify the main idea of longer selections

Because of the great quantity of material included in a book, understanding the main idea of longer selections such as chapters and articles seems more difficult than understanding a single paragraph. Longer selections have several major ideas contributing to the main point and many paragraphs of supporting details. To pull the ideas together under one central theme, an additional twist to the three-question strategy is necessary: simplify the material by organizing paragraphs or sections into manageable categories. These categories represent the major supporting details. Then decide how each subsection contributes to the whole.

1. Establish the topic.
   Ask "Who or what is this about?"
   Consider what the title and first paragraphs suggest about the topic.
2. Identify the key supporting points.
   Ask "What are the major details?"
   Group paragraphs or sections into categories that represent major support. Use headings and subheadings as a guide.
3. Focus on the message.
   Ask "What is the point the author is trying to make about the topic?"
   Review the categories you have identified as major supporting details. What point do they make about the topic?

PERSONAL FEEDBACK 1   Name _____

1. Describe the theme or main idea of a movie that you have seen recently, one that you liked, and give reasons for your positive evaluation.

   Movie Title: _____

   Theme or Main Idea: _____

   Reasons for Positive Evaluation: _____

2. What do you think was the main point of the movie?

   _____

   _____

3. Was there anything you did not understand about the main idea? _____

   _____

   _____

   Tear out and submit to your instructor.

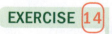
EXERCISE 14   Search the Internet for articles on dreaming. Select an article that interests you, and use the expanded three-question strategy above to determine the topic, the major supporting details, and the main idea. Write them on a separate sheet of paper.

SUMMARY POINTS

1 What are topics, main ideas, and major and minor supporting details? (page 114)

A topic is the general subject of a reading selection. It tells who or what the selection is about.

A main idea is the point the author is making about the topic. The main idea might also be called the thesis, main point, central focus, gist, controlling idea, or central thought.

Major supporting details explain and elaborate on the main idea.

Minor supporting details provide further explanation of the major details. They are sometimes the link that helps readers remember the material, but they are not the most important items.

2 How can I identify the topic? (page 115)

Read the passage and ask "Who or what is this about?" Think of a general word or phrase that describes the details in the passage.

3 How can I recognize a stated main idea? (pages 120 and 128)

Ask "What point is the author making about the topic?" If the main idea is stated directly in the passage, you will find a sentence that mirrors your answer. A stated main idea will be broad enough to include the details in the passage yet narrow enough that it doesn't imply more than the details relate. A stated main idea can be placed anywhere in a paragraph or longer selection, but the most common locations are at the beginning or end. Always think through the main idea yourself before searching for a sentence that states it. Remember, only about half of textbook paragraphs contain a direct statement of the main idea.

4 How can I identify supporting details? (page 124)

Supporting details are narrow and add information that explains the main idea. Think about the diagram on page 114 of this chapter while sorting details from main ideas and topics. Also remember the umbrella diagram: Details fit under the umbrella of the topic and main idea.

5 How can I master topic and main idea questions on tests? (page 126)

Incorrect answers to both types of questions usually take two forms: They are either too narrow or too broad. Answers that are too narrow don't cover all of the details in the passage. Answers that are too broad imply information that is not in the passage at all. Occasionally, a test writer will include a distractor that sounds important but is completely unrelated to the passage. Don't let those fool you!

6 What is the three-question strategy for identifying the main idea? (page 128)

1. Establish the topic. Ask "Who or what is this about?"
2. Identify the key supporting terms. Ask "What are the major details?" Remember that details are more narrow than the topic or main idea. Ask yourself what explanatory information is given.
3. Focus on the message of the topic. Ask "What is the point the author is trying to make about the topic?" Your answer should be a complete sentence of your own that is broad enough to cover the details and focused enough not to imply more than is in the passage.

This strategy should be used whether the main idea is stated in the passage or not.

7 How can I identify unstated main ideas? (page 133)

Use the three-question strategy! The thinking process for finding a main idea is the same whether there is a sentence in the passage that expresses it or not. Ask "Who or what is the passage about?" "What are the key details?" and "What point is the author making about the topic?" The answer will be implied rather than directly stated in a sentence within the passage. Think like a detective putting all the evidence together to solve a crime.

8 How can I identify the main idea of longer selections? (page 140)

Break the material into subsections and determine how the subsections support the whole. Apply the expanded three-question strategy to the entire selection.

COLLABORATIVE PROBLEM SOLVING

Form a five-member group and select one of the following questions. Brainstorm and then outline your major points on a transparency. Choose a member to present the group findings to the class.

➤ Why is prior knowledge the best single predictor of reading comprehension?

➤ Why is comprehension better when the main idea is stated at the beginning of a test passage?

➤ Describe a passage that you might write that would have the main idea stated at the end.

➤ Why should the main idea of a passage be stated in a sentence rather than a phrase? Give examples.

MyReadingLab

MyReadingLab (MRL) www.myreadinglab.com

➤ For support in meeting this chapter's objectives, log in to **www.myreadinglab.com** and select "Main Idea."

THE READING WORKSHOP

If reading a novel, biography, or other book is part of your course experience, refer to The Reading Workshop: Thinking, Talking, and Writing about Books in Appendix 5 for suggestions.

SELECTION 1   Psychology

"Dreams say what they mean, but they don't say it in daytime language."

Gail Godwin

In studies conducted worldwide, modern dream scientists have found that dreams vary according to age, gender, and culture. Women tend to have more dreams of children, whereas men dream more of aggression, weapons, and tools. Americans are frequently embarrassed by nakedness in dreams, but such dreams rarely occur in cultures of people wearing fewer clothes. Mexican American college students dream of death more often than do Anglo American students, perhaps because death is more a part of life in Latin American cultures. The findings of such cross-cultural research support the hypothesis that dreams reflect life events that are important to the dreamer.

THINKING BEFORE READING

Preview for content, activate your schema, and anticipate what you will learn.

Did you dream last night?

What dream or dreams have you had recently?

Can you explain the meaning of any of your dreams?

I think this reading will tell me _____.

VOCABULARY PREVIEW

Are you familiar with these words?

unconscious	paradox	convenient	symbolizes	bullied
idling	depriving	ascribed	critical	synchronized

Which word has the same root as *chronological*?

What is the definition of the prefix in *unconscious*?

Is the phrase "jumbo shrimp" a *paradox*?

Your instructor may choose to give a true-false vocabulary review before or after reading.

THINKING DURING READING

As you read, use the six thinking strategies of a good reader: predict, picture, relate, monitor, correct, and annotate.

SLEEPING AND DREAMING

The time when we are most obviously unconscious is when we are asleep. Yet we have dreams during that time. This implies that something is going on in our brain.

Is all sleep the same? Are there stages in sleep? When do humans dream? How can you tell if a person is dreaming? Why do people have dreams, anyway? These are the
5   questions to be answered in this section.

Reader's TIP Reading and Studying Psychology

- Seek to understand abstract terms and confusing concepts through the concrete examples that illustrate them.
- Relate psychological theories to yourself and visualize people you know as examples.
- Memorize key terms with definitions and examples, especially for multiple-choice tests.
- Test yourself by turning each boldface heading into a question, and recite your answer.
- Because much of psychology is about theories, connect the names of researchers with their theories. Learn characteristics and examples for each theory.
- Compare and contrast theories. For example, how do the social learning theorists differ from the behaviorists?
- Reduce your notes to visual diagrams. For example, to study personality theories, draw charts to list the comparative elements.

Researchers have learned more about sleep and dreaming in the past twenty-five years than in all of history up to that time. One major reason for this is the discovery that when people are asleep there are changes in the activity of their brain and eyes. These changes can be recorded.

10   Beth Smith lies down to sleep after a hard day. She drifts off. At first she is in a light kind of sleep. Her brain waves, if recorded on a brain-wave machine, show a pattern that is definitely different than when she is awake. After less than an hour, two things happen to Beth. Her brain waves change, so that they now look pretty much the way they do when she is awake. Yet she is still asleep. Also, although her eyelids are closed, her eyes begin to
15   move about rapidly under the lids. This lasts for twenty minutes. Then Beth returns to the sleep of easy brain waves and no eye movement.

Basically, there are two kinds of sleep. One is Rapid Eye Movement (REM) sleep. In this, the brain waves are similar to those of a waking person, and the eyes move about rapidly under the closed lids. The other kind of sleep is Non-Rapid Eye Movement sleep.
20   You can guess what that's like, right? Stop for a moment and describe REM and non-REM sleep to yourself.

REM sleep is also called *paradoxical sleep.* A paradox is something that seems contradictory within itself. What is the paradox about REM sleep? That the sleeper's brain waves would lead you to believe the person is awake, but in fact the person is asleep.

25   Now, the interesting thing is this. Suppose Beth is showing non-REM sleep. We wake her up and say: "Wake up, Beth! What are you dreaming?"

"Uh . . . nothing," Beth mumbles.

Disappointed, we let her go back to sleep. Later on, Beth begins to show REM sleep. Again, we wake her up. "What are you dreaming, Beth?"
30   "Uh . . . this man has ridden a camel into Mom's office. It's too big. The camel fills up the whole office. The man riding him is an Arab." She goes on with her dream.

Dreaming happens mainly in REM sleep. This is very convenient for researchers. They get volunteers to sleep in a bed in the laboratory. An electronic sensing device that registers eye movement is placed on the eyelids of the volunteers. Thus the researcher can tell
35   exactly when the volunteer is showing REM sleep.

"Wake up, volunteer! What are you dreaming?"

WHAT HAS BEEN LEARNED ABOUT DREAMING?

Everyone dreams about 20 percent of the time they are sleeping—that is, they show REM sleep about that much. Even people who say they never dream show about 20 percent REM sleep. If these "nondreamers" do their sleeping in a laboratory where the researcher
40 can wake them up, it turns out that they dream as much as others. They just don't remember the dreams in the morning, perhaps because memories for dreams fade fast and they are slow waking up.

People go back and forth between REM and non-REM sleep during the night. If something happens in their environment while they are sleeping, people may fit this into the
45 dream. Did you ever have the experience of someone calling you in the morning, but at first you thought it was part of a dream?

Events in daily life sometimes occur in symbolic form in dreams. For example, a boy was having a lot of difficulty on the school playground because a bigger boy kept bullying him. That night the smaller boy dreamed of being alone and unarmed in the
50 African grass country, facing a lion. The lion symbolizes the bully. At other times the dreaded event from daily life simply occurs in a dream in its real-life form—the boy dreams of being bullied by the bigger boy. How and when dream symbols are used is not yet understood.

WHY DO WE DREAM?

Do people actually need to dream? Or is it just the brain "idling its motor"? It's possible
55 that dreams are unimportant, just an accidental part of REM sleep.

One experimenter waked volunteers each time they started REM sleep. This meant that he was also depriving them of their dreams. When they showed non-REM sleep, he let them sleep on. Notice that by itself this experiment wouldn't prove much, even if effects did occur. Why? Because the effects might result from just being waked up all the
60 time, rather than from just not being allowed to dream. The experimenters realized this, so they used a second group of volunteers. These were waked exactly as much as the first group, but no attention was paid to whether it was REM or non-REM sleep. Thus any differences could be ascribed to lack of REM sleep periods in the one group.

There were differences. People who were deprived of most of their REM sleep for
65 three nights in a row became irritable and somewhat disrupted in their actions. When on

the fourth night they were allowed to sleep on, so they could have REM sleep, they had it about 30 percent of the time instead of the usual 20 percent. Apparently they were "catching up" on their REM sleep. It looks as though people do, indeed, need REM sleep. The critical question is: Is it the REM sleep that they need or the dreams? Do we have
70 REM sleep because it brings dreaming, or is dreaming just an accidental aspect of the needed REM sleep? We don't know.

Why do people dream, then? We don't know that either. It does seem that REM sleep is necessary. But are dreams? What do they accomplish? Some theorists have suggested that we use dreaming to solve emotional problems, some have suggested that memories
75 are stored in the brain during sleep time and dream time. Some even suggest this is a way of keeping our two eyes synchronized. Tomorrow we may know the answer. The discovery of rapid eye movements during dreaming has opened up the world of dreams for research. Notice that the researchers here do something interesting. They go from an observable behavior—the eye movements—to an internal condition—the dream. The
80 discovery of REM sleep helps bridge the gap between mental processes and the outside world.

(1,124 words)

—From *Psychology: What It Is/How to Use It*,
by David Watson

THINKING AND WRITING AFTER READING

RECALL Self-test your understanding.

Your instructor may choose to give you a true-false comprehension review.

REACT Why are sleep and dreaming important research topics for psychologists?

_____

_____

REFLECT Describe and try to interpret one of your recent or recurring dreams.

_____

_____

THINK CRITICALLY Would you predict any correlation between a good night's sleep and a good quality of life? Why or why not? Write your answer on a separate sheet of paper.

THINK AND WRITE Researchers suggest that dreams differ according to age, gender, and culture. Do sleep patterns show similar differences? How would you predict that sleep patterns differ according to age, gender, and culture? _____

_____

_____

MAIN IDEA Answer the following questions concerning the selection.

1. Who or what is the topic of the selection? _____

2. What point is the author trying to make? _____

_____

EXTENDED WRITING   Review "Sleeping and Dreaming" and write a one-paragraph summary of the selection. The purpose of the summary is to condense the selection to the most important points so that someone who has not read it can understand its basic content. Your first sentence will state the main idea. The remainder of the paragraph will reiterate the major supporting details that the author used to develop the main idea. Introduce the details in the same order they appear in the selection. Do not include any of your own opinions or experiences in the summary, but remember to use your own words. A well-developed summary will probably contain between 10 and 12 sentences.

Interpret THE QUOTE

Now that you have finished reading the selection, "Sleeping and Dreaming," go back to the beginning of the selection and read the opening quote again. What does Godwin mean when she says that dreams "say what they mean"? What is the difference between daytime language and the language of dreams? Answer both questions on a separate piece of paper.

Name _____

Date _____

COMPREHENSION QUESTIONS

Answer the following with *a, b, c,* or *d,* or fill in the blank. In order to help analyze your strengths and weaknesses, the question types are indicated.

Main Idea _____ 1. The best statement of the main idea of this selection is

    a. People become irritable when they do not have an adequate amount of dreaming.

    b. Through the discovery of REM, researchers have begun to learn about sleeping and dreaming, but many questions remain unanswered.

    c. Sleep is an observable behavior, whereas dreaming is an internal condition reflecting the mental processes.

    d. Dreams follow an irregular pattern, with people moving back and forth between REM and non-REM sleep all during the night.

Detail _____ 2. During REM sleep a person experiences

    a. different brain waves than when awake.

    b. the same brain waves as when awake.

    c. eye movement under closed lids.

    d. both *b* and *c*.

Inference _____ 3. REM sleep is called paradoxical sleep because _____

_____

Detail _____ 4. Dreaming occurs

    a. during REM and non-REM sleep.

    b. during REM sleep.

    c. only during non-REM sleep.

    d. as people go back and forth between REM and non-REM sleep.

Detail _____ 5. Some people probably cannot remember dreams because

    a. they awaken in the middle of a dream.

    b. they are nondreamers.

    c. they experience only 20 percent REM sleep.

    d. they are slow waking up.

Inference _____ 6. The author implies that dreams do all of the following *except*

    a. symbolically reflect real-life problems.

    b. include experiences in the environment.

    c. relieve tension and irritability.

    d. normally occur in the last two hours of sleep.

Detail _____ 7. According to the passage, after several nights of interrupted REM sleep, people need to

    a. sleep longer.

    b. have a higher percent of REM sleep at the next sleeping time.

    c. have a higher percentage of non-REM sleep.

    d. sleep more frequently for brief periods of time.

Answer the following with *T* (true), *F* (false), or *CT* (can't tell).

Inference _____ 8. Research shows that dreams are unimportant and just an acciden-tal part of REM sleep.

Inference _____ 9. The author feels that the discovery of rapid eye movement is the most significant finding thus far in dream research.

Inference _____ 10. Dreams help people store memories.

VOCABULARY

Answer the following with *a, b, c,* or *d* for the word or phrase that best defines the boldface word as used in the selection. The number in parentheses indicates the line of the passage in which the word appears.

_____ 1. "most obviously **unconscious**" (1)

    a. alert
    b. daydreaming
    c. half-knowing
    d. not aware

_____ 2. "a **paradox** is" (22)

    a. mystery
    b. error
    c. contradictory truth
    d. reasoning

_____ 3. "**convenient** for researchers" (32)

    a. logical
    b. easy to use
    c. necessary
    d. cooperative

_____ 4. "**symbolizes** the bully" (50)

    a. warns
    b. summarizes
    c. represents
    d. suspects

_____ 5. "**bullied** by the bigger boy" (52)

    a. intimidated
    b. befriended
    c. joined
    d. recognized

_____ 6. "**idling** its motor" (54)

    a. exhausting
    b. running without power
    c. withdrawing
    d. renewing

_____ 7. "**depriving** them of" (57)

    a. irritating
    b. educating
    c. encouraging
    d. preventing

_____ 8. "**ascribed** to lack of" (63)

    a. convened
    b. remembered
    c. credited
    d. returned

_____ 9. "the **critical** question is" (69)

    a. first
    b. general
    c. crucial
    d. most frequent

_____ 10. "keeping our two eyes **synchronized**" (76)

    a. working simultaneously
    b. working vigorously
    c. focused
    d. slightly crossed

Your instructor may choose to give a true-false vocabulary review.

VOCABULARY ENRICHMENT

A. An acronym is an invented word formed by the initial letters of a compound term. REM, for example, is pronounced as a word that rhymes with *them*, rather than pronouncing the three letters separately to indicate *rapid eye movement*. Write an *A* beside the following letters that are pronounced as words and thus are acronyms.

_____ 1. HUD   _____ 3. FBI   _____ 5. NAFTA

_____ 2. UNICEF   _____ 4. CIA   _____ 6. radar

B. Study the following easily confused words, and circle the one that is correct in each sentence.

conscience: sense of right or wrong   **its:** ownership or possessive
conscious: awareness of self   **it's:** contraction of *it is*

to: toward
too: more than enough
two: the number 2

7. Let your (**conscience, conscious**) be your guide when faced with the temptation to oversleep and cut class.

8. Over a lifetime, (**its, it's**) estimated we spend 25 years sleeping.

9. Sleeping for five hours is (**to, too, two**) little for most people.

C. Use the context clues in the following sentences to write the meaning of the boldface psychology terms.

10. Nightmares frequently reflect the frustration and **anxiety** felt in daily life.

    _____

11. After years of practice, we **condition** ourselves to get up by the alarm clock.

    _____

12. With the birth of the second child, the first child's desire for a bottle at bedtime was a sign of **regression.** _____

    _____

13. Saying that you are too busy to sleep is only **rationalizing.**

    _____

14. Dream therapy offers a **permissive** setting for revealing haunting and embarrassing nightmares. _____

15. Adequate sleep **reinforces** the immune system's ability to fight disease.

    _____

ASSESS YOUR LEARNING

Review confusing questions, seek clarification, and make notes in your text to help you remember new information and vocabulary.

SELECTION 2   Literature: Short Story

"The trouble with lying and deceiving is that their efficiency depends entirely upon a clear notion of the truth that the liar and deceiver wishes to hide."

Hannah Arendt

Jack Ritchie, born John George Reitci, was stationed in the Central Pacific during World War II. There, to pass the time, he read large numbers of crime stories and mystery fiction. Following the war, and with the help of a literary agent, he became a prolific short story writer whose work appeared in a wide variety of periodicals.

THINKING BEFORE READING

Preview the selection for clues to content. Activate your schema, and anticipate what you will learn.

What do you know about murder-for-hire?

How does a crime of passion differ from one that is premeditated?

I'll read this to find out _____.

VOCABULARY PREVIEW

Are you familiar with these words?

decanter	morbid	insight	davenport	authentic
commission	incorruptible	fortitude	pertinent	commiserate

Are *morbid* thoughts the same as irrational thoughts?

What is the difference between *insight* and *oversight*?

Your instructor may choose to give a true-false vocabulary review before or after reading.

((•—|Scan this QR
code to hear
this reading.

THINKING DURING READING

As you read, use the six thinking strategies of a good reader: predict, picture, relate, monitor, correct, and annotate.

SHATTER PROOF

He was a soft-faced man wearing rimless glasses, but he handled the automatic with unmistakable competence.

I was rather surprised at my calmness when I learned the reason for his presence. "It's a pity to die in ignorance," I said, "Who hired you to kill me?"

5   His voice was mild. "I could be an enemy in my own right."

I had been making a drink in my study when I had heard him and turned. Now I finished pouring from the decanter. "I know the enemies I've made and you are a stranger. Was it my wife?"

SELECTION 2

Reader's TIP — Reading and Studying a Short Story

Ask yourself the following questions as you read a short story:

- How would you describe the main character? What other **characters** are well-developed? What is the purpose of the "flat" characters? What do the characters learn? How do the characters change?
- What is the main **conflict** in the story? What are the steps in the development of the **plot**? What is the **climax**? What is the **resolution**?
- What is the **theme** of the story? What universal truth did you learn from the story?
- When and where is the story set? How does the **setting** affect the theme?
- Who is telling the story? How does this **point of view** affect the message?
- What is the **tone** of the author? What **mood** is the author trying to create?
- What **symbols** provide vivid images that enrich the theme?
- What is your evaluation of the author's work?

He smiled. "Quite correct. Her motive must be obvious."

10 "Yes," I said. "I have money and apparently she wants it. All of it."

He regarded me objectively. "Your age is?"

"Fifty-three."

"And your wife is?"

"Twenty-two."

15 He clicked his tongue. "You were foolish to expect anything permanent, Mr. Williams."

I sipped the whiskey. "I expected a divorce after a year or two and a painful settlement. But not death."

"Your wife is a beautiful woman, but greedy, Mr. Williams. I'm surprised that you

20 never noticed."

My eyes went to the gun. "I assume you have killed before?"

"Yes."

"And obviously you enjoy it."

He nodded. "A morbid pleasure, I admit. But I do."

25 I watched him and waited. Finally I said, "You have been here more than two minutes and I am still alive."

"There is no hurry, Mr. Williams," he said softly.

"Ah, then the actual killing is not your greatest joy. You must savor the preceding moments."

30 "You have insight, Mr. Williams."

"And as long as I keep you entertained, in one manner or another, I remain alive?"

"Within a time limit, of course."

"Naturally. A drink, Mr. . . . ?"

"Smith requires no strain on the memory. Yes, thank you. But please allow me to see

35 what you are doing when you prepare it."

"It's hardly likely that I would have poison conveniently at hand for just such an occasion."

"Hardly likely, but still possible."

He watched me while I made his drink and then took an easy chair.

40   I sat on the davenport. "Where would my wife be at this moment?"

"At a party, Mr. Williams. There will be a dozen people to swear that she never left their sight during the time of your murder."

"I will be shot by a burglar? An intruder?"

He put his drink on the cocktail table in front of him. "Yes. After I shoot you, I shall, of
45   course, wash this glass and return it to your liquor cabinet. And when I leave I shall wipe all fingerprints from the doorknobs I've touched."

"You will take a few trifles with you? To make the burglar-intruder story more authentic?"

"That will not be necessary, Mr. Williams. The police will assume that the burglar
50   panicked after he killed you and fled empty-handed."

"That picture on the east wall," I said. "It's worth thirty thousand."

His eyes went to it for a moment and then quickly returned to me. "It is tempting, Mr. Williams, but I desire to possess nothing that will even remotely link me to you. I appreciate art, and especially its monetary value, but not to the extent where I will risk
55   the electric chair." Then he smiled. "Or were you perhaps offering me the painting? In exchange for your life?"

"It was a thought."

He shook his head. "I'm sorry, Mr. Williams. Once I accept a commission, I am not dissuaded. It is a matter of professional pride."

60   I put my drink on the table. "Are you waiting for me to show fear, Mr. Smith?"

"You will show it."

"And then you will kill me?"

His eyes flickered. "It is a strain, isn't it, Mr. Williams? To be afraid and not to dare show it."

65   "Do you expect your victims to beg?" I asked.

"They do. In one manner or another."

"They appeal to your humanity? And that is hopeless?"

"It is hopeless."

"They offer you money?"

70   "Very often."

"Is that hopeless too?"

"So far it has been, Mr. Williams."

"Behind the picture I pointed out to you, Mr. Smith, there is a wall safe."

He gave the painting another brief glance. "Yes."

75   "It contains five thousand dollars."

"That is a lot of money, Mr. Williams."

I picked up my glass and went to the painting. I opened the safe, selected a brown envelope, and then finished my drink. I put the empty glass in the safe and twirled the knob.

80   Smith's eyes were drawn to the envelope. "Bring that here, please."

I put the envelope on the cocktail table in front of him.

He looked at it for a few moments and then up at me. "Did you actually think you could buy your life?"

I lit a cigarette. "No. You are, shall we say, incorruptible."

85   He frowned slightly. "But still you brought me the five thousand?"

I picked up the envelope and tapped its contents out on the table. "Old receipts. All completely valueless to you."

He showed the color of irritation. "What do you think this has possibly gained you?"

"The opportunity to go to the safe and put your glass inside it."

90   His eyes flicked to the glass in front of him. "That was yours. Not mine."

I smiled. "It was your glass, Mr. Smith. And I imagine that the police will wonder what an empty glass is doing in my safe. I rather think, especially since this will be a case of murder, that they will have the intelligence to take fingerprints."

His eyes narrowed. "I haven't taken my eyes off you for a moment. You couldn't have

95 switched our glasses."

"No? I seem to recall that at least twice you looked at the painting."

Automatically he looked in that direction again. "Only for a second or two."

"It was enough."

He was perspiring faintly. "I say it was impossible."

100   "Then I'm afraid you will be greatly surprised when the police come for you. And after a little time you will have the delightful opportunity of facing death in the electric chair. You will share your victims' anticipation of death with the addition of a great deal more time in which to let your imagination play with the topic. I'm sure you've read accounts of executions in the electric chair?"

105   His finger seemed to tighten on the trigger.

"I wonder how you'll go," I said. "You've probably pictured yourself meeting death with calmness and fortitude. But that is a common comforting delusion, Mr. Smith. You will more likely have to be dragged. . . ."

His voice was level. "Open that safe or I'll kill you." I laughed. "Really now, Mr. Smith,

110 we both know that obviously you will kill me if I *do* open the safe."

A half a minute went by before he spoke. "What do you intend to do with the glass?"

"If you don't murder me—and I rather think you won't now—I will take it to a private detective agency and have your fingerprints reproduced. I will put them, along with a

115   note containing pertinent information, inside a sealed envelope. And I will leave instructions that in the event I die violently, even if the occurrence appears accidental, the envelope be forwarded to the police."

Smith stared at me and then he took a breath. "All that won't be necessary. I will leave now and you will never see me again."

120   I shook my head. "I prefer my plan. It provides protection for my future."

He was thoughtful. "Why don't you go direct to the police?"

"I have my reasons."

His eyes went down to his gun and then slowly he put it in his pocket. An idea came to him. "Your wife could very easily hire someone else to kill you."

125   "Yes. She could do that."

"I would be accused of your death. I could go to the electric chair."

"I imagine so. Unless. . . ."

Smith waited.

"Unless, of course, she were unable to hire anyone."

130   "But there are probably a half dozen other. . . ." He stopped.

I smiled. "Did my wife tell you where she is now?"

"Just that she'd be at a place called the Petersons. She will leave at eleven."

"Eleven? A good time. It will be very dark tonight. Do you know the Petersons' address?"

135   He stared at me. "No."

"In Bridgehampton," I said, and I gave him the house number.

Our eyes held for half a minute.

"It's something you must do," I said softly. "For your own protection."

He buttoned his coat slowly. "And where will you be at eleven, Mr. Williams?"

140   "At my club, probably playing cards with five or six friends. They will no doubt commiserate with me when I receive word that my wife has been . . . shot?"

"It all depends on the circumstances and the opportunity." He smiled thinly. "Did you ever love her?"

I picked up a jade figurine and examined it. "I was extremely fond of this piece when

145   I first bought it. Now it bores me. I will replace it with another."

When he was gone there was just enough time to take the glass to a detective agency before I went on to the club.

Not the glass in the safe, of course. It held nothing but my own fingerprints.

I took the one that Mr. Smith left on the cocktail table when he departed.

150   The prints of Mr. Smith's fingers developed quite clearly.

(1,588 words)

—"Shatter Proof" by Jack Ritchie,
from *Manhunt Magazine*

THINKING AND WRITING AFTER READING

RECALL   Self-test your understanding.

Your instructor may choose to give you a true-false comprehension review.

REACT   Why do you think Mr. Williams will take the glass with the killer's finger prints to the detective agency before going to the club? _____

_____

REFLECT   How did Mr. Williams manage to trick and blackmail the killer? _____

_____

THINKING CRITICALLY Why did the author not end the story with the glass in the safe and the killer saying he would leave? Would it still have been a clever short story if it had ended at that point? _____

_____

THINK AND WRITE Irony is a twist that leads to the unexpected happening. In this story, what is the ironic twist for each of the three: Mr. Williams, the professional killer, and Mrs. Williams? _____

_____

EXTENDED WRITING Make a list of Mr. Smith's traits. Are there any that you admire? Are there any you do not admire? Use the list to write a character sketch. Your purpose is to describe the aspects of Mr. Smith that his actions in this story demonstrate. Support your conclusions about him with evidence from the story. As you write, explain why you think certain traits are admirable and why others are not.

Interpret THE QUOTE

Now that you have finished reading the selection, "Shatter Proof," go back to the beginning of the selection and read the opening quote again. On a separate sheet of paper, explain the meaning of the quote. Do you think that Mr. Williams' deception was effective? Explain why.

Name ————————————————

Date ————————————————

COMPREHENSION QUESTIONS

Answer the following with *a, b, c,* or *d.* In order to help you analyze your strengths and weaknesses, the question types are indicated.

Main Idea ———— 1. The best statement of the main idea of the selection is

    a. Mr. Williams cleverly tricks a professional killer to change his own fate.
    b. Mr. Williams wanted to kill his wife and finally found a way to do it.
    c. Murder is a random game of chance.
    d. Dishonest people in polite society commit serious crimes and get away with it.

Inference ———— 2. The killer does not shoot Mr. Williams immediately because

    a. he wants more money.
    b. he takes pleasure in being entertained by the victim.
    c. he wants to give Mrs. Williams more time to establish her alibi.
    d. he does not enjoy killing but wants Mr. Williams to beg for his life.

Inference ———— 3. The main purpose for Mr. Williams' pointing to the painting and presenting the envelope was

    a. to switch the glasses.
    b. to divert the killer's eyes.
    c. to buy his life with the money.
    d. to get the $5,000 out of the safe.

Inference ———— 4. The killer did not shoot Mr. Williams because

    a. he had professional pride in accepting a commission.
    b. he believed Mr. Williams would give him the glass if he killed Mrs. Williams.
    c. he believed that Mrs. Williams also knew the combination to the safe.
    d. he believed he was trapped by the fingerprints in the safe.

Inference ———— 5. The killer will shoot Mrs. Williams because

    a. she might send someone else to kill Mr. Williams.
    b. he wants the glass returned by Mr. Williams.
    c. he plans to blame Mr. Williams for the murder.
    d. he realizes that he will not get any money from Mrs. Williams.

Inference ———— 6. Mr. Williams uses the jade figurine to describe

    a. his love for his wife.
    b. his present lack of interest in his wife.
    c. his long hatred for his wife.
    d. his wife's greed for money.

Inference   _____   7. The reader can most likely conclude that

      a. Mr. Williams will be convicted of his wife's murder.

      b. Mr. Williams will go to the police.

      c. The killer will not kill Mrs. Williams.

      d. Mr. Williams will keep the killer's fingerprints for his own protection.

Answer the following with *T* (true) or *F* (false).

Inference   _____   8. The reader can conclude that the professional killer's real name is Mr. Smith.

Detail   _____   9. Mr. Williams married a woman less than half his age.

Detail   _____ 10. Mr. Williams discovered that the killer's weakness or vulnerable point was his fear of conviction and the electric chair.

VOCABULARY

Answer the following with *a*, *b*, *c*, or *d* for the word or phrase that best defines the boldface word as used in the selection. The number in parentheses indicates the line of the passage in which the word appears.

_____ 1. "from the **decanter**" (7)

    a. bowl

    b. glass

    c. vase

    d. ornamental bottle

_____ 2. "**morbid** pleasure"(24)

    a. healthy

    b. abnormal

    c. guilty

    d. happy

_____ 3. "you have **insight**" (30)

    a. time

    b. money

    c. education

    d. understanding

_____ 4. "sat on the **davenport**" (40)

    a. sofa

    b. table

    c. liquor cabinet

    d. bed

_____ 5. "story more **authentic**" (47–48)

    a. fake

    b. interesting

    c. slow

    d. genuine

_____ 6. "accept a **commission**" (58)

    a. client

    b. fee

    c. painting

    d. vote

_____ 7. "You are ... **incorruptible**" (84)

    a. not open to bribery

    b. dishonest

    c. clumsy

    d. innocent

_____ 8. "calmness and **fortitude**" (107)

    a. protest

    b. temper

    c. happiness

    d. courage

_____ 9. "containing **pertinent** information" (115)

    a. relevant

    b. insignificant

    c. misleading

    d. misspelled

_____ 10. "**commiserate** with me" (140–141)

    a. laugh

    b. sympathize

    c. wonder

    d. approve

Your instructor may choose to give a true-false vocabulary review.

VOCABULARY ENRICHMENT

A. Use the indicated prefix to write words from the word bank that complete each sentence in the groups.

in: not, in, into   **Word Bank:** incorruptible   insight   intruder

1. His wife had planned for Mr. Williams' murder to look like the act of a surprised _____ rather than a premeditated action.

2. Mr. Williams' _____ was that the hired gun did not particularly care for the act of killing.

3. Since the killer would not accept Mr. Williams' offer of a valuable painting in exchange for his life, Mr. Williams referred to him as _____.

pro: before, for   **Word Bank:** professional   protection   provided

4. Mr. Williams was able to convince the hit man to kill Mrs. Williams for his own _____.

5. Although unsettled by Mr. Williams' trick, the man stayed calm and collected because he was a _____ in his field.

6. Had Mr. Williams become a murder victim, his wife would probably have been _____ with a substantial estate.

re: back, again   **Word Bank:** remain   remotely   return

7. Mr. Williams kept his would-be killer occupied as long as possible in order to _____ alive.

8. The murderer's initial plan was to shoot Mr. Williams, wash the glass he had used, and _____ it to the liquor cabinet.

9. Mr. Williams' offer of the painting was rejected partly because the criminal wanted no part of anything that would even _____ link him to the victim.

B. Use the context clues in the sentences to write the meaning of the boldface words.

10. **Narratives** never preach, but rather deliver a message to our emotions, senses, and imagination through a powerful shared experience.

_____

_____

11. The **theme** of a story about a college tennis champion might be that the journey to the top, including the hard work and discipline, was more meaningful than the final victory. _____

_____

12. Poisoned apples and talking mirrors may not seem realistic in a modern telephone conversation; however, in the context of Snow White, we easily find both **plausible.** _____

_____

13. E. M. Forster said that "The king died, and the queen died," is a narrative, but changing this to "The king died, and the queen died of grief," creates a **plot.** _____

_____

14. The **suspense** of a narrative is based on conflict, which perhaps starts out as mild and intensifies as each incident occurs. _____

_____

_____

15. Good writers select incidents and details that give **unity** to the story and advance the central theme. _____

_____

ASSESS YOUR LEARNING

Review confusing questions, seek clarification, and make notes in your text to help you remember new information and vocabulary.

SELECTION 3 History

"An individual who breaks a law that conscience tells him is unjust, and who willingly accepts the penalty of imprisonment in order to arouse the conscience of the community over its injustice, is in reality expressing the highest respect for the law."

Martin Luther King, Jr.

A critical event in the struggle for equal rights occurred in Montgomery, Alabama, in 1955. Rosa Parks, a black seamstress who was returning from work and tired, sat down on a bus in a section reserved for whites. When asked to get up, she refused. Parks was arrested and ordered to stand trial. Black civil rights officials seized the issue and responded with a boycott of the bus system. Organizational meetings for the boycott were held in a Montgomery Baptist church where the young 27-year-old minister, Martin Luther King, Jr., took an active role in the protest. Soon the talented and articulate Dr. King emerged as the leading spokesman for the protest and for the civil and economic concerns of black Americans.

THINKING BEFORE READING

Preview for clues to the content. Activate your prior knowledge. Anticipate what is coming and think about your purpose for reading.

In what city is the Martin Luther King, Jr. homeplace and national memorial?

Where did Dr. King make his "I Have a Dream" speech?

What world leader inspired Dr. King's nonviolent tactics?

I want to learn _____.

VOCABULARY PREVIEW

Are you familiar with these words?

sweltering	centennial	oppressive	podium	resonant
galvanized	spurious	dire	recanted	compelled

What is a *centenarian*?

At what temperature do you *swelter*?

How do *compel, repel,* and *expel* differ?

Your instructor may chose to give a true-false vocabulary review before or after reading.

THINKING DURING READING

As you read, use the six thinking strategies of a good reader: predict, picture, relate, monitor, correct, and annotate.

Reader's **TIP**   **Reading and Studying History**

- Know the *who*, *what*, *when*, *where*, and *why* for people, places, documents, and events.
- Seek to understand the cause-and-effect relationship among events and their causes, results, and consequences.
- Use time lines to familiarize yourself with chronologies to get an overall picture of parallel or overlapping events.
- Learn significant dates to provide a framework for grouping and understanding events.
- Look at maps of the region being studied.
- Distinguish between fact and opinion, and compare your conclusions with the historian's interpretation.

THE DREAM OF NONVIOLENT REFORM

Perspiring in the sweltering heat of a Washington August afternoon, Martin Luther King, Jr., looked down from the steps of the Lincoln Memorial at the largest assembly ever congregated in the United States. Well over 200,000 people, 70 percent of them blacks, jammed the mile-long mall that swept away to the Washington Monument. Angry yet

5   hopeful, they had come to the nation's capital in 1963, the centennial of the Emancipation Proclamation, to personify black demands for equality in society. But the speakers and singers who preceded King had not been particularly effective, the heat and humidity were oppressive, and the great crowd was starting to thin around the edges. As he mounted the podium, King sensed this restlessness and the need for a focus. At first his

10 deep voice was husky, but it soon became resonant with a purpose that quieted and transfixed the multitude and the millions of television viewers. King's eloquence dramatized the anguish of black history. One hundred years after slavery, he pointed out, the black was still "an exile in his own land." It was the future, however, that mattered. "I have a dream," he cried repeatedly, as he sketched his vision of freedom, justice, and harmony.

15 At the end of his speech King prophesied that one day all people would be able to join together in singing the words of an old Negro spiritual: "Free at last! Free at last! Thank God Almighty, we are free at last." There was an awed silence, then an ear-shattering roar: the crowd was applauding wildly. King had galvanized the massive assembly. At that moment he stood at the crest of a mounting wave of African American protest. Yet, as

20 King must have known, his dream would have an agonizing birth. Just five years after his Washington address, he lay dead on the balcony of a Memphis motel, the victim of the violence he had devoted his life to overcoming.

. . .

The Poor People's March was set for June 1968, but the whirlwind pace King had kept since the beginning of the decade allowed him only occasional participation in the

25 planning. One of the detours took him to Memphis, where a garbage strike threatened to evolve into a racial encounter of crisis proportions. Local black leaders wanted King to organize a peaceful demonstration, but once again he had difficulty working with Black Power militants. Uncontrollable black looters, arsonists, and street fighters were another source of difficulty. On March 28, they had transformed a nonviolent march into an orgy

30 of destruction that had provoked an even greater measure of police brutality. As a self-styled "riot preventer," King was sick at heart. If Memphis exploded, he feared, the approaching summer of 1968 would be chaos. Already, black leaders like Harlem congressman

Adam Clayton Powell were arousing the urban masses and, as part of their campaign, making references to "Martin Loser King" and his Uncle Tom tactics. Nonviolence, King
35 felt, was on trial in Memphis.

On April 3, 1968, on the eve of the crucial Memphis march, King addressed a capacity crowd at the Masonic Temple located in that city. His mood was strangely somber and introspective. "Like anybody," he mused, "I would like to live a long life." But longevity, he added, was not his chief concern; he would rather do God's will. Some of his aides
40 were reminded of the great Washington rally of 1963, where King had expressed his belief that "if a man hasn't discovered something that he will die for, he isn't fit to live!" The following evening, on the way to yet another mass meeting, King walked onto the balcony of his hotel room and leaned over the railing to talk with a colleague. A moment later he crumpled to the ground. An assassin's bullet, fired from a hotel room across the
45 street, had pierced his skull. The killer, arrested two months later and identified as James Earl Ray, was a white drifter with a long criminal record.

Following Ray's confession, investigations of King's murder continued until 1977. Exhaustive reviews of the evidence seemed to prove conclusively that Ray had acted alone

50　in the assassination, and there was no conspiracy. The research did reveal that the Federal Bureau of Investigation, under orders of its director, J. Edgar Hoover, had complicated the last six years of King's life with a program of systematic harassment on the spurious grounds that he was under the influence of the Communist party. The conspiracy theory surrounding King's death reemerged in the 1990's when James Earl Ray, in prison and in dire health, recanted his confession. Talk of Ray being brought to trial—there had been 55　none due to his confession—ended abruptly when Ray died in early 1998.

　　The murder of Martin Luther King, Jr., moved the American people as had few events in recent years. The immediate response in all but the most prejudiced white minds was shame. Millions of whites felt compelled to apologize to black people as a whole and went to their churches for services honoring King. But even among the mourners, white and 60　black eyes did not meet easily. Everyone seemed to recognize that, with King's death, a powerful influence for interracial compassion and understanding had been eliminated— the basis of ordered change and reform.

(878 words)

—*From These Beginnings,* Sixth Edition, Volume Two, by Roderick Nash and Gregory Graves

THINKING AND WRITING AFTER READING

RECALL　Self-test your understanding.

Your instructor may choose to give you a true-false comprehension review.

REACT　Aside from their stated reasons, why do you think the FBI would spend six years tracking Dr. King? _____

_____

REFLECT　What seemed to be the differences in philosophy among the civil rights leaders? _____

_____

THINK CRITICALLY　Why was Martin Luther King, Jr.'s birthday made a national holiday? _____

_____

THINK AND WRITE　Events often call for ordinary men and women to do extraordinary things. How were Rosa Parks and Martin Luther King, Jr. both ordinary and extraordinary? How did events converge to change their destinies and our history?

_____

_____

MAIN IDEA

1. What is the topic of the first paragraph? _____

2. What is the topic of the last paragraph? _____

_____

EXTENDED WRITING Take a moment to think of someone you highly respect. This person might be a historical figure like Dr. King, a living political or human rights leader, or someone you know personally. Write a well-developed paragraph that explains why you respect this person. Give examples of this person's actions, beliefs, or behavior that support your explanations.

Interpret THE QUOTE

Now that you have finished reading the selection, "The Dream of Nonviolent Reform," go back to the beginning of the selection and read the opening quote again. Under what circumstances does Martin Luther King, Jr. believe it is acceptable to break the law? On a separate piece of paper, explain why you agree or disagree with Dr. King's views on breaking laws.

SELECTION

3

Name _____

Date _____

COMPREHENSION QUESTIONS

Answer the following with *a*, *b*, *c*, or *d*, or fill in the blank. In order to help you analyze your strengths and weaknesses, the question types are indicated.

Main Idea _____ 1. The best statement of the main idea of the selection is:

    a. Dr. King started the civil rights movement with his "I Have a Dream" speech in Washington.

    b. Though his life was taken violently, Dr. King was a moving speaker and a major force in the nonviolent movement for civil rights.

    c. Dr. King was killed violently by a drifter.

    d. Dr. King controlled the violence in Memphis but was killed for doing so.

Detail _____ 2. The primary reason over 200,000 people had congregated in Washington in 1963 was

    a. to hear Dr. King speak.

    b. to urge legislators to pass the Emancipation Proclamation.

    c. to show strength in demanding equal treatment for African Americans in society.

    d. to honor Lincoln for freeing the slaves.

Detail _____ 3. In his "I Have a Dream" speech, Dr. King's major thrust is to

    a. recall the hardships of the past.

    b. blame society for prejudice and hatred.

    c. ask God for forgiveness and strength.

    d. focus on the possibilities of the future.

Inference _____ 4. The author implies that

    a. Black Power militants did not agree with Dr. King's tactics.

    b. Dr. King and Black Power militants shared the same philosophy and strategies.

    c. Adam Clayton Powell supported Dr. King's tactics.

    d. little friction existed among the different leaders supporting civil rights.

Inference _____ 5. Dr. King felt that nonviolence was on trial in Memphis because

_____

_____

_____

Inference _____ 6. The author suggests all of the following *except*

    a. Dr. King was willing to die for his cause.

    b. Dr. King had a premonition that he would not live a long life.

    c. Dr. King knew that fighting for his cause was dangerous.

    d. Dr. King was willing to back off from his nonviolent stand to get the support of other civil rights leaders.

Detail _____ 7. The author indicates that evidence suggests that
   a. Ray acted alone.
   b. Ray was part of a conspiracy.
   c. J. Edgar Hoover was involved in Dr. King's death.
   d. Ray was not the man who fired the shots from the hotel room.

Answer the following with *T* (true) or *F* (false).

Inference _____ 8. After Dr. King's death, the American people realized that he was indeed the "riot preventer."

Detail _____ 9. The garbage strike in Memphis was in June 1968.

Detail _____ 10. Ray was brought to trial after he took back his confession.

VOCABULARY

Answer the following with *a, b, c,* or *d* for the word or phrase that best defines the boldface word as used in the selection. The number in parentheses indicates the line of the passage in which the word appears.

_____ 1. "**sweltering** heat" (1)
   a. never-ending
   b. humid and sweaty
   c. permanent
   d. oncoming

_____ 2. "the **centennial** of the Emancipation Proclamation" (5)
   a. 10-year celebration
   b. 50-year celebration
   c. 100-year celebration
   d. 200-year celebration

_____ 3. "heat and humidity were **oppressive**" (7–8)
   a. overpowering
   b. surprising
   c. brief
   d. energizing

_____ 4. "mounted the **podium**" (9)
   a. stairway
   b. top of the monument
   c. steps
   d. speaker's stand

_____ 5. "**resonant** with a purpose" (10)
   a. sensitive
   b. hoarse
   c. forceful and loud
   d. repetitious

_____ 6. "**galvanized** the massive assembly" (18)
   a. stopped
   b. excited
   c. frightened
   d. shamed

_____ 7. "on the **spurious** grounds" (51)
   a. false
   b. evil
   c. criminal
   d. socialistic

_____ 8. "in **dire** health" (54)
   a. fair
   b. uncertain
   c. questionable
   d. terrible

_____ 9. "**recanted** his confession" (54)
   a. emphasized
   b. questioned
   c. regretted
   d. took back

_____ 10. "**compelled** to apologize" (58)
   a. nervous
   b. obliged
   c. angered
   d. manipulated

Your instructor may choose to give a true-false vocabulary review.

VOCABULARY ENRICHMENT

A. Use the indicated root to form words to complete each sentence.

voc, vok: voice, call

1. Dr. King's message of freedom and love for all mankind _____ a feeling of hope for racial unity in his audience.

2. Dr. King's brave manner of speaking out against injustice has inspired future generations to be more _____ about prejudice.

3. Dr. King's persuasive _____ included simple words like *dream* and *justice*.

gress, grad, gred: step, degree

4. Dr. King's inspiring words are often quoted to _____ in commencement speeches.

5. While Dr. King used peaceful methods of conflict resolution, Black Power militants tended to use more _____ tactics.

6. While many advocates for civil rights wanted instant change, Dr. King recognized that lasting change would be more _____.

spec, spect: see, watch

7. Over 200,000 _____ observed Dr. King's speech on the steps of the Lincoln Memorial.

8. An _____ of the assassination scene indicated that Dr. King had been shot from the window of a neighboring hotel.

9. The Memphis march was intended to be a _____ that would call national attention to the Civil Rights Movement.

B. Use context clues and mark *a, b, c,* or *d* for the meaning closest to that of the boldface word.

_____   10. The fight for racial equality **signifies** a larger struggle for all human rights.
   a. indicates
   b. simplifies
   c. reduces
   d. warns of

_____   11. Sit-ins by **diligent** believers in racial equality resulted in the desegregation of public facilities in a hundred southern cities.
   a. convincing
   b. hard-working
   c. older
   d. talkative

_____ 12. The Civil Rights movement accomplished a **tangible** result when the Supreme Court ruled the Alabama segregated bus seating law unconstitutional.

    a. sizable

    b. tremendous

    c. actual

    d. movable

C. Study the following easily confused words, and circle the one that is correct in each sentence.

thorough: careful	**straight:** not curving	**loose:** not tight
threw: tossed	**strait:** narrow passage of water	**lose:** misplace
through: by means of		

13. Dr. King's "Letter from a Birmingham City Jail" did a (**thorough, threw, through**) job in explaining his vision to a group of Alabama clergymen.

14. Dr. King's doctrine of passive resistance required followers to stare and walk (**straight, strait**) ahead when confronted by violence.

15. Police often let attack dogs run (**loose, lose**) to menace Civil Rights protesters.

ASSESS YOUR LEARNING

Review confusing questions, seek clarification, and make notes in your text to help you remember new information and vocabulary.

PERSONAL FEEDBACK 2   **Name** _____

1. Review your responses to the three longer reading selections. Summarize and comment on your error patterns. _____

_____

_____

2. What selection, short or long, has held your attention the best? Why do you think it did so? _____

_____

_____

3. What unforeseen difficulties have you already encountered this term that have interfered with your ability to study? _____

_____

_____

Tear out and submit to your instructor.

VOCABULARY LESSON

Before and After

Study the prefixes, words, and sentences.

| **Prefixes** | *ante*: before | *pre*: before | *post*: after |

Words with *ante* = *before*

Can *antenuptial* counseling strengthen marriages? Is an entry an *anteroom*?

- Antebellum: existing before the war

  The *antebellum* home with the white columns was built before the Civil War.

- Antecede: to go before

  Your good name can *antecede* your presence.

- Antecedent: word coming before the pronoun to which the pronoun refers

  The name *Valerie* is the *antecedent* of *her* in the sentence.

- Antediluvian: belonging to the time before the flood; very old

  She ignored the advice and regarded it as *antediluvian*.

- Antennae: feelers on the head of an insect used as organs of touch

  The insect's *antennae* inspected the food.

- Antescript: a note added before something such as a prefix to a letter

  The *antescript* indicated why the letter would be late arriving.

Words with *pre* = *before*

Can a *prefix predict* the meaning of a new word?

- Preamble: an introduction

  Schoolchildren learn the *Preamble* to the Constitution.

- Precede: to go before

  Queen Elizabeth should *precede* Prince Philip at state events.

- Predecessor: one who came before another in office

  Her *predecessor* helped orient the new chairperson to the job.

- Preeminent: supreme, before all others

  Our professor is the *preeminent* scholar in contemporary Russian literature.

- Prelude: a musical or dramatic introduction

  As the *prelude* began, the remaining ticket holders were seated in the audience.

- Premonition: a forewarning or omen

  When I heard the dog bark, I had a *premonition* that trouble was near.

- Prejudice: judgment before proof is given

  A lawyer tries to avoid choosing a potential juror who shows signs of *prejudice*.

- Precocious: having early development

  The *precocious* child could read at 2 years of age.

Words with *post* = *after*

Is the time ante meridian or *post* meridian?

- Posterity: descendants who come after

  Leave a gift for *posterity* and donate money to the college library.

- Posthumous: after death

  The *posthumous* award was given to the widow of the soldier.

- Postnatal: the time immediately after birth

  A *postnatal* examination monitors the health of the new mother.

- Postpone: delay or set the date back

  Let's *postpone* the meeting until tomorrow after lunch.

- Postscript: a note added to a letter after it has been signed

  Karen scribbled an afterthought in the *postscript* to her long letter.

Review

Part I

Choose an appropriate word from the list to complete each of the following sentences.

precocious	premonition	antebellum	prelude	postscript
predecessor	posthumous	preamble	postponed	preeminent

1. The ambassador is a _____ scholar in the history of Nigeria.

2. Shorten the _____ and begin the main point of your speech.

3. As a _____ athlete, the young Tiger Woods golfed on TV with adults.

4. The threat of a tornado _____ the game for three hours.

5. A _____ award honors a dead hero.

6. The couple restored the _____ home to its original 1850s appearance.

7. The musical _____ introduced the song to follow.

8. George W. Bush was the immediate _____ of Barack Obama.

9. A superstitious person would see a black cat as a _____ of danger.

10. Sara's letter ended with her quickly remembered thoughts in a _____.

Part II

Answer the following with *T* (true) or *F* (false).

_____ 11. A prejudiced listener has trouble fairly evaluating both sides.

_____ 12. An antediluvian outfit is up to date.

_____ 13. A postnatal exam checks the growth of the fetus.

_____ 14. Antemeridian refers to the afternoon.

_____ 15. The antennae of an insect are usually attached to its tail.

_____ 16. The antescript is positioned in the main body of the letter.

_____ 17. An antecedent is a person, place, or thing.

_____ 18. Antinuptial arguments occur after the wedding day.

_____ 19. A presumed appointment needs to be double-checked for certainty.

_____ 20. Environmental regulations consider both the present and posterity.

Selecting a Book

The next time you are in the market for a good read, you might spend some time browsing the shelves of a bookstore or library, or perhaps you will do your browsing on the Web. Whichever method you use, the chances of success are greater if you exercise your critical thinking skills. Like clothing and groceries, books are products—and the presentation matters. Book covers and quick descriptions are slick marketing tools designed by experts to entice you to make a purchase through pictures, testimonials, and exaggeration. Cut through the hype and decide if the book will be of interest to you.

Any one book might be sold with several different covers to appeal to a variety of audiences. The testimonials by other authors are carefully selected to present a positive image, and customer ratings should also be viewed with an analytical mind. Summary blurbs and excerpts are chosen to present the most appealing aspects of the book. Remember that exciting advertising can make even boring books look good.

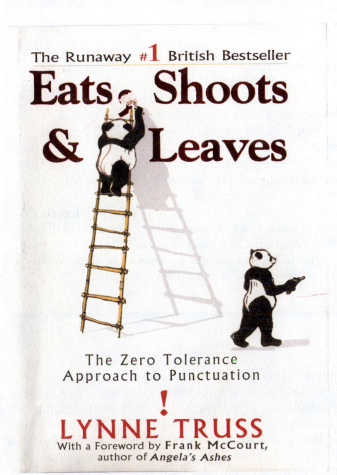

The Runaway #1 British Bestseller

Eats, Shoots & Leaves

The Zero Tolerance Approach to Punctuation

!

LYNNE TRUSS

With a Foreword by Frank McCourt, author of *Angela's Ashes*

A panda walks into a café. He orders a sandwich, eats it, then draws a gun and fires two shots in the air.

"Why?" asks the confused waiter, as the panda makes towards the exit. The panda produces a badly punctuated wildlife manual and tosses it over his shoulder.

"I'm a panda," he says, at the door. "Look it up."

The waiter turns to the relevant entry and, sure enough, finds an explanation.

"**Panda.** Large black-and-white bear-like mammal, native to China. Eats, shoots and leaves."

So, punctuation really does matter, even if it is only occasionally a matter of life and death.

Sticklers unite!
What people are saying about *Eats, Shoots & Leaves*

"If Lynne Truss were Roman Catholic I'd nominate her for sainthood. As it is, thousands of English teachers from Maine to Maui will be calling down blessings on her merry, learned head."
—FRANK MCCOURT, author of *Angela's Ashes*

"There is a multitude of us riding this planet for whom apostrophe catastrophes, quotation bloatation, mad dashes, and other comma-tose errors squeak like chalk across the blackboard of our sensibilities. At last we who are punctilious about punctuation have a manifesto, and it is titled *Eats, Shoots & Leaves*."
—RICHARD LEDERER, author of *A Man of My Words* and *Anguished English*

"At long last, a worthy tribute to punctuation's stepchildren: the neglected semi-colon, the enigmatic ellipsis and the mad dash. Punc-rock on!"
—JAMES LIPTON, author of *An Exaltation of Larks* and writer and host of *Inside the Actors Studio*

ISBN 1-592-40087-6

51750

9 781592 400874

EAN

173

EXERCISE 1 Refer to the preceding figure to answer the following questions.

1. Is this book on the British Best Sellers list? _____
   _____

2. What is the book's topic? _____

3. Why is the comma misplaced in the panda anecdote? How does it alter the
   meaning of the sentence? _____
   _____
   _____

4. Is this book an example of fiction or nonfiction? (See the definitions that
   follow if you are not sure.) Justify your response. _____
   _____
   _____

Reader's TIP   Selecting a Book

After locating a book that looks interesting, investigate further using these strategies.

- Read the blurbs introducing the book. Do they entice you? Is it the kind of book you have enjoyed in the past?
- Read the first page and at least one other page if possible. Most bookstore websites allow a peek inside the book. Do you like the writing style? Is it comfortable for you to read? Does the first page grab your attention?
- Read about the author. Have you enjoyed other books by the author? Have friends recommended the author? If the book is nonfiction, what are the author's credentials?
- If nonfiction, review the table of contents and scan the index. Is this material that you want to learn more about? Look at the illustrations and read the captions. Are you intrigued?
- Glance at the testimonials or customer reviews? Are they consistent? Do the reasons given address your personal concerns?

Consult Best-Seller Lists

If you want to know what books other people are buying, consult a best-seller list. Your bookstore or your city newspaper may publish one. If not, the *New York Times* Best Sellers list is nationally respected. Such lists are sometimes divided into best-selling fiction and nonfiction, and then further divided into hardbound books—which are published first and cost more—and paperbacks. Similar to a listing of top-grossing movies, a ranking on a best-seller list indicates quantity, but not necessarily quality. Bookstores often post their own lists of local best-selling suggestions.

Sample a Variety of Fiction and Nonfiction

Fiction is writing that has been invented by the imagination. The **novel,** the literary form for the imaginative and pleasurable stories of contemporary fiction, is longer than a short story but presents the same elements of **plot**, **character**, **theme**, **setting**, and **tone**.

Nonfiction is a piece of writing based on true events. The label of *nonfiction* includes biographies and books about travel, art, music, decorating, computers, cooking, and other special interests. Some are historical works in which dialogue may be invented based on known facts about the actual people and events of a given time period. Such books can be difficult to distinguish from fiction.

EXERCISE 2   Visit a local bookstore or log on to an online bookstore and pretend you have $100 to spend on books. Review both fiction and nonfiction books and make your choices. Record the title and author of each book you select, as well as a one- or two-sentence summary of what you think the book will be about and why you may want to read it.

5 Supporting Details and Organizational Patterns

Learning Objectives

From this chapter, readers will learn:

1 To distinguish major and minor details
2 The roles of major and minor details
3 To attend to details in written directions
4 To identify seven common organizational patterns by using transitional words and graphic organizers
5 To mark the text using the organizational pattern as a guide
6 The clues to recognizing the organizational pattern

Everyday Reading Skills: Selecting Magazines

WHAT IS A DETAIL?

Details develop, explain, and prove the main idea. They are the facts, descriptions, and reasons that convince the reader and make the material interesting. Details answer questions and paint visual images so the reader has an experience with the author and sees what the author sees and understands. For example, in a passage on the validity of movie reviews, the supporting details might include information on the rating scale, the qualifications of the raters, and the influence of the production companies on the eventual reviews.

Details can be ranked by their levels of importance in supporting a topic. Some details offer major support and elaboration, whereas others merely provide illustrations to relate the material to the reader's prior knowledge and make visualizing easier. All details play a part in our enjoyment of reading, but it is necessary to recognize their varying levels of importance.

Recognize Levels of Importance

To organize related words or ideas into levels of importance, the general topic is stated first, followed by subcategories of details, which may be further subdivided into specific examples. Outlines, diagrams, and **graphic organizers** can be used to help organize information into levels of importance.

EXAMPLE Notice that by using an outline and a diagram, the following list of words can be unscrambled to show relationships and levels of importance:

horses	grass	botany
zoology	cows	ants
bees	rabbits	entomology
branches of biology	flowers	mosquitoes
trees		

Branches of Biology

  Botany

    grass

    flowers

    trees

  Zoology

    horses

    cows

    rabbits

    Entomology

    ants

    bees

    mosquitoes

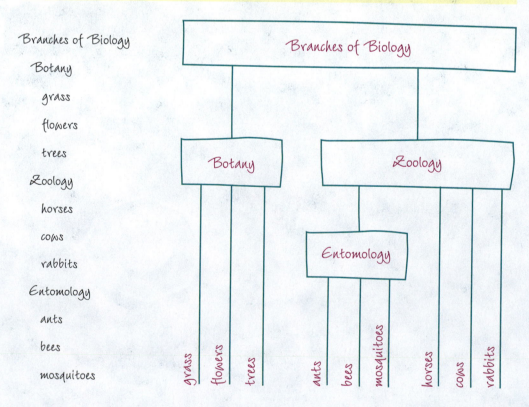

EXERCISE 1 Major ideas and supporting details have been mixed together in the following lists of words. Think about how the ideas should be organized, and insert them in the outline or diagram form provided. The main idea or topic of each list appears either on the line above the outline or in the top box of the diagram.

List 1

radio, television, advertising media, broadcast, direct mail, internet, print, news-papers, magazines

Advertising media

  I. _Print_ _____

   A. _____

   B. _____

   C. _____

  II. _____

   A. _____

   B. _____

   C. _____

List 2

Maine, North Carolina, Southeastern, states in regions of the United States, New Mexico, Southwestern, Arizona, Rhode Island, Georgia, Connecticut, Florida, Northeastern

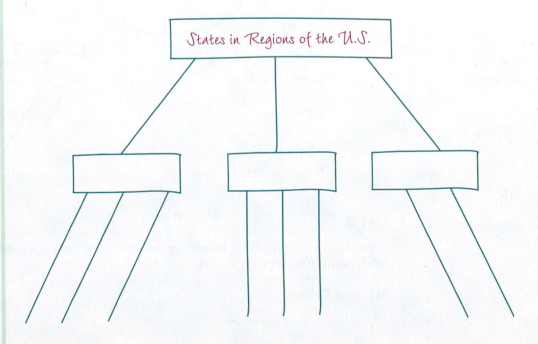

States in Regions of the U.S.

List 3

honest, personality, appearance, description of a person, shy, well-dressed, blond, straightforward, tall

Description of a Person

    I. _____

       A. _____

       B. _____

       C. _____

   II. _____

       A. _____

       B. _____

       C. _____

List 4

salsa, pasta, soy sauce, Mexican, ethnic foods, olive oil, fortune cookie, tacos, guacamole, Italian, egg rolls, Chinese

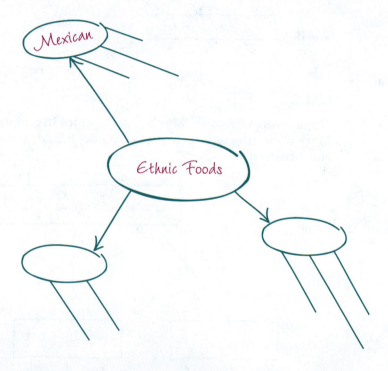

List 5

speeding, misdemeanor, felony, types of crime, murder, disorderly conduct, rape, gambling, armed robbery

Types of Crime

    I. _____

       A. _____

       B. _____

       C. _____

II. _____
    A. _____
    B. _____
    C. _____

List 6

compass, digging tools, hoe, tools, machete, straight edge, cutting tools, measuring tools, axe, gauge, jigsaw, spade, shovel

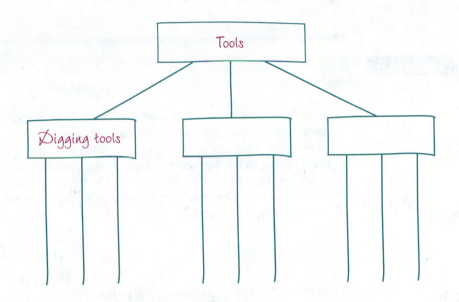

The Roles of Major and Minor Details

Learning Objective 2

The roles of major and minor details

The outlines and diagrams on the preceding pages show that all details are not of equal importance. When reading textbooks, you may sometimes feel you are receiving an overload of details. Not only is it impossible to remember all of them, but doing so can be a waste of time. With practice, you will learn that some details are major and should be remembered, whereas others are of only minor significance in supporting the main idea. How do you determine the importance of a particular detail? It depends on what point the author is making, and it depends on *what information is essential to develop, explain, or prove that point*.

For example, in a passage about communication by sound, the reason a bird sings would be of major significance and gives primary support for the main idea, whereas the particular species of bird would be a minor detail the author included for secondary support. In a passage on the limitations of acupuncture, the date of origin of the technique would most likely be a minor detail, providing a secondary level of support. However, if the focus of the passage were on the history of acupuncture, the date of origin would be a major detail, giving primary support to the main idea.

Minor details add interest, help the reader understand by giving examples, create visual images, and generally fill out a passage. Perhaps the author could make the point without them, but minor details tend to enhance the quality of the work. Major details, however, directly support the main idea regardless of whether it is directly or indirectly stated, and they are vital to your understanding the passage.

> ## Reader's TIP — Distinguishing Major and Minor Details
>
> To determine which details give major or minor support, first identify the author's main point and then ask yourself the following questions.
>
> 1. What details are needed to explain or prove the main idea? (These are major details that give primary support.)
> 2. What details are included just to make the passage more interesting? (These are minor details that provide a secondary level of support.)

EXAMPLE   Read the following paragraph. First determine the main point and then decide which details are major and which are minor.

> John Quincy Adams was a chip off the old family glacier. Short (5 feet 7 inches; 1.7 meters), thickset, and billiard-bald, he was even more frigidly austere than his presidential father, John Adams. Shunning people, he often went for early morning swims, sometimes stark naked, in the then pure Potomac River. Essentially a closeted thinker rather than a politician, he was irritable, sarcastic, and tactless. Yet few men have ever come to the presidency with a more brilliant record in statecraft, especially in foreign affairs. He ranks as one of the most successful secretaries of state, yet one of the least successful presidents.
>
> —*The American Pageant*
> by Thomas Bailey and David Kennedy

1. What point is the author trying to make? _____

   _____

2. Are the following details major or minor in their support of the author's point?

   _____ a. He was 5 feet 7 inches tall.

   _____ b. He was thickset and bald.

   _____ c. He was a closeted thinker rather than a politician.

   _____ d. He swam naked in the Potomac River.

   _____ e. He came to the presidency with a brilliant record in statecraft.

EXPLANATION   The author's main point is that John Quincy Adams had been a brilliant secretary of state but was a socially inept politician and thus one of the least successful presidents. Items *a* and *b* on appearance are minor details that add interest but lend only secondary support. Item *c* is a major detail because it shows Adams's isolation as a socially inept politician. Swimming naked (*d*) is an interesting minor detail, and the last item (*e*) is a major detail because it develops the main point.

Transitional Words to Signal Levels of Importance. Sometimes the following connecting words signal the importance of details:

Major (primary support):   *first / second   last / in addition*
Minor (secondary support):   *for example / to illustrate*

 For each of the following topics, three details are given. Determine which details offer major (primary) support to the topic and which offer minor (secondary) support. Write the appropriate word in the blanks.

1. Reducing the Fur Trade

_____ a. Through advertising and publicity stunts, PETA, the world's largest animal rights group, has done much to convince the public that wearing fur is cruel.

_____ b. Over the last fifteen years people have come to realize the suffering of animals, and the fur industry has declined dramatically.

_____ c. For example, Tyra Banks and Cindy Crawford will not model fur.

2. Dorothea Dix's Humanitarian Reform

_____ a. After visiting a jail to teach a Sunday school class to the female inmates and finding female patients in a mental hospital freezing in unheated, filthy cells, Dix started a lifelong campaign to improve conditions in such institutions.

_____ b. From 1845 to 1885 she was directly responsible for establishing thirty-three mental hospitals at home and abroad.

_____ c. Dix was born in Maine but moved to Boston at the age of 12 to live with her grandmother.

3. Diet of an Armadillo

_____ a. The armadillo enjoys scorpions, tarantulas, and grasshoppers, but its favorite food is ants, including the eggs and larvae.

_____ b. If pursued, the armadillo can outrun a human and quickly dig itself into the ground.

_____ c. Sometimes it will eat fungus and wild berries or catch a lazy lizard, but the belief that the armadillo raids henhouses is unfounded.

4. Characteristics of the Millennium Generation (Born 1977–2002)

_____ a. This group is also called Generation Y because it followed Generation X.

_____ b. Members of this group have known digital technology all of their lives and are comfortable with it.

_____ c. Millennials place a high value on making their jobs fit around their families and personal lives.

5. Larceny-theft

_____ a. Tires, wheels, hubcaps, radar detectors, stereos, CD players, cassette tapes, compact discs, and cellular phones account for many of the items reported stolen.

_____ b. Larceny-theft is the most frequently reported major crime.

_____ c. Larceny-theft may be the most underreported crime category, because small thefts rarely come to the attention of the police.

6. Preterm Neonates

_____ a. The immature development of preterm neonates makes them unusually sensitive to stimuli in their environment.

_____ b. Preterm neonates can easily be overwhelmed by the sights, sounds, and sensations they experience, and their breathing may be interrupted or their heart rates may slow.

_____ c. Such behavior is quite disconcerting to parents.

EXERCISE 3 Distinguishing between major and minor details is important, whether you are studying a single paragraph, a chapter, or a whole book. After reading each of the following passages, first identify the author's main point. Then determine which of the details listed are major and which are minor in supporting that point. The skills you will use apply equally to these short readings and to the larger units of text you will be studying in college textbooks.

Passage 1

PRICE SETTING

The DeBeers Company of South Africa, a syndicate that controls most of the sales of raw diamonds, maximizes profits by determining what quantity of raw diamonds to offer on the world raw-diamond market. DeBeers markets diamonds through an unusual marketing procedure called a sight. About three weeks before each sight, DeBeers sends notices to the 300 largest diamond purchasers, who are asked to send in requests in carats for the amount of diamonds they wish to buy. Two days before the sight (held in London, Luzerne, and Kimberley, South Africa), the buyers are informed how many carats they have been allocated—an amount often below the quantity requested. At the sight each buyer is handed a container of raw diamonds. Buyers who refuse to purchase would run the risk of not being invited back. The market price of diamonds is regulated by the number of diamonds offered in each sight.

—*Essentials of Economics,* Fourth Edition, by Paul Gregory

1. What point is the author trying to make? _____

_____

2. Which details are major and which are minor in supporting the author's point?

_____ a. The sight is held in London, Luzerne, and Kimberley.

_____ b. DeBeers invites the 300 largest diamond buyers to the sight.

_____ c. The buyers are offered fewer diamonds than the quantity they requested.

Passage 2

HEALTH FOOD?

When 35 million people in the United States gave their loved ones boxes of chocolates last Valentine's Day, they knew they were giving sweet comfort—but health food? Chocolate candy is certainly a significant source of fat and sugar calories, but recent research suggests that chocolate itself—the dark, bitter powder made from the seeds within cacao pods—may also be a significant source of protective molecules. Medical scientists have known for some time that many things that go wrong with our bodies can be traced to destructive molecules called *free radicals*. Many free radicals contain oxygen in a form that reacts strongly with, and damages, various biological molecules and their cellular structures. This process is called *oxidative stress*. So what's a person to do? Well, maybe eat more chocolate!

—*Biology: Life on Earth,* Sixth Edition,
by Teresa Audesirk, Gerald Audesirk, and Bruce Byers

1. What point is the author trying to make? _____

_____

2. Which details are major and which are minor in supporting the author's point?

_____ a. Free radicals damage biological molecules and their cellular structure.

_____ b. About 35 million people in the United States gave chocolates on Valentine's Day.

_____ c. Chocolate is a source of fat and sugar calories.

Passage 3

GENDER AND COLLEGE PERFORMANCE

I registered for a calculus course my first year at DePauw. Even twenty years ago I was not timid, so on the very first day I raised my hand and asked a question. I still have a vivid memory of the professor rolling his eyes, hitting his head with his hand in frustration, and announcing to everyone, "Why do they expect me to teach calculus to girls?" I never asked another question. Several weeks later I went to a football game, but I had forgotten to bring my ID. My calculus professor was at the gate checking IDs, so I went up to him and said, "I forgot my ID but you know me, I'm in your class." He looked right at me and said, "I don't remember you in my class." I couldn't believe that someone who changed my life and whom I remember to this day didn't even recognize me.

—Patricia Ireland, quoted in *Failing at Fairness: How America's Schools Cheat Girls,*
by Myra and David Sadker

1. What point is the author trying to make? _____

_____

2. Which details are major and which are minor in supporting the author's point?

_____ a. The author registered for a calculus course in her first year of college.

_____ b. When the author asked a question in class, her calculus professor responded in frustration, "Why do they expect me to teach calculus to girls?"

_____ c. The author attended a football game at which her calculus professor worked the gate checking IDs.

Passage 4

ASTEROIDS

Besides the eight major planets, thousands of smaller planetoids are also part of the solar system. These minor planets are called asteroids. There are more than 10,000 known asteroids, but many others are far too small to be seen even through the best telescopes. Most are found between the orbits of Jupiter and Mars, where the gravitational force of Jupiter prevented them from combining to form a single larger planet. The largest asteroid is only about 1000 km across.

—*Earth's Dynamic Systems*, Ninth Edition,
by W. Kenneth Hamblin and Eric H. Christiansen

1. What point is the author trying to make? _____

_____

_____

2. Which details are major and which are minor in supporting the author's point?

_____ a. There are more than 10,000 known asteroids.

_____ b. There are eight major planets.

_____ c. The minor planets of the solar system are called asteroids.

Passage 5

INTEREST

When you deposit money in a bank—for example, in a savings account—you are permitting the bank to use your money. The bank may use the deposited money to lend customers the money to buy cars or make renovations on their homes. The bank pays you for the privilege of using your money. The amount paid to you is called interest. If you are the one borrowing money from the bank, the amount you pay for the privilege of using that money is also called interest.

—From Aufmann/Barker/Lockwood, *Basic College Mathematics*,
8th Edition. © 2006 Brooks/Cole, a part of Cengage Learning, Inc.
Reproduced by permission. www.cengage.com/permissions

1. What point is the author trying to make? _____

_____

2. Which details are major and which are minor in supporting the author's point?

_____ a. The bank lends money to customers who want to purchase cars or renovate their homes.

_____ b. The bank pays you for the privilege of using your money.

_____ c. When you deposit money in a bank you are permitting the bank to use your money.

Passage 6

Most of us have relieved stress by engaging in aggressive physical activity. Chopping wood when angry is one example. Exercise performed as an immediate response can help alleviate stress symptoms. However, a regular exercise program yields even more substantial benefits. Try to engage in at least 25 minutes of aerobic exercise three or four times a week. But simply walking up stairs, parking farther away from your destination, or standing rather than sitting helps to conserve and replenish your adaptation energy stores. Although it may not improve your aerobic capacity, a quiet walk can refresh your mind and calm your stress response. Plan walking breaks alone or with friends. Stretch after prolonged periods of study at your desk. A short period of physical exercise may provide the break you really need.

—*Health: The Basics*, Sixth Edition,
by Rebecca J. Donatelle

1. What point is the author trying to make? _____

_____

2. Which details are major and which are minor in supporting the author's point?

_____ a. Chopping wood when angry is an example of exercise used as stress relief.

_____ b. Exercise performed as an immediate response to stress can help alleviate stress symptoms.

_____ c. Walking with friends can be beneficial.

Follow Detailed Directions

Learning Objective 3

Attend to details in written directions

Some of the normal rules of reading change dramatically when the task is to follow printed directions. Suddenly, all details are of equal importance, and you must switch gears to accomplish this new task. For example, every detail requires attention when you read the directions for a science experiment, a nursing procedure, or a computer program. You cannot read directions as you would a newspaper article.

Readers are not accustomed to attending to every single detail. For most reading, understanding the general idea and important details is adequate. However, this strategy does not work well when you are assembling a bicycle or following travel directions to a party. Confronted with a set of directions, you recognize that the task is different, even tedious, and then commit to reading step by step, sometimes even word by word and phrase by phrase. Consult any diagram that accompanies the directions, and read aloud if necessary. Remember that some people are better than others at visualizing graphic designs, so consider finding a partner if you think you need help.

EXAMPLE

Select a friend and follow these directions together for calculating pulse rate.

1. Select a pulse point that is comfortable for you and the other person. You can take pulse rate on the inner surface of the wrist, in the fold of the arm opposite the elbow, on the side of the throat a few inches from the center, or in the bend of the leg behind the knee.
2. Press two or three fingers gently down over the selected pulse point. Do not use the thumb because it has a pulse of its own that could be mistaken for the client's pulse.

Reader's TIP — Following Directions

- Change your mindset from normal reading and commit to a different kind of task.
- Read to get an overview so you have a general idea of the task and can make a plan.
- Assemble the necessary equipment, estimate the time, and find a helper if needed.
- Read each step sequentially, and do as directed. Move from word to word and phrase to phrase for a clear understanding. Read aloud if necessary.
- Use numbers, letters, and guide words such as *first, next, before, after, then*, and *now* to maintain sequence. Insert your own numbers if steps are not sequenced.
- Visualize the process. Consult the diagram. Draw your own diagram if none exists.
- Think logically and keep your goal in mind.

3. Once the pulsations are felt, use the second hand on your watch to count the pulsations for 30 seconds.
4. Multiply the number of pulsations by two to calculate the pulse rate per minute. Write down the rate.
5. Wait a few minutes and repeat the procedure to obtain a second pulse rate. Write down the rate.
6. If the difference in the two pulse rates is more than two counts, repeat the procedure using a different pulse point. Write down this rate.

EXPLANATION   An overview of these directions indicates that you need a watch with a second hand, paper and a pen, and a willing friend. Find a comfortable pulsation point and calculate the pulse rate. Evaluate your results by considering that a normal resting pulse rate for an adult is 80 pulsations per minute with a range from 60 to 100.

EXERCISE 4

Directions 1

Use the following directions to put numbers and signs on the line below.

_____

1. Put the number 8 in the middle of the line.
2. On the left end of the line, write a 5 and on the right end put a 7.
3. Equidistant between the 8 and the 7, write down the sum of the two numbers.
4. Equidistant between the number on the far left of the line and the number in the middle, write down the sum of all the numbers on the line.
5. On either side of the number in the middle of the line insert a minus.
6. To the right of the first number on the line and to the left of the last number, insert a plus.
7. Put an equals sign after the last number on the line and use the signs to calculate the total of the numbers listed. What is your total? _____

Directions 2

The American College of Sports Medicine (ACSM) recommends that you know how to determine your target heart rate in order to get the full benefit of exercise. Your **target heart rate** is the rate at which your heart should beat during any aerobic exercise such as running, cycling, fast walking, or participating in an aerobics class. According to the ACSM, you should reach your target rate and then maintain it for 20 minutes or more to achieve cardiovascular fitness. The intensity level varies for different individuals. A sedentary person might begin at the 60% level and gradually work up to 70%, whereas athletes and very fit individuals might work at the 85% level. The ACSM suggests that you calculate both 50% and 85% of your maximum heart rate. This will give you the low and high ends of the range within which your heart rate should stay.

To calculate your target heart rate:

	Example
Subtract your age from 220. This is your maximum heart rate.	$220 - 20 = 200$
Multiply your maximum heart rate by 50%. This is the low end of your range.	$200(0.50) = 100$
Divide the low end by 6. This is your low 10-second heart rate.	$100 \div 6 \approx 17$
Multiply your maximum heart rate by 85%. This is the high end of your range.	$200(0.85) = 170$
Divide the high end by 6. This is your high 10-second heart rate.	$170 \div 6 \approx 28$

1. Why are the low end and high end divided by 6 in order to determine the low and high 10-second heart rates? _____

_____

_____

2. Calculate your target heart rate, both the low and high end of your range.

_____

—From Aufmann/Barker/Lockwood, 8th Edition.
© 2006 Brooks/Cole, a part of Cengage Learning, Inc.
Reproduced by permission. www.cengage.com/permissions

Directions 3

> When in the Course of human Events, it becomes necessary for
> one People to dissolve the Political Bands which have connected
> them with another, and to assume, among the Powers of the Earth,
> the separate and equal Station to which the Laws of Nature and of
> Nature's God entitle them, a descent Respect to the Opinions of
> Mankind requires that they should declare the causes which impel
> them to the Separation.

Printed above is the first paragraph of the U.S. Declaration of Independence. As you can see, the rules for use of capital letters were different in 1776 than they are today.

Select any one of the first 20 words. Count the letters in it and call that number "*n*." Move ahead *n* words, beginning with the word after your selected word. When you reach that *n*th word, count its letters and move ahead as many words as the new letter count. Continue in this manner, counting letters and moving ahead words, until you stop on a word that is beyond the fourth line.

On what word did you stop? _____

—Martin Gardner, "Some Math Magic Tricks with
Numbers," *Games Magazine*, May 1999

Directions 4

Use the compass directions and the grid to complete the following exercise.

1. Begin in the southwest corner of cell X, and draw a line that extends north 4 cells.
2. Retrace this line south 2 cells, and then draw east 3 cells. Draw north 1 cell.
3. Draw a straight line northeast to the north center of this cell. Draw another straight line to the southeast corner of the cell.
4. Draw due east 1 cell and repeat step 3.
5. Draw south 3 cells. Draw west 6 cells.
6. Draw an oval in each of the full cells directly south of those in which you have drawn partial triangles.
7. Draw a line west to east across the center of the cell directly south of the cell between the ovals.

What have you drawn? _____

Write additional directions to complete the figure? _____

_____

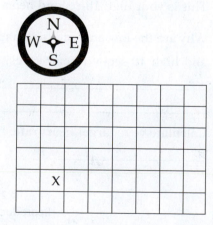

> **BRAIN BOOSTER**
>
> **Brains Like Patterns**
> Human brains are designed to notice patterns because patterns are how we make sense of our world. We learn through repeated experience that a toy pushed off the table falls to the floor, so we expect that to happen every time. When we see an incomplete circle, our brains attempt to complete it. If we miss a word in a spoken sentence, we fill the blank with something that makes sense. Each time the pattern repeats, our neuronal network grows larger and stronger. Use this natural feature of your brain to your advantage when reading. Look for the pattern the author used to organize the information. When you see the pattern, you can make better sense of the author's message.

PATTERNS OF ORGANIZATION

Learning Objective 4

Identify seven organizational patterns by using transitional words and graphic organizers.

The logical presentation of details in textbooks tends to form several identifiable patterns. For example, introductory psychology texts tend to list many definitions and examples, whereas history texts present events in time order with numerous cause-and-effect conclusions. Recognizing these patterns helps you to read more efficiently and take notes for later study. They are blueprints for organizing your thinking.

Each organizational pattern can be predicted by key terms that signal the structure. Learn to use the patterns to mark your text and take notes for later study. Your markings and your notes are an organization of main ideas and major supporting details. The following are examples of the organizational patterns found most frequently in textbooks.

Simple Listing

To organize and condense material for the reader, introductory texts often enumerate key ideas. The listing technique may be used within one paragraph, or it may be used over three or four pages to pull material together. With a simple listing pattern, the items are of equal value, and thus the order in which they are presented is of no importance.

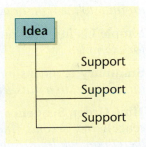

Consider an addition problem:

Does the order of the numbers change the sum?

$$
\begin{array}{r}
4 \\
7 \\
2 \\
5 \\
+\,9 \\
\hline
\end{array}
\qquad\qquad
\begin{array}{r}
9 \\
4 \\
5 \\
2 \\
+\,7 \\
\hline
\end{array}
$$

Likewise, the order of details in a simple list pattern does not change the main point nor influence the reader's understanding of the passage.

Reader's TIP — Patterns of Organization and Signal Words

Recognizing the function of a signal word (transition) in a sentence, paragraph, or longer selection offers a clue to the author's pattern of organization. For example, *because* suggests a reason is being given, and the pattern might be cause and effect.

Addition (providing additional information): *furthermore, again, also, further, moreover, besides, likewise*

Cause and Effect (showing one element as producing or causing a result or effect): *because, for this reason, consequently, hence, as a result, thus, due to, therefore*

Classification (dividing items into groups or categories): *groups, categories, elements, classes, parts*

Comparison (listing similarities among items): *in a similar way, similar, parallels, likewise, in a like manner*

Contrast (listing differences among items): *on the other hand, bigger than, but, however, conversely, on the contrary, although, nevertheless*

Definition (initially defining a concept and expanding with examples and restatements): *can be defined, means, for example, like*

Description (listing characteristics or details): *is, as, like, could be described*

Generalization and Example (explaining with examples to illustrate): *to restate, that is, for example, to illustrate, for instance*

Location or Spatial Order (identifying the whereabouts of objects): *next to, near, below, above, close by, within, without, adjacent to, beside, around, to the right or left side, opposite*

Simple Listing (randomly listing items in a series): *also, another, several, for example*

Summary (condensing major points): *in conclusion, briefly, to sum up, in short, in a nutshell*

Time Order, Sequence, or Narration (listing events in order of occurrence): *first, second, finally, after, before, next, later, now, at last, until, thereupon, while, during*

Transitional Words to Signal Listing. Listed items usually begin with general phrases, such as these:

Many of the items included were . . .

A number of factors were . . .

Signal words used as transitional words to link ideas include:

in addition	*also*	*several*	*for example*	*a number of*

Also used are numbers such as *one, two, three* (or *first, second, third*) or positions such as *next, last,* or *finally,* where numerical order is not relevant.

Mark Your Text. After reading a listing, circle the topic of the list, that is, the words that best describe what the list contains. Next, insert numbers for each listed item and underline any key words that help explain the details listed. The following is an example of this technique.

EXAMPLE **INTERVIEWING FOR A JOB**

There are (several tips) one should remember (when interviewing for a job.) Be sure to arrive
on time and remember there is no excuse for being late. Attend to appearance and dress
to look like a successful company employee. Also, do not smoke, chew gum, or accept
candy, even if it is offered.

EXPLANATION Your Notes on "Interviewing for a Job" would be as follows:

Topic: Tips for job interviewing

1. Arrive on time.

2. Attend to appearance.

3. Don't smoke, chew gum, or eat.

EXERCISE 5 For each of the following paragraphs, mark your text as if for later study. After reading, insert a topic onto the blank at the beginning of the passage. Take notes by first recording the topic and then listing the items. Respond with *T* (true) or *F* (false) to the comprehension items.

Passage 1

College students may be especially vulnerable because they are in a period of transition in which they are often away from home for the first time, striking out on their own, and forging new relationships. From the moment they start packing for school, these transitions cause them to face key developmental tasks as their lives begin to make dramatic changes, such as achieving emotional independence from family, choosing and preparing for a career, preparing for a major relationship, commitment, and/or family life; facing economic independence; and developing their own values and ethical system. These tasks require the college student to develop new social roles and modify old ones. Such changes can result in role strain as they attempt to form a new identity and lead to chronic stress responses.

—*Health: The Basics*, Sixth Edition,
by Rebecca J. Donatelle

1. Mark your text; then take notes.

Topic: _____

    (1) _____

    (2) _____

    (3) _____

    (4) _____

    (5) _____

_____ 2. Establishing financial independence is the largest source of stress for college students.

_____ 3. The many transitions involved in the lives of college students can make them more vulnerable to stress.

Passage 2

_____

During elections to Congress there are a number of advantages of incumbency (being currently in office). One big one is that incumbents can issue "official" statements or make "official" trips to their district. They can get a lot of free publicity that their opponents would have to pay for. For another advantage, members of the House have office and staff budgets of approximately $350,000 a year; senators are given at least that and often considerably more if their states are large. Both receive 32 government-paid round trips to their districts each year. Also, facilities for making television or radio tapes are available in Washington at a low cost. In addition, there is the *frank*, the privilege of free official mailing enjoyed by Congress. Two hundred million pieces of mail, much of it quite partisan, are sent free under the frank every year.

        —*The Basics of American Politics,* by Gary Wasserman

1. Mark your text; then take notes.

Topic: _____

    (1) _____

    (2) _____

    (3) _____

    (4) _____

    (5) _____

_____ 2. A *frank* privilege is a government-paid trip home.

_____ 3. Incumbents receive publicity paid for by taxpayers.

Classification

In order to simplify a complex topic, authors frequently begin introductory paragraphs by stating that the information that follows is divided into a certain number of groups or categories. The divisions are then named and the parts are explained.

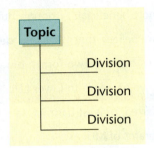

Transitional Words to Signal Classification. Signal words often used for classification are the following:

two divisions   *three groups*   *four elements*   *five classes*

Mark Your Text. After reading, circle the group that will be classified and the number of categories you can expect. Underline any key words that help explain the major details listed. The following is an example of this technique.

EXAMPLE

FIVE KINGDOMS

Today most scientists believe that living things should be divided into five kingdoms. We begin by describing the largest groups, the kingdoms, and then discuss various representatives at lower levels in the taxonomic scheme. The five kingdoms generally accepted by biologists are monera, protista, fungi, plantae, and animalia.

—*Biology: The World of Life*, Seventh Edition, by Robert Wallace

EXERCISE 6

For each of the following paragraphs, mark your text as if for later study. After reading, insert a topic onto the blank at the beginning of the passage. Take notes by first recording the topic and then listing relevant supporting items. Respond with *T* (true), *F* (false), or *CT* (can't tell) to the comprehension items.

Passage 1

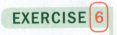

Two main categories of fats

Fat cells consist of chains of carbon and hydrogen atoms. Those that are unable to hold any more hydrogen in their chemical structure are labeled **saturated fats.** They generally come from animal sources, such as meats and dairy products, and are solid at room temperature.

*Two types of
unsaturated fats*

Unsaturated fats, which come from plants and include most vegetable oils, are generally liquid at room temperature and have room for additional hydrogen atoms in their chemical structure. The terms *monounsaturated fat* (MUFA) and *polyunsaturated fat* (PUFA) refer to the relative number of hydrogen atoms that are missing. Peanut and olive oils are high in monounsaturated fats, whereas corn, sunflower, and safflower oils are high in polyunsaturated fats.

*Which type is
healthier?*

There is currently a great deal of controversy about which type of unsaturated fat is most beneficial. Although nutritional researchers in the 1980s favored PUFAs, today many believe that they may decrease beneficial HDL levels while reducing LDL levels. PUFAs come in two forms: omega-3 fatty acids and omega-6 fatty acids. MUFAs, such as olive oil, seem to lower LDL levels and increase HDL levels and thus are currently the preferred, or least harmful, fats. Nevertheless, a tablespoon of olive oil gives you a hefty 10 grams of MUFAs.

—*Health: The Basics*, by Rebecca J. Donatelle

1. Mark your text; then take notes.

   Topic: _____

   (1) _____

   (a) _____

   (b) _____

   i. _____

   ii. _____

   _____

_____ 2. Butter is an example of an unsaturated fat.

_____ 3. Fats are labeled according to the number of carbon atoms in their chemical structure.

Passage 2

_____

Three types

Three types of planets formed in our solar system. The inner planets are small and made mostly of silicates and iron metal. The outer planets are large and made largely of gaseous hydrogen and helium. The icy planets also lie in the outer solar system but are small and have surfaces dominated by water ice.

—*Earth's Dynamic Systems*, Ninth Edition,
by W. Kenneth Hamblin and Eric H. Christiansen

1. Mark your text; then take notes.

   Topic: _____

   (1) _____

   (2) _____

   _____

   (3) _____

   _____

_____ 2. The icy planets are smaller than the outer planets.

_____ 3. The outer planets differ from the icy planets only in terms of size.

Definitions with Examples

In each introductory course, you enter a completely new field with its own unique concepts and ideas. These courses frequently seem to be the hardest because of the overload of information presented. In a single beginning course, you are expected to survey the field from one end to the other. Beyond simply learning vocabulary, you must learn the terminology for major ideas that create a framework for the entire course. You must create a new schema. For example, in an introductory psychology textbook, several paragraphs might be devoted to describing *schizophrenia, paranoia,* or a *manic-depressive cycle*. To remember these terms, you would mark your text and take notes defining the conditions. You would also include examples to help you visualize the terms.

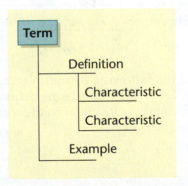

Transitional Words to Signal Definition and Examples. The new terms or concepts may appear as headings, or they may appear in quotation marks, boldface, or italics. Connecting words include the following:

for example	*in this case*	*to illustrate*
more specifically	*in more precise terms*	*in one instance*

Mark Your Text. After reading the definition of a new term, circle the term and then underline the *key defining words*. A word of caution here: Only underline *key* words. Refrain from underlining sentence after sentence, which leaves you with too much highlighted material for later reference. Mark *Ex* by the example that best helps you remember the term. The following paragraph illustrates this technique.

EXAMPLE   **DISPLACEMENT**

Father spanks son, who kicks the dog, who chases the cat. (Displacement) is the shifting of response from one object to another. The boss has yelled at the father, the father is angry at the boss but can't express it safely, so he displaces his anger to his son and spanks him. The son is angry at his father, but can't express it safely, so he displaces his anger to the dog and kicks it. The dog is "angry" at the son but can't express it safely, so he displaces his "anger" to the cat and chases it. In the mechanism of displacement, a feeling is displaced to a safer substitute.

—From Morris Holland, *Psychology*, 1E © 1974 Wadsworth,
a part of Cengage Learning, Inc. Reproduced
by permission. www.cengage.com/permissions

Take Notes. For your study notes, jot down the term, define it in your own words, and list an example. Frequently, you will need to condense several sentences into a short phrase for your notes. If you think the text uses a clear and concise definition, it is permissible to use the same words, but don't let yourself fall into the "delayed learning" trap. If you simply copy textbook words that you do not understand, you won't be any better off weeks later when you study your notes for a midterm or final exam. The appropriate time to understand the term is when you first study and take notes on it.

Your notes on displacement might look like this:

Displacement: *Shifting the expression of a feeling from one object to another safe substitute*

Example: *Son angry at father, so kicks dog*

EXERCISE 7   Read the following paragraphs and write a topic for the beginning of each passage. Circle the terms being defined, underline key phrases, and then write notes for later study. Respond to the comprehension items with *T* (true) or *F* (false).

Passage 1

_____

Large waves, known as seismic sea waves or by the Japanese term tsunami, originate from disturbances on the ocean floor. They are also commonly referred to as tidal waves, but they have no relationship with tides at all. **Tsunamis** can be caused by volcanic eruptions, submarine landslides, or even meteorite impact, but most result from earthquakes that displace the ocean floor. It is not surprising then that most tsunamis occur in the Pacific Ocean, which is circled by active volcanoes and intense seismicity, both of which result from a series of subduction zones surrounding the Pacific. For example, in 1999 a magnitude 7.1 earthquake triggered in a subduction zone north of New Guinea created a tsunami that was 15 m high. When it struck the shore, it swept 2200 people to their deaths.

—*Earth's Dynamic Systems,* Ninth Edition,
by W. Kenneth Hamblin and Eric H. Christiansen

1. Mark your text; then take notes.

   Tsunamis: _____

   _____

   Example: _____

   _____

_____ 2. Most tsunamis occur in the Pacific Ocean because of its size, depth, and temperature.

_____ 3. Tsunamis are also referred to as tidal waves because they are dependent on the ebb and flow of tides.

Passage 2

_____

Most forget that there is also supposed to be a Type B, defined not by the personality traits its members possess but by the traits they lack. Type B people are the shadowy opposites of Type A people. They are those who are not so very Type A. They do not wear out their fingers punching that elevator button. They do not allow a slow car in the fast lane to drive their hearts to fatal distraction; in fact, they are at the wheel of that slow car.

—"Life as Type A" by James Gleick. From *Faster, the Acceleration of Just About Everything*

1. Mark your text; then take notes.

   Type B People: _____

   _____

   Example: _____

   _____

_____ 2. The author suggests that Type B behavior is defined more by what *isn't* than by what *is* (i.e., angry, impolite, rushed).

_____ 3. The author implies that Type A people are unlikely to demonstrate patience.

Description

Description is similar to listing; the characteristics that make up a description are no more than a definition or a simple list of details.

Transitional Words to Signal Description. *Look for a list of defining details.*

Mark Your Text. Circle the item being described and then underline the *key characteristic*. Only underline *key* words. The following paragraph illustrates this technique.

Item or issue
— Characteristic
— Characteristic
— Characteristic

EXAMPLE **LIZARDS**

(Lizards) are the <u>most successful</u> living group of reptiles. There are <u>3,100 different species</u>[1] of lizards in comparison to the snakes, which have 2,000 species. Lizards range in <u>size</u>[2] from a gecko at <u>1.2 inches</u> to monitor lizards at <u>15 feet</u>. The <u>speed</u>[3] of a lizard <u>varies</u> with where it lives. The <u>desert lizard is the fastest.</u>

Take Notes. After marking your text, jot down the topic and underline the key characteristics. Your notes on the previous paragraph would be as follows:

Topic: Lizards

1. Most successful reptiles—3,100 different species

2. Size varies—gecko at 1.2 inches to monitor lizards at 15 feet

3. Speed varies—desert lizard fastest

EXERCISE 8 Read the following paragraphs and write a topic for the beginning of each passage. Circle the item being described, underline key phrases, and then write notes for later study. Respond to the comprehension items with *T* (true) or *F* (false).

Passage 1

_____

Vertebrates of class Mammalia have hair, a characteristic as diagnostic as the feathers of birds. Hair insulates the body, helping the animal maintain a warm and constant body temperature. Mammals are endothermic, and their active metabolism is supported by an efficient respiratory system. Mammary glands that produce milk are as distinctively mammalian as hair. All mammalian mothers nourish their babies with milk. Most mammals are born rather than hatched, and mammals have larger brains than other vertebrates of equivalent size.

—From *Biology,* Fourth Edition, by Neil Campbell

1. Mark your text; then take notes.

    Topic: _____

    (1) _____

    (2) _____

(3) _____

(4) _____

(5) _____

_____ 2. Apes are mammals.

_____ 3. According to this information, chickens would be characterized as mammals.

Passage 2

_____

The shark is one of the most fabled, feared, and least understood large animals on earth. They have well-developed jaws and teeth and are reported to be totally humorless. The shark has a very short intestine and a large liver that helps with buoyancy. The body shape itself is quite streamlined, an important adaptation for coping with resistance.

—*Biology: World of Life*, Seventh Edition,
by Robert Wallace

1. Mark your text; then take notes.

   Topic: _____

   (1) _____

   (2) _____

   (3) _____

   (4) _____

_____ 2. The author exhibits a sense of humor in claiming that sharks have none.

_____ 3. The shark's liver helps it float.

BRAIN BOOSTER

Human brains need other human brains

Instead of growing vicious claws or sharp teeth, humans grew large brains. The problems associated with giving birth to babies with adult-size heads, however, necessitate long childhoods during which brains and heads can grow. Long childhoods require the protection of adults from predators and other dangers that might kill a child. Long ago, humans learned to band together for the safety of everyone. Relationships with other humans were (and are) vital to survival and learning. Living in a group resulted in the development of emotions and the ability to read the emotions of other. What does this have to do with succeeding in college? Working cooperatively with other students and your professors is advantageous to you and everyone in your class. Embrace it! Make cooperating with others work for you.

Time Order, Sequence, or Narration

Items in time order, sequence, or narration are listed in the order in which they occurred or in a specifically planned order in which they must develop. Changing the order would change the results. For example, events in history are typically organized in time order or narration. Novels, biographies, and anecdotes are usually developed chronologically, and instructions and directions are usually developed in sequence.

A diagram or graphic organizer like the one below is a helpful tool for sorting details and especially for future study.

Topic:	
When did it happen?	What happened?

Transitional Words to Signal Time Order or Sequence. Signal words often used for time order or sequence include:

first	*second*	*afterward*	*after*		*before*	*when*
until	*at last*	*next*	*most important*		*finally*	*(dates)*

Mark Your Text. After reading a time-ordered or sequenced section, first circle the topic and time indicators, such as dates or words like *later* or *the next year*. Insert numbers for each important stage and underline key words that explain each one. By its nature, history is full of time-ordered or chronological events. Be aware that every event is not of equal significance. History textbooks include many details that help you visualize but that you do not need to remember. Use the subheadings in the text to help you judge the importance of events.

EXAMPLE   **THE LOUISIANA PURCHASE**

The events surrounding the Louisiana Purchase occurred as follows: In 1795 Spain granted western farmers the right to ship their produce down the Mississippi River to New Orleans, where their cargoes of corn, whiskey, and pork were loaded aboard ships bound for the East Coast and foreign ports. In 1800, however, Spain secretly ceded the Louisiana territory to France and closed the port of New Orleans to American farmers, who exploded with anger. The president sent James Monroe to France to purchase the land. Circumstances played into American hands when, also in 1800, slaves rebelled in Haiti, and France had to send troops to fight. After meeting with a determined resistance and mosquitoes carrying yellow fever, Napoleon exclaimed, "Damn sugar, damn coffee, damn colonies." He was then ready to sell. Finally, in 1803, the United States officially purchased all of the <u>Louisiana Province</u>, a territory extending from Canada to the Gulf of Mexico and westward as far as the Rocky Mountains. The American negotiators agreed on a price of $15 million, or about 4 cents an acre.

—*America and Its People*, Third Edition,
by James Martin et al.

Take Notes. After marking your text, jot down the topic and number the items that are relevant. Be brief. If these items need explanation, put key words underneath the item or in parentheses beside it. Your notes on the previous paragraph would be as follows:

Topic: *Louisiana Purchase*

When did it happen?	What happened?
1795	1. Spain allowed shipping
1800	2. Sold to France, which stopped shipping
	3. France failed to win in Haiti
1803	4. U.S. bought all land

EXERCISE 9 Read the following paragraphs and mark your text by writing a topic at the beginning of the passage, circling indicators of time, and underlining what happened. Then write notes for later study. Respond to the comprehension items with *T* (true) or *F* (false).

Passage 1

She was the twentieth child in a black family of 22 in Clarksville, Tennessee. A weak and sickly infant, she was continually afflicted with childhood diseases, and at four she contracted polio. She was unable to walk without steel braces until she was nine and she continued to wear a supportive device in her shoes until age 11.

Both she and her mother were strong believers that fate was not something you had to resign yourself to, but that people could create their own vision and destiny. Together mother and daughter began a training program for those skinny, wobbly legs. Soon she was running. With renewed energy she began to formulate her own goals with a strategy plan. It did not take long until she was the fastest kid on the block . . . and then in the city, in the state, and even the nation.

At age 16 she qualified for the U.S. Olympic team and in 1956 she won a bronze medal in the 100-meter dash. In the 1960 Olympic Games she won three gold medals, for the 100- and 200-meter events and the 400-meter relay. In all three races she broke world records and established herself as the fastest woman on earth.

When asked how she did it, Wilma Rudolph answered, "No one has a life where everything that happened was good. I think the thing that made my life good for me is that I never looked back. I've always been positive no matter what happened."

—Interpersonal Skills for Leadership, Second Edition,
by Susan Fritz, et al.

1. Mark your text; then take notes.

Topic: _____

When did it happen?	What happened?
Childhood	
Age 16	
1956	
1960	

_____ 2. Wilma Rudolph began her vigorous training program in the hope of obtaining a college scholarship to Tennessee State University.

_____ 3. Rudolph views her success as a direct result of optimism in the face of hardship.

Passage 2

Let us consider the deadly Ebola virus as an example of an emerging virus. Ebola outbreaks have occurred several times during the past few decades. The virus was first identified in 1976 in Zaire and Sudan (outbreaks that killed more than 400 people). During the 2000–2001 outbreak in Uganda several hundred people were infected, with a fatality rate of about 50%.

Early symptoms to Ebola infection resemble those of influenza or dysentery. Within about three days of infection, victims develop a fever and weakness, followed by a rash and vomiting. The victim hemorrhages internally, and bleeds from the mouth, eyes, ears, and other body openings. Internal organs shut down, and 50% to 90% of victims die within one to two weeks after infection. The disease is spread by contact with infected body fluids. Like many RNA viruses, Ebola makes frequent mistakes when it duplicates its RNA. The resulting high mutation rate leads to the rapid development of new strains, making it difficult for researchers to develop an effective vaccine.

—From Solomon, Berg, and Martin,
Biology (with InfoTrac), 6th ed. © 2002 Brooks/Cole,
a part of Cengage Learning, Inc. Reproduced by
permission. www.cengage.com/permissions

1. Mark your text; then take notes.

Topic: _____

When did it happen?	What happened?
_____	1. _____
_____	2. _____
	3. _____
	4. _____
	5. _____
	6. _____

_____ 2. According to the passage, there has been difficulty creating an effective vaccine to prevent the spread of Ebola because the majority of research funding is committed to finding a cure for HIV.

_____ 3. The passage suggests that, in its early stages, Ebola might be mistaken for the common flu.

Comparison and Contrast

Another pattern you will find in introductory texts is one that relates items according to existing comparisons and contrasts. To enrich your understanding of a topic, items are paired and then similarities or differences are listed.

Topic

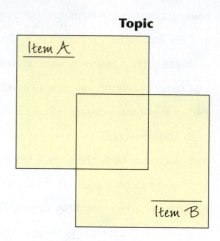

Transitional Words to Signal Comparison and Contrast. Signal words often used for comparison or contrast include:

Comparison: *similar* *like* *in the same way* *likewise*

Contrast: *different* *on the other hand* *nevertheless* *however*
  although *instead* *conversely* *but*

Mark Your Text. After reading the passage, record the topic and then write an abbreviation for similarities or differences in the margin. Circle the items being discussed, and underline key words. The following paragraph illustrates the technique.

EXAMPLE **CHICAGO AND CLEVELAND**

Diff.
Sim.
Sim.

Chicago, at the southern tip of Lake Michigan, is a port city and an important commercial and industrial center of the Midwest. It is also an important educational, cultural, and recreational center, drawing thousands to its concert halls, art museums, and sports arenas. Cleveland, on the south shore of Lake Erie, is also a port city and a commercial and industrial center important to its area. Like Chicago, it has several important colleges and universities, a distinguished symphony orchestra, one of the fine art museums of the world, and many recreational centers. The location of the two cities undoubtedly contributed to their growth, but this similarity is not sufficient to explain their wide social diversity.

—*Short Essays*, Seventh Edition, by Gerald Levin

Take Notes. First, write in the topics being discussed. Then write the similarities and differences in the appropriate positions in the diagram. Some passages will be mostly comparisons and some will be mostly contrasts. The following illustration is an example.

Topic: *Chicago and Cleveland*

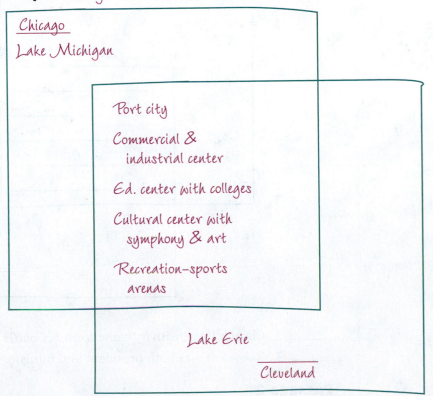

Chicago
Lake Michigan

Port city

Commercial & industrial center

Ed. center with colleges

Cultural center with symphony & art

Recreation–sports arenas

Lake Erie

Cleveland

EXERCISE 10

Read the paragraphs and write the topic at the beginning of the passage. Use an abbreviation to mark similarities or differences, underline key phrases, and then take notes for later study. Respond with *T* (true) or *F* (false) to the comprehension items.

Passage 1

During World War II, Roosevelt was president of the United States and Churchill was prime minister of England. Both men had similar styles of leadership and were skilled in the uses of power. When in office, Roosevelt asked Congress for broad executive powers to deal with a national emergency even before war was declared. Similarly, Churchill immediately centralized the war in his own hands by becoming both the prime minister and the defense minister. Both leaders had magnetic personalities that drew people to them. Roosevelt was sensitive to people and their dreams, perhaps having learned from his own battle with polio. Churchill was fired with imagination and a love of language. Both were gifted speakers, Roosevelt with his homey illustrations and Churchill with his emotion and vivid imagery.

1. Mark your text and then take notes. Describe each of the political leaders.

Topic: _____

_____ 2. Churchill's sensitivity came from his battle with polio.

_____ 3. Roosevelt was both president and minister of defense.

Passage 2

People talk about a new economy—one where the Internet is supposed to change everything. Now some even question whether a "new economy" exists, and if so, how it differs from the old economy.

new

The new economy is less concerned with physical goods. Almost 93 million workers (80 percent of the workforce) do not spend their days making things. Instead they work in jobs that require them to move things, process or generate information, or provide services to people. *old* In the old economy, information flow was <u>physical</u>: cash, checks, invoices, reports, and face-to-face meetings. But in the new economy, information in all its forms becomes digital.

old In the old economy, geography played a key role in determining who competed with whom. *new* In the new economy, distance and time differences have vanished. Besides compressing distance, the Internet compresses time. In the new economy, the ability to innovate and get to market faster is a key competitive advantage. Consider this: In less than 18 months after its launch, Hotmail had signed up 12 million subscribers. A few days later its founders sold the company to Microsoft for $400 million in Microsoft stock. Today, with 50 million registered users, Hotmail is the largest Web-based e-mail service in the world.

old In the old economy, setting up a nursery to sell plants might involve leasing a shed, buying various types of trees and plants, and more. But on the Internet, setting up a nursery can be as simple as registering a domain name, hiring an artist to design some Web pages, and making arrangements with a plant wholesaler. In short, barriers to entry for companies selling over the Internet are virtually nonexistent. *new*

—*Business Today*, Tenth Edition,
by Michael Mescon et al.

1. Mark your text; then take notes.

Topic: _____

_____ 2. At the time of its purchase by Microsoft, Hotmail had 50 million subscribers.

_____ 3. The author suggests that online nurseries do not need to house their own plants.

Cause and Effect

In this pattern, one of several factors, or causes, is shown to lead to or result in certain events, or effects. Cause-and-effect patterns can be complex, because a single effect can have multiple causes and one cause can have many effects.

Topic:	
Cause → Why did it happen?	**Effect** What happened?
→	
→	
→	

Transitional Words to Signal Cause and Effect. Signal words often used to indicate cause and effect include:

for this reason	*consequently*	*on that account*	*thus*
hence	*because*	*made*	*therefore*

Mark Your Text. Circle the topic, and remember there can be many causes and many effects. Therefore, give both labels and numbers to the causes and effects, as well as underlining key words to explain the items. The following paragraph illustrates the technique.

EXAMPLE   **EARLY JOBS**

Cause: (1) summer and (2) after-school jobs

Effects:
1. Money management
2. Skills
3. Belief in work
   a. Anxiety over free time
   b. Guilt over non-work activity

Aside from basic money management, what did I actually learn from all my summer and after-school jobs? Each one may have given me some small skills but the cumulative effect was to deepen my belief that work was the essential aspect of grown-up life. Even now, I am sometimes filled with anxieties at the prospect of stretches of *free time*. When I do not immediately rush to fill that time with work, I have to fight off *guilt*, struggling mentally against a picture of a Real Grown-up shaking a finger at me, someone with the droning voice of our high school career counselor, but with firm overtones of former employers, teachers, even my mother. "This," the voice beats relentlessly into my ear, "is your preparation for life."

—"Blooming: A Small-Town Girlhood," by Susan Allen Toth

Take Notes. Write the topic and then write headings to label causes and effects. List and number the causes and effects and add key words that are needed to explain. Note that an effect may also be the cause of something else. Arrows can indicate these relationships. Here is an example.

Topic: *Effects of Early Jobs*

Cause → Why did it happen?	Effect What happened?
Summer and after-school jobs → → →	*1. Money mgt.* *2. Skills* *3. Belief in work as essential to adult life* ↓ *4. Anxiety over fun time; guilt over non-work*

EXERCISE 11   Read the following paragraphs. For each one, write the topic in the answer blank, label the causes and effects, underline key terms, and then take notes for later study. Respond with *T* (True) or *F* (False) to the comprehension items.

Passage 1

_____

Insects perform many roles vital to human life. Without bees and other insects, for instance, many flowering plants would never be pollinated—a prerequisite to producing crops such as apples, citrus fruits, berries, and cucumbers. Many beetles, ants, and flies are important decomposers, breaking down the dead bodies of plants and animals.

Nevertheless, people have devoted more time to killing insects than to praising them. It is perhaps unduly gloomy to conclude that we are losing the battle against insects, who will one day inherit the earth, but those who believe this have good reason for their opinion.

Insects destroy more than 10% of all crops in the United States, but the damage is even worse in the tropics, where hot weather throughout the year permits insects to grow and reproduce faster. In Kenya, officials estimate that insects destroy 75% of the nation's crops. A locust swarm in Africa may be 30 meters deep along a front 1500 meters long, and will consume every fragment of plant material in its path, leaving hundreds of square kilometers of country devastated.

Pesticides have not solved the insect problem. This is partly because pesticides act as selective pressures for the evolution of resistant strains of insects, which evolve too fast for expensive pesticide research to keep up.

—From Arms and Camp, *Biology: A Journey into Life*, 2nd ed. © Brooks/Cole, a part of Cengage Learning, Inc. Reproduced by permission. www.cengage.com/permissions

1. Mark your text; then take notes.

Topic:_____

Cause → Why did it happen?	Effect What happened?
_____ →	_____
_____	
_____ →	_____
_____ →	_____
	_____

_____ 2. Bees are considered decomposers.

_____ 3. Locusts can probably be eradicated in Africa with pesticides.

Passage 2

Americans are also more conscious of what they are eating. The desire to reduce cholesterol intake has caused a shift away from red meat and dairy products. The trend was substantial enough to cause beef producers to band together and mount an educational campaign to convince consumers that beef is healthful. The trend to healthier foods has primarily affected product rather than promotional strategies. Producers of dairy foods are coming out with lines of low-cholesterol products, cereal companies with high-fiber products, and liquor manufacturers with lower alcohol lines to reflect the trend away from hard liquor.

The combined effects of better medical care and greater health awareness have resulted in increased longevity in the past twenty years. From 1970 to 1990, life expectancy of the average American went from 70 to 76 years reaching 80 by the turn of the century.

—*Consumer Behavior and Marketing Action,* Fourth Edition, by Henry Assael

1. Mark your text; then take notes.

Topic: _____

Cause → Why did it happen?	Effect What happened?
_____ _____ →	_____
→	_____
→	_____
→	_____

_____ 2. Americans are eating fewer dairy products.

_____ 3. Eating beef tends to lower cholesterol levels.

Clues to the Organizational Pattern

As shown in the previous explanations, readers have several clues to the organizational pattern of the material they are reading. Active readers use all of the clues rather than just one because they focus on the meaning.

1. *Transitional words:* For example, repeated words, such as *because, as a result, therefore, for this reason,* suggest a cause-and-effect pattern. Be careful, though! Some signal words may be used in several different patterns.

2. *Diagrams or graphic organizers:* If the details fit into the diagram, the reader has more evidence that the predicted pattern is correct.

3. *Relationship among the details and the main idea:* This is the most reliable evidence a reader has to determine the organizational pattern, because it directly reflects the meaning of the material.

Mixed Patterns. In longer reading selections, authors often mix patterns. For example, a simple list pattern may be used in the introductory paragraph, a definition pattern in another paragraph, and a cause-and-effect pattern in yet another. Rather than be confused by this, readers should keep in mind the overall pattern—the pattern that best develops the author's main point.

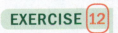 **EXERCISE 12**

Read the following beginning portions of paragraphs. Predict the dominant pattern(s) of organization to be used by the author. Select from the following list:

Simple listing	Definition	Description
Time order	Narration	Comparison-Contrast
Cause and effect		

1. Many psychologists believe that the basic structure of human personality is represented by five broad factors, known as the Big Five. They are neuroticism, extroversion, openness, agreeableness, and conscientiousness.

   —*Human Relations,* Eighth Edition,
   by Andrew J. DuBrin

   Organizational pattern: _____

2. In some regions, such as Europe and South Asia, it is common for people to cluster in villages and towns; this contrasts with the dispersed settlement pattern of rural North America, where people tend to scatter across the countryside in individual farms and homesteads.

   —*Diversity and Globalization,* Second Edition,
   by Les Rowntree et al.

   Organizational pattern: _____

3. To remain financially sound, Mega Music used the services of *headhunters.* They are paid recruiters who match hiring companies with employees or executives in order to find a new CEO. The headhunter found a young energetic Yankee named Bill Black. (A *Yankee* is a person from the northeastern region of the United States. The name originated during the Civil War because Yankees were soldiers from the north.)

   —*Choices: A Basic Writing Guide with Readings,* Third Edition,
   by Kate Mangelsdorf and Evelyn Posey

   Organizational pattern: _____

4. At last all the preparations for my wedding were almost completed and the day was fixed for August 21 of this year 1745. On the eve of the 21st we moved from the Summer to the Winter Palace.

   —*Sources of the West: Readings in Western Civilization,*
   Sixth Edition, edited by Mark A. Kishlansky

   Organizational pattern: _____

5. If the people in your life treat you in an undesirable way, you're going to want to figure out what you are doing to reinforce, elicit, or allow that treatment. If you're involved in a relationship in which someone is consistently abusive, exploitive, or insensitive toward you, find out what you're doing to encourage that behavior, so that you can realign the relationship in a more healthy direction.

   —*Celebrity Writing in America: A Thematic Reader for Composition,*
   by William Vesterman

   Organizational pattern: _____

6. *Comets* are small ice bodies that formed in the outer solar system. Some have elliptical orbits that take them near the Sun.

   —*Earth's Dynamic Systems,* Ninth Edition,
   by W. Kenneth Hamblin and Eric H. Christiansen

Organizational pattern: _____

7. She holds a tall iced coffee in one hand, and her blond hair is piled high in a ponytail. Headphones hang above the stools, and computer screens are embedded in the countertop.

—Adapted from Alison Overholt, "Thinking Outside the Cup,"
Fast Company Issue 84 (July 2004)

Organizational pattern: _____

8. Within moments of sitting or lying down and pushing the "power" button, viewers report feeling more relaxed. Because the relaxation occurs quickly, people are conditioned to associate viewing with rest and lack of tension.

—Robert Kubey and Mihaly Csikszentmihalyi,
"Television Addiction Is No Mere Metaphor,"
Scientific American, February 2002.

Organizational pattern: _____

9. A new cycle began in October when peasants prepared the ground for the planting of winter crops. In November came the slaughter of excess livestock because there was usually insufficient food to keep animals all winter. In February and March, the land was plowed for spring crops—oats, barley, peas, beans, and lentils.

—*Western Civilization I: To 1715*, Fifth Edition,
by Jackson J. Spielvogel

Organizational pattern: _____

10. According to crime reports, individuals were the most common target of robbers. Banks, gas stations, convenience stores, and other businesses were the second most common target. Residential robberies accounted for only 13.5% of the total.

—*Criminal Justice Today: An Introductory Text for the
Twenty-First Century,* Eighth Edition, by Frank Schmalleger

Organizational pattern: _____

SUMMARY POINTS

1 How can I distinguish major and minor details? (page 178)
Recognize the varying levels of importance among ideas. Use diagrams and outlines to visualize them.

2 What are the roles of major and minor details? (page 181)
Major details are essential to support, explain, develop, or prove the main point.
Minor details provide interesting and memorable examples of the major details but provide secondary support of the main idea.

3 How can I follow written directions accurately? (page 187)

Attend carefully to all of the details. Every detail is of the same importance in written directions, unlike in typical prose.

4 How can I identify the seven common organizational patterns? (page 191)

Use the transitional words typically used with each pattern. Picture the graphic organizer for the pattern to see if the details fit.

Simple listing: Items of equal value are listed in a passage. Their order does not matter.

Classification: The divisions or categories are named and the parts are explained.

Definition with examples: A new term is defined and examples are added for clarification.

Description: This pattern is like a simple list of characteristics that describe something such as an object or person.

Time order or sequence: Events and when they occurred are the focus of the passage.

Comparison or contrast: Items are compared or contrasted to show how they are alike or different.

Cause and effect: Events and their causes are the focus of the passage.

5 How can the pattern help me mark my text? (page 193)

Recognizing the pattern requires that the reader look more carefully for the important details. A system of circling, underlining, and numbering makes sense when the pattern is determined. For example, in a time order pattern, it makes sense to circle the time indicators and underline what happened.

6 What are the clues to recognizing the organizational pattern? (page 213)

Transitional words, graphic organizers, and the relationship among the details and the main idea are the best clues to the organizational pattern.

COLLABORATIVE PROBLEM SOLVING

Form a five-member group and select one of the following activities. Brainstorm and then outline your major points on a transparency. Choose a member to present the group findings to the class.

➤ Write step-by-step directions for leaving your classroom and going to a place on campus to eat lunch.

➤ Create a diagram that shows several categories and subcategories for elected state government officials.

➤ Create a list or diagram of ideas that compares and contrasts your college with another college in the state.

➤ Provide two opening sentences stating the main idea for passages with a simple listing pattern of organization and two for a sequence pattern.

MyReadingLab

MyReadingLab (MRL) www.myreadinglab.com

➤ For support in meeting this chapter's objectives, log in to **www.myreadinglab.com** and select "Supporting Details" and "Patterns of Organization."

THE READING WORKSHOP

If reading a novel, biography, or other book is part of your course experience, refer to The Reading Workshop: Thinking, Talking, and Writing about Books in Appendix 5 for suggestions.

PERSONAL FEEDBACK 1

Name _____

1. In this class, who would you feel comfortable calling for assignment information?

   _____

   _____

2. What organizations have you joined? _____

   _____

   _____

3. What campus events or social functions have you attended? _____

   _____

   _____

4. What volunteer work have you recently done on or off campus? _____

   _____

   _____

5. What would make you feel bonded to your college? _____

   _____

   _____

Tear out and submit to your instructor.

SELECTION 1   Psychology

"Three grand essentials to happiness in this life are something to do, something to love, and something to hope for."

Joseph Addison

Many factors within our control contribute to good emotional health. One such factor is the social support or help provided in time of need by a spouse, friends, colleagues, and family. Research indicates that social support can have a positive influence on the body's immune system, reduce the impact of stress, and increase the probability of recovering from illnesses. How strong is your social network, and what other factors should you consider?

THINKING BEFORE READING

Preview for content and organizational clues. Activate your schema and anticipate what you will learn.

What is the happiest part of your day?

Why do you like hugs?

I think this will say _____

VOCABULARY PREVIEW

Are you familiar with these words?

pervasive	encounters	excessive	timidity	frailties
chronic	perspective	profoundly	competence	self-transcendence

What does the prefix *per* in *pervasive* and *perspective* mean?

How long does a *chronic* illness last?

Do you suffer from *timidity*?

Your instructor may choose to give a true-false vocabulary review before or after reading.

THINKING DURING READING

As you read, use the six thinking strategies of a good reader: predict, picture, relate, monitor, correct, and annotate.

BECOMING HEALTHY

How can you grow and eventually become fully functioning? How can you achieve that ideal stage of psychological health? You cannot be healthy simply by trying to be healthy; you cannot be happy simply by deciding to be happy.

Refer to the
Reader's **TIP**
for **Psychology** on
page 144.

Pleasure, happiness, and self-actualization cannot be effectively pursued; instead,
5   they ensue, or automatically result, from your having satisfied a need, attained a goal,
or grown toward health. Your deciding to be happy will not make you happy; happiness
follows from what you *do*.

THREE THINGS TO AVOID

You have unpleasant feelings sometimes and this is quite natural. But if your unpleasant
feelings are pervasive, unending, and tend to color your whole emotional life, then you
10   want to stop feeling so bad. We are all sometimes blue, but if you are blue most of the
time, then you want to change. As you grow toward health, you tend to experience fewer
and fewer persistent unpleasant feelings. Three of these unpleasant feelings are doubt,
dread, and depression.

Doubt. Self-doubt makes you feel worthless, stupid, and dull. Many persons have
15   excessive doubts about their physical appearance; they consider themselves unattractive,
ugly, and unlovable. They then retreat from dating and other interpersonal encounters
and remain highly self-conscious about their appearance. Other persons have excessive
doubts about their intelligence; they consider themselves uninteresting, ordinary, and
dull. They act with great shyness and timidity when among other people, believing that
20   no one would want to listen to their ideas. Excessive self-doubt, in general, comes from a
feeling that other people will not find you acceptable in some way; this feeling leads you
not to accept yourself. Understanding yourself and others is one way to avoid self-doubt;
you will discover that your frailties and fears are not unique. Being loved and prized by
someone is another way to escape excessive self-doubt; to be wholly accepted by some-
25   one else makes it easier for you to accept yourself.

Dread. Dread is a feeling of anxiety or worry. You feel afraid, but you are not sure
why. Dread makes you feel nervous, high-strung, restless, and irritable. The tension that
you feel may show up physically in nail-biting, in crying spells, in chain-smoking, in frequent headaches or neck aches, or in chronic fatigue. The persistent feeling of dread is
30   a message, and the message is this: Relax, reduce the pressures in your life, and try to
resolve some of your conflicts.

Relaxing is something you may have to practice and learn how to do. Here is something
for you to try: Go to a quiet darkened room. Sit or lie in a comfortable position. Begin breathing deeply and slowly while you try to empty your mind of thoughts. Beginning with your
35   feet, tighten and then relax your muscles one by one, until all of the muscles of your body
are relatively relaxed. Then close your eyes and imagine yourself floating in a tub of warm
water. The pressures of your life can sometimes be reduced by getting away from them for
a while—take a break and change your scene. For a change of pace take a walk every day
or do some light reading. You can sometimes be helped in working out your problems and
40   conflicts by talking to other people about them. As you listen to yourself, you may gain some
insights. The feedback of other people may also give you a new perspective. Expressing your
feelings to other people often in itself reduces the tension that you feel.

Depression. When you are depressed, you feel profoundly unhappy, blue, and sad.
You are moody and pessimistic; you don't feel that things will get better in the near future.
45   You tend not to do things; your energy level is low. Things that once were significant now
seem rather pointless. The persistent feeling of depression is a message, and the message
is this: Become active, get to work, begin to be involved. Get a part-time job, start a project, volunteer as a helper in a clinic or community agency, join a club—do something.
Depression is the opposite of involvement.

THREE THINGS TO DO

50   What you do and what happens to you are under your control. You are in charge. And
what you do will determine whether you grow toward health or whether you stay as you
are now. While you cannot attain psychological health by pursuing it directly, you can

grow in the direction of health through certain kinds of experiences, and these experiences are under your control. Some experiences move you toward health; some move you
55 away from health. To learn about yourself and others, to love and to be loved, and to live actively and productively—all are growth-producing.

Learn. To learn about others you must be involved with them. You must have a relationship with them of mutual trust. For how can I learn about you unless you trust me enough to disclose your "inner self" to me? And how can you trust me unless I am willing to
60 reveal myself to you? You can help me understand myself, if I trust what you say about me.

Self-understanding cannot easily be achieved in isolation; other people help us to define who we are. Our impression of ourselves depends upon how other people consistently react to us. My self-understanding and my knowledge of you thus depend upon our relationship. If we do not have a trustful relationship, you may hide yourself from me.
65 You may "mystify" me by trying to create an impression that you are different from what you really are. But if you allow me to know you, then you help me understand myself. Knowing others and understanding yourself leads to self-acceptance. You discover that the qualities in yourself that you have rejected are not unique to yourself; others are very similar to you. And as you are accepted by others, you are led to accept yourself. Self-
70 understanding and self-acceptance are experiences of growth that make possible a state of self-actualization.

Love. Experiences that confirm or validate who you are are health-producing experiences. Being loved by another is the most profound validation of yourself; for to be loved means that someone knows you, that they accept the way you are, and that they value
75 and prize you. To be loved, and therefore validated, is health-producing because it leads you to know, accept, and value yourself. And if you can do this, you are better able to function in life and more likely to experience a continual feeling of well-being.

The capacity for love is a symptom of health. The ability to love depends upon the extent to which you value yourself, have faith in your own powers, and are not afraid of
80 giving yourself.

Live. Living fully implies involvement with the world. When you actively do things, you experience your self, your power, and your capacity. When you become intensely involved in a job, hobby, cause, or other person, you tend to lose self-consciousness, develop feelings of competence, and invest yourself in something "outside your own

85   skin." You have feelings of purpose and meaningfulness and may taste the satisfaction of what has been called "meaning fulfillment." When you become absorbed in
something outside yourself, you begin to experience a kind of self-transcendence, ac-
companied by a feeling of well-being. Thus the experience of active involvement is a
growth experience.

(1,225 words)

—From Morris Holland, *Psychology*, 1E. © 1974
Wadsworth, a part of Cengage Learning, Inc. Reproduced
by permission. www.cengage.com/permissions

THINKING AND WRITING AFTER READING

RECALL   Self-test your understanding.

Your instructor may choose to give you a true-false comprehension review.

REACT   How does someone you know well create unhappiness? _____

_____

REFLECT   What makes you depressed? _____

_____

THINK CRITICALLY   Discuss how learning can help you achieve good health. Write
your answer on a separate sheet of paper.

THINK AND WRITE   Describe your own social network and explain how its members

contribute to your well-being. _____

_____

_____

EXTENDED WRITING   Write a personal narrative to be read by your professor that
describes a time in your life when the support of a friend, teacher, family member, or other person helped you through an emotionally difficult situation. If this
is too personal, focus your narrative on how you lent support for someone else
during a difficult time. Remember to include how you felt about being the one
who helped.

DETAILS AND ORGANIZATIONAL PATTERNS   Mark the following as major (*M*) or minor
(*m*) details in support of the author's main point.

_____   1. Self-doubt makes you feel worthless, stupid, and dull.

_____   2. Tension may show up physically in nail-biting or headaches.

_____   3. Learn about others.

_____   4. Join a club to beat depression.

_____   5. Live fully and be involved with the world.

6. What is the purpose of the first paragraph? _____

_____

7. What is the pattern of organization of the section entitled *Three Things to Avoid*? _____

8. What is the pattern of organization of the section entitled *Three Things to Do*? _____

Interpret THE QUOTE

Now that you have finished reading the selection, "Becoming Healthy," go back to the beginning of the selection and read the opening quote again. Do you agree with Addison's three essentials to happiness? On a separate sheet of paper, list five essentials that bring you personal happiness.

Name ———————————————

Date ———————————————

COMPREHENSION QUESTIONS

Answer the following with *a, b, c,* or *d,* or fill in the blank. In order to help you analyze your strengths and weaknesses, the question types are indicated.

Main Idea ———— 1. The best statement of the main idea of this selection is:

    a. Negative and unpleasant feelings are natural but tend to ruin your emotional life.

    b. You can achieve health and happiness by avoiding negative feelings and focusing on certain positive experiences.

    c. In achieving good health, love and learning are more important than money.

    d. Pleasure, happiness, and self-actualization result as you grow toward health.

Inference ———— 2. The author's attitude toward becoming healthy is

    a. optimistic.

    b. pessimistic.

    c. sarcastic.

    d. sympathetic.

Inference ———— 3. The author believes that

    a. happiness can be pursued.

    b. happiness follows positive action.

    c. deciding to be happy can make you happy.

    d. setting realistic goals brings happiness.

Inference ———— 4. The author suggests that relaxation is a cure for

    a. self-doubt.

    b. anxiety.

    c. depression.

    d. timidity.

Inference   5. The author suggests that shyness is primarily a reflection of

——————————————————————————

Detail ———— 6. The author views learning as

    a. getting a college degree.

    b. becoming involved in new hobbies.

    c. finding out about yourself and others.

    d. always actively pursuing knowledge.

Inference ———— 7. The author feels that being loved

    a. is more important than loving.

    b. is not as important as involvement with the world.

    c. is the single key to good health.

    d. gives a feeling of self-worth.

Answer the following with *T* (true), *F* (false), or *CT* (can't tell).

Inference ———— 8. The author is more concerned with the psychological than the physiological contributions to health.

Inference _____ 9. According to the author, involvement and activity help to prevent depression.

Detail _____ 10. Shy people can benefit from associating with self-confident, aggressive friends.

VOCABULARY

Answer the following with *a, b, c,* or *d* for the word or phrase that best defines the boldface word as used in the selection. The number in parentheses indicates the line of the passage in which the word appears.

_____ 1. "unpleasant feelings are **pervasive**" (9)

a. upsetting
b. uncharacteristic
c. surprising
d. widespread

_____ 2. "other interpersonal **encounters**" (16)

a. meetings
b. groups
c. friendships
d. circumstances

_____ 3. "have **excessive** doubts" (17)

a. endless
b. needless
c. more than usual
d. inferior

_____ 4. "shyness and **timidity**" (19)

a. nervousness
b. meekness
c. unreasonableness
d. inconsistency

_____ 5. "your **frailties** and fears" (23)

a. expectations
b. unusual features
c. hopes
d. weaknesses

_____ 6. "**chronic** fatigue" (29)

a. constant
b. unwanted
c. difficult
d. nervous

_____ 7. "give you a new **perspective**" (41)

a. interest
b. view
c. tension
d. desire

_____ 8. "feel **profoundly** unhappy" (43)

a. slightly
b. briefly
c. deeply
d. frankly

_____ 9. "feelings of **competence**" (84)

a. love
b. ability
c. belonging
d. need

_____ 10. "a kind of **self-transcendence**" (87)

a. excelling
b. rejection
c. inner analysis
d. admiration

Your instructor may choose to give a true-false vocabulary review.

VOCABULARY ENRICHMENT

A. The purpose of many invented words is to form shorter expressions that carry the same meaning. Acronyms are words made from the initial letters of other words. Blends are words formed by combining parts of other words. *Abbreviations* are shortened forms of longer words. Write the definitions and elongated forms of the following words.

scu·ba \ˈskü-bə\ *n, often attrib* [self-contained underwater breathing apparatus] (1952) : an apparatus utilizing a portable supply of compressed gas (as air) supplied at a regulated pressure and used for breathing while swimming underwater

> Source: By permission. From Merriam-Webster's *Collegiate*® *Dictionary, Eleventh Edition.* © 2011 by Merriam Webster Incorporated (www.Merriam-Webster.com).

(acronyms)

1. *Scuba* means _____

2. It comes from _____

Medi·care \ˈme-di-ˌker\ *n* [blend of *medical* and *care*] (1955) : a government program of medical care esp. for the aged

> Source: By permission. From Merriam-Webster's *Collegiate*® *Dictionary, Eleventh Edition.* © 2011 by Merriam Webster Incorporated (www.Merriam-Webster.com).

(blends)

3. *Medicare* means _____

4. It comes from _____

¹ad \ˈad\ *n, often attrib* (1841)   **1 :** ADVERTISEMENT 2   **2 :** ADVERTISING
²ad *n* (1928) : ADVANTAGE 4

> Source: By permission. From Merriam-Webster's *Collegiate*® *Dictionary, Eleventh Edition.* © 2011 by Merriam Webster Incorporated (www.Merriam-Webster.com).

(abbreviations)

5. *Ad* means _____

6. It comes from _____

B. Use an unabridged dictionary in your college library to find the definitions and origins of the following words.

Achilles' heel

7. Definition: _____

8. Origin: _____

_____

maudlin

9. Definition: _____

10. Origin: _____

babel

11. Definition: _____

12. Origin: _____

_____

C. Circle the similar-sounding word that is correct in each sentence.

anecdote: story	**access:** entrance	**moral:** honorable
antidote: medicine	**excess:** more than needed	**morale:** spirit

13. The professor told an amusing (**anecdote**, **antidote**) about Queen Elizabeth.

14. The new key will give you easy (**access**, **excess**) to the computer room.

15. After the positive test grades were announced, the class (**moral**, **morale**) was high.

ASSESS YOUR LEARNING

Review confusing questions, seek clarification, and make notes in your text to help you remember new information and vocabulary.

SELECTION 2   Criminal Justice

Refer to the *Reader's* **TIP** for **Criminal Justice** on page 63.

"… every time I learn something new, it pushes some old stuff out of my brain. Remember when I took that home winemaking course, and I forgot how to drive?"
—Matt Groening, *The Simpsons*, spoken by the character Homer

The National Highway Traffic Safety Administration reported that in 2009 (the latest statistics available at the time of this writing), 10,839 people died in car accidents involving alcohol-impaired driving in the United States. That number represented 32% of all traffic deaths that year and an average death rate of one person every 50 minutes. The numbers are staggering, especially considering that such accidents are preventable. Add to these statistics the traffic deaths related to other causes of impaired driving—substance abuse, cell phone use, and sleep deprivation—and one might reasonably fear getting in a car at all. What efforts to encourage responsible driving are working? What else can be done?

THINKING BEFORE READING

Preview for content and organizational clues. Activate your schema and anticipate what you will learn.

Do you know someone who has been arrested for drunk driving?

What are the penalties for drunk driving in your state?

What do you think the penalties should be?

I'll read this to find out _____

_____

VOCABULARY PREVIEW

Are you familiar with these words?

hors d'oeuvres	sobriety	manacles	arraignment	negotiates
triumphant	dysfunctional	registry	trepidation	subsidiary

Does *sobriety* have something to do with being sober?

Is *trepidation* an uncomfortable feeling?

Does *dysfunctional* mean functioning badly?

Your instructor may choose to give a true-false vocabulary review before or after reading.

THINKING DURING READING

As you read, use the six thinking strategies of a good reader: predict, picture, relate, monitor, correct, and annotate.

DRINKING, DRIVING AND PAYING

Here's what can happen: You attend a small dinner party at your brother's house with your 80-year-old mother, your visiting 74-year-old second cousin from Holland and assorted other family members. As per family custom, you enjoy hors d'oeuvres and several glasses of wine over a lovely meal full of conversation and laughter.

((•⃝ Scan this QR code to hear this reading.

5   Around 9 o'clock, after a couple of small cups of coffee, and a little more wine, a thimble's worth of Scotch, you prepare to leave, and do so. Ten minutes later, on a quiet country road near a small town, you notice flashing blue lights behind you; you stop, and you are spoken to by a young officer who asks if you have been drinking.

"Yes," you say, "I had a couple glasses of wine at a family dinner."

10   You are asked to step out of the car for some "field sobriety tests." You do so, and perform the tests, and feel you have done quite well—except the one where you have to stand on one foot with your arms spread for 30 seconds, and . . . oops . . . you have to touch down a couple of times to keep your balance—no big deal.

He asks if you are willing to take a Breathalyzer: if you refuse, you will receive an au-
15   tomatic six-month suspended license. You agree, somewhat hopefully: you blow into the tube—very well, and slowly. He repeats the process. There is a pause, and the young man says, rather abruptly: "Put your hands behind your back. You have the right to remain silent. . . ." You feel the cold hardness of your new manacles, and the hardness of the back seat of the police cruiser, which is made of plastic.

20   You arrive at the police station, where you are processed and re-Breathalyzed twice—"point 08," you hear the officer say. In your state it's the lowest measurable illegal amount. It used to be .10. Your license is taken away. You are allowed to make phone calls—"as many as you want"—the first to your son, who has just arrived home from college to an empty house because your wife is away. (You were hurrying to get home
25   to greet him.)

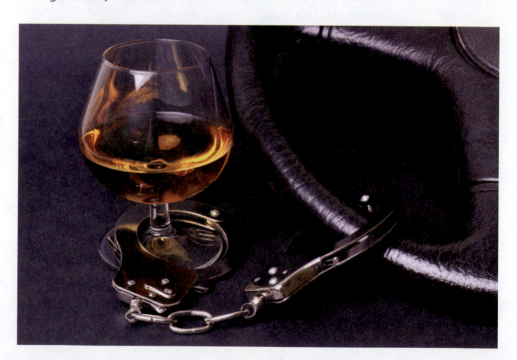

You pay your own bail, $40, and call your brother, who agrees to pick you up. While you wait, you are put in a jail cell, and you lie on a shiny aluminum "bed" under a bright yellow light, feeling dumb and criminal, in the company of a gleaming metal toilet. You use it.

30   You are picked up, and sleep at your brother's house—badly. In the morning, you are "arraigned." After the arraignment of many fellow criminals, your case is heard, and you agree to return two weeks later with a lawyer. Later that day, you have to get your mother and brother-in-law to help you get your car, which was towed: you pay the man $134 for his trouble.

35   Two weeks later, you are back in court with your brother-in-law lawyer to learn your fate. He negotiates, in about a minute, a 24D, Continuance Without a Finding, and the

judge reads you your sentence: 45 (more) days' suspended license; one year's probation; 16 weekly alcohol-education classes, including two A.A. meetings and a "victim-impact movie." You thank him. You feel triumphant! On your way out, you pay your fines and
40   court fees: $600. Outside it is a beautiful day, April 1, and you are not in jail!

A week later, you attend your first alcohol education class. You bring a money order (required) for $200, the first installment of $571. You are not allowed to drink 24 hours before each class. You watch an Al Franken movie about a dysfunctional alcoholic family.

For the next 45 days, you do not drive. You ride your bike to work. You get a ride to
45   Easter dinner at your mother's house. You pay your nephew to drive you in your own car to pick up your son from college in Connecticut. (You forget to ask permission from your probation officer to leave the state.)

When your 45 days are up, you go to the registry, wait in line and pay to get your license back—$500. You start to drive again, with a vague sense of trepidation. In the
50   summer, you return to court twice to request permission to leave the county on family vacations. Granted.

By August, you have completed all 16 classes, and have only seven more monthly checks of $65 to send to your probation officer. In November, a note from your car-insurance company informs you that your policy has been canceled: you call, and they say
55   you can reapply with a subsidiary. Your premium more than doubles.

This is what can happen. And while all this is happening, you find yourself thinking more and more about something else that could have happened: you could have crashed and killed someone, including yourself.

(824 words)

—*New York Times,* December 3, 2010
by David Updike

THINKING AND WRITING AFTER READING

RECALL   Self-test your understanding.

Your instructor may choose to give you a true-false comprehension review.

REACT   Do you think the author's punishment was fair? Why? _____

_____

REFLECT   Do you think the author will drink "several glasses of wine … and a

thimble's worth of Scotch" before driving again? _____

THINKING CRITICALLY   Total the monetary costs of Updike's drinking and driving

mistake and list the other punishments given by the court. _____

_____

THINK AND WRITE   Are you surprised at the amount of money this episode cost the

author? Explain why or why not. _____

EXTENDED WRITING   Do you think that this article would convince someone not to drive when intoxicated? Write a letter that could be sent to a friend that you know drives under the influence of alcohol or drugs. Your purpose is to remind him or her of the possible consequences and urge your friend to make a wiser choice. Use evidence from the reading selection and from your own knowledge to support your point.

DETAILS AND ORGANIZATIONAL PATTERNS

1. Why did Updike describe the other guests at dinner that night? _____

_____

2. What is the overall pattern of organization used in this selection? _____

3. List four transitional words or phrases used in this selection that indicate time.

    Answers could include _____

    _____

4. What is the organizational pattern used in the paragraph beginning at Line 14 about the author's Breathalyzer test? _____

Mark the following as major (*M*) or minor (*m*) details in support of the author's main point.

_____ 5. The author had several glasses of wine at dinner.

_____ 6. Updike's elderly mother and second cousin from Holland were with him at the dinner party.

_____ 7. He slept badly the night of the incident.

_____ 8. Altogether, the dollar cost of this incident was quite high.

Interpret THE QUOTE

Go back to the beginning of the selection and read the opening quote again. On a separate sheet of paper, explain how Homer's comment relates to Updike's story.

Name ————————————————

Date ————————————————

COMPREHENSION QUESTIONS

Answer the following with *a*, *b*, *c*, or *d*, or fill in the blank. In order to help you analyze your strengths and weaknesses, the question types are indicated.

Main Idea _____ 1. The best statement of the main idea of this selection is
  a. Drinking and driving can be costly both financially and because of the possibility of killing someone.
  b. No one should drink and drive.
  c. All of Updike's Breathalyzer tests registered an illegal blood alcohol level.
  d. This was a humiliating experience for the author.

Detail _____ 2. Updike's blood alcohol level at the police station was
  a. .10
  b. .45
  c. .40
  d. .08

Detail _____ 3. Which of the following was NOT a result of his drinking and driving?
  a. His car was towed.
  b. He attended alcohol education classes.
  c. He did community service.
  d. His drivers' license was suspended.

Inference _____ 4. Updike agreed to take the Breathalyzer test because _____.
  a. he was too drunk to make careful decisions
  b. he thought he could avoid the automatic six-month suspended license
  c. he was completely certain he would pass it
  d. he had taken one in another incident without any bad consequences

Main Idea _____ 5. Which of the following best describes the topic of this article?
  a. What to do when stopped by the police
  b. Field sobriety tests
  c. A poor example for the author's son
  d. The costs of drinking and driving

Detail _____ 6. Where did Updike spend the night after his arrest?
  a. In a jail cell
  b. At his home
  c. With his 80-year-old mother
  d. At his brother's house

Inference _____ 7. We can reasonably infer from the selection that _____.
  a. Updike was sorry for what he had done
  b. Updike was angry about the punishments he was given
  c. Updike had been arrested for drunk driving before this incident
  d. Updike had additional punishment for leaving the state without notifying his probation officer

Inference _____ 8. The author hinted that the officer stopped him on the road that night because he was speeding.

Inference _____ 9. If this event had occurred before the law changed, Updike would not have been charged with DUI.

Detail _____ 10. Updike's punishment included a jail sentence.

VOCABULARY

Answer the following with *a*, *b*, *c*, or *d* for the word or phrase that best defines the boldface word used in the selection. The number in parentheses indicates the line of the passage in which the word appears. In addition to the context clues, use a dictionary to more precisely define the technical terms.

_____ 1. "enjoy **hors d'oeuvres**" (5)

    a. drinks
    b. desserts
    c. appetizers
    d. side dishes

_____ 2. "field **sobriety** tests" (10)

    a. condition of skillfulness
    b. addiction
    c. state of being drunk
    d. opposite of drunkenness

_____ 3. "your new **manacles**" (18)

    a. handcuffs
    b. seat cushions
    c. boots
    d. surroundings

_____ 4. "After the **arraignment**" (31)

    a. arrangement
    b. sentencing
    c. legal accusation
    d. arrest

_____ 5. "He **negotiates**" (36)

    a. hesitates
    b. bargains
    c. thinks
    d. punishes

_____ 6. "You feel **triumphant**!" (39)

    a. defeated
    b. unfairly treated
    c. amazed
    d. successful

_____ 7. "**dysfunctional** alcoholic family" (43)

    a. working badly
    b. abusive
    c. addicted
    d. unhappy

_____ 8. "go to the **registry**" (48)

    a. the police station
    b. place where license records are kept
    c. driver's license bureau
    d. bank

_____ 9. "sense of **trepidation**" (49)

    a. hopelessness
    b. freedom
    c. fear
    d. humility

_____ 10. "with a **subsidiary**" (55)

    a. larger company
    b. individual person
    c. subcategory
    d. a smaller company owned by a larger one

Your instructor may choose to give a true-false vocabulary review.

VOCABULARY ENRICHMENT

Transitional Words

Transitions are signal words that connect parts of sentences and lead readers to anticipate a continuation or a change in the writer's thoughts. They are the same signal words that suggest patterns of organization and are categorized as follows:

Signal *Addition*: in addition   furthermore   moreover

Signal *Examples*: for example   for instance   to illustrate   such as

Signal *Time*: first   secondly   finally   last   afterward

Signal *Comparison*: similarly   likewise   in the same manner

Signal *Contrast*: however   but   nevertheless   whereas   on the contrary   conversely   in contrast

Signal *Cause and Effect*: thus   consequently   therefore   as a result

Choose a signal word from the following words to complete the sentences:

however	consequently	for example	likewise	furthermore

1. Betty Shabazz, the widow of Malcolm X, recognized the value of a college education; _____, she returned to college to earn a doctorate and became a college teacher and administrator.

2. Anthropologists must be persistent. _____, Louis and Mary Leakey initially found primitive tools in Olduvai Gorge, but it was 28 years later that Mary discovered the first skull.

3. His real name was Samuel Langhorne Clemens; _____, millions know him as Mark Twain.

4. Plant hormones that regulate growth include auxins and gibberellins. _____, humans have important growth hormones.

5. People enjoy eating steaks rare. _____, some people use raw steak to cover an open wound, as did the ancient Egyptians.

nevertheless	therefore	in this case	similarly	moreover

6. Some vitamins act as antioxidants, which means they neutralize free radicals and _____ reduce the risk of cancer.

7. _____, despite the benefits of antioxidants, new research shows a danger because some minerals in multivitamins cause vitamin C to be released as a free radical.

8. More research on vitamins should be done. _____, doctors should be cautious in recommending vitamins that may not be needed.

9. At least five people were dead from botulism. _____, the poison could be traced to a swollen can of food that should have been discarded.

10. Hornwort is a bryophyta. _____, liverwort is also a bryophyta.

on the other hand	for this reason	second
as an illustration	by the same token	

11. A cut in the skin breaks the protective covering around the body and _____ can be dangerous.

12. To give CPR, first lift the neck and tilt the chin upward to open the airway. _____, check for breathing by holding your ear to the victim's mouth.

13. Dogs can be conditioned to respond to smell. _____, humans will sometimes salivate when smelling cookies baking.

14. Abnormal pituitary secretions can cause sudden increases in hormone production. Acromegaly, _____, is a condition known as dwarfism.

15. Plants store glucose in starch granules. Animals, _____, store glucose in glycogen molecules.

ASSESS YOUR LEARNING

Review confusing questions, seek clarification, and make notes in your text to help you remember new information and vocabulary.

SELECTION
3

SELECTION 3   History

A Short History of Medicine
2000 BCE–"Here, eat this root."
1000 BCE–"That root is heathen, say this prayer."
1850 CE–"That prayer is superstition, drink this potion."
1940 CE–"That potion is snake oil, swallow this pill."
1985 CE–"That pill is ineffective, take this antibiotic."
2000 CE–"That antibiotic is artificial. Here, eat this root."

—Author Unknown

Unfortunately, it is likely that you know someone who has firsthand experience with cancer. You may have fought this difficult, yet all too common disease yourself or with someone close to you. According to the American Cancer Society and the Cancer Research Institute, cancer is the second leading cause of death in the United States. Some people mistakenly believe that cancer is a modern disease, but historic records show that it is a health issue that has afflicted people for more than 3,600 years. This article describes historical explanations of cancer. It provides useful information for the general reader and for readers interested in health science careers.

THINKING BEFORE READING

Preview for content and organizational clues. Activate your schema and anticipate what you will learn.

How have people explained the causes of cancer throughout history?

What progress has modern medicine made in understanding cancer?

I think this will say that _____.

VOCABULARY PREVIEW

Are you familiar with these words?

oncology	pathology	osteosarcoma	carcinoma	autopsy
lymph	chronic	trauma	mutations	carcinogens

Is *oncology* the study of cancer?

Is *pathology* the study of diseases?

Are *osteosarcoma* and *carcinoma* types of cancer?

How might an *autopsy* help oncologists and pathologists learn more about cancer?

Your instructor may choose to give a true-false vocabulary review before or after reading.

Refer to the
Reader's **TIP**
for **History** on
page 162.

SELECTION 3

THINKING DURING READING

As you read, use the six thinking strategies of a good reader: predict, picture, relate, monitor, correct, and annotate.

THE HISTORY OF CANCER

Webster's *Encyclopedic Unabridged Dictionary of the English Language* defines *cancer* as "a malignant and invasive growth or tumor." It can affect nearly any organ or system of the body—bones, blood, skin, brain, breast, colon, etc. For thousands of years, people have struggled to explain this deadly disease. Physicians both ancient and modern have used 5 whatever tools and techniques available to understand its causes so that they could treat it more effectively. Along with advances in medical knowledge, the fields of oncology (study of tumors) and pathology (study of diseases) have grown.

OLDEST DESCRIPTIONS OF CANCER

Some of the earliest evidence of cancer is found among fossilized bone tumors, human mummies in ancient Egypt, and ancient manuscripts. Bone remains of mummies have 10 revealed growths suggestive of the bone cancer, osteosarcoma. In other cases, bony skull destruction as seen in cancer of the head and neck has been found.

Our oldest description of cancer (although the team *cancer* was not used) was discovered in Egypt and dates back to approximately 1600 BCE. The Edwin Smith Papyrus, or writing, describes 8 cases of tumors or ulcers of the breast that were treated by cauter-15 ization, with a tool called "the fire drill." The writing says about the disease, "There is no treatment."

ORIGIN OF THE WORD CANCER

The origin of the word *cancer* is credited to the Greek physician Hippocrates (460–370 BCE), considered the "Father of Medicine." Hippocrates used the terms *carcinos* and *carcinoma* to describe non-ulcer-forming and ulcer-forming tumors. In Greek these words refer to 20 a crab, most likely applied to the disease because the finger-like spreading projections from a cancer called to mind the shape of a crab. Carcinoma is the most common type of cancer.

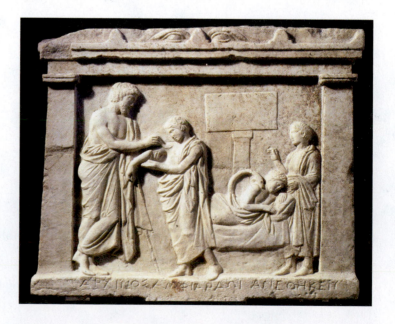

CHANGING THEORIES OF CANCER CAUSES

From the earliest times, physicians have wondered about the cause of cancer. The Egyptians blamed cancers on the Gods.

25   **Humoral Theory:** Hippocrates believed that the body contained 4 *humors* (body fluids)—blood, phlegm, yellow bile, and black bile. A balance of these fluids resulted in a state of health. Any excesses or deficiencies caused disease. An excess of black bile collecting in various body sites was thought to cause cancer. This theory of cancer was passed on by the Romans and was embraced by the influential doctor Galen's medical teaching,

30   which remained the unchallenged standard through the Middle Ages for over 1300 years. During this period, the study of the body, including autopsies (examining a body after death) was prohibited for religious reasons, thus limiting knowledge.

    Lymph Theory: Among theories that replaced the humoral theory of cancer was cancer's formation by another fluid, lymph. Life was believed to consist of continuous and

35   appropriate movement of the fluid parts through solids. Of all the fluids, the most important were blood and lymph. Stahl and Hofman theorized that cancer was composed of fermenting and degenerating lymph varying in density, acidity, and alkalinity. The lymph theory gained rapid support. John Hunter (1723–1792) agreed that tumors grow from lymph constantly thrown out by the blood.

40   **Blastema Theory:** In 1838, German pathologist Johannes Muller demonstrated that cancer is made up of cells and not lymph, but he was of the opinion that cancer cells did not arise from normal cells. Muller proposed that cancer cells arose from budding elements (blastema) between normal tissues. His student, Rudolph Virchow (1821–1902), the famous German pathologist, determined that all cells, including cancer cells, are de-

45   rived from other cells.

    Chronic Irritation: Virchow proposed that chronic irritation was the cause of cancer, but he falsely believed that cancers "spread like a liquid." A German surgeon, Karl Thiersch, showed that cancers metastasize through the spread of malignant cells and not through some unidentified fluid.

50   **Trauma:** Despite advances in the understanding of cancer, from the late 1800s until the 1920s, cancer was thought by some to be caused by trauma. This belief was maintained despite the failure to cause cancer in experimental animals by injury.

    Parasite Theory: A Nobel Prize was wrongly awarded in 1926 for scientific research documenting stomach cancer being caused by a certain worm. With the inability to con-

55   firm this research, scientists lost interest in the parasite theory.

MODERN DAY CARCINOGENS

More recently, other causes of cancer were discovered and documented. In 1911 Peyton Rous, at the Rockefeller Institute in New York, described a sarcoma in chickens caused by what later became known as the Rous sarcoma virus. He was awarded the Nobel Prize for that work in 1968. In 1915 cancer was induced in laboratory animals for the first time by a

60   chemical, coal tar, applied to rabbit skin at Tokyo University. One hundred and fifty years had passed since the most destructive source of chemical carcinogens known to man, tobacco, was first identified in London by the astute clinician John Hill. It was to be many years until tobacco was "rediscovered" as a carcinogen.

    Today we recognize and avoid many specific substances that cause cancer: coal tars

65   and their derivatives such as benzene, some hydrocarbons, aniline (a substance used to make dyes), asbestos, and others. Radiation from a variety of sources, including the sun, is known to lead to cancer. To ensure the public's safety, the government has set occupational standards for many substances, such as benzene, asbestos, hydrocarbons in the air, arsenic in drinking water, radiation, and so on.

70   Several viruses are now linked to cancer:

- Long-standing liver infection with the hepatitis virus can lead to cancer of the liver.

- A variety of the herpes virus, the Epstein-Barr virus, causes infectious mononucleosis and has been implicated in non-Hodgkin's lymphomas and nasopharyngeal cancer.

75
- The human immunodeficiency virus (HIV) is associated with an increased risk of developing several cancers, especially Kaposi's Sarcoma and non-Hodgkin's lymphoma.

- Human papilloma viruses (HPVs) have been linked to cancers of the cervix, vulva, and penis.

Many of these associations were recognized long before scientists understood the mechanism by which the cancer was produced.

TWENTIETH-CENTURY UNDERSTANDING OF CANCER

80   By the middle of the 20th century, scientists had in their hands the instruments needed to begin solving the complex problems of chemistry and biology presented by cancer. James Watson and Francis Crick, who received the Nobel Prize for their work, had discovered the exact chemical structure of DNA, the basic material in genes.

    DNA was found to be the basis of the genetic code that gives orders to all cells. After
85 learning how to translate this code, scientists were able to understand how genes worked and how they could be damaged by mutations (changes or mistakes in genes). These modern techniques of chemistry and biology answered many complex questions about cancer.

    Scientists already knew that cancer could be caused by chemicals, radiation, and vi-
90 ruses, and that sometimes cancer seemed to run in families. But, as our understanding of DNA and genes increased, we learned that it was the damage to DNA by chemicals and radiation or introduction of new DNA sequences by viruses that often led to the development of cancer. It became possible to pinpoint the exact site of the damage to a specific gene.

95   Further, scientists discovered that sometimes defective genes are inherited and that sometimes these inherited genes are defective at the same points that chemicals exerted their effect. In other words, most carcinogens caused genetic damage (mutations), mutations led to abnormal groups of cells (called clones), mutant clones evolved to even more malignant clones over time, and the cancer progressed by more and more genetic dam-
100 age and mutations. Normal cells with damaged DNA die; cancer cells with damaged DNA do not. The recent discovery of this critical difference answers many questions that have troubled scientists for many years.

    Slowly, medical scientists are identifying genes that are damaged by chemicals or radiation and the genes that, when inherited, can lead to cancer. The recent discovery of
105 two genes that cause some breast cancers, BRCA1 and BRCA2, represents considerable promise because many people who have a higher probability of developing breast cancer can now be identified.

    Other genes have been discovered that are associated with some cancers that run in families, such as cancers of the colon, rectum, kidney, ovary, esophagus, lymph nodes,
110 and pancreas and skin melanoma. Familial cancer is not nearly as common as spontaneous cancer, causing less than 15% of all cancers, but it is important to understand these cancers because with continued research in genetics we may be able to identify persons at very high risk.

SUMMARY

The growth in our knowledge of cancer biology and cancer treatment and prevention
115 has been staggering in recent years. Oncologists, pathologists and other scientists have learned more about cancer in the last decade of the 20th century than has been learned

in all the centuries preceding. This does not change the fact, however, that all scientific knowledge is based on the knowledge already acquired by the hard work and discovery of our predecessors.

(1,473 words)

—Adapted and reprinted by the permission of the American Cancer Society, Inc. from www.cancer.org. All rights reserved.

THINKING AND WRITING AFTER READING

RECALL Self-test your understanding.

Your instructor may choose to give you a true-false comprehension review.

REACT How does greater knowledge of cancer's history influence your understanding of the disease today? _____

REFLECT How does current understanding of the causes of the disease affect treatment methods? _____

_____

THINKING CRITICALLY The article mentions that in the Middle Ages medical science was restricted because of religious objections to autopsies. In what ways do religious beliefs affect medical research today? Write your answer on a separate sheet of paper.

THINK AND WRITE Name two examples and explain how the invention of new equipment or technology affected advances in medical knowledge. _____

_____

_____

EXTENDED WRITING What details in this article reveal the historical and present day understanding of cancer? In what way is scientific understanding the same or different? In a 2 or 3 paragraph essay, use the information in this selection to compare and contrast the knowledge of the more distant past and of the twentieth century. Start by completing a graphic organizer for comparison and contrast.

DETAILS AND ORGANIZATIONAL PATTERNS

1. What is the purpose of the first section? _____

_____

2. What two patterns of organization are used throughout this selection?

_____

_____

3. Which pattern best reflects the main point of this selection? (Hint: Consider the title when you answer.) _____

4. What pattern is used in paragraph 1? _____

Mark the following as major (*M*) or minor (*m*) details in support of the author's main point.

_____ 5. The humoral theory, which lasted for more than 1300 years, explained cancer as stemming from an imbalance in bodily fluids.

_____ 6. The government has set occupational standards on certain cancer-causing substances to ensure public safety.

_____ 7. More recent discoveries connect some cancers to viruses.

_____ 8. Twentieth-century scientists have shown cancer to be linked to genetic mutations in DNA.

Interpret THE QUOTE

Now that you have finished reading the selection, "The History of Cancer," go back to the beginning of the selection and read the opening quote again. What does the quote imply about advances in medical science? Do you agree with the author of the quote? Explain. It may be helpful to begin with a list of ways in which the quote is accurate and ways in which it is inaccurate. Write your responses on a separate sheet of paper.

Name ——————————————————

Date ——————————————————

COMPREHENSION QUESTIONS

Answer the following with *a, b, c,* or *d,* or fill in the blank. In order to help you analyze your strengths and weaknesses, the question types are indicated.

Main Idea   _____   1. The best statement of the main idea of this selection is:

   a. People once thought that cancer was caused by traumatic injuries.
   b. Scientists today know that cancer can be caused by viruses and by genetic mutations.
   c. Cancer can affect almost any part of the body.
   d. Understanding of cancer has changed with scientific advances throughout history.

Detail   _____   2. The theory that dominated for more than 1300 years was the

   a. Humoral Theory
   b. Lymph Theory
   c. Chronic Irritation Theory
   d. Parasite Theory

Detail   _____   3. According to the article, _____ is the most common type of cancer.

   a. breast cancer
   b. colon cancer
   c. carcinoma
   d. osteosarcoma

Inference   _____   4. The details in the article suggest that

   a. medical science has made significant progress in determining the causes of cancer.
   b. despite apparent advances we know little more today than we did centuries ago.
   c. the Lymph Theory is still accepted today.
   d. the Egyptians considered breast cancer untreatable.

Main Idea   _____   5. The main point of the section under the heading "Twentieth-Century Understanding of Cancer" is

   a. new instruments made further advances in medical science possible.
   b. the discovery of DNA led to the knowledge that genetic mutations are a critical cause of cancer.
   c. scientists discovered that viruses are the cause of some cancers.
   d. colon cancer has been linked with specific genes that run in families.

Detail   _____   6. _____ is considered the "Father or Medicine."

   a. Virchow
   b. Johannes Muller
   c. James Watson
   d. Hippocrates

Inference ———— 7. We can infer from the selection that

    a. genetic research has little affect on curing cancer.

    b. further discovery of genes associated with cancer will enable doctors to better treat patients with a family history of certain cancers.

    c. before the discovery of DNA, scientists did not consider family history as a factor in cancer.

    d. radiation is less damaging to genes than chemicals.

Inference Answer the following with *T* (true), *F* (false), or *CT* (can't tell).

———— 8. The ancient Egyptians had little scientific knowledge of cancer.

Detail ———— 9. According to the article, tobacco is the most destructive known source of chemical carcinogens.

Detail ————10. It is only in the last 50 years that tobacco has been linked to cancer.

VOCABULARY

Answer the following with *a, b, c,* or *d* for the word or phrase that best defines the boldface word used in the selection. The number in parentheses indicates the line of the passage in which the word appears. In addition to the context clues, use a dictionary to more precisely define the technical terms.

———— 1. "the fields of **oncology**" (6)

    a. research in history

    b. scientific research

    c. study of tumors

    d. study of disease

———— 2. "the fields of … **pathology**" (7)

    a. research in medicine

    b. scientific research

    c. cancer research

    d. study of diseases

———— 3. "suggestive of … **osteosarcoma**" (10)

    a. breast cancer

    b. brain cancer

    c. bone cancer

    d. blood cancer

———— 4. "Hippocrates used … **carcinoma** to" (18)

    a. a bone disease

    b. a disease spread by contact with crabs

    c. a condition common to ancient Egyptians

    d. non-ulcer and ulcer-forming tumors

———— 5. "including **autopsies**" (31)

    a. laboratory tests

    b. examinations of a crime scene

    c. methods used often in the Middle Ages

    d. examinations of bodies after death

———— 6. "**Lymph** Theory" (33)

    a. a body fluid that is discharged into the blood

    b. blood

    c. a type of tumor

    d. another word for "cancer"

———— 7. "**Chronic** Irritation" (46)

    a. painful

    b. occurring often

    c. pleasant

    d. spreading

———— 8. "caused by **trauma**" (51)

    a. poor eating habits

    b. injury to living tissue

    c. smoking

    d. lack of exercise

_____ 9. "of chemical **carcinogens**" (61)

a. cures
b. explanations
c. cancer-causing agents
d. reports

_____10. "damaged by **mutations**" (86)

a. radiation
b. injuries
c. chemicals
d. changes in genes

Your instructor may choose to give a true-false vocabulary review.

VOCABULARY ENRICHMENT

A. Study the similar-sounding words, then circle the one that is correct in each sentence.

alter: change	**coarse:** not smooth	**dual:** two
altar: platform in church	**course:** studies or path	**duel:** fight

1. You must (**alter, altar**) your study habits to make better grades.

2. To change a (**coarse, course**), you must go through a drop-add procedure.

3. The two senators fought a (**dual, duel**) at dawn.

B. Use context clues to mark *a, b, c,* or *d* for for the meaning closest to that of the boldface word.

_____ 4. From listening to her talk about the trip, I got **vicarious** pleasure and felt as if I had been there.

a. selfish
b. enormous
c. secret
d. secondhand

_____ 5. The **cardiac** patient was waiting in surgery for a bypass operation.

a. rested
b. cancer
c. emotion
d. heart

_____ 6. Because of his **phobia**, he did not want to climb to the top of the tower and look down.

a. rash
b. fear
c. disease
d. mood

C. Use the indicated root to write words to complete each sentence in the groups.

vis, vid: see

7. When she plays tennis, she wears a _____ to keep the sun out of her eyes.

8. From the description you have given me, I cannot _____ the actor's face.

9. The rip was so well-mended that the hole is now _____.

   tin, ten, tent: hold, hold together

10. We cannot _____ the trip without stopping for gas.

11. The _____ crew cleans the floors at night when no one is in the building.

12. She has been _____ at her present job for a long time and is thus seeking other employment.

    clud, clus: shut

13. She gradually became a _____ by staying in the house and not receiving visitors.

14. To _____ the interview, the manager stood up and shook her hand.

15. A correct address should _____ the zip code.

ASSESS YOUR LEARNING

Review confusing questions, seek clarification, and make notes in your text to help you remember new information and vocabulary.

PERSONAL FEEDBACK 2   Name _____

1. Approximately how much time do you spend each day studying for this class?

   _____

   _____

2. Where do you typically study? _____

   _____

3. How do you manage telephone calls and texts during your scheduled study time?

   _____

4. Describe a time this week when you have procrastinated.

   _____

5. What were the consequences of your procrastination?

   _____

   Tear out and submit to your instructor.

VOCABULARY LESSON

One Too Many

Study the prefixes, words, and sentences.

Prefixes	*mono, mon*: one	*bi, bin, bis*: two	*poly*: many

Words with *mono* or *mon* = *one*

Can a *monomaniac* be addicted to the Internet? Can a *monotone* put you to sleep?

- Monarchy: a government with only one ruler

  The power of the English *monarchy* has changed since the time of Elizabeth I.

- Monocle: an eyeglass for only one eye

  An 1800s *monocle* was more difficult to wear than the eyeglasses of today.

- Monogamy: marriage to one person only

  In the United States, *monogamy* is the legally accepted form of marriage.

- Monologue: a discourse by one person

  Jay Leno starts his late night show with a humorous *monologue*.

- Monochromatic: only one color

  A home decorated in beige has a *monochromatic* color scheme.

- Monotony: sameness

  Talking to customers breaks the *monotony* of working as a cashier.

Words with *bi, bin,* or *bis* = *two*

With cheap concert seats, carry *binoculars*. Are *biweekly* meetings every two weeks?

- Bimonthly: occurs every two months

  Regular *bimonthly* reports are required six times each year.

- Bifocal: having two lenses

  Initial use of *bifocal* lenses can be a difficult adjustment.

- Bigamy: marrying one person while already married to another

  Bigamy is illegal in the United States.

- Bilingual: using two languages

  In the United States most *bilingual* speakers know Spanish as well as English.

- Bipartisan: representing two parties

  A *bipartisan* committee would include both Democrats and Republicans.

- Biennial: something that occurs at two-year intervals or lasts two years

  Rather than every year, the class decided to have *biennial* reunions.

Words with *poly = many*

Can a *polytechnic* institute offer classes? Does the city have *polyethnic* districts?

- Polygon: closed figure with many angles

  A square is a *polygon* with four equal sides.

- Polyglot: a linguist who knows many languages

  Having lived abroad extensively, the student returned home a *polyglot*.

- Polygamy: custom of having more than one spouse at the same time.

  In cultures with *polygamy*, the additional wives function as servants.

- Polyandry: custom of having more than one husband at the same time.

  Polyandry is the exclusively female version of polygamy.

- Polychromatic: having many colors

  The *polychromatic* fabric emphasized reds and blues on a yellow background.

- Polydactyl: having more than the normal number of fingers or toes.

  The *polydactyl* abnormality was evident in three family members.

- Polymorphic: having many forms

  A *polymorphic* cartoon character can change from a cat to a tiger.

Review

Part I

Answer the following with (*T*) true or (*F*) false.

_____ 1. A polyglot is more than bilingual.

_____ 2. Two people talk to each other in a monologue.

_____ 3. A black piano has a monochromatic surface.

_____ 4. Bimonthly meetings occur twice each month.

_____ 5. Bipartisan politics suggests two parties willing to negotiate.

_____ 6. The biennial reports were due every January and July.

_____ 7. If white is a color, the U.S. flag is polychromatic.

_____ 8. An exclusively Italian area constitutes a polyethnic neighborhood.

_____ 9. Exciting people tend to enjoy monotony.

_____ 10. Bifocal lenses contain two separate eyeglass prescriptions.

Part II

Choose the best word from the list to fit the following descriptions.

monarch	monocle	monogamy	bilingual	polymorphic
bigamy	monotone	polyandry	polygon	polydactyl

11. More than ten toes _____

12. One tone of voice _____

13. Having two wives _____

14. Having two or more husbands _____

15. One eyeglass _____

16. Many forms _____

17. Speaking two languages _____

18. A queen _____

19. One spouse _____

20. A rectangle _____

Selecting Magazines

Visit the magazine section of a large local bookstore, and you will see specialty magazines on an amazing array of topics, from decorating to alternative medicine to scuba diving. Browse through the magazines to make your purchase choices. Publishers know that covers sell magazines, so check out the contents before spending your money.

News Magazines

News magazines are similar to newspapers in that they cover current events and areas of special interest, such as business, science and technology, and the arts. Because they are usually published weekly, they cannot cover breaking stories with the same immediacy as newspapers and television. What they can offer, however, is more detail and an analysis of events.

There are three main news magazines in the United States: *Time, Newsweek,* and *U.S. News & World Report*. They all contain the following elements:

News Stories. News magazine stories present the same 5 W's and H as newspapers do, but they include more details, use more colorful and dramatic language, and add amusing or touching anecdotes.

Feature Stories. The feature story for the week is usually displayed prominently on the cover to attract your attention. Most features include background information so you can understand how the current situation came to be. Colorful pictures, graphs, and survey results enrich the stories.

Editorials. The topics of these opinion essays in news magazines appeal to a broader national readership than those found in most newspapers. Rather than be isolated on a particular page, the editorials often appear beside the related stories.

Essays. News magazines also include essays that can either cover very serious matters or be whimsical and humorous. These pieces can be written by professional journalists, politicians, or readers—anyone who has an opinion or experience they want to share.

Critiques. News magazines include critiques or reviews of new movies, plays, music CDs, and books that summarize the work, state the critic's opinion, and predict the impact of the work.

EXERCISE 1

Review current copies of *Time, Newsweek, People,* and *U.S. News & World Report* in your college library or bookstore to answer the following questions.

1. Which magazine would you prefer to subscribe to and why?

2. What is the feature story in each, and why is each noteworthy?

3. Is *People* a news magazine? How would you categorize the stories in *People*?

Specialty Magazines

Specialty magazines cover almost every imaginable subject: fashion, business, technology, decorating, hobbies, health, and entertainment. Within these many categories, such publications can be very precise in their focus—not any type of guitar, but acoustic guitars. Although much of the content and terminology (jargon) may be difficult to follow for a new reader, there are usually columns and articles devoted to beginners.

Feature Articles. Feature articles are highlighted on the cover and in the table of contents. If you don't find the catchy summaries to be interesting, the articles probably won't be, either. Sometimes, rather than one feature story, a featured theme is addressed throughout an entire issue.

Letters to the Editor. If you are unfamiliar with a particular magazine, read the Letters to the Editor section. These letters, sent in by readers, will refer to past stories and can give you an idea of the audience to which the magazine appeals.

Brief News Updates. Most magazines begin with short summaries that are comparable to headline news updates on television and radio. No more than a paragraph or two in length, these updates cover news in the field on upcoming events, research findings, celebrity news, products, and trends.

Regular Columns. Columns appear regularly in magazines and are usually written by the same columnists each time, although guest writers can contribute as well. The columns are editorials about a current issue, event, or person in the magazine's field of interest, and reflect the writer's own biases.

Advertisements. Magazines make most of their revenue through selling advertising pages. Be aware that an advertisement for a particular product does not imply an endorsement of that product by the magazine. Conflicts of interest can arise between the editorial content of a magazine and its major advertisers. If a major advertiser's products and services always receive overwhelmingly positive reviews, take extra care to decide for yourself whether the findings are warranted based on the material presented. With some magazines, particularly fashion magazines, ask yourself if the publication is more interested in informing its readers or in maintaining advertising dollars.

> ### Reader's TIP Choosing a Magazine
>
> - Read the lead article headlines and the table of contents to find articles of interest to you.
> - Flip through the magazine and read article titles and boxed article excerpts.
> - Read several Letters to the Editor.
> - Decide, purchase, and enjoy!

 **EXERCISE 2**   Select four specialty magazines that you would like to subscribe to if money were not an issue. For each magazine list the following:

1. Evaluate the quality of the feature articles.

2. Estimate the ratio or percentage of news and feature stories to advertisements.

3. Which regular articles particularly appeal to you?

What Makes Work Satisfying?

To find out what one is fitted to do, and to secure an opportunity to do it, is the key to happiness.

—John Dewey

If you ask a student why he or she is attending college, it is very likely the answer will have something to do with getting a good job. A college degree offers graduates more choices in the job market, allows for work in the fields they love, and promises greater financial rewards. Some jobs that once were held by workers with high school diplomas or even less schooling, now require at least a 2-year college degree if not a Bachelor's degree. According to the Bureau of Labor Statistics data shown below, education pays off in lower unemployment rates and higher earnings.

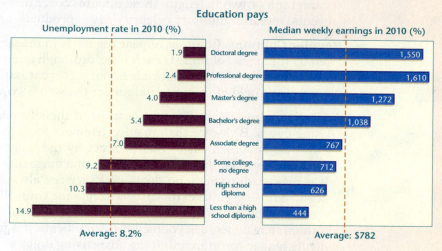

Note: Data are 2010 annual averages for persons age 25 and over. Earnings are for full-time wage and salary workers.

Source: Bureau of Labor Statistics, Current Population Survey.
www.bls.gov/emp/ep_chart_001.htm

Clearly, preparing for future work is a reasonable and practical aim for college students. While some students begin college with a definite career goal in mind, others are uncertain about the right direction for them. Fortunately, college offers opportunities to explore fields of study and work that were unknown to the typical freshman before setting foot on campus. College also provides time and resources to seriously examine what will make work satisfying for a lifetime.

The selections in this Casebook offer perspectives on what work is and what makes it rewarding. As you read, think about your goals, your values, and how they point you to a career that is more than a job, one that provides a lifetime of satisfaction.

Begin by reading the list of job characteristics. The last item, "other," is reserved for anything that is important to you but not included in the list. Next, rank the items from 1 to 20 in order of their importance to you. Write the characteristic that is most important to you on Line 1 and so on down to the one of least importance to you on Line 20.

WHAT IS MOST IMPORTANT TO ME IN A CAREER?

Job Characteristic	Level of Personal Importance
Challenge	1. _____
Compatible co-workers	2. _____
Creativity	3. _____
Fair supervisor	4. _____
Feeling of accomplishment; good use of abilities	5. _____
Free time available away from the job	6. _____
Job security	7. _____
Level of interaction with others	8. _____
Opportunity to improve society	9. _____
Opportunity for work travel	10. _____
Pride in the company	11. _____
Public recognition	12. _____
Room for advancement	13. _____
Salary and benefits	14. _____
Service to others	15. _____
Status of the job field or position	16. _____
Variety	17. _____
Work hours	18. _____
Working conditions (safety, comfort, indoors, outdoors)	19. _____
Other (specify):	20. _____

Reader's TIP Reading and Studying Poetry

As the poet A. E. Housman said, "Poetry is not the thing said but the way of saying it." Poetry is very "dense" writing in that every word is important to the meaning. As much care must be taken to absorb each word as the poet took to select it. Poems are also personal and can be interpreted differently by each reader.

- Read the poem aloud several times to hear its rhythm, possible rhyme, and the sounds of its letters.
- React emotionally to what you have read. Don't think too much at first nor discount anything that comes to mind no matter how irrelevant it seems.
  Feelings: What emotions did you feel as you read?
  Visual images: What mental pictures came to mind?
  Associations: What memories does the poem bring to mind?
- Examine and "translate" the figurative expressions and difficult vocabulary
- Use the clues in the poem and your prior knowledge to infer the meaning.

The two poems that follow present very different views of work. Use the steps in the Reader's Tip to read and respond to them. Use the chart that follows the poems to record your responses.

I HEAR AMERICA SINGING
BY WALT WHITMAN (1819–1892)

I hear America singing, the varied carols I hear,
Those of mechanics, each one singing his as it should be blithe and strong,
The carpenter singing his as he measures his plank or beam,
The mason singing his as he makes ready for work, or leaves off work,
The boatman singing what belongs to him in his boat, the deckhand singing on the
   steamboat deck,
The shoemaker singing as he sits on his bench, the hatter singing as he stands,
The wood-cutter's song, the ploughboy's on his way in the morning, or at noon
   intermission or at sundown,
The delicious singing of the mother, or of the young wife at work, or of the girl sewing
   or washing,
Each singing what belongs to him or her and to none else,
The day what belongs to the day—at night the party of young fellows, robust, friendly,
Singing with open mouths their strong melodious songs.

—Selected Poems (1991)

WHAT WORK IS
BY PHILIP LEVINE (B.1928)

We stand in the rain in a long line
waiting at Ford Highland Park. For work.
You know what work is—if you're
old enough to read this you know what
work is, although you may not do it.
Forget you. This is about waiting,
shifting from one foot to another.
Feeling the light rain falling like mist
into your hair, blurring your vision
until you think you see your own brother
ahead of you, maybe ten places.
You rub your glasses with your fingers,
and of course it's someone else's brother,
narrower across the shoulders than
yours but with the same sad slouch, the grin
that does not hide the stubbornness,
the sad refusal to give in to
rain, to the hours of wasted waiting,
to the knowledge that somewhere ahead
a man is waiting who will say, "No,
we're not hiring today," for any
reason he wants. You love your brother,

now suddenly you can hardly stand
the love flooding you for your brother,
who's not beside you or behind or
ahead because he's home trying to
sleep off a miserable night shift
at Cadillac so he can get up
before noon to study his German.
Works eight hours a night so he can sing
Wagner, the opera you hate most,
the worst music ever invented.
How long has it been since you told him
you loved him, held his wide shoulders,
opened your eyes wide and said those words,
and maybe kissed his cheek? You've never
done something so simple, so obvious,
not because you're too young or too dumb,
not because you're jealous or even mean
or incapable of crying in
the presence of another man, no,
just because you don't know what work is.

—From *What Work Is* (Knopf, 1991)

"I Hear America Singing"	"What Work Is"
Feelings:	Feelings:
Visual images:	Visual images:
Associations/memories:	Associations/memories:
Figurative language/difficult vocabulary:	Figurative language/difficult vocabulary:

What does the poet think about why people work?

_____

_____

_____

_____

_____

What does the poet think about why people work?

_____

_____

_____

_____

_____

Which poem better expresses your ideas about why people work? Explain?

_____

_____

Perhaps you are familiar with the saying "Money doesn't buy happiness." A typical response, though, is "Maybe not, but it sure doesn't hurt" or "I'd like to find out for myself." How big a part does salary have in job satisfaction? Some studies show that people are happiest when their work helps others. Imagine that you won enough money in the lottery to support you and your family in style for the rest of your life. Would you be happy? Would you want to work if you didn't have to? Consider another situation: You are offered two positions, one provides a very rewarding salary but requires work that you find boring, and the other offers a lower but sustainable salary doing work that you know you would find interesting and worthwhile. Which would you choose?

Reader's TIP — Reading and Studying a News or Feature Article

- Preview the headline and photographs.
- Find the facts: *who, what, when, were, why* and *how.*
- Consider how the angle or focus of a feature story differs from a straight news story.
- Evaluate the credibility of the sources cited.
- When reading a feature story, observe the number of facts compared with the number of opinions.
- Look for bias or judgment on the part of the reporter.

For more suggestions on reading news and feature articles in the newspaper, refer to the Everyday Reading Skills on page 73.

JOB SATISFACTION VS. A BIG PAYCHECK

Does earning a higher salary make you happier?

It's an issue that tugs at many of us: the tradeoff between a satisfying job and a satisfying paycheck. Students have to ponder the question when considering a college major or embarking on a career. Workers are concerned about it when weighing a promotion that would bring longer hours and more stress along with higher pay.

5   In many ways, achieving the right balance depends on one's values, priorities, family obligations and spending habits. But according to a recent study in the Proceedings of the National Academy of Sciences, there is something of a magic number when it comes to income and happiness.

Beyond household income of $75,000 a year, money "does nothing for happiness,
10   enjoyment, sadness or stress," the study concluded.

It's not so much that money buys you happiness but that lack of money buys you misery, said Daniel Kahneman, a professor emeritus of psychology at Princeton and one of the authors of the study. "The lack of money," he said, "no longer hurts you after $75,000."

Where you live and the cost of living there has only a small influence on that number,
15   he added. (That may be a revelation to some Manhattanites.)

The study, which analyzed Gallup data of 450,000 randomly selected Americans, did find that one's "life evaluation"—a self-assessment of one's life—continued rising well above $75,000. But this is not the same as experiencing day-to-day happiness.

"Many people want to make a lot of money, but the benefits of having a high income are ambiguous," said Professor Kahneman, who is also a Nobel laureate in economics. When you are wealthy you are able to buy more pleasures, he said, but a recent study suggests that wealthier people "seem to be less able to savor the small things in life."

That said, some people seem almost hardwired to want to make money. A 2007 article in *The Journal of Happiness Studies* reported that college freshmen who stated that they wanted a high salary by and large achieved that goal 20 years later. The article said that "individuals with strong financial aspirations are socially inclined, confident, ambitious, politically conservative, traditional, conventional, and relatively less able academically, but not psychologically distressed."

People who sought high incomes were more likely to major in things like business, engineering and economics, it said, while people for whom high income was not paramount gravitated toward the liberal arts and social sciences.

"Wanting money is not a recipe for disaster, but wanting money and not getting it—that's a good recipe for disaster," Professor Kahneman said. People who want to become performing artists are likely to be unhappy, because most will fail, he said. Becoming a wealthy rock star is a common dream when you are young, but when you are in college, you should try to take a longer-term view, he said.

These days, of course, many people are worried about whether they will get a job at all, let alone become rock stars. Understandably, the recession is causing more people to place the financial rewards of a career first, said Nicholas Lore, founder of the Rockport Institute, a career coaching firm, and author of "The Pathfinder."

But this could backfire as people who initially pursue a field because of the salary realize that the work is unsatisfying. Mr. Lore has recently coached a lawyer who decided to forgo his high pay in favor of teaching law, an investment banker who

45   decided to switch to a green energy company and a dentist who decided to become a schoolteacher.

It all depends on priorities, Mr. Lore said. Some people are willing to make lifestyle changes because the intrinsic rewards of following a passion or making a difference are more important than a high salary in an unenjoyable career, he said.

50   In the end, people should pursue what they're interested in, said Daniel H. Pink, author of "Drive: The Surprising Truth About What Motivates Us." Looking at lists of careers with the highest salaries tends to be a fool's game, he said.

"It's very hard to game the system, in the sense that situations and conditions change so quickly that a field that is hot today might be only lukewarm in 5 or 10 years," he said.

55   "It might even be nonexistent."

Let's say you see that accountants are getting decent salaries directly out of college, he said, but you don't really like accounting. "Chances are you're not going to be very good at accounting," and your salary will reflect that, he said. "Generally, people flourish when they're doing something they like and what they're good at."

60   For his part, Mr. Lore said he was concerned that current economic woes might force people into poor career choices.

"I would prefer that the economy was doing better and people were more adventurous because it often has an enormous effect on the quality of their life," he said. Many people equate success with a high income, but, "How can someone say they're successful

65   if they're not happy doing their work? To me, that's not success."

COMPREHENSION QUESTIONS

Answer the following questions with true (*T*) or false (*F*).

_____ 1. According to a recent study, people are happier if they make $100,000 per year than if they make $75,000 per year.

_____ 2. An article cited in the selection reported that most college freshmen who said they wanted jobs with high salaries achieved them in the next 20 years.

_____ 3. The selection suggests that majoring in social sciences or liberal arts is likely to result in higher salaries.

_____ 4. Lower-salaried positions are more likely if you major in business or engineering.

_____ 5. Nicholas Lore and Daniel Pink would agree that the best route to happiness in one's job is to make choices based on interest rather than salary.

THINKING AND WRITING AFTER READING

REACT   Which college courses interest you most? In which do you excel? _____

_____

REFLECT As you consider your college major, will you decide based on your interests and ability or on the potential to earn a higher salary? Explain your answer.

_____

_____

THINK AND WRITE What advice would you give a younger sibling about choosing a college major and ultimately a career?_____

_____

COMPARE The article says that "life evaluation," an assessment of one's life, is different from day-to-day happiness. Do you agree? How might they be different or similar? _____

_____

DEFINE What factors constitute happiness in one's job? Consider what you have read in this selection as well as the job characteristics you ranked by level of importance at the beginning of this Casebook. _____

_____

This selection is an adaptation and update of an article written by Dr. Rene Dawis and published in a professional reference, Encyclopedia of Career Change and Work Issues. *The article appeared in its present form on a website sponsored by* The Career Key, *a career advice firm. The previous selections in this Casebook have explored the nature of work and studies that reveal aspects of work that people find satisfying. In this article, you will find advice based on professional experience about how to identify the kind of work that is likely to be personally fulfilling.*

Reader's TIP   Reading and Studying Business

- Activate your schema with the introductory profiles and boxed material that describe an actual company with a current business dilemma. These illustrate the chapter concepts.
- Connect business theories with a real company's problems or solutions to make learning easier. Use the business illustrations to visualize the concepts.
- Cross-reference your reading with the illustrative photographs, tables, flow charts, figures, and copies of real advertisements. Sketch your own models of business and marketing processes and concepts. Use these visual learning tools to enhance your learning.
- Use the exercises to reinforce chapter topics, strengthen your research skills, and expand your knowledge. An instructional software disk may come with your text with practice quizzes and other instructional help.
- Use the tips that suggest how to market yourself by applying the chapter's concepts in your career search. For example, tips may offer advice on how to identify and access the major employment pipelines (*distribution channels*) for your product (you) in your career search.

EIGHT STEPS TO FINDING FULFILLMENT IN THE WORK PLACE

According to a 2010 survey of U.S. households by The Conference Board, job dissatisfaction is widespread among workers of all ages across all income brackets. The study found that "only 45 percent of those surveyed say they are satisfied with their jobs, down from 61.1 percent in 1987, the first year in which the survey was conducted."

5   With worker dissatisfaction so high and increasing, how can you avoid it? Or, if you are working and dissatisfied, what can you do about it?

First, it is important to know that there are different kinds of job satisfaction. The surveys just described investigated *overall job satisfaction*. This is when a person considers the whole job and everything about it. Overall job satisfaction is actually a combination of
10   *intrinsic* and *extrinsic* job satisfaction:

- *Intrinsic job satisfaction* is when workers consider only *the kind of work they do*, the tasks that make up the job.

- *Extrinsic job satisfaction* is when workers consider *the conditions of work,* such as their pay, coworkers, and supervisor.

These two types of satisfaction are different, and it helps to look at jobs from both points of view. For example, if you are dissatisfied with your current job, ask yourself, "To what extent is it *due to the kind of work* I am doing?" and "To what extent is it due to *the conditions of my work*?" If it is primarily the kind of work you are doing, it is *intrinsic* job dis-
15 satisfaction. This calls for a different solution than if your dissatisfaction is *extrinsic* in nature.

And, second, you want to recognize that job satisfaction is influenced by *job expectations*—what people look for or require from a job such as job security, pay, prestige, or independence. And, that some people have higher expectations for work than others. What expectations do you have for your work? How strong are they? These are the
20 ten job expectations that workers mention most frequently:

1. *Type of work:* the kind of work that makes the best use of one's abilities and gives one a feeling of accomplishment.
2. *Security:* having a job that provides a steady employment.
3. *Company:* working for a company that has a good reputation, that one can be proud of working for.
4. *Advancement:* being able to progress in one's job or career, having the chance to advance in the company.
5. *Coworkers:* having coworkers who are competent and congenial.
6. *Pay:* being paid at least enough to meet one's needs, and being paid fairly in comparison to others.
7. *Supervision:* having an immediate supervisor who is competent, considerate, and fair.
8. *Hours:* having working hours that allow one enough time with family and/or time to pursue other strong interests and live one's preferred lifestyle.
9. *Benefits:* having benefits that meet one's needs and compare well with those of others.
10. *Working Conditions:* having physical working conditions that are safe, not injurious to health, not stressful, and even comfortable.

What can you do to maximize your job satisfaction? Based on research and the experience of professional career specialists, here are eight recommendations:

1. *Know yourself.* Know what is important to you and what is not. What kinds of work tasks or activities are attractive to you? Be clear about what you expect from or require of a job. Write your ideas down. Then, you will know what to look for when choosing among jobs or careers.

   Review the "ten job expectations" listed above that are most frequently mentioned by workers and rank their importance to you. Are there others, not mentioned, like autonomy or prestige, that are important to you?

   Also, learn more about yourself through career counseling sources. For example, take tests or inventories that measure your abilities, interests, values and personality. Review your academic interests and strengths. Examine the activities you enjoy in your leisure time. Talk with a friend, family member or professional career counselor. Identify the skills you possess and those expected by employers. Write an autobiography and identify the themes that represent who you are. Lastly, write a personal mission statement. In it write: what you want to be, what you want to accomplish in life, and what values or principles you want to guide you.

2. *Learn about jobs that are most likely to meet your expectations.* Career counselors and online sites offer resources to help you identify occupations that fit your personality and provide accurate information about each of them.

3. *Consider consulting a professional career counselor.*

4. *Do not allow your job dissatisfactions to go unresolved for long.* Job satisfactions and dissatisfactions are barometers of your adjustment to work. They may lead to something worse—job loss, accidents, even mental illness. Depression, anxiety, worry, tension, and interpersonal problems can result from, or be made worse by job dissatisfaction. In fact, job satisfaction was found to be the best predictor of how long you live ... better than a doctor's rating of physical functioning, use of tobacco, or genetic inheritance. So, it is important to work out a solution if your job is making you unhappy.

5. *Have realistic expectations for work.* Overall job satisfaction is a trade-off (like many things in life). You should not expect 100% satisfaction or 0% dissatisfaction. There are usually dissatisfactions even in the best jobs. And, in today's work world you cannot expect your company to look out for you; you have to take the initiative yourself.

6. *Look separately at the kind of work you are doing versus the conditions of work* (pay, supervisor, coworkers, company, physical working conditions). If you are becoming increasingly dissatisfied with the kind of work you are doing, you should consider a career change. If you are dissatisfied with the conditions of work, you might be able to set matters right by negotiating with your supervisor or your coworkers, or by changing companies.

7. *Look down the road at your possible career progress.* Present dissatisfactions might be worth bearing if you see your career progressing.

8. *Examine your values—what is most important to you.* You have to answer this question honestly: How important is your job, your career to you? Only when this question is answered can you put your job satisfaction or dissatisfaction in proper perspective.

—From The Career Key website, 2001, www.careerkey.org

COMPREHENSION QUESTIONS

Answer the following questions with true (*T*) or false (*F*) or write a response.

_____ 1. According to the most recent Conference Board survey more workers are unhappy with their jobs than were reported in 1987.

_____ 2. The level of satisfaction with one's salary is an example of *intrinsic job satisfaction.*

_____ 3. *Extrinsic job satisfaction* refers to aspects of work such as safety conditions, vacation time, and relationships with co-workers.

_____ 4. The author believes that workers would be happier with their jobs if they analyzed their expectations and sought positions that are likely to match them.

_____ 5. The author recommends changing careers if dissatisfaction is due to the kind of work one is doing, but attempting to negotiate change within the present job if the problem is the working conditions.

THINKING AND WRITING AFTER READING

REACT   The article states that job satisfaction is a better predictor of life expectancy than tobacco use or family history. What effect does this have on how you will plan for a career?

REFLECT   How does this quote from Confucius, the ancient Chinese philosopher, relate to the ideas in this article: *Choose a job you love, and you will never have to work a day in your life?*

THINK AND WRITE   Select the quote that best illustrates your beliefs about work and explain why you chose it:

Far and away the best prize that life has to offer is the chance to work hard at work worth doing.

Theodore Roosevelt

All labor that uplifts humanity has dignity and importance and should be undertaken with painstaking excellence.

Martin Luther King, Jr.

I think the person who takes a job in order to live—that is to say, for the money—has turned himself into a slave.

Joseph Campbell

Laziness may appear attractive, but work gives satisfaction.

Anne Frank

There is joy in work. There is no happiness except in the realization that we have accomplished something.

Henry Ford

COMPARE   Examine the way you ranked the importance of job characteristics at the beginning of this Casebook and the rankings of survey participants shown in Selection 3. What are the similarities and differences? Were any of your top five in the survey's top five? Did any of your top ten not appear at all in the survey's top ten?

DEFINE   Divide the top ten job expectations listed in this article into two groups—extrinsic and intrinsic factors. Do the same with the top ten in your personal list.

EXTENDED WRITING   Now that you have read and thought about several selections on work and the qualities that make work satisfying, follow the advice given in the last selection: Write a personal mission statement. In it write what you want to be, what you want to accomplish in life, and what values or principles you want to guide you. Use ideas, discoveries, and advice from the activities and readings in this Casebook to inform your thinking.

6 Textbook Learning

Learning Objectives

From this chapter, readers will learn:

1. To use active methods to aid recall
2. To annotate texts during the reading stage
3. To use the Cornell method of notetaking
4. When and how to write a summary
5. To make outline notes
6. To make notes using mapping

Everyday Reading Skills: Reading Reference Materials

EXPECT TO LEARN FROM READING

Expect to know something after you have read a textbook assignment. Don't just watch the words go by. Use learning strategies to select key elements and to prepare for remembering. In chapter five, we discussed two such strategies—marking the text and taking notes. In this chapter, our discussion of those strategies continues with coverage of annotating, summarizing, outlining, and mapping.

The process of reading, marking, and organizing textbook information takes time. Many students ask, "How much do I need to do?" The answer to that question is, "Typically, the more you do, the more you learn." In other words, it is better to read the text than not to read the text. What's more, it is better to read and mark than only to read. Finally, it is better to read, mark, and take notes in some form (summary, Cornell notes, outline, or map) than just to read and mark. Your choices depend on the amount of time you can dedicate to learning. "Time on task" is a critical element in college success.

ANNOTATING

Annotating is a system of marking that includes underlining and notations. It is the first and most basic step for all of the other organizing strategies.

When to Annotate

Annotate during reading but after a complete thought is presented. Many students tend to mark too much, and overmarking wastes valuable review time. Wait until a complete thought has been presented to separate the most important ideas from the least important ones. Such a thought unit may be as short as one paragraph or as long as an entire section under a subheading. Marking the text is a key part of Stage Two-Integrating Knowledge. The annotations record what is important enough to include in your notes later, and the thinking involved helps keep your mind from wandering.

How to Annotate

The word *annotate* is used to suggest a notation system for selecting important ideas that goes beyond straight lines and includes numbers, circles, stars, and written comments, such as marginal notes, questions, and key words. With practice, students tend to form their own notation systems, which may include a variation of the following examples.

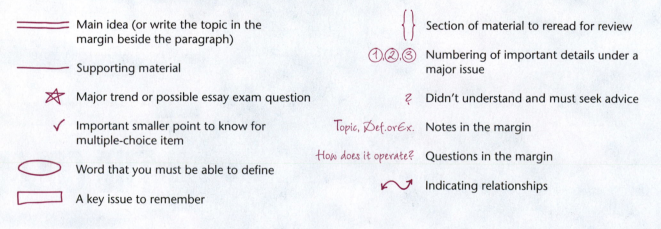

═══ Main idea (or write the topic in the margin beside the paragraph)	{ } Section of material to reread for review
──── Supporting material	①,②,③ Numbering of important details under a major issue
☆ Major trend or possible essay exam question	¿ Didn't understand and must seek advice
✓ Important smaller point to know for multiple-choice item	*Topic, Def.or Ex.* Notes in the margin
⬭ Word that you must be able to define	*How does it operate?* Questions in the margin
▭ A key issue to remember	∿ Indicating relationships

Unless you are reading a library book, annotate for study reading. For example, have you been annotating throughout this text as you have been reading? (The correct answer to this question should be yes!) If your instructor were to say at this moment, "Take fifteen minutes to review for a quiz on the last two chapters," could you quickly review your annotations? Remember, you can waste time reading for the purpose of learning if you do not annotate.

BRAIN BOOSTER

Sleeping Body, Busy Brain

An experiment that has been done many times always gives the same results: Math students were taught a way to solve a set of problems but were told there was also an easier method. Twelve hours after the math lesson, 20 percent of the students discovered the easier method on their own. If the learners had 8 hours of sleep during the 12 hours, 60 percent discovered the trick! It appears that our brains use time when the rest of the body is sleeping to consolidate the information it has processed earlier. Although just putting a book under the pillow while you sleep won't help, reading, studying the material, and then sleeping will.

—Adapted from John J. Medina, *Brain Rules*.
© 2008 John J. Medina. Pear Press: Seattle, WA

EXAMPLE The following passage was taken from a college psychology textbook. Do you recognize the definition and example organizational pattern and that the details are presented in order of increasing importance? Notice how the passage was annotated and how the annotations became the basis for the notetaking examples on the following pages.

HOW WE REMEMBER: REHEARSAL

Def.

3 Strategies

An important technique for keeping information in short-term memory and increasing the chances of long-term retention is rehearsal, the review or practice of material while you are learning it. Some strategies for rehearsing are more effective than others.

Def. ①

Maintenance rehearsal involves merely the rote repetition of the material. You are taking advantage of maintenance rehearsal when you look up a phone number and then

Ex.

repeat it over and over to keep it in short-term memory until you no longer need it. This kind of rehearsal is fine for keeping information in short-term memory, but it will not always lead to long-term retention.

Def. ②

A better strategy if you want to remember for the long haul is elaborative rehearsal. Elaboration involves associating new information with material that has already been stored or with other new facts. Suppose, for example, that you are studying the hypothalamus. Simply memorizing the definition of the hypothalamus is unlikely to help much. But if you can elaborate the concept of the hypothalamus, you are more likely to remember it.

Ex.

For example, knowing that hypo means "under" tells you its location, under the thalamus. Many students try to pare down what they are learning to the bare essentials, but in fact, knowing more details about something makes it more memorable; that is what elaboration means.

Def. ③

A related strategy for prolonging retention is (**deep processing**) or the processing of meaning. If you process only the physical or sensory features, such as how the word hypothalamus is spelled and how it sounds, your processing will be shallow even if it is elaborated. If you recognize patterns and assign labels to objects or events ("The hypothalamus is below the thalamus"), your processing will be somewhat deeper. If you fully analyze the meaning of what you are trying to remember (for example, by encoding the functions and importance of the hypothalamus), your processing will be deeper yet.

Ex.

—Adapted from *Psychology*, Tenth edition, by
Carole Wade and Carol Tavris

The learner's task is not just to read but also to earmark relevant ideas for future study. To be an efficient learner, do not waste time.

EXERCISE 1 Read the following passage and use the suggested annotations on page 264 to organize the material and mark key ideas for later study. Respond with *T* (true) or *F* (false) to the comprehension items.

SPATIAL DISTANCES

The way in which you treat space, a field of study called **proxemics**, communicates a wide variety of messages. Edward Hall distinguishes four distances that define the type of relationship between people and identifies the various messages that each distance communicates.

In **intimate distance**, ranging from actual touching to 18 inches, the presence of the other individual is unmistakable. Each person experiences the sound, smell, and feel of the other's breath. You use intimate distance for love-making and wrestling, for comforting and protecting. This distance is so short that most people do not consider it proper in public.

Personal distance refers to the protective "bubble" that defines your personal space, which measures from 18 inches to 4 feet. This imaginary bubble keeps you protected and untouched by others. You can still hold or grasp another person at this distance—but only by extending your arms—allowing you to take certain individuals such as loved ones into your protective bubble. At the outer limit of personal distance, you can touch another person only if both of you extend your arms.

At **social distance**, ranging from 4 to 12 feet, you lose the visual detail you have at personal distance. You conduct impersonal business and interact at a social gathering at this distance. The more distance you maintain in your interactions, the more formal they appear. Many people in executive and management positions place their desks so that they are assured of at least this distance from employees.

Public distance, measuring from 12 to more than 25 feet, protects you. At this distance, you can take defensive action if threatened. On a public bus or train, for example, you might keep at least this distance from a drunkard. Although you lose fine details of the face and eyes at this distance, you are close enough to see what is happening.

—*Essentials of Human Communication*, Fourth Edition,
by Joseph A. DeVito

Check your annotations with a study buddy. Could you study the essentials from the annotations without rereading the passage?

_____   1. Intimate distance is appropriate for social gatherings.

_____   2. The greater the social distance, the more formal the interaction appears.

NOTETAKING

Notetaking involves using your own words and separate paper to condense the key ideas you have marked in your text while annotating. Simply jotting these ideas down on paper is notetaking, but putting notes into an organized form makes them clearer and easier to use for study purposes. Four common forms are presented in the following pages.

When to Take Notes

Take notes from textbooks in the "Recall" stage, after reading and annotating. Take notes from lectures while the speaker talks, and revise later. Record major topics and supporting details, but avoid trying to write everything.

The Cornell Method of Notetaking

Learning Objective 3

How to use the Cornell method

The Cornell method, one of the most popular systems of notetaking, includes the following steps:

1. Draw a line down your paper 2.5 inches from the left edge to create a wide margin for key words and a wider area on the right for explanatory details. (Some students prefer to follow the more formal guidelines for Cornell notes and write complete sentences in this column.)
2. After reading and annotating a selection, review your annotations and write the key details in the left-hand column. Use your marginal notes as a guide.
3. Write the explanatory details in the right-hand column. Use phrases or complete sentences, as in the more formal style. Align the details on the right with their labels on the left. Use your text markings as a guide.

You will probably notice that as you create your notes you are also correcting your annotations. You may find that you failed to mark important information or that you annotated too much. To study Cornell-style notes, cover the details in the right-hand column and use the labels in the left-hand column to quiz yourself or a study partner.

Abbreviations.   Use shortcuts. Develop your own system of abbreviations for notetaking for both textbook and lecture notes. Some students mix shorthand symbols with their regular writing.

The following is an example of how the Cornell method might be used to organize notes for future study on the passage about rehearsal strategies.

How We Remember: Rehearsal	
Rehearsal *Def.*	*Important for memory. Some strategies more effective than others* *Review of material while learning*
3 Strategies *Maintenance rehearsal* *Def.* *Ex.*	*Okay for short-term memory* *Rote repetition* *Repeating a phone number only as long as you need it*
Elaborative rehearsal *Def.* *Ex.*	*More effective; details aid memory* *Associating new information with existing information* *Hypothalamus: hypo- means below; the hypothalamus is below the thalamus*
Deep processing *Def.* *Ex.*	*Most effective method* *Processing the meaning; adding labels, recognizing patterns* *Associate the hypothalamus with its purpose and importance*

When to Use Cornell-Style Notes.   This method is useful for textbook study and class lectures. The marginal topic notes placed on the left are particularly helpful in organizing the study of a large body of material for a midterm or final exam.

 Read the following passage about population growth in poorer nations. Annotate it, then use the Cornell method to take notes for future use. Write your notes in the box that follows the selection. Respond with *T* (true) or *F* (false) to the comprehension items.

POPULATION GROWTH

Why do people in the countries that can least afford it have so many children? We must take the role of the other so we can understand the world as *they* see it. As our culture does for us, their culture provides a perspective on life that guides their choices. Let's consider three reasons why bearing many children plays a central role in the lives of millions upon millions of poor people around the world.

First is the status of parenthood. In the least industrialized nations, motherhood is the most prized status a woman can achieve. The more children a woman bears, the more she is thought to have achieved the purpose for which she was born. Similarly, a man proves his manhood by fathering children. The more children he fathers, especially sons, the better—for through them his name lives on.

Second, the community supports this view; many people share values and closely identify with one another. Children are viewed as a sign of God's blessing. Accordingly, a couple should have many children. By producing children, people reflect the values of their community and achieve status. The barren woman, not the woman with a dozen children, is to be pitied.

These factors certainly provide strong motivations for bearing many children. Yet, there is a third incentive. For poor people in the least industrialized nations, children are economic assets. These people have no Social Security or medical and unemployment insurance. This motivates them to bear *more* children, not fewer, for when parents become sick or too old to work—or when no work is to be found—they rely on their children to take care of them. The more children they have, the broader their base of support. Moreover, children begin contributing to the family income at a young age.

To those of us who live in the most industrialized nations, it seems irrational to have many children. And *for us it would be*. Understanding life from the framework of people who are living it, however—the essence of the symbolic interactionist perspective—reveals how it makes perfect sense to have many children. For example, consider the following incident, reported by a government worker in India:

> Thaman Singh (a very poor man, a water carrier) . . . welcomed me inside his home, gave me a cup of tea (with milk and "market" sugar, as he proudly pointed out later), and said: "You were trying to convince me that I shouldn't have any more sons. Now, you see, I have six sons and two daughters and I sit at home in leisure. They are grown up and they bring me money. One even works outside the village as a laborer. *You told me I was a poor man and couldn't support a large family. Now, you see, because of my large family I am a rich man.*"

Conflict theorists offer a different view of why women in the poor nations bear so many children. They would argue that these women have values that support male dominance. To father many children, especially sons, demonstrates virility, giving a man valued status in the community. From a conflict perspective, then, the reason poor people have so many children is that men control women's reproductive choices.

—From James M. Henslin, *Sociology: A Down-to-Earth Approach*, 7th ed. © 2007 (excerpt from pages 583–585). Reproduced by permission of Pearson Education, Inc.

_____ 1. In poor countries throughout the world, poverty tends to increase rather than decrease the desire for a large number of children.

_____ 2. A barren woman is a mother.

_____ 3. In the least industrialized nations, an inability to bear children results in lower status for a woman.

_____ 4. For poor people in the least industrialized countries, children are viewed as their social security for old age.

Summarizing

A **summary** is a short, concise method of stating the main idea and significant supporting details of the material. Think of it as the key words and phrases linked by complete sentences and presented in paragraphs.

When to Summarize. Professors frequently ask students to take notes in the form of a summary on assigned readings. Such readings, which are usually in the library or on the Internet, might include chapters from related texts, short stories, research articles from periodicals, or scholarly essays from books or periodicals. The preparation of a written summary can demonstrate to the professor that you have a clear understanding of the main points of the assignment. A summary can provide you with reference notes for later study; and it can be useful when you are compiling information from several sources for a long research paper.

Reader's TIP   How to Write a Summary

- Remember your purpose; be brief.
- In the text, underline the key ideas you want to include.
- Begin your summary with a general statement, the main idea, that unites the key ideas.
- Include the key ideas that support the general statement. Link these ideas in sentences, and show their significance.
- Delete irrelevant or trivial information.
- Delete redundant information.
- Use your own words to show your understanding of the material. Don't try to camouflage a lack of comprehension by copying from the original.
- Do not include your opinions or anything that is not in the original.

How to Summarize.   When you write a summary, put the ideas into your own words. If you need to quote an author directly, place quotation marks around the *exact* wording to avoid plagiarism. Keep in mind the purpose of your summary. The way you will use the information will influence the number of details you include. Generally, be brief but make your point. A summary is usually just one paragraph. A summary should never be as long as the piece it is summarizing!

EXAMPLE   The following is a summary of the passage on rehearsal strategies (p. 265). Notice that the first sentence states the main ideas and the others concisely state the major supporting details.

How We Remember: Rehearsal

Rehearsal, repeated review of material while learning it, is important to establishing memory. Some rehearsal strategies are more effective than others. Maintenance rehearsal is simple, rote repetition like what one does when repeating a telephone number for only as long as the number is needed. This is adequate for short-term memory. The next strategy, elaborative rehearsal, is more effective. It involves associating the new information with existing knowledge. For example, recognizing that hypo- means "below" is helpful in remembering that the hypothalamus is below the thalamus. The most effective rehearsal method is deep processing. In this method, meaning is developed by adding labels and recognizing patterns. Connecting the hypothalamus with its function and importance provides a more lasting memory.

EXERCISE 3   Annotate the following passage and then write a summary of it. Include only the most important details in your summary and exclude the irrelevant ones. For example, this passage is dramatized by an anecdote, but does the information belong in the summary? Respond with *T* (true) or *F* (false) to the comprehension items.

RATTLESNAKE SURPRISE

David Chiszar, a professor in the psychology department at the University of Colorado, got a big surprise when he walked into his laboratory in 1995. His laboratory shelves are lined with dozens of glass cases; behind the glass, the subjects of Dr. Chiszar's research coil a safe distance from the professor and any visitors brave enough to enter. Although most are eerily silent, an occasional research subject emits a dry, rattling sound when the professor passes by. Dr. Chiszar is a herpetologist—in particular, he studies snakes. The day of the surprise, he went to the glass case that held a 14-year-old female timber rattlesnake. Timber rattlesnakes are poisonous but relatively unaggressive snakes that are found only in the eastern half of the United States. Severe declines in timber rattlesnake populations have led several states, including New York and Massachusetts, to list it as a threatened or endangered species, making it illegal to harass, kill, or collect timber rattlesnakes.

Dr. Chiszar had raised this timber rattlesnake since she was a two-day-old baby, not much bigger than an earthworm. Now, as he peered into her cage, he was astonished to see a tiny rattlesnake baby next to the $2\frac{1}{2}$-foot-long female snake. Even though she had never been in contact with a male snake, she had given birth to a male timber rattlesnake. Like other pit vipers, timber rattlesnakes don't lay eggs, but bear their young alive. Genetic studies showed that the baby snake really was the offspring of the 14-year-old rattler and that he didn't have a "father" in the usual sense of the word.

Although it may surprise you, such events are not all that rare in the world of reptiles, some birds, and insects. In fact, some species of whiptail lizards and geckos lack males entirely. The females of these species routinely produce offspring without the requirement for fertilization.

—*Biology: Life on Earth,* Sixth Edition, by Teresa Audesirk,
Gerald Audesirk, and Bruce Byers

Written Summary

Timber rattlesnakes _____

_____

_____

_____

_____ 1. The female timber rattlesnake produced a male offspring without any contact with a male.

_____ 2. The 14-year-old mother rattlesnake had been isolated in captivity since it was two days old.

EXERCISE 4   Annotate the following passage and write a summary of it. Respond with *T* (true) or *F* (false) to the comprehension items.

YOUTH IN CRISIS

Problems in the home, the school, and the neighborhood have placed a significant portion of American youth at risk. Youths considered at risk are those who engage in dangerous conduct such as drug abuse, alcohol use, and precocious sexuality. Although it is impossible to determine precisely the number of at-risk youths in the United States, one estimate is that 25 percent of the population under age 17, or about 17 million youths, are in this category. The most pressing problems facing American youth revolve around four issues.

Poverty. Though the number of American children living in poverty is dropping, the U.S. Census Bureau finds that there are still more than 12 million indigent children (the Census Bureau defines poverty as an income below $13,290 a year, or the equivalent of $1,108 a month for a family of three). While the percentage of children living in poverty in America is at its lowest level since 1979, the percentage of poor children in working families continues to climb, with 77 percent of poor children living in families where someone is working; this indicates that many working families are still struggling to stay afloat.

Family Problems. Divorce strikes about half of all new marriages, and many families sacrifice time with each other to afford more affluent lifestyles. Research shows that children are being polarized into two distinct economic groups: those in affluent, two-earner, married-couple households and those in poor, single-parent households.

Urban Decay. Adolescents living in deteriorated urban areas are prevented from having productive and happy lives. Many die from random bullets and drive-by shootings. Some are homeless and living on the street, where they are at risk of drug addiction and sexually transmitted diseases (STDs) including AIDS. One study of street kids in New York City found that 37 percent earned money through prostitution and almost one-third had contracted an STD.

Inadequate Education. The U.S. educational system seems to be failing many young people. We are lagging behind other developed nations in critical areas such as science and mathematics. The rate of *retention* (being forced to repeat a grade) is far higher than it should be. Retention rates are associated with another major problem: dropping out. It is estimated that about 14 percent of all eligible youths do not finish high school. In addition, poor and minority-group children attend the most under-funded schools, receive inadequate educational opportunities, and have the fewest opportunities to achieve conventional success.

—From Larry J. Siegel, *Juvenile Delinquency,* 1st ed. © 2002 Wadsworth, a part of Cengage Learning, Inc. Reproduced by permission. www.cengage.com/permissions

Written Summary

Begin with a general statement about youth in crisis. Link the key ideas and do not include irrelevant information.

_____

_____

_____

_____

_____

_____

_____ 1. The author suggests that children who experience any of the four at-risk factors have a higher probability of becoming drug or alcohol abusers than those without such experiences.

_____ 2. The author suggests that having a job is not a guarantee of avoiding poverty.

EXERCISE 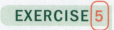 Annotate the following passage and write a summary of it. Respond with *T* (true) or *F* (false) to the comprehension items.

BUSINESS ETIQUETTE

A major component of managing your impression is practicing good etiquette. **Business etiquette** is a special code of behavior required in work situations. *Manners* has an equivalent meaning. Both manners and etiquette generally refer to behaving in a refined and acceptable manner. Business etiquette is much more than knowing how to use the correct utensil or how to dress in a given situation. Businesspeople today must know how to be at ease with strangers and with groups, be able to offer congratulations smoothly, know how to make introductions, and know how to conduct themselves at company social functions. Studying etiquette is important because knowing and using proper business etiquette contributes to individual and business success. People who are considerate of the feelings of others, and companies who are courteous toward customers, are more likely to succeed than their rude counterparts.

Business etiquette includes many aspects of interpersonal relations in organizations. What is considered proper etiquette and manners in the workplace changes over time and may vary with the situation. At one time, addressing one's superior by his or her first name was considered brash. Today it is commonplace behavior. A sampling of etiquette guidelines is nevertheless helpful. A general principle of being considerate of the feelings of work associates is more important than any one act of etiquette or courtesy.

ETIQUETTE FOR WORK BEHAVIOR AND CLOTHING

General work etiquette includes all aspects of performing in the work environment, such as completing work on time, punctuality, being a good team player, listening to others, and following through. For instance, having the courtesy to complete a project when it is due demonstrates good manners and respect for the work of others.

Clothing might be considered part of general work behavior. The casual standards in the information technology field, along with dress-down days, have created confusion about proper office attire. A general rule is that *casual* should not be interpreted as sloppy, such as torn jeans or a stained sweatshirt. Many companies have moved back toward emphasizing traditional business attire, such as suits for men and women. In many work situations, dressing more formally may constitute proper etiquette.

INTRODUCING PEOPLE

The basic rule for introductions is to present the lower-ranking person to the higher-ranking person regardless of age or sex. "Ms. Barker (the CEO), I would like you to meet my new coworker, Reggie Taylor." If the two people being introduced are of equal rank, mention the older one first. Providing a little information about the person being introduced is considered good manners. When introducing one person to the group, present the group to the individual. "Sid Foster, this is our information systems team." When being introduced to a person, concentrate on the name and repeat it soon, thus enhancing learning. A fundamental display of good manners is to remember people's names and to pronounce them correctly. When dealing with people senior to you or of higher rank, call them by their last name and title until told otherwise. (Maybe Ms. Barker, above, will tell you, "Please call me Kathy.")

It is good manners and good etiquette to remember the names of work associates to whom you are introduced, even if you see them only occasionally. If you forget the name of a person, it is better to admit this than to guess and come up with the wrong name. Just say, "I apologize, but I have forgotten your name. Tell me once more, and I will not forget your name again."

A major change in introducing people is that men and women are now both expected to extend their right hand when being introduced. Give a firm, but not overpowering, handshake, and establish eye contact with the person you are greeting.

—*Human Relations: Interpersonal, Job-Oriented Skills*, Eighth Edition, by Andrew J. DuBrin

Written Summary

Begin with a general statement about business etiquette. Link the key ideas and do not include irrelevant information.

_____
_____
_____
_____
_____
_____
_____

_____ 1. The passage indicates that *etiquette* and *manners* have about the same meaning.

_____ 2. In introductions, present the higher ranking person to the lower ranking one.

Outlining

Learning Objective 5
Make outline notes

Outlining is a form of notetaking that gives a quick display of key issues and essential supporting details. Outlining uses indentations, numbers, and letters to show levels of importance. The outline forces you to sort out significant details and decide

Reader's TIP Creating an Outline

The following is the format for a model outline. Notice how the numbers, letters, and indentations show the importance of an idea.

Main Point or Topic

I. Primary supporting idea

   A. Secondary supporting detail

   B. Secondary supporting detail

   C. Secondary supporting detail

II. Primary supporting idea #2

   A. Secondary supporting detail

   B. Secondary supporting detail

      1. Minor supporting detail or example

      2. Minor supporting detail or example

III. Primary supporting idea #3

   A. Secondary supporting detail

   B. Secondary supporting detail

on levels of importance. Being able to outline shows that you understand main ideas and can distinguish between major and minor supporting details.

When to Outline. Outlining can be used to take notes on a textbook chapter or a class lecture or for brainstorming the answer for a possible essay question.

How to Outline. Letters, numbers, and indentations are used in an outline to show levels of importance. In a standard outline, Roman numerals mark items of greatest importance and letters indicate supporting details. The greater distance from the left margin an item is listed, the less significance it is afforded. Your outline need not be picture perfect, but it should use indentation and some form of enumeration. Always remember that you are outlining to save time for later study and review. Don't cram all your facts on half a sheet of paper when you need several sheets. Give yourself plenty of room to write. You want to be able to look back quickly to get a clear picture of what is important and what supports it.

When taking notes in outline form, be brief and to the point. Use phrases rather than sentences. Record the main points, including key explanatory words, but leave out the insignificant details or "fillers."

Remember, making a picture-perfect outline is not critical; the important thing is to distinguish between the primary supporting ideas and the secondary supporting details. In an informal study outline, you can show the same levels of importance with indentations and bullets.

EXAMPLE   The following example shows how the passage on rehearsal strategies (see p. 265) might be outlined for future study. Again, notice how the annotations were used to create the outline.

> How We Remember: Rehearsal
>
> I. Rehearsal
>
>   A. Def: Review of material while learning
>
>   B. Important for memory
>
>   C. Some strategies more effective than others
>
> II. Maintenance rehearsal
>
>   A. Def: Rote repetition
>
>   B. Ex: Repeating a phone number only as long as it is needed
>
>   C. Okay for short-term memory
>
> III. Elaborative rehearsal
>
>   A. Def: Associating new information with existing information
>
>   B. Ex: Hypo- means "below", so the hypothalamus is below the thalamus
>
>   C. Details make this strategy more effective
>
> IV. Deep processing
>
>   A. Def: Developing meaning by adding labels and recognizing patterns
>
>   B. Ex: Associating the hypothalamus with its purpose and importance
>
>   C. Most effective method

EXPLANATION   Reviewing the outline provides all the information needed to study the material. For active review, try reproducing your outline notes from memory, or make a copy, cut it up, and reconstruct the parts in the appropriate order.

EXERCISE 6   Make a study outline for the following material. Annotate first, and then organize your notes into an informal outline with numbers or bullets.

THE SIX TYPES OF LOVE

EROS: BEAUTY AND SENSUALITY

Erotic love focuses on beauty and physical attractiveness, sometimes to the exclusion of qualities you might consider more important and more lasting. The erotic lover has an idealized image of beauty that is unattainable in reality. Consequently, the erotic lover often feels unfulfilled. In defense of eros, however, it should be noted that both male and female eros lovers have the highest levels of reward and satisfaction when compared with all other types of lovers (Morrow, Clark, & Brock 1995).

LUDUS: ENTERTAINMENT AND EXCITEMENT

Ludus love is seen as fun, a game to be played. To the ludic lover, love is not to be taken too seriously; emotions are to be held in check lest they get out of hand and make trouble. Passions never rise to the point at which they get out of control. A ludic lover is self-controlled and consciously aware of the need to manage love rather than to allow it to control him or her. The ludic lover is manipulative, and the extent of one's ludic tendencies has been found to correlate with the use of verbal sexual coercion (Sarwer, Kalichman, Johnson, Early, et al. 1993). Ludic-oriented sexually coercive men also experience less happiness, friendship, and trust in their relationships than do noncoercive men (Kalichman, Sarwer, Johnson, & Ali 1993). Ludic lover tendencies in women are likewise related to a dissatisfaction with life (Yancey & Berglass 1991).

STORGE LOVE: PEACEFUL AND SLOW

Like ludus love, **storge love** lacks passion and intensity. Storgic lovers do not set out to find lovers but to establish a companion-like relationship with someone they know and with whom they can share interests and activities. Storgic love develops over a period of time rather than in one mad burst of passion. Sex in storgic relationships comes late, and when it comes it assumes no great importance. Storgic love is sometimes difficult to separate from friendship; it is often characterized by the same qualities that characterize friendship: mutual caring, compassion, respect, and concern for the other person.

PRAGMA: PRACTICAL AND TRADITIONAL

The **pragma lover** is practical and wants compatibility and a relationship in which important needs and desires will be satisfied. In its extreme, pragma may be seen in the person who writes down the qualities wanted in a mate and actively goes about seeking someone who matches up. The pragma lover is concerned with the social qualifications of a potential mate even more than personal qualities; family and background are extremely important to the pragma lover, who relies not so much on feelings as on logic. The pragma lover views love as a necessity—or as a useful relationship—that makes the rest of life easier. The pragma lover therefore asks such questions about a potential mate as, "Will this person earn a good living?" "Can this person cook?" and "Will this person help me advance in my career?"

MANIC LOVE: ELATION AND DEPRESSION

The quality of mania that separates it from other types of love is the extremes of its highs and lows, its ups and downs. The **manic lover** loves intensely and at the same time worries intensely about and fears the loss of the love. With little provocation, for example, the manic lover may experience extreme jealousy. Manic love is obsessive; the manic lover has to possess the beloved completely—in all ways, at all times. In return, the manic lover wishes to be possessed, to be loved intensely. It seems almost as if the manic lover is driven to these extremes by some outside force or perhaps by some inner obsession that cannot be controlled.

AGAPE: COMPASSIONATE AND SELFLESS

Agape is a compassionate, egoless, self-giving love. Agape is nonrational and nondiscriminative. Agape creates value and virtue through love rather than bestowing love only on that which is valuable and virtuous. The agapic lover loves even people with whom he or she has no close ties. This lover loves the stranger on the road, and the fact that they will probably never meet again has nothing to do with it. Jesus, Buddha, and Gandhi practiced and preached this unqualified love. Agape is a spiritual love, offered without concern for personal reward or gain. The agapic lover loves without expecting that the love will be returned or reciprocated. For women, agape is the only love style positively related to their own life satisfaction (Yancy & Berglass 1991).

—*Human Communication*, Sixth Edition,
by Joseph A. DeVito

Six Types of Love

I. Eros: Beauty and Sensuality

A. Focus: _____

B. _____

C. _____

D. _____

II. Ludus: Entertainment and Excitement

A. Focus: _____

B. _____

C. _____

D. _____

III. Storge: Peaceful and Slow

A. Focus: _____

B. _____

C. _____

D. _____

IV. Pragma: Practical and Traditional

A. Focus: _____

B. _____

C. _____

D. _____

V. Manic: Elation and Depression

A. Focus: _____

B. _____

C. _____

D. _____

VI. Agape: Compassionate and Selfless

A. Focus: _____

B. _____

C. _____

D. _____

 **EXERCISE 7**   Make a study outline for the following material. Annotate first, and then organize your notes into an informal outline with numbers or bullets.

DRUG TESTS

Employers bear a crushing economic burden—estimates run as high as $100 billion—owing to drug and alcohol abuse by employees. These costs arise from high turnover, poor work performance, absenteeism, increased medical claims, low morale, theft, and other factors.

The drug-abusing employee is late three times as often as his coworkers, asks for time off twice as often, has two and one-half times as many absences of eight or more days, is five times more likely to file a workers' compensation claim, and is involved in accidents more than three times as often.

Typical on-the-job symptoms of drug abuse are inability to pay attention, difficulty with simple arithmetic, prolonged trips to the restroom, frequent absenteeism, poor personal hygiene, lapses in memory, and inattention to detail.

Given the social gravity and bottom-line expense of the drug problem, it is understandable that most American companies now screen for drug abuse during the pre-employment process. In most cases, this testing takes place as an ordinary and relatively inexpensive part of the pre-employment physical.

—Interviewing for Success,
by Arthur H. Bell and Dayle M. Smith

Drug Abuse by Employees

I. Costs to Employers

A. _____

B. _____

C. _____

D. _____

E. _____

F. _____

G. _____

II. Symptoms of Drug-Abusing Employees

A. _____

B. _____

C. _____

D. _____

E. _____

F. _____

G. _____

BRAIN BOOSTER

Stress: Crouching Tigers versus Looming Deadlines

Stress is an aroused physical state in which adrenaline is released to help us react; next, cortisol kicks in to calm us down. Stress is designed to keep us from being eaten by the crouching tiger. It is when adrenaline levels stay high for an extended period, like when we worry for weeks over the research paper that determines passing or failing, that stress is harmful. Chronic stress scars our blood vessels, reduces our ability to fight illness, and inhibits learning. It can actually disconnect neural networks and prevent the growth of new ones. The worst damage is done when we feel powerless. What to do? Exercise and proper amounts of sleep can help. Some people find meditation and prayer effective. Just as important, however, is to establish a can-do attitude. Analyze the situation and take control! Decide on small steps that give you power over your situation: Look at the index in your textbook for term paper topics, begin searching for materials, make notes, plan your paper, draft one section at a time—and seek guidance when you need it. Chronic stress is history!

EXERCISE  8   Make a study outline for the following material. Annotate first, and then organize your notes into an informal outline with numbers or bullets.

BUILDING SKILLS TO REDUCE STRESS

Dealing with stress involves assessing all aspects of a stressor, examining your response and how you can change it, and learning to cope. Often we cannot change the requirements at our college, assignments in class, or unexpected stressors. Inevitably, we will be stuck in classes that bore us and for which we find no application in real life. We feel powerless when a loved one dies. Although the facts cannot be changed, we can change our reactions to them.

ASSESSING YOUR STRESSORS

After recognizing a stressor evaluate it. Can you alter the circumstances to reduce the amount of distress you are experiencing or must you change your behavior and reactions to reduce stress levels? For example, you may have five term papers due for five different courses during the semester, but your professors are unlikely to drop such requirements. However, you can change your behavior by beginning the papers early and spacing them over time to avoid last-minute panic.

CHANGING YOUR RESPONSES

Changing your responses requires practice and emotional control. If your roommate is habitually messy and this causes you stress, you can choose from among several responses. You can express your anger by yelling; you can pick up the mess and leave a nasty note; or you can defuse the situation with humor. The first reaction that comes to mind is not always the best. Stop before reacting to gain the time you need to find an appropriate response. Ask yourself, "What is to be gained from my response?"

LEARNING TO COPE

Everyone copes with stress in different ways. Some people drink or take drugs; others seek help from counselors; and still others try to forget about it or engage in positive activities, such as exercise. **Stress inoculation,** one of the newer techniques, helps people prepare for stressful events ahead of time. For example, suppose you are petrified about speaking in front of a class. Practicing in front of friends or in front of a video camera may inoculate you and prevent your freezing up on the day of the presentation. Some health experts compare stress inoculation to a vaccine given to protect against a disease. Regardless of how you cope with a situation, your conscious effort to deal with it is an important step in stress management.

DOWNSHIFTING

Today's lifestyles are hectic and pressure-packed, and stress often comes from trying to keep up. Many people are questioning whether "having it all" is worth it, and they are taking a step back and simplifying their lives. This trend is known as **downshifting.** Moving from a large urban area to a smaller town, exchanging the expensive SUV for a modest four-door sedan, and a host of other changes in lifestyle typify downshifting. Some dedicated downshifters have given up television, phones, and even computers.

Downshifting involves a fundamental alteration in values and honest introspection about what is important in life. When you consider any form of downshift or perhaps even start your career this way, it's important to move slowly and consider the following.

a. *Determine your ultimate goal.* What is most important to you, and what will you need to reach that goal? What can you do without? Where do you want to live?

b. *Make a short-term and a long-term plan for simplifying your life.* Set up your plan in doable steps, and work slowly toward each step. Begin saying no to requests for your time, and determine those people with whom it is important for you to spend time.

c. *Complete a financial inventory.* How much money will you need to do the things you want to do? Will you live alone or share costs with roommates? Do you need a car, or can you rely on public transportation? Pay off credit cards and eliminate existing debt, or consider debt consolidation. Get used to paying with cash.

—*Health: The Basics,* Sixth Edition,
by Rebecca J. Donatelle

Building Skills to Reduce Stress

    I. Assessing Your Stressors

        A. _____

        B. _____

        C. _____

    II. Changing Your Responses

        A. _____

        B. _____

    III. Learning to Cope

        A. _____

        B. _____

        C. _____

    IV. Downshifting

        A. _____

        B. _____

Mapping

Learning Objective 6

Make notes using mapping

Mapping visually condenses material to show relationships. A map is a diagram that places important topics in a central location and connects major points and supporting details in a visual display that shows degrees of importance. The previous study methods are linear in nature, whereas mapping uses space in a free and graphic manner.

When to Map.   A map provides a quick reference for overviewing a chapter to stimulate prior knowledge, emphasize relationships, and aid recall. College students use maps or charts to reduce information for memorizing from lecture notes and the text.

How to Map.   To prepare a map, do the following:

1. Draw a circle or a box in the middle of a page, and in it write the subject or topic of the material.
2. Determine the main ideas that support the subject, and write them on lines radiating from the central circle or box.
3. Determine the significant details, and write them on lines attached to each main idea. The number of details you include will depend on the material and your purpose.

Maps are not restricted to any one pattern but can be formed in a variety of creative shapes, as the following diagrams illustrate.

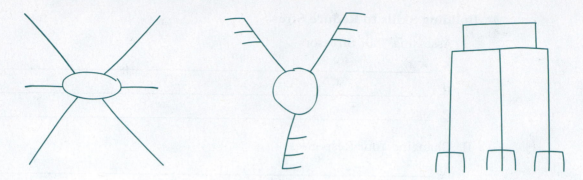

The following is an example of how the passage on rehearsal strategies might be mapped for future study. Many forms and shapes are acceptable as long as the connections represent the correct relationships among major and minor details.

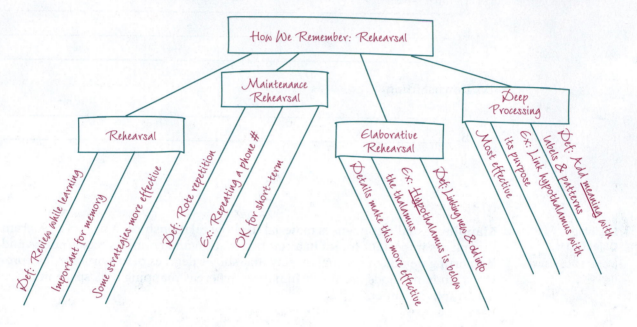

EXPLANATION   Mapping works best when only a few major details are displayed. The same active study methods suggested for outline notes work well for maps: Recreate the map from memory, or make a copy, cut it up, and reconstruct it like a jigsaw puzzle.

EXERCISE 9   Read the following passage and map the key ideas. The structure of the map is provided. Insert the topic first, then arrange the supporting ideas to radiate appropriately.

RELIEF FOR INJURIES

For the past several hundred years many injuries were treated with heat—steaming baths where leisurely soaking was encouraged, hot water bottles, or electric heating pads or wraps. It was assumed that since heat speeded up metabolism, it would also speed the healing process. Today's researchers have proved that just the opposite is true. . . . Heat does speed up body processes but it also stimulates injured tissue and dilates blood vessels.

In turn, this causes swelling to increase and enlarges the pools of blood and fluid, actually slowing healing. Even if there is no injury, heat after exercising can cause aches and pains. A quick, cool shower is recommended after your jog rather than a hot tub.

Four basic first aid procedures are used in treating the majority of runners' injuries.

STOP ACTIVITY

The first and most critical is to stop jogging as soon as the symptom appears. About the only pain you can run through is a side stitch. Joggers who insist on running with pain or walking off an injury usually incur further harm. Even though the pain does not become more intense, continuing the activity may aggravate the injury and prolong healing.

APPLY COLD

Cold packs are now universally accepted as the best first aid for virtually any jogging injury and constitute the second step in treatment. Chilling numbs the pain and minimizes swelling and inflammation by constricting blood and lymph vessels. Apply cold packs at least twice a day until the swelling and tenderness disappear. The ice pack should not be left in place longer than 30 minutes at one time. Muscle cramps are one of the few conditions associated with jogging where heat instead of cold should be applied.

IMMOBILIZE AND ELEVATE

Injuries that would benefit from being immobilized and/or given additional support should be wrapped with an elastic Ace-type bandage. This wrapping should be snug, but not tight enough to inhibit blood circulation. This third step should be taken before the final step of elevating the injured body part. Elevation not only helps drain fluid from the area, but also prevents blood and fluid from rushing to the area, thereby causing further swelling.

— *Jogging Everyone,* by Charles Williams
and Clancy Moore

EXERCISE    Read the following passage and map the key ideas. The structure of the map is provided. Insert the topic first, then arrange the supporting ideas to radiate appropriately.

TYPES OF CRIME

In the United States, the Federal Bureau of Investigation gathers information on criminal offenses and regularly reports the results in a publication called *Crime in the United States*. Two major types of crime make up the FBI "crime index."

Crimes against the person are *crimes that direct violence or the threat of violence against others*. Such violent crimes include murder and manslaughter (legally defined as "the willful killing of one human being by another"), aggravated assault ("an unlawful attack by one person upon another for the purpose of inflicting severe or aggravated bodily injury"), forcible rape ("the carnal knowledge of a female forcibly and against her will"), and robbery ("taking or attempting to take anything of value from the care, custody, or control of a person or persons by force or threat of force or violence and/or putting the victim in fear").

Crimes against property encompass *crimes that involve theft of property belonging to others*. Property crimes include burglary ("the unlawful entry of a structure to commit a [serious crime] or a theft"), larceny-theft ("the unlawful taking, carrying, leading, or riding away of property from the possession of another"), auto theft ("the theft or attempted theft of a motor vehicle"), and arson ("any willful or malicious burning or attempt to burn the personal property of another").

A third category of offenses, not included in major crime indexes, is **victimless crimes**, *violations of law in which there are no readily apparent victims*. Also called "crimes without complaint," they include illegal drug use, prostitution, and gambling. The term "victimless crime" is misleading, however. How victimless is a crime when young people have to steal to support a drug habit? What about a young pregnant woman who smokes crack and permanently harms her baby? Perhaps it is more correct to say that people who commit such crimes are both offenders and victims.

—*Sociology*, Tenth Edition,
by John J. Macionis

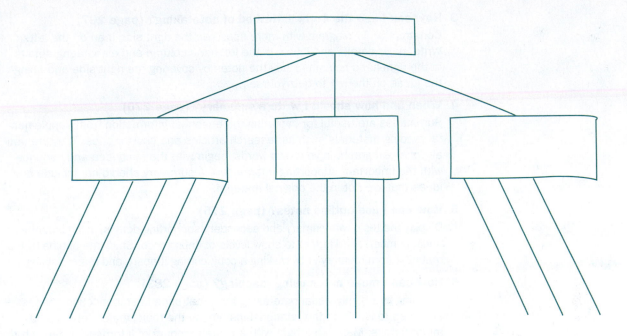

 **EXERCISE 11**   On a separate sheet of paper, make a study map or chart to diagram the essential information in the passage titled *The Six Types of Love* (see Exercise 6).

TAKE ORGANIZED LECTURE NOTES

Develop an efficient system for organizing class lectures. Professors speak rapidly yet expect students to remember important information. The Cornell method uses marginal notes to emphasize main points, whereas the outline format shows importance through indentation. Whichever system you use, allow yourself plenty of room to write. Considering your investment in college, paper is inexpensive. Use a pen, not a pencil, to avoid smudges. Try writing on only one side of the paper so you can backtrack later to add information when the professor summarizes. Compare your lecture notes with those of other students. Why would some professors say, "I can tell how much a student understood by looking at his or her lecture notes"?

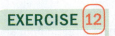 **EXERCISE 12**   Choose a study buddy and divide the work in order to compare the two notetaking systems, the Cornell method and the modified outline format. Ask permission and, if possible, both of you visit a history, psychology, sociology, or political science class. One of you should take notes using the Cornell method and the other using an informal version of the outline format. After class, compare notes and decide which method works better for you.

SUMMARY POINTS

1 What active methods can be used to assist recall? (page 264)
Annotating while reading and making notes after reading are very effective recall methods.

2 How can I effectively annotate my textbooks? (page 264)
Use a system of circling, underlining, consistent symbols, and marginal notes.

3 How can I use the Cornell Method of notetaking? (page 267)

Construct a "T" diagram with more space on the right side than on the left. Write major details and labels in the left-hand column and elaborating details in the right-hand column. Study the notes by covering the right side and using the ideas on the left to quiz yourself.

4 When and how should I write a summary? (page 270)

Summaries are useful for capturing the essential information from supplemental reading materials such as research articles and short stories. They are usually one paragraph. In your own words, begin with the main idea and continue with the important supporting information. A summary should not include any ideas that are not in the original material.

5 How can I use outline notes? (page 275)

Display the topic with primary and secondary supporting details, using indentations, numbers, and letters to show levels of importance. Study the outline by recreating it from memory or by making a copy, cutting it apart, and reassembling it.

6 How can I make notes using mapping? (page 283)

Mapping is a highly visual notetaking form that uses interconnecting shapes and lines to illustrate the relationships among the topic, major details, and minor details. Maps work best with a limited amount of information. Study by drawing the map from memory, or by making a copy, cutting it into parts, and putting it back together like a jigsaw puzzle.

COLLABORATIVE   PROBLEM SOLVING

Form a five-member group and select one of the following activities. Brainstorm and then outline your major points on a transparency. Choose a member to present the group findings to the class.

➤ List ten tips for taking good lecture notes.

➤ List ten items you can purchase that will help you get organized for successful study.

➤ List ten shorthand terms or abbreviations that will help you take lecture notes rapidly.

➤ List ten reasons not to cut a class.

MyReadingLab

MyReadingLab (MRL) www.myreadinglab.com

➤ For support in meeting this chapter's objectives, log in to **www.myreadinglab.com** and select "Outlining and Summarizing" and "Note Taking and Textbook Highlighting."

THE READING WORKSHOP

If reading a novel, biography, or other book is part of your course experience, refer to The Reading Workshop: Thinking, Talking, and Writing about Books in Appendix 5 for suggestions.

PERSONAL FEEDBACK 1   Name _____

1. What format do you prefer for notetaking? Why? _____
   _____
   _____

2. What has been your experience with marking your texts (annotating)? How would
   you evaluate your annotating in light of what you learned in this chapter? _____
   _____
   _____

3. Why should you take notes on one side of a notebook page only? _____
   _____
   _____

4. What value do you see in making notes from your textbook reading? _____
   _____
   _____

5. What do you feel are the five major differences in academic expectations between
   high school and college? _____
   _____
   _____

Tear out and submit to your instructor.

SELECTION 1 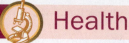 Health

> "People's behavior makes sense if you think about it in terms of their goals, needs, and motives."
> —Thomas Mann

Dr. Bernard Suran reports in the Florida Bar News *that when asked, "Would you like to become a better person?" most people surprisingly respond with a resounding "maybe" rather than an enthusiastic "of course." Why bother to change if life is not holding your feet to the fire in a reaction to circumstances? Genuine change is difficult, requiring a firm commitment and an organized plan. Dr. Suran says, "What motivates best is the realm of possibility, if we allow ourselves to consider the prospect of becoming even more awesome than we already are."*

THINKING BEFORE READING

Preview for content and organizational clues. Activate your schema and anticipate what you will learn.

What circumstances can give people the impetus to change unwanted behaviors?

What is a positive reinforcement?

How do Olympic athletes use imagery and psychology to excel?

I think this will say that _____.

VOCABULARY PREVIEW

Are you familiar with these words?

coaxed	acknowledgment	languish	vigilance	commitment
scenario	inducement	premise	irrational	resort

How can someone be *coaxed* into a *commitment* they do not want to make?

What *scenario* might cause someone to resort to an extreme lifestyle change?

Your instructor may choose to give a true-false vocabulary review before or after reading.

THINKING DURING READING

As you read, use the six thinking strategies of a good reader: predict, picture, relate, monitor, correct, and annotate.

ANNOTATING

Annotate the selection in order to make an outline of significant elements in behavior change.

Reader's TIP — Reading and Studying Health

- Use learning aids provided within the text. Such items might include running glossaries on pages, checklists, discussion and application questions, and summaries.
- Answer any marginal questions placed within a chapter.
- Review and understand procedures by following the graphics provided.
- Design your own concept cards (see Chapter 3) to help learn new vocabulary.
- Draw simple figures or symbols to aid your understanding and recall of concepts.

BEHAVIOR CHANGE

Mark Twain said that "habit is habit, and not to be flung out the window by anyone, but coaxed downstairs a step at a time." The chances of successfully changing negative behavior improve when you make gradual changes that give you time to unlearn negative patterns and to substitute positive ones.

STAGING FOR CHANGE

5   On any given day, countless numbers of us get out of bed and resolve to begin to change a given behavior "today." Whether it be losing weight, drinking less, exercising more, being nicer to others, managing time better, or some other change in a negative behavior, we start out with high expectations. In a short time, however, a vast majority of people fail and are soon doing whatever it was they thought they shouldn't be doing.

10   After considerable research, Dr. James Prochaska and Dr. Carlos DiClimente believe that behavior changes usually do not succeed if they start with the change itself. Instead, they believe that we must go through a series of "stages" to adequately prepare, or ready, ourselves for that eventual change.

Precontemplation. People in the precontemplation stage have no current intention
15   of changing. They may have tried to change a behavior before and may have all but given up, or they may just be in denial and unaware of any problem.

Contemplation. In the contemplation stage, the person recognizes that he or she has a problem and begins to think about the need to change. Despite this acknowledgment, people can languish in this stage for years, knowing that they have a problem but never
20   finding the time or energy to make the change.

Preparation. Most people in this stage are close to taking action. They've thought about several things they might do and may even have come up with a plan.

Action. In the action stage, the individual begins to follow the action plan he or she has put together. Unfortunately, too many people start behavior change here rather than

25 going through the first three stages. Without a plan, without enlisting the help of others, or without a realistic goal, failure is likely.

Maintenance. Maintenance requires vigilance, attention to detail, and long-term commitment. Many people reach their goals, only to relax and slip back into the undesired behavior.

30 **Termination.** In this stage, the behavior is so ingrained that the current level of vigilance may be unnecessary. The new behavior has become an essential part of daily living.

CHOOSING A BEHAVIOR-CHANGE STRATEGY

Once you have analyzed all the factors that influence what you do, you must decide which behavior-change technique will work best for you. These techniques include

35 shaping, visualization, modeling, controlling the situation, reinforcement, and changing self-talk.

Shaping.

Regardless of how motivated you are, some behaviors are almost impossible to change immediately. To reach your goal, you may need to take a number of individual steps, each designed to change one small piece of the larger behavior. This process is known as shaping.

40 For example, suppose that you have not exercised for a while. You decide that you want to get into shape, and your goal is to jog three to four miles every other day. So you start slowly and build up to your desired fitness level gradually.

Visualization.

Mental practice and rehearsal can help change unhealthy behaviors into healthy ones. Athletes and others use a technique known as imagined rehearsal to reach their goals.

45 By visualizing their planned action ahead of time, they are better prepared when they put themselves to the test.

For example, suppose you want to ask someone out on a date. Imagine the setting (walking together to class) for the action. Then practice exactly what you're going to say ("Minh, there's a great concert this Sunday and I was wondering if") in your mind and out

50 loud. Mentally anticipate different responses ("Oh, I'd love to, but I'm busy that evening") and what you will say in reaction ("How about if I call you sometime this week?"). Careful mental and verbal rehearsal—you could even try out your scenario on a friend—will greatly improve the likelihood of success.

Modeling.

Modeling, or learning behaviors through careful observation of other people, is one of
55 the most effective strategies for changing behavior. For example, suppose that you have
trouble talking to people you don't know very well. One of the easiest ways to improve
your communication skills is to select friends whose "gift of gab" you envy. Observe their
social skills. Do they talk more or listen more? How do people respond to them? Why are
they such good communicators?

Controlling the Situation.

60 Sometimes, the right setting or right group of people will positively influence your behaviors. Many situations and occasions trigger certain actions. The term **situational inducement**
refers to an attempt to influence a behavior by using situations and occasions to control it.

    For example, you may be more apt to stop smoking if you work in a smoke-free
office, a positive situational inducement. By carefully considering which settings will help
65 and which will hurt your effort to change, you will improve your chances for change.

Reinforcement.

A **positive reinforcement** is a reward that is given to increase the likelihood that a behavior change will occur. Each of us is motivated by different reinforcers. Although a special
T-shirt may be a positive reinforcer for young adults entering a race, it would not be for a
40-year-old runner who dislikes message-bearing T-shirts.

Changing Self-Talk

70 **Self-talk,** or the way you think and talk to yourself, can also play a role in modifying
health-related behaviors. Here are some cognitive procedures for changing self-talk.

    Rational-Emotive Therapy—This form of cognitive therapy or self-directed behav-
ior change is based on the premise that there is a close connection between what
people say to themselves and how they feel. According to psychologist Albert Ellis, most
75 emotional problems and related behaviors stem from irrational statements that people
make to themselves when events in their lives are different from what they would like
them to be.

    For example, suppose that after doing poorly on an exam, you say to yourself, "I can't
believe I flunked that easy exam. I'm so stupid." By changing this irrational, "catastrophic"
80 self-talk into rational, positive statements about what is really going on, you can increase
the likelihood that positive behaviors will occur. Positive self-talk might be phrased as follows: "I really didn't study enough for that exam, and I'm not surprised I didn't do very
well. I'm certainly not stupid. I just need to prepare better for the next test." Such self-talk
will help you to recover quickly from disappointment and take positive steps to correct
85 the situation.

A contestant on the popular NBC series, *The Biggest Loser*, posted a weight loss of 154 pounds. On this show, success is rewarded with public recognition and sometimes with product endorsements.

Meichenbaum's Self-Instructional Methods—Behavioral psychologist Donald Meichenbaum is perhaps best known for a process known as stress inoculation, which subjects clients to extreme stressors in a laboratory environment. Before a stressful event (e.g., going to the doctor), clients practice individual coping skills (e.g., deep breathing

90   exercises) and self-instruction (e.g., "I'll feel better once I know what's causing my pain"). Meichenbaum demonstrated that clients who practiced coping techniques and self-instruction were less likely to resort to negative behaviors in difficult situations. In Meichenbaum's behavioral therapies, clients are encouraged to give themselves "self-instructions" ("Slow down, don't rush") and "positive affirmations" ("My speech is going

95   fine—I'm almost done!") instead of self-defeating thoughts ("I'm talking too fast—my speech is terrible") whenever a situation seems to be getting out of control.

Blocking/Thought Stopping—By purposefully blocking or stopping negative thoughts, a person can concentrate on taking positive steps toward behavior change. For example, suppose you are preoccupied with your ex-partner, who has recently deserted

100   you for someone else. You consciously stop dwelling on the situation and force yourself to think about something more pleasant (e.g., dinner tomorrow with your best friend). By refusing to dwell on negative images and forcing yourself to focus elsewhere, you can save wasted energy, time, and emotional resources and move on to positive change.

(1,321 words)

—*Health: the Basics*, Fifth Edition,
by Rebecca J. Donatelle

STUDY OUTLINE

Use your annotations to make an outline of significant elements in behavior change.

THINKING AND WRITING AFTER READING

RECALL   Self-test your understanding.

Your instructor may choose to give you a true-false comprehension review.

REACT   Why are positive role models important for success? How has your behavior been affected by negative role models? Who has been a positive role model for you? _____

_____

REFLECT   Why are people reluctant to initiate behavior change? How do past experiences temper enthusiasm? _____

_____

THINK CRITICALLY   What behavior would you most like to change? Outline your plan for success.

THINK AND WRITE   Why do we engage in negative self-talk? How can negative self-talk be self-defeating and positive talk be uplifting? What does self-talk say about the power of language? How would you like to change your own self-talk?

_____

_____

_____

EXTENDED WRITING   Scholarly journal articles usually begin with an abstract. An abstract is a summary, usually one paragraph, that concisely presents the main point and supporting details. Researchers read the abstract to determine if the article contains information that fits their purpose. If so, they read the article carefully. If not, they move on to other articles. Use your outline of this selection to write a summary that could be used as an abstract for researchers.

Interpret THE QUOTE

Now that you have finished reading the selection, "Behavior Change," go back to the beginning of the selection and read the opening quote again. Do you agree that people's behavior is shaped by their goals, needs, and motives? On a separate sheet of paper, list five personal goals and, for each goal, explain how your behavior is related to it.

Name _____

Date _____

COMPREHENSION QUESTIONS

Answer the following with *a, b, c,* or *d,* or fill in the blank. In order to help you analyze your strengths and weaknesses, the question types are indicated.

Main Idea   _____   1. The best statement of the main idea of the selection is:

    a. Behavior change is the science of learning new, positive patterns to replace previous negative actions.
    b. Successful behavior change begins with precontemplation, and then other stages follow.
    c. Shaping, visualization, and modeling are the significant strategies for behavior change.
    d. Successful behavior change begins with adequate preparation and continues with a variety of strategies and techniques to gradually alter thoughts and actions.

Inference   2. What did Mark Twain mean by saying, "habit is habit, and not to be flung out the window by anyone, but coaxed downstairs a step at a time"? _____

_____

_____

Inference   _____   3. Establishing realistic goals, identifying rewards for milestones, and seeking support from friends is the stage of change labeled

    a. precontemplation.
    b. contemplation.
    c. preparation.
    d. termination.

Detail   _____   4. The strategy of learning behaviors through watching other people is called

    a. shaping.
    b. visualization.
    c. modeling.
    d. reinforcement.

Inference   _____   5. To achieve a weight loss goal, not making your usual weekly purchase of M & M's is an example of the behavior-changing strategy called

    a. shaping.
    b. modeling.
    c. controlling the situation.
    d. reinforcement.

Detail   _____   6. Rational-emotive therapy is based on the premise that

    a. feelings are manipulated by what we tell ourselves.
    b. coping techniques such as deep breathing can reduce stress.
    c. forcing yourself to focus elsewhere removes the negative thought.
    d. language is more powerful than thought.

Inference _____ 7. For a weight loss goal, replacing thoughts of chocolate candy with thoughts of the Friday night basketball game is an example of

    a. rational-emotive therapy.

    b. self-instruction.

    c. Meichenbaum's coping strategy.

    d. blocking.

Answer the following with *T* (true), *F* (false), or *CT* (can't tell).

Detail _____ 8. Prochaska and DiClimente believe that failure occurs when people start with the change itself.

Detail _____ 9. In Meichenbaum's self-instructional method, clients pretend to experience the dreaded event in order to practice coping skills.

Detail _____ 10. Visualization is the observation and imitation of positive behaviors of others.

VOCABULARY

Answer the following with *a*, *b*, *c*, or *d* for the word or phrase that best defines the boldface word used in the selection. The number in parentheses indicates the line of the passage in which the word appears.

_____ 1. "**coaxed** downstairs" (2)

    a. forced

    b. persuaded

    c. thrown

    d. scattered

_____ 2. "Despite this **acknowledgment**" (18)

    a. denial

    b. fulfillment

    c. opportunity

    d. admission

_____ 3. "people can **languish**" (19)

    a. pine away

    b. progress

    c. contemplate

    d. evolve

_____ 4. "requires **vigilance**" (27)

    a. courage

    b. watchfulness

    c. intelligence

    d. energy

_____ 5. "long-term **commitment**" (28)

    a. confidence

    b. frustration

    c. management

    d. obligation

_____ 6. "try out your **scenario**" (52)

    a. enactment

    b. dream

    c. argument

    d. sentences

_____ 7. "situational **inducement**" (61)

    a. stop

    b. error

    c. enticement

    d. replacement

_____ 8. "based on the **premise**" (73)

    a. hope

    b. feeling

    c. idea

    d. emotion

_____ 9. "**irrational** statements" (75)

    a. illogical

    b. angry

    c. hateful

    d. threatening

_____ 10. "**resort to** negative behaviors" (92)

    a. escape through

    b. go back to

    c. hide under

    d. yearn for

Your instructor may choose to give a true-false vocabulary review.

VOCABULARY ENRICHMENT

A. **Context Clues:** Select the word from the list that best completes the sentences.

coaxed	acknowledgment	languish	vigilance	commitment
scenario	inducement	premise	irrational	resort

1. Without becoming a "warrior against pleasure," you do not want to silently watch a friend _____ to undesired behaviors.

2. Money can be a strong and effective _____ to motivate behavior changes.

3. Denial can cause people to _____ in a state of indecision and fail to embrace change.

4. Entering the termination stage is an _____ that maintenance has been successful.

5. During the contemplation stage of change, a gentle nudge from a friend may have _____ the contemplator to get started.

6. Emotive therapy or self-talk can calm the nerves and help prevent _____ behavior.

7. Without proper _____, a dieter can slip back into old habits of snacking and not exercising.

8. Significant others can assist a loved one in making a _____ to lasting change.

9. If you accept the _____ that positive reinforcements promote change, seek to individualize incentives for maximum motivation.

10. Write a _____ in which you are tempted to revert to your old bad habits, but instead you skillfully conquer the demons.

B. **Thesaurus:** Use a thesaurus, either the computer or book version, to find four alternative words for each of the following:

1. indication _____

2. habit _____

3. beginning _____

4. agreement _____

5. respect _____

ASSESS YOUR LEARNING

Review confusing questions, seek clarification, and make notes in your text to help you remember new information and vocabulary.

"A hero is an ordinary individual who finds the strength to persevere and endure in spite of overwhelming obstacles."

—Christopher Reeve

The Holocaust created by Nazi desires for power during the 1930s and 40s resulted in the deaths of an estimated 11–17 million non-military people—6 million Jews (two-thirds of the population of European Jews), plus Romani, gay, and disabled people, Jehovah's Witnesses, prisoners of war, and Polish and Soviet civilians. Much has been written about the horrors of that time, yet even today stories of the heroes who risked their own lives to save others are surfacing to give inspiration and hope. Some of those heroes have been reluctant to talk about their experiences, but some are now sharing their stories, encouraged by the next generations of their families and families of those they saved. Perhaps their accounts can lend courage to future heroes.

THINKING BEFORE READING

Preview the selection for content and organizational clues. Activate your schema and anticipate what you will learn.

What do you know about the Holocaust? Where did it occur? Why?

Do you know anyone who is a Holocaust survivor, or have you seen stories about Holocaust survivors?

Do you think you would take action to save innocent people you thought were threatened with death?

I'll read this to find out _____

_____.

VOCABULARY PREVIEW

Are you familiar with these words?

oblivious	anti-Semitism	gentile	disparaged	distraught
succumbed	daunting	sentimental	trivial	solace

Are individuals still *oblivious* to the inhumane treatment of large groups of people?

Have you ever *succumbed* to a desire to do something you knew was not the best course of action?

What gives you *solace* when you are sad?

Your instructor may choose to give a true-false vocabulary review before or after reading.

THINKING DURING READING

As you read, use the six thinking strategies of a good reader: predict, picture, relate, monitor, correct, and annotate.

ANNOTATING AND TAKING NOTES

Annotate as you read, and then make Cornell notes to track the events described in this personal narrative.

FINDING A HERO AMID FADING MEMORIES

Refer to the
Reader's **TIP**
for **History** on
page 162

It's been nearly 70 years since my mother and her sisters climbed aboard a train and left their small village in what was then Czechoslovakia. No wonder their memories have faded.

"I remember very well how we had to feed the geese," my mother says.

"Our maid actually used to feed the geese," says Josi, her sister.

5 "And laundry . . . it was taken to the river to be rinsed," my mother recalls.

"I don't remember ever anybody taking things to the river," Josi objects.

And so it goes.

My mother is 83. Aunt Josi was the eldest of the three—she just turned 85. When we gathered in London recently for her birthday party, I had a rare opportunity to ask the two

10 sisters, side by side, about their memories. (Elli, the youngest, died of cancer some years ago.) Despite the conflicts, both sisters agree that theirs was a happy childhood:

"In the winter we skated on the river and we skied and sledded," my mother says. "In the summertime, we went to the woods and picked berries, and it was a very beautiful life."

15 Josi, Alice and Elli were born in Trstena, a village in a mountainous region near the Polish border. The three girls left home on June 29, 1939, on a special train—a *kindertransport*—arranged to protect children from the advancing Nazis. They were taken to London, where my aunts Josi and Elli stayed. (My mother later ventured to the U.S., and settled in Washington, D.C.)

20 My mother's family was quite religious—though of course the sisters disagree about exactly to what extent. There weren't many Jews in Trstena, they say. My mother was the only Jewish child in her class, and she felt self-conscious as the Catholic students recited daily prayers. But she and Josi say they were mostly oblivious to anti-Semitism.

They played with gentile friends, though my aunt says some of their parents told dark

25 tales. "Horrific stories of what the Jews did—killed a child at Passover, drank the blood and—such horrible things! It showed later, when the Nazis came around. Our great friends . . . turned against all of us."

Even as the Nazis drew near, the children still were not really aware of the threat. But their parents had been warned. My mother's uncle worked for one of the grand spas in

30 what is now Slovakia, and the company posted him to Berlin. He saw firsthand what was happening, and he warned his sister to get the children out of the country.

"My mother started to sew and prepare all the clothes for us," my mother remembers. "She just sat at that sewing machine and sewed and sewed." My mother still has her flowered orange dress, an embroidered nightgown and a pair of pajamas with the letter A (for

35 Alice) on the breast pocket.

SELECTION 2

When the day of departure arrived, my aunt says the tension was obvious. "In the bedroom, our father was sitting on the edge of the bed and he was crying. And I [had] never seen him cry before," Josi says.

Most of the villagers had disparaged the idea of sending the children away. But my
40 grandparents took their girls to Bratislava and put them on the train. Josi was about to turn 16, my mother was 14 and Elli, the youngest, was 10. My grandmother, naturally, was distraught.

"We kept on saying, 'Take Elli off the train,'" my mother recalls. "We said, 'Keep her! Keep her!'"And her conflicted mother almost succumbed—taking the tiny girl off the
45 train—before finally putting her back on—the last time my grandmother would ever see her daughters.

The train was there only because of a young British stockbroker named Nicholas Winton. Just 29 at the time, he'd been planning to go on a ski trip to Switzerland when a friend asked him to come to Prague instead to help refugees fleeing Hitler's advancing army.
50 Winton went and became alarmed about the fate of Jewish children if the Nazis invaded— as he knew they would. He set to work organizing the *kindertransport* and ultimately saved more than 650 children, including my mother and her sisters.

Nicholas Winton.

In the decades that have passed since then, many of those who were rescued have grown old and died. But Winton is still alive. At 99, he lives on his own in a snug house
55 with a lush garden near Maidenhead, west of London. His living room is filled with photographs of himself with prominent figures, including Prince Charles and President Clinton. Winton has given up needlepoint in the past couple of years, but he still enjoys bridge. And he gets around—his driving permit is valid until he's 101.

Winton is Sir Nicholas now; he was knighted in 2002. As we settle in his living room, I ask
60 Sir Nicholas what made him undertake a project as daunting as resettling unaccompanied children in a foreign country.

"Nobody had tried to do anything for the children because everybody had said, 'No country is going to allow children in without their parents,' " he says. "But nobody had tried."

65 Winton says the first challenge was finding countries willing to help. "America was the one hope I had of taking a lot, and they didn't take any," he remembers.

England opened its doors as long as Winton and fellow volunteers could find guardians for each child. Hundreds were rescued, though Winton didn't get to know them—not for 50 years. It wasn't until 1988 that Winton had his first encounter with some of those
70 whom he had saved. The setting was a British television program called *That's Life.* The host displayed a scrapbook that lists the names of the rescued children, and she pointed to the woman seated beside Winton.

"Vera Gissing is here with us tonight and I should tell you that you are actually sitting next to Nicholas Winton," she said.

75 The woman beside Winton embraced him; he wiped away a tear. The host asked, "Is there anyone in our audience tonight who owes their life to Nicholas Winton? If so, could you stand up, please?"

The entire audience rose. Just behind Winton stood my aunts, Elli and Josi. "He got up and he looked around absolutely—absolutely—amazed," Josi says.

80 When I ask Winton about this deeply moving moment, he declines to be sentimental. To some degree, Winton feels that too much has been made of his efforts. What seemed to him like a brief interlude in his life has overshadowed everything else. And Winton feels his story has been exaggerated in the retelling. Maybe that's because people so desperately need heroes.

"It's nothing I can do about it—what you and the press make of it. And all this is
85 something quite outside my life," he says.

For example, one often-repeated aspect of the story is that Winton was so modest that he never told anyone of his work on the *kindertransport*—that it only came to light when his wife discovered a cache of papers in the attic. But Winton says he did try to interest several institutions in his papers and finally gave up.

90   That aspect of the story may seem trivial, but it seems to trouble Winton.

"It becomes very difficult at times," he says, "because every time the newspapers say anything, they add a little bit of their own. It makes me completely disbelieve in history." But he's philosophical. "*Si non e vero, e ben travato,* as Mother used to say," he says with a chuckle. "If it's not true, it's a damn good story."

95   Winton's saga has become as hazy in some details as have the memories that my mother and her sister have of their childhood. But one thing is clear to me. If it weren't for this man, none of us would be here—not my mother, not my daughter, not me.

Pointing to my mother, I say, "She's a child, and I'm a grandchild." Then, pointing to my 10-year-old daughter, I add, "And that's your great-grandchild."

100   "Yes, I know," he replies.

In fact, with his contemporaries gone, Winton says he draws solace from his Czech children. As for my mother and my aunt, they take comfort in the fact that their parents knew they had saved their children as they were deported to a concentration camp in 1942.

"I'm sure when they were taken away, they must have thought what a great thing 105 they did to part . . . with the children, and save their lives," Josi says.

That seems clear as my mother reads from the last letter she received from her father.

"I am happy you are over there because for us it is not good any more," he wrote. "We will come through and you mustn't worry about us. But I am very happy that you are not here. If you were, I would have many more worries. God keep you well and I always 110 pray that in the next new year, we should be happier."

We don't know exactly where or how my grandparents died—that knowledge is lost forever. Only a drop in the ocean of losses—of family and memory and stories from that era.

(1,537 words)

—By Kim Masters, October 11, 2008. Story
broadcast on "Weekend Edition Saturday,"
National Public Radio.

Note: Nicholas Winton celebrated his 102nd birthday on May 19, 2011.

THINKING AND WRITING AFTER READING

RECALL Self-test your understanding.

Your instructor may choose to give you a true-false comprehension review.

REACT What emotions did you experience as you read this account?

REFLECT What were the reasons and personal qualities that caused Winton to try to do something to save Jewish children?

THINKING CRITICALLY   Do you think Winton would have eventually taken action to save these children if his friend hadn't persuaded him to cancel the ski trip? Is acting heroically partly due to simply being in a certain place at a certain time?

THINK AND WRITE   What qualities and conditions make someone heroic? Make a list and include examples of people you consider to be heroes.

EXTENDED WRITING   Do an Internet search to find stories about "Holocaust rescuers." Select one person who especially interests you. In one paragraph, write a brief account of the person's story, and in a second paragraph, write your thoughts and reactions. Be sure to include the URL of the source of your information and the date you retrieved it.

Interpret THE QUOTE

Go back to the beginning of the selection and read the opening quote again. Do you agree with Christopher Reeve that heroes are just like everyone else and that all that it takes is persistence? Explain your opinions on a separate sheet of paper.

Name _____

Date _____

SELECTION 2

COMPREHENSION QUESTIONS

Answer the following with *a, b, c,* or *d,* or fill in the blank. In order to help you analyze your strengths and weaknesses, the question types are indicated.

Main Idea _____ 1. Which statement best expresses the author's main point?

    a. Kim Masters' mother was one of the children rescued by Nicholas Winton.

    b. The Holocaust was a horror that we should never allow to be repeated.

    c. Nicholas Winton's bravery was featured on a British TV show called "That's Life."

    d. Nicholas Winton is a hero who rescued hundreds of Jewish children from the Holocaust, including the author's mother and two aunts.

Detail _____ 2. The *kindertransport* was _____.

    a. a special train to carry children

    b. a bus used to take children to safety

    c. a special school for Jewish children

    d. a method for transporting skiers up the slopes

Detail _____ 3. Which is NOT a true statement about the three sisters?

    a. Josi was the oldest

    b. Elli was the youngest.

    c. All three sisters settled permanently in England.

    d. Alice is the author's mother.

Inference _____ 4. Based on the sisters' recollections, it is reasonable to infer that____.

    a. very few of the people living in Trstena were devoutly religious.

    b. the majority of Trstena residents in 1939 were Catholic.

    c. the girls had an unhappy childhood before the Nazis came.

    d. the girls had very few friends as young children.

Main Idea _____ 5. Which of the following best describes the topic of this article?

    a. Nicholas Winton's rescue of Jewish children in the late 1930s

    b. The author's mother and her childhood home

    c. The Nazis' arrival in Czechoslovakia

    d. The Holocaust

Detail _____ 6. The first challenge Winton faced in getting the children out safely was _____.

    a. selecting the children who would be transported.

    b. convincing the parents to send their children away.

    c. securing the money to transport the children.

    d. finding countries who would receive the children.

Inference _____ 7. The details suggest that _____.

    a. the author's grandparents survived the concentration camp and died of natural causes.

    b. Winton received funding from organizations in the United States.

    c. Winton was not well-educated nor financially well off as a young man.

    d. the author's grandparents perished in a Nazi concentration camp.

Inference _____ 8. The author's grandparents were able to communicate with the children for a few years after they were taken from home.

Inference _____ 9. The audience attending the television show honoring Winton consisted entirely of the children Winton saved and their descendants.

Inference _____ 10. Winton thinks of the children he saved and their families as his own.

VOCABULARY

Answer the following with *a, b, c,* or *d* for the word or phrase that best defines the boldface word used in the selection. The number in parentheses indicates the line of the passage in which the word appears. In addition to the context clues, use a dictionary to more precisely define the technical terms.

_____ 1. "**oblivious** to anti-Semitism" (23)

    a. uncaring
    b. unaware
    c. hateful
    d. knowledgeable

_____ 2. "oblivious to **anti-Semitism**" (23)

    a. showing favoritism to Jews
    b. opposed to religion
    c. religious practices
    d. against Jews

_____ 3. "with **gentile** friends" (24)

    a. non Jewish
    b. Jewish
    c. neighborhood
    d. kind

_____ 4. "**disparaged** the idea" (39)

    a. approved
    b. preferred
    c. discredited
    d. liked

_____ 6. "mother almost **succumbed!**" (44)

    a. gave in
    b. fell
    c. cried
    d. laughed

_____ 7. "project as **daunting**" (60)

    a. expensive
    b. dangerous
    c. fearfully difficult
    d. worthwhile

_____ 8. "declines to be **sentimental**" (80)

    a. emotional
    b. angry
    c. bitter
    d. happy

_____ 9. "may seem **trivial**" (90)

    a. crucial
    b. sad
    c. unfortunate
    d. unimportant

_____ 5. "was **distraught**" (42)
   a. proud
   b. deeply upset
   c. distrustful
   d. relieved

_____ 10. "he draws **solace** from" (101)
   a. income
   b. pride
   c. comfort
   d. misfortune

Your instructor may choose to give a true-false vocabulary review.

VOCABULARY ENRICHMENT

A. Study the following definitions and then circle the similar-sounding word that is correct in each sentence.

conscience: sense of right and wrong	**fair:** just or right
conscious: aware	**fare:** fee for transportation

1. Heroes are often made when people act out of (conscience, conscious) in spite of the dangers they might face.

2. Nicholas Winton feels that the attention given to his role in the *kindertransport* is not quite (fair, fare) because it gives too much credit to just one phase of his life.

B. **Analogies:** Supply a word that completes each analogy, then state the relationship that has been established.

3. *Knife* is to *cut* as *gun* is to _____

   Relationship? _____

4. *Old* is to *ancient* as *new* is to _____

   Relationship? _____

5. *Eye* is to *see* as *ear* is to _____

   Relationship? _____

6. *Go* is to *come* as *sell* is to _____

   Relationship? _____

7. *State* is to *governor* as *city* is to _____

   Relationship? _____

8. *Skin* is to *person* as *fur* is to _____

   Relationship? _____

9. *Smart* is to *intelligent* as *chilly* is to _____

   Relationship? _____

10. *Razor* is to *sharp* as *cement* is to _____

    Relationship? _____

11. *Winter* is to *summer* as *wet* is to _____

    Relationship? _____

C. **Words from Literature:** The names of certain characters in literature have dropped their capital letters and taken on special meaning in the English language. The following are from Spanish and English literature, respectively. Read the entries to determine their definitions and origins.

quix·ot·ic \kwik-'sä-tik\ *adj* [Don *Quixote*] (1718) **1 :** foolishly impractical esp. in the pursuit of ideals; *esp* **:** marked by rash lofty romantic ideas or extravagantly chivalrous action **2 :** CAPRICIOUS, UNPREDICTABLE   *syn* see IMAGINARY — **quix·ot·i·cal** \-ti-kəl\ *adj* — **quix·ot·i·cal·ly** \-ti-k(ə-)lē\ *adv*

Source: By permission. From *Merriam-Webster's Collegiate*® *Dictionary, 11th Edition.* © 2011 by Merriam-Webster Incorporated (www.Merriam-Webster.com).

12. *Quixotic* means _____.

13. The origin of the word is _____.

Lil·li·put \'li-li-(ˌ)pət\ *n* (1726) **:** an island in Swift's *Gulliver's Travels* where the inhabitants are six inches tall
Lil·li·pu·tian \ˌli-lə-'pyü-shən\ *adj* (1726) **1 :** of, relating to, or characteristic of the Lilliputians or the island of Lilliput **2** *often not cap* **a** **:** SMALL, MINIATURE ⟨a ∼ camera⟩ **b :** PETTY
Lilliputian *n* (1726) **1 :** an inhabitant of Lilliput **2** *often not cap* **:** one resembling a Lilliputian; *esp* **:** an undersized individual

Source: By permission. From *Merriam-Webster's Collegiate*® *Dictionary, 11th Edition.* © 2011 by Merriam-Webster Incorporated (www.Merriam-Webster.com).

14. *Lilliputian* means _____.

15. The origin of the word is _____.

ASSESS YOUR LEARNING

Review confusing questions, seek clarification, and make notes in your text to help you remember new information and vocabulary.

SELECTION 3 Communication

> "An eye can threaten like a loaded and leveled gun, or it can insult like hissing or kicking; or, in its altered mood, by beams of kindness, it can make the heart dance for joy."
> —Ralph Waldo Emerson

We draw conclusions about people through what their eyes communicate. A lifted eyebrow suggests surprise, and a narrowed gaze hints at skepticism. We say "Look me straight in the eye" to search for truth. On the other hand, a furtive glance arouses suspicion. To both lubricate and protect the eyes, we normally blink an average of fifteen times a minute, but excessive blinking can cause us to question sincerity. The eyes have been called the "mirrors of the soul." How accurate are we in reading the eyes?

THINKING BEFORE READING

Preview for content and organizational clues. Activate your schema and anticipate what you will learn.

Why does the expression "The couple locked eyes" suggest romance?

When speaking to a group, do you make eye contact with each member of the audience?

When do your pupils become dilated?

After reading this I will probably know _____.

VOCABULARY PREVIEW

Are you familiar with these words?

duration	gaze	perceive	compensate	avert
auditory	intuitive	dilated	constricted	profound

Why do you want to be *compensated* for your hard work?

How is *intuitive* related to *intuition*?

Is a *profound* statement worthy of remembering?

Your instructor may choose to give a true-false vocabulary review before or after reading.

THINKING DURING READING

As you read, use the six thinking strategies of a good reader: predict, picture, relate, monitor, correct, and annotate.

MAPPING

Annotate the selection and then use mapping to create notes to prepare for an essay exam.

Reader's TIP   Reading and Studying Communication

Ask yourself the following questions as you read a communications text.

- How can I improve as a communicator and a conversationalist?
- How do I react to other people? Am I open to new ideas?
- How can I become a more valuable group member or a more productive group leader?
- Am I afraid to speak in public? How can I lessen that fear?
- What actions and expressions should be avoided in opening and closing a speech?

EYE COMMUNICATION

Scan this QR code to hear this reading.

The messages communicated by the eyes vary depending on the duration, direction, and quality of the eye behavior. For example, in every culture there are rather strict, though unstated, rules for the proper duration for eye contact. In much of England and the United States, for example, the average length of gaze is 2.95 seconds. The
5 average length of mutual gaze (two persons gazing at each other) is 1.18 seconds. When eye contact falls short of this amount, you may think the person is uninterested, shy, or preoccupied. When the appropriate amount of time is exceeded, you may perceive this as showing high interest.

10   In much of the United States direct eye contact is considered an expression of honesty and forthrightness. But the Japanese often view this as a lack of respect. The Japanese will glance at the other person's face rarely and then only for very short periods. In many Hispanic cultures, direct eye contact signifies a certain equality and so should be avoided by, say, children when speaking to a person in authority. Try visualizing the potential mis-understandings that eye communication alone could create when people from Tokyo, San

15   Francisco, and San Juan try to communicate.

    The direction of the eye also communicates. Generally, in communicating with an-other person, you would glance alternatively at the other person's face, then away, then again at the face, and so on. When these directional rules are broken, different mean-ings are communicated—abnormally high or low interest, self-consciousness, nervousness

20   over the interaction, and so on. The quality—how wide or how narrow your eyes get dur-ing interaction—also communicates meaning, especially interest level and such emotions as surprise, fear, and disgust.

EYE CONTACT

You use eye contact to serve several important functions. You can use eye contact to *monitor feedback.* For example, when you talk with someone, you look at the person

25   intently, as if to say, "Well, what do you think?" or "React to what I've just said." You also look at speakers to let them know that you're listening. Studies show that listeners gaze at speakers more than speakers gaze at listeners. The percentage of interaction time spent gazing while listening, for example, ranges from 62 percent to 75 percent; the percent-age of time spent gazing while talking, however, ranges from 38 percent to 41 percent.

30   When these percentages are reversed—when a speaker gazes at the listener for longer than "normal" periods or when a listener gazes at the speaker for shorter than "normal" periods—the conversational interaction becomes awkward. You may wish to try this with a friend. Even with mutual awareness, you'll notice the discomfort caused by this seem-ingly minor communication change.

35   When you speak with two or three other people, you maintain eye contact to *secure the attention and interest* of your listeners. When someone fails to pay attention you will increase attention. When making an especially important point, you would look intently at your listeners—assuming what nonverbal researchers call "visual dominance behavior"— almost as a way of preventing them from devoting any attention to anything but what

40   you're saying.

    Eye communication can also *regulate or control the conversation.* For example, with eye movements you can inform the other person that the channel of communication is open and that she or he should now speak. A clear example of this occurs in the col-lege classroom, where the instructor asks a question and then locks eyes with a student.

45 Without any verbal message, it's assumed that the student should answer the question. Similarly, when you're nearing the end of what you want to say, you'll probably focus eye contact on the person you think wants to speak next and then turn over the conversation to that person.

Eye communication also helps *signal the nature of the relationship* between two
50 people—for example, one of positive or negative regard. In the United States when you like someone, you increase your eye contact. When eye contact exceeds 60 percent in an interaction, the people are probably more interested in each other than in the verbal messages being exchanged.

Eye contact in the higher primates is often used to *signal status and aggression.*
55 Among many younger people, prolonged eye contact from a stranger is taken to signify aggressiveness and has frequently prompted physical violence, just because one person looked perhaps a little longer than is considered normal in that specific culture. A less extreme way to assert one's position is with visual dominance behavior. The average person maintains a higher level of eye contact while listening and a lower level while speaking.
60 When people want to signal dominance, they may reverse this pattern and maintain a high level of eye contact while talking but a much lower level while listening. Another way people try to signal dominance is to lower their eyebrows. Research does support this general interpretation of behavior. For example, faces with lowered eyebrows, in both cartoons and photographs, were judged to communicate greater dominance than raised
65 eyebrows. Eye movements may also signal whether the relationship between two people is amorous, hostile, or indifferent.

Eye movements are often used to *compensate for increased physical distance.* By making eye contact, we overcome psychologically the physical distance between us. When we catch someone's eye at a party, for example, we become psychologically close even
70 though we may be separated by considerable physical distance. Eye contact and other expressions of psychological closeness, such as self-disclosure and intimacy, have been found to vary in proportion to each other.

EYE AVOIDANCE

The eyes, sociologist Erving Goffman observed in *Interaction Ritual* (1967), are "great intruders." When you avoid eye contact or avert your glance, you allow others to maintain
75 their privacy. You probably do this when you see a couple arguing in the street or on a bus. You turn your eyes away as if to say, "I don't mean to intrude; I respect your privacy." Goffman refers to this behavior as **civil inattention**.

Eye avoidance can also signal lack of interest—in a person, a conversation, or some visual stimulus. At times, like the ostrich, we hide our eyes to try to cut off unpleasant
80 stimuli. Notice, for example, how quickly people close their eyes in the face of some

extreme unpleasantness. Interestingly enough, even if the unpleasantness is auditory, we tend to shut it out by closing our eyes. At other times, we close our eyes to block out visual stimuli and thus heighten our other senses; for example we often listen to music with our eyes closed. Lovers often close their eyes while kissing, and many people prefer to make
85 love in a dark or dimly lit room.

PUPIL DILATION

In the fifteenth and sixteenth centuries, Italian women used to put drops of belladonna (which literally means "beautiful woman") into their eyes to enlarge the pupils so that they would look more attractive. Contemporary research supports the intuitive logic of these women; dilated pupils are in fact judged more attractive than constricted ones.

90   In one study, photographs of women were retouched. In one set of photographs, the pupils were enlarged, and in the other they were made smaller. Men were then asked to judge the women's personalities from the photographs. The photos of women with small pupils drew responses such as cold, hard, and selfish; those with dilated pupils drew responses such as feminine and soft. However, the male observers could not verbalize the
95 reasons for the different perceptions. **Pupil dilation** and reactions to changes in the pupil size of others both seem to function below the level of conscious awareness.

Pupil size also reveals your interest and level of emotional arousal. Your pupils enlarge when you're interested in something or when you're emotionally aroused. When homosexuals and heterosexuals were shown pictures of nude bodies, the homosexuals' pupils
100 dilated more when viewing same-sex bodies. These papillary responses are unconscious and are even observed in persons with profound mental retardation. Perhaps we judge dilated pupils more attractive because we judge them as indicative of a person's interest in us. That may be why models, Beanie Babies, and Teletubbies have exceptionally large pupils.

105   Although belladonna is no longer used, the cosmetics industry has made millions selling eye enhancers—eye shadow, eyeliner, false eyelashes, and tinted contact lenses that change eye color. These items function (ideally, at least) to draw attention to these most powerful communicators.

(1,394 words)

—From Joseph A. DeVito, *The Interpersonal Communication Book,* 12th edition. Published by Allyn and Bacon/Merrill Education, Boston, MA. Copyright © 2009 by Pearson Education. Adapted by permission of the publisher.

STUDY NOTES

Use your annotations to make a map of significant elements in behavior change.

THINKING AND WRITING AFTER READING

RECALL Self-test your understanding.

Your instructor may choose to give you a true-false comprehension review.

REACT Why do you feel uncomfortable when locked in a mutual gaze for more than 1.18 seconds? _____

_____

REFLECT Try the suggested experiment of adjusting the percentage of interaction time for gazing. With another student, first let the speaker gaze for 62 to 75 percent of the time, and then have the speaker gaze for only 38 to 41 percent of the time. Next, try the same percentages for the listener. Describe the difficulties and your reactions. _____

_____

THINK CRITICALLY How do college instructors use eye contact to enhance instruction? Give examples of a variety of effective strategies that you have observed. _____

_____

THINK AND WRITE Why do you agree or disagree that the eyes are the "mirrors to the soul"? Give examples of when you feel you have been both correct and incorrect in "reading the eyes." _____

_____

_____

EXTENDED WRITING College professors often ask essay questions on tests. They expect clear, concise answers that demonstrate knowledge of the topic and directly answer the question. Successful students predict possible essay questions and practice answering them. If you have not done so already, create a map that illustrates the main points and key details of this selection. Use your map notes to write an answer to the following question that might be asked on an essay test:

> *In one paragraph, describe at least four of the six functions of eye contact that are explained in "Eye Communication." Include an example in your description of each function.*

Interpret THE QUOTE

Now that you have finished reading the selection, "Eye Communication," go back to the beginning of the selection and read the opening quote again. On a separate sheet of paper, describe what Emerson means when he says that an eye can "threaten like a loaded and leveled gun." Also, describe two situations in which you used your eyes to communicate joy or anger.

Name _____

Date _____

SELECTION 3

COMPREHENSION QUESTIONS

Answer the following with *a, b, c,* or *d,* or fill in the blank. In order to help you analyze your strengths and weaknesses, the question types are indicated.

Main Idea   _____   1. The best statement of the main idea of the selection is:

a. Eye contact in different cultures varies according to duration, direction, and quality.
b. Eye contact communicates several different messages that vary according to duration, direction, and quality.
c. When the rules are broken for eye contact, the messages can range from self-consciousness to fear and disgust.
d. The appropriateness of eye contact can be measured in the length of seconds of duration and the percentage of time gazing while listening.

Detail   _____   2. Direct eye contact is considered a sign of equality in

a. Japan.
b. England.
c. the United States.
d. Latin America.

Detail   _____   3. For a speaker to be considered within the "normal" range, an appropriate percentage of time spent gazing while talking is

a. 39 percent.
b. 45 percent.
c. 62 percent.
d. 75 percent.

Inference   _____   4. The author suggests that in the United States a short duration of eye contact will most likely be interpreted as

a. aggression.
b. status for the speaker.
c. love interest.
d. inattention.

Inference   5. In what cases might civil inattention be inappropriate? _____

_____

_____

Detail   _____   6. Belladonna was all of the following *except*

a. eye drops used by Italian women.
b. a fifteenth- and sixteenth-century beauty enhancer.
c. eye medication with beautifying side effects.
d. an Italian word meaning "beautiful woman."

Detail _____ 7. According to research findings discussed in the passage, the general viewer's pupil dilation reactions when viewing pictures of nude bodies were all of the following *except*

    a. varying in emotional arousal for different groups.
    b. emotionally arousing for homosexuals viewing same-sex pictures.
    c. emotionally arousing for heterosexuals viewing same-sex pictures.
    d. made without conscious awareness.

Answer the following with *T* (true), *F* (false), or *CT* (can't tell).

Detail _____ 8. In referring to the quality of eye communication, the author is describing how wide or narrow the eyes are during interaction.

Detail _____ 9. The eyes can silently be used by a speaker to indicate the next to speak.

Detail _____ 10. A high level of eye contact by the listener shows a lack of status for the speaker.

SELECTION
3

VOCABULARY

Answer the following with *a, b, c,* or *d* for the word or phrase that best defines the boldface word as used in the selection. The number in parentheses indicates the line of the passage in which the word appears.

_____ 1. "depending on the **duration**" (1)

    a. strength
    b. length
    c. ability
    d. meaning

_____ 2. "length of **gaze**" (4)

    a. look
    b. clarity
    c. direction
    d. quality

_____ 3. "may **perceive** this" (7)

    a. deny
    b. dismiss
    c. object to
    d. recognize

_____ 4. "used to **compensate** for" (67)

    a. calculate
    b. make up
    c. detract
    d. vary

_____ 5. "**avert** your glance" (74)

    a. turn toward
    b. intensify
    c. extend
    d. turn away

_____ 6. "unpleasantness is **auditory**" (81)

    a. seen
    b. imagined
    c. heard
    d. real

_____ 7. "**intuitive** logic" (88)

    a. instinctive
    b. ancient
    c. stylish
    d. historic

_____ 8. "**dilated** pupils" (89)

    a. colored
    b. narrowed
    c. enlarged
    d. painted

_____ 9. "**constricted** ones" (89)

    a. narrowed
    b. enlarged
    c. closed
    d. unadorned

_____ 10. "**profound** mental retardation" (101)

    a. slight
    b. deep
    c. recent
    d. confusing

Your instructor may choose to give a true-false vocabulary review.

VOCABULARY ENRICHMENT

A. Use context clues and word parts to determine the meaning of the boldface words from a popular communications textbook.

1. When speaking, avoid **adaptors,** such as scratching your face while speaking, that interfere with effective communication. _____ _____

2. Be specific and use examples to clarify points so that your audience is not confused by **ambiguity**. _____

3. Express **empathy** as a listener by actively involving your face to reflect the feelings that you think the speaker is experiencing. _____ _____

4. Use a **euphemism** when appropriate. Rather than saying "I am sorry your father died," say "I am sorry he passed away." _____ _____

5. In using a **feedforward** to alert your listener, be brief and always follow through on what you promised. _____ _____

6. In an interpersonal conflict, stick to the specific topic and avoid **gunnysacking** previous grievances. _____ _____

7. In analyzing the supplied information, the speaker solved the problem by **deduction**. _____

8. In a conversation, be sensitive to the **leave-taking cues** of others and politely end the exchange. _____ _____

9. **Emphatic communication**—"Hello," "How are you?" and "I'm fine"—is traditional in American culture. _____ _____

10. Those who study **proxemics** in foreign countries find variations in the accepted distances for personal interaction and even the organization of space in homes and offices. _____ _____

B. **Analogies:** Supply a word that completes each analogy, then state the relationship that has been established.

11. *Music* is to *piano* as *explosion* is to _____

    Relationship? _____

12. *Whale* is to *mammal* as *ant* is to _____

    Relationship? _____

13. *Bones* are to *leg* as *freckles* are to _____

    Relationship? _____

14. *Attract* is to *repel* as *pretty* is to _____

    Relationship? _____

15. *Tiger* is to *meat* as *cow* is to _____

    Relationship? _____

SELECTION 3

ASSESS YOUR LEARNING

Review confusing questions, seek clarification, and make notes in your text to help you remember new information and vocabulary.

PERSONAL FEEDBACK 2   Name _____

1. List three questions that you have asked in any of your classes during the past two

   weeks. _____

   _____

   _____

2. What routine do you usually follow at night to get ready for the next day at school?

   _____

   _____

3. What has pleasantly surprised you about your college experience? _____

   _____

   _____

4. How did you waste time this past week? _____

   _____

   _____

Tear out and submit to your instructor.

VOCABULARY LESSON

See, Hear, and Voice Your Concerns

Study the roots, words, and sentences.

Roots	Vis, vid: see	aud, aus: hear or listen	voc, vok: voice or call

Words with **vis** or **vid** = **see**

What did Julius Caesar mean by, "Veni, *vidi*, vici,"? Can *invisible* ink be seen?

- Visible: can be seen

  On clear nights, stars are more *visible* in the countryside than in cities.

- Visionary: one who sees visions or dreams of the future

  Be both a *visionary* and a good businessperson to create a successful company.

- Visor: a brim to protect the eyes so you can see better

  Wear a *visor* for tennis so the sun doesn't interfere with your performance.

- Evident: can easily be seen

  The solution was *evident* to those who had previously encountered the problem.

- Visa: a passport endorsement giving the bearer the right to enter a country

  Prior to visiting certain countries, tourists must apply for a *visa*.

- Vista: a view from a distance

  The *vista* from a mountaintop on an autumn day can be breathtaking.

- Envision: to see in one's mind

  Try to *envision* the furniture in the empty room.

Words with **aud** or **aus** = **hear** or **listen**

Does an *audience* sit in an *auditorium*? Can *inaudible* words be heard?

- Audible: can be heard

  Because she speaks so softly, her voice is barely *audible*.

- Audition: a hearing to try out for a role

  The actor nervously began the *audition* for a part in the Broadway musical.

- Audio: sound made by electronic or mechanical reproduction

  The *audio* on my television is not clear.

- Auditory: relating to hearing

  The *auditory* nerves are damaged and thus hearing is impaired.

- Audit: a formal examination of accounts made by an accountant

  Citizens fear an *audit* by the Internal Revenue Service.

Words with *voc* or *vok* = *voice* or *call*

How can you *voice* your ideas on *vocabulary*? Are *vocal* people heard?

- Evoke: call out from the past

  The ceremony was designed to *evoke* the memory of past heroes.

- Vocation: a call to serve in a particular profession

  Although my plans may change, I am preparing for a *vocation* in nursing.

- Vociferous: making a noisy outcry

  The opponent's remarks drew *vociferous* objections.

- Avocation: a hobby or second calling

  My money comes from banking, but music is my *avocation*.

- Convocation: an assembly or calling together

  The *convocation* celebrated the 75th anniversary of the college.

- Invocation: solemn prayer or divine blessing

  The religious service began with an *invocation*.

- Invoke: to call forth

  The witness *invoked* the Fifth Amendment to avoid answering questions.

Review

Part I

Choose the best word from the list to complete each of the following sentences.

invocation	audience	vocation	vista	visor
vocal	convocation	audit	avocation	visa

1. If customers are _____, they can make their complaints heard.

2. From the cruise ship, the travelers could see a mountain _____.

3. Our chorus sang at the _____ honoring our new college president.

4. A company _____ indicated funds were incorrectly allocated.

5. The _____ clapped after the performance.

6. The priest gave a brief _____ at the beginning of the assembly.

7. A _____ is required to enter Israel.

8. Recreational golfing can become a serious and challenging _____.

9. After thirty years, the electrical engineer retired from his lifelong _____.

10. Wear a _____ to protect your eyes from the sun.

Part II

Answer the following with *T* (true) or *F* (false).

_____11. Parents invoke their authority to get their children to go to bed.

_____12. A vociferous group is quiet and orderly.

_____13. A visionary might seek to make a dream become a reality.

_____14. The taillights on a motor vehicle should be visible at night.

_____15. To promote a cause, activists usually want a vocal spokesperson.

_____16. For most people, gardening is an avocation rather than a vocation.

_____17. Landing a part in a play usually requires an audition.

_____18. Financial records are reviewed in a company audit.

_____19. The person who provokes an argument is called a troublemaker.

_____20. Teens usually prefer background music to be inaudible.

Reading and Organizing Research Materials

Whether you are researching a topic for a term paper or an automobile purchase decision, you want to find relevant and reliable data to support your final conclusions and recommendations. The material you use for support will depend on your project, your goals, and the research tools available to you.

The first step is to find the information you seek. The next step is to record the information in a usable form for your ultimate purpose.

Locating Information

Academic research today is easier than ever. Today, the collections of libraries all over the world are a mouse click or two away. Whether you go to the library building or access the library from a home or school computer, you will use the Internet to locate its holdings. Review the Everyday Reading Skills feature on page 25 for suggestions about conducting research on the Internet.

Begin with Encyclopedias

Encyclopedias will provide you with background information about your topic, define key words used in the field, and, in certain cases, mention important researchers in the area under consideration. Many different encyclopedias are available for specific topics, such as the *Encyclopedia of African American Religions*, *Encyclopedia of Earth Sciences*, and *The Cambridge Encyclopedia of Astronomy*. For college research, general encyclopedias such as *Americana*, *Colliers*, and *Britannica* may be helpful in your preliminary efforts at defining your research topic, but they will probably not include enough in-depth information to support your premise.

Your college or university library probably has a subscription to several encyclopedias on the Web. Some popular ones are the following:

Encarta	encarta.msn.com
Encyclopedia Britannica	britannica.com
Grolier	go.grolier.com

Keep in mind that free general encyclopedias online are not as comprehensive as subscription-based online encyclopedias or encyclopedias in print. Try www.freeality.com/encyclop.htm or www.encyclopedia.com for hot links to other online sources.

EXERCISE 1 Visit your college library and locate two specialty encyclopedias, excluding general encyclopedias such as the *Encyclopedia Britannica*. It may be possible to do this remotely from the library link at your college's website. Take notes on an interesting entry from each and share the notes with your classmates.

Use Indexes to Scholarly and Popular Publications

Most research topics can be approached from the viewpoints of several academic disciplines. For example, sexual assault can be addressed from a legal, medical, sociological, psychological, or educational vantage point. Decide on the academic

323

discipline for your research paper, and ask a reference librarian to help you select an appropriate index. Then use the index to locate appropriate articles in the *periodical literature*. **Periodical** is a term used to describe all publications that come out on a regular schedule. They include popular magazines and scholarly journals.

Articles in **popular sources** (usually newspapers and magazines) are aimed at the general public and written by professional journalists who are usually not specialists in the field. On the other hand, articles in **scholarly journals** contain research results of experts and always include a **bibliography**, a list of the sources consulted by the author of the article. For most college research, you will need to use primarily scholarly journals.

Many articles that you find in indexes will not be relevant to your specific needs. Use the information that appears in the index entries to save time and make decisions. Each entry will display a **citation** to the article that includes the title, author(s), name of the periodical, volume and page numbers, issue date, and descriptive notes or key search terms. Usually the entry will also include an abstract.

If the article title and the date look appropriate to your search, read the abstract. The **abstract** is a short paragraph that summarizes the article, stating the premise the authors set out to prove, the subjects or location of the project, and the conclusions. If the abstract sounds as if the article will be relevant to your research, print the entry page or record the information so you can locate a copy of the article. In some cases the database provides a link to the complete text of the article. However, remember that the best articles for your topic may not be available electronically, but they may be easily accessible in the library collection.

Organizing the Information

When you have located material that fits your purpose, handle it the way you would handle textbook information. Many students choose to print the articles to read later. If you have a printed copy, annotate while you read just as you would if you were reading a textbook, and then take notes. If you read the source material on the computer screen, you must skip the annotations and go directly to the notetaking process.

When taking notes for an academic paper, put the ideas into your own words. By doing this, you will be less likely to use the author's phrasing when you write your paper. Avoiding plagiarism is extremely important. Record page numbers, urls, and all other source information. These details will be necessary when you

U.S. House of Representatives

cite the references in your final paper. This habit will also make it much easier for you to find the source again if necessary.

Make it a habit to put your notes in a clear, well-organized form such as those forms discussed in this chapter. Use the form that best suits the material and your preferences—Cornell, summarizing, outlining, or mapping.

EXERCISE 2 Answer the following questions based on the Internet article "The U.S. House of Representatives."

1. Would the Internet article be relevant if you were making a class presentation on the U.S. Congress? Yes. _____

_____

2. What kinds of information will you find on this site? _____

_____

_____

_____

3. Is the information reliable? How do you know? (*Hint*: Review the definitions and parts of a Web address in Chapter 1, page 25) _____

_____

_____

4. Use one of the notetaking forms you learned in this chapter—Cornell, summarizing, outlining, or mapping—to make notes from this article. Remember to cite the complete URL as the source.

7

Text-Taking Strategies

Learning Objectives

From this chapter, readers will learn:

1 How content tests and standardized tests differ
2 General pre-test strategies
3 Strategies to use during a test
4 Strategies to use after a test
5 How to improve scores on standardized reading tests
6 Strategies for answering five major question types on reading tests
7 Hints for answering multiple-choice and true-false questions
8 Strategies for essay exams

Everyday Reading Skills: Using Mnemonics

ACHIEVE YOUR HIGHEST POTENTIAL

Learning Objective 1

The difference between content tests and standardized tests

Are you now at the midpoint of your courses and preparing to take tests? High test scores should reflect your knowledge and ability, not your use of tricks or gimmicks. The best and most essential preparation for any test, of course, is learning the material. Awareness of test-taking strategies, however, can help you achieve your highest potential.

In college you face basically two types of tests: content exams and standardized tests. A **content exam** measures your knowledge on a subject that you have been studying. For example, the final exam in Psychology 101 measures your understanding and retention of what was taught throughout the course. The score becomes a major part of your final grade in the course. A **standardized test**, in contrast, measures your mastery of a skill that has developed over a long period of time, such as reading or mathematics. The scores on standardized tests usually help you qualify for entering or exiting specific college programs.

This chapter will help you improve your test scores by becoming aware of what is expected in the test-taking situation. Many of the following suggestions are obvious, but it is surprising how frequently students overlook them. Some relate to your physical and mental readiness for peak performance, whereas others explore means for coping with the challenging demands of the testing situation. Technical aspects of test construction are presented with opportunities for application and practice. Awareness and practice can indeed improve test scores and give you that winning edge!

BE PREPARED

EXERCISE 1 Read the passage, then write *agree* or *disagree* for the statements that follow.

Learning Objective 2

General pre-test strategies

Ed was earning money for college by working at a local convenience store in the late afternoon and early evening. On Wednesday night his boss asked him to work long past midnight for an employee who had called in sick. Because Ed needed money for his car payments, he agreed. He did not tell his boss that he had an important test early the next morning.

Thursday morning Ed slept through the alarm but fortunately was awakened by the telephone a half-hour later. He arrived at the exam as the test booklets were being distributed, having missed the professor's introductory remarks and responses to students' questions. Ed spent the first part of the test settling down mentally and physically. He was surprised by some of the material on the test. As he began to read and answer questions, he worried that he would not do well.

_____ 1. Ed was mentally alert after a good night's sleep.

Ed made a poor decision in not telling his boss that he needed adequate sleep on the night before his big test. Being alert rather than drowsy can make the difference in correctly answering one item or more. That correct item, for example, could make the difference in a failing score of 68 or a passing score of 70. Don't take chances when the stakes are high. Being alert can make a difference. *Set yourself up for success, and get plenty of sleep the night before a test.*

_____ 2. Because Ed arrived while the test was being distributed, his lateness did not work against him.

Ed could not immediately begin to work on the test because he had to calm himself first. If you arrive late and flustered, you lose valuable time and begin at a disadvantage.

Do your nerves a favor and avoid close calls. *Arrive five or ten minutes early for a test, and get settled.* Find a seat, greet your friends, and take out a pen or pencil.

_____ 3. Ed knew what to expect on the test.

Ed expressed surprise over some of the material on the test. Always check to be sure you know exactly what the test will cover. Know the format of the test. Will it be essay or multiple choice? Study with the format in mind. *Know what to expect on the test.*

_____ 4. Ed had probably asked how the test would be scored.

Because Ed arrived late and missed the professor's introductory remarks, he probably did not know about the scoring. Sometimes, but not very often, guessing is penalized in the scoring. When scores are based on answering all questions, you are better off guessing than leaving items blank. To be safe, ask if omitted items count against you. Also, sometimes some items are worth more points than others; this information is usually stated on the test itself. *Be aware of how the test will be scored.*

_____ 5. Ed approached the test with a positive mental attitude.

Ed had unnecessarily hurt himself and thus lost confidence. Preparation breeds self-confidence, and the lack of it breeds anxiety. Be prepared and plan for success. Give yourself good reasons to be optimistic. *Have confidence in your abilities.*

BRAIN BOOSTER

Balance Memorization and Application

Information from the senses goes generally to the back cortex area of the brain. Creativity and decision-making occur in the front cortex. The two parts are connected by very important bundles of nerves called *fasiculi*. How does this biological structure affect college students? The answer has to do with the connection between learning facts and making use of them. Some students memorize information and feel they have studied well, but professors expect students to apply knowledge rather than just repeat it. Strengthening the connections between the back and front cortex requires learning material first, and then using it in new situations. Don't stop with memorizing information; practice applying it.

—Adapted from James E. Zull, *The Art of Changing the Brain*.
© 2002 Stylus Publishing, LLC. Sterling, VA.

STAY ALERT

EXERCISE 2   Read the passage, then write *agree* or *disagree* for the statements that follow.

Learning Objective 3

Strategies to use during a test

After reading the first passage on the comprehension test, Julie realized that she had no idea what she had read. She had seen all the words, but her mind was not on the message. She was excited and wanted to do well, but she was having trouble focusing on the material. She moved to the questions, hoping—erroneously—that they would provide clues to the meaning. They did not, and so she began rereading the passage with greater determination.

Julie finally gained control over the test and was doing fine until her classmates began to leave. She panicked. She was not finished, but others were turning in their tests. She was stuck on an item that she had reread three times. She looked at her watch and saw she had ten minutes left. That would be plenty of time to finish the last passage, if she could only regain her composure.

———— 1. Julie was unable to concentrate when she began the test.

Julie could not initially focus her attention and comprehend the material. She was anxious and excited. *Concentration is essential for comprehension.* If you are distracted, take a few deep breaths to relax and get your mind on track. Tune out internal and external distractions, and focus on the meaning. Visualize the message and relate it to what you already know. *Follow directions,* and proceed with confidence. Use your pen as a pacer to concentrate on the passage. (For more on this technique of rhythmically following the words, see Chapter 8.) If anxiety is a consistent problem, seek help from the campus counseling center.

———— 2. Julie was smart to wear a watch to the test.

Time is usually a major consideration on a test, so always wear *and use* a watch. *Size up the task and schedule your time.* Look over all parts of the test when you receive it. Determine the number of sections to be covered and allocate your time accordingly. Check periodically to see if you are meeting your time goals.

On a midterm or final exam, the number of points for each item sometimes varies greatly. Spend the most time on the items that yield the most points.

———— 3. Julie should be sure of her answer to each item before moving to another.

Do not waste time that you may need later by pondering an especially difficult question. Mark the item with a dot and move on to the rest of the test. If you have a few minutes at the end, return to the marked items. *On a test every minute counts, so work rapidly.* Be aggressive and alert in moving through the test.

———— 4. Changing an answer usually makes it wrong.

If you have time at the end of the test, *go back to the items you were unsure about.* If careful rethinking indicates another response, change your answer. Research shows that scores can be improved by making such changes.[1]

———— 5. Students who finish a test early make the best grades.

The evidence indicates no correlation between high scores and the time taken to complete a test.[2] Speed does not always equal accuracy. *Don't be intimidated by students who finish early.* Schedule your time and meet your goals.

SEEK FEEDBACK

Learning Objective 4

Strategies to use after a test

After a test, investigate your errors, if possible. On many standardized tests, only the score is reported, so you are unable to review the test itself. But when feedback is available, take advantage of the opportunity. Analyze your mistakes so you can learn from them and avoid repeating the same errors. Wrong answers give you valuable diagnostic information. If you do not understand the error in

[1]Marshal A. Geiger, "Changing Multiple-Choice Answers: Do Students Accurately Perceive Their Performance?" *Journal of Experimental Educating* 59 (1991): 250–257.

[2]Robert K. Bridges, "Order of Finish, Time to Completion, and Performance on Course-Based Objective Examinations: A Systematic Analysis of Their Relationship on Both Individual Exam Scores and Total Score Across Three Exams," Annual Meeting of the Eastern Psychological Association, Baltimore, MD, April 1982.

> **BRAIN BOOSTER**
>
> **Turn Mistakes Into Successes**
>
> Mistaken information exists in neuronal networks just like correct information does. Unless you do something about them, the mistakes will persist. That is why the "after-test" discussion is so important. To change the erroneous neuronal networks, uncover the reason for your mistake. Ask for help understanding the correct answer and connect it to what you already know. Build this understanding into a new or expanded neuronal network by repeating the correct information and using it. Instead of focusing on the mistake, focus on the new learning you have created and reinforce it.

your thinking, seek advice from another student or the professor. Never merely look at your grade and forget the test if feedback is available.

STANDARDIZED READING TESTS

Learning Objective 5

Improving scores on standardized reading tests

Students take standardized reading comprehension tests for a variety of reasons. Tests such as the SAT or the ACT are required for admission to many colleges. Computerized tests such as the Compass are used by many colleges for placement. Some states require additional testing for entering students, such as the CLAST in Florida. In Georgia, students must take a test with a reading component, the Regents Exam, before they are allowed to graduate.

PERSONAL FEEDBACK 1   **Name** _____

1. Depending on which test you were required to take, what were your scores on the SAT, the ACT, or a college placement test? _____

   _____

2. How do you feel you could improve your scores if you took the test again? _____

   _____

3. What state- or college-mandated tests will you need to take before college graduation?

   _____

   _____

4. What skills are included in those mandated tests? _____

   _____

5. Review the comprehension questions you missed in previous chapters. What question types do you tend to miss most often? Why? _____

   _____

   Tear out and submit to your instructor.

Thus, for college students, performing well on standardized tests can be critical to success.

The following strategies will help you perform better on standardized reading tests.

Read to Comprehend

Read for the main idea of the passage. Don't fixate on details. Read to understand the author's message. Students ask, "Should I read the questions first and then the passage?" Experts differ in their opinions, but most advise reading the passage first and then answering the questions. If you read the questions first, you have five or six purposes for reading. Reading thus becomes fragmented and lacks focus. Read with one purpose: to understand the main idea rather than initially focusing on details.

Interact

Use the thinking strategies of good readers to interact with the passage. Predict the topic and activate your schema. Visualize the message and relate it to what you already know. Monitor and self-correct. Apply what you already know about the reading process to each test passage.

Anticipate

Anticipate what is coming. Test passages are frequently untitled and thus offer no clue to content. To activate your schema before reading, glance at the passage for a repeated word, name, or date that might signal its subject.

Read the first sentence carefully. Reread if necessary. The first sentence usually sets the stage for what is to come. It sometimes states the central theme or simply stimulates your curiosity. In any case, the first sentence starts you thinking about what you will be reading. Continue to anticipate throughout the passage. Some of your guesses will be right and some will be wrong. Double-check information and self-monitor.

Relax

Don't allow yourself to feel rushed. Work with control and confidence. That anxious, pressured feeling tends to occur at the beginning, middle, and end of a test. In the beginning, you are worried about not being able to concentrate immediately and thus having to reread. In the middle, you may be upset because you are only half finished, which is where you should be. When the first student finishes the test, you may again feel rushed and lose your concentration. To combat this feeling, use your pen as a pointer to focus your attention both mentally and physically on the printed page. Plan your time, relax, and concentrate.

Read to Learn

Test passages are not always dull. They may never compete with steamy novels, but some are quite interesting and informative. Rather than reading with the artificial purpose of only answering questions, read to learn and enjoy. You may surprise yourself!

Recall

Pull the passage together before pulling it apart. Remind yourself of the author's main point, rather than wait for questions to prod you. This final monitoring step in the reading process takes only a few seconds.

EXERCISE 3

Using the suggestions just outlined, read the following passage as if it were part of a reading comprehension test. The handwritten side notes will help make you aware of a few aspects of your thinking.

A What? How could she get out of there?

One of the most remarkable women in world history, famed for her vices as well as for her strong and able rule, governed China from about 660 to 705. The Empress Wu began her career as a concubine in the harem of the third T'ang emperor. When the emperor died, Wu and all the other concubines, according to custom, had their heads shaved and entered a Buddhist convent. Here they were expected to pass the remainder of their lives. Wu, however, was too intelligent and beautiful—as well as too unscrupulous—to accept such a fate. Within a year she had won the new emperor's heart and had become his concubine. According to a hostile tradition, she first met the new emperor in a lavatory when he was paying a ceremonial visit to the convent.

Where? Wu accused empress and took power

Evil?

Wu rose steadily in the new emperor's favor until, after accusing the empress of engaging in sorcery, murdering her baby daughter, and plotting to poison her husband, she was herself installed as empress. According to the official history of the age, "The whole sovereign power passed into her hands. Life and death, reward and punishment, were determined by her word. The Son of Heaven merely sat upon his throne with hands folded."

Puppets?

After the death of the emperor twenty years later, Wu installed two of her sons as successive puppets. She ruthlessly employed secret police and informers to suppress conspiracies against her. Finally, in 690 at the age of sixty-two, she usurped the imperial title and became the only woman ever to rule China in name as well as in fact.

Full power

Evil monks wanting power manipulated scripture.

Does the author think it's O.K.?

To legitimize her usurpation, the empress was aided by a group of unscrupulous Buddhist monks, one of whom is reputed to have been her lover. They discovered in Buddhist scriptures a prophecy that a pious woman was destined to be reborn as the ruler of an empire that would inaugurate a better age and to which all countries would be subject. Not only did the monks identify Wu as the woman in the prophecy, but they acclaimed her as a divine incarnation of the Buddha. The T'ang capital was renamed the Divine Capital, and Wu assumed a special title—"Holy Mother Divine Imperial One."

Surprise!

Expanded empire Weaknesses?

Despite her ruthlessness—understandable in the totally unprecedented situation of a woman seeking successfully to rule a great empire—the Empress Wu was an able ruler who consolidated the T'ang Dynasty. She not only avenged earlier Sui and T'ang defeats at the hands of the northern Koreans who had been subject to the Han, but she made all of Korea a loyal vassal state of China. Yet because she was a woman and a usurper, she found little favor with Chinese Confucian historians. They played up her vices, particularly her many favorites and lovers whom she rewarded with unprecedented honors.

Lover?

One too many Downfall

Among those who gained great influence over the aging empress was a peddler of cosmetics, famous for his virility, who was first made abbot of a Buddhist monastery, then palace architect, and finally commander-in-chief of the armies on the northern frontier. At the age of seventy-two, her favorites—and reputed lovers—were two young brothers of a type known as "white faces" (men who were physically attractive but otherwise of no account), whose powdered and rouged faces were a common sight around the palace. When the empress appointed a younger brother of her two favorites to an important governorship, her leading ministers successfully conspired to put her son back on the throne. The two brothers were decapitated in the palace and the Empress Wu, the founder and only member of the Wu Dynasty, was forced to abdicate.

—*Civilization Past and Present*, Eighth Edition, by Walter Wallbank et al.

UNDERSTAND MAJOR QUESTION TYPES

Test questions follow certain predictable patterns. For example, almost all passages are followed by one question on the main idea. Learn to recognize the types of questions and understand how they are constructed. What techniques does the test writer use when creating correct answers and incorrect distractors?

Learning Objective 6

Answering the five major question types on standardized reading tests

Well-written distractors are tempting incorrect responses that draw attention, cause confusion, and thus force the test taker to use knowledge and logic. This section discusses each major question type, offers insight into their construction, and gives you an opportunity to play the role of test writer.

Main Idea Questions

Main idea questions ask you to identify the author's main point. These questions are often stated in one of the following forms:

The best statement of the main idea is . . .

The best title for this passage is . . .

The author is primarily concerned with . . .

The central theme of the passage is . . .

Incorrect responses to main idea items fall into two categories: (1) Some are too broad or general. They suggest that the passage includes much more than it actually does. For example, for a passage describing the hibernation of goldfish in a pond during the winter, the title "Fish" would be much too general to describe the specific topic. (2) Other incorrect answers are too narrow. They focus on details within the passage that support the main idea. The details may be attention-getting and interesting, but they do not describe the central focus. They are tempting, however, because they are direct statements from the passage.

If you have difficulty understanding the main idea of a passage, reread the first and last sentences. Sometimes, but not always, one of these sentences will give you an overview or focus.

EXAMPLE   Answer the following main idea items on the passage about Empress Wu. Then read the handwritten remarks describing the student's thinking involved in judging whether a response is correct.

_____ 1. The best statement of the main idea of this passage is:

a. Buddhist monks bring Wu to power.

(Important detail, but the focus is on her.)

b. Women in China were not equal to men.

(Too broad and general, or not really covered.)

c. Empress Wu's ambition for her young lovers leads to her downfall.

(Very interesting, but a detail.)

d. Empress Wu ruthlessly usurped power but became an able ruler of a great empire.

(Yes, includes all major points and sounds great!)

_____ 2. Which is the best title for this passage?

a. Confucians Defeat Wu

(Detail.)

b. Empress Wu and Her Lovers

(Very interesting, but a detail.)

c. Empress Wu, Ruler of China

(Sounds best.)

d. Rulers of China

(Too broad; this passage is about only one woman.)

EXERCISE 4   For further practice on main idea items, read the following passage and answer the two questions. After each possible answer, write why you did or did not choose that response. For main idea distractors, the reasons might be that the incorrect response is *too broad, too narrow, a detail*, or *not in the passage*.

In the United States, every state has laws prohibiting some type of relatives from marrying each other. Today there is universal agreement when it comes to prohibiting mother–son marriage and preventing full siblings from marrying, but the laws vary when it comes to more distant relatives. Thirty states prohibit first cousins from marrying, while twenty do not. Furthermore, the prohibitions are not limited to people related by birth. A dozen states forbid some types of in-laws from intermarrying.

—*Cultural Anthropology: The Human Challenge,*
Eleventh Edition, by William A. Haviland et al.

_____ 1. The best title for this passage is:

a. Marriage Laws _____

b. Marriage Prohibitions Among Relatives in the United States

_____

c. Mother–Son Marriage Prohibitions _____

_____

d. Cultural Taboos Forbidding Intermarrying _____

_____

_____ 2. The best statement of the main idea of this passage is:

a. There is no disagreement with preventing marriage between

brothers and sisters. _____

_____

b. Twenty states allow first cousins to marry. _____

c. There are laws forbidding citizens from marrying relatives in

every state in the U.S. _____

d. Intermarriage results in increased health problems for the

children of such marriages. _____

Detail Questions

Detail questions check your ability to understand material that is directly stated in the passage. To find or double-check an answer, note a key word in the question and then quickly glance at the passage for that word or synonym. When you locate the term, reread the sentence for clarification. Detail questions fall in the following patterns:

The author states that . . .

According to the author . . .

According to the passage . . .

All of the following are true except . . .

A person, term, or place is . . .

Incorrect answers to detail questions tend to be false statements. Test writers like to use pompous or catchy phrases stated directly from the passage as distractors. Such phrases may sound authoritative but mean nothing.

EXAMPLE   Answer the following detail question on the passage about Empress Wu (see page 333). Then note the handwritten remarks reflecting the thinking involved in judging whether a response is correct.

_____ 1. Empress Wu did all the following *except*

(Note the use of "except"; look for the only false item to be the correct answer.)

    a. consolidate the T'ang Dynasty.

(True, this is stated in the fifth paragraph.)

    b. accuse the empress of sorcery.

(True, this is stated in the second paragraph.)

    c. appoint the brother of a young favorite to an important governorship.

(True, this is stated in the last paragraph.)

    d. poison her husband.

(She did not do this, so this is the correct answer.)

EXERCISE 5   For further practice on details, read the following passage and answer the detail question. Indicate beside each response why you did or did not choose the item.

Be quite sure that there isn't a woman who cannot be won, and make up your mind that you will win her. Only you must prepare the ground. Sooner would the birds cease their song in the springtime, or the grasshopper be silent in the summer, . . . than a woman resist the tender wooing of a youthful lover. . . .

In the first place, it's best to send her a letter, just to pave the way. In it you should tell her how you dote on her; pay her pretty compliments and say all the nice things lovers always say. . . . And promise, promise, promise. Promises will cost you nothing. Everyone's a millionaire where promises are concerned. . . .

If she refuses your letter and sends it back unread, don't give up; hope for the best and try again.

—From *The Love Books of Ovid*,
translated by J. Lewis May

_____ 1. The author recommends the following to capture the heart of a young woman:

   a. Playing hard to get. _____

   b. Flattery. _____

   c. Total honesty. _____

   d. Gifts. _____

Inference Questions

An inference is something that is suggested but not directly stated. Clues in the passage lead you to make assumptions and draw conclusions. Items testing implied meaning deal with the attitudes and feelings of the writer that emerge as if from behind or between words. Favorable and unfavorable descriptions suggest positive and negative opinions toward a subject. Sarcastic remarks indicate the motivation of characters. Look for clues that help you develop logical assumptions. Inference questions may be stated in one of the following forms:

The author believes (or feels or implies) . . .

It can be inferred (deduced from clues) from the passage . . .

The passage (or author) suggests . . .

It can be concluded from the passage that . . .

   Base your conclusion on both what is known and what is suggested. Incorrect responses to implied meaning items tend to be false statements that lack logical support.

EXAMPLE   Answer the following inference questions on the passage about Empress Wu. Then note the handwritten remarks reflecting the thinking involved in judging whether a response is correct.

_____ 1. The author implies that Empress Wu

   a. was a devout Buddhist.

   (She was aided by Buddhists, but her religious preference is not suggested.)

   b. killed the first empress's baby daughter.

   (No; she accused the former empress of doing this.)

   c. let her vices lead to her downfall.

   (True, rewarding her young lovers probably hurt the empire.)

   d. conquered Korea to satisfy the Confucian historians.

   (She did conquer Korea, but it is not suggested that she tried to satisfy the Confucian historians.)

EXERCISE 6   For further practice on inference, read the following passage and answer the inference question. In the blank, indicate the reason for your answer choice.

[We were invited to a banquet with Attila.] When the hour arrived we went to Attila's palace, along with the embassy from the western Romans, and stood on the threshold of the hall in the presence of Attila. The cup-bearers gave us a cup, according to the national custom, that we might pray before we sat down. Having tasted the cup, we proceeded to take our seats, all the chairs being ranged along the walls of the room on either side. Attila sat in the middle on a couch; a second couch was set behind him, and from it steps led up to his bed, which was covered with linen sheets and coverlets. . . .

[First the king and his guests pledged one another with the wine.] When this ceremony was over the cup-bearers retired and tables, large enough for three or four, or even more, to sit at, were placed next the table of Attila, so that each could take of the food on the dishes without leaving his seat. The attendant of Attila first entered with a dish full of meat, and behind him came the other attendants with bread and other dishes, which they laid on the tables. A luxurious meal, served on a silver plate, had been made ready for us and the other guests, but Attila ate nothing but meat on a wooden platter. In everything else, too, he showed himself temperate; his cup was of wood, while to the guests were given goblets of gold and silver. His dress, too, was quite simple, affecting only to be clean.

—Priscus, quoted in *Western Civilization, Volume 1: To 1715*, Fifth Edition, by Jackson J. Spielvogel

_____ 1. The author implies that

    a. although luxuries are available to him, Attila chooses a simpler lifestyle.

    b. Attila ordered a victory feast for his leaders before a day of battle.

    c. the Roman peasants were starving while the food and drink flowed at Attila's palace.

    d. while he enjoys the banquet, the author is also fearful of Attila.

    Reason for choice: _____

    _____

    _____

    _____

Purpose Questions

The purpose of a passage is not usually stated. Instead, it is implied and is related to the main idea. In responding to a purpose item, you are answering the question, "What was the author's purpose in writing this material?" You might restate this question as, "What did the author do to or for me, the reader?"

EXAMPLE   Reading comprehension tests tend to include three basic types of passages, each of which suggests a separate set of purposes. Study the outline of the three types shown in the Reader's Tip box, and answer the question on the Empress Wu passage. Then note the handwritten remarks reflecting the thinking involved in judging whether an answer is correct.

_____ 1. The purpose of the passage on Empress Wu is

    a. to argue.

      (No side is taken.)

    b. to explain.

      (Yes, because the material is factual, like a textbook.)

Reader's TIP   Types of Test Passages

Factual Passages

What? Science, sociology, psychology, or history articles

How to Read? Read for the main idea, and do not get bogged down in details. Remember, you can look back.

Author's Purpose?

- To inform
- To explain
- To describe

Example: Textbooks

Opinion Passages

What? Articles with a particular point of view on a topic

How to Read? Read to determine the author's opinion on the subject. Then judge the value of the support included and decide whether you agree or disagree.

Author's Purpose?

- To argue
- To persuade
- To condemn
- To ridicule

Example: Newspaper editorials

Fiction Passages

What? Articles that tell a story

How to Read? Read to understand what the characters are thinking and why they act as they do.

Author's Purpose?

- To entertain
- To narrate
- To describe
- To shock

Examples: Novels and short stories

c. to condemn.

(The reading is not judgmental.)

d. to persuade.

(No point of view is argued.)

EXERCISE 7 For further practice, read the following passage and answer the purpose question. In the blank, indicate the reason for your answer choice.

During the Victorian age women were often considered frail and delicate creatures, at least partly because they seemed prone to fainting spells. Did they faint because of their "inner natures" or for some other reason? Consider the fact that many of these women wore extremely tight corsets to give them tiny waists. In fact, the corsets were so tight that women could only take shallow breaths—if they took a deep breath, they ran the risk of being stabbed by the whale-bone "stays" in the corset. These stays were thin and very sharp, and not only could they cause a bloody wound, but they could also puncture a lung! One consequence of continued shallow breathing is dizziness—hence the fainting spells common among stylish Victorian women.

—*Psychology: The Brain, The Person, The World,* Second Edition,
by Stephen M. Kosslyn and Robin S. Rosenberg

_____ 1. The author's primary purpose in this passage is

    a. to argue.

    b. to condemn.

    c. to entertain.

    d. to explain.

    Reason for response: _____

    _____

    _____

Vocabulary Questions

Vocabulary items test your general word knowledge as well as your ability to figure out meaning by using context clues. Vocabulary items are usually stated as follows.

As used in the passage, the best definition of _____ is . . .

    Both word knowledge and context are necessary for a correct response. Go back and reread the sentence before the word, the sentence with the word, and the sentence after the word to be sure that you understand the context and are not misled by unusual meanings. Be suspicious of common words such as *industry,* which seems simple on the surface but can have multiple meanings.

EXAMPLE   Answer the following vocabulary question on the passage about Empress Wu. Then note the handwritten remarks reflecting the thinking involved in judging whether an answer is correct.

_____ 1. As used in the third paragraph of the passage, the best definition of *usurped* is

    (Reread the sentence. Look also at the use of "usurpation" in the fourth paragraph.)

    a. earned.

    (This is too positive to describe her ruthless behavior.)

    b. won.

    (Again, this is too positive for her negative actions.)

    c. bought.

    (No payoff is suggested.)

    d. seized.

    (Yes, she took control and then tried to make it legal.)

EXERCISE 8   For further practice, read the following passage and answer the vocabulary question. In the blank, indicate the reason for your answer choice.

> Pennsylvania plans to begin paying the relatives of organ donors $300 toward funeral expenses. It would be the first jurisdiction in the country to reward organ donation. Indeed, it might even be violating a 1984 federal law that declares organs a national resource not subject to compensation. Already there are voices opposing the very idea of pricing a kidney.
>
> —"Yes, Let's Pay for Organs,"
> by Charles Krauthammer

_____ 1. As used in the passage, the best definition of *compensation* is

     a. discussion.

     b. regulation.

     c. authority.

     d. payment.

     Reason for choice: _____

     _____

     _____

     _____

     _____

     _____

HINTS FOR TAKING MULTIPLE-CHOICE AND TRUE-FALSE TESTS

Learning Objective 7

Approaches to multiple-choice and true-false questions

Study the following hints and answer the items on the passage about Empress Wu with *a, b, c,* or *d,* or *T* (true) or *F* (false) before reading the explanation in italics.

Read All Options

Even if the first answer seems undisputedly correct, read all the options. Be careful, and consider each answer. Multiple-choice tests usually ask for the *best* answer, not for any one that is reasonable.

_____ 1. The author suggests that

     a. the empress wanted the emperor dead.

     b. the sons of the empress were disobedient.

     c. Wu's sons plotted against the emperor.

     d. the emperor gave the empress immense power.

     (Although the first option may be tempting, the last answer is implied by the quote describing her power and thus is correct.)

Predict the Correct Answer

As you read the stem (or beginning) of a multiple-choice item, anticipate what you would write for a correct response. Develop an answer in your mind before you read the options, and then look for a choice that corresponds to your thinking.

_____ 2. At the end of her reign, the Empress Wu was

    a. decapitated.
    b. married.
    c. pushed from power.
    d. imprisoned.
    (It says in the last sentence that she "was forced to abdicate."
    The third option most closely matches this answer.)

Avoid Answers with "100 Percent" Words

All and *never* mean 100 percent, without exception. In a true-false question, a response containing either word is seldom correct. Rarely can a statement be so definitely inclusive or exclusive. Other "100 percent" words to avoid are *no, none, only, every, always,* and *must.*

_____ 3. Empress Wu was hated by all the Chinese Confucian historians.
    (All means 100 percent, and thus is too inclusive. Surely one or two
    Confucians might not have felt so strongly against Wu.)

Consider Answers with Qualifying Words

Words such as *sometimes* and *seldom* suggest frequency but do not go so far as to say *all* or *none.* Such qualifying words can mean more than none and less than all. By being so indefinite, they are difficult to dispute. Therefore, qualifiers are more likely to be included in a correct response to a true-false question. Other qualifiers are *few, much, often, may, many, some, perhaps,* and *generally.*

_____ 4. Empress Wu was hated by many of the Chinese Confucian historians.
    (The phrases "she found little favor" with Confucians and "They
    played up her vices" suggest dislike. The statement is true.)

Do Not Overanalyze

Try to follow the thinking of the test writer rather than overanalyze minute points. Don't make the question harder than it is. Use your common sense, and answer what you think was intended.

_____ 5. Empress Wu fought Korea and won.
    (Of course Empress Wu was not standing on the front line of battle
    with a sword, but as the leader of China she was ultimately respon-
    sible for the victory. Thus the answer is true.)

True Statements Must Be True Without Exception

A statement is either totally true or it is incorrect. Adding an incorrect *and, but,* or *because* phrase to a true statement makes it false and thus an unacceptable answer. If a statement is half true and half false, mark it false.

_____ 6. The Chinese Confucian historians plotted against Empress Wu because they were concerned about the welfare of the poor people of China.
(It is true that the Confucians plotted against Wu, but their reasons for doing so are not stated. The statement is half true and half false, so it is false.)

If Two Options Are Synonymous, Eliminate Both

If two items say basically the same thing but only one answer is possible, then neither can be correct. Eliminate the two and spend your time on the others.

_____ 7. The purpose of this passage is

   a. to argue.
   b. to persuade.
   c. to inform.
   d. to entertain.
(Because "argue" and "persuade" are basically synonyms, you can eliminate both and move on to other options.)

Figure Out the Difference Between Similar Options

If two similar options appear, frequently one of them will be correct. Study the choices to see the subtle difference intended by the test maker.

_____ 8. Empress Wu was

   a. supported by many Buddhists.
   b. supported by all the Buddhists.
   c. beloved by the poor.
   d. the greatest ruler of the T'ang Dynasty.
(The last two answers are not suggested. Close inspection shows that the word all *is the only difference between the first and second answers and is the reason that the second is untrue. Thus the first answer, with the qualifying word, is correct.)*

Use Logical Reasoning When Two Answers Are Correct

Some tests include the option *all of the above* and *none of the above*. If you see that two of the answers are correct and are unsure about a third, *all of the above* would be a logical response.

_____ 9. Empress Wu was a

   a. concubine.
   b. mother.
   c. wife.
   d. all of the above.
(If you recall that Wu was a concubine and a mother but are not sure that she was a wife, "all of the above" would be your logical option because you know that two of the choices are correct.)

Look Suspiciously at Directly Quoted Pompous Phrases

In searching for distractors, test makers sometimes quote a pompous phrase from the passage that doesn't make much sense. Such a phrase may include lofty, ornate, and seemingly important language from the passage, yet still be incorrect. However, you may read the phrase and think, "Oh yes, I saw that in the passage. It sounds good, so it must be right." Be sure authoritative phrases make sense before choosing them.

_____10. Wu was installed as empress because

        a. the Son of Heaven folded his hands.
        b. the imperial title was suppressed in conspiracy.
        c. the prophecy in Buddhist scriptures identified her by name.
        d. the brilliant conniving of an ambitious woman was successful.
        (The first two are pompous and do not make sense. The third is false because of the phrase "by name." The last is the correct answer.)

Simplify Double Negatives by Canceling Out Both

Double negatives are confusing and time-consuming to unravel. Simplify a double-negative statement by first canceling out both negatives. Then reread the statement without the confusion of the two negatives, and decide on the accuracy of the statement.

_____11. Empress Wu was not unscrupulous.
        (Cancel out the two negatives, not *and* un. *Reread the sentence without the negatives: "Empress Wu was scrupulous." This is a false statement.)*

Certain Responses Are Neither True nor False

For some items, you are not given the clues necessary for judging their accuracy. There is not sufficient evidence to indicate whether they are true or false.

_____12. Empress Wu was loved by the Chinese people.
        (The passage does not provide clues to indicate that she was loved or not loved by the Chinese people.)

Validate True Responses

If you are told that all the answers are correct except one, verify each response and, by the process of elimination, find the one that does not fit.

_____13. Empress Wu was all of the following *except*

        a. a scheming concubine.
        b. a ruthless woman.
        c. the first woman to rule China.
        d. the founder of the T'ang Dynasty.
        (Always note the "except" and look for the response that is false. The first three answers are true and the last is untrue, so it is the correct answer.)

Recognize Flaws in Test Making

Professionally developed reading tests are usually well-constructed and do not contain obvious clues to the correct answers. However, some teacher-made tests are hastily written and thus may have errors in test making that can help you find the correct answer. Do not, however, rely on these flaws to make a big difference in your score, for such errors should not occur on a well-constructed test.

Grammar. Eliminate responses that do not have subject-verb agreement. The tense of the verb as well as modifiers such as *a* or *an* can also give clues to the correct response.

_____14. Wu's ambition was to become an

    a. concubine.
    b. empress.
    c. lover.
    d. Buddhist.
    (*The* an *suggests an answer that starts with a vowel. Thus "empress" is the obvious answer.*)

Clues from Other Parts of the Test. Information in one part of the test may help you with an uncertain answer in another section.

_____15. During Wu's reign, China defeated

    a. Vietnam.
    b. India.
    c. Russia.
    d. Korea.
    (*A previous question mentions the conquest of Korea.*)

Length. On poorly constructed tests, longer answers are more frequently correct.

_____16. The author suggests that Wu promoted the cosmetics peddler to commander-in-chief because he

    a. was a good soldier.
    b. knew how to sell.
    c. had been a Buddhist monk.
    d. was her lover and she wanted to give him favors.
    (*In an effort to be totally correct without question, the test maker has written the last—and longest—answer.*)

Absurd Ideas and Emotional Words. Avoid distractors that contain absurd ideas or emotional words. The test maker probably got tired of trying to think of distractors and in a moment of weakness included a nonsense answer.

_____17. As used in the passage, the best definition of *concubine* is

    a. wife.
    b. child.
    c. mistress.
    d. dog.
    (*The last answer is totally absurd. The test maker should take a break.*)

HINTS FOR TAKING ESSAY EXAMS

Learning Objective 8

Strategies for answering essay questions

In many ways, essay tests are more demanding than multiple-choice tests. Rather than simply recognizing correct answers, you must recall, create, and organize. You face a blank sheet of paper instead of a list of options, and, to write an appropriate response, you must remember ideas and present them in a logical and well-organized manner. The following suggestions can help you respond effectively.

Predict and Practice

Predict possible essay items by using the table of contents and subheadings of your text to form questions. Practice brainstorming to answer these questions. Review old exams for insight into both the questions and the kinds of answers that received good marks. Outline answers to possible exam questions. Do as much thinking as possible to prepare yourself to take the test before you sit down to begin writing.

Reword the Statement or Question

Sometimes the statement or question you are asked to discuss is written in a confusing or pompous manner. Be sure you understand the meaning, then rephrase it in your own words. If it is a statement, put it in the form of a question. If it is a question, simplify it and, if possible, divide it into parts.

Decide on the approach you will use in making your response. Will you define, describe, explain, or compare? For example, suppose you were asked to support the following statement:

> Wu rose to power through unscrupulous deception, and she fell through her own vice and weaknesses.

First rephrase the statement as a question, using words such as *why, what,* or *how*:

> *How did Wu rise to power through unscrupulous deception and fall through her own vice and weaknesses?*

The question really contains two parts, which you can list separately:

1. *How did Wu rise to power through unscrupulous deception?*
2. *How did Wu fall from power through her own vice and weaknesses?*

How will you answer the question? Use two approaches:

1. List her unscrupulous acts of deception that put her in power.
2. Explain the reasons for her fall.

Notice Key Words

Following is a list of key words of instruction that appear in essay questions, with hints for responding to each word.

Compare: List the similarities.

Contrast: Note the differences.

Criticize: State your opinion and stress weaknesses.

Define: State the meaning and use examples so the term is understood.

Describe: State the characteristics so the image is vivid.

Diagram: Make a drawing that demonstrates relationships.

Discuss: Define the issue and elaborate on the advantages and disadvantages.

Evaluate: State positive and negative views and make a judgment.

Explain: Show cause and effect and give reasons.

Illustrate: Provide examples.

Interpret: Explain your own understanding of and opinions on a topic.

Justify: Give proof or reasons to support an opinion.

List: Record a series of numbered items.

Outline: Sketch the main points with their significant supporting details.

Prove: Use facts to support an opinion.

Relate: Connect items and show how one influences another.

Review: Give an overview with a summary.

Summarize: Retell the main points.

Trace: Move sequentially from one event to another.

Answer the Question

Answer the question that is asked—not some other question. This may seem obvious, but students frequently get off track. Do not write a summary of the material, include irrelevant information, or repeat the same idea over and over again. Focus on the question and write with purpose.

The following is an example of an incorrect response to the question about Wu's rise and fall. It is a summary of the material rather than a direct answer:

> Empress Wu became the only woman to rule China in name as well as fact. Her rule lasted for 45 years. She began her rise to power as a concubine of the third T'ang emperor.

Organize Your Answer

Think before you write. This is perhaps the most important step in test taking, but it is the one you may least want to take the time to do. Plan what you are going to say before you say it.

Brainstorm Ideas.   Reread the question and jot down words or phrases to indicate the ideas you want to include in the answer. Number your ideas in the order in which you want to discuss them. On reconsidering, you may find that some of your brainstorming ideas overlap and others are examples of larger ideas. This is a chance for you to look at your possibilities and come up with a plan. When you use a plan, the writing is a lot easier and more logical.

Establish your purpose in the first sentence, and direct your writing specifically to answer the question. List specific details that support, explain, prove, and develop your point. In a concluding sentence, reemphasize your arguments and restate your purpose. Divide your writing with numbers or subheadings whenever possible, because they simplify the answer for the reader and show the organization. If time runs short, use an outline or a diagram to express your remaining ideas.

The following example shows the plan for answering the question on Empress Wu. The brainstormed ideas have already been organized into a concise, working outline. Remember to think before you write; that is the most important step.

<u>Rise</u>

1. Left convent
2. Plots against wife (sorcery, daughter, poison)
3. Made empress
4. After his death—2 sons
5. Took power
6. Monks made her divine ruler

<u>Fall</u>

1. Made ministers mad
2. Rewarding lovers & fav⌐
   – Cosmetics peddler
   – Young brothers (gove⌐

Use a Formal Writing Style

A college professor, not your best friend, will be reading and gr⌐
swer. Be respectful, direct, and formal. Do not use slang expressi⌐
phrases such as *as you know* or *well*. They may be appropriate i⌐
but not in formal writing.

Avoid empty words and thought. Adjectives such as *good, intere*⌐
say little. Be direct and descriptive in your writing.

State your thesis or main point, supply proof, and use transiti⌐
tie your ideas together. Words such as *first, second,* and *finally* add⌐
help to organize your answer. Other terms, such as *however* and *in*⌐
a shift in thought. Remember, you are pulling ideas together, so u⌐
words to help the reader see relationships.

The following example illustrates a poor response to the questi⌐
Wu. Note the total lack of organization, the weak language, the sla⌐
the failure to use transition words in this paragraph.

Empress Wu was very sneaky. She did many dishonest things. She t⌐
lies about the empress that were so bad that the emperor dumped the⌐
empress. Well, then Wu rose like a bird to fill the new shoes.

Be Aware of Appearance

Research has shown that, on the average, essays written in a c⌐
receive a grade-level higher score than essays written so⌐
Be particular about appearance and be considerate of the rea⌐
correct grammar, punctuation, and spelling.

Write to Earn Points

Essay exam grades seem much more subjective and mysterious⌐
test grades. Some students feel they deserve to pass for filling⌐
They wonder what they did wrong when their paper is return⌐

Professors use objective measures to grade essay test⌐
to cover a certain number of points for a passing score. If⌐
minimum number of points, the paper fails. Answer an⌐
points; do not waste your time including personal experien⌐
Stick to the question, and demonstrate to the professor that⌐

The professor will use the following checklist to score⌐
Wu. A checklist such as this is often called a **rubric**.

---

[3]Charles A. Sloan and Iris McGinnis, "The Effects of Handwriting⌐
School Essays," Eric No. ED 220 836, 1978.

Diagram: Make a drawing that demonstrates relationships.

Discuss: Define the issue and elaborate on the advantages and disadvantages.

Evaluate: State positive and negative views and make a judgment.

Explain: Show cause and effect and give reasons.

Illustrate: Provide examples.

Interpret: Explain your own understanding of and opinions on a topic.

Justify: Give proof or reasons to support an opinion.

List: Record a series of numbered items.

Outline: Sketch the main points with their significant supporting details.

Prove: Use facts to support an opinion.

Relate: Connect items and show how one influences another.

Review: Give an overview with a summary.

Summarize: Retell the main points.

Trace: Move sequentially from one event to another.

Answer the Question

Answer the question that is asked—not some other question. This may seem obvious, but students frequently get off track. Do not write a summary of the material, include irrelevant information, or repeat the same idea over and over again. Focus on the question and write with purpose.

The following is an example of an incorrect response to the question about Wu's rise and fall. It is a summary of the material rather than a direct answer:

> Empress Wu became the only woman to rule China in name as well as fact. Her rule lasted for 45 years. She began her rise to power as a concubine ~~~~~~~ one third T'ang emperor.

Org~~~~~~~ Your Answer

~~Th~~ink before you write. This is perhaps the most important step in test taking, but it is the one you may least want to take the time to do. Plan what you are going to say before you say it.

Brainstorm Ideas. Reread the question and jot down words or phrases to indicate the ideas you want to include in the answer. Number your ideas in the order in which you want to discuss them. On reconsidering, you may find that some of your brainstorming ideas overlap and others are examples of larger ideas. This is a chance for you to look at your possibilities and come up with a plan. When you use a plan, the writing is a lot easier and more logical.

Establish your purpose in the first sentence, and direct your writing specifically to answer the question. List specific details that support, explain, prove, and develop your point. In a concluding sentence, reemphasize your arguments and restate your purpose. Divide your writing with numbers or subheadings whenever possible, because they simplify the answer for the reader and show the organization. If time runs short, use an outline or a diagram to express your remaining ideas.

The following example shows the plan for answering the question on Empress Wu. The brainstormed ideas have already been organized into a concise, working outline. Remember to think before you write; that is the most important step.

<u>Rise</u>

1. Left convent
2. Plots against wife (sorcery, daughter, poison)
3. Made empress
4. After his death—2 sons
5. Took power
6. Monks made her divine ruler

<u>Fall</u>

1. Made ministers mad
2. Rewarding lovers & favorites
   - Cosmetics peddler
   - Young brothers (governorship)

Use a Formal Writing Style

A college professor, not your best friend, will be reading and grading your answer. Be respectful, direct, and formal. Do not use slang expressions. Do not use phrases such as *as you know* or *well*. They may be appropriate in conversation but not in formal writing.

Avoid empty words and thought. Adjectives such as *good, interesting,* and *nice* say little. Be direct and descriptive in your writing.

State your thesis or main point, supply proof, and use transitional phrases to tie your ideas together. Words such as *first, second,* and *finally* add transition and help to organize your answer. Other terms, such as *however* and *in contrast,* show a shift in thought. Remember, you are pulling ideas together, so use phrases and words to help the reader see relationships.

The following example illustrates a poor response to the question on Empress Wu. Note the total lack of organization, the weak language, the slang phrase, and the failure to use transition words in this paragraph.

Empress Wu was very sneaky. She did many dishonest things. She told lies about the empress that were so bad that the emperor dumped the empress. Well, then Wu rose like a bird to fill the new shoes.

Be Aware of Appearance

Research has shown that, on the average, essays ——— receive a grade-level higher score than essays w—n in a clear, legible hand. Be particular about appearance and be considerate of th— somewhat illegibly.[3] correct grammar, punctuation, and spelling.   Proofread for

Write to Earn Points

Essay exam grades seem much more subjective and mysterious than multiple-choice test grades. Some students feel they deserve to pass for filling the page with writing. They wonder what they did wrong when their paper is returned with a low score.

Professors use objective measures to grade essay tests. They look for you to cover a certain number of points for a passing score. If you do not make the minimum number of points, the paper fails. Answer an essay question to earn points; do not waste your time including personal experiences or irrelevant facts. Stick to the question, and demonstrate to the professor that you know the material.

The professor will use the following checklist to score the essay on Empress Wu. A checklist such as this is often called a **rubric**.

---

[3]Charles A. Sloan and Iris McGinnis, "The Effects of Handwriting on Teachers' Grading of High School Essays," Eric No. ED 220 836, 1978.

Rise (60 points)

1. Left convent
2. Plots against wife
3. Installed as empress
4. Sons on throne
5. Took power
6. Monks made her divine

Fall (40 points)

1. Ministers angry
2. Rewarding lovers
3. Examples—peddler and brothers

Grades

All passing exams must have items on both her rise and her fall.

C = Minimum of 5 items

B = Minimum of 6 items

A = Minimum of 7 items

Read an "A" Paper for Feedback

When your professor returns a multiple-choice exam, reread the items. Use what you know about test construction to analyze your errors to figure out what you did wrong. An essay exam, however, is not so easy to review. Sometimes essay exams have only a grade on the front and no other comment. The professor may discuss in class what was needed for an "A" answer, but without your seeing it pulled together, a perfect paper is difficult to visualize.

Ask your classmates or professor to see an "A" paper. If it's yours, share it with others. The "A" paper becomes a model from which you can learn. Compare this paper with your own, and draw conclusions about the professor's expectations. Study and learn from the model so you will not repeat your mistakes.

 **EXERCISE 9** Read and assign a grade of *A, B, C, D,* or *F* to each of the following essay responses to the Empress Wu question. Explain your reasons for each grade and include any suggestions you would offer to the student who wrote the paper.

Paper 1

Empress Wu did many bad things in order to get the power. The things she did were against the people in power. She did not want to stay with the Buddhists because she wanted to be with the new emperor. He died and her sons became puppets. She worked against the people who did not like her.

She was finally forced out of power because she had lovers. One of the lovers became a governor. The two brothers that she liked were decapitated. She fell from power and thus was no longer the empress.

Paper 2

Empress Wu rose to power through tricks and deception. She was intelligent enough to devise a way to meet the new emperor, get him attracted to her, and thus escape her lifetime sentence in the convent. She rose in the new emperor's favor and plotted dishonestly against his wife. Wu falsely accused the emperor's wife of sorcery, murdering her own daughter, and plotting to poison her husband. Wu was soon made empress and given great power. When the emperor died, she ruled through her two sons. Finally, she took the throne herself. Buddhist monks helped her devise a scheme using the scriptures to validate her power. They said she was a divine incarnation of the Buddha.

Wu fell from power because of her weakness for men as lovers. She rewarded her lovers with power and thus angered her ministers. She made a cosmetics peddler an abbot, architect, and then commander–in–chief. Her final appointment of a younger brother of two of her favorites to an important governorship was too much for the ministers. They forced her from power.

Remember: Brainstorm before you write. Jot down the ideas you will use to answer the question and number them. Stick to the question, organize your response, and use logic.

PERSONAL FEEDBACK 2　　　Name _____

1. Do you prefer multiple-choice or essay exams? Why? _____
   _____

2. Have you ever outlined a possible essay question before a test? If so, how did this
   help you prepare for the test? _____
   _____

3. Describe the best paper you have ever written. _____
   _____

4. Grading essay responses is more subjective than grading multiple-choice items.
   What system do you think professors use to arrive at accurate grades? _____
   _____

   Tear out and submit to your instructor.

SUMMARY POINTS

1　How do content tests and standardized tests differ? (page 328)
Content tests measure understanding and recall of concepts covered in a particular course, such as history or psychology. Standardized tests measure ability to apply skills, such as reading or mathematics, which are acquired over a period of time.

2　What general strategies will help me before a test? (page 328)
Arrive at the test well-rested and on time. Know what material will be covered, what types of questions will be included, and how the test will be scored. Thorough preparation inspires well-earned confidence in your ability to do well.

3　What strategies can I use during a test? (page 329)
Concentrate and manage your time wisely. Review your answers and change the ones you are sure are incorrect.

4 **What strategies should I use after a test? (page 330)**
Analyze your errors and ask for help if you don't understand your mistakes.

5 **How can I improve my scores on standardized reading tests? (page 331)**
Read for the main idea, interact with the passage, anticipate the next point, relax, read to learn, and take a moment to recall the main point before answering the questions.

6 **What strategies can I use to answer the major questions types on reading tests? (page 334)**
Main idea: Use the three-question strategy discussed in Chapter 4.
Detail: Verify your answer by looking back in the passage.
Inference: Use logic and the clues in the passage that support your answer.
Purpose: The type of passage suggests the author's purpose in writing. Determine whether the passage type is factual, opinion, or fiction.
Vocabulary: Reread the sentences surrounding the word, and use the context clues to determine its meaning.

7 **What hints can help me approach multiple-choice and true-false questions? (page 341)**
Read all answer choices and select the one that matches your prediction. Look for "100 Percent" words and qualifying words. Use logic to eliminate incorrect answers and recognize flaws in test making.

8 **What strategies will help me answer essay questions? (page 346)**
Prepare by predicting questions and practicing answering them. At the test, analyze the question carefully so you can answer it directly. Brainstorm and organize your ideas before writing. Pay attention to the style and appearance of your answer, and be sure to address all parts of the question to earn maximum credit. When the test is returned, examine an "A" paper.

COLLABORATIVE PROBLEM SOLVING

Form a five-member group and select one of the following activities. Brainstorm and then outline your major points. Choose a member to present the group's findings.

➤ List ten feelings you have when you begin to take an important test.

➤ List ten tips for successfully writing essay exam responses in a history course.

➤ List ten reasons why you would not want to take a course that only had one test, the final exam.

➤ List standardized tests that you or your classmates may have to take in the future. Include tests for admission to professional schools, for graduate schools, and for jobs.

MyReadingLab

MyReadingLab (MRL) www.myreadinglab.com

➤ For support in meeting this chapter's objectives, log in to **www.myreadinglab.com** and select "Memorization and Concentration" and "Test Taking."

THE READING WORKSHOP

If reading a novel, biography, or other book is part of your course experience, refer to The Reading Workshop: Thinking, Talking, and Writing about Books in Appendix 5 for suggestions.

VOCABULARY LESSON

Call Out and Remember to Send

Study the roots, words, and sentences.

> **Roots**   *claim, clam*: declare, call out   *mem*: remember   *mitt, miss*: send

Words with *claim* or *clam* = *declare* or *call out*

Can an *exclamation* point end a sentence? What is *unclaimed* freight?

- Clamor: a racket

  The suitcases made a *clamor* as they fell off the rack.

- Reclaim: regain or demand the return of

  After recovering from an injury, the tennis star *reclaimed* the championship.

- Disclaim: cut off, deny

  If you insult the host, I will *disclaim* ever knowing you.

- Exclaim: cry out

  At the celebration, the patriots *exclaimed* in their joy of victory.

- Irreclaimable: cannot be restored

  The moving company declared that the broken furniture was *irreclaimable*.

- Proclamation: a notice to the public

  A *proclamation* concerning taxation was published in the newspaper.

- Claimant: one who makes a claim

  The *claimant* told the insurance company a tree hit the car in a hurricane.

Words with *mem* = *remember*

Are most *memos* short? Do holidays jog *unremembered* feelings?

- Memento: something to make one remember

  The small statue is a *memento* of my trip to Italy.

- Memoir: a record to remember

  The soldier's *memoirs* gave a personal perspective to the war.

- Memorandum: a note or reminder

  Because a *memorandum* is a business correspondence, make it short.

- Memorable: worth remembering

  With the family together, Thanksgiving dinner was a *memorable* event.

- Memorabilia: things valued for the memories associated with them.

  Elvis *memorabilia* are sold at Graceland.

- Commemorate: to observe and remember

  Display a flag to *commemorate* Independence Day.

- Memorial: a reminder of a distinguished person or a great event

  The fountain was a *memorial* to the founder of the city.

Words with *mit* or *miss* = send

Do you *admit* errors? Will you *permit* me to use you as a reference?

- Missile: something sent through the air

  The *missile* was directed toward enemy territory.

- Emissary: a messenger sent on a mission

  She sent an *emissary* to the French government.

- Remiss: careless

  I would be *remiss* if I did not remind you that the gates close at midnight.

- Remit: pay

  The phone company asked me to *remit* another thirty dollars.

- Submit: surrender

  He had to *submit* to a body search at the airport.

- Emit: to send out

  The car seems to be *emitting* pollution.

Review

Part I

Answer the following with *T* (true) or *F* (false).

_____ 1. An exhaust emissions check measures auto pollution.

_____ 2. Veterans Day commemorates those who served our country.

_____ 3. To receive an insurance payment, the claimant must suffer a loss.

_____ 4. Irreclaimable goods are fixed rather than replaced.

_____ 5. A "We are not responsible for" statement is a company disclaimer.

_____ 6. To reclaim checked goods, you usually need a ticket.

_____ 7. To be remiss is to neglect a duty.

_____ 8. A memoir is nonfiction.

_____ 9. Olympic memorabilia include collectors' pins for the events.

_____ 10. If you remit money, you refuse to pay.

Part II

Choose the best word from the list as a synonym for the following.

memorandum	emissary	proclamation	exclamation	memoir
clamor	memorial	remittance	missile	memento

11. book   _____

12. Washington Monument   _____

13. person   _____

14. keepsake   _____

15. correspondence   _____

16. noise   _____

17. explosive   _____

18. official announcement   _____

19. cry   _____

20. payment   _____

Using Mnemonics

Mnemonics is a technique that helps you organize and recall. It works by stimulating your senses through pictures, sounds, rhythms, and other mental "tricks" to create extrasensory "handles" or hooks that make it easier for your brain to arrange and retrieve information. Given a list of twelve nouns to remember, students who link them in a story remember more than students who just try to memorize them as unrelated items. Weaving such a story is called *narrative chaining,* because the technique links, organizes, and gives meaning to unrelated items. The following are suggested mnemonic techniques for college learning.

Reading Out Loud

Although you may not think of this as a mnemonic, you use additional senses when you read out loud. Memory experts explain that your eyes *see* the material on the page, and your ears *hear* the information. Your mouth, tongue, lips, and throat *feel* the sensation of speaking the words. This is particularly effective for studying lecture notes after class or before an exam.

Writing It Down

Writing works in a similar way to reading aloud, because you feel your hand transcribing the information. Thus summarizing, annotating, notetaking, outlining, and mapping add sensory steps to learning. Always take class lecture notes to reinforce the spoken information.

Creating Acronyms

Create **acronyms**—using the first letter of each word you want to remember. A well-known example of this technique is using HOMES to remember the great lakes: *H*uron, *O*ntario, *M*ichigan, *E*rie, *S*uperior.

Creating Acrostics

Form a sentence in which the first letter of each word corresponds to the first letter of each word in a list you want to remember. For example, *members must jump unless neighbors enlist very soon* is an **acrostic** for remembering the eight planets in our solar system: *M*ercury, *M*ars, *J*upiter, *U*ranus, *N*eptune, *E*arth, *V*enus, *S*aturn. If you need to remember the planets in the order they orbit the sun, create a different sentence. Silly and unusual acrostics can be easy to remember.

Using Rhythms, Rhymes, and Jingles

Use rhythms, rhymes, and jingles to create additional handles for your brain to use to process and retrieve. Most students never forget the year Christopher Columbus came to America because they learned the rhythmic rhyme, "In fourteen-hundred-and-ninety-two/Columbus sailed the ocean blue."

Making Associations

Make a connection between seemingly unrelated ideas by using pictures, nonsense ideas, or connected bits of logic. For example, two easily confused words are *stationary*, which means standing still, and *stationery*, meaning letter-writing paper. To remember the difference, note that *station<u>a</u>ry* is spelled with an "a," which relates to the "a" in *st<u>a</u>nding still*; *station<u>e</u>ry* is spelled with an "e," which relates to *l<u>e</u>tters*.

Conjuring Mental Images

Create a picture, perhaps a funny picture, just as you would on a vocabulary concept card. Picture a *voracious* reader as a shark greedily eating a book.

Using Key Word Images

To learn foreign language vocabulary, use the sound of the new word to relate to an image of a known word. For example, the Spanish word for horse is *caballo*, which is pronounced *cab-eye-yo*. Associate *eye* as the key word and picture a horse with only one large eye looking into a taxi cab.

EXERCISE 1

1. Create an association to remember that *cereal* is a breakfast food and *serial* is a numerical order. _____

   _____

2. Create an acrostic to remember the elements that make up the vast majority of molecules in living things: carbon, hydrogen, nitrogen, oxygen, phosphorus, and sulfur. _____

   _____

3. Create a rhyme or jingle to remember that World War II ended in 1945.

   _____

   _____

Reader's TIP Remembering Information

- Hook information to mental signs that are easy to remember.
- Link information to other information you already know.
- Sense information by touching, writing, or speaking.
- Rehearse information by writing and speaking to yourself.

8

Efficient Reading

Learning Objectives

From this chapter, readers will learn:

1 To determine individual reading rate
2 The average reading for college students
3 Methods to increase reading rate

Everyday Reading Skills: Managing Workplace Reading

WHAT IS YOUR READING RATE?

Learning Objective 1
Determine individual reading rate

If you are not zipping through a book at 1,000 words per minute, does it mean you are a slow reader? No, of course not. You do not need to be reading as fast as you can turn the pages. Yet many college students are concerned about their reading rates. This chapter explains factors that contribute to a fast or slow reading rate and suggests techniques that can help you improve your reading efficiency.

EXERCISE 1

Read the following selection at your normal reading speed. Time your reading so you can calculate your words-per-minute rate. Use a stopwatch or a watch with a second hand. Record your starting time in minutes and seconds. When you have completed the selection, record your finishing time in minutes and seconds. Answer the questions that follow, and use the chart to determine your rate.

Starting time: _____ *minutes* _____ *seconds*

CHILDREN MAY BE HAZARDOUS TO YOUR HAPPINESS

It's the American dream—getting married, buying a home, and settling down to have children. Everyone knows that parenthood is one of the great joys of life and that it contributes greatly to one's happiness and sense of well-being. But in that regard, everyone may be wrong: Research shows that not only does having children not necessarily produce increased happiness, but it may actually reduce it.

Sociologist Robin Simon, who studied thousands of American families, summarized her findings this way: "Parents experience lower levels of emotional well-being, less frequent positive emotions and more frequent negative emotions than their childless peers. In fact, no group of parents—married, single, step or even empty nest—reported significantly greater emotional well-being than people who never had children."

Of course, parenthood is not without its rewards. Despite lower levels of happiness, parents also report more purpose, more meaning, and ultimately more satisfaction with life than nonparents. But research data do not show that children bring greater happiness to their parents.

Why, then, does the belief that children bring great happiness persist, then? One possible reason is that we learn them from our parents. People who believe that parenting is a satisfying, life-enhancing experience are more likely to have children than are people who don't. The former group has more children to whom to pass on their beliefs, while the latter group's less rosy perspective is less likely to get transmitted to the subsequent generation.

Another reason for people's continued faith in the joys of parenting has to do with selective recall. When people conjure up memories of their parenting experiences, they are likely to focus on the relatively rare best of times: a baby's first words or first smile, a fun day at the park, or graduation day. The stresses of parenthood—nighttime feedings, dirty diapers, fighting siblings, piles of dirty laundry, and so forth—may be much more common but tend to recede into the background when parents reflect back on the experience.

So when parents are asked whether having children enriched their lives, they tend to respond in the affirmative. But when parents' current sense of well-being is actually measured at various points in time, the truth emerges: Parents are not actually happier than people who do not have children, and on some measures the parents actually seem to do worse. Again, the culprit seems to be the day-to-day stresses that parenthood brings. On any given day, parents have fewer freedoms, more worries, and more domestic drudgery to deal with than do their childless peers.

Ultimately, of course, many worthwhile pursuits in life, such as marriage or a career (not to mention pursuing a college education), bring their fair share of daily hassles and headaches. The hope is that in the balance the occasional moments of joy and accomplishment make it all worthwhile.

(472 words)

—Development Across the Life Span, Sixth Edition,
by Robert S. Feldman

Finishing time: _____ *minutes* _____ *seconds*

Reading time in seconds = _____

Words per minute = _____ *(see Time Chart)*

TIME CHART

Time in Seconds and Minutes	Words per Minute
60 (1 min.)	472
80	354
90	315
100	283
110	257
120 (2 min.)	236
130	218
140	202
150	189
160	177
170	167
180 (3 min.)	157
190	149

Answer the following with *T* (true) or *F* (false).

_____ 1. The author assumes that most people think being a parent brings happiness.

_____ 2. Robin Simon's study showed that people with children are happier than childless people.

_____ 3. This article mentioned no benefits to having children.

_____ 4. According to the article, one reason for a belief in the greater joys of parenthood is that people tend to recall the pleasant experiences and forget the unpleasant ones.

_____ 5. The author is trying to convince readers not to have children.

What Is an Average Reading Rate?

Learning Objective 2

Average reading rate for college students

Rate calculations vary according to the difficulty of the material. Research indicates, however, that on relatively easy material, the average adult reading speed is approximately 250 words per minute at 70 percent comprehension. For college students, the rate is sometimes estimated at closer to 300 words per minute.

Because this selection was not particularly difficult, the average adult reading speed of 250 words per minute at 70 percent comprehension would apply. If you are reading below this rate, you may have trouble finishing standardized tests and finishing assignments. The suggestions in this chapter can help you become a more efficient reader.

HOW CAN YOU INCREASE YOUR READING SPEED?

Learning Objective 3

Apply methods to increase reading rate

Be Aggressive—Attack!

Grab that book, sit up straight, and try to get some work done. Don't be a passive reader who watches the words go by but lacks understanding and involvement. Be active. Look for meaning with a strong intellectual curiosity, and try to get something out of what you read. Drive for the main idea.

Faster reading does not mean poorer comprehension. Moderate gains in speed usually result in improved comprehension because you are concentrating and thinking more.

The following exercises will help increase your awareness of speed and give you a sense of haste. Time yourself on each exercise and then compare your time with those of other members of the class. If possible, do these exercises as a class or group, with one person calling out the time at five-second intervals.

PERSONAL FEEDBACK 1   **Name** _____

1. When you read the timed reading, how many times did you have to reread? _____
   _____

2. If your mind wandered during the timed reading, what were you thinking about?
   _____
   _____

3. Describe why reading speed is or is not a problem for you. _____
   _____

4. What kind of easy reading would you choose for practicing and improving your
   reading rate? _____
   _____

Tear out and submit to your instructor.

EXERCISE 2   In the following lists, the key word is in boldface in the column at the left. It is then repeated in the group of words to the right. As rapidly as possible, locate the identical word, check it, and then move to the next line. Try to do most of this visually rather than saying each word to yourself. When you have finished each list, record your time and compare your performance with that of fellow classmates.

List 1

1. **lip**	lid	long	left	lip	lap
2. **stand**	start	stand	strong	torn	stop
3. **wander**	willow	wanton	waiting	wander	worry
4. **vain**	vale	vain	vane	vague	value

5. **most**	mort	most	might	host	mast
6. **divide**	divine	devoted	divide	have	doing
7. **someone**	somewhere	someone	sooner	somehow	somebody
8. **week**	weak	meek	week	leak	seek
9. **hazy**	hazy	hazard	hamper	lazy	dizzy
10. **mold**	mole	mound	mold	mind	hold
11. **sight**	height	right	might	sight	light
12. **aide**	aid	aide	add	also	hide
13. **reform**	remake	reclaim	malformed	reform	form
14. **bubble**	raffle	baffle	bubble	rubber	blubber
15. **scarce**	source	sacred	scarce	scorn	serious
16. **fabulous**	famous	fabulous	fashion	false	fasten
17. **reservation**	preservation	occupation	realization	reservation	reserve
18. **reality**	really	reaction	finality	reality	rational
19. **tranquilizer**	transfer	relaxation	tranquilizer	transcribe	transit
20. **phenomena**	pneumonia	phenomena	paralysis	feminine	phrases

Time in seconds = _____

List 2

1. **wing**	wig	wring	wing	with	ring
2. **cram**	crash	carry	ram	ham	cram
3. **like**	mike	like	land	load	hike
4. **sandal**	saddle	sandal	ramble	soften	sweet
5. **prime**	proud	prim	prime	prissy	rime
6. **manage**	mingle	manager	mangle	manner	manage
7. **rash**	rash	rush	race	lush	rich
8. **trace**	trance	trace	trade	train	trail
9. **saline**	saloon	salmon	saline	short	slowly
10. **revenge**	regain	ravenous	rancid	revamp	revenge
11. **tired**	tried	trend	tread	tired	torn
12. **withdrawn**	without	withdraw	within	withdrawn	witness
13. **powerful**	power	potential	powerful	potent	palate
14. **indignant**	indigenous	indigent	distinguish	indignant	indulge
15. **remember**	dismember	remain	reminisce	remission	remember
16. **condescending**	condemning	condense	concise	coherent	condescending
17. **magnanimous**	magnificent	magnanimous	magnetic	malformed	magnify
18. **humorous**	human	hormone	hammock	hammer	humorous
19. **civilization**	civilized	citizenry	civic	civilization	centered
20. **ingenious**	ingenuous	injurious	ingenious	ignoble	engine

Time in seconds = _____

Concentrate

Our eyes cannot actually read. We read with our minds. Thus getting information from the printed page ultimately comes down to concentration. The faster you read, the harder you must concentrate. It is like driving a car at 75 miles per hour as opposed to 35 miles per hour. You are covering more ground at 75, and it requires total concentration if you are to keep the car on the road. Faster reading is direct, purposeful, and attentive. There is no time to think about anything except what you are reading.

As Professor Clayton Pinette at the University of Maine says, "Concentration requires lots of energy. Health, rest, and physical and mental well-being are necessary for good concentration. Rest breaks are important and so are personal rewards."[1]

Both external and internal distractions interfere with concentration. External distractions are the physical things around you. Are you in a quiet place? Is the television going? Can you hear people talking on the telephone? Are you being interrupted by someone asking you questions? You can control most external distractions by prior planning. Be careful in selecting your time and place to study. Choose a quiet place and start at a reasonable hour. Set yourself up for success.

Internal distractions, however, are much more difficult to control. They are the thoughts in your mind that keep you from concentrating. Again, prior planning will help. Keep a "To Do" list as described in Chapter 1. Making a list and knowing that you will check back over it will help you stop worrying about your duties and responsibilities. Make an effort to spend more time *doing* something than *worrying* about something.

Visualizing can also help concentration. If you are reading about ostriches, visualize ostriches. As much as possible, try to see what you read as a movie. Use your imagination and all five of your senses to improve your comprehension.

EXERCISE 3

In the lists here, the key word is in boldface. Among the words to the right, locate and mark the one most similar in meaning to the key word. In this exercise, you are not just looking at the shapes of words, but you are looking quickly for meaning. This will help you think fast and effectively. When you have finished each list, record your time, check your answers, and compare your performance with those of others in the class.

List 1

1. recall	read	guide	remember	fail	forgive
2. sanitary	new	fine	equal	clean	straight
3. physician	health	doctor	coward	elder	teacher
4. motor	car	horse	wagon	shine	engine
5. first	primary	last	finally	only	hard
6. look	stick	serve	glance	open	wait
7. usual	common	neat	best	cruel	kindness
8. quick	noisy	near	fast	finish	give
9. annoy	logic	make	win	disturb	set
10. shout	cry	action	most	fear	force
11. friend	family	mother	soldier	farmer	comrade
12. carry	plan	instruct	take	deal	rank
13. sincere	style	genuine	safe	future	simple
14. valuable	dear	unstable	truthful	ancient	broken
15. diminish	season	promote	forward	reduce	marry
16. anxious	appear	sight	nervous	mean	helpful
17. liquid	clear	running	pipes	kitchen	fluid
18. prestige	program	status	mission	natural	report
19. core	side	nation	heart	event	process
20. harness	control	appear	build	mark	attend

Time in seconds = _____

---

[1]Clayton Pinette, personal communication, February 1994.

List 2

1. ill	sin	die	skill	sick	mind
2. calm	envy	breeze	peaceful	early	far
3. nice	pleasant	needed	new	smooth	plastic
4. emotion	drain	feeling	heat	silent	search
5. close	cost	tall	mild	flow	near
6. gun	knife	rifle	handle	metal	hold
7. expert	rule	sort	believer	follower	specialist
8. obtain	get	feature	delay	injure	adapt
9. discuss	sense	divide	order	talk	find
10. moisture	dampness	sample	screen	dark	dirty
11. village	mountain	town	river	country	moving
12. bravery	origin	voluntary	courage	means	social
13. loyal	client	faithful	definite	legal	scale
14. convert	swim	chief	movement	policy	change
15. celebrate	attain	learn	century	rejoice	statement
16. argument	fund	quarrel	meeting	democracy	voice
17. preserve	opportunity	solar	system	save	signal
18. hilarious	funny	horrible	drama	sensible	even
19. imitate	difficult	confer	strike	language	copy
20. danger	general	fair	position	risk	army

Time in seconds = _____

Stop Regressions

A regression is the act of going back and rereading what you have just finished. Does this ever happen to you? Certainly some textbook material is so complex that it requires a second reading, but most of us regress even when the material is not that complicated. The problem is simply "sleeping on the job." Your mind takes a nap or starts thinking about something else while your eyes keep moving across the page. Hence halfway down the page, you wonder, "What am I reading?" and you plod back to reread and find out. Then, after an alert rereading, the meaning is clear, but you have lost valuable time.

Regression can be a habit. You know you can always go back and reread. Break yourself of the habit. The next time you catch yourself going back to reread because your mind has been wandering say, "Halt, I'm going to keep on reading." This will put more pressure on you to pay attention the first time.

Sleeping through only one or two paragraphs in an entire chapter probably won't hurt your comprehension that much. Sleeping through much more than that, however, could be a problem. Remember, reading the assignment twice takes double the time. Try to reread only when it is necessary because of the complexity of the material.

Avoid Vocalization

Vocalization means moving your lips as you read. It takes additional time and is generally a sign of an immature reader. A trick suggested by specialists to stop lip movement is to put a slip of paper in your mouth. If the paper moves, your lips are moving, and you are thus alerted to stop the habit.

Subvocalization refers to the little voice in your head that reads out loud for you. Even though you are not moving your lips or making any sounds, you hear the words in your mind as you read. Some experts say that subvocalization is necessary for difficult material, and others say that fast readers are totally visual and do not need to subvocalize. The truth is probably between the two. You may find that in easy reading you can eliminate some of your subvocalization and only hear the key words, whereas on more difficult textbook material, subvocalization reinforces the words and gives you better reading comprehension. Because your work will be primarily with textbook reading, do not concern yourself with subvocalization at this time. In fact, sometimes you may need to read particularly difficult textbook passages aloud in order to understand them fully.

Expand Fixations

Your eyes must stop for you to read. These stops, which last for a fraction of a second, are called **fixations.** If you are reading a page that has twelve words to a line and you need to stop at each word, you have made twelve fixations, each of which takes a fraction of a second. If, however, you can read two words with each fixation, you will make only half the stops and thus increase your total reading speed.

You might say, "How can I do this?" and the answer has to do with peripheral vision. To illustrate, hold up your finger and try to look only at that finger. As you can see, such limited vision is impossible. Because of peripheral vision, you can see many other things in the room besides your finger. Research has shown that the average reader can see approximately 2.5 words per fixation.

Read the following phrase:

in the barn

Did you make three fixations, one on each word, or did you fixate once? Now read the following word:

entertainment

How many fixations did you make? Probably one, but as a beginning reader in elementary school, you most likely read the word with four fixations, one for each syllable. Your use of one fixation for *entertainment* dramatizes the progress you have already made as a reader and indicates the ability of the eyes to take in a number of letters at one time. The phrase *in the barn* has nine letters, whereas *entertainment* has thirteen. Does it make any sense to stop three times to read nine letters and once to read thirteen? Again, the reason we do so is habit. If you never expected or tried to read more than one word per fixation, that is all you are able to do.

The key to expanding your fixations is to read phrases or thought units. Some words seem to go together automatically and some don't. Words need to be grouped according to thought units. Your fixation point, as shown in the following example, will be under and between the words forming the thought unit, so your peripheral vision can pick up what is on either side of the point.

Read the following paragraph by fixating at each indicated point. Notice how the words have been divided into phrase units.

FASTER READING

A faster   reading speed   is developed   through practice
·   ·   ·   ·
and concentration.   Your reading rate   also depends
·   ·   ·
on how much   you know   about a subject.
·   ·   ·

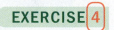 **EXERCISE 4**   In the following lists, the key phrase is in boldface. Among the words on the line below, locate and mark the phrase that is most similar in meaning to the key phrase. Record your time, check your answers, and compare your performance with those of others in the class. This exercise will help you increase your eye span and grasp meaning quickly from phrases.

List 1

1. **to have your own**
   wish for more   share with others   keep for yourself   be harmed by fire
2. **finish a task**
   lessen the impact   clean the attic   turn on the lights   complete a job
3. **sing a song**
   hum a tune   work for pleasure   leave for vacation   wish on a star
4. **manage a business**
   lose your job   lock the door   seek employment   run a company
5. **sit for a while**
   make ends meet   rest in a chair   learn new ways   fall into bed
6. **clear and concise**
   engaging in conversation   ordering a change   easy to understand   complex and difficult
7. **reach a goal**
   achieve an objective   call a meeting   change your mind   open a hearing
8. **free your mind**
   leave a spot   clear the head   turn the motor   remember a date
9. **walk down the road**
   meet in the car   support rapid transit   call the taxi   stroll in the street
10. **hold some money back**
    rush to the bank   drop a dime   accumulate savings   remain at work

Time in seconds = _____

List 2

1. **sense a disaster**
   sleep with ease   feel danger near   yearn for adventure   seek your fortune
2. **hurry to leave**
   walk in the rain   spill the coffee   lower the rent   rush out the door
3. **seek legal advice**
   engage an attorney   earn a living   move your address   give to charity
4. **forget to call**
   scream and yell   open an account   send by mail   neglect to phone
5. **offer your services**
   get in the way   ask to help   quit your job   waste your time
6. **listen to music**
   play in a band   buy a piano   hear a tune   turn off the radio
7. **notice a change**
   see a difference   buy a new shirt   work on a project   meet new people
8. **lose money gambling**
   pay for a product   not win a bet   cut expenses   make an offer
9. **clean up a spill**
   go in the kitchen   add more water   wipe away a stain   tear a rag
10. **leap with delight**
    sing a high note   turn the page   ask for help   jump for joy

Time in seconds = _____

Use a Pen as a Pacer

Using a pen to follow the words in a smooth, flowing line can help you set a rhythmical pace for your reading. In elementary school you were probably taught never to point at words, so this advice may be contrary to what you have learned. However, it can be an effective speed-reading technique.

The technique of using a pen as a pacer is demonstrated in the following paragraph. Use a pen to trace the lines shown, so it goes from one side of the column to the other and returns in a Z pattern. Because you are trying to read several words at a fixation, it is not necessary for your pen to go to the extreme end of either side of the column. After you have finished, answer the comprehension questions with T (true) or F (false) and compare your speed with that of others.

EXAMPLE   **BREAKING FOR MEMORY**

Researchers have found that taking a series
of short breaks during a long
study period can enhance memory
and thus improve your recall
of the information. The breaks should be
a complete rest from the task
and should be no longer than
ten minutes. You may choose
to break every forty or fifty minutes.
During your break, you will experience
what experts call memory consolidation
as the new information is linked
and organized into knowledge networks.
According to some experts, deep breathing
and relaxation exercises can also help
by improving the flow of oxygen to the brain.

(100 words)

Time in seconds = _____

_____ 1. Fifty-minute breaks are recommended during long study periods.

_____ 2. Memory consolidation means improving the flow of oxygen to the brain.

EXPLANATION   The answers are (1) *false* and (2) *false*. Although it may seem awkward at first, practice using a pen to read in a Z pattern on light material such as newspaper or magazine articles to get accustomed to the technique. It will not only force you to move your eyes faster, it will also improve your concentration and keep you alert and awake.

Try using your pen as a pacer for the first five or ten minutes of your reading to become familiar with the feeling of a faster, rhythmical pace. When you tire, stop the technique, but try to keep reading at the same pace. If, later in the reading, you feel yourself slowing down, resume the technique until you have regained the pace. This is a simple technique that does not involve expensive machines or complicated instruction, and *it works!* Pacing with the *Z* pattern *will* increase your reading speed.

EXERCISE 5

Read the following passages (using your pen as a pacer in the *Z* pattern in Passages 1, 2, and 3). Answer the comprehension questions with *T* (true) or *F* (false), then record your reading time and compare your performance with that of other students.

Passage 1

NATURAL GAS SAFETY

Natural gas is odorless so, in the early days of using natural gas to heat buildings and cook, someone would occasionally light a match without realizing that a gas leak had filled the air with gas. Poof! Inventors quickly began designing devices that would detect the presence of natural gas in the air and sound an alarm. However, the best solution was not a detection device. Instead, a gas that could be easily smelled was added to the odorless natural gas so that a leak could be detected easily by a human's built-in gas detector, the nose!

(98 words)

—*A Creative Problem Solver's Toolbox,* by Richard Fobes

Time in seconds = _____

_____ 1. Another gas was mixed with natural gas to create a smell.

_____ 2. Originally natural gas was odorless.

Passage 2

NETIQUETTE

The rules and guidelines for acceptable behavior on the Net are called netiquette. Be careful to say what you mean and to say it with care. You cannot double-click and take it back. Keep your messages short and to the point. People who receive hundreds of e-mails each day are more likely to respond to short ones. Although you are hidden from view, appearances are important. Proofread your messages. Other people will judge your intelligence   and education   by the spelling,   grammar,   punctuation, and clarity   of your messages.   If you   want your messages   to be taken seriously,   present your   best face.

(100 words)

—Computer Confluence: Exploring Tomorrow's Technology,
Third Edition, by George Beekman

Time in seconds = _____

_____ 1. According to the author, once a message is sent you can double-click and retract it.

_____ 2. The author suggests that grammar and punctuation are not important in e-mail messages to close friends.

Passage 3

TYPING KEYBOARD

The earliest typewriters   usually jammed   when a key
was pressed   too soon   after the previous key
was released.   Most people   weren't willing
to tolerate   this flaw,   so early typewriters
were used   mostly by blind people   and others
who couldn't write   easily by hand.   Christopher Sholes
created a clever   supporting enhancement   that overcame
this jamming tendency.   He arranged   the letters
on the keys   awkwardly!   He put   the frequently
typed letters   E, T, O, N, R, and I   on keys
that required   finger movement   to reach them,
and assigned   frequently typed   pairs of letters,
such as E and D,   to the same finger.   His innovation worked!
It successfully   slowed down   a person's typing speed,
thereby reducing   the tendency for   his typewriters to jam.
Unfortunately,   because Sholes' typewriters   became so popular,
this awkward   keyboard arrangement   is the one
we still   use today!

(139 words)

—The Creative Problem Solver's Toolbox, by Richard Fobes

Time in seconds = _____

_____ 1. Our present typing keyboard was adopted to enhance speed.

_____ 2. Early typewriters were used by blind people.

Passage 4

I HAVE A SENSE OF HUMOR

According to the journalist Norman Cousins, laughing is internal jogging, and when you laugh, you are exercising all your internal organs. Not only does laughter feel good, it is essential to good health and a sense of well-being. Cousins has good reason to believe this. Some years ago he was diagnosed with a terminal illness and given just two months to live. Instead of spending his precious time remaining in the hospital, he checked into a hotel and watched, read, or listened to every humorous movie, book, and audiotape he could get his hands on. He virtually laughed himself well. Many years later, still in excellent health, Cousins was convinced, as were his doctors, that laughter accounted for his recovery! In fact, the medical school at UCLA invited him to join its faculty to teach interns how to lighten up.

Cousins' amazing story holds a lesson for all of us. We can all stand to lighten up a little—to find the genuine humor in an embarrassing moment, in a mistake, in a situation that is so serious that we need to laugh to keep from crying. Humor at its best means being able to laugh at yourself. Look for opportunities to see the lighter side of life and to share the experience of being human with others who can laugh with you, not at you. Cultivate the habit of walking on the "light" side of life.

(237 words)

—*The Career Fitness Program: Exercising Your Options,*
Seventh Edition, by Diane Sukiennik et al.

Time in seconds = _____

_____ 1. Norman Cousins had humorous movies, books, and tapes brought to his hospital room to speed his recovery.

_____ 2. Cousins was invited to teach student interns about humor.

Passage 5

DWARF PLANETS

What is a planet? We've been asking that question at least since Greek astronomers came up with the word to describe the bright points of light that seemed to wander among fixed stars. Our solar system's planet count has soared as high as 15 before it was decided that some discoveries were different and should be called asteroids.

Many disagreed in 1930 when Pluto was added as our solar system's ninth planet. The debate flared again in 2005 when Eris—about the same size as Pluto—was found deep in a zone beyond Neptune called the Kuiper Belt. Was it the 10th planet? Or are Eris and Pluto examples of an intriguing, new kind of world?

The International Astronomical Union decided in 2006 that a new system of classification was needed to describe these new worlds, which are more developed than asteroids, but different than the known planets. Pluto, Eris and the asteroid Ceres became the first dwarf planets. Unlike planets, dwarf planets lack the gravitational muscle to sweep up or scatter objects near their orbits. They end up orbiting the sun in zones of similar objects such as the asteroid and Kuiper belts.

Our solar system's planet count now stands at eight. But the lively debate continues as we enter another exciting decade of exploration and discoveries.

(220 words)

—Retrieved 5/15/2011 http://solarsystem.nasa.gov/planets/profile.cfm?Object=Dwarf

Time in seconds = _____

_____ 1. The word *planet* was given to these celestial objects by the Greeks.

_____ 2. Pluto, Eris, and Ceres are now considered dwarf planets.

Preview Before Reading

Do not start reading without looking over the material and thinking about what you need to accomplish. Think about the title and glance over the material looking for key words and phrases. Read the boldface and italic type. Decide what you think the selection is going to be about and what you want to know when you finish it. A few minutes spent on such an initial survey will help you read more purposefully and thus more quickly.

Activate your schema. What is your prior knowledge on the subject? Pull out your computer chip and prepare to add new information or change existing ideas.

Set a Time Goal for an Assignment

For each of your textbooks, estimate the approximate number of words per page. Write this estimate in the front of your book so you can refer to it during the course. Knowing your reading rate, you can approximate how many minutes it will take you to read a page. Remember, your speed will vary with different textbooks according to the difficulty of the material. Toward the middle of the book, as you become more familiar with the subject, you will read faster than you did in the beginning.

Each time you sit down to do an assignment, count the number of pages you need to complete. Calculate the amount of time it will probably take you, and then look at the clock and write down your projected finishing time. Make your goal realistic and pace yourself so you can achieve it. Having an expectation will help you speed up your reading and improve your concentration. Do not become an all-night victim of Parkinson's law, which states that the job expands to fit the time available. Don't allow yourself all night or all weekend to read twenty-five pages. Set a goal and then try to meet it. Rather than leisurely sauntering through an assignment, develop a sense of urgency.

Be Flexible

Inefficient readers are overconscientious, too often giving equal time to all words and all types of reading. As mentioned, you should be able to read a newspaper article in much less time than it would take you to read a science or economics passage, especially if you have already heard the news highlights on television or radio. Textbooks are more difficult and less familiar than news stories. Don't read everything at the same rate. Be willing to switch gears and select the appropriate speed for the job.

Sometimes you may need to look over material for a detail or a specific point. In this case, don't read all the words. Skim until your eyes locate the information you need and then move on to the next task. This is a case of adjusting your speed to your purpose. For example, if you are told to read a history chapter for an exam, read it carefully and spend some time studying it. But if you have been told to write a half-page summary of five articles in the library, you can probably just skim the material for the main ideas and a few supporting details. Again, adjust your speed to your purpose.

Practice

You cannot improve your running speed unless you get out and run. The same is true with reading. To learn to read faster, practice faster reading techniques every day. As the following paragraph explains, *wishing* and *willing* are not the same:

The *wish* to learn is diffuse and general. The *will* to learn is concentrated and specific. The wish to learn means that we repeat a thing again and again hoping for something to happen. The will to learn means that we dig down and analyze, that we try to find out exactly what is wrong and exactly how to put it right.

—*Streamline Your Mind,* by James Mursell

SUMMARY POINTS

1 What is my reading rate? (page 358)

The timed readings and charts helped you see your reading rate. With a little effort, you can determine your rate while reading any material. Count the number of words in the passage, and divide by the number of seconds it took you to read it. Convert the answer to minutes by dividing by 60. Remember that your rate will vary depending on your familiarity with the subject and your purpose for reading.

2 What is the average reading rate for college students? (page 359)

It is about 300 words per minute. How did your rate compare?

3 What methods will help me increase my reading rate? (page 360)

Reading faster requires being an active, aggressive reader. Concentrate on finding meaning, stop regressions, avoid vocalization, expand fixations, use a pen as a pacer, preview, and set a time goal. Adjust your speed to achieve your purpose, and practice!

 **COLLABORATIVE PROBLEM SOLVING**

Form a five-member group and select one of the following activities. Brainstorm and then outline your major points on a transparency. Choose a member to present the group findings to the class.

➤ Create a "Top Ten" list of suggestions for improving your reading speed.

➤ Create a "Top Ten" list of reasons why students have trouble concentrating on what they are reading.

➤ List reasons why prior knowledge influences reading rate.

➤ List reasons why you should not expect to read a textbook at the same reading rate as a novel.

MyReadingLab

MyReadingLab (MRL) www.myreadinglab.com

➤ For support in meeting this chapter's objectives, log in to **www.myreadinglab.com** and select "Reading Rate."

THE READING WORKSHOP

If reading a novel, biography, or other book is part of your course experience, refer to The Reading Workshop: Thinking, Talking, and Writing about Books in Appendix 5 for suggestions.

TIMED READING 1 Business

Preparing for an interview can be challenging. Interviewees often practice answering questions and think about how to present themselves in the best possible light for the jobs they are seeking. Occasionally, a question might be asked that not only borders on the personal but might actually be against the law.

Use your pen as a pacer and time your reading of the following selection.

Starting time: _____ minutes _____ seconds

Refer to the
Reader's **TIP**
for **Reading and
Studying Business**
on page 259.

WHEN INTERVIEW QUESTIONS TURN ILLEGAL

You're probably aware that interviewers are not supposed to ask you certain questions. There are five areas of special sensitivity in selection interviewing. Our goal here is twofold: to point out these illegal areas of questions, and to suggest strategic ways to handle them if they occur in your interview.

5   Our aim here is not to turn you into a "legal eagle" on constant alert for any cause to accuse or sue an interviewing company. In truth, many instances of illegal interview questions (such as, "Are you married?") occur in the course of ordinary getting-to-know-you small talk during an interview and aren't intended by the interviewer as an intrusion into your privacy. But innocent or not, illegal interview questions can land a company in court
10   when a job seeker claims discrimination in the interview process.

Learning to avoid illegal questions as an interviewer and handling them well as an interviewee is the focus of what follows.

WHO MAKES THE RULES FOR INTERVIEW QUESTIONS?

No single federal, state, or local agency or court defines for all cases which interview questions are legal or illegal. Instead, a plethora of court rulings, legislative decisions,
15   agency regulations, and constitutional laws combine to produce the often confusing and frequently changing list of what you can and can't ask a job applicant.

HOW TO ANSWER DIFFICULT QUESTIONS

Following are our suggestions for some of the more difficult areas in which the employer must exercise caution when asking questions—and you must be equally careful in how or if you answer.

MARITAL CIRCUMSTANCES

20   Courts have ruled that it's none of the company's business how many children an applicant has; whether he or she is married, single, divorced, or engaged; whether the applicant plans to become pregnant at any time in the future; how the applicant's spouse or partner feels about overnight travel; or what plans the applicant has made for child care during the workday.

25   Managers stumble into trouble in this area when making small talk, especially of a disclosing or "sharing" nature with the candidate. Manager: "My wife and I have lived here for about 10 years. We love it—especially the school system. Do you have kids?" Innocent? Of course. But if relations turn litigious, the manager will have to admit in court that he inquired about children as part of the selection interview.

WHAT TO DO

30   If you are asked an illegal question in this area, you can give a general response, said graciously: "I would prefer to stick to job-related questions." Or you can be more pointed: "Are children a requirement for this position?" And, of course, you can always decide simply to play along, but as minimally as possible: "Yes, we have one child. Shall we talk about your requirements for this position?"

AGE

35   To prevent age discrimination in hiring, courts have disallowed these sorts of questions: "How old are you?" "In what year were you born?" "When did you graduate from high school?" and so forth. You do have the right to ask whether the applicant meets the legal age requirements for work in your city or state.

Managers stray into trouble here when they talk about the average age of their work-
40   force in relation to the candidate: "Our typical employee is probably 8 to 10 years older than you. Do you anticipate problems managing people older than yourself?" You can imagine the later court scene. *Manager:* "But, Your Honor, I never asked her age!" *Candidate/plaintiff:* "My age seemed to be one of his key concerns about my ability to manage." Verdict goes to the plaintiff, with back pay, damages, and court costs.

WHAT TO DO

45   If asked an illegal question having to do with your age, you can respond, with a smile: "Age has never been a consideration for me in my work life." Or you can turn the knife a bit: "Is my age being considered as part of my application?" And, of course, you can simply answer, if you wish: "I'm 27, but my age hasn't been a consideration in past jobs."

DISABILITIES

50   Companies are forbidden by law from asking an applicant if he or she has mental or physical disabilities. Nor can they inquire about the nature or severity of disabilities, no matter how apparent they seem in the hiring process. Any physical or mental requirements a company establishes as a prerequisite for hiring must be based on "business necessity" and the safe performance of the job.

55   Managers are misled here by their best intentions: "We have many people with disabilities working for us and we support their needs in every way possible. For example, we could overcome the problem you have with your hands by giving you an automated speech recognition word processor." If the candidate with disabilities does not get the job, the manager's assumptions about the candidate's typing abilities could come back to
60   haunt in an expensive way.

WHAT TO DO

If you are asked an illegal question having to do with disabilities, you can refer the interviewer to Americans with Disabilities Act (ADA) guidelines: "I believe that under current ADA law you can't make this issue a part of the hiring process." Or you can take the edge off a bit with a general answer: "I know of nothing that will prevent me from fulfilling the
65   job requirements of this position."

SEX AND PHYSICAL APPEARANCE

An employer cannot ask questions about the person's gender unless the job specifications strictly require either a male or a female. The burden of proof is on the employer to demonstrate that only a man or a woman can do the job. Employers should beware: Courts and the Equal Employment Opportunity Commission have interpreted very narrowly the notion that

70 only one gender can perform a particular job. In addition, employers should avoid questions about the person's physical appearance, including height, weight, grooming, and dress, unless these bear clearly upon job requirements.

Again, a manager's small talk in the job interview is the unhappy hunting ground for mistakes in this area of questioning. *Manager to a woman applicant:* "We have a fitness 75 facility here at the plant. But you seem to be pretty fit already." Oops.

WHAT TO DO

If quizzed about matters of gender or physical appearance, you can respond in a general way: "I'm fully prepared to take on these job responsibilities, and I don't think gender or appearance plays a role." Or you can return the question with a question: "Are gender and appearance being considered as part of this hiring process?" These responses need 80 not be said in a snarlish way (though the interviewer may well deserve your anger). You can preserve your chances for the job by handling the questions professionally.

CITIZENSHIP AND NATIONAL ORIGIN

A company cannot legally inquire into the applicant's place of birth, ancestry, native language, spouse's or parents' birthplace, or residence. Nor can an employer ask directly, "Are you a U.S. citizen?" or "Do you have naturalization papers?" Prior to the decision 85 to hire, these questions may tend to reveal racial or ethnic factors that may bias the employer. Companies should request names or *persons* to notify in case of an emergency rather than specifying *relatives*. Employers should not require that the applicant's photograph be submitted prior to the hiring decision.

Managers often misstep into this pitfall when inquiring about a candidate's second 90 language capability. *Manager:* "You say on your resume that you speak Spanish fluently. Did you grow up in Mexico?" A person's land of birth cannot be grounds for a hiring decision. Clearly, this question strays into legally hazardous areas.

WHAT TO DO

If asked about your national origin, you can answer "My family history and heritage are getting us off the topic, don't you think? I would rather talk about job requirements."

95 Or you can be more direct: "I assume that where my parents came from isn't one of the requirements for this job."

(1,318 words)

—*Interviewing for Success,* by Arthur H. Bell and
Dayle M. Smith

Finishing time: _____ *minutes* _____ *seconds*

Total time: _____ *minutes* _____ *seconds*

Rate = words per minute _____ *(see time chart)*

TIME CHART

Time in Seconds and Minutes	Words per Minute	Time in Seconds and Minutes	Words per Minute
180 (3 min.)	439	340	233
220	359	350	226
230	344	360 (6 min.)	220
240 (4 min.)	329	370	214
250	316	380	208
260	304	390	203
270	293	400	197
280	282	410	193
300 (5 min.)	263	420 (7 min.)	188
310	255	430	184
320	247	440	180
330	239	450	176

Answer the following with *T* (true) or *F* (false).

_____ 1. According to the passage, the list of legal and illegal interview questions frequently changes with new regulations.

_____ 2. Illegal interview questions often request personal information.

_____ 3. Interviewers cannot legally ask questions regarding whether or not an applicant is a parent.

_____ 4. Companies may ask questions about an applicant's physical disabilities if they relate to job safety.

_____ 5. If the company offers a child care program for employees, the interviewer may ask about the number of children who might participate.

_____ 6. It is not permissible for an interviewer to ask whether or not an applicant is a U.S. citizen.

_____ 7. School administrators are permitted to ask questions regarding planned pregnancies of teacher applicants, since a maternity leave would directly affect schoolchildren.

_____ 8. While interviewers cannot directly ask an applicant's age, they can ask when the applicant graduated from high school.

_____ 9. Employers have the right to ask whether or not job applicants meet the legal age requirements for work in their city or state.

_____ 10. The reader can conclude that many of the questions that have been determined to be illegal were found to be so on the basis that the answers to such questions could be used to discriminate against job applicants.

THINK AND WRITE

Why might it not be in the best interests of job applicants to tell their interviewers

they are asking illegal questions? _____

_____

_____

_____

Do you crave foods that you know are not good for you and struggle to resist them? Scientists have discovered biological reasons for those cravings, and so have food manufacturers. New methods of making processed food appeal to us are based on brain chemistry.

Use your pen as a pacer and time your reading of the following selection.

Starting time: _____ minutes _____ seconds

THE DARK SIDE OF FOOD SCIENCE

Refer to the
Reader's **TIP**
for **Health** on
page 291.

Show me a chicken nugget and I will show you the world. The world that is, of highly palatable foods engineered by the food industry to go down easily while also stimulating us to crave more.

Commercial foods like chicken nuggets, French fries, chips, crackers, cookies and
5 pastries are designed to be virtually *irresistible*. And, for a lot of reasons most of us don't fully understand, they are.

There's a "biological basis for why it's so hard for millions of Americans to resist food," former FDA commissioner David Kessler, MD, explained in a recent National Public Radio (NPR) interview. For many of us, one of the most salient stimuli in our environment is food.
10 And how do you make food even more salient? Fat, sugar and salt."

Of course, fat, sugar and salt have been around as kitchen staples for centuries, but it wasn't until the past few decades that they became as abundant and cheap as they are now. And during the course of those same few decades, food manufacturers have been busily leveraging science and technology to enhance their products—manipulating food
15 in ways that not only play on our innate fondness for sugar, salt and fat, but also dramatically boost their overall taste, texture, aroma and appearance.

Think about the flavor of beef infused into McDonald's signature French fries, the creamy filling injected into a Twinkie or the fake crosshatched grill marks stamped onto a KFC grilled chicken breast, and you begin to get the idea. The stuff regularly served

20 up at every chain restaurant, gas station and food court amounts to an edible—and irresistible—amusement park. And it's all fueled by food science and technology.

    "When we were kids," recalls Kessler, "it was enough to put sugar in water, add a little coloring and get a relatively simple sensory experience called Kool-Aid. Since then, food makers have upped the ante." Today we've got Flamin' Hot Cheetos and Double
25 Chocolate Strawberry Cake Krispy Kreme doughnuts.

    We need to have a better understanding about what we're up against. That starts with a brief lesson in food technology.

THIS IS YOUR BRAIN ON PROCESSED FOOD

The human brain has many attributes, but resisting Krispy Kreme doughnuts is not one of them. "The most salient foods are those with fat, sugar and salt," Kessler reminds us. "The
30 advantage those foods have is that they are hardwired from our taste receptors directly into our brains."

    Being attracted to high-calorie foods worked to our advantage when food was scarce and humans had to hunt and gather for a living, explains Christopher Dehner, PhD, a professor of clinical psychology at Columbia University's Obesity Research Center. "The
35 problem is that, today, the food never runs out." On the contrary, it's dangled in front of us around the clock.

    The taste preferences that food-product designers play upon today evolved over many thousands of years as a survival mechanism, notes Dana Small, PhD, a brain researcher at Yale University School of Medicine. They were a means for our ancestors to
40 identify which foods had the dense caloric value their bodies needed to support huge daily energy expenditures. Hardwired as they are, these preferences aren't something from which we can easily free ourselves.

    "You may not even like the taste of a sugary treat initially," Small says, "but as long as it has a major caloric impact, the brain will keep you coming back for more."
45 That's why we are more easily triggered to want cake than to want carrots. "Carrots are better for you, but they have fewer calories," Small explains. And from the human body's instinctive, short-term perspective, calories are more essential than nutrients for survival.

    In generations past when sugar, fat, and even salt were less available, this instinct was
50 not as hard to resist. But thanks to the growth of fast-food restaurants and processed foods the cue for a high-calorie treat may now confront us several times a day.

    The chemicals in our brains are not designed to help us resist. "For each of us it's going to be different," says Kessler, "but the food industry knows that layering fat on top of sugar on top of salt makes the food that much harder for the brain to resist."

A SENSORY EXPLOSION

55 But taste isn't everything. Manufacturers also work hard to develop mouth-watering aromas and carefully engineered textures. They also invest in ad campaigns that equate their products with happiness and success. "The more multisensory the stimuli," says Kessler, "the greater the reward and the stronger the emotional cues."

    Companies are willing to pay big bucks for "sensory science," the kind of in-depth
60 research that tells them exactly how to design a product that appeals to all the senses. No one knows this better than Gail Vance Civille, founder and president of Sensory Spectrum, a New Jersey-based consumer research firm. Civille tests consumer reactions across a range of different sensory areas.

    In the all-important area of taste, for example, what used to be a simple question of
65 sweet versus savory has evolved into a complex science that the food industry calls "flavor dynamics."

    Take a basic chocolate bar. The expert tasters at Sensory Spectrum identified a wide range of flavors in a basic chocolate bar—everything from winey, woody, nutty, citrusy, floral, alkaline and sourness to flavors of soap, cardboard, casein, cooked milk, spray-dried

70 milk and developed milk. A client can then take this information and tweak its formulas to boost certain flavors and suppress others.

Civille and her colleagues will also evaluate a product's texture. Food manufacturers are always searching for the perfect "mouthfeel," which is why fat is so prevalent in processed food. Fat not only bestows crunch, creaminess and contrast, but it also blends

75 flavors and even acts as a lubricant, allowing people to eat faster.

Another texture trick is to presoften food by mashing it. "Processed food is basically prechewed," notes Kessler. This allows us to eat things like chicken tenders more quickly and easily, which can lead to unconscious eating and overeating.

"We used to have foods that took more work," Civille explained in a recent NPR inter-

80 view. "We used to have foods that we chewed 15 times and 20 times and 30 times before we swallowed. Now, there's rarely a food out there, outside of a sweet, chewy candy, that you have to chew more than 12 times before it's gone.

BREAKING THE CYCLE

With two-thirds of Americans now overweight, it's safe to say that our processed-food addiction is messing with our metabolisms as well as our brains.

85 A number of health experts, including Kessler, assert that food companies are actively capitalizing on our genetically hardwired impulses. Food scientists like Civille, meanwhile, argue that the food industry is simply giving people what they want. They may both be right.

Civille, for her part, says she does not believe the food industry is consciously trying to "design food to trick, track or coerce consumers." But she does agree with Kessler that

90 government and media both have a role to play in helping to educate consumers about what goes into the processed foods we consume and how some of that pleasure-boosting science and technology can work against us.

Regulations, incentives and information campaigns may all be a long time coming, though. In the meantime, here are some tips that you can use to curb your consumption

95 of processed foods.

Create Structure. The Achilles' heel of a healthy diet, says Kessler, is being caught off-guard—hungry and at the mercy of your environment. Instead, plan what you're going to eat and when. Meals and snacks should be eaten at regular intervals, and they should be appealing enough to keep you satisfied, but predictable enough that your

100 senses don't feel overstimulated.

Eat Substantial Foods. Foods made from ingredients that race willy-nilly through your digestive system, like simple sugars and refined flours, are not as satisfying as foods that digest more gradually. Protein has the best staying power, taking 2.5 times longer to digest than simple sugars. High-fiber foods, like legumes, fruits, veggies and whole grains, also leave

105 the body feeling full longer because they add volume to meals and take longer to digest.

> "It's not that you can't ever have another serving of French fries. The goal is to reclaim control over what you eat and when, and to stay conscious of your entire eating experience—before, during and after."

Re-size Portions. In a culture of supersized portions, it's easy to forget how much it really takes to feel satisfied (vs. stuffed). To regain a sense of portion control, try eating only half your normal amount of food at a single meal. Then pay close attention to how your body feels 30 minutes later. Notice how you feel 90 minutes later. For most people, a

110 just-right meal is one that staves off hunger for about four hours; a just-right snack keeps you satisfied about two hours, says Kessler, who calls this practice "just-right eating."

Get Comfortable with Eating Real Food. A lot of people opt for easy-to-eat processed foods because "they don't like to be embarrassed when they eat," says Civille. "They don't want to get something stuck in their teeth, and they don't like to be eating

115 complicated foods in public." In the United States, many otherwise-civilized adults aren't confident of proper knife-and-fork techniques, which may incline them toward bite-size, hand-held and nuggetized foods. If you don't yet feel confident eating real foods and enjoying them in all their lovely messiness, make a point of developing that confidence.

Change Your Relationship with Food. Instead of looking at food as if it's your
120 friend, try and deactivate those emotional connections, says Kessler: "1 look at food that's highly processed and I say, It's only going to make me want more." In much the same way we changed our view of tobacco from a sexy to a decidedly unsexy thing, he adds, we can try to do the same with processed food.

Don't Bring It Into the House. If your pantry is full of processed foods, some part
125 of you will be constantly aware of their presence. Those foods will "call out to you," says Kessler, and just seeing them, or even knowing they are there on the shelf, may be enough to activate your brain and trigger cravings.

Don't Resort to Deprivation. It's not that you can't ever have another serving of French fries. In fact, Kessler argues, adopting a mindset of deprivation will just trigger
130 more intense cravings. The goal is to reclaim control over what you eat and when, and to stay conscious of your entire eating experience—before, during and after.

Ultimately, taking back your mind and metabolism means becoming more aware of not only what you eat but also what drives you to eat it. Self-awareness is the greatest tool people can wield against the assault of processed foods, says Kessler.

135 But remember: Self-awareness doesn't mean self-denial. It means learning how to delight in foods that are good for you, and how to enjoy less healthy edible pleasures in moderation, on occasion, when you consciously decide to.

"By consciously paying attention to the pleasures of taste and the experience of eating, you can deepen the reward value of any food you choose," says Kessler, "so choose well."

(1920 words)

—From *Experience Life Magazine,*
October 2010, by Catherine Guthrie

Finishing time: _____ minutes _____ seconds

Total time: _____ minutes _____ seconds

Rate = words per minute _____ (see time chart)

TIME CHART

Time in Seconds and Minutes	Words per Minute	Time in Seconds and Minutes	Words per Minute
180 (3 min.)	640	460	250
200	576	480 (8 min.)	240
220	524	500	230
240 (4 min.)	480	520	222
260	443	540 (9 min.)	213
280	411	560	206
300 (5 min.)	384	580	199
320	360	600 (10 min.)	192
340	339	620	186
360 (6 min.)	320	640	180
380	303	660 (11 min.)	175
400	288	680	169
420 (7 min.)	274	700	165
440	262	720 (12 min.)	160

Answer the following with *T* (true) or *F* (false).

_____ 1. This article consists entirely of the author's opinions about food.

_____ 2. According to the selection, humans tend to crave sugar, fat, and salt because our brains are designed to prefer high-calorie foods.

_____ 3. The author assumes that early humans expended more energy each day than most people today.

_____ 4. According to the article, an attraction to fatty, sugary food is mainly the result of poor childhood habits.

_____ 5. To make processed foods more appealing, manufacturers adjust flavors with additives.

_____ 6. Food scientists have developed methods to change texture, but they cannot yet adjust the smells of foods.

_____ 7. Experienced tasters can identify flavors of wood, wine, and even soap in a chocolate bar.

_____ 8. Civille noted that today's foods require more chewing than the foods of 40–50 years ago.

_____ 9. Manufacturers sometimes include more fat in foods so they are eaten faster, and thus people eat more.

_____ 10. The article suggests that processed foods contribute to poorer health.

Comprehension = (% correct) _____

THINK AND WRITE

Based on the information in this article, do you have a healthy relationship with food? If you do, provide details that support your claim. If you don't, list changes you could make to achieve a better diet. _____

_____

_____

_____

TIMED READING 3 Mathematics

Are arithmetic and mathematics the same? Webster defines arithmetic as "the method or process of computation with figures: the most elementary branch of mathematics." Mathematics, on the other hand, is not so easily captured: "the science of numbers and their operations, interrelations, combinations, generalizations, and abstractions and of space configurations and their structure, measurement, transformations, and generalizations."

Mathematics emerged about the same time as reading and writing, probably in Sumeria about 5,000 years ago, to fulfill the need to measure and communicate time, distance, and quantity. It is both a language and a tool for problem solving that spans all academic disciplines. Like reading and writing, it is basic to learning and using knowledge and a way of understanding the world. Mathematics is considered by many to be beautiful and elegant. Do you agree?

Use your pen as a pacer and time your reading of the following selection.

Starting time: _____ minutes _____ seconds

FROM FISH TO INFINITY

I have a friend who gets a tremendous kick out of science, even though he's an artist. Whenever we get together all he wants to do is chat about the latest thing in evolution or quantum mechanics. But when it comes to math, he feels at sea, and it saddens him. The strange symbols keep him out. He says he doesn't even know how to pronounce them.

5   In fact, his alienation runs a lot deeper. He's not sure what mathematicians do all day, or what they mean when they say a proof is elegant. Sometimes we joke that I just should sit him down and teach him everything, starting with 1 + 1 = 2 and going as far as we can.

Crazy as it sounds, over the next several weeks I'm going to try to do something close to that. I'll be writing about the elements of mathematics, from pre-school to grad
10   school, for anyone out there who'd like to have a second chance at the subject—but this time from an adult perspective. It's not intended to be remedial. The goal is to give you a better feeling for what math is all about and why it's so enthralling to those who get it.

So, let's begin with pre-school.

The best introduction to numbers I've ever seen—the clearest and funniest explana-
15   tion of what they are and why we need them—appears in a "Sesame Street" video called "123 Count With Me." Humphrey, an amiable but dim-witted fellow with pink fur and a green nose, is working the lunch shift at The Furry Arms hotel, when he takes a call from a room full of penguins. Humphrey listens carefully and then calls out their order to the kitchen: "Fish, fish, fish, fish, fish, fish." This prompts Ernie to enlighten him about the
20   virtues of the number six.

Children learn from this that numbers are wonderful shortcuts. Instead of saying the word "fish" exactly as many times as there are penguins, Humphrey could use the more powerful concept of "six."

As adults, however, we might notice a potential downside to numbers. Sure, they are
25   great time savers, but at a serious cost in abstraction. Six is more ethereal than six fish, precisely because it's more general. It applies to six of anything: six plates, six penguins, six utterances of the word "fish." It's the ineffable thing they all have in common.

Viewed in this light, numbers start to seem a bit mysterious. They apparently exist in some sort of Platonic realm, a level above reality. In that respect they are more like other
30   lofty concepts such as truth and justice, and less like the ordinary objects of daily life.

Reader's TIP — Reading and Studying Mathematics Textbooks

Mathematics is a way of thinking. It is as basic a tool for understanding the world as reading and writing.

- Learn the language of mathematics, which is often expressed in symbols and specialized vocabulary.

Devote a section of your class notebook to mathematical expressions and their meanings.

Translate symbols into words. Here are the most basic examples:

+	Plus sign, read "plus." *Example:* "3 + 5" is read "three plus five."
−	Minus sign, read "minus." *Example:* "5 − 3" is read, "five minus three."
× or ( ) or •	Multiplication sign, read "times" or "multiplied by." *Example:* "5 × 3" is read "five times three" or "five multiplied by three."
÷	Division sign, read "divided by." *Example:* "3 ÷ 5" is read "three divided by five."
=	Equal sign, read "equals."

Specialized mathematical vocabulary:

Examples: *ratio, percentage, slope, intercept, algorithm, integer*

Read mathematical expressions using the correct words. For example:

$-2(a^2 + b)$ reads as "negative two (also can be read "minus two") times the sum of a squared plus b or "the sum of a^2 and b multiplied by negative two"

- Use a strategy to attack word problems:

Read carefully to understand exactly what the problem is asking. Translate the problem into mathematical language. The following words are often used to indicate mathematical operations:

The phrases *more than, increase, total of* imply addition.

Less than, decrease, and *difference between* mean to subtract.

Split into equal parts, half, quotient mean to divide.

Groups of, product, twice, triple mean to multiply.

- Mathematics textbooks are dense and detailed.

Pay attention to headings and subheadings to understand the topics being discussed. Bold and italic type often indicate an important term. Read and study the examples.

Read especially difficult parts aloud.

Do as many example problems as necessary to feel confident that you can do them without help.

Upon further reflection, their philosophical status becomes even murkier. Where exactly do numbers come from? Did humanity invent them? Or discover them?

A further subtlety is that numbers (and all mathematical ideas, for that matter) have lives of their own. We can't control them. Even though they exist in our minds, 35 once we decide what we mean by them we have no say in how they behave. They obey certain laws and have certain properties, personalities, and ways of combining with one another, and there's nothing we can do about it except watch and try to understand. In that sense they are eerily reminiscent of atoms and stars, the things of this world, which are likewise subject to laws beyond our control . . . except that those things exist 40 outside our heads.

This dual aspect of numbers—as part-heaven, and part-earth—is perhaps the most paradoxical thing about them, and the feature that makes them so useful. It is what the physicist Eugene Wigner had in mind when he wrote of "the unreasonable effectiveness of mathematics in the natural sciences."

45 In case it's not clear what I mean about the lives of numbers and their uncontrollable behavior, let's go back to the The Furry Arms. Suppose that Humphrey suddenly gets a call on another line, from a room occupied by as many penguins as before, also clamoring for fish. After taking both calls, what should Humphrey yell out to the kitchen? If he hasn't learned anything, he could shout "fish" once for each penguin. 50 Or, using his numbers, he could tell the cook he needs six orders of fish for the first room and six more for the second room. But what he really needs is a new concept: addition. Once he's mastered it, he'll proudly say he needs six plus six (or, if he's a show-off, 12) fish.

The creative process here is the same as the one that gave us numbers in the first 55 place. Just as numbers are a shortcut for counting by ones, addition is a shortcut for counting by any amount. This is how mathematics grows. The right abstraction leads to new insight, and new power.

Before long, even Humphrey might realize he can keep counting forever.

Yet despite this infinite vista, there are always constraints on our creativity. We can 60 decide what we mean by things like 6 and +, but once we do, the results of equations like 6 + 6 are beyond our control. In mathematics, we'll see in the coming weeks, our freedom lies in the questions we ask—and in how we pursue them.

(891 words)

—"From Fish to Infinity," *The New York Times*, January 31, 2010, by Steven Strogatz

Finishing time: _____ *minutes* _____ *seconds*

Total time: _____ *minutes* _____ *seconds*

Rate = words per minute _____ *(see time chart)*

READING 3

TIME CHART

Time in Seconds and Minutes	Words per Minute	Time in Seconds and Minutes	Words per Minute
120 (2 min.)	446	240 (4 min.)	223
140	382	260	206
160	334	280	191
180 (3 min.)	297	300 (5 min.)	178
200	267	320	167
220	243	340	157

Answer the following with *T* (true) or *F* (false).

_____ 1. The fish example from the children's television show, Sesame Street, is used to show the usefulness of numbers.

_____ 2. This selection explains who invented numbers.

_____ 3. Strogatz says that numbers are uncontrollable.

_____ 4. Strogatz states that numbers do not obey any laws, in other words, they are unpredictable.

_____ 5. This selection introduces the idea of counting by ones and also the idea of addition.

Comprehension = (% correct) _____

THINK AND WRITE

If you were continuing Strogatz's blog, what examples might you use to illustrate subtraction, multiplication, and division? _____

_____

Managing Workplace Reading

Everyone works at some point. Perhaps you had a full-time job before you entered college, or perhaps you work part time when you are not studying. In any event, all occupations demand some amount of reading. In fact, companies frequently hire expensive consultants to advise employees on efficient methods for meeting workplace reading demands. Typically, these consultants first urge employees to put their reading demands in perspective and set priorities. Memos, for example, may need to be read immediately, but annual reports can probably wait until later. As a next step, the experts strongly suggest handling a piece of paper only once. Their advice is "Do not open a letter and then set it aside to be handled later. If you open a letter, read it and take action." The three action options are: respond to it, throw it in the trash, or file it to be used later with other material on the same subject.

Reader's **TIP**   **Managing Workplace Reading**

- Set priorities before reading.
- Strive to handle a piece of paper only once.
- Respond to it, discard it in a paper recycling bin, or file it.

Types of Workplace Reading

Work-related documents usually make points quickly, have a serious tone, and are written to inform rather than to entertain. The importance of a document is determined by the way in which the information it contains can affect your job performance, so only you can set priorities.

E-mail

In many workplaces, communication is done mainly by e-mail. This can be an efficient and convenient way to transmit information, discuss ideas, and issue work orders. Sometimes the number of e-mails that employees must process takes an excessive amount of time. Experienced employees use several time-saving methods to manage their e-mail.

First, they disable the tone that signals an incoming message and read their e-mail only two or three times a day. Second, they read messages once and immediately respond, delete, or file as needed; they try to have no messages in their inboxes at the end of the day. Third, they store important messages in folders with logical names.

For responding to e-mail, experts advise employees to keep their messages brief, polite, and not to "reply to all" unless it is necessary; to re-read outgoing messages before sending them; and to avoid rushing with an e-mail response to an important message by sending a courteous, one-sentence e-mail saying they will reply at a later time.

Specific types of workplace reading such as those described below are often sent to employees via e-mail.

Memos

A memo is a brief message used to update co-workers, announce meetings, ask questions, request assistance, or announce decisions. Memos are written in a concise, direct style and can be formal or informal, depending on the sender's level of seniority and the sender's relationship with the recipient. Used correctly, memos are intended for internal messages among company employees and are not generally used for communicating with those outside the organization. They are frequently sent by e-mail.

Memos are usually only a few sentences long but can sometimes continue for several pages. The most important information is given at the beginning (see the illustration below). Notice dates, times, places, and requests for a response or action. Special formatting such as numbered or bulleted lists may be applied to other important items to make them stand out.

1. What is the reason for the memo? _____

_____

2. What is the necessary action? _____

TO:	Market Designs Personnel
FROM:	Sergio Rodriguez, Director of Personnel Services
DATE:	November 1, 2011
CC:	Veronica Menser, General Manager
RE:	Direct Deposit of Paychecks

Please note that beginning with the second pay period in December, all nonsalaried employees will have the option of direct deposit of their paychecks. In order to take advantage of this option, you must fill out a Direct Deposit Request Form (sample is attached) and return it to the Accounting Department by no later than November 15. Implementation of the direct deposit option will be delayed one month for those employees who submit their requests after that date. If you have any questions, please contact me at extension 225.

Letters

A letter is somewhat more formal than a memo and therefore more appropriate for communication outside a company. Use a letter to give or request information, to congratulate or express appreciation, to register complaints, or to emphasize an action. Like memos, business letters are relatively short and written in a concise, direct manner.

Newsletters

Newsletters are documents published by businesses, organizations, clubs, or schools that combine news, editorial columns, letters, stories, and graphics on subjects of interest to group members. They look like mini-newspapers or multi-page stapled letters. The purpose of a newsletter is to build group spirit, bind members together, recognize member achievement, and chronicle group events. Each member of the particular group usually receives the newsletter.

Newsletters are basically *propaganda* (persuasive public relations information) for the organization. They tend to report on the past and rarely have any critical information that demands action. If there is a table of contents, use it to guide your reading. If not, read the headings and beginning paragraphs to determine what you care to read.

Reader's TIP — Reading Newsletters

- Read selectively. You may want to read all of the newsletter or none of it.
- Read critically. You cannot consider the information in a newsletter to be objective, because it contains information beneficial only to the company or organization. Unflattering information is not included, so the coverage is not balanced.
- Note items that are highlighted; set off by numbers, bullets, or capital letters; or that appear in boldface or italic type.

Minutes

Minutes, sometimes called meeting notes, are the official record of business meetings. The minutes include the topics discussed, decisions made, votes tallied, and action taken. Groups rely on the minutes as a reminder, so it is very important that the people present at the meeting review them for accuracy. Any errors should be reported and corrected quickly to avoid future confusion and, perhaps, costly mistakes.

9 Analytical Reasoning

Learning Objectives

From this chapter, readers will learn:

1 To identify the elements of analytical thinking
2 How the thinking strategies of successful and unsuccessful students differ
3 To apply analytical thinking strategies when reading graphic illustrations

Everyday Reading Skills: Reading Direct Mail Advertisements

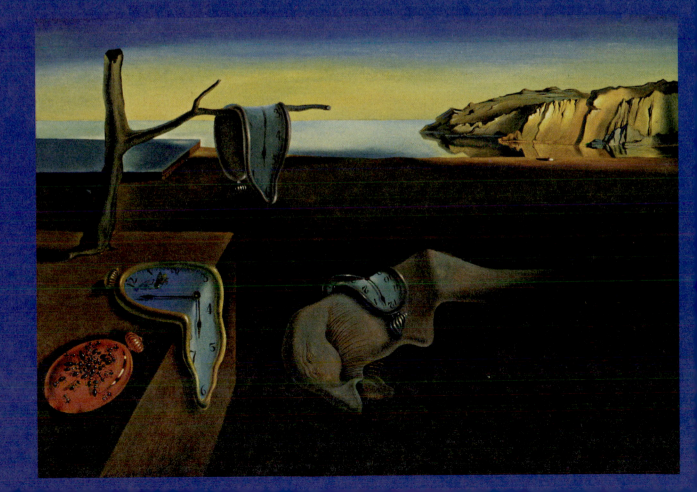

IDENTIFY ANALYTICAL THINKING

According to researchers, good thinkers have developed a logical and sequential pattern of working through complex material, whereas poor thinkers lack this habit of analysis. Good thinkers work persistently, believing they will find answers. They draw on their old knowledge to solve new problems and thus relate, interpret, and integrate what they already know with what they want to learn. Poor thinkers, in contrast, merely collect facts and are unaware of relationships. They cannot put old and new information together to draw conclusions. They seem to have no logical method for problem solving.

Mastering each new college subject offers you both immediate and future benefits. For example, after you struggle through and finally understand an introductory biology text, those same new habits of thinking transfer to the next biology course, which then will be easier to understand. You can also apply these thinking skills to new and different tasks. For instance, the very act of thinking through the complexities of biology will make it easier for you to tackle chemistry and physics. Thinking, like everything else, requires practice, and the more you do, the better you become. You gradually develop the ability to educate yourself.

Two researchers, Bloom and Broder, studied both academically successful and academically unsuccessful college students at the University of Chicago.[1] They described the thinking processes of each (see the lists that follow).

Before reading further, think of a student you know personally who is not successful in school. Check to see if the following characteristics describe that student.

An Unsuccessful Student

1. Has no method of attacking new material.
2. Misunderstands or skips directions.
3. Fails to keep the purpose in mind.
4. Is unable to apply present knowledge to new situations.
5. Is passive in thinking and answers questions on the basis of few clues.
6. Uses "impression" or "feeling" to arrive at answers.
7. Is careless in considering details and jumps around from one to another.
8. After making a superficial attempt to reason, gives up and guesses.

Who do you know who is a very successful student? How many of the following characteristics describe that student?

A Successful Student

1. Is careful and systematic in attacking the problem.
2. Can read directions and immediately choose a point at which to begin reasoning.
3. Keeps sight of goals while thinking through the problem.
4. Pulls out key terms and tries to simplify the material.
5. Breaks larger problems into smaller subproblems.
6. Is active and aggressive in seeking meaning.
7. Applies relevant old knowledge to the problem.
8. Is persistent and careful in seeking solutions.

What kind of student are you? Go back to both lists and circle the characteristics that apply to you.

---

[1]B. S. Bloom and L. Broder, *Problem-Solving Process of College Students* (Chicago: University of Chicago Press, 1950).

Successful students aggressively and systematically attack their studying, and they persist to a logical conclusion. As you can see, Bloom and Broder's list of characteristics might just as easily apply to successful problem solving in everyday life as to success in the academic world. These characteristics thus contribute not only to college success but to the long-lasting personal success that is the ultimate reason for going to college. Start developing them!

PERSONAL FEEDBACK) 1   Name _____

1. What does *delayed gratification* mean and how does it apply to college? _____
   _____
   _____

2. What causes you the most stress? _____
   _____
   _____

3. Describe a problem at home, work, or school that you enjoyed attacking and solving
   systematically. _____
   _____
   _____

4. What do you feel is your greatest problem-solving strength? _____
   _____
   _____

Tear out and submit to your instructor.

Engage in Problem Solving

Another researcher, Arthur Whimbey, studied good and poor readers. He noted two prominent features of poor college readers.

> First, there is one-shot thinking rather than extended, sequential construction of understanding; and second, there is a willingness to allow gaps of knowledge to exist, in effect, an attitude of indifference toward achieving an accurate and complete comprehension of situations and relations.[2]

Whimbey and other researchers believe that all students can learn the characteristic behaviors of good readers by increasing their analytical reasoning skills through problem solving. Through analytical reasoning they break problems into

---

[2]Arthur Whimbey, *Intelligence Can Be Taught* (New York: E. P. Dutton, 1975), 55.

small parts and use logic to arrive at a solution. Breaking a complex word problem into sequential steps for solution requires thinking skills similar to those used in breaking a paragraph down to get a main idea, draw a conclusion, or trace the details of a process.

EXAMPLE   Read the following word problem and think about how you would figure out the answer.

> Mary is shorter than Carol but taller than Kathy. Sue is taller than Mary but shorter than Carol. Which girl is tallest?

Although the problem may seem rather confusing at first reading, when it is broken down in sequential steps, the answer is simple. The best way to solve this problem is to draw a **diagram** so you can visualize the relative height of each girl. Reread the problem and place each girl in a position on a vertical line.

Mary is shorter than Carol,	Carol Mary
but taller than Kathy.	Carol Mary Kathy
Sue is taller than Mary, but shorter than Carol.	Carol Sue Mary Kathy

EXPLANATION   The diagram indicates that the tallest girl is Carol.

Whimbey found that analytical reasoning skills can be taught through practice. He devised a variety of word problems similar to those that follow to help students learn. The thinking strategies used to solve these problems apply in every academic task, not just in reading textbooks. Break each problem in the exercise into parts and work sequentially toward a solution. You may want to do the first exercise with someone else so you can discuss the steps leading to a solution, then try the rest on your own.

BRAIN BOOSTER

Male and Female Brains

Culture and environment obviously are important in shaping gender roles. However, neuroscience reveals that there are biological differences in male and female brains that influence thinking and behavior. Females have two X chromosomes, each containing 1500 genes. Males have 1 X chromosome and 1 Y chromosome, which contain 100 genes. Many of the genes on the X chromosome govern verbal skills and other aspects of thinking. For this reason and others involving chemical differences, females generally tend to be better at seeing details and males tend to excel at recognizing the gist of a situation.

How do these general observations apply to problem solving? Working groups are often more successful at finding solutions when they are made up of both males and females. Test this when forming teams to complete the exercises in this chapter.

—Adapted from John J. Medina, Brain Rules.
© 2008 John J. Medina. Pear Press: Seattle, WA.

EXERCISE 1   Collaborate with a study buddy to answer the following questions. Share your steps in thinking with each other.

_____ 1. Which set of letters is different from the other three?

   a. GHIF   b. MNOK   c. RSTQ   d. CDEB

_____ 2. Face the south and turn to your right. Make another right turn and then an about-face. In which direction are you now facing?

_____ 3. According to the pattern, which letters should come next in the series?

   KL   NO   QR   T __   __   __

_____ 4. A train arrived at its destination at 7:45, which was 3 hours and 50 minutes after its departure. What time was its departure?

_____ 5. According to the pattern, which numbers should come next in the series?

   1   2   4   5   7   8   10   11   __   __   __

_____ 6. Write the word *manage*. If deleting the first three letters or the last three letters leaves an actual word, circle the second *a* in the original word. If not, circle the first *a*.

_____ 7. According to the pattern, what numbers should come next in the series?

   1   6   11   16   21   __   __   __

8. Sylvia needed dental work in a small town with only two dentists. She met them both. Dr. Drill had beautiful teeth, but Dr. Fill's teeth needed work. Using logic, which dentist should Sylvia choose?

_____

_____

9. Ellen, Carolyn, and Betsy each finished the road race at a different time. Their last names, not in order, are King, Wilson, and Harris. Wilson finished before Harris but after King. Betsy came in before Carolyn, and Ellen was last. What are the last names of Betsy and Ellen?

_____

10. Fran, Sally, and Marsha collect old books from different countries. Together they have a total of eighteen books. Six of the books are from Spain, with one more than that being the total from India and one less being the total from Holland. Sally has two books from Spain, and Fran has an equal number from India. Marsha has twice as many books from India as Fran has. Both Marsha and Fran have only one book each from Holland, and Fran has only one from Spain. How many books does Sally have? How many does Marsha have?

_____

	Holland	Spain	India	**Total**
Fran	1	1	2	4
Sally	3	2	1	6
Marsha	1	3	4	8
Total	5	6	7	18

Do you prefer working alone or do you benefit more from working with a study buddy? _____

ANALYTICAL REASONING IN TEXTBOOKS

Learning Objective 3

Apply analytical thinking strategies when reading graphic illustrations

Apply analytical reasoning to every page of every textbook you read. Reading is problem solving, and reading is thinking. Get in the habit of working through complex ideas carefully and systematically. Simplify the material, and break it into smaller, more manageable ideas. Draw on what you already know, and actively and aggressively seek to understand.

To help you visualize complex ideas, textbooks frequently include maps, charts, diagrams, and graphs. These illustrations condense a lot of information into one picture. Refer to such graphic illustrations while you read; the material will then be easier to understand.

This chapter presents exercises on graphic illustrations and problems that require logical and sequential thinking. Before doing the exercises, read the hints in the Reader's Tip.

Reader's TIP — Thinking About Maps, Charts, Graphs, and Diagrams

1. Read the title to determine the subject.
2. Read any information in italics or boldface.
3. Read the footnotes to determine the source of the information.
4. Read the labels to determine what each mark, arrow, figure, or design means.
5. Figure out the legend, the key on a map that shows what the markings represent.
6. Notice numbers indicating units of measurement, such as percentages, dollars, thousands, millions, or billions.
7. Notice trends and extremes. What is the average, and what are the highs and lows?
8. Refer back and forth to the text to follow a process or label parts.
9. Draw conclusions based on the information.
10. Do not read more into the illustration than is supported by fact. In other words, don't draw conclusions that cannot be proved.

EXERCISE 2   Make notes or diagrams to help you solve the following problems.

1. Which set of letters differs from the other three? _____

   _____

   a. ABCD   b. EFGH   c. IJKL   d. MNOP

2. What number would be next in this sequence?

   _____

   3   4   6   9   13

   —The Great Book of Math Teasers, by Robert Muller

3. **The nine-dot problem:** Without lifting your pencil from the paper, draw no more than four straight lines that will cross through all nine dots.

   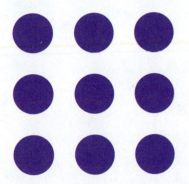

   —Conceptual Blockbusting: A Guide to Better Ideas, Fourth edition, by James L. Adams

4. **The matchstick problem:** Move two matches to form four squares of equal size.

   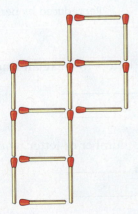

   —Basic Psychology, by Howard H. Kendler

5. **Analogy:** What word completes the analogy?

Merchant: Sell : : Customer: _____

Lawyer: Client : : Doctor: _____

6. **String problem:** You are in the situation depicted below and given the task of tying the two strings together. If you hold one string, the other is out of reach. Can you do it?

_____

_____

_____

—From Richard J. Gerrig and Philip G. Zimbardo, *Psychology & Life,* 17th ed., figure 8.13D (page 266) and figure 18.14D (page 268). ©2005 Pearson Education, Inc. Reproduced by permission of Pearson Education, Inc.

7. **Anagram:** Rearrange the letters to make an English word.

RWAET _____

KEROJ _____

8. **Series completion:** What number or letter would be next in each series?

1 2 8 3 4 6 5 6 _____

A B M C D M _____

—Items 5, 7, 8 from Wayne Weiten, 6th ed.
©2005 Wadsworth, a part of Cengage Learning, Inc.
Reproduced by permission. www.cengage.com/permissions

EXERCISE  3   Collaborate with a study buddy to answer the following questions.

Earnings of Full-time U.S. Women Workers as a Percentage of Men's Earnings
The gender gap in earnings means that women are more likely to be at the low end of the income scale.

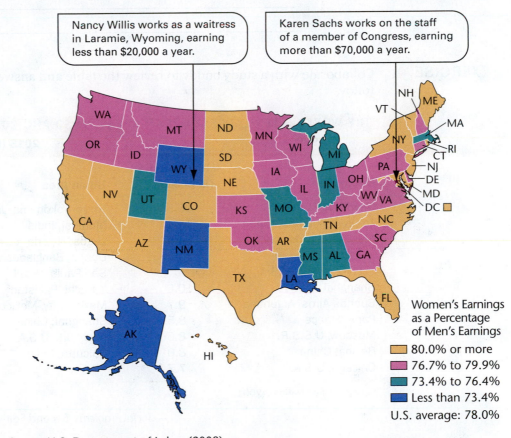

Nancy Willis works as a waitress in Laramie, Wyoming, earning less than $20,000 a year.

Karen Sachs works on the staff of a member of Congress, earning more than $70,000 a year.

Women's Earnings as a Percentage of Men's Earnings

- 80.0% or more
- 76.7% to 79.9%
- 73.4% to 76.4%
- Less than 73.4%

U.S. average: 78.0%

Source: U.S. Department of Labor (2008).

—*Social Problems*, Fourth Edition, by John Macionis

The purpose of the map is to show _____

_____

Use the map to answer the following with *T* (true), *F* (false), or *CT* (can't tell).

_____ 1. Average earnings of women across the United States is 90% of average earnings of men.

_____ 2. Women's earnings in Texas compare more favorably to men's than they do in Michigan.

_____ 3. The average salary for women is less than 73.4% of the average for men in only four states.

_____ 4. In more than half the states, the average salary for women is 76.7% of men's or higher.

_____ 5. The average salary for women working full-time in Wyoming is $20,000 a year.

6. Although the map does not show reasons, why do you think women generally make less money than men? _____

_____

_____

_____

EXERCISE 4

Collaborate with a study buddy to review the table and answer the questions that follow.

THE WORLD'S TEN LARGEST URBAN AREAS, 1980 AND 2015

1980		2015 (Projected)	
Urban Area	**Population (in Millions)**	**Urban Area**	**Population (in Millions)**
New York, U.S.A.	16.5	Tokyo–Yokohama, Japan	26.4
Tokyo–Yokohama, Japan	14.4	Mumbai, India	26.1
Mexico City, Mexico	14.0	Lagos, Nigeria	23.2
Los Angeles–Long Beach, U.S.A.	10.6	Dhaka, Bangladesh	21.1
Shanghai, China	10.0	São Paulo, Brazil	20.4
Buenos Aires, Argentina	9.7	Karachi, Pakistan	19.2
Paris, France	8.5	Mexico City, Mexico	19.2
Moscow, U.S.S.R.	8.0	Shanghai, China	18.0
Beijing, China	8.0	New York, U.S.A.	17.4
Chicago, U.S.A.	7.7	Calcutta, India	17.3

Source: United Nations (2001).

—*Social Problems,* Second Edition, by John J. Macionis

The purpose of this table is _____

_____

Use the table to answer the following with *T* (true), *F* (false), or *CT* (can't tell).

_____ 1. The number of U.S. metropolitan areas ranking in the world's ten largest urban areas of population drops from three to one in the thirty-five-year period projected by the table.

_____ 2. The New York City metropolitan area would increase in population but fall from first place to last in the ranking of the world's ten largest urban areas of population over the thirty-five-year period shown.

_____ 3. Only four metropolitan areas listed in the top ten for 1980 are also listed in the world's ten largest urban areas of population in 2015.

_____ 4. In the year 2006, the Tokyo metropolitan area had over 20 million people.

_____ 5. The reader can assume that the population of Mumbai will have to have more than doubled from 1980 to meet its projection for 2015.

6. The table does not show the reasons for population growth. Why do you think the six areas listed after Tokyo in 2015 are expected to have such a dramatic increase in population and no European area is listed on the 2015 chart?

_____

_____

EXERCISE 5

Graphs That Spin

Graphs are an excellent way to depict trends and illustrate changes over time. Readers can easily see increases and decreases in a graph when the same data presented in a list of numbers are more difficult to absorb. However, graphs also present an opportunity to dramatize or minimize the trends. Readers must pay close attention to the time frame and the scale to interpret the data.

(A)

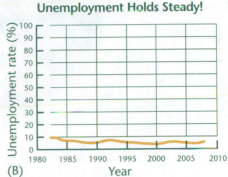

(B)

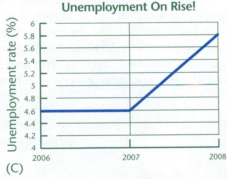

(C)

Do Statistics Lie?

Analysts can "spin" their data to encourage readers to reach various conclusions. These three graphs are based on the same factual data. Yet the way we construct each graph suggests a different reality. The scale used in graph (A) gives the impression that over time, unemployment has gone down. Graph (B) changes the scale to flatten the line, thus giving the impression that the unemployment rate has changed little. Graph (C) presents the data only for the years 2006 through 2008, giving the impression that the unemployment rate is going up.

Source: Data from U.S. Department of Labor (2009).

—_Social Problems,_ Fourth Edition, by John Macionis

The purpose of these graphs is to _____

_____

_____

Use the graphs to answer the following with _T_ (true), _F_ (false), or _CT_ (can't tell).

_____ 1. Graphs A and B show unemployment rates over the same period of time.

_____ 2. The three graphs report different unemployment rates for 2008.

_____ 3. The high unemployment rates in 1982–1983 were due to cheap labor opportunities overseas.

_____ 4. The scale showing unemployment rate in Graph A shows a smaller range than the scale in Graph C.

_____ 5. From 1980 to 2008, the lowest unemployment rate occurred in 2000.

EXERCISE 6   Collaborate to study the pie graphs and to answer the questions.

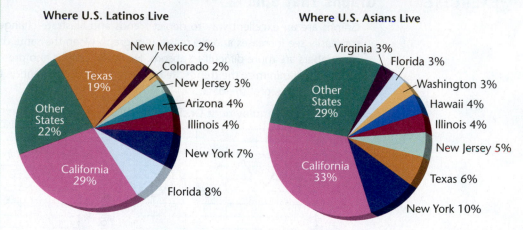

—*Source*: By L. Morris. Based on *Statistical Abstract of the United States*: 2010, Table 19.

Today, Latinos are the largest minority group in the United States. About 29 million people trace their origins to Mexico, 4 million to Puerto Rico, 1 to 2 million to Cuba, and about 8 million to Central or South America. As shown, two-thirds of Latinos live in just four states: California, Texas, Florida, and New York. Likewise, Asian Americans come to the Unites States from many nations: China, India, the Philippines, Vietnam, Korea, Japan, and other countries. Today, nearly half of this very diverse group lives in three states: California, New York, and Texas.

—Adapted from, *Essentials of Sociology: A Down-to-Earth Approach*, Ninth Edition, by James M. Henslin

The purpose of these graphs is _____

_____

Use the pie graphs to answer the following with *T* (true), *F* (false), or *CT* (can't tell).

_____ 1. Over 25% of Latino Americans live in Texas and Florida.

_____ 2. The majority of Puerto Rican Americans live in Florida.

_____ 3. Hawaii and Illinois are home to an equal proportion of the Asian American population.

_____ 4. The same number of Latino and Asian Americans live in Illinois.

_____ 5. Arizona is the home state of 4% of the Latino American population but none of the Asian American population.

6. Although the graphs do not reveal this information, why do you think that California has the largest proportion of both Latino and Asian Americans? _____

_____

_____

_____

EXERCISE 7   Collaborate to study the bar graph and to answer the questions.

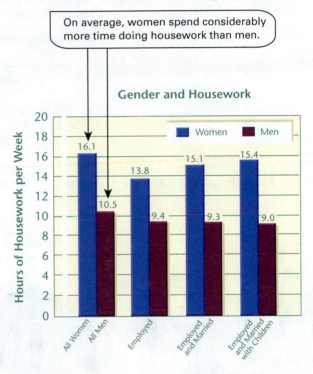

On average, women spend considerably more time doing housework than men.

Gender and Housework

—*Source*: Bureau of Labor Statistics (2009)

GENDER AND HOUSEWORK

Just as patriarchy gives men control of the workplace, it also assigns women most of the housework. In Japan, probably the most patriarchal of all high-income nations, women do almost all the shopping, cooking, cleaning, and child care. In the United States, where having two incomes is the norm among married couples, women still do most of the housework (or pay other women to do it). The bar graph shows that the amount of housework people do depends on whether they are single or married and working for pay or staying at home. But in every one of the categories, women spend a lot more time doing housework than men—one of the reasons that housework is sometimes called women's "second shift."

—*Social Problems*, Fourth Edition, by John Macionis

The purpose of this graph is _____

_____

_____

Use the bar graph to answer the following with *T* (true), *F* (false), or *CT* (can't tell).

_____ 1. The graph indicates that employed, married men do less housework if they have children.

_____ 2. Employed married women do more housework if they have children.

_____ 3. The amount of time men spend on housework varies by less than one hour per week regardless of employment or household status.

_____ 4. The number of hours men and women spend on housework has changed significantly over the last 50 years.

_____ 5. According to the data in the graph, women do more housework than men regardless of employment or family status.

6. How would you explain the greater amount of housework done by women? _____

_____

_____

_____

EXERCISE 8   Read the passage and use the drawing to help visualize your thoughts.

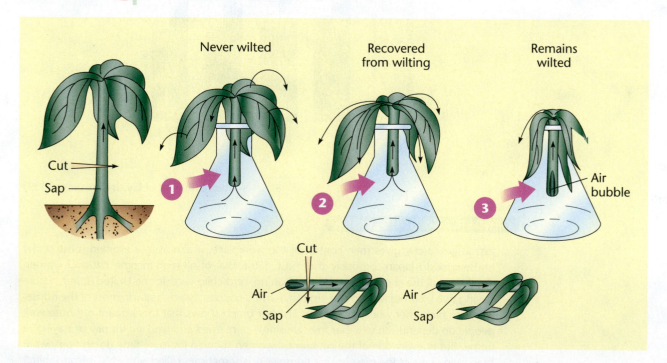

THE KINDEST CUT

After thanking the donor for a bouquet of flowers and sniffing them appreciatively, the next step is to find a vase and put them in water. The florist usually sends a message to cut off an inch or two of stem first; purists even instruct that this should be done while the stem is immersed in water.

Three stems were cut from the same plant at the same time. Stem 1 was placed in water immediately. Stem 2 was left for half an hour, and then a two-inch length was cut off the bottom end. It was then placed in water. Stem 3 was also left for half an hour and then placed in water without further treatment.

Stem 3 is distinctly wilted, whereas the other two look normal.

The figure shows why Stems 1 and 2 have fared so much better: in both, the column of water in the xylem is continuous with the water in the container. As the leaves transpire, the water lost from the plant is replaced by pulling more water into the xylem from the container. While Stems 2 and 3 were left out of water, transpiration from the leaves pulled the water column in the xylem up into the stem, leaving room for air to enter the base of the xylem. Cutting Stem 2 the second time removed this air-filled xylem, permitting the water still in the xylem to link up with the water in the container. However, Stem 3 was left with an air bubble at the base of its xylem, which blocks the entry of water from the container. As the leaves transpire, they lose water faster than the dwindling xylem contents can replace it. Water is pulled out of other cells in the leaves until they no longer fill their walls. Without this internal support the walls buckle and the plant wilts.

—From Arms and Camp, *Biology: A Journey into Life*, 2nd ed.
© 1991 Brooks/Cole, a part of Cengage Learning, Inc.
Reproduced by permission. www.cengage.com/permissions

Use the passage and the diagram to answer the following questions with *T* (true) or *F* (false).

_____ 1. Stem 2 would not be receiving water unless it had been cut a second time.

_____ 2. The flow of water in Stem 1 is not blocked by an air bubble.

_____ 3. The xylem is in the stem of the plant.

_____ 4. The xylem of Stem 2 was blocked before the second cut.

_____ 5. If cut immediately above the air bubble and placed in water, Stem 3 might recover freshness.

EXERCISE 9   Answer the following questions from an interpersonal communications textbook, and then analyze your responses in order to learn about your listening skills. Compare your results with those of your classmates.

ASSESSING YOUR LISTENING SKILLS

The purpose of this questionnaire is to assess your listening skills. Respond to each statement with a number as follows: 1 for always false, 2 for usually false, 3 for sometimes false, 4 for usually true, and 5 for always true.

_____ 1. I have a difficult time separating important and unimportant ideas when I listen to others.

_____ 2. I check new information against what I already know when I listen to others.

_____ 3. I have an idea what others will say when I listen to them.

_____ 4. I am sensitive to others' feelings when I listen to them.

_____ 5. I think about what I am going to say next when I listen to others.

_____ 6. I focus on the process of communication that is occurring between me and others when I listen to them.

_____ 7. I cannot wait for others to finish talking so I can take my turn.

_____   8. I try to understand the meanings that are being created when I communicate with others.

_____   9. I focus on determining whether others understand what I said when they are talking.

_____   10. I ask others to elaborate when I am not sure what they mean.

SCORING

To find your score, first reverse your responses for the odd-numbered items. (If you wrote 1, make it 5; if you wrote 2, make it 4; if you wrote 3, leave it as 3; if you wrote 4, make it 2; if you wrote 5, make it 1.) Next, add the numbers next to each statement. Scores range from 10 to 50. The higher your score, the better your listening skill.

—*Interpersonal Communication*, Third Edition, by
Steven Beebe, Susan Beebe, and Mark Redmond

Write a brief description of the strengths and weaknesses of your listening skills.

I am _____

_____

_____

EXERCISE 10   Experience the specialization of the cerebral hemispheres by performing the following activity. Then respond to the True-False items.

RIGHT AND LEFT HEMISPHERE FUNCTIONS

Get a meter stick or yardstick. Try balancing it vertically on the end of your left index finger, as shown in the drawing. Then try balancing it on your right index finger. Most people are better with their dominant hand—the right for right-handers, for example. Is this true for you?

Now try this: Begin reciting the ABCs out loud as fast as you can while balancing the stick with your left hand. Do you have less trouble this time? Why should that be? The right hemisphere controls the act of balancing with the left hand. However, your left hemisphere, though poor at controlling the left hand, still tries to coordinate your balancing efforts. When you distract the left hemisphere with a steady stream of talk, the right hemisphere can orchestrate more efficient balancing with your left hand without interference.

—From Samuel E. Wood and Ellen R. Wood, *The World of Psychology,* 4th ed. © 2002 (from page 62). Reproduced by permission of Pearson Education, Inc.

———— 1. To successfully balance the yardstick, right-handers want the right hemisphere to be in control.

———— 2. To successfully balance the yardstick, right-handers use talk to distract the left hemisphere so that the right hemisphere can take control for balance.

SUMMARY POINTS

1 What are the elements of analytical thinking? (page 390)

Good analytical thinkers work persistently in a logical and sequential pattern, drawing on old knowledge to solve new problems while they relate, interpret, and integrate what they know with what they are learning.

2 How do the thinking strategies of successful and unsuccessful students differ? (page 390)

Successful students systematically identify goals and break larger problems into smaller parts. They pull out key terms and simplify problems. They are persistent, active, and aggressive. They apply relevant old knowledge to create new solutions.

Unsuccessful students engage in one-shot thinking and allow gaps of knowledge to exist. They fail to work with purpose and have no method of attacking new material. They are passive, careless in considering details, superficial in reasoning, and allow impressions to reign rather than logic.

3 What analytical thinking strategies should I apply when reading graphic illustrations? (page 394)

Graphic illustrations such as graphs, charts, maps, and diagrams condense complicated information into a graphic representation to highlight differences and allow for quick comparisons. Read the title and legend to understand the topic, and study the details carefully. Notice trends, and use prior knowledge and logic to interpret the information.

COLLABORATIVE PROBLEM SOLVING

Form a five-member group and select one of the following activities. Brainstorm and then outline your major points on a transparency. Choose a member to present the group findings to the class.

➤ Record the month in which each class member was born. Create a bar graph showing the number of class birthdays in each month. Put the months on the horizontal line and indicate the number of birthdays in each month on the vertical line.

➤ Record the month in which each class member was born. Create a bar graph showing the number of class birthdays in each month. Indicate the number of birthdays on the horizontal line and put the months on the vertical line.

➤ Record the date of the month on which each class member was born. Create a bar graph showing the number of class birthdays on each date. Put the dates on the horizontal line and indicate the number of birthdays on each date on the vertical line.

➤ Record the date of the month on which each class member was born. Create a bar graph showing the number of class birthdays on each date. Indicate the number of birthdays on the horizontal line and put the dates on the vertical line.

MyReadingLab

MyReadingLab (MRL) www.myreadinglab.com

➤ For support in meeting this chapter's objectives, log in to **www.myreadinglab.com** and select "Graphs and Visual Aids."

THE READING WORKSHOP

If reading a novel, biography, or other book is part of your course experience, refer to The Reading Workshop: Thinking, Talking, and Writing about Books in Appendix 5 for suggestions.

SELECTION 1 🧪 Science

"Like the linkage of the oppositions of continent and ocean in the thermal exchanges of the atmosphere, our linked system of oppositions can generate good harvests and tornadoes, tourist paradises and hurricanes, as well as a global warming and a new Ice Age."

—William I. Thompson

Hurricane specialists can accurately forecast the path of a hurricane with just an 85-mile margin of error when a hurricane is 24 hours away. Forecasting the strength of the storm, however, is more difficult. A Category 5 monster could wallop a community that was expecting a weaker Category 1 tropical storm. Computers cannot accurately show the details of the storm's eye, which changes in shape and intensity as it moves over water and thunderstorms build. The need for accurate forecasting is vital to build the public trust necessary for defensive preparations and forced evacuations.

THINKING BEFORE READING

Preview for content and organizational clues. Activate your schema and anticipate what you will learn.

What type of natural disaster most threatens your area?

What was the name of last year's most destructive hurricane?

How are hurricanes named?

This selection will probably tell me _____.

VOCABULARY PREVIEW

Are you familiar with these words?

tranquil	rotary	precipitation	deceptive	liberated
aloft	barrage	debris	torrential	advent

What does the prefix in *advent* mean?

Why is the pronunciation of *debris* unexpected?

What is the opposite of *torrential*?

Your instructor may choose to give a true-false vocabulary review before or after reading.

THINKING DURING READING

As you read, use the six thinking strategies of a good reader: predict, picture, relate, monitor, correct, and annotate.

SELECTION

1

Refer to the
Reader's **TIP**
for **Science** on
page 49.

PROFILE OF A HURRICANE

Most of us view the weather in the tropics with favor. Places like Hawaii and the islands of the Caribbean are known for their lack of significant day-to-day variations. Warm breezes, steady temperatures, and rains that come as heavy but brief tropical showers are expected. It is ironic that these relatively tranquil regions sometimes produce the most violent storms on Earth.

5   These intense tropical storms are known in various parts of the world by different names. In the western Pacific, they are called *typhoons,* and in the Indian Ocean, including the Bay of Bengal and Arabian Sea, they are simply called *cyclones.* In the following discussion, these storms will be referred to as hurricanes. The term *hurricane* is derived from Huracan, a Carib god of evil.

10   Although many tropical disturbances develop each year, only a few reach hurricane status. By international agreement a hurricane has wind speeds of at least 119 kilometers[1] per hour and a rotary circulation. Mature hurricanes average about 600 kilometers across, although they can range in diameter from 100 kilometers up to about 1500 kilometers. From the outer edge of the hurricane to the center, the barometric pressure has some-
15   times dropped 60 millibars, from 1010 to 950 millibars. The lowest pressures ever recorded in the western hemisphere are associated with these storms.

At the very center of the storm is the eye of the hurricane. This well-known feature is a zone where precipitation ceases and winds subside. The eye offers a brief but deceptive break from the extreme weather in the enormous curving wall clouds that surround it. The
20   air within the eye gradually descends and heats by compression, making it the warmest part of the storm. Although many people believe that the eye is characterized by clear blue skies, this is usually not the case because the subsidence in the eye is seldom strong enough to produce cloudless conditions. Although the sky appears much brighter in this region, scattered clouds at various levels are common.

25   A hurricane is a heat engine that is fueled by the latent heat liberated when huge quantities of water vapor condense. The amount of energy produced by a typical hurricane in just a single day is truly immense—roughly equivalent to the entire electrical energy production of the United States in a year.

Hurricanes develop most often in the late summer when ocean waters have reached
30   temperatures of 27°C or higher and are thus able to provide the necessary heat and

THE 20 DEADLIEST U.S. HURRICANES, 1900–2005

Ranking	Hurricane	Year	Category	Deaths
1.	Texas (Galveston)	1900	4	8000*
2.	Florida (Lake Okeechobee)	1928	4	1836
3.	Katrina	2005	4	1300**
4.	Florida (Keys)/S. Texas	1919	4	600†
5.	New England	1938	3	600
6.	Florida (Keys)	1935	5	408
7. (tie)	Audrey (SW Louisiana/Texas)	1957	4	390
7. (tie)	NE United States	1944	3	390†
9.	Louisiana (Grand Isle)	1909	4	350
10. (tie)	Louisiana (New Orleans)	1915	4	275
10. (tie)	Texas (Galveston)	1915	4	275
12.	Camille (Mississippi/Louisiana)	1969	5	256

*May actually have been as high as 10,000 to 12,000.

**Estimated figure.

†Over 500 of these lost on ships at sea; 600 to 900 estimated deaths.

†Some 344 of these lost on ships at sea.

[1]1 kilometer is equal to approximately 0.62 mile.

moisture to the air. This ocean-water temperature requirement is thought to account for the fact that hurricanes do not form over the relatively cool waters of the South Atlantic and the eastern South Pacific.

35 Hurricanes diminish in intensity whenever they (1) move over ocean waters that cannot supply warm, moist tropical air, (2) move onto land, or (3) reach a location where the large-scale flow aloft is unfavorable. In addition, because the land is usually cooler than the ocean, the low-level air is chilled rather than warmed. Moreover, the increased surface roughness over land results in a rapid reduction in surface wind speeds.

STORM SURGE

40 Without question, the most devastating damage in the coastal zone is caused by the storm surge. It not only accounts for a large share of coastal property losses, but it is also responsible for 90 percent of all hurricane-caused deaths. A storm surge is a dome of water 65 to 80 kilometers wide that sweeps across the coast near the point where the eye makes landfall. If all wave activity were smoothed out, the storm surge is the height of the water above normal tide level. In addition, tremendous wave activity is superimposed on the surge. We can

45 easily imagine the damage that this surge of water could inflict on low-lying coastal areas.

WIND DAMAGE

Destruction caused by wind is perhaps the most obvious of the classes of hurricane damage. For some structures, the force of the wind is sufficient to cause total ruin. Mobile homes are particularly vulnerable. In addition, the strong winds can create a dangerous barrage of flying debris.

INLAND FLOODING

50 The torrential rains that accompany most hurricanes represent a third significant threat—flooding. Whereas the effects of storm surge and strong winds are concentrated in coastal areas, heavy rains may affect places hundreds of kilometers from the coast for several days after the storm has lost its hurricane-force winds.

DETECTING HURRICANES

The advent of weather satellites has largely solved the problem of detecting tropical
55 storms and has significantly improved monitoring. However, satellites are remote sensors, and it is not unusual for wind-speed estimates to be off by tens of kilometers per hour.

(773 words)

—*The Atmosphere,* 7th Edition,
by Frederick Lutgens and Edward Tarbuck

Note: On September 13, 2008, Hurricane Ike made U.S. landfall at Galveston, Texas, within a few miles of Houston. Ike devastated Galveston Island and Bolivar Peninsula and spread its fury north all the way into Ohio and beyond. Although Ike was a Category 2 storm at landfall, its large size and estimated 15-ft. storm surge accounted for its place as the third costliest tropical cyclone in U.S. and Atlantic basin history, behind Andrew in 1992 and Katrina in 2005. Ike is blamed for 158 deaths. (Data from the National Hurricane Center, updated May 3, 2010.) In August, 2011, Hurricane Irene caused devastating flooding from its landfall in Puerto Rico all the way north along the U.S. Atlantic Coast and into Eastern Canada and is blamed for an estimated 56 deaths and $10.1 billion in damages.

THINKING AND WRITING AFTER READING

RECALL Self-test your understanding.

Your instructor may choose to give you a true-false comprehension review.

REACT Why are mobile homes particularly vulnerable to hurricane damage?

_____

_____

REFLECT Under what conditions might an area benefit from a hurricane?

_____

_____

_____

THINKING CRITICALLY Considering the factors involved in the development of a hurricane, why are Florida and the east coast so vulnerable to hurricanes? Write your answer on a separate sheet of paper.

THINK AND WRITE Why is accurate forecasting to build the public trust necessary for defensive preparations and forced evacuations? Describe the possible short-term and long-term results of inaccurate forecasting. _____

_____

_____

EXTENDED WRITING Create the script for a television or radio segment to be broadcast near the beginning of hurricane season. Your purpose is to use facts to persuade citizens to evacuate coastal areas ahead of a major storm. In addition to the information in the reading selection, your instructor might require further research to support your paper.

ANALYTICAL REASONING

Use the table on page 408 to answer the following items with *T* (true) or *F* (false).

_____ 1. Most of the deadliest U.S. hurricanes occurred before 1970.

_____ 2. According to the table, Katrina was the deadliest hurricane of 2005.

_____ 3. More than three times as many people were killed in the Galveston hurricane of 1900 than were estimated to be killed by Katrina.

_____ 4. According to the chart, category 5 hurricanes cause more deaths than category 4 storms.

_____ 5. From the list of the deadliest hurricanes, two have been in the northeastern United States.

Interpret THE QUOTE

Now that you have finished reading the selection, "Profile of a Hurricane," go back to the beginning of the selection and read the opening quote again. What does the quote say about opposites? On a separate sheet of paper, list three situations in which something positive happens as a result of something negative, or something negative happens as a result of something positive.

Name _____

Date _____

COMPREHENSION QUESTIONS

Answer the following with *a, b, c,* or *d,* or fill in the blank. In order to help you analyze your strengths and weaknesses, the question types are indicated.

Main Idea _____ 1. The best statement of the main idea of the selection is:
   a. Calm places can produce intense tropical storms.
   b. Hurricanes cause intense damage and leave many people homeless each year.
   c. A hurricane is an intense tropical storm that develops over warm tropical waters and can cause extreme damage from winds and water on land.
   d. A hurricane is a heat engine that produces electricity.

Detail _____ 2. By international agreement, a hurricane is defined by all of the following *except*
   a. wind speed of 119 kilometers per hour.
   b. rotary circulation.
   c. a drop in barometric pressure.
   d. an eye with a clear blue sky.

Detail _____ 3. The eye of a hurricane
   a. has the most damaging winds.
   b. produces torrential rains.
   c. is the warmest part of the storm.
   d. signals the end of the storm.

Inference _____ 4. According to the passage, hurricanes probably begin developing in late summer because
   a. the season will soon be changing to autumn.
   b. the ocean water temperature is highest.
   c. cool winds from the South Atlantic reach the Caribbean.
   d. typhoons and cyclones occur during the winter.

Detail _____ 5. All of the following will diminish the intensity of a hurricane *except*
   a. cold ocean water.
   b. land.
   c. warm ocean air.
   d. cold land air.

Detail 6. What is the purpose of the table on page 408? _____

_____

_____

Detail _____ 7. The storm surge is characterized by all of the following *except*
   a. it pushes ocean water across coastal property.
   b. it occurs near where the eye of the hurricane hits land.
   c. it always occurs at low tide.
   d. it surges and floods.

Answer the following with *T* (true), *F* (false), or *CT* (can't tell).

Inference _____ 8. The author implies that typhoons, cyclones, and hurricanes are all about the same.

Detail _____ 9. High winds from a hurricane usually kill more people than the storm surges.

Detail _____ 10. The storm surge can be as much as 80 kilometers high.

VOCABULARY

Answer the following with *a*, *b*, *c*, or *d* for the word or phrase that best defines the boldface word as used in the selection. The number in parentheses indicates the line of the passage in which the word appears.

_____ 1. "**tranquil** regions" (4)

    a. warm
    b. calm
    c. breezy
    d. tropical

_____ 2. "**rotary** circulation" (12)

    a. intense
    b. random
    c. rapid
    d. circular

_____ 3. "**precipitation** ceases" (18)

    a. rain
    b. heat
    c. temperature
    d. winds

_____ 4. "**deceptive** break" (18)

    a. fearful
    b. uneventful
    c. turbulent
    d. deceiving

_____ 5. "heat **liberated**" (25)

    a. added
    b. freed
    c. mixed
    d. multiplied

_____ 6. "large-scale flow **aloft**" (36)

    a. below
    b. around
    c. overhead
    d. downhill

_____ 7. "dangerous **barrage**" (49)

    a. circle
    b. wall
    c. blast
    d. barrier

_____ 8. "flying **debris**" (49)

    a. dirt
    b. insects
    c. water
    d. trash

_____ 9. "**torrential** rains" (50)

    a. sudden
    b. frequent
    c. annoying
    d. fierce

_____ 10. "**advent** of weather satellites" (54)

    a. advertisement
    b. appearance
    c. location
    d. idea

Your instructor may choose to give a true-false vocabulary review.

VOCABULARY ENRICHMENT

Context Clues

Select the word from the list that best completes each sentence.

tranquil	rotary	precipitation	deceptive	liberated
aloft	barrage	debris	torrential	advent

1. After the storm, the shore was littered with _____.

2. When the summer tourists come to Maine, the small coastal towns are no longer _____.

3. _____ women do not mind speaking out on issues, even when their opinions are unpopular.

4. Five days of _____ rain created flooding in the fields and threatened the livestock.

5. The forecast for the evening is for _____ in the form of snow or sleet.

6. With the _____ of more accurate hurricane forecasting, people are hoping for fewer evacuations.

7. The pickpocket had a _____ way of smiling and asking unsuspecting tourists for directions.

8. The scientists sent a weather balloon _____ to record data for the experiment.

9. The speaker was hit by a _____ of questions about where evacuees would be housed.

10. The _____ fan above the bed moves the air enough to keep the room cool on moderate spring nights.

ASSESS YOUR LEARNING

Review confusing questions, seek clarification, and make notes in your text to help you remember new information and vocabulary.

SELECTION 2 Sociology

"Almost all the ideas we have about being a man or being a woman are so burdened with pain, anxiety, fear and self-doubt. For many of us, the confusion around this question is excruciating."

—Andrew Cohen

The ever changing issues of gender, and their accompanying status concerns, affect social institutions by solving some problems and usually creating others. For example, in the 1960s women were underrepresented in the colleges. Advocates for women voiced concerns. In 2005 approximately 213,000 more women than men graduated with bachelor's degrees from colleges in the United States. [In 2011 the graduation numbers were expected to further widen to 273,000 more women than men.] Are these numbers a victory for advocacy, or do they define another problem? In another social institution, marriage, the ages are shifting upward. In 1960 the median age for a first marriage was 20 for women and 22 for men. In 2010 the median age was 26 for women and 28 for men. How does this significant shift in age affect the institution, the status of the members, and the culture?

THINKING BEFORE READING

Preview for content and organizational clues. Activate your schema and anticipate what you will learn.

How do parents encourage different behaviors for sons and daughters?

How do teachers treat females and males differently?

What jobs tend to be typically male or typically female?

I think this selection will say that _____.

VOCABULARY PREVIEW

Are you familiar with these words?

humdrum	conventional	stereotypes	bias	banning
spectators	subtle	competence	pout	rural

Do you live in a *rural* area?

Is there a political *bias* in elections?

Does it take *competence* to fly an airplane?

Your instructor may choose to give a true-false vocabulary review before or after reading.

THINKING DURING READING

As you read, use the six thinking strategies of a good reader: predict, picture, relate, monitor, correct, and annotate.

Reader's TIP   Reading and Studying Sociology

- Think broadly about society and social organizations. Search for the historical reasons for human behavior and organizational structures. Make cause-and-effect connections among history, culture, and social organizations.
- Compare and contrast customs and social behaviors across cultures.
- Remain open-minded and be tolerant of cultural differences. Avoid biased value judgments.
- Think objectively and scientifically to evaluate the problems of society.

GENDER AND SOCIAL INSTITUTIONS

((•─ **Scan this QR code to hear this reading.**

At countless bridal showers, women celebrate a friend's upcoming marriage by showering her with useful gifts. But the scene is very different at bachelor parties, where men give their friend one last fling before he must settle down to the humdrum routines of married life. We find the same pattern among singles: Contrast the positive image of a carefree
5   bachelor with the negative one of the lonely spinster.

On the face of it, it seems that marriage is a *solution* for women and a *problem* for men. But is this really the case? Research indicates that in general, marriage is good for people, not only raising levels of personal happiness but improving health and boosting income, too. But researcher Jessie Bernard points out that the benefits of traditional mar-
10   riage are greater for men than for women. Bernard claims that there is no better prescription for a man's long life, good health, and overall happiness than having a wife devoted to caring for him and keeping an orderly home. That is why divorced men are less happy than divorced women and are more eager to remarry.

But for many women, Bernard continues, marriage reduces happiness and increases
15   the risk of depression or other personality disorders. Why? Bernard explains that the problem is not marriage in general but the fact that conventional marriage places men in charge and saddles women with most of the housework.

In the past, marriages based on conventional ideas about gender were more common than they are today. So why have women always seemed so eager to marry? Bernard
20   explains that at a time when women were all but shut out of the labor force, "landing a man" was the only way a woman could gain economic security.

Today, however, women with more economic opportunity also have more choices about marriage. This is one reason that more couples are sharing responsibilities more equally. As Bernard sees it, breaking away from conventional ideas about gender is making
25   both women and men happier and healthier.

GENDER AND EDUCATION

By the time they begin school, children have learned a great deal about gender from books. Children's books used to be full of gender stereotypes, showing girls and women mostly in the home while boys and men did almost everything else outside the home. Newer children's books present the two sexes in a more balanced way, although some
30   antifemale bias remains.

And what of school itself? Today's primary and secondary schools do a pretty good job of providing equal education to both boys and girls. In addition, 57 percent of all college students are now women, and some professional schools (such as law) now graduate as

many women as men. Even so, gender stereotyping still steers women toward college ma-
35 jors in English, dance, drama, or sociology while pushing men toward physics, economics,
biology, mathematics, and computer science.

Gender is at work on the playing fields as much as in the classroom. In the past, ex-
tracurricular athletics was a male world in which females were expected to watch instead
of play. In 1972, Congress passed Title IX, the Educational Amendment to the Civil Rights
40 Act, banning sex discrimination in any educational program receiving federal funding. In
recent years, colleges and universities have also tried to provide an equal number of sports
to both women and men. Even so, men benefit from higher-paid coaches and enjoy larger
crowds of spectators. In short, despite the federal policy outlawing gender bias, in few
athletic programs is gender equality a reality.

GENDER AND THE MASS MEDIA

45 With some 250 million television sets in the United States and people watching an average
of four-and-one-half hours of TV each day (U.S. Bureau of the Census, 2006), who can
doubt the importance of the mass media in shaping how we think and act? What messages about gender do we find on TV?

When television became popular in the 1950s, almost all the starring roles belonged to
50 men. Only in recent decades have television shows featured women as central characters.
But we still find fewer women than men cast as talented athletes, successful executives,
brilliant detectives, and skilled surgeons. More often than not, women have supporting
roles as wives, assistants, and secretaries. Music videos also come in for criticism: Performing groups are mostly all men, and when women do appear on stage, they are there
55 for little more than their sex appeal. And today's song lyrics reinforce men's power over
women.

What about advertising? In the early years of television, advertisers targeted wom-
en during the day because so many women were at-home wives (the fact that most of
the commercials advertised laundry and household products is the reason daytime TV dra-
60 mas are still called "soap operas"). On television and in newspaper and magazine advertising, most ads continue to use male models to pitch products such as automobiles, banking
services, travel, and alcoholic beverages to men and female models to sell products such as
clothing, cosmetics, cleaning products, and food to women. Ads have always been more
likely to show men in offices or in rugged outdoor scenes and women in the home.
65 Gender biases in advertising can be subtle. Research shows that ads almost always
present men as taller than women, and women (but never men) often lie on sofas and
beds or sit on the floor like children.

In addition, men's facial expressions suggest competence and authority, whereas
women laugh, pout, or strike childlike poses. Finally, the men featured in advertising focus
70 on the products they are promoting; women, as often as not, pay attention to men.

GENDER AND THE MILITARY

Women have been part of the military since the Revolutionary War. During World War II,
when the government officially opened the military to both sexes, women made up
just 2 percent of the armed forces. By the Gulf War in 1991, that share rose to almost
7 percent, and 5 of the 148 soldiers killed were women. Women have been 15 percent of
75 the U.S. military fighting in Iraq, and 62 women are included among the 3,000 fatalities
(as of January 6, 2007).

Today, almost all military assignments are open to women. But there is still resistance
to expanding the role of women in the military. The traditional explanation for limiting
women's opportunities is the claim that women are not as strong as men, although this
80 argument makes much less sense in a high-technology military that depends less and less
on muscle power. The real reason people oppose women in the military has to do with
gender itself. Many people have difficulty with the idea of women—whom our culture
defines as nurturers—being put in a position to kill and be killed.

Women and Men in the U.S. Labor Force

Over the last fifty years, the share of men in the labor force has gone down (with men retiring earlier and living longer), while the share of women working for income has gone up rapidly.

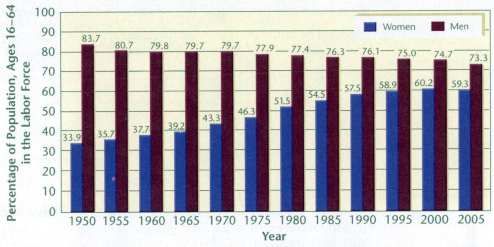

—*Source*: U.S. Department of Labor (2006).

GENDER AND WORK

Many people still think of different kinds of jobs as either "men's work" or "women's
85   work." A century ago in the United States, in fact, most people did not think women should work at all, at least not for pay. Back then, as the saying used to be, "a woman's place is in the home," and in 1900, just one woman in five worked for income. By 2005, as the graph above shows, this share jumped to three in five (59 percent), even as the share of adult men in the labor force declined. About three-fourths of women in today's labor
90   force work full time (U.S. Department of Labor, 2006).

What accounts for this dramatic rise in the share of working women? Many factors are involved. At the beginning of the twentieth century, a majority of the U.S. population lived in rural areas largely without electric power, where women typically spent long hours cooking, doing housework, and raising large families. Today's typical home has a host of
95   appliances, including washers, vacuums, and microwaves, that have dramatically reduced the time needed for housework.

In addition, today's average woman has just two children, half the number that was typical a century ago. Having young children does not prevent most women from working: Fifty-nine percent of married women with children under age six work, as do 76 percent of married
100   women with children six to seventeen years old. From another angle, more than half of today's married couples have both partners working for income (U.S. Census Bureau, 2005).

Even though more women now work for pay, the range of jobs open to them is still limited, and our society still labels most jobs as either feminine or masculine. Work that our society has defined as "masculine" involves physical danger (such as firefighting and
105   police work), strength and endurance (construction work and truck driving), and leadership roles (clergy, judges, and business executives). Work defined as "feminine" includes support positions (secretarial work or medical assisting) or occupations requiring nurturing skills (child care and teaching young children).

Gender discrimination was outlawed by the federal Equal Pay Act of 1963 and Title VII
110   of the Civil Rights Act of 1964. This means that employers cannot discriminate between men and women in hiring or pay. But gender inequality is deeply rooted in U.S. society; officials investigate thousands of discrimination complaints every year, and few doubt that the real number of cases of discrimination is far higher.

(1525 words)

—*Social Problems*, Third Edition, by John J. Macionis

THINKING AND WRITING AFTER READING

RECALL Self-test your understanding.

Your instructor may choose to give you a true-false comprehension review.

REACT The author is harsh in criticizing gender stereotyping. How have you been persuaded to think about a "masculine job" or a "feminine job"? Did any of the stereotyping stick?_____

_____

REFLECT Why do economic opportunities drive something as basic as the relationship between a husband and wife?_____

_____

THINKING CRITICALLY In recent years, young brides have been going to Las Vegas or Miami for exciting bachelorette parties with their close girlfriends. How does this mark a change in culture? What does it imply about a breaking away of conventional ideas? Why do you think this change is occurring? _____

_____

THINK AND WRITE Statistically the people who live in the greatest poverty in the United States are single mothers with children. What can be done to empower them? How did they get into their impoverished situation? Are they victims of gender discrimination? How can such situations be prevented? How can they gain financial independence? _____

_____

EXTENDED WRITING A recent news story surfaced about a couple who had made a considered decision to keep their baby's gender a secret from all but a very few trusted relatives. Their purpose was to shield the child from gender discrimination. While this is an extreme solution, it illustrates a concern of many parents. What are your opinions about child-rearing practices that reinforce traditional gender roles? Write a statement of your opinions that takes into account the many aspects of society that shape gender roles—clothing, hair styles, chores, toys, nursery décor, sports activities, behavior expectations—and also considers outcomes mentioned in the selection. Should parents help children embrace the traditional gender roles or help their children reshape them?

Interpret THE QUOTE

Now that you have finished reading the selection, "Gender and Social Institutions," go back to the beginning of the selection and read the opening quote again. Do you agree that how we think of ourselves in terms of our gender is "burdened with pain, anxiety, fear, and self-doubt"? On a separate sheet of paper, write a paragraph on what you think it means to be a man or woman.

Name _____

Date _____

COMPREHENSION QUESTIONS

Answer the following with *a, b, c,* or *d,* or fill in the blank. In order to help you analyze your strengths and weaknesses, the question types are indicated.

Main Idea _____ 1. The best statement of the main idea of the selection is:

    a. Current research indicates that women have nearly achieved social equality with males.

    b. Bias against women continues to be promoted by societal institutions.

    c. The majority of Americans believe that women and men deserve equal pay.

    d. Mothers and fathers in the United States remain unbiased in their parenting duties.

Inference _____ 2. The author's primary objection to bachelor parties in comparison with bridal showers is that

    a. women give gifts to the couple to be used in the marriage.

    b. women are eager to solve problems through marriage.

    c. men "celebrate" a loss rather than a positive gain.

    d. men raise their levels of personal happiness through marriage.

Inference _____ 3. The author would consider a conventional idea about marriage to be all of the following *except*

    a. women doing the laundry.

    b. men washing the dishes.

    c. women cooking breakfast.

    d. men working to provide income.

Detail _____ 4. Despite the passage of Title IX in 1972, the author feels that colleges still discriminate against women by

    a. giving women little chance to play.

    b. banning sex discrimination in any educational program receiving federal funding.

    c. the number of spectators who show up to watch the games.

    d. paying coaches for male sports more than coaches for female sports.

Detail _____ 5. Daytime television dramas are called "soap operas" because

    a. they appeal to at-home wives.

    b. the content is soapy with gossip and sex.

    c. women were targeted during the day.

    d. most began by advertising cleaning products.

Inference _____ 6. The author suggests that women still face limited opportunities in the military primarily because of

    a. the physical demands of military assignments.

    b. the high technology now used by the military.

    c. the public perception of the role of women.

    d. the inability of women to perform many military maneuvers.

Inference _____ 7. The reader can conclude that sociologists consider all of the following social institutions *except*

a. the family.
b. the schools.
c. recreation.
d. work.

Answer the following with *T* (true) or *F* (false).

Detail _____ 8. According to the passage, 80 percent of women with children under the age of six work outside the home.

Inference _____ 9. The author suggests that economic opportunity for women is the primary and underlying reason for the weakening of conventional ideas about gender and marriage.

Inference _____ 10. The author implies that a help wanted advertisement cannot legally specify the desire for a male or female applicant.

Answer the following with *T* (true) or *F* (false), referring to the graph on page 417.

_____ 1. In 1955 the percentage of men in the labor force was more than twice the percentage of women.

_____ 2. In this graph, if you were 16 years old in 2000 and without a job, you were considered a nonworker.

_____ 3. From 1950 to 2005, the increase in the number of women in the workforce was more than twice as much as the decline in the number of men working.

_____ 4. From 1950 to 1965, the decrease in men working was 5 percentage points.

_____ 5. For every year indicated on the graph, women showed an increase in their percentage of the workforce.

VOCABULARY

Answer the following with *a*, *b*, *c*, or *d* for the word or phrase that best defines the boldface word used in the selection. The number in parentheses indicates the line of the passage in which the word appears.

_____ 1. "**humdrum** routines" (3)

a. inspiring
b. dull
c. connected
d. wonderful

_____ 2. "**conventional** ideas" (18)

a. novel
b. institutional
c. strange
d. traditional

_____ 3. "gender **stereotypes**" (27)

a. typical representations
b. caricatures
c. editorial cartoons
d. tendencies

_____ 4. "antifemale **bias**" (30)

a. basis
b. prejudice
c. inference
d. happenings

_____ 5. "**banning** sex discrimination"
(40)
    a. highlighting
    b. prohibiting
    c. exposing
    d. hiding

_____ 8. "suggest **competence**"
(68)
    a. completeness
    b. ownership
    c. skill
    d. total helplessness

_____ 6. "crowds of **spectators**" (43)
    a. players
    b. owners
    c. scouts
    d. onlookers

_____ 9. "women laugh, **pout**" (69)
    a. talk
    b. tease
    c. smile
    d. show displeasure

_____ 7. "can be **subtle**" (65)
    a. easy to identify
    b. costly
    c. obvious
    d. hard to understand

_____ 10. "**rural** areas" (93)
    a. foreign
    b. elegant
    c. city
    d. country

Your instructor may choose to give a true-false vocabulary review.

VOCABULARY ENRICHMENT

Context Clues

Select the word from the list that best completes each sentence.

humdrum	conventional	stereotypes	bias	banning
spectators	subtle	competence	pout	rural

1. People in _____ India value sons because they can work in the fields.

2. Does a cultural _____ exist regarding women in combat?

3. Advertisers often place males in roles that suggest _____ and authority.

4. It could be said that people following the same routines day after day may be leading a _____ sort of existence.

5. _____ career choices for women were once largely limited to professions such as teaching and nursing.

6. The superior positioning of male actors and models in advertisements may be a more _____ example of gender bias.

7. _____ reinforce the myths that all women are good cooks and love housework.

8. Although laws have been passed _____ sex discrimination in the workplace, women continue to be underrepresented in boardrooms across America.

9. In many cases, the number of _____ at men's college sports events greatly exceeds those in attendance at women's games.

10. Television is full of examples of females who _____ to get what they want instead of simply stating their wishes.

Thesaurus

Use a thesaurus, either a computer or a book version, to find three alternative words or phrases for each of the following. Answers may vary according to the thesaurus used.

11. primary _____

12. devoted _____

13. restrict _____

14. nurturing _____

15. dramatic _____

ASSESS YOUR LEARNING

Review confusing questions. Seek clarification and make notes in your text to help you remember new information and vocabulary. Use visuals such as symbols, diagrams, and pictures to reinforce your learning.

"Shoot for the moon. Even if you miss, you'll land among the stars."

—Brian Littrell

What makes workers tick? Surprisingly, money is not the only motivator. Different workers are motivated by different factors. Motivation to work hard can be inspired by the recognition that comes with a simple thank you, an award, or a public acknowledgment for a job well done. For employees who enjoy learning and find repetition dull, new projects and new challenges stimulate enthusiasm for work. Self-starting employees thrive in a flexible environment; they do not like to be micromanaged. To become a successful manager, the trick is to find the appropriate motivator for each employee.

THINKING BEFORE READING

Preview for content and organizational clues. Activate your schema and anticipate what you will learn.

Why are you motivated to make good grades in college?

If you were a millionaire, would you get a college degree?

This selection will probably tell me _____.

VOCABULARY PREVIEW

Are you familiar with these words?

stifled	inspire	proponent	premise	pinnacle
crux	deemphasis	hygienic	grievances	verbalizing

How do the prefixes *pre* and *pro* differ?

Are people who get to the *pinnacle* usually inspired?

What committees in your college are set up to hear student *grievances*?

Your instructor may give a true-false vocabulary review before or after reading.

THINKING DURING READING

As you read, use the six thinking strategies of a good reader: predict, picture, relate, monitor, correct, and annotate.

MOTIVATING YOURSELF

"It is asking too much to suggest that people motivate themselves in the work environment. Motivation should come from the supervisor, special rewards, or the job itself."

Many people would disagree with the preceding quotation. They would claim that self-motivation is an absolute necessity in many work environments. They would also

Refer to the
Reader's **TIP**
for **Business** on
page 259.

SELECTION 3

5 claim that the more you can learn about motivation, the more you understand yourself and, as a result, the more you will be in a position to inspire your own efforts.

Let's assume that you find yourself in a job where things are not going well. You feel stifled and "boxed in." You may, for example, be much more capable than the job demands. Perhaps too, the pay and benefits are only average, your immediate supervisor
10 is difficult to deal with, and some other factors are not ideal. Even so, you consider the organization a good one and you recognize that by earning promotions your long-term future can be excellent.

How can you inspire yourself to do a better-than-average job despite the temporary handicaps? How can you motivate yourself to live close to your potential despite a nega-
15 tive environment? How can you keep your attitude from showing? How can you keep from injuring important human relationships?

There are many theories or schools of thought on why people are motivated to achieve high productivity on the job. Most of these are studied by managers so that they will be in a better position to motivate the employees who work for them. In this chapter we are
20 going to reverse the procedure. We are going to show you how to motivate yourself. *If your supervisor can be trained to motivate you, why can't you learn to motivate yourself?*

THEORY 1: SELF-IMAGE PSYCHOLOGY

This is frequently called the PsychoCybernetics School. The proponent of this theory is Dr. Maxwell Maltz, a plastic surgeon. The basic idea is that, in order to be properly

motivated to achieve certain goals, an individual must recognize the *need* for a good self-
25 image. Dr. Maltz discovered in his work as a plastic surgeon that some patients became
much more self-confident and far more motivated after having their faces greatly improved. Why? Maltz came to the conclusion that the image the individual had of himself
(or herself) *inside* was more motivating than the changes he had made *outside*. In short,
the way an individual *thinks* he or she looks can be more important than the way he or
30 she actually looks to others.

How Can You Use This Theory to Motivate Yourself? Learn to picture yourself
in a more complimentary way. First, research has shown that most people who have
poor self-images actually *do* look better to others than they do to themselves. If this is
true of you, you might try concentrating on your strong features instead of the weak
35 ones, thus developing a more positive outlook and a better self-image.

Second, you might consider improving yourself on the outside as well as on the
inside. You may not want to go as far as plastic surgery, but you could change your hair-
style, dress differently, lose or gain weight, exercise, and many other things. According
to the theory, however, unless you recognize and accept the improvement, nothing may
40 happen. PsychoCybernetics is, of course, a do-it-yourself project. You do all the work—
and you get all the credit, too!

THEORY 2: MASLOW'S HIERARCHY OF NEEDS

This is a very old theory developed by Abraham Maslow in his book *Motivation and Personality*. The premise here is that you have certain needs that must be fulfilled if you are to be
properly motivated. These needs are built one on top of the other as in a pyramid.

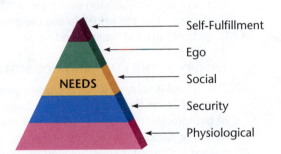

45 The bottom need is physiological—food, good health. The next is safety and security.
The third from the bottom is social needs: one needs to be accepted and enjoy the company of others. Next are ego needs—recognition from others. Finally, at the pinnacle, is
one's need for self-fulfillment or self-realization.

The crux of this theory is that the bottom needs must be fulfilled before the oth-
50 ers come into play. In other words, you must satisfy your need for food and security
before social needs become motivating. You must satisfy social and ego needs before self-
fulfillment is possible.

How Can You Use This Idea to Motivate Yourself to Reach Goals? If you believe Maslow is right, it would be self-defeating to reverse the pyramid or "skip over"
55 unsatisfied needs to reach others. Chances are good, however, that your first two
needs are being adequately satisfied so you could make a greater effort to meet new
people and make new friends. This could, in turn, help to satisfy your ego needs.
With both your social and ego needs better satisfied you might be inspired to attempt
greater creative efforts which could eventually lead you to greater self-realization.

THEORY 3: PSYCHOLOGICAL ADVANTAGE

60 This school was founded by Saul W. Gellerman. It contends that people constantly seek
to serve their own self-interests, which change as they grow older. People can make their

jobs work for them to give them a psychological advantage over other people at the same level. The way to create a psychological advantage in a starting job that is beneath your capacity is to learn all there is about that job. That way, you can use the job as a springboard to something better, a position that will give you more freedom and responsibility.

65   **How Could You Use This to Inspire Yourself?** The best way, perhaps, is to be a little selfish about your job. Work for the organization and yourself at the same time. Instead of letting your job control you, perhaps pulling you and your attitude down, use it as a launching pad. Use it to build human relations that will be important later on. Study the structure of your organization so you will understand the lines of pro-
70 gression better than the other employees. Study the leadership style of your supervisor and others so that you will have a better one when your turn comes.

THEORY 4: MOTIVATION-HYGIENIC SCHOOL

This theory was developed by Professor Frederick Herzberg. Basically it claims that undesirable environmental factors (physical working conditions) can be dissatisfiers. Factors of achievement, recognition, and freedom, on the other hand, are satisfiers. All working
75 environments have both negative and positive factors.

    How Can You Take Advantage of This Theory? People who maintain positive attitudes under difficult circumstances do so through attitude control. They concentrate *only* on the positive factors in their environment. You can, for instance, refuse to recognize the demotivating factors in your job and concentrate only on those things
80 that will satisfy your needs better.

    This could mean a deemphasis on physical factors and more emphasis on psychological factors such as social, ego, and self-fulfillment needs. One individual puts it this way: "I work in a very old building with poor facilities. Even so I have learned that I can be happy there because of the work I do and the great people I work with. One quickly gets used to
85 fancy buildings and facilities and begins to take them for granted anyway."

THEORY 5: THE MAINTENANCE-MOTIVATION THEORY

This school is much like Herzberg's hygienic approach and was developed by M. Scott Myers of Texas Instruments, Inc. His research found that employees usually fall into one of two groups: motivation-seekers and maintenance-seekers. In short, some people look for those factors that are motivating to them and are constantly pushing themselves
90 toward fulfillment. Others are concerned with just staying where they are. Maintenance-seekers spend much time talking about working conditions, wages, recreational programs, grievances, and similar matters and do little or nothing to motivate themselves. Motivation-seekers, on the other hand, look beyond such matters.

    How Might You Use This to Improve Your Own Motivation? The obvious answer
95 is, of course, to keep yourself out of the maintenance-seeker classification. To do this you should try not to overassociate with those in the maintenance classification. Without your knowing it, they could pull you into their camp. Try also to talk about positive things instead of being a complainer. Verbalizing negative factors often intensifies the dissatisfaction one feels. Turn your attention to things you can achieve on the job—not to the negative factors.

(1,338 words)

—*Your Attitude Is Showing,* Ninth Edition,
by Elwood N. Chapman and Sharon Lund O'Neil

THINKING AND WRITING AFTER READING

RECALL   Self-test your understanding.

Your instructor may choose to give you a true-false comprehension review.

REACT   If you could have plastic surgery, what would you have done and what do you think it would do for you? _____

_____

REFLECT   For each of Maslow's five levels of needs, name and describe a person you know who fits the level. _____

_____

THINKING CRITICALLY   Why would a plastic surgeon be the author of a book on self-image and motivation? Write your answer on a separate sheet of paper.

THINK AND WRITE   Assuming that your salary is appealing and that you are willing to work, describe what you would consider the perfect work environment for you. What factors would be strong motivators, and what factors would be disincentives? _____

_____

EXTENDED WRITING   Review the five motivational theories presented in the selection. Which one best explains what is likely to encourage you to achieve? Write a "message to self" that identifies an important personal goal and lays out specific plans to achieve it using the elements of that theory.

ANALYTICAL REASONING

Use your analytical reasoning skills on the following business problem.

After having worked for the same corporation for over three years, Norman decided that he had made a major mistake. He had been accepted into a formal management training program directly out of college. He had received his first supervisory role before his first year was up, but after that nothing else happened. He had been on a plateau for over two years. In recent months he had been feeling extremely frustrated, stifled, and somewhat hostile. He admitted that his attitude was showing. He admitted that his personal productivity had stagnated.

Norman knew the primary reason for his lack of upward progress. His company had been going through a consolidation process and had put a freeze on hiring new employees. Very few middle- and upper-management positions were opening. Nevertheless, Norman finally came to the uncomfortable conclusion that he had to do something about his situation. He had to force some kind of action, even if it was difficult.

He then sat down and listed the advantages and disadvantages of his role with the company:

Advantages	Disadvantages
Good geographical location	Corporation not expanding
Good benefits	Salary only fair
Job security	Limited learning opportunities
Good personnel policies	Overconservative management
Good physical working conditions	Poor supervisor
Little commuting time	Already made some human relations mistakes

Good home neighborhood   Limited opportunities for upward
Enjoyable type of work   communication with management
                                                     Boring fellow supervisors

After carefully going over the pros and cons of his job—and considering his three-year investment—Norman decided he had the following options:

1. Go to the personnel department and discuss his frustration about being on a plateau.
2. Submit a written request for a transfer involving a promotion.
3. Start a serious search for a new job in a new company.
4. Resign with two weeks' notice and start looking for a new job.
5. Talk to his supervisor and ask for more responsibility.
6. Motivate himself so that management will recognize a change in attitude and consider him for the next promotion.
7. Relax, continue present efforts, and wait it out.
8. Motivate himself for three months. Then if nothing happens, resign.
9. After telling his boss his intentions, go to the president of the company with the problem.
10. Go to the president of the company to discuss his personal progress.

Assume you are Norman. First, on a separate sheet of paper, list which of the listed options you would consider. Second, put them in the order in which you would undertake them. Third, add any steps you would take that are not on the list. Fourth, justify your decisions.

Interpret THE QUOTE

Now that you have finished reading the selection, "Motivating Yourself," go back to the beginning of the selection and read the opening quote again. How does the quote relate to motivation? On a separate sheet of paper, list three situations in your life when motivation helped you achieve a goal. Also, list three situations in which you could use motivation to reach a goal.

Name _____

Date _____

COMPREHENSION QUESTIONS

Answer the following with *a, b, c,* or *d* or fill in the blank. In order to help you analyze your strengths and weaknesses, the question types are indicated.

Main Idea   _____ 1. The best statement of the main idea is:

    a. Motivation comes from within and cannot be taught.

    b. People can use different theories of motivation to motivate themselves.

    c. People who are not motivated lose their jobs.

    d. Motivation in an organization is the responsibility of management.

Inference   _____ 2. The purpose of this selection is to

    a. improve management.

    b. criticize supervisors.

    c. encourage self-motivation.

    d. analyze mistakes.

Detail   _____ 3. According to Maltz's theory, many people make mistakes by

    a. thinking they look worse than others think they do.

    b. trying to look as good as others.

    c. thinking they look better than they do.

    d. trying to hide their weaknesses from others.

Inference   _____ 4. In Maslow's hierarchy of needs, winning sales trophies satisfies the

    a. security need.

    b. social need.

    c. ego need.

    d. self-fulfillment need.

Inference   _____ 5. Gellerman's theory of psychological advantage is based primarily on

    a. competition.

    b. self-interest.

    c. group cooperation.

    d. the needs of management.

Inference   _____ 6. According to the motivation-hygienic theory, a person should

    a. work only in a positive environment.

    b. motivate supervisors to clean up the environment.

    c. ignore the negative factors in the environment and focus on the positive factors.

    d. seek a job with only positive factors.

Inference   7. According to the maintenance-motivation theory, someone who wants to stay in a position for a few more years until retirement is a

_____

Answer the following with *T* (true) or *F* (false).

Inference _____ 8. The author seems to agree with the quotation on lines 1 and 2 at the beginning of the selection.

Inference _____ 9. In Maslow's hierarchy, the need to feel that you are using all of your talents to the best of your ability is the self-fulfillment need.

Inference _____ 10. Maltz's theory is exactly the opposite of Herzberg's theory.

VOCABULARY

Answer the following with *a, b, c,* or *d* for the word or phrase that best defines the boldface word used in the selection. The number in parentheses indicates the line of the passage in which the word appears.

_____ 1. "feel **stifled**"
(8)

    a. useless
    b. smothered
    c. angry
    d. sick

_____ 2. "**inspire** yourself"
(13)

    a. motivate
    b. force
    c. command
    d. instruct

_____ 3. "**proponent** of this theory" (22)

    a. scholar
    b. attacker
    c. advocate
    d. manager

_____ 4. "The **premise** here" (43)

    a. signal
    b. mistake
    c. meaning
    d. supposition

_____ 5. "at the **pinnacle**" (47)

    a. bottom
    b. crucial time
    c. peak
    d. most noticeable point

_____ 6. "The **crux** of this theory" (49)

    a. crucial point
    b. beginning
    c. solution
    d. reward

_____ 7. "**deemphasis** on physical factors" (81)

    a. renewed response
    b. less stress
    c. complete drop
    d. minor stress

_____ 8. "**hygienic** approach" (86)

    a. scientific
    b. analytical
    c. healthful
    d. resourceful

_____ 9. "**grievances**, and similar matters" (92)

    a. successes
    b. contests
    c. enrichments
    d. complaints

_____ 10. "**Verbalizing** negative factors" (98)

    a. hiding
    b. talking about
    c. overlooking
    d. remembering

Your instructor may choose to give a true-false vocabulary review.

VOCABULARY ENRICHMENT

A. Study these easily confused words and circle the correct one for each sentence.

wares: goods sold	**decent:** morally good	**allusion:** reference
wears: puts on clothes	**descent:** move downward	in literature
where: a place	**dissent:** disagreement	**illusion:** false idea

1. The (**wares, wears**) of the company were posted on the website before customers received catalogs.

2. The (**decent, descent, dissent**) between the two employees grew into a major confrontation that hurt company morale.

3. He is operating under the (**allusion, illusion**) that I am going to write the corporate report and then let him take credit for it.

B. Refer to Appendix 2 and use the doubling rule to form the following words.

4. regret + ing = _____

5. swim + ing = _____

6. excel + ent = _____

7. ship + ed = _____

C. Suffixes: Use the boldface suffix to supply an appropriate word for each group of sentences.

ment: act of, state of, result of action

8. Like another _____ to the constitution, theories of motivating can change as researchers document new results with innovative techniques.

9. Just as the mind needs stimulation, an energetic worker needs to eat the right foods so the body gets the proper _____.

10. My _____ with the manager was postponed until tomorrow at two o'clock.

ence: action, state, quality

11. The therapist showed great _____ in working with the man for hours to achieve a tiny degree of success.

12. While previous authoritarian managers may have valued _____ in following orders, now managers want workers who can problem-solve and share in decision making.

13. A capable and nurturing manager can have a great _____ on your success in a company.

able, ible: can do

14. Highly motivated employees seek extra responsibility and make themselves highly _____ to corporate decision makers.

15. Being a _____ employee means meeting deadlines and getting to meetings on time with the necessary information.

ASSESS YOUR LEARNING

Review confusing questions, seek clarification, and make notes in your text to help you remember new information and vocabulary.

VOCABULARY LESSON

Turn and Throw

Study the roots, words, and sentences.

Roots	*vers, vert:* turn	*jac, jec, ject:* throw, lie

Words with *vers* or *vert* = *turn*

Is sex in *advertisements controversial*? Is the coat *reversible*?

- Convert: win over; persuade

  With mind-controlling strategies, the student was *converted* to a cult.

- Revert: turn back to

  Reformed smokers are frequently tempted to *revert* to old habits.

- Divert: turn away from

  The driver's attention was *diverted* by the accident on the roadside.

- Invert: turn upside down

  If you want to divide a fraction, you need to *invert* and multiply.

- Averse: turned against

  They were divorced, but she was not *averse* to seeing him at parties.

- Introvert: shy and quiet; introspective

  Being an *introvert*, the writer rejected offers to read his poems in public.

- Extrovert: outgoing; gregarious

  An *extrovert* like Oprah Winfrey enjoys the energy of a large studio audience.

- Ambivert: having both introverted and extroverted tendencies

  Most *ambiverts* enjoy both being with people and having some quiet time.

- Pervert: turned to an improper use

  Because of a shoe fetish, the thief was regarded as *perverted*.

- Obverse: facing the opponent; front surface

  The head of the president was depicted on the *obverse* side of the coin.

- Conversant: knowledgeable about a subject

  After another semester of economics, I hope to be more *conversant* on the euro.

- Versatile: having many skills; can turn from one thing to another

  A *versatile* jacket can be worn with several different pants and shirts.

- Subversive: undermining

  The terrorists were engaged in *subversive* activities.

- Vertigo: a dizzy spell when things seem to be turning

  Avoid roller-coasters if you have a tendency toward *vertigo*.

- Version: an adaptation or translation of the original form

  The children's *version* of the Bible had pictures and large print.

- Versus: against

  The next trial was *State of Texas versus John Doe*.

- Vortex: both a whirling and a suction motion, as in a whirlpool

  Watching the whirling water from the cliff, he threw a log into the *vortex*.

Words with *jac, jec, ject = throw or lie*

Do you have an *objection* to leaving early? Does *rejection* hurt?

- Inject: insert

  Students appreciate professors who *inject* humor into lectures.

- Eject: to throw out

  If the plane is on fire, the fighter pilot can push the *eject* button.

- Dejected: low in spirits

  After failing two tests, the *dejected* student finally sought help in the lab.

- Adjacent: next to

  Consumers save time when a dry cleaner is *adjacent* to a grocery store.

- Conjecture: to form an opinion; guess

  The statement that the new president will step down is merely *conjecture*.

- Interject: throw a word in between others

  Because renters were talking, I could not *interject* a word about a deposit.

- Projection: thrown or caused to appear on a surface or space

  We decided to screen our videos in another classroom where the *projection* equipment was better.

- Abject: degraded

  In the Rio Barrio the children live in *abject* poverty.

Review

Part I

Answer the following with (*T*) true or (*F*) false.

_____ 1. A conjecture is a fact rather than an opinion.

_____ 2. If a proposal is rejected, it is no longer under consideration.

_____ 3. Subversive activity is clearly evident.

_____ 4. Water in the vortex sprays up like a fountain.

_____ 5. If it is stated as *Wiley versus Rogers*, the two sides are in opposition.

_____ 6. If you are conversant in Spanish history, you know the subject well.

_____ 7. A versatile athlete can play several sports well.

_____ 8. If you invert a cup of coffee, the liquid is likely to spill.

_____ 9. A dejected worker is not a happy employee.

_____10. A controversial topic draws little disagreement.

Part II

Select the word from the list that best completes each sentence.

diverted	averse	projections	pervert	extroverted
converted	vertigo	version	adjacent	introverted

1. Inner ear problems can cause loss of balance and _____.

2. The _____ sculptor enjoyed his meditative time alone outdoors.

3. The developer _____ the stream to build on the property.

4. The _____ professor gave lively lectures and enjoyed students.

5. The sex offender's unacceptable behavior labeled him as a _____.

6. By remodeling with glass windows, the porch was _____ to a usable room.

7. Unfortunately I can hear the TV in the room _____ to mine.

8. The population _____ for 2025 will influence mass-transit decisions.

9. The sign indicates the home owners are _____ to smoking on the premises.

10. Did you hear the rock singer or the movie star _____ of the story?

Reading Direct Mail Advertisements

How much "junk" mail do you receive each week? If you have no interest in a piece of advertising, put it in a recycle bin or throw it away. If you are interested, always remember the old saying, "If it sounds too good to be true, it probably is."

Do not succumb to the glitz. Recognize that if you do not really need the product or service, saving 40 percent will not be beneficial. If you are intrigued, however, read to clarify your total commitment and exactly what you will receive in return. Read the fine print.

Credit Cards

Credit card promotions (see figure on facing page) have become such a problem at colleges that some institutions are banning the advertisers from their campuses. You have probably already received many promotions saying that you are preapproved for a certain credit limit. Some students, enticed by the easy credit and low monthly payments, charge themselves into serious debt with crippling finance charges that take years to repay. Thus the misuse of credit cards can be deadly.

Proper use of a credit card, however, can be extremely convenient. Before committing to one, know first that you have the means and the discipline to pay your bill before the due date. If always paid promptly, your only cost for this financial convenience will be the annual fee, which is typically $50 or less (and for many cards there is no annual fee).

Reader's TIP — Evaluating a Credit Card Offer

- How much is the annual fee for the card?
- What is the finance charge rate? Annual rates typically run from 18% to 22%, so finance charges can add up quickly.
- Does the rate start low and change after an initial introductory period? The balance may be subject to a higher interest rate after the initial period as the low rate expires.
- Why do you need it? If you already have one card, why do you need another one?

---

1. How long will the introductory rate be available on the Hamilton Premier MasterCard advertised on page 437? _____

2. After the introductory period, what is the best annual percentage rate (APR) you could get if your account balance is less than $2,500? _____

3. If your application is transferred to Hamilton Southwest, what is the highest fixed annual percentage rate (APR) you might have to pay? _____

(NOTE: ALL OF THIS INFORMATION IS VALID EVEN IF THE OFFER INDICATES YOU HAVE BEEN PRE-APPROVED)

3.99%
Introductory APR

THE CARD YOU'VE BEEN WAITING FOR
THE BENEFITS YOU NEED
THE RATE YOU WANT

Dear Stephanie Albert,

This card is not for everyone. It's for people like you who are just starting out and have already demonstrated responsibility with their credit. Because you've shown that kind of special care, Hamilton Bank can make this special offer to you—a Hamilton Premier MasterCard.

The rate shown above is one of the lowest of any major credit card issuer. There's no gimmick here—the fixed rate of 3.99% is yours for nine months and will not increase if the Prime Rate changes.* After nine months, you'll still save with a variable Annual Percentage Rate as low as Prime +5.49%—right now that's only 13.24%.*

This rate saves you money on new purchases and on outstanding balances, too. Move those high rate balances to your Hamilton Premier MasterCard—who knows how much you'll save?

With a Hamilton Premier MasterCard, you'll also enjoy these benefits:
- Credit line up to $100,000
- No annual fee
- Optional Travel Accident Insurance, Lost Luggage Insurance, Auto Rental Insurance, Credit Card Registration and Merchandise Protection

*By filling out the following application, you agree that we reserve the right, based upon your evaluation, to open a Hamilton Standard MasterCard account if you do not qualify for a Hamilton Premier MasterCard account or, if you do not qualify, not to open any account. If we do not open an account, we may submit your application to our subsidiary, Hamilton Southwest, which will consider you for an Excel or Regular MasterCard account with the pricing terms shown below.

HAMILTON BANK SUMMARY OF TERMS

Annual Percentage Rate for Purchases	Variable Rate Information
Preferred Pricing: 3.99% Introductory APR for 9 months. Thereafter, for Hamilton MasterCard: 13.24% if your balances are greater than or equal to $2,500/15.24% if your balances are less than $2,500. For Hamilton MasterCard: 17.24%. *Non-Preferred Pricing:* 22.74%	Annual Percentage Rate is fixed at 3.99% for the first 9 months your account is open. Thereafter, your Annual Percentage Rate may vary. For Hamilton Premier MasterCard, the rate is determined monthly by adding 5.49% if your balances are greater than or equal to $2,500 or 7.49% if balances are less than $2,500 (for Hamilton Standard MasterCard: 9.49% for all balances), to the Prime Rate as published in *The Wall Street Journal*. *Non-Preferred Pricing:* Your Annual Percentage Rate may vary. The rate is determined monthly by adding 14.99% to the Prime Rate. This rate will not be lower than 19.8%.

HAMILTON SOUTHWEST SUMMARY OF TERMS

Annual Percentage Rate for Purchases	Variable Rate Information
Preferred Pricing: For Excel MasterCard: 23.15%. For Regular MasterCard: 27.15%. These rates will not be lower than 21.9% or higher than 29.9% *Non-Preferred Pricing:* Fixed 29.9% APR.	*Preferred Pricing:* Your Annual Percentage Rate may vary. For Excel MasterCard accounts, the rate is determined quarterly by adding 15.4% to the Prime Rate as published in *The Wall Street Journal*. For Regular MasterCard accounts, the rate is determined quarterly by adding 19.4% to the Prime Rate.

10 Inference

Learning Objectives

From this chapter, readers will learn:

1 To define *inference*
2 To explain why authors might imply meaning rather than state it directly
3 To use prior knowledge to make inferences
4 To recognize slanted language as a clue to meaning
5 To draw reasonable conclusions

Everyday Reading Skills: Reading Newspaper Editorials

WHAT IS AN INFERENCE?

An *inference* is a meaning that is suggested rather than directly stated. Inferences are implied through clues that lead the reader to make assumptions and draw conclusions. For example, instead of making a direct statement, "These people are rich and influential," an author could imply that idea by describing a palatial residence, expensive heirlooms, and prominent friends. Understanding an inference is what we mean by "reading between the lines," because the suggestion, rather than the actual words, carries the meaning.

Inference from Cartoons

Cartoons and jokes require you to read between the lines and make a connection. They are funny because of the unstated rather than the stated. When listeners catch on to a joke, it simply means they have made the connection and recognized the unstated inference. For example, what inference makes the following joke funny?

> *Sam:* Do you know how to save a politician from drowning?
> *Joe:* No.
> *Sam:* Good.

Taxpayers like to dislike politicians, and this joke falls into that category. As a rule, when you have to explain the inference in a joke, the fun is lost. You want your audience to make the connection and laugh uproariously.

EXAMPLE   Look at the following cartoon. What is being implied?

"Anyway, to make a long story short, the medical examiner who performed your autopsy was fired."

EXPLANATION   The implication in this cartoon is that the medical examiner made a huge mistake and declared the man dead, but he was actually alive. Frequently, a point that takes some figuring out and taps our imagination has a greater impact on us than one that is obviously stated.

EXERCISE 1   The following cartoon contains many details that imply meaning. Use the details to figure out the meaning of the cartoon and answer the questions.

© Rob Shepperson

1. What are the people in line hoping to do in "Retirement Park?" _____
   _____
   _____

2. What is the significance of the setting sun in the background? _____
   _____
   _____

3. Why do the people waiting in line look so distressed? _____
   _____

4. What message does this cartoon have for young people? _____
   _____

5. What are many older people doing now to supplement their retirement
   income? _____
   _____
   _____

6. What is the main point of the cartoon? _____
   _____

Recognizing Suggested Meaning

In reading, as in everyday life, information may or may not be stated outright. For example, someone's death would seem to be a fact beyond question. An author could simply state, "He is dead," but often it is more complicated than that. In literature and in poetry, such a fact might be divulged in a more dramatic manner, and the reader is left to put the clues together and figure out what happened. Read the following excerpt from a story about a shipwrecked crew's struggle to shore. What clues tell you that the oiler is dead?

> In the shallows, face downward, lay the oiler. His forehead touched sand that was periodically, between each wave, clear of the sea.
>
> —*The Open Boat,* by Stephen Crane

The oiler's head is face down in the shallow water. When the waves rush in to shore, his face is in the water, and when they wash out, his face or forehead touches the sand. He is bobbing at the water's edge like a dead fish and cannot possibly be alive with his face constantly underwater or buried in the sand. The man must be dead, but the author doesn't directly state that.

Two paragraphs later in the story the author writes:

> The welcome of the land to the men from the sea was warm and generous; but a still and dripping shape was carried slowly up the beach, and the land's welcome for it could only be the different and sinister hospitality of the grave.
>
> —*The Open Boat,* by Stephen Crane

The "still and dripping shape" and the "sinister hospitality of the grave" support your interpretation of the clues, even though the author still has not directly stated, "The oiler is dead." Implying the idea is perhaps more forceful than making a direct statement.

Connecting with Prior Knowledge

Authors, like cartoonists, use inferences that require linking old knowledge to what is being read at the time. Clues that imply meaning may draw on an assumed knowledge of history, current issues, or social concerns. Just as in making the connection to understand the punch line of a joke, the reader must make a connection in order to understand the inference.

EXAMPLE   **A TURNING POINT**

> More than 3,000 people were killed, thousands more were wounded, and the loss of property was unprecedented in the worst terrorist attack in history. The events horrified people around the world who understood that two symbols of American global financial and military dominance had been singled out in a carefully planned and executed mission of destruction. The event was immediately compared to the Japanese attack on Pearl Harbor in 1941.
>
> —*Civilization in the West,* Fifth Edition, by Mark Kishlansky, Patrick Geary, and Patricia O'Brien

1. What was the symbol of financial dominance that is not named here? Where was the attack?
2. What is the symbol of military dominance? Where was the destruction?

3. When did these terrorist attacks occur?

4. Why was the attack compared to the Japanese attack on Pearl Harbor in 1941?

PERSONAL FEEDBACK) 1   **Name** _____

1. Who supplied your references for college admission or for your last job? _____

_____

_____

_____

2. What professor would you ask to write you a letter of reference for an award or scholarship? Why would you choose that particular professor? _____

_____

_____

3. What preparation have you done for next term? What courses do you plan to take and why? _____

_____

_____

Tear out and submit to your instructor.

EXPLANATION   The symbol of financial dominance was the twin towers of the World Trade Center in New York City. The symbol of military dominance was the Pentagon in Washington, D.C. The attacks occurred on September 11, 2001, when terrorists hijacked passenger planes and used them to bomb buildings. The attacks precipitated a war, just as the Japanese attack on Pearl Harbor brought the United States into World War II. The following exercise illustrates how authors expect readers to connect with prior knowledge.

EXERCISE 2   Link prior knowledge to answer the questions that follow each passage.

Passage 1

THE BEGINNING OF THE SHOOTING

After seeing the light in the North Church, Paul Revere and William Dawes rode through the countryside alerting the colonists that British troops were moving across the back bay. In Concord and Lexington, trained militiamen were waiting to respond.

Where and approximately when was this? _____

_____

_____

Passage 2

FOOT BINDING

Foot binding was a form of violence against women. The woman's tiny feet, which made it difficult for her to walk, were a "marker" of status, indicating that her husband was wealthy and did not need her labor. It also made her dependent on him.

—*Essentials of Sociology: A Down-to-Earth Approach,* Fourth Edition, by James Henslin

Although not directly stated, foot binding was practiced in what country?

_____

Passage 3

TELLING THE STORY

The account of that morning some weeks later belongs to history. Three planes take off during the night of 6 August from Tinian in the Mariana Islands. Paul Tibbets is the group's commander. Eatherly opens the formation. There are no bombs in his plane; as for the others, no one suspects what a terrible device is hidden inside the *Enola Gay.* A bigger contrivance, they think, nothing more. Eatherly's job is to pinpoint the target with maximum accuracy. He must establish whether weather conditions allow for the center to be Hiroshima, Kokura or Nagasaki, or whether they should continue towards secondary targets. He tells the story of that morning's events in a voice devoid of emotion which suggests that the recitation is the thousandth one.

—"The Man from Hiroshima," by Maurizio Chierici, *Granta #22,* Autumn 1987

1. What is the "bigger contrivance"? _____

_____

2. What was the mission assignment of Tibbets and Eatherly? _____

_____

Recognizing Slanted Language

Learning Objective 4

Recognize slanted language as a clue to meaning.

Writers choose words to manipulate the reader and thus to control the reader's attitude toward a subject. Such words are referred to as having a particular **connotation** or **slant.** The dictionary definition of a word is its *denotation,* but the feeling or emotion surrounding a word is its *connotation.* For example, a real estate agent showing a rundown house to a prospective buyer might refer to the house as "neglected" rather than "deteriorated." Both words mean rundown. *Neglected* sounds as if a few things have been forgotten, whereas *deteriorated* sounds as if the place is rotting away and falling apart.

Some words in our society seem to have an automatic positive or negative slant. Words such as *socialist, cult member,* and *welfare state* have a negative emotional effect; words such as *the American worker, democracy,* and *everyday people* have a positive effect. The overall result of using slanted language is to shift the reader's attitude toward the point of view, positive or negative, advocated by the author. Recognizing slanted language provides another clue to the author's meaning.

EXERCISE 3   Label the following phrases as either *P* (slanted positively) or *N* (slanted negatively).

_____ 1. warm and winning ways

_____ 2. an engaging smile

_____ 3. appearing remote and self-involved

_____ 4. a cunning salesperson

_____ 5. candid and open

_____ 6. the picture of efficiency

_____ 7. weak and sickly

_____ 8. words like daggers

_____ 9. a loose cannon

_____10. spoken without thinking

_____11. not the sharpest knife in the drawer

_____12. a creased brow

_____13. an exasperated look

_____14. wise beyond her years

_____15. a nurturing mother

_____16. an easy mark

_____17. a hostile takeover

_____18. a dream fulfilled

_____19. the promise of tomorrow

_____20. the brotherhood of man

EXERCISE 4   Indicate whether the boldface words in the following passages are *P* (positive) or *N* (negative), and explain your answer.

_____ 1. Opponents forecast that the increased labor cost from a large

minimum-wage hike would jeopardize hundreds of thousands

of **unskilled jobs.** _____

_____

—*Microeconomics for Today*, Fourth Edition,
by Irvin B. Tucker

_____ 2. One of the best *Candid Camera* illustrations of the subtle power of

social situations to control behavior is the "elevator caper." A per-

son riding a rigged elevator first obeys the usual silent rule to face

the front, but when a group of other passengers all face the rear,

the **hapless victim** follows the group and faces the rear as well.

_____

—*Life-Span Development*, Ninth Edition,
by John W. Santrock

_____ 3. In the United States and other **highly developed** countries, infectious disease accounts for about 4% to 8% of deaths, compared with death rates of 30% to 50% in developing regions. _____

_____

_____

—*Biology*, Sixth Edition, by Eldra P. Solomon et al.

_____ 4. Early on in your approach to cooking—or in running a restaurant—you have to determine whether or not you are willing to commit fully and completely to the idea of **the pursuit of excellence.** I have always looked at it this way: if you strive for perfection—an all out assault on total perfection—at the very least you will hit a high level of excellence, and then you might be able to sleep at night. _____

_____

—*Introduction to Hospitality,* Fourth Edition, by John R. Walker

_____ 5. Finding Mozart a job was not easy. Most of his prospective employers thought that he was too young and too talented ("**overqualified**" is the word we would use today) for a normal position. Indeed, any music director would have been threatened by this brash and brilliant youngster. _____

_____

—*Understanding Music,* Fourth Edition,
by Jeremy Yudkin

EXERCISE 5   Write a word or phrase with a positive connotation that could be substituted for each of the following negative words. For example, positive substitutes for the word *criticism* might be *feedback* and *advice*. Answers may vary.

1. strange _____

2. wild _____

3. shy _____

4. bossy _____

5. skinny _____

6. nosy _____

7. hyperactive _____

8. slow _____

9. old _____

10. tree-hugger _____

Drawing Conclusions

Learning Objective 5

Draw reasonable conclusions

Readers use both stated and unstated ideas to draw logical conclusions. They use the facts, the hints, and their prior knowledge to piece together meaning. The facts and clues lead to assumptions, which then lead to conclusions. Read the following passage and explain how the conclusion is suggested.

EXAMPLE

MY HOUSE

My master still went to school every day and, coming home, he'd still bottle himself up in his study. When he had visitors he'd continue to complain about his job.

I still had nothing to eat so I did not become very fat but I was healthy enough. I didn't become sick like Kuro and, always, I took things as they came. I still didn't try to catch rats, and I still hated Osan, the maid. I still didn't have a name but you can't always have what you want. I resigned myself to continue living here at the home of this schoolteacher.

—Excerpt from *I Am a Cat,* by Natsume Soseki

Conclusion: The narrator of the book is a cat.

What clues suggest this conclusion? _____

EXPLANATION   The term *my master* may lead to an initial suspicion of a pet, and "try to catch rats" clearly suggests a cat. The option of continuing to live in the home supports the idea of a cat. The book, as you might guess, is titled *I Am a Cat.*

EXERCISE 6

In passages 1 through 3, identify the clues that lead to the stated conclusions. In passages 4 and 5, state the conclusion and identify the clues.

Passage 1

CULTS: THE PEOPLE'S TEMPLE

A **cult** is usually united by total rejection of society and extreme devotion to the cult's leader. The People's Temple is a dramatic example. In the 1970s their leader, Jim Jones, preached racial harmony, helped the poor, established drug-rehabilitation programs, staged protest demonstrations against social injustices, and helped elect sympathetic politicians. He moved his cult from San Francisco to Jonestown, Guyana, because, he said, evil people in the United States would try to destroy the Temple. He told his flock that to build a just society required a living God—namely, himself. To prove his deity, he "healed parishioners by appearing to draw forth cancers" (which actually were bloody chicken gizzards). He claimed that he had extraordinary sexual gifts, required Temple members to turn over all their possessions to him, and insisted that they call him "Dad" or "Father."

Then the People's Temple shocked the world. In November 1978 more than 900 members committed mass suicide at the order of their leader.

—*Sociology,* Third Edition, by Alex Thio

Conclusion: Jim Jones brainwashed cult members into total submission.

What clues suggest this conclusion? _____

_____

_____

_____

Passage 2

THE TOBACCO CRAZE

The first European smoker, Rodrigo de Jerez, was with Columbus. Jerez was jailed by the Spanish Inquisition for seven years because of his bad habit, but he was the wave of the future. Slowly, inexorably, the practice of "drinking" tobacco smoke spread throughout Europe. James I, who found smoking "loathsome" and forbade it in his presence, could not stop it. Nor could the Sultan of Turkey, who threatened to execute puffers.

The lure of the exotic—the trendy—has always been potent among the leisured classes, and some European physicians seized on tobacco as a miracle drug—"the holy, healing herb," "a sovereign remedy to all diseases"—prescribing it liberally to their patients. Throughout the 1500s, the Spanish were pleased to meet Europe's demand from their West Indian plantations.

—*The American Past,* Fifth Edition, by Joseph Conlin

Conclusion: Although initially rejected by political leaders, tobacco became an accepted and sought after commodity.

What clues suggest this conclusion? _____

_____

_____

Passage 3

NICHOLAS II (1894–1917)

Last of the Romanov tsars, Nicholas II was in almost every respect an unfortunate man. Besides having been influenced by a reactionary father and a strong-willed mother, he was dull, weak, stubborn, insensitive, and totally devoid of the qualities required for successfully administering a great empire. The day following his coronation, in conformity with tradition, he scheduled a banquet celebration for the people of the capital. A huge throng, possibly half a million souls, turned out for the great event. At one point the crowd surged forward and more than a thousand people were trampled to death. But Nicholas and the tsarina attended a ball at the French embassy that night and apparently spent a most enjoyable evening.

—*A History of the Western World,* by Solomon Modell

Conclusion: Nicholas and the tsarina had a total lack of concern for the welfare of the people.

What clues suggest this conclusion? _____

_____

_____

Passage 4

THE FUTURE OF M-COMMERCE

M-commerce has everything to do with speed and location, with short requests for information and prompt, relevant replies. Consider a scenario from the near future. Customers entering a butcher shop are offered a discount for waving their cell phone through an infrared sensor that records the telephone's number. Business at the store is brisk throughout the day. But near closing time, the butcher is anxious to get rid of some prime cuts of Argentine beef.

— *Business Today,* Tenth Edition,
by Michael Mescon et al.

What conclusion does the author imply? _____

_____

_____

What clues suggest this conclusion? _____

_____

_____

Passage 5

LANDMINES

Cheap and easy to deploy, many fighting forces routinely use mines to defend a frontier, deny opponents the use of a road, and many other purposes. Often these landmines remain active long after the fighting has ceased, posing a significant threat to the safety of the civilian population. The magnitude and horror of this problem sparked a grassroots effort to ban landmines.

The campaign received a major boost in 1996 when Diana, Princess of Wales, joined in the effort, going to places most affected by land mines, comforting victims, and bringing the issue to the attention of millions. When Princess Diana died in a car crash in August 1997, sorrow often turned into commitments to support her charitable interests, including the effort to ban mines. Only a few nations remain opposed to the landmine convention.

—*American Government,*
by Karen O'Connor and Larry Sabato

What conclusion does the author imply? _____

_____

_____

What clues suggest this conclusion? _____

_____

_____

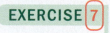

Use a combination of inference skills to read the following passages and answer the questions.

Passage 1

TEXAS TOUGH

Lyndon Baines Johnson was a complex man—shrewd, arrogant, intelligent, sensitive, vulgar, vain, and occasionally cruel. He loved power, and he knew where it was, how to get it, and how to use it. "I'm a powerful sonofabitch," he told two Texas congressmen in 1958 when he was the most powerful legislator on Capitol Hill. Everything about Johnson seemed to emphasize or enhance his power. He was physically large, and seemed even bigger than he was, and he used his size to persuade people. The "Johnson Method" involved "pressing the flesh"—a back-slapping, hugging sort of camaraderie. He also used symbols of power adroitly, especially the telephone which had replaced the sword and pen as the symbol of power. "No gunman," remarked one historian, "ever held a Colt. 44 so easily" as Johnson handled a telephone.

A legislative genius, Johnson had little experience in foreign affairs. Reared in the poverty of the Texas hill country, educated at a small teachers' college, and concerned politically with domestic issues, before becoming president LBJ had expressed little interest in foreign affairs. "Foreigners are not like the folks I am used to," he often said, and whether it was a joke or not he meant it. He was particularly uncomfortable around foreign dignitaries and ambassadors, often receiving them in groups and scarcely paying attention to them. "Why do I have to see them?" he once asked. "They're [Secretary of State] Dean Rusk's clients, not mine."

—America and Its People, Third Edition, by James Martin et al.

Answer with *T* (true) or *F* (false).

_____ 1. LBJ had an enormous ego.

_____ 2. LBJ used the telephone to influence votes.

_____ 3. LBJ quickly learned to perform in international situations.

_____ 4. LBJ's background is reflected in both his genius and his flaws.

_____ 5. LBJ was the right person to be president during the Vietnam War.

_____ 6. The phrase *replaced the sword* suggests a negative connotation.

Passage 2

THE REIGN OF LOUIS XVI (1774–1793)

A plain, fat, rather stupid young man, who loved to hunt and tinker with locks, Louis XVI succeeded his grandfather (whose one legitimate son, Louis XVI's father, died in 1765) at the age of twenty. His modesty and inherent kindness did not serve him well. He was far too simple, possessed an almost total lack of self-confidence, and could be made to change his mind with relative ease. His wife, Marie Antoinette, an Austrian princess, was pretty, not well educated, shallow, and selfish. Totally unconcerned with the people's welfare, she devoted herself to jewels and costly clothes, gambling and flirtation, masques and balls. Not completely satisfied with court life, she insisted on interfering in governmental affairs and sabotaged, to the extent that she could, whatever chance existed for the reformation of French life. Her liberal emperor-brother, Joseph II of Austria, reprimanded her, but his words went unheeded.

—*A History of the Western World,* by Solomon Modell

Answer with *T* (true) or *F* (false).

———— 1. Louis XVI and his wife were probably loved and respected by his people.

———— 2. Despite his wife's influence, Louis XVI had many of the qualities of a great leader.

———— 3. Louis XVI was firm in his decisions.

———— 4. Marie Antoinette's extravagance was probably resented by the people.

———— 5. Joseph II understood the possible repercussions of Marie Antoinette's actions.

———— 6. The reformation of French life would probably have been a benefit to the people.

———— 7. The phrase *tinker with locks* suggests hard work.

Passage 3

"LIZZIE BORDEN TOOK AN AX"

Andrew [Borden] was rich, but he didn't live like a wealthy man. Instead of living alongside the other prosperous Fall River citizens in the elite neighborhood known as The Hill, Andrew resided in an area near the business district called the flats. He liked to save time as well as money, and from the flats he could conveniently walk to work. For his daughters Lizzie and Emma, whose eyes and dreams focused on The Hill, life in the flats was an intolerable embarrassment. Their house was a grim, boxlike structure that lacked comfort and privacy. Since Andrew believed that running water on each floor was a wasteful luxury, the only washing facilities were a cold-water faucet in the kitchen and a laundry room water tap in the cellar. Also in the cellar was the toilet in the house. To make matters worse, the house was not connected to the Fall River gas main. Andrew preferred to use kerosene to light his house. Although it did not provide as good light or burn as cleanly as gas, it was less expensive. To save even more money, he and his family frequently sat in the dark.

The Borden home was far from happy. Lizzie and Emma, ages thirty-two and forty-two in 1892, strongly disliked their stepmother Abby and resented Andrew's penny-pinching ways. Lizzie especially felt alienated from the world around her. Although Fall River was the largest cotton-manufacturing town in America, it offered few opportunities for the unmarried daughter of a prosperous man. Society expected a woman of Lizzie's social position to marry, and while she waited for a proper suitor, her only respectable social outlets were church and community service. So Lizzie taught a Sunday School class and was active in the Woman's Christian Temperance Union, the Ladies' Fruit and Flower Mission, and other organizations. She kept herself busy, but she wasn't happy.

In August 1892, strange things started to happen in the Borden home. They began after Lizzie and Emma learned that Andrew had secretly changed his will. Abby became violently ill. Abby told a neighborhood doctor that she had been poisoned, but Andrew refused to listen to her wild ideas. Shortly thereafter, Lizzie went shopping for prussic acid, a deadly poison she said she needed to clean her sealskin cape. When a Fall River druggist refused her request, she left the store in an agitated state. Later in the day, she told a friend that she feared an unknown enemy of her father's was after him. "I'm afraid somebody will do something," she said.

On August 4, 1892, the maid Bridget awoke early and ill, but she still managed to prepare a large breakfast of johnnycakes, fresh-baked bread, ginger and oatmeal cookies with raisins, and some three-day-old mutton and hot mutton soup. After eating a hearty meal, Andrew left for work. Bridget also left to do some work outside. This left Abby and Lizzie in the house alone. Then somebody did something very specific and very grisly. As Abby was bent over making the bed in the guest room, someone moved into the room unobserved and killed her with an ax.

Andrew came home for lunch earlier than usual. He asked Lizzie where Abby was, and she said she didn't know. Unconcerned, Andrew, who was not feeling well, lay down on the parlor sofa for a nap. He never awoke. Like Abby, he was slaughtered by someone with an ax. Lizzie "discovered" his body, still lying on the sofa. She called Bridget, who had taken the back stairs to her attic room: "Come down quick; father's dead; somebody came in and killed him."

Experts have examined and reexamined the crime, and most have reached the same conclusion: Lizzie killed her father and stepmother. In fact, Lizzie was tried for the gruesome murders. However, despite a preponderance of evidence, an all male jury found her not guilty. Their verdict was unanimous and was arrived at without debate or disagreement. A woman of Lizzie's social position, they affirmed, simply could not have committed such a terrible crime.

Even before the trial started, newspaper and magazine writers had judged Lizzie innocent for much the same reasons. As one expert on the case noted, "Americans were certain that well-brought-up daughters could not commit murder with a hatchet on sunny summer mornings."

Jurors and editorialists alike judged Lizzie according to their preconceived notions of Victorian womanhood. They believed that such a woman was gentle, docile, and physically frail, short on analytical ability but long on nurturing instincts.

Too uncoordinated and weak to accurately swing an ax and too gentle and unintelligent to coldly plan a double murder, women of Lizzie's background simply had to be innocent because of their basic innocence.

—*America and Its People*, Third Edition,
by James Martin et al.

Answer with *T* (true) or *F* (false).

———— 1. Andrew Borden's family suffered from his efforts to save money.

———— 2. Abby was probably correct in telling the doctor that her illness was due to poison.

———— 3. Andrew was killed when he discovered his wife dead.

———— 4. The jury did not carefully consider the evidence against Lizzie.

———— 5. The Victorian stereotyping of women worked in Lizzie's favor.

———— 6. The author believes that Lizzie was not guilty.

———— 7. The quotation marks around the word *discovered* change the connotation of the word.

PERSONAL FEEDBACK 2   Name _____

1. What characteristics do you have that are important for leadership? _____
   _____

2. During this term, what have your leadership roles been? _____
   _____

3. As the term has progressed, how has your thinking about college changed? _____
   _____

4. How are your friends and loved ones affecting your academic success? _____
   _____

5. What is most irritating about your roommates or people you live with? _____
   _____

6. What will you remember most from this class? _____
   _____

Tear out and submit to your instructor.

SUMMARY POINTS

1 What is an inference? (page 440)
An inference is an implied meaning that is not directly stated but can be deduced from clues in the passage. Inferences require linking old knowledge to what is being read at the time.

2 Why do authors sometimes suggest rather than state meaning? (page 442)
Requiring the reader to infer the author's meaning is often more dramatic and interesting than stating it outright.

3 What is the role of prior knowledge in making inferences? (page 442)
Authors provide clues to their intended meaning but also make assumptions about the reader's prior knowledge of the subject. Therefore, it is important to recognize what you already know and fill in any missing knowledge to understand the clues.

4 How does slanted language relate to understanding the author's meaning? (page 444)
Slanted language manipulates the reader's attitude toward a subject in a positive or negative manner. Recognizing slanted language is another clue the reader has to the author's intended meaning.

5 How can I draw reasonable conclusions? (page 447)
Pay close attention to the details in the passage that provide clues to the author's meaning. Activate prior knowledge that relates to the topic and use logic to connect it to the clues. Making a reasonable inference requires the reader's prior knowledge and recognition of the details provided by the author.

COLLABORATIVE   PROBLEM SOLVING

Form a five-member group and select one of the following activities. Brainstorm and then outline your major points on a transparency. Choose a member to present the group findings to the class.

➤ Use details, dialogue, and characters to create a cartoon about poorly performing public high schools that blames *teachers* for the problems.

➤ Use details, dialogue, and characters to create a cartoon about poorly performing public high schools that blames *students* for the problems.

➤ Use details, dialogue, and characters to create a cartoon about poorly performing public high schools that blames *parents* for the problems.

➤ Use details, dialogue, and characters to create a cartoon about poorly performing public high schools that blames a *lack of money* for the problems.

MyReadingLab

MyReadingLab (MRL) www.myreadinglab.com

➤ For support in meeting this chapter's objectives, log in to **www.myreadinglab.com** and select "Inference."

THE READING WORKSHOP

If reading a novel, biography, or other book is part of your course experience, refer to The Reading Workshop: Thinking, Talking, and Writing about Books in Appendix 5 for suggestions.

SELECTION 1 # Literature: Short Story

"Deception is a cruel act . . . It often has many players on different stages that corrode the soul."

—Donna A. Favors

The training to be a physician is long, rigorous, and expensive. Most young doctors finally emerge in their 30s, ready for a job and burdened with debt. However, their financial opportunities appear rosy. Based on almost 3,000 replies to Physicians Search, doctors with three years of experience in practice are making money. On the high end of the salary range, the survey indicates the following yearly base salaries without benefits or bonuses for these specialties: psychiatrist at $189,000; family practice physician at $197,000; pediatrician at $201,000; emergency medicine at $250,000; dermatologist at $407,000; plastic surgeon at $411,000; radiologist at $429,000; cardiologist at $450,000; oncologist at $473,000; neurosurgeon at $713,000. Thus, for someone who is oriented toward science and gifted in medicine, the choices of a specialty are compelling. How does a young doctor decide, even with the special training needed, which is the best career path to pursue?

THINKING BEFORE READING

Preview the selection for content and organizational clues. Activate your schema and anticipate the story.

How much medical attention do prisoners receive?

What types of crime do FBI agents investigate?

After reading this, I will probably know _____ .

VOCABULARY PREVIEW

Are you familiar with these words?

deceptively	acknowledged	extradition	financier	limp
manipulations	distracting	stashed	extracted	trance

Have you ever had a tooth *extracted*?

Do you think driving while talking on a cell phone is *distracting*?

Do you sometimes feel as though you are in a *trance*?

Your instructor may choose to give a true-false vocabulary review before or after reading.

THINKING DURING READING

As you read, use the six thinking strategies of a good reader: predict, picture, relate, monitor, correct, and annotate.

SELECTION

1

Refer to the
Reader's **TIP**
for **Short Story** on
page 152.

((•—[Scan this QR
code to hear
this reading.

THE BEST PLACE

Dr. Jason Whitney saw the two federal agents enter the crowded restaurant. Their rumpled suits and stubble-covered cheeks betrayed the fact that they had been too busy to think of appearances for some time. They moved wearily toward him along the line of booths against the wall, looking for an empty one. When they reached the booth where the
5   young doctor was sitting alone, he spoke to the agent he recognized, a deceptively soft-looking man in his forties.

"Hello, Tom. Have a seat." He indicated the place opposite him with a sweep of his hand. "There probably aren't any empty booths at this hour. A lot of people stop here for breakfast on their way to work."

10   Tom Campbell slid heavily into the booth and was followed by his look-alike companion. "I'd like you to meet my partner, Joe Moffet, Dr. . . . Dr. . . ." Campbell snapped his fingers, trying to dislodge the name from his memory.

"Whitney. Jason Whitney," the doctor offered with a smile, not the least offended at not being remembered.

15   "Yeah, that's right," Campbell acknowledged with a nod as Joe Moffet and the young doctor clasped hands briefly.

"You men look like you've had a hard night," the doctor said.

"You can say that again," Campbell answered. "We haven't been out of our clothes in two days. Just brought a man back from Spain."

20   "Extradition?"

Campbell gave a wry smile. "You could call it that. Our man was staying in Andorra, that little postage-stamp country on the border between Spain and France. They'd have let him stay there until his money ran out, which would've taken a couple of thousand years or so. We have no treaty with them."

25   "So what happened?"

"The usual. We pretended we'd lost interest in him and waited for him to get careless. When he made the mistake of taking a walk too close to the Spanish border, we were ready. Next thing he knew, Joe and I each had one of his arms and were marching him past the Spanish customhouse. We tossed him into a car and rushed him to a plane we had waiting
30   at one of our bases. The Spanish authorities pretended they didn't see a thing."

"Seems like a lot of trouble and expense over just one man," Dr. Whitney said.

"It was Henry Hammond." Campbell had a touch of pride in his tone.

A waitress came to take their breakfast orders. As soon as she was gone, the doctor repeated the name. "Henry Hammond . . . It *does* sound a bit familiar. Should I know the name?"

35   "He's the big-shot financier who jumped bail and skipped the country a couple of years ago. He'd built himself an empire, using phony balance sheets and illegal manipulations. He got away with just about every nickel from his companies' treasuries."

"Oh, yes, now I remember. It made quite a splash in the papers at the time. What did you do with him?"

40   "Dropped him off at your place ten minutes ago," Campbell said.

The second agent, Joe Moffet, had been sitting quietly, but now he twisted his face into a puzzled expression and said, "Huh?"

Campbell turned to him. "The doctor is in charge of the infirmary at the Federal House of Detention on West Street," he explained. "He'll probably be giving our friend a
45   physical examination today."

"I check all new prisoners," Dr. Whitney agreed.

The waitress returned with their orders. They didn't say much until they had settled back to enjoy their coffee. Then the conversation returned to Henry Hammond.

"Do you think he'll return the money he stole?" the doctor asked.

50   "That's something you'll have to ask Hammond. We couldn't get a word out of him all the way across the Atlantic. He probably has it safely stashed away in a couple of dozen Swiss banks. One thing's sure—no one will ever see it again unless he wants them to."

"I wonder what makes a man decide to be a criminal?" the doctor mused.

55 Campbell shrugged. "Who knows? People don't always do the things you'd expect, or fit into patterns the way you think they should. Take yourself, for instance. What's a bright young guy like you doing in the Public Health Service? There's no military draft anymore, so you didn't choose it as an alternative service the way doctors and dentists have in the past. I'll bet you could have had your pick of the private hospitals."

60 "Yes, I probably could have, but I'm happy where I am. I think it's the best place for me. If I didn't, I'd go somewhere else or do something else. That's the way you feel about your job, isn't it, Tom? That active police work is the best occupation for you?"

"You certainly have Tom figured out," Joe Moffet said. "And you put it into words better than he does, too. He's turned down two promotions in the last year. He could have a comfortable desk job in D.C., but he prefers to transport fugitives. Everyone thinks he's 65 crazy, but he says he's happy where he is."

They exchanged small talk for a few more minutes, then left the restaurant together. They paused to say good-bye on the sidewalk outside, and Tom Campbell's face clouded with confusion and embarrassment. "I'm terribly sorry, Doctor, but I—uh—I've forgotten your name again."

70 Jason Whitney smiled. "That's all right. You'd be surprised how many people have trouble remembering me. The next time you're at the House of Detention stop by my office to say hello. I always have a pot of coffee on the hot plate." He turned to the other agent. "That goes for you, too, Mr. Moffet. Stop in any time. It's been nice meeting you."

Jason Whitney waited until ten that morning before having Henry Hammond called 75 to the infirmary. He chose that time because the morning sick call had been taken care of by then, and his assistants were enjoying a coffee break.

"Good morning, Mr. Hammond. I'm Dr. Whitney, the Chief Medical Officer here. I'm in charge of the health and physical well-being of you and the other prisoners. It's my job to examine each new arrival and determine whether or not he'll require treatment of any kind."

80 Hammond nodded his understanding. He had dark circles under his eyes and stood nervously in the doorway of the infirmary. He clenched and unclenched his right fist in an uneven rhythm, and his eyes swept back and forth, taking in all the cabinets and equipment. It was obvious his sudden arrest and transportation to the United States had been a severe shock.

"Step this way, please," Whitney said, leading the way to a side room.

85 Here there were bare white walls and the only furniture was an examination table for the patient. There was nothing that might prove distracting.

"Lie down, please. I'm going to take your blood pressure. I'm sure you've had it done before."

The doctor wrapped the instrument around Hammond's arm, and squeezed the bulb 90 to pump air into it.

"Be as quiet as you can. I want the lowest reading possible. Relax as much as you can and try not to think of anything in particular."

Whitney busied himself with the instrument.

"Your reading is a bit high, Mr. Hammond. I think you're a little too tense. If you 95 don't mind, I'll show you how to relax. Just close your eyes. That's right, close your eyes and relax the eyelids. I think you can get the feeling of complete relaxation if you'll follow my suggestions. Relax your eyelids completely. Now turn your attention to your arms. Let them become completely limp. Think of them as a pair of limp rags and when I lift them let them fall back to the table just as a couple of limp rags would. That's very good. Now 100 we'll do the same with your legs. See, you're much more relaxed and at ease now.

"I'll just take your blood pressure again and see how well you've done. Oh, that's very good. That's very, very good. You're far more relaxed than before. Let's try it again, Mr. Hammond, and this time keep your eyes closed all the while. That will aid the relaxation process.

"Okay, now, relax your eyes. Now your arms. Let them become as limp as rags. Now your 105 legs. Relax them. Just relax your whole body. Let your whole body go limp. Let your whole body become heavy. Get completely comfortable. Now, if you are truly relaxed, you will find that your eyelids won't open. Relax your eyelids and body completely. When you feel you're completely relaxed you may try to open your eyes. If you are completely relaxed, they won't open. If you cannot open your eyes, you will be completely relaxed. That's fine. Now try to

110 open your eyes. See—you cannot open them. You are completely, deeply relaxed and you cannot open your eyes. Your arms and legs are heavy and limp and you cannot lift or move them."

As quickly and easily as that, without once using the words sleep or hypnosis,
Dr. Jason Whitney placed Henry Hammond into a deep trance.

In the next half hour he deepened the trance still further, then extracted from Hammond
115 the code numbers and balances of ten secret bank accounts. Immediately before allowing the
man to wake up, he directed Hammond to forget forever that the secret accounts had ever
existed. "And you will never be able to remember my name," he told him.

That reminded Whitney of Agent Tom Campbell. When he had hypnotized Campbell
a year before and instructed the man to keep him informed about criminals with hidden
120 money; he had neglected to order him always to come to the restaurant alone. He would
have to rectify that oversight at the first opportunity.

As Hammond left the infirmary to return to his cell, Dr. Whitney watched him walk
away and felt a wave of satisfaction. This *was* the best place for him. He didn't have to
work the long hours a hospital might have demanded, and he was collecting far, far more
125 money in a single year than his professional hypnotist parents had earned in their lifetimes.

(1,714 words)

—by A. F. Oreshnik

THINKING AND WRITING AFTER READING

RECALL Self-test your understanding.

Your instructor may choose to give you a true-false comprehension review.

REACT At what point in the story did you guess what was going to happen?

_____

_____

REFLECT Why is the blood pressure deception an excellent choice for Dr. Whitney?

_____

THINKING CRITICALLY What factors must combine to make Dr. Whitney's scheme a

perfect and profitable crime? _____

_____

THINK AND WRITE   Define *irony*, and describe how it applies to three of the characters.

_____

_____

EXTENDED WRITING   Do you think Dr. Whitney has committed the perfect crime or is there a chance he will be caught? Create a follow-up to this story in which Dr. Whitney's scheme is discovered and verified. Think first about the possible weaknesses in his scheme that are suggested in the story and that you can imagine. Who might suspect him? How might evidence be gathered? Then, write the story featuring a trap to reveal clear evidence that will convict Dr. Whitney.

INFERENCE QUESTIONS

1. What does the author mean by the phrase "a deceptively soft-looking man"?

_____

_____

_____

_____

2. What is the irony in Jason Whitney's statement to the agents, "I wonder what makes a man decide to be a criminal?" _____

_____

3. Why does Dr. Whitney never mention the words *sleep* and *hypnosis*? _____

_____

4. What can be inferred from Dr. Whitney's remark to Tom Campbell, "You'd be surprised how many people have trouble remembering me"? _____

_____

_____

5. Why did Dr. Whitney wait until his assistants were on their coffee break before meeting with Henry Hammond? _____

_____

Interpret THE QUOTE

Now that you have finished reading the selection, "The Best Place," go back to the beginning of the selection and read the opening quote again. On a separate sheet of paper, explain the acts of deception that are most apparent in the story. Who were the players in this deception?

Name ——————————————————

Date ——————————————————

COMPREHENSION QUESTIONS

Answer the following with *a, b, c,* or *d,* or fill in the blank. In order to help you analyze your strengths and weaknesses, the question types are indicated.

Main Idea ——————— 1. The cliché that best reflects the main idea of this selection is:

    a. Crime does not pay.
    b. Honesty is the best policy.
    c. You can't judge a book by its cover.
    d. A penny saved is a penny earned.

Detail ——————— 2. Dr. Whitney is not offended when Agent Campbell fails to recall his name because

    a. Dr. Whitney is a modest man.
    b. Dr. Whitney does not want to embarrass the agent.
    c. Dr. Whitney has hypnotized Agent Campbell and told him to for-get the name.
    d. Dr. Whitney knows Agent Campbell usually has trouble remem-bering names.

Inference ——————— 3. Dr. Whitney needs to maintain a relationship with Agent Campbell because

    a. Campbell is his source for criminals with money.
    b. he considers Campbell a friend.
    c. Dr. Whitney and Agent Campbell are partners in crime.
    d. both men are employed by the same federal agency.

Inference ——————— 4. The irony of the story is that

    a. Hammond is guilty.
    b. Hammond was captured by the FBI.
    c. Dr. Whitney is a criminal.
    d. Joe Moffet believes his partner.

Inference ——————— 5. The reader can most likely conclude that Tom Campbell turned down two promotions because

    a. he was hypnotized to do so.
    b. he enjoys the travel in transporting fugitives.
    c. he did not want to move to D.C.
    d. he makes more money in his present job of transporting fugitives.

Inference ——————— 6. The reader can conclude that Henry Hammond was most likely arrested

    a. inside Spain.
    b. by Spanish customs officials.
    c. during the night when officials were not watching.
    d. while still in Andorra.

Inference ——————— 7. The author uses the story's title, *The Best Place,* to apply ironically to the situations in the lives of:

    a. Dr. Whitney and Tom Campbell.
    b. Tom Campbell and Joe Moffet.

c. Dr. Whitney, Tom Campbell, and Joe Moffet.

d. Dr. Whitney, Tom Campbell, Joe Moffet, and Henry Hammond.

Answer the following with *T* (true) or *F* (false).

Inference   _____   8. The reader can conclude that Dr. Whitney most likely got his job in the Federal House of Detention by accident.

Inference   _____   9. The reader can conclude that the FBI agents question Dr. Whitney about his job choice because they are suspicious of him.

Inference   _____ 10. The reader can conclude that Henry Hammond's blood pressure was high.

VOCABULARY

Answer the following with *a, b, c,* or *d* for the word or phrase that best defines the boldface word used in the selection. The number in parentheses indicates the line of the passage in which the word appears.

_____ 1. "**deceptively** soft-look-ing" (5)

a. honestly

b. misleadingly

c. plainly

d. happily

_____ 2. "**acknowledged** with" (15)

a. smiled

b. remembered

c. recognized

d. choked

_____ 3. "**Extradition**" (20)

a. exile

b. forced removal

c. relation

d. stay

_____ 4. "big-shot **financier**" (34)

a. drug lord

b. criminal

c. waiter

d. money manager

_____ 5. "illegal **manipulations**" (36–37)

a. schemes

b. money

c. adjustments

d. companies

_____ 6. "safely **stashed**" (51)

a. sent

b. found

c. buried

d. hidden

_____ 7. "prove **distracting**" (86)

a. examining

b. comforting

c. drawing attention elsewhere

d. truthful

_____ 8. "completely **limp**" (98)

a. lifeless

b. rigid

c. clean

d. tense

_____ 9. "a deep **trance**" (114)

a. sleeplike state

b. alertness

c. awareness

d. panic

_____ 10. "**extracted** from" (114)

a. followed

b. removed

c. made up

d. helped

Your instructor may choose to give a true-false vocabulary review.

VOCABULARY ENRICHMENT

Idiom

An **idiom** is a phrase used mainly in conversation that has meaning other than the literal meaning of the words themselves. For example, the phrase "My eyes were bigger than my stomach" is an idiom. The exact, literal meaning of the words is anatomically impossible. In our culture, however, the phrase is a creative way of saying, "I took more food on my plate than I can possibly eat." Other languages may not have this exact same expression, but they may have different idioms to express the same idea. Students who learn English as a second language find our idioms confusing when they look for an exact translation.

Idioms are slang phrases, clichés, and regional expressions. Their popularity changes with the times. Grandparents may use idioms that would make a college student shudder. Professional writers try to avoid idioms because they are considered informal.

Write the meaning of the boldface idioms in the following sentences.

1. Thomas's first-born son is **a chip off the old block**. _____

_____

2. It was getting late, and the mother decided to **hit the road** with her children.

_____

3. With that inappropriate comment to his students, the professor really **crossed the line**. _____

_____

4. Many inventors and entrepreneurs are experts at **thinking outside the box**.

_____

_____

5. Her father can be demanding and outspoken, but Suzanne knows that **his bark is worse than his bite**. _____

_____

6. Cynthia's dog has taken obedience class three times yet remains untrained; he is definitely **not the sharpest knife in the drawer**. _____

_____

7. When she learned that her son had made online purchases using her debit card, the mother **raked him over the coals**. _____

_____

8. After seeing the negative effects of his dishonesty, the student vowed to **turn over a new leaf** and turn in only his own work. _____

_____

9. The new coach is in favor of discipline and hard work; he makes his players **toe the line**. _____

10. Students who have jobs and attend college full-time often find themselves **burning the candle at both ends**. _____

_____

ASSESS YOUR LEARNING

Review confusing questions, seek clarification, and make notes in your text to help you remember the new information and vocabulary.

SELECTION 2 Literature: Short Story

> ". . . I have been married for forty-seven years and not once have we had an argument serious enough to consider divorce; murder, yes, but divorce, never."
>
> —Jack Benny

The term alchemist conjures up visions of medieval wizards who mixed chemistry with the supernatural. The occult art or pseudoscience of alchemy was veiled in magic and superstition. The exceedingly optimistic goals of alchemists were to transmute or turn base metals into gold, to create a potion to cure all ills, and to discover an elixir to extend life. Alchemists were both sought after and persecuted for their secrets. Today these first practitioners of chemistry might be seen as New Age spiritualists exploring homeopathy, aromatherapy, or astrology.

THINKING BEFORE READING

Preview the selection for content and organizational clues. Activate your schema and anticipate the story.

What is an alchemist?

Were alchemists viewed positively or negatively? Why?

After reading this, I will probably know _____ .

VOCABULARY PREVIEW

Are you familiar with these words?

alchemist	baser metals	autopsy	insomnia	hot grog

Can chemists turn *baser metals* into gold?

What ingredients are in *hot grog*?

Your instructor may choose to give a true-false vocabulary review before or after reading.

THINKING DURING READING

As you read, use the six thinking strategies of a good reader: predict, picture, relate, monitor, correct, and annotate.

THE ALCHEMIST'S SECRET

Refer to the
Reader's TIP
for a **Short Story**
on page 152.

Sitting quietly in his little herb shop on a crooked street in the shadow of Notre Dame, Doctor Maximus did not look like a very remarkable man. But he was. Five hundred years before, he might have busied himself changing the baser metals into gold. But in Paris of the nineties, it is said, he worked at a more subtle alchemy. He changed dreams into

5 realities—provided, of course, you could pay.

    The man who came into the gaslit shop this early October evening in 1891 was prepared to pay. He stood just inside the door, blotting his forehead with a silk handkerchief

although actually the weather was rather cool. He was holding a heart-shaped package tightly under one arm. "You are Monsieur le Doctor Maximus?"

10   The Doctor bowed respectfully.

"I have a problem," said the visitor nervously. "I am told you might help me with it."

"Indeed?" said the Doctor mildly. "Who told you that?"

The newcomer glanced around uneasily at the dim shelves, the leathery tortoise dangling from a string, the small stuffed crocodile with its dust-filmed eyes. "Last night we 15   had a dinner guest. A foreign diplomat. First secretary of the—"

"Ah, yes, Pechkoff. It is true I did him a small service."

"He was not very specific, you understand. But after a few glasses of cognac he talked rather freely. I got the impression . . ."

"Yes?"

20   "That if it weren't for your—er—assistance he would still be married, most unhappily, to his first wife."

Doctor Maximus took off his glasses and polished the spotless lenses. "She died, I believe, poor woman. Quite suddenly."

"Yes," said the visitor, "she did. So suddenly that there was an autopsy. But they dis-
25   covered nothing wrong."

"Of course not," said Doctor Maximus, smiling gently.

"My wife," said the visitor with a certain agitation, "is a very beautiful woman. Natu-
rally, she has many admirers. She has always ignored them until recently, but now there is one—I don't know which one—a younger man, no doubt. She admits it! She demands
30   that I make some settlement. I will not—"

Doctor Maximus raised his hand. "The details," he murmured, "do not concern me."

The visitor's face was tight and dangerous. "I am not a man to be made a fool of!"

"No," said the Doctor, "I can see that."

"Madame," said the visitor abruptly, "is very fond of candy." He unwrapped the heart-
35   shaped package and placed it on the counter. It was a box of chocolates. "I thought per-
haps you might—ah—improve the candies at your convenience and then post them to her. She would be very pleased. I have even prepared a card to enclose." He took out a small rectangle of cardboard. On it was printed in neat capitals: FROM AN ADMIRER.

Doctor Maximus took the card and sighed. "My fees are not inconsiderable."

40   "I did not expect them to be," the visitor said stiffly. He did not flinch when the price was named. He paid it, in gold coins. He blotted his forehead once more with the silk handkerchief. "Will you be able to send the candy tonight?"

"Perhaps," said the Doctor noncommittally. "We shall see. And where should it be sent?"

45   "Ah, yes," said the visitor. "Of course." And he gave Madame's name and address.

Doctor Maximus wrote the information on a slip of paper. Then he scribbled three digits on another slip and handed it over. "You sir, are customer 322. If there are any difficulties, kindly refer to that number. Not," he added, "that there will be any."

With one hand on the doorknob, the visitor hesitated. "It won't be—" he wet his
50   lips—"it won't be painful, will it?"

"Not at all," said Dr. Maximus. He peered over his spectacles in a benign and sympathetic fashion. "You seem rather upset. Do you want me to give you something to make you sleep?"

"No, thank you," said his visitor nervously. "I have my own prescription for insomnia: a hot grog before going to bed."

55   "Ah, yes," said Dr. Maximus. "An excellent habit."

"Good night," said the visitor, opening the door into the narrow, ill-lit street.

"Good-bye," murmured Dr. Maximus.

Taking the box of chocolates in one hand and the slip of paper in the other, he went into the little room at the rear of the shop. From the shelf above his test tubes and retorts
60   he took a big black book, opened it, and looked at the record of the previous transaction. There it was, entered only that afternoon in his spidery handwriting: *Customer 321. Complaint: the usual. Remedy: six drops of the elixir, to be administered in husband's hot grog at bedtime . . .*

Dr. Maximus sighed. Then, being a man who honored his commitments, he opened
65   the box of chocolates and went to work. There was no great rush. He would post the parcel in the morning.

In the herb shop, as in life, you got just about what you paid for. But his motto was, First come, first served.

(867 words)

—by Arthur Gordon

THINKING AND WRITING AFTER READING

Inference Questions

1. Where did the couple learn of Dr. Maximus? _____

_____

2. How was Dr. Maximus connected to Pechkoff's wife? _____

_____

3. Why was the husband who drank grog unhappy with his wife? _____

_____

4. How did Dr. Maximus realize that the husband was his next victim? _____

_____

_____

5. What can be concluded about Customer 321? _____

6. Why is the motto "First come, first served" ironic in this story? _____

_____

_____

7. Why is the phrase "being a man who honored his commitments" sarcastic?

_____

_____

8. What is the theme of this story? _____

_____

THINK AND WRITE

Considering the three goals of alchemists, why do you think they were both sought after and persecuted for their secrets? _____

_____

_____

EXTENDED WRITING As a result of the dishonesty of some large companies and business people, ethics has become a very important aspect of training in business schools. What do you think constitutes ethical practice in business? What do you expect from a company or store with which you do business? Write a 1-2 page section on the qualities of an ethical business person that could be included in a business management textbook. Use the qualities you think are important as headings. Elaborate, explain, and give examples under each heading.

Interpret THE QUOTE

Now that you have finished reading the selection, "The Alchemist's Secret," go back to the beginning of the selection and read the opening quote again. What can you infer from Jack Benny's quote about his marriage? On a separate sheet of paper, explain how this quote relates to the relationship between the husband and wife depicted in the story.

VOCABULARY ENRICHMENT

Literary Devices

A. **Personification.** In personification, an inanimate object is given human characteristics. Personification can embellish an image and create a mood. In the sentence "The wind sang through the trees," the word *sang* gives the wind a human characteristic that adds a soft, gentle mood to the message.

   Write the meaning, mood, or feeling the boldface personification adds to the message in the following sentences.

1. As the alchemist scraped the bar of gold, her skin **crawled**. _____

_____

2. The glowing fireplace was the **heart** of the tiny shop selling health remedies.

_____

3. The sun **kissed** the window and brightened the dark laboratory. _____
_____

4. The shelves **stretched** to make room for more new youth potions. _____
_____

5. As he reached for the poison potion, the stars **flirted** with the drifting sand.
_____

B. **Irony.** Irony is saying one thing but meaning another. It may be used to show humor or to be sarcastic and ridicule others. The trick in irony is to be able to recognize that the speaker does not really mean what he or she says. The context in which the statement is made gives clues to the speaker's true attitude. Gullible people have trouble picking up irony and are subsequently sometimes fooled and embarrassed. For example, after a basketball game, someone may say to a player who scored only once in seventeen tries, "You're a great shot." Here irony is used to ridicule the poor shooting.

Complete the story in each of the following sentences by choosing the response that best shows irony.

_____ 6. Each time the professor called on Larry to answer a question, he gave the wrong response. After class Frances said to Larry,
    a. "We need to study hard."
    b. "Here's the guy with the brains."
    c. "I hope you weren't embarrassed."

_____ 7. Sue missed only one item on a chemistry exam that almost everyone else failed. When congratulated, Sue retorted,
    a. "Maybe next time I'll study."
    b. "I'm glad I studied."
    c. "My major is chemistry."

_____ 8. As newlyweds, Betsy and Fred moved to a tiny New York apartment. When their parents came to visit, a sign on the door said,
    a. "Welcome to our new place."
    b. "Welcome to the Caribbean Hilton."
    c. "Welcome to our friends and family."

_____ 9. Because George's apartment was so dirty, his friends called him
    a. the Slob.
    b. George the Unclean.
    c. Mother's Helper.

_____ 10. Chris was known to be cheap, so friends started calling him
    a. Mr. Rockefeller.
    b. Mr. Scrooge.
    c. Mr. Chips.

ASSESS YOUR LEARNING

Review confusing questions, seek clarification, and make notes in your text to help you remember the new information and vocabulary.

SELECTION 3 Literature: Short Story

"Diamonds are nothing more than chunks of coal that stuck to their jobs."

—Malcolm Forbes

Diamonds have value because they sparkle and are cherished in the marketplace. That value, or price, is determined by the four Cs of diamonds: cut, clarity, color, and carat weight. If you are searching for specific prices, the range varies. For example, one company lists its one-carat round cut diamonds from $5,000 to $17,000 according to clarity and color. Another company offers one-carat stones with the same round cut for $3,000 to $16,000. For three-carat diamonds with round cuts, the range is $14,000 to $112,000 or $7,000 to $41,000. High prices make diamonds particularly attractive to thieves. Stones are also difficult to trace and easy to sell on the black market. Robbing a jewelry store may be easier than robbing a bank, and some people may think that both produce sure money.

THINKING BEFORE READING

Preview for content and organizational clues. Activate your schema and anticipate the author's opinion.

What factors contribute to the appeal and the price of diamonds?

Why are stolen diamonds easy to resell without being traced?

After reading this, I will probably want to _____ .

VOCABULARY PREVIEW

Are you familiar with these words?

strolled	fashion-plate	reluctantly	commotion	cooler
previous	mingled	dapper	confirmed	wading

Is Beyoncé a *fashion-plate*?

Do you *reluctantly* go to the doctor?

When was the last time you *mingled* with people you didn't know?

Your instructor may choose to give a true-false vocabulary review before or after reading.

THINKING DURING READING

As you read, use the six thinking strategies of a good reader: predict, picture, relate, monitor, correct, and annotate.

A DEAL IN DIAMONDS

Refer to the
Reader's **TIP**
for a **Short Story** on
page 152.

It was seeing a girl toss a penny into the plaza fountain that gave Pete Hopkins the idea. He was always on the lookout for money-making ideas, and they were getting tougher to find all the time. But as he looked up from the fountain to the open window of the Downtown Diamond Exchange, he thought he had found a good one at last.

5   He strolled over to the phone booth at the other side of the plaza and called Johnny Stoop. Johnny was the classiest dude Pete knew—a real fashion-plate who could walk into a store and have the clerks falling over themselves to wait on him. Better yet, he had no record here in the east. And it was doubtful if the cops could link him to the long list of felonies he had committed ten years ago in California.

10   "Johnny? This is Pete. Glad I caught you in."

"I'm always in during the daytime, Pete boy. In fact, I was just getting up."

"I got a job for us, Johnny, if you're interested."

"What sort?"

"Meet me at the Birchbark Bar and we'll talk about it."

15   "How soon?"

"An hour?"

Johnny Stoop groaned. "Make it two. I gotta shower and eat breakfast."

"Okay, two. See you."

The Birchbark Bar was a quiet place in the afternoons—perfect for the sort of meet-
20   ing Pete wanted. He took a booth near the back and ordered a beer. Johnny was only ten minutes late and he walked into the place as if he were casing it for a robbery or a girl he might pick up. Finally he settled, almost reluctantly, for Pete's booth.

"So what's the story?"

The bartender was on the phone yelling at somebody about a delivery, and the rest
25   of the place was empty. Pete started talking. "The Downtown Diamond Exchange. I think we can rip it off for a quick handful of stones. Might be good for fifty grand."

Johnny Stoop grunted, obviously interested. "How do we do it?"

"*You* do it. I wait outside."

"Great! And I'm the one the cops grab!"

30   "The cops don't grab anyone. You stroll in, just like Dapper Dan, and ask to see a tray of diamonds. You know where the place is, on the fourth floor. Go at noon, when there's always a few customers around. I'll create a commotion in the hall, and you snatch up a handful of stones."

"What do I do—swallow them like the gypsy kids used to do?"

35   "Nothing so crude. The cops are wise to that, anyway. You throw them out the window."

"Like hell I do!"

"I'm serious, Johnny."

"They don't even keep their windows open. They got air conditioning, haven't they?"

40   "I saw the window open today. You know all this energy-conservation stuff—turn off the air conditioner and open the windows. Well, they're doing it. They probably figure four flights up nobody's goin' to get in that way. But something can get *out*—the diamonds."

"It sounds crazy, Pete."

45   "Listen, you toss the diamonds through the window from the counter. That's maybe ten feet away." He was making a quick pencil sketch of the office as he talked. "See, the window's behind the counter, and you're in front of it. They never suspect that you threw 'em out the window because you're never near the window. They search you, they question you, but then they gotta let you go. There are other people in the store, other
50   suspects. And nobody saw you take them."

"So the diamonds go out the window. But you're not outside to catch them. You're in the hall creating a diversion. So what happens to the stones?"

"This is the clever part. Directly beneath the window, four stories down, is the fountain in the plaza. It's big enough so the diamonds can't miss it. They fall into the fountain
55   and they're as safe as in a bank vault till we decide to get them. Nobody noticed them hit the water because the fountain is splashing. And nobody sees them *in* the water because they're clear. They're like glass."

"Yeah," Johnny agreed. "Unless the sun—"

"The sun don't reach the bottom of the pool. You could look right at 'em and not
60 notice 'em—unless you knew they were there. We'll know, and we'll come back for them
tomorrow night, or the next."

Johnny was nodding. "I'm in. When do we pull it off?"

Pete smiled and raised his glass of beer. "Tomorrow."

On the following day, Johnny Stoop entered the fourth floor offices of the Downtown
65 Diamond Exchange at exactly 12:15. The uniformed guard who was always at the door
gave him no more than a passing glance. Pete watched it all from the busy hallway outside,
getting a clear view through the thick glass doors that ran from floor to ceiling.

As soon as he saw the clerk produce a tray of diamonds for Johnny, he glanced across
the office at the window. It was open about halfway, as it had been the previous day. Pete
70 started walking toward the door, touched the thick glass handle, and fell over in an apparent faint. The guard inside the door heard him fall and came out to offer assistance.

"What's the matter, mister? You okay?"

"I—I can't—breathe . . ."

He raised his head and asked for a glass of water. Already one of the clerks had come
75 around the counter to see what the trouble was.

Pete sat up and drank the water, putting on a good act. "I just fainted, I guess."

"Let me get you a chair," one clerk said.

"No, I think I'd better just go home." He brushed off his suit and thanked them. "I'll
be back when I'm feeling better." He hadn't dared to look at Johnny, and he hoped the
80 diamonds had gone out the window as planned.

He took the elevator downstairs and strolled across the plaza to the fountain. There
was always a crowd around it at noon—secretaries eating their lunches out of brown-paper
bags, young men casually chatting with them. He mingled unnoticed and worked his way
to the edge of the pool. But it was a big area, and through the rippling water he couldn't be
85 certain he saw anything except the scattering of pennies and nickels at the bottom. Well, he
hadn't expected to see the diamonds anyway, so he wasn't disappointed.

He waited an hour, then decided the police must still be questioning Johnny. The best
thing to do was to head for his apartment and wait for a call.

It came two hours later.

90   "That was a close one," Johnny said. "They finally let me go, but they still might be following me."

"Did you do it?"

"Sure I did it! What do you think they held me for? They were goin' crazy in there. But I can't talk now. Let's meet at the Birchbark in an hour. I'll make sure I'm not followed."

95   Pete took the same booth at the rear of the Birchbark and ordered his usual beer. When Johnny arrived the dapper man was smiling. "I think we pulled it off, Pete. Damn if we didn't pull it off!"

"What'd you tell them?"

"That I didn't see a thing. Sure, I'd asked for the tray of stones, but then when there 100 was the commotion in the hall I went to see what it was along with everyone else. There were four customers in the place and they couldn't really pin it on any one of us. But they searched us all, and even took us downtown to be X-rayed, to be certain we hadn't swallowed the stones."

"I was wondering what took you so long."

105   "I was lucky to be out as soon as I was. A couple of the others acted more suspicious than me, and that was a break. One of them even had an arrest record for a stolen car." He said it in a superior manner. "The dumb cops figure anyone who stole a car would steal diamonds."

"I hope they didn't get too good a look at me. I'm the one who caused the commo-110 tion, and they just gotta figure I'm involved."

"Don't worry. We'll pick up the diamonds tonight and get out of town for a while."

"How many stones were there?" Pete asked expectantly.

"Five. And all beauties."

The evening papers confirmed it. They placed the value of the five missing diamonds 115 at $65,000. And the police had no clue.

They went back to the plaza around midnight, but Pete didn't like the feel of it. "They might be wise," he told Johnny. "Let's wait a night, in case the cops are still snoopin' around up there. Hell, the stones are safe where they are."

The following night, when the story had already disappeared from the papers, re-120 placed by a bank robbery, they returned to the plaza once more. This time they waited till three A.M., when even the late crowd from the bars had scattered for home. Johnny carried a flashlight and Pete wore wading boots. He'd already considered the possibility that one or two of the diamonds might not be found, but even so they'd be far ahead of the game.

125   The fountain was turned off at night, and the calmness of the water made the search easier. Wading in the shallow water, Pete found two of the gems almost at once. It took another ten minutes to find the third one, and he was ready to quit then. "Let's take what we got, Johnny."

The flashlight bobbed. "No, no. Keep looking. Find us at least one more."

130   Suddenly they were pinned in the glare of a spotlight, and a voice shouted, "Hold it right there! We're police officers!"

"Damn!" Johnny dropped the flashlight and started to run, but already the two cops were out of their squad car. One of them pulled his gun and Johnny stopped in his tracks. Pete climbed from the pool and stood with his hands up.

135   "You got us, officer," he said.

"Damn right we got you," the cop with the gun growled.

"The coins in that fountain go to charity every month. Anybody that would steal them has to be pretty low. I hope the judge gives you both ninety days in the cooler. Now up against the car while we search you!"

(1,000 words)

—by Edward D. Hoch, from *Ellery Queen's Mystery Magazine*

THINKING AND WRITING AFTER READING

RECALL   Self-test your understanding.

Your instructor may choose to give you a true-false comprehension review.

REACT   Greed prompted the robbery, but how did excessive greed figure into the arrest? _____

_____

REFLECT   What do you think Pete and Johnny did to escape charges for the dia-mond robbery when the police caught them?_____

_____

THINKING CRITICALLY   This story was first published in 1975. What modern changes in building construction and security might make such a heist far less probable today? Write your answer on a separate sheet of paper.

THINK AND WRITE   What better or "safer" plan might have been devised for getting diamonds out of the fountain? Explain your ideas. _____

_____

EXTENDED WRITING   Search the Internet for information on buying a good quality diamond. Write a letter to a friend who wants to buy a diamond engagement ring. Provide solid advice based on your research about how to select the best quality diamond. Your letter should include an explanation of the "4-Cs."

INFERENCE QUESTIONS

1. Why does Pete want Johnny rather than himself to steal the diamonds?

   _____

   _____

2. Why does Pete's plan call for retrieving the diamonds a night or two after

   they are stolen? _____

   _____

   _____

3. What is the meaning of the phrase "Dapper Dan"? _____

   _____

4. Why was Johnny not arrested as a suspect in the crime? _____

   _____

   _____

5. What is suggested by the phrase "Pete didn't like the feel of it"? _____

   _____

   _____

Interpret THE QUOTE

Now that you have finished reading the selection, "A Deal in Diamonds," go back to the beginning of the selection and read the opening quote again. In the story, Pete and Johnny go to great lengths to steal the diamonds, yet what does Malcolm Forbes' quote say about the value of diamonds? On a separate sheet of paper, list three things (other than diamonds) that become valuable over time, and explain why.

Name ————————————————

Date ————————————————

COMPREHENSION QUESTIONS

Answer the following *T* (true) or *F* (false).

Inference _____ 1. The diamond heist could have taken place in New York but not in Las Vegas.

Inference _____ 2. Johnny Stoop would have been detained longer by the police if the robbery had been in California.

Inference _____ 3. Pete gambled correctly that office workers having lunch around the fountain would not see the falling diamonds.

Inference _____ 4. The irony of the story is that the police arrested the right men for the wrong reasons.

Inference _____ 5. The reader can conclude that Johnny and Pete will be charged with the diamond robbery.

Inference _____ 6. The security guard was suspicious of Pete's fainting spell.

Inference _____ 7. The reader can conclude that one of the suspected Diamond Exchange customers confessed to a previous arrest.

Inference _____ 8. The two men were worried that the police might find the diamonds in the fountain if they waited longer than a night or two to collect them.

Detail _____ 9. Pete and Johnny found four of the diamonds before they were arrested.

Inference _____ 10. The police officers suspected that they had apprehended the men responsible for the diamond theft.

VOCABULARY

Answer the following with *a, b, c,* or *d* for the word or phrase that best defines the boldface word used in the selection. The number in parentheses indicates the line of the passage in which the word appears.

_____ 1. "**strolled** over" (5)
    a. walked slowly
    b. called
    c. walked quickly
    d. looked

_____ 3. "almost **reluctantly**" (22)
    a. happily
    b. willingly
    c. quietly
    d. unenthusiastically

_____ 2. "a real **fashion-plate**" (6)
    a. set of dinner dishes
    b. well-dressed person
    c. jerk
    d. criminal

_____ 4. "create a **commotion**" (32)
    a. play
    b. job
    c. interest
    d. disturbance

SELECTION 3

_____ 5. "**previous** day" (69)
   a. subsequent
   b. prior
   c. following
   d. later

_____ 6. "He **mingled**" (83)
   a. blended
   b. walked
   c. talked
   d. shopped

_____ 7. "**dapper** man" (96)
   a. grubby
   b. smelly
   c. elegant
   d. happy

_____ 8. "**confirmed** it" (114)
   a. reported
   b. proved
   c. valued
   d. ignored

_____ 9. "**Wading** in" (126)
   a. walking
   b. looking
   c. finding
   d. hiding

_____ 10. "in the **cooler**" (138)
   a. refrigerator
   b. freezer
   c. drink
   d. jail

Your instructor may choose to give a true-false vocabulary review.

VOCABULARY ENRICHMENT

Figurative Language

Writers and speakers use figurative language to spark the imagination and make the message more sensual and visual. The words create images in the mind and activate associations stored in memory. Figurative language is challenging, because figuring out the meaning demands logical and creative thinking.

A. **Simile.** A simile uses the words *like* or *as* to compare two unlike things. The purpose of a simile is to strengthen the message by adding a visual image. Similes usually dramatize the characteristics of nouns. As a reader, you must figure out the unique characteristic the simile is describing. In the sentence, "The new teacher stood like a statue in front of the class," what does the simile add to the meaning? "Like a statue" describes the teacher as "stiff and unmoving." The simile adds humor and visual interest to the sentence.

Write the meaning of the boldface similes in the following sentences.

1. The boys were **like two peas in a pod** working on their handheld electronic devices. _____

2. My grandmother claims to be **as old as the hills**. _____

3. Her face was **as fresh as the morning dew.** _____

4. When he walked into the arcade, the little boy smiled **like a fox in a henhouse**. _____

5. Looking for the missing check was **like trying to find a needle in a haystack**. _____

B. **Metaphor.** Whereas a simile uses the words *like* or *as* to compare two unlike things, a metaphor does not use those words but instead states the comparison directly. For example, "The soccer player was a tiger" is a metaphor that dramatizes the player's aggressive spirit. If the statement had been, "The girl plays soccer like a tiger," the figure of speech would be a simile, but the meaning would remain the same.

Write the meaning of the boldface metaphors in the following sentences.

6. Superman is **made of steel**. _____

7. Her words were **daggers** directed toward his heart. _____
_____

8. She was a **willow** in the winds of time. _____
_____

9. The woman had **built a wall** between herself and others. _____
_____

10. He was her **world**. _____

ASSESS YOUR LEARNING

Review confusing questions, seek clarification, and make notes in your textbook to help you remember the new information and vocabulary.

VOCABULARY LESSON

Come Together, Hold Together, and Shut

Study the roots, words, and sentences.

Roots *greg*: come together, group	*clud, clus*: shut
ten, tent, tain, tinu: hold together, hold	

Words with *greg* = come together, group

Does a *congregation* sing hymns? Have men's clubs *desegregated*?

- Congregate: to flock together

  Students usually *congregate* in the gym prior to the first class period.

- Gregarious: outgoing; enjoying groups

  Gregarious people enjoy parties.

- Aggregation: a collection or union

  The steering committee was an *aggregation* of members of six sororities.

- Egregious: conspicuous; the worst of the group

  The *egregious* error was easy to detect but costly to fix.

- Segregate: to separate from the group

  Before eating M&Ms, do you *segregate* the red ones?

Words with *ten, tent, tain, tinu* = hold together, hold

Will a lock secure the *contents*? Is daily *maintenance* needed?

- Tenant: one who holds a lease on a house or apartment

  The present *tenant* pays his rent early.

- Tenacity: quality of holding together for a purpose

  Do you have the drive and *tenacity* to run for public office?

- Contented: easy in mind or satisfied

  A *contented* dog is usually one that is well fed.

- Contentment: satisfaction with one's lot

  Money is not essential for *contentment*, but it does help.

- Intent: purpose, concentration, holding one's mind on a single matter

  What is the *intent* of this lengthy proposal?

- Retain: to hold secure

  With a majority in the Senate, the Republicans can *retain* power.

- Continuously: without stopping

  In summer, the Niagara River flows *continuously* over Horseshoe Falls.

- Tenable: able to be held or defended

  Paying for the damage is a *tenable* resolution to the accident.

- Untenable: cannot be held

  Continuing a relationship after being abused is *untenable*.

- Discontented: not content

  I am *discontented* with my grades, because I know I can do better.

Words with *clud* or *clus* = shut

Should *conclusive* evidence result in a conviction? Is your *conclusion* final?

- Recluse: one who shuts himself or herself away from others, a hermit

  The *recluse* left the island only to get provisions.

- Exclude: to shut out

  Do not *exclude* your friends from your joys or sorrows.

- Inclusive: counting everything

  The quoted price is *inclusive* of tax and shipping.

- Seclude: to remove, shut off

  In order to recuperate, he wanted to *seclude* himself from visitors.

- Preclude: to close beforehand or hinder

  Having a mobile phone does not *preclude* the need for an answering machine on your home telephone.

Review

Part I

Answer the following with true (*T*) or false (*F*).

_____ 1. Gregarious students are usually shy.

_____ 2. If you segregate your socks by color, you mix them in one group.

_____ 3. When students congregate in the doorway, entrance can be difficult.

_____ 4. An egregious boor is usually a desirable companion.

_____ 5. Desegregated schools bring together students of different backgrounds.

_____ 6. Contented babies cry excessively.

_____ 7. If you retain your job, you keep your position.

_____ 8. A winning lawyer has a tenable case.

_____ 9. To seclude yourself is to join the group for the celebration.

_____10. An inclusive organization welcomes entry to many.

Part II

Choose the word from the list that is a synonym for the following.

| intent | tenacity | contents | recluse | conclusion |
| maintenance | aggregation | tenant | congregation | contentment |

11. hermit _____

12. renter _____

13. happiness _____

14. collection _____

15. purpose _____

16. final statement _____

17. flock _____

18. determination _____

19. upkeep _____

20. belongings _____

Reading Newspaper Editorials

Editorials. Unlike news stories, **editorials** are one of the few types of articles in newspapers that are subjective—that is, they express the opinion of a person or organization. A newspaper's editorial pages feature the views of its management and editors. Issues discussed in these pieces are usually related to particular local, national, or international news stories.

Although the style of editorials varies as widely as people's opinions, the basic format is usually the same: Two or three brief paragraphs describe a scene or provide historical background leading up to the main theme the writer intends to discuss. After stating a position, the writer follows up with examples, data, and analysis to support the position. Once the case has been made, alternative ideas and solutions may be provided and may also include the writer's prediction of what will happen if the current situation is not changed. The final paragraphs summarize and restate the main idea of the editorial.

Remember that editorials *always express opinions,* and regardless of how persuasive the writer's argument might be, you are free to reject it. Newspapers encourage readers to express their own opinions—either for or against editorials—in the Letters to the Editor section. Selected letters are published in the newspaper, usually in the same section with the editorials, and they often feature the views of readers who disagree with recent editorials or with the way in which a news story has been reported.

Reader's **TIP**   Reading an Editorial

While reading an editorial, ask yourself the following questions:

- What event prompted the editorial?
- What is the thesis or opinion being promoted by the author?
- Do the details prove the thesis?
- Is the author liberal or conservative?
- What is left out?
- Are the sources, facts, and other support credible?

EXERCISE 1   Read the following editorial to answer the questions.

1. What event does the writer describe to introduce the main idea? _____
   _____
   _____

2. What is the writer's main idea? _____
   _____

Tuesday, April 25, 2011

EDITORIAL PAGE

Political Poverty

In a recent speech to the Linville Chamber of Commerce, Mayor Anderson praised the city council for its "new direction" and its efforts to eliminate city programs that "throw money" at social problems. The audience found this statement to their liking and responded enthusiastically.

However, one phrase in the mayor's speech was quite revealing. He believes it is wrong to expect "governments . . . to take over the upbringing of all who choose the low road to poverty."

What sort of misguided thinking is this—not only to blame those who are "grossly neglected" (as the Mayor characterized them) and who have "special needs for their predicaments," but to further stigmatize them by calling theirs "the low road"?

People do not choose poverty. People do not choose the obstacles they must overcome any more than they choose the family into which they are born. The physically challenged, the culturally deprived, and those lacking sufficient education can certainly take the responsibility for changing their circumstances, but cannot be blamed for those circumstances—no matter how convenient it may be for addressing the city's fiscal difficulties.

A moral society bears responsibility for providing aid and education to the less fortunate. We all contribute to this effort by paying our taxes. However, all too often our culture also rushes to blame victims for their own predicaments. This is because we have an unrealistic sense of our own immunity and invulnerability, believing we can avoid or surmount any challenge—in other words, always thinking "that could never happen to me." Perhaps we would feel more humble if we were the ones trying to overcome catastrophic illness without adequate medical care, trying to find a job without the skills provided by a sound public education system, or trying to feed a family on a minimum-wage salary. In such circumstances, the luxury of being as smug and self-assured as the mayor, the city council, and the Chamber members are would certainly be lost.

Proponents of this so-called new direction absolve themselves too easily of moral responsibility when the low road that they have chosen is one of convenience and callous indifference toward those already burdened and less fortunate than themselves.

3. What one example does the writer give that would help the mayor better understand this position? _____

_____

4. Is the author liberal or conservative? _____

5. Is the main idea supported primarily by facts or opinions? _____

EXERCISE 2

Locate an editorial that interests you in a local, city, or national newspaper. Cut out the editorial and answer the following questions:

1. What event prompted the editorial? _____

2. What is the author's opinion on the issue? _____

3. Do the details prove the thesis? Are they credible? _____

4. What has been left out? _____

11 Critical Reading

Learning Objectives

From this chapter, readers will learn:

1 Strategies for critical reading
2 To recognize an author's purpose or intent
3 To identify an author's point of view or bias
4 To recognize the author's tone
5 To distinguish fact from opinion
6 To recognize valid and invalid support for arguments

Everyday Reading Skills: Evaluating Internet Information

WHAT DO CRITICAL READERS DO?

Learning Objective 1

Strategies for critical reading

Critical readers do not accept the idea that "If it's in print, it must be true." They do not immediately accept the thinking of others. Rather, they use direct statements, inferences, prior knowledge, and language clues to assess and evaluate. They think for themselves, analyze written material in their search for truth, and then decide how accurate and relevant the printed words are.

Recognize the Author's Purpose or Intent

Learning Objective 2

Recognize the author's purpose

Authors write with a particular **purpose** or **intent** in mind. For example, you might be instructed to write a scientific paper on environmental pollution with the ultimate purpose of inspiring classmates to recycle. In writing the paper, you must both educate and persuade, but your overriding goal is persuasion. Therefore, you will choose and use only the facts that support your argument. Your critical reading audience will then carefully evaluate your scientific support, recognizing that your purpose was to persuade and not really to educate, and thus decide whether to recycle all or some combination of paper, glass, aluminum, and plastic. The author's reason for writing can alert the reader to be accepting or suspicious. These are three common purposes for writing:

- **To inform.** Authors use facts to inform, to explain, to educate, and to enlighten. The purpose of textbooks is usually to inform or explain, but sometimes an author might venture into persuasion, particularly on topics such as smoking or recycling.
- **To persuade.** Authors use a combination of facts and opinions to persuade, to argue, to condemn, and to ridicule. Editorials in newspapers are written to argue a point and persuade the reader.
- **To entertain.** Authors use fiction and nonfiction to entertain, to narrate, to describe, and to shock. Novels, short stories, and essays are written to entertain. Sometimes an author may adopt a guise of humor in order to entertain and achieve a special result.

EXAMPLE   For each of the following topic sentences, decide whether the author's main purpose is to inform (*I*), to persuade (*P*), or to entertain (*E*).

_____ 1. Telling secrets in the form of public confessions on television talk shows is detrimental to building healthy, satisfying relationships. Such talk shows reveal the worst in human behavior and should be taken off the air.

_____ 2. Self-disclosure in communication means revealing information about yourself, usually in exchange for information about the other person.

_____ 3. Daytime viewers don't seem too surprised to find that Sam has been married to two other women while he has been dating Lucinda, who is carrying his third child and is having an affair with Sam's best friend.

EXPLANATION   The purpose of the first sentence is to persuade the reader to condemn such programs for the harm they can cause the participants. The purpose of the second sentence is simply to inform or educate by giving a definition. The last sentence exaggerates in order to entertain.

EXERCISE 1   Identify the main purpose of each of the following as to inform (*I*), to persuade (*P*), or to entertain (*E*).

_____ 1. Lucy and Rachel were both 11 years old when they met in the textile mill for work. When they were not changing the bobbins on the spinning machines, they could laugh with each other and dream of trips back home.

_____ 2. Samuel Slater opened a new textile mill in Rhode Island in 1790 and employed seven boys and two girls between the ages of 7 and 12. The children were whipped with a leather strap and sprayed with water to keep them awake and alert. Consolidating such a workforce under one roof, the children could produce three times as much as whole families working at home.

_____ 3. The textile mills of the late eighteenth century in America were not unlike the sweatshops of Central America today. Children were employed for pennies under the supervision of an adult who was concerned about profit. Today, however, enlightened Americans are buying the product of the labor of foreign children. Perhaps Americans should think before buying.

_____ 4. To be successful in the future, retail companies must embrace e-commerce and establish creative websites that are easy for customers to use. Learn to use the Internet for advertising, marketing, and retailing.

_____ 5. In response to a drop in profits, Gap Inc. opened Old Navy stores targeted at discount shoppers. This created a three-tiered organization. The company's Banana Republic is designed to appeal to high-end shoppers, The Gap to a middle market searching for quality casual clothing, and Old Navy for the bargain hunters.

_____ 6. She quickened her pace as the footsteps behind her became louder. Was he following her, or did he just happen to be turning down Grove Street, too?

EXERCISE 2   Read the passages and identify the author's purpose for each by responding with *a, b, c,* or *d*.

Passage 1

KEEP YOUR EYES ON FINLAND

Despite its small size and relative isolation in the Arctic Circle, Finland leads the pack in mobile phone technology and its applications. The country is a laboratory of eager users and will soon pioneer the use of so-called third-generation mobile phones that boast lightning-quick access to the Internet. Part of the reason for Finland's advancement is its geography. When telecommunications developed in the 1970s, Finns were more inclined to pursue wireless options because the costs of running cable to isolated pockets of a vast and frozen nation were daunting. Thus wireless technology became a priority for the government and the private sector.

—*Business Today,* Tenth Edition,
by Michael Mescon et al.

_____ 1. The primary purpose of this passage is to

      a. support fast mobile phone access to the Internet.
      b. explain why Finland is the leader in mobile phone technology.
      c. argue against Finland's leadership in mobile phone technology.
      d. compare cable phones with wireless options.

_____ 2. The author describes Finland as a "vast and frozen nation" in order to

      a. compliment the Finns on their struggle with nature.
      b. show that employment is difficult and the industry provides jobs.
      c. explain the cause-and-effect relationship that has motivated excellence in the industry.
      d. show how Finns have reduced spending to increase profits.

Passage 2

JANE ADDAMS

Without knowing why, Jane Addams opened her eyes. It was pitch-black in her bedroom, and at first, she heard nothing more than the muted night noises of the Chicago streets surrounding Hull House. Then she saw what had disturbed her sleep. A burglar had pried open the second-story window and was rifling her bureau drawers. Jane spoke quietly, "Don't make a noise." The man whirled around, then prepared to leap out the window. "You'll be hurt if you go that way," Jane calmly observed. A conversation ensued in the darkness. Addams learned that the intruder was not a professional thief, but simply a desperate man who could find no employment that winter of 1890 and had turned to crime to survive. Hull House had been founded the previous fall as a social "settlement" to serve just such people. It testified to Jane Addams's belief that only unfavorable circumstances stood between the innate dignity and worth of every individual and their realization. Moreover, Addams believed that as a well-to-do, cultivated lady she had a special responsibility for alleviating the social ills accompanying the nation's growth. So she was in earnest when she promised her unexpected visitor that if he would come back the next morning, she would try to help. The burglar agreed, walked down the main stairs, and left by the front door. At 9 A.M. he returned to learn that Jane Addams had found him a job.

—From These Beginnings, Sixth Edition,
by Roderick Nash and Edward Graves

_____ 1. The primary purpose of this passage is to

      a. explain how Hull House operated on a daily basis.
      b. illustrate Jane Addams's courage and commitment to her cause.
      c. argue the need for social settlements to assist the needy.
      d. educate the public on the reasons for crime.

_____ 2. The author implies that Hull House was designed primarily to serve

      a. drug users.
      b. the mentally ill.
      c. criminals after release from jail.
      d. people down on their luck.

Passage 3

POPULARITY OF PART-TIMERS

Some experts claim that full-time, core employees are paid for eight hours of work but actually work closer to six or seven. This discrepancy is because it may take ten minutes or more for them to get ready to work, two fifteen-minute breaks are required, and often employees start getting ready to leave before the end of their work day. In contrast, part-timers employed for four hours may actually work at top performance for almost the entire period.

Part-time workers can be divided into three classifications: (1) full-time students who seek "peak period" jobs for approximately twenty hours per week to help with educational expenses, (2) housewives who seek part-time work so they can devote more time to children, and (3) retired people who wish to supplement their retirement incomes.

Many supervisors claim that part-timers are a welcome challenge when it comes to weaving them into the general mix of employees. They like the enthusiasm, energy, and flexibility they bring with them. Others claim that the high turnover rate of part-timers negates their advantages. All agree that it takes additional time and energy from the supervisor to convert part-timers into productive members of a work team.

—*Supervisor's Survival Kit: Your First Step into Management,* Ninth Edition, by Elwood N. Chapman and Cliff Goodwin

_____ 1. The primary purpose of this passage is to

     a. condemn society's reliance on part-time workers.
     b. explain the downside of relying on part-timers in the workforce.
     c. discuss methods employees can use to increase the productivity of part-time workers.
     d. discuss the pros and cons of part-time work for both employers and employees.

_____ 2. The author implies that

     a. employers are split in their opinions of the advantages of part-time workers.
     b. full-time workers put in fewer hours because part-timers are more committed to getting the job done.
     c. part-time work can be considered to range from twenty to forty hours per week.
     d. the majority of part-time employees are students.

Recognize the Author's Point of View or Bias

Learning Objective 3

Identify the author's point of view

If you were reading an article analyzing George W. Bush's achievements as president, you might ask, "Is this written by a Republican or a Democrat?" The answer would help you understand the point of view or bias from which the author is writing and thus help you evaluate the accuracy and relevance of the message.

Point of view refers to the opinions and beliefs of the author or of the reader, and a critical reader must recognize how those beliefs influence the message. Students sometimes find the term *point of view* confusing because, when discussing literature, point of view refers to the narrative voice the author is using: first, second, or third person. In this chapter, however, point of view refers to an opinion or position on a subject. For example, if you were reading an article on UFOs you would ask, "Does the author write from the point of view of a believer or a nonbeliever in aliens?"

Bias is a word closely related to point of view. However, the term *bias* tends to be associated with prejudice, and thus it has a negative connotation. A bias, like a point of view, is an opinion or a judgment. Either may be based on solid facts or on incorrect information, but a bias suggests that an author leans to one side, unequally presenting evidence and arguments. All authors write from a certain point of view, but not all authors have the same degree of bias.

Because both writers and readers are people with opinions, their biases interact on the printed page. Thus critical readers need to recognize an author's bias or point of view as well as their own. For example, a reader might fail to understand an author's position on legalizing prostitution because the reader is totally opposed to the idea. In such a case, the reader's bias or point of view on the subject can interfere with comprehension.

EXAMPLE   Respond to the following statement by describing the author's point of view or bias, as well as your own.

> African animals are endangered and should not be killed for their fur to make coats. Minks, however, are a different story and should be considered separately. Minks are farmed animals that are produced only for their fur.

Explain the author's point of view/bias. _____

Explain your own position on the topic. _____

EXPLANATION   The author implies that minks are not endangered and should be used in making fur coats. Your position may be the same, or you may think that being on the endangered list is not the only issue. You may feel that animals should not be used for clothing.

EXERCISE 3   The following statements adamantly express only one side of an issue. Read each statement and mark whether you agree (*A*) or disagree (*D*). Then describe the point of view/bias of the author and your own position.

_____ 1. Citizens deserve to be protected from pornography on the Internet. Although pictures of child pornography are now prohibited on the Internet, lessons on how to seduce grade school children are perfectly legal in chat rooms and news groups. First Amendment rights should not outweigh our need to protect the population from deviant behaviors.

Explain the author's point of view/bias. _____

_____

Explain your own point of view/bias. _____

_____

_____ 2. Reproductive technology has outpaced the law and is in need of record keeping. In a fertility laboratory, the sperm of one anonymous donor is united with the egg of another anonymous donor. Then the fertilized product is implanted into a hopeful parent who never knows the identity of either donor. Considering that such donors usually make multiple contributions, how can children be sure in future years that they are not marrying brothers or sisters?

Explain the author's point of view/bias. _____

_____

Explain your own point of view/bias. _____

_____

_____ 3. An overwhelming amount of this nation's land is owned by the government in the form of national parks and forests. This is especially true in the West. Much of this land is not needed for public recreation and could be sold to private enterprise, with the proceeds going to pay off part of the national debt.

Explain the author's point of view/bias. _____

_____

Explain your own point of view/bias. _____

_____

_____ 4. Is a parent responsible for a child's actions? Because some parents neglect their parental duties when signs of danger are obvious, public interest in parental duty laws is increasing. Under such laws, parents can no longer look the other way while society suffers the consequences.

Explain the author's point of view/bias. _____

_____

Explain your own point of view/bias. _____

_____

_____ 5. Cities that have teen curfews violate the rights of responsible teens. Those teens who obey are forced to curtail wholesome activities while violators continue as if there were no curfew.

Explain the author's point of view/bias. _____

_____

Explain your own point of view/bias. _____

_____

EXERCISE 4 Read the following description of Napoleon Bonaparte from a freshman history textbook. Keep in mind that Napoleon is generally considered one of the great heroes of France and one of the greatest conquerors of the world. Does this passage say exactly what you would expect? Analyze the author's point of view, and answer the questions that follow with *T* (true) or *F* (false).

Passage 1

Napoleon was a short, swarthy, handsome man with remarkable, magnetic eyes. Slender as a youth, he exhibited a tendency toward obesity as he grew older. He was high-strung, and his manners were coarse. Militarily, he has been both denigrated and extolled. On the one hand, his success has been attributed to luck and the great skill of his professional lieutenants; on the other, he has been compared with the greatest conquerors of the past. Politically, he combined the shrewdness of a Machiavellian despot with the majesty of a "sun king." It is generally conceded that he was one of the giants of history. He had an exalted belief in his own destiny, but as an utter cynic and misanthrope felt only contempt for the human race. He once exclaimed, "What do a million men matter to such as I?" The world was Napoleon's oyster. He considered himself emancipated from moral scruples. Yet this man, who despised humanity, was worshiped by the millions he held in such contempt. To his soldiers he was the invincible hero, a supreme ruler over men, literally a *demi-god*. He came from nowhere, but was endowed with an extraordinary mind and the charisma required for masterful leadership. He used democracy to destroy democracy. He employed the slogans of revolution to fasten his hold on nations. His great empire collapsed, but his name will never be forgotten.

—*A History of the Western World,*
by Solomon Modell

_____ 1. The author wants to present Napoleon as a demigod.

_____ 2. The author shows Napoleon as the greatest military leader in history.

_____ 3. The author feels that Napoleon effectively used propaganda for his own benefit.

_____ 4. The author wants to show the differences between the public and the private views of Napoleon.

_____ 5. The author feels that Napoleon adhered to a strict moral code.

_____ 6. The author feels that Napoleon matured into a handsome, well-mannered gentleman.

_____ 7. The author believes that Napoleon's success was due primarily to good luck.

_____ 8. The author feels that Napoleon had little regard for the average person.

_____ 9. The author feels that Napoleon is undeserving of a prominent place in history.

_____ 10. The author feels that Napoleon used ruthless tactics to get what he wanted.

The author gives a cynical description of Napoleon. For example, he relates a quote attributed to Napoleon that shows him in an unfavorable light. The critical reader needs to be aware that other accounts show Napoleon as a great leader who was concerned for his soldiers and wanted the best for France.

Read Passage 2 for a somewhat different view of Napoleon. Then answer the questions that follow.

Passage 2

Few men in Western history have compelled the attention of the world as Napoleon Bonaparte did during the fifteen years of his absolutist rule in France. Schooled in France and at the military academy in Paris, he possessed a mind congenial to the ideas of the Enlightenment—creative, imaginative, and ready to perceive things anew. His primary interests were history, law, and mathematics. His particular strengths as a leader lay in his ability to conceive of financial, legal, or military plans and then to master their every detail; his capacity for inspiring others, even those initially opposed to him; and his belief in himself as the destined savior of the French. That last conviction eventually became the obsession that led to Napoleon's undoing. But supreme self-confidence was just what the French government lacked since the first days of the revolution. Napoleon believed both in himself and in France. That latter belief was the tonic France now needed, and Napoleon proceeded to administer it in liberally revivifying doses.

—Western Civilizations,
by Edward McNall Berns et al.

_____ 1. This author has a more positive opinion of Napoleon than did the previous author.

_____ 2. This author believes that Napoleon's initial self-confidence was unwelcome in France.

_____ 3. This author suggests that Napoleon developed a mental obsession about being a destined savior that led to his decline.

_____ 4. This author does not imply that Napoleon hated humanity.

_____ 5. This author believes that Napoleon failed to attend to details and thus lost power.

Recognize the Author's Tone

Learning Objective 4

Recognize the author's tone

The author's **tone** describes the writer's attitude toward the subject. An easy trick to distinguish tone is to think of tone of voice. When someone is speaking, voice sounds usually indicate whether the person is angry, romantic, or joyful. In reading, however, you cannot hear the voice, but you can pick up clues from the choice of words and details.

As a critical reader, tune in to the author's tone, and thus let attitude become a part of evaluating the message. For example, an optimistic tone on water pollution might make you suspicious that the author has overlooked information, whereas an extremely pessimistic article on the same subject might overwhelm you, causing you to discount valuable information.

EXAMPLE   Identify the tone of the following passage.

Hillary Clinton has shattered glass ceilings and paved the way to better lives for women in the U.S. and around the world. Her remarkable history is testament to her most heartfelt cause, assuring rights for women and girls. Not only is she a stellar role model—from a stunning speech at a college graduation that landed her on the cover of *Life* magazine in 1974, to strong First Lady, to the nation's first female presidential candidate to be taken seriously, to tough-bargaining Secretary of State—but all along she has not wavered from her fight to better the lives of women and girls worldwide.

_____ 1. The author's tone is

a. critical.
b. nostalgic.
c. admiring.

EXPLANATION   Details and slanted language such as "shattered glass ceilings," "paved the way for women," "her remarkable history," and "stellar role model" reveal the author's admiration for Hillary Clinton.

Reader's TIP Recognizing the Author's Tone

The following list of words with explanations can describe an author's tone or attitude:

- **absurd, farcical, ridiculous**: laughable or a joke
- **ambivalent, apathetic, detached**: not caring
- **angry, bitter, hateful**: feeling bad and upset about the topic
- **arrogant, condescending**: acting conceited or above others
- **awestruck, admiring, wondering**: filled with wonder
- **cheerful, joyous, happy**: feeling good about the topic
- **compassionate, sympathetic**: feeling sorrow at the distress of others
- **complex**: intricate, complicated, and entangled with confusing parts
- **congratulatory, celebratory**: honoring an achievement or festive occasion
- **cruel, malicious**: meanspirited
- **cynical**: expecting the worst from people
- **depressed, melancholy**: sad, dejected, or having low spirits
- **disapproving**: judging unfavorably
- **distressed**: suffering strain, misery, or agony
- **evasive, abstruse**: avoiding or confusing the issue
- **formal**: using an official style
- **frustrated**: blocked from a goal
- **gentle**: kind or of a high social class
- **ghoulish, grim**: robbing graves or feeding on corpses; stern and forbidding
- **hard**: unfeeling, strict, and unrelenting
- **humorous, jovial, comic, playful, amused**: being funny
- **incredulous**: unbelieving
- **indignant**: outraged
- **intense, impassioned**: extremely involved, zealous, or agitated
- **ironic**: the opposite of what is expected; a twist at the end
- **irreverent**: lack of respect for authority
- **mocking, scornful, caustic, condemning**: ridiculing the topic
- **objective, factual, straightforward, critical**: using facts without emotions
- **obsequious**: fawning for attention
- **optimistic**: looking on the bright side
- **outspoken**: speaking one's mind on issues
- **pathetic**: moving one to compassion or pity
- **pessimistic**: looking on the negative side
- **prayerful**: religiously thankful
- **reticent**: shy and not speaking out
- **reverent**: showing respect
- **righteous**: morally correct
- **romantic, intimate, loving**: expressing love or affection
- **sarcastic**: saying one thing and meaning another
- **satiric**: using irony, wit, and sarcasm to discredit or ridicule

- **sensational**: overdramatized or overhyped
- **sentimental, nostalgic**: remembering the good old days
- **serious, sincere, earnest, solemn**: being honest and concerned
- **straightforward**: forthright
- **subjective, opinionated**: expressing opinions and feelings
- **tragic**: regrettable or deplorable mistake
- **uneasy**: restless or uncertain
- **vindictive**: seeking revenge

EXERCISE 5   Mark the letter that identifies the tone for each of the following sentences.

_____ 1. Baseball was invented as an urban game in order for owners to make money, players to become arrogant, and spectators to drink overpriced beer.

  a. objective
  b. nostalgic
  c. cynical

_____ 2. The Puritans came to the new land for religious freedom, yet they allowed their followers little freedom. Anne Hutchinson was banished from the colony for preaching that salvation can come through good works.

  a. optimistic
  b. ironic
  c. sentimental

_____ 3. When I study now, I'm in a lab with fifty noisy computers. What happened to the quiet chair in a corner with a table for your books, papers, and pencils?

  a. objective
  b. cheerful
  c. nostalgic

_____ 4. According to a recent study in a book called _Living Well_, sexually active partners who do not use contraceptives stand an 85 percent chance of conceiving within a year.

  a. subjective
  b. objective
  c. sarcastic

_____ 5. If given the funding, scientists could trace most aggressive behavior, crime, and violence to either too much testosterone or low blood sugar.

  a. sentimental
  b. subjective
  c. objective

_____ 6. On hot summer days, the health risks increase as auto exhaust from rush hour traffic pollutes the air, threatens our lungs, and damages the ozone layer.

  a. disapproving
  b. reverent
  c. incredulous

_____ 7. Aging can be isolating and lonely. As mobility becomes more limited, the elderly patiently wait for the excitement of a friend's call or a child's next visit.

  a. evasive
  b. righteous
  c. sympathetic

_____ 8. Is the top of the world as crowded as Times Square? According to official records, the greatest number of people to reach the summit of Mount Everest on a single day is 89. The number of corpses still remaining on Everest is 120.

  a. sarcastic
  b. optimistic
  c. indignant

EXERCISE 6   Read the passages and answer the questions that follow by writing in the blanks or answering with *a, b, c,* or *d.*

Passage 1

TECHNO-BORES

Techno-bores are like chemically altered bores in that their condition (infatuation with technology—often computers) blinds them to the possibility that *your* reality simply isn't theirs. Details about the latest software or synthesizer are lost on you.

The curious thing about computer-obsessed bores is that their behavior appears to have been directly influenced by the machines they love—you can see little floppy disks spinning in their eyes when they speak; their sentences come out in a robotic cadence. Don't even consider launching a personal question in the direction of a techno-bore—you may cause a short circuit.

—"The Ten Most Memorable Bores,"
by Margot Mifflin

1. What is the tone of the passage? _____

2. What clues reveal the author's tone? _____

_____

Passage 2

STONE CRABS

One of the more regrettable circumstances attendant upon the tourist invasion of Dade County, Florida, of recent winters, was the discovery by visitors of the stone crab.

The home folks in Dade County, Florida, have long esteemed the stone crab, the greatest of native delicacies, and can remember when they were so numerous that a man could dip a foot anywhere in Biscayne Bay and come up with a stone crab hanging on each toe. Or lacking the energy to dunk a pedal he could buy more stone crabs for a few bits than a horse could lug.

Since the winter visitors got on to the stone crab, however, the crustaceans have become scarce and costly. They now sell by the karat. They are so expensive that the home folks are inclined to leave them off their menus. The visitors eat more of the stone crab nowadays and this is all the more deplorable when you reflect that stone crabs are really too good for visitors. A certificate of at least four years residence in Dade County should be required of every person desiring stone crabs.

—"The Brighter Side," by Damon Runyon

_____ 1. The author's tone is

     a. bitter.
     b. serious.
     c. humorous.
     d. sympathetic.

_____ 2. The author's primary purpose is to

     a. educate.
     b. entertain.
     c. narrate.
     d. shock.

Passage 3

TAKING THE TEST

For the next two weeks I ate bacon cheeseburgers almost daily, a series of last meals. Every time the phone rang, at home or at the office, I felt an electric anxiety. My doctor had promised he would not call, but I kept hoping he'd break our agreement and phone to say I was negative. That way I could sleep at night. He didn't call. I grew more obsessed daily. Even though for hours at a time I'd forget to anticipate my test results, my fear would ambush me like a bowel-loosening punch in the gut. I told myself that I wouldn't die the very day the doctor told me the bad news. My HIV-positive friends, and those who had been diagnosed with AIDS, were still alive—mostly. They'd coped. I'd cope too. Cold comfort.

—"Taking the Test," by David Groff

_____ 1. The author's tone is

     a. bitter.
     b. fearful.
     c. sarcastic.
     d. intellectual.

_____ 2. The author's primary purpose is

     a. to argue.
     b. to criticize.
     c. to describe.
     d. to entertain.

Passage 4

ZOO DOO

Sometimes, companies don't realize how valuable their by-products are. For example, most zoos don't realize that one of their by-products—their occupants' manure—can be an excellent source of additional revenue. Sales of the fragrant by-product can be substantial. So far, novelty sales have been the largest, with tiny containers of Zoo Doo (and even "Love, Love Me Doo" valentines) available in 160 zoo stores and 700 additional retail outlets. For the long-term market, Zoo-Doo looks to organic gardeners who buy 15 to 70 pounds of manure at a time. Zoo-Doo is already planning a "Dung of the Month" club to reach this lucrative by-products market.

—Principles of Marketing, Ninth Edition,
by Philip Kotler and Gary Armstrong

_____ 1. The authors' tone is

    a. cynical.
    b. disapproving.
    c. incredulous.
    d. playful.

_____ 2. The authors' primary purpose is

    a. to argue.
    b. to criticize.
    c. to educate.
    d. to narrate.

Passage 5

COSTCO

But this isn't a story about Wal-Mart. It's about Costco, the red-hot warehouse retailer that competes head-on with Wal-Mart's Sam's Club. Sam's Club is huge. With more than 550 stores and $40 billion in revenues, if Sam's Club were a separate company, it would be the seventh-largest U.S. retailer. But when it comes to warehouse retailing, it's Costco that's the bully, not the other way around.

With about the same number of members but 50 fewer stores, Costco outsells Sam's Club by 50 percent. Its $60 billion in sales makes Costco the nation's third-largest retailer, behind only Wal-Mart and Home Depot and one step ahead of Target. And unlike Wal-Mart and Sam's Club, Costco is growing at a torrid pace. In just the past four years, Costco's sales have surged 55 percent; profits are up 57 percent. Costco's same-store sales are growing at more than twice the rate of Wal-Mart's. How is Costco beating Sam's Club at its own low-price game? The two retailers are very similar in many ways. But inside the store, Costco adds a certain merchandising magic that Sam's Club just can't match.

—Marketing, An Introduction, Ninth Edition,
by Gary Armstrong and Philip Kotler

_____ 1. The author's tone is

    a. admiring.
    b. nostalgic.
    c. serious.
    d. amused.

_____ 2. The author's primary purpose is

    a. to entertain.
    b. to criticize.
    c. to narrate.
    d. to convince.

Passage 6

DECIMAL NOTATION

The set of arithmetic numbers, or nonnegative rational numbers, consists of the whole numbers 0, 1, 2, 3, 4, 5, 6, 7, 8, 9, 10, and so on, and fractions like 1/2, 2/3, 7/8, 17/10, and so on. Note that we can write the whole numbers using fraction notation. For example, 3 can be written as 3/1 We studied the use of fraction notation for arithmetic numbers in Chapter 2.

In Chapter 3, we will study the use of *decimal notation*. The word *decimal* comes from the Latin word *decima,* meaning a tenth part. Although we are using different notation, we are still considering the nonnegative rational numbers. Using decimal notation, we can write 0.875 for 7/8; for example, or 48.97 for 48 97/100.

—*Developmental Mathematics: College Mathematics and Introductory Algebra,* Seventh Edition, by Marvin L. Bittinger and Judith A. Beecher

_____ 1. The author's tone is

   a. satiric.
   b. objective.
   c. irreverent.
   d. cheerful.

_____ 2. The author's primary purpose is

   a. to narrate.
   b. to argue.
   c. to instruct.
   d. to describe.

Passage 7

THE GIFT

To pull the metal splinter from my palm
my father recited a story in a low voice.
I watched his lovely face and not the blade.
Before the story ended, he'd removed
the iron sliver I thought I'd die from.

I can't remember the tale,
but hear his voice still, a well
of dark water, a prayer.
And I recall his hands,
two measures of tenderness
he laid against my face,
the flames of discipline
he raised above my head.

Had you entered that afternoon
you would have thought you saw a man
planting something in a boy's palm,
a silver tear, a tiny flame.
Had you followed that boy
you would have arrived here,
where I bend over my wife's right hand.

Look how I shave her thumbnail down
so carefully she feels no pain.
Watch as I lift the splinter out.
I was seven when my father
took my hand like this,
and I did not hold that shard
between my fingers and think,
Metal that will bury me,
christen it Little Assassin,
Ore Going Deep for My Heart.
And I did not lift up my wound and cry,
Death visited here!
I did what a child does
when he's given something to keep.
I kissed my father.

—*The Gift*, by Li-Young Lee

_____ 1. The author's tone is

    a. loving.
    b. humorous.
    c. irreverent.
    d. cheerful.

_____ 2. The author's primary purpose is

    a. to narrate.
    b. to criticize.
    c. to instruct.
    d. to entertain.

Distinguish Fact from Opinion

Learning Objective 5
Distinguish facts and opinions

The reader who cannot distinguish between fact and opinion will always remain gullible. By contrast, the critical reader realizes that most writing contains a combination of facts and opinions and is able to tell one from the other. A **fact** is a statement that can be proven true or false, whereas an **opinion** is a statement of feeling or belief that cannot be proven right or wrong.

EXAMPLE Mark the following stand-alone statements as *F* (fact) or *O* (opinion).

_____ 1. George Washington was the first president of the United States.

_____ 2. George Washington was the best president of the United States.

_____ 3. The author states that George Washington was the best president of the United States.

_____ 4. It is a fact that George Washington was the best president of the United States.

The first and third are statements of fact that can be proven, but the second and fourth are opinions, even though the fourth tries to present itself as a fact. In psychology, for example, it is a fact that Freud believed the personality is divided into three parts; however, it is only an opinion that there are three parts of the human personality. Others may believe the personality should be divided into two parts or ten parts.

Dr. Beatrice Mendez-Egle, a professor at the University of Texas–Pan American, further clarifies the distinction between fact and opinion with the following definitions and table.

A **fact** is an observation that can be supported with incontrovertible evidence. An **opinion,** on the other hand, is a commentary, position, or observation based on fact but that represents a personal judgment or interpretation of these facts.

Fact	Opinion
3/4 of the students in this class are making A's.	This class is really smart.
The temperature in the class is 78°.	This classroom is always hot and stuffy!
Facebook has over 800 million active users.	Everybody uses Facebook; it is the best way to communicate.

The first two opinions are clearly judgments that would probably be obvious to most readers. The third opinion, however, is mixed with fact; and thus the judgment portion of "doesn't deserve to be president" needs the sharp eye of a critical reader to recognize it as an opinion. In order to achieve a certain purpose, a writer can support a particular bias or point of view and attempt to confuse the reader by blending facts and opinions so that both sound like facts.

EXERCISE 7 Mark the following statements from textbooks as *F* (fact) or *O* (opinion).

_____ 1. I maintain it is much safer to be feared than loved, if you have to do without one of the two.

—Machiavelli, quoted in *Western Civilization,* Fifth Edition, by Jackson J. Spielvogel

_____ 2. Everyone complains about federal, state, and local taxes.

—*We the People: An Introduction to American Politics,* Fourth Edition, by Benjamin Ginsberg et al.

_____ 3. The technical name for our gigantic social insurance program is Old Age, Survivors, and Disability Health Insurance, or OASDHI.

—*Micro Economics for Today,* Fourth Edition, by Irvin B. Tucker

_____ 4. At first, young children were barred from the factories, and older ones were allowed to work only a partial adult shift.

—*A Brief History of Western Civilization,* Fourth Edition, by Mark Kishlansky et al.

_____ 5. Taxi drivers have been found to have unusually large hippocampi (a brain structure that plays a special role in spatial memory)—and the longer a driver has worked, the larger they are.

—*Psychology*, Second Edition, by Steven M. Kosslyn and Rogin S. Rosenberg

_____ 6. Leopold Mozart, father of the illustrious Wolfgang Amadeus Mozart, sacrificed his own considerable career to further that of his son.

—*Understanding Music,* Fourth Edition, by Jeremy Yudkin

_____ 7. English, the language of globalization, is both savior and villain in Europe.

—*Diversity and Globalization: Western World Geography*, Second Edition, by Les Rowntree et al.

_____ 8. In the 1920s, Cleveland, Ohio, and Chicago, Illinois, were among the first major cities to perform crime surveys.

—*Criminal Justice,* by James A. Fagin

_____ 9. Longshoremen, who are on their feet all day and lift, push, and carry heavy cargo, have about half the risk of fatal heart attack as coworkers like crane drivers and clerks.

—*Life-Span Development,* Ninth Edition, by John W. Santrock

_____ 10. Self-confidence, perhaps more than any other factor, is the secret to success and happiness.

—*The Career Fitness Program,* Seventh Edition, by Diane Sukiennik et al.

EXERCISE 8 The following passage from a history textbook describes Thomas Jefferson. Notice the mixture of facts and opinions the author uses to develop a view of Thomas Jefferson. Mark the items that follow as (*F*) fact or (*O*) opinion.

Jefferson hardly seemed cut out for politics. Although in some ways a typical, pleasure-loving southern planter, he had in him something of the Spartan. He grew tobacco, but did not smoke, and he partook only sparingly of meat and alcohol. Unlike most planters he never hunted or gambled, though he was a fine horseman and enjoyed dancing, music, and other social diversions. His practical interests ranged enormously—from architecture and geology to natural history and scientific farming—yet he displayed little interest in managing men. Controversy dismayed him, and he tended to avoid it by assigning to some thicker-skinned associate the task of attacking his enemies. Nevertheless, he wanted to have a say in shaping the future of the country, and once engaged, he fought stubbornly and at times deviously to get and hold power.

—*The American Nation,* Tenth Edition, by John Garraty and Mark Carnes

_____ 1. Jefferson hardly seemed cut out for politics.

_____ 2. Jefferson was a typical, pleasure-loving southern planter.

_____ 3. Jefferson grew tobacco, but did not smoke.

_____ 4. Controversy dismayed Jefferson.

_____ 5. Jefferson fought deviously to get and hold power.

Recognize Valid and Invalid Support for Arguments

Learning Objective 6

Recognize valid and invalid support

When evaluating persuasive writing, critical readers realize that support for an argument or a position can be in the form of both facts and opinions. For example, valid reasons for a career change or a vacation destination can be a combination of both facts and feelings. The trick is to recognize which reasons validly support the point and which merely confuse the issue with an illusion of support.

A **fallacy** is an error in reasoning that can give an illusion of support. On the surface, a fallacy can appear to add support, but closer inspection shows it to be unrelated and illogical. For example, valid reasons for buying running shoes might be comfort and price, whereas invalid reasons might be that "everybody has them" and a sports figure said to buy them.

Fallacies are particularly prevalent in **propaganda,** a form of writing designed to convince the reader by whatever means possible. Propaganda can be used to support a political cause, advertise a product, or engender enthusiasm for a college event.

Experts have identified and labeled over 200 fallacies or tricks of persuasion. The following list describes some of the most common ones.

Testimonials: Celebrities who are not experts state support.

> *Example:* Tiger Woods appears in television advertisements endorsing a particular credit card.

Bandwagon: You will be left out if you do not join the crowd.

> *Example:* All the voters in the district support Henson for senator.

Transfer: A famous person is associated with an argument.

> *Example:* George Washington indicated in a quote that he would have agreed with us on this issue.

Straw Person: A simplistic exaggeration is set up to represent the argument.

> *Example:* The professor replied, "If I delay the exam, you'll expect me to change the due dates of all papers and assignments."

Misleading Analogy: Two things are compared as similar that are actually distinctly different.

> *Example:* Studying is like taking a shower; most of the material goes down the drain.

Circular Reasoning: The conclusion is supported by restating it.

> *Example:* Papers must be turned in on time because papers cannot be turned in late.

EXERCISE 9

Identify the fallacy in each of the following statements, using (a) testimonial, (b) bandwagon, (c) transfer, (d) straw person, (e) misleading analogy, (f) circular reasoning.

_____ 1. Purchase her new novel, *Growing Up Latino,* which is written in the tradition of outstanding novelist Richard Rodriguez, who wrote *Hunger of Memory: The Education of Richard Rodriguez.*

_____ 2. The first semester of college is like the premiere of a Batman movie because both require the use of imagination.

_____ 3. Customs booklets warn that Cuban cigars are not legally allowed in the United States because the government will not let you bring them into the country.

_____ 4. Pele, the famous soccer player who led Brazil to three World Cup championships, recommends multivitamins by Zip to add energy to your life and strength to your body.

_____ 5. Purchase tickets immediately because everyone in school has signed up for the event and it will soon be sold out.

_____ 6. A student who is late for class would probably be late for a job interview and thus be a failure.

_____ 7. Use the cosmetics advertised by Jennifer Lopez because she says they work for her.

_____ 8. Writing a term paper is like brewing coffee when your crushed beans turn into a flow of ideas.

_____ 9. Join a club to meet new friends because you will meet people that you do not know.

_____10. George W. Bush pointed out that the first president of the United States was another George W.

EXERCISE 10

To practice your critical thinking skills, read the passages and answer the questions that follow.

Passage 1

BEETHOVEN'S WORK HABITS

As Beethoven grew older and withdrew more and more from society, he became wholly absorbed in his art. He would habitually miss meals, forget or ignore invitations, and work long into the night. He himself described his "ceaseless occupations." Beethoven felt the strongest urge to produce the music within him, and yet he suffered the same creative anxiety as lesser mortals. "For some time past I have been carrying about with me the idea of three great works. . . . These I must get rid of: two symphonies, each different from the other, and also different from all my other symphonies, and an oratorio. . . . I dread beginning works of such magnitude. Once I have begun, then all goes well."

We are fortunate in possessing many of the sketchbooks in which Beethoven worked out his musical ideas. They present a vivid picture of the composer at work.

—*Understanding Music,* Fourth Edition, by Jeremy Yudkin

Answer the following with *T* (true) or *F* (false) or with *a, b, c,* or *d.*

_____ 1. The author wishes to show Beethoven as both a preoccupied genius and a person who dreaded a big project.

_____ 2. The author suggests that the sketchbooks reveal some of the thought processes of Beethoven.

_____ 3. The author's tone is condemning.

_____ 4. The author conveys an appreciation for Beethoven as a creative artist.

_____ 5. The author implies that Beethoven did not write down his symphonies until they were completed in his head.

_____ 6. Each of the following words has a negative connotation *except*

   a. vivid
   b. withdrew
   c. anxiety
   d. dread

Mark the following statements as *F* (fact) or *O* (opinion).

_____ 7. "He became wholly absorbed in his art."

_____ 8. "He would habitually miss meals . . . and work long into the night."

_____ 9. "Beethoven felt the strongest urge to produce the music within him, and yet he suffered the same creative anxiety as lesser mortals."

Passage 2

ALEXANDER THE LEADER

The army was crossing a desert of sand. The sun was already blazing down upon them, but they were struggling on under the necessity of reaching water, which was still far away. Alexander, like everyone else, was tormented by thirst, but he was nonetheless marching on foot at the head of his men. It was all he could do to keep going, but he did so, and the result (as always) was that the men were better able to endure their misery when they saw that it was equally shared. As they toiled on, a party of light infantry which had gone off looking for water found some—just a wretched little trickle collected in a shallow gully. They scooped up with difficulty what they could and hurried back, with their priceless treasure, to Alexander. Then, just before they reached him, they tipped the water into a helmet and gave it to him. Alexander, with a word of thanks for the gift, took the helmet and, giving it full view of his troops, poured the water on the ground. So extraordinary was the effect of this action that the water wasted by Alexander was as good as a drink for every man in the army. I cannot praise this act too highly. It was a proof, if anything was, not only of his power of endurance, but also of his genius for leadership.

—From *The Campaigns of Alexander* by Arrian,
translated by Aubrey de Sélincourt.

Answer the following with *T* (true) or *F* (false).

_____ 1. The author's purpose is to compliment Alexander's troops for giving him the treasured water.

     2. The author implies that part of Alexander's success as a leader was his understanding and endurance of the same hardships as his soldiers.

     3. The author implies that Alexander was willing to die of thirst with his soldiers.

     4. The author's tone is respectful of Alexander.

     5. The reader can conclude that this account could contribute to the positive propaganda about Alexander.

     6. In using the words *extraordinary* and *genius,* the author intends a positive slant.

Mark the following statements as *F* (fact) or *O* (opinion).

     7. "The army was crossing a desert of sand."

     8. "Alexander, with a word of thanks for the gift, took the helmet and, giving it full view of his troops, poured the water on the ground."

     9. "It was a proof, if anything was, not only of his power of endurance, but also of his genius for leadership."

Passage 3

OPTIMISM

One measure of how helpless or effective you feel is where you stand on optimism-pessimism. How do you characteristically explain negative and positive events? Perhaps you have known students whose *attributional style* is negative—who attribute poor performance to their lack of ability ("I can't do this") or to situations enduringly beyond their control ("There is nothing I can do about it"). Such students are more likely to persist in getting low grades than are students who adopt the more hopeful attitude that effort, good study habits, and self-discipline can make a difference. Although mere fantasies tend not to fuel motivation and success, genuine positive expectations do.

In their study of professional achievement, psychologists Martin Seligman and Peter Schulman compared sales made by new life insurance representatives who were more or less optimistic in their outlooks. Those who put an optimistic spin on their setbacks—seeing them as flukes or as a means to learning a new approach, rather than viewing them as signs of incompetence—sold more policies during their first year and were half as likely to quit. Seligman's finding came to life for him when Bob Dell, one of the optimistic recruits who began selling for Metropolitan Life after taking Seligman's optimism test, later dialed him up and sold him a policy.

Health, too, benefits from a basic optimism. A depressed hopelessness dampens the body's disease-fighting immune system. In repeated studies, optimists have outlived pessimists or lived with fewer illnesses.

—David G. Myers, *Psychology,* 7th Edition. Copyright 2004 by Worth Publishers Inc. Reproduced with permission of Worth Publishers Inc. in the format Textbook via Copyright Clearance Center

Answer the following with *T* (true) or *F* (false).

     1. The author's purpose is to discuss a positive relationship between optimism and achievement.

     2. The author's tone in telling the Bob Dell story is humorous.

_____ 3. The author indicates that pessimists are likely to receive lower grades than optimists.

_____ 4. According to the passage, optimistic students can achieve better grades even without good study habits and self-discipline.

_____ 5. The author suggests that pessimism affects motivation but does not physically affect the body.

_____ 6. The author implies that an optimist would believe that "It happens when it happens."

Mark the following statements as *F* (fact) or *O* (opinion).

_____ 7. "In their study of professional achievement, Seligman and Peter Schulman compared sales made by new life insurance representatives . . . ".

_____ 8. "Those who put an optimistic spin on their setbacks . . . sold more policies during their first year and were half as likely to quit."

_____ 9. "In repeated studies, optimists have outlived pessimists or lived with fewer illnesses."

Passage 4

SIMPLICITY

Clutter is the disease of American writing. We are a society strangling in unnecessary words, circular constructions, pompous frills and meaningless jargon.

Who can understand the clotted language of everyday American commerce: the memo, the corporation report, the business letter, the notice from the bank explaining its latest "simplified" statement? What member of an insurance or medical plan can decipher the brochure explaining his costs and benefits? What father or mother can put together a child's toy from the instructions on the box? Our national tendency is to inflate and thereby sound important. The airline pilot who announces that he is presently anticipating experiencing considerable precipitation wouldn't think of saying it may rain. The sentence is too simple—there must be something wrong with it.

But the secret of good writing is to strip every sentence to its cleanest components. Every word that serves no function, every long word that could be a short word, every adverb that carries the same meaning that's already in the verb, every passive construction that leaves the reader unsure of who is doing what—these are the thousand and one adulterants that weaken the strength of a sentence. And they usually occur in proportion to education and rank.

During the 1960s the president of my university wrote a letter to mollify the alumni after a spell of campus unrest. "You are probably aware," he began, "that we have been experiencing very considerable potentially explosive expressions of dissatisfaction on issues only partially related." He meant that the students had been hassling them about different things. I was far more upset by the president's English than by the students' potentially explosive expressions of dissatisfaction. I would have preferred the presidential approach taken by Franklin D. Roosevelt when he tried to convert into English his own government's memos, such as this blackout order of 1942:

> Such preparations shall be made as will completely obscure all Federal buildings and non-Federal buildings occupied by the Federal government during an air raid for any period of time from visibility by reason of internal or external illumination.

"Tell them," Roosevelt said, "that in buildings where they have to keep the work going to put something across the windows."

—From "Simplicity" from *On Writing Well,* Seventh Edition, by William Zinsser. Published by Collins, an imprint of HarperCollins Publishers. Copyright © 1976, 1980, 1988, 1990, 1994, 1998, 2001, and 2006 by William K. Zinsser. Reprinted by permission of the author.

Answer the following with *T* (true) or *F* (false) or with *a, b, c,* or *d*.

_____ 1. The author's main purpose is to criticize wordy writing.

_____ 2. The author quotes Franklin D. Roosevelt to show how simply the blackout order could have been stated.

_____ 3. The author quotes the president of his university to show that educated people usually communicate clearly.

_____ 4. The author feels that the airline pilot avoids using the word *storm* because it may frighten the passengers.

_____ 5. The overall tone of the passage is serious.

_____ 6. All of the following words are negatively slanted *except*

    a. clutter.
    b. jargon.
    c. decipher.
    d. brochure.

Mark the following statements as *F* (fact) or *O* (opinion).

_____ 7. "Clutter is the disease of American writing."

_____ 8. "We are a society strangling in unnecessary words . . . ".

_____ 9. ". . . the secret of good writing is to strip every sentence to its cleanest components."

Passage 5

THEODORE ROOSEVELT AND THE ROUGH RIDERS

Brimming with enthusiasm, perhaps a bit innocent in their naiveté, the Rough Riders viewed Cuba as a land of stars, a place to win great honors or die in the pursuit. Like many of his men, TR believed "that the nearing future held . . . many chances of death, of honor and renown." And he was ready. Dressed in a Brooks Brothers uniform made especially for him and with several extra pairs of spectacles sewn in the lining of his Rough Rider hat, Roosevelt prepared to "meet his destiny."

In a land of beauty, death often came swiftly. As the Rough Riders and other soldiers moved inland toward Santiago, snipers fired upon them. The high-speed Mauser bullets seemed to come out of nowhere, making a *z-z-z-z-z-eu* as they moved through the air or a loud *chug* as they hit flesh. Since the Spanish snipers used smokeless gunpowder, no puffs of smoke betrayed their positions.

During the first day in Cuba, the Rough Riders experienced the "blood, sweat and tears" of warfare. Dr. Church looked "like a kid who had gotten his hands and arms into a bucket of thick red paint." Some men died, and others lay where they had been shot, dying. The reality of war strikes different men differently. It horrifies some, terrifies others, and enrages still others. Sheer exhilaration was the best way to describe Roosevelt's response to death and danger. Even sniper fire could not keep TR from jumping up and down with excitement.

On July 1, 1898, the Rough Riders faced their sternest task. Moving from the coast toward Santiago along the Camino Real, the main arm of the United States forces encountered an entrenched enemy. Spread out along the San Juan Heights, Spanish forces commanded a splendid position. As American troops emerged from a stretch of jungle, they found themselves in a dangerous position. Once again the sky seemed to be raining Mauser bullets and shrapnel. Clearly the Heights had to be taken. Each hour of delay meant more American casualties.

The Rough Riders were deployed to the right to prepare to assault Kettle Hill. Once in position, they faced an agonizing wait for orders to charge. Most soldiers hunched behind cover. Bucky O'Neill, however, casually strolled up and down in front of his troops, chain-smoked cigarettes, and shouted encouragement. A sergeant implored him to take cover. "Sergeant," Bucky remarked, "the Spanish bullet isn't made that will kill me." Hardly had he finished the statement when a Mauser bullet ripped into his mouth and burst out of the back of his head. Even before he fell, Roosevelt wrote, Bucky's "wild and gallant soul has gone out into the darkness."

—*America and Its People,* Third Edition,
by James Martin et al.

Answer the following with *T* (true) or *F* (false) or with *a, b, c,* or *d.*

_____ 1. The author's main purpose is to persuade.

_____ 2. The author feels that the Rough Riders had a glorified view of war.

_____ 3. The author shows sarcasm in mentioning the "Brooks Brothers uniform."

_____ 4. In view of his subsequent death, Bucky O'Neill's remark about a Spanish bullet was ironic.

_____ 5. The overall tone of the passage is humorous.

_____ 6. Which of the following phrases is negatively slanted?

   a. sheer exhilaration
   b. jumping up and down
   c. sternest task
   d. casually strolled

Mark the following statements as *F* (fact) or *O* (opinion).

_____ 7. ". . . the Spanish snipers used smokeless gunpowder. . . .".

_____ 8. "Dr. Church looked 'like a kid who had gotten his hands and arms into a bucket of thick red paint.'"

_____ 9. "Some men died, and others lay where they had been shot, dying."

Passage 6

SHYNESS AS A NEW DISEASE

A fast-growing number of people are doing something they would not have thought of doing before: going to their doctors for a prescription drug to cure their shyness.

In the past, many people knew that they were shy, but it never crossed their minds that shyness was a pathology, a disease that requires medical treatment. Recently, though, a number of social forces have converged to turn shyness into a mental disorder. First, in 1980, the psychiatric profession labeled extreme shyness as a *social phobia* or *social anxiety disorder*. At that time, the condition was regarded as a *rare* disorder, as it involved experiencing not only a distracting nervousness at parties or before giving a speech but also a powerful desire to avoid these social situations altogether. Next, some movie stars, big-name athletes, and other celebrities appeared on talk shows, in magazines, and on other media to disclose their struggles with shyness. Finally, the pharmaceutical company Smith Kline Beecham entered the picture by advertising and selling its antidepressant Paxil as a medicine for shyness. And thus, Americans were left with the impression that shyness is far more serious and widespread than they had ever realized.

As a result, many people today regard shyness as a disease, a medical problem serious enough to require treatment with a drug. But shyness is a serious problem only for a very few—those who are extremely bashful or truly incapacitated by fears of others' disapproval and need relief through the use of psychoactive drugs. For the majority, however, shyness is only a mild problem. According to a recent survey, nearly half of all Americans consider themselves shy and still manage to carry on a normal social life. Also consider the fact that many of these Americans may actually not be shy at all. In American culture today, it is difficult *not* to feel shy given the ubiquitous media full of immodest and even brazen talkers, just as it is difficult not to feel fat with the media presentation of extremely thin beauties.

In short, what was once considered a personality trait is now labeled as a disease and treated with drugs.

—From *Sociology: A Brief Introduction*, Sixth Edition, by Alex Thio.

Answer the following with *T* (true) or *F* (false) or with *a*, *b*, *c*, or *d*.

_____ 1. The author's primary purpose is to discuss solutions for shyness.

_____ 2. The author's overall tone is skeptical.

_____ 3. The author writes from the point of view of a shy person who has sought treatment.

_____ 4. The author suggests that Smith Kline Beecham had a role in perception of shyness as a treatable disease.

_____ 5. The words *pathology* and *disorder* convey negative connotations regarding shyness.

_____ 6. All of the following words are positively slanted *except*

  a. movie stars.
  b. big-name athletes.
  c. celebrities.
  d. ubiquitous media.

Mark the following statements as *F* (fact) or *O* (opinion).

_____ 7. "In 1980s, the psychiatric profession labeled extreme shyness as a *social phobia* or *social anxiety disorder*."

_____ 8. "Americans were left with the impression that shyness is far more serious and widespread than they had ever realized."

_____ 9. "In American culture today, it is difficult *not* to feel shy. . . ."

SUMMARY POINTS

1 What strategies do critical readers use? (page 484)

Critical readers think for themselves, analyze, and evaluate the accuracy of the printed word before accepting it. They recognize the author's purpose, point of view, and tone. They know the difference between facts and opinions and recognize valid and invalid support for arguments.

2 How do critical readers recognize an author's purpose? (page 484)

Critical readers consider the publication, the words used, and the support given. They know that common goals are to inform, persuade, or entertain. They realize that an author may have more than one purpose but that there is usually one purpose that dominates.

3 How do critical readers recognize the author's point of view or bias? (page 487)

Point of view refers to the author's opinion on the topic. Bias is similar but generally has a negative connotation. To determine the author's point of view, critical readers notice the words and supporting evidence given. They also acknowledge that their own opinions might influence their understanding of the author's point of view.

4 How do critical readers recognize the author's tone? (page 491)

Tone refers to the author's attitude toward the subject. Tone is revealed in the words and details the writer uses to make the point.

5 How do critical readers distinguish between facts and opinions? (page 498)

Facts can be proven true or false while opinions are statements of opinion and cannot be proven true or false. Critical readers evaluate supporting evidence so as not to be taken in by an argument that sounds strong but consists primarily of opinions or limited facts selected to support the point.

6 How do critical readers recognize valid and invalid support for arguments? (page 501)

Critical readers are acquainted with various forms of logical fallacies or errors in reasoning so they can identify them when reading a persuasive selection. Critical readers use this knowledge and their awareness of facts and opinions to analyze the validity of an argument. Likewise, they use the same strategies to avoid falling prey to propaganda, which is designed to convince in any way possible.

COLLABORATIVE   PROBLEM SOLVING

Form a five-member group and select one of the following activities. Brainstorm and then outline your major points on a transparency. Choose a member to present the group findings to the class.

➤ List five facts and five opinions that could be used to support the argument that people should not smoke.

➤ Write five different statements regarding rap music, each with one of the following tones: humorous, angry, ironic, sarcastic, and nostalgic.

➤ Create a fallacy for each of the six types listed in this chapter: testimonial, bandwagon, transfer, straw person, misleading analogy, and circular reasoning.

➤ List five points that you would make in an argument for capital punishment and five points that you would make in an argument against capital punishment.

MyReadingLab

MyReadingLab (MRL) www.myreadinglab.com

➤ For support in meeting this chapter's objectives, log in to **www.myreadinglab.com** and select "Critical Thinking."

THE READING WORKSHOP

If reading a novel, biography, or other book is part of your course experience, refer to The Reading Workshop: Thinking, Talking, and Writing about Books in Appendix 5 for suggestions.

SELECTION 1 Literature: Short Story

The emotional, sexual, and psychological stereotyping of females begins when the doctor says, "It's a girl."

—Shirley Chisholm

Irony is a literary technique used to entertain or educate a reader. Irony occurs when there is a contrast between what is said or expected and what actually happens. There are three basic types of irony: verbal, dramatic, and situational. In verbal irony, you say one thing when you mean another. Sarcasm is a type of verbal irony when you mean the precise opposite of what you say. The second type of irony, dramatic irony, occurs when the reader has information that the characters do not. For example, in Romeo and Juliet the reader knows that Juliet is not dead but Romeo thinks she is dead. The third type of irony is situational irony, in which both the characters and the audience are unaware of certain important information. This type of irony results in surprise endings to stories as the characters and the reader both become aware of the missing information.

THINKING BEFORE READING

Preview for content and organizational clues. Activate your schema and anticipate what you will learn.

Why were British colonists in India in the early 1900s?

Why do people scream at the unexpected?

What makes you scream?

I think this story will be about _____.

VOCABULARY PREVIEW

Are you familiar with these words?

colonial	attachés	naturalist	veranda	spacious
contracting	summons	impulse	commotion	forfeit

What is an *attaché* case?

What type of science does a *naturalist* study?

What happens to your money if you *forfeit* a deposit?

Your instructor may give a true-false vocabulary review before or after reading.

THINKING DURING READING

As you read, use the six thinking strategies of a good reader: predict, picture, relate, monitor, correct, and annotate.

SELECTION

1

Refer to the
Reader's **TIP**
for **Short Story** on
page 152.

THE DINNER PARTY

The country is India. A colonial official and his wife are giving a large dinner party. They are seated with their guests—army officers and government attachés and their wives, and a visiting American naturalist—in their spacious dining room, which has a bare marble floor, open rafters, and wide glass doors opening onto a veranda. A spirited discussion springs
5   up between a young girl who insists that women have outgrown the jumping-on-a-chair-at-the-sight-of-a-mouse era and a colonel who says they have not.

"A woman's unfailing reaction in any crisis," the colonel says, "is to scream. And while a man may feel like it, he has that ounce more of nerve control than a woman has. And that last ounce is what counts."

10   The American does not join in the argument but watches the other guests. As he looks, he sees a strange expression come over the face of the hostess. She is staring straight ahead, her muscles contracting slightly. With a slight gesture she summons the servant standing behind her chair and whispers to him. The servant's eyes widen, and he quickly leaves the room.

15   Of the guests, none except the American notices this or sees the servant place a bowl of milk on the veranda just outside the open doors.

The American comes to with a start. In India, milk in a bowl means only one thing—bait for a snake. He realizes there must be a cobra in the room. He looks up at the rafters—the likeliest place—but they are bare. Three corners of the room are empty, and
20   in the fourth the servants are waiting to serve the next course. There is only one place left—under the table.

His first impulse is to jump back and warn the others, but he knows the commotion would frighten the cobra into striking. He speaks quickly, the tone of his voice so arresting that it sobers everyone.

25   "I want to know just what control everyone at this table has. I will count three hundred—that's five minutes—and not one of you is to move a muscle. Those who move will forfeit fifty rupees. Ready!"

The twenty people sit like stone images while he counts. He is saying ". . . two hundred and eighty . . ." when, out of the corner of his eye, he sees the cobra emerge and
30   make for the bowl of milk. Screams ring out as he jumps to slam the veranda doors safely shut.

"You were right, Colonel!" the host exclaims. "A man has just shown us an example of perfect control."

"Just a minute," the American says, turning to the hostess. "Mrs. Wynnes, how did you know that cobra was in the room?"

A faint smile lights up the woman's face as she replies: "Because it was crawling across my foot."

(466 words)

—"The Dinner Party," by Mona Gardner,
Saturday Review of Literature

THINKING AND WRITING AFTER READING

RECALL Self-test your understanding.

Your instructor may choose to give you a true-false comprehension review.

REACT How would this incident have affected you? _____

_____

REFLECT How did Mrs. Wynnes and the American act as a team? What might have

happened if each had acted in a different manner? _____

_____

THINKING CRITICALLY What do you think the young girl will say to the colonel after the incident? How do you think the colonel and the guests replied? How does the author feel about the gender argument? Write your answer on a separate sheet of paper.

THINK AND WRITE How does the situational irony in this story entertain and edu-

cate? How is irony used to attack a bias? _____

_____

EXTENDED WRITING This short story dramatically disproves the colonel's claim that women react emotionally in a crisis by screaming. What gender stereotypes still exist? Select one or more gender stereotypes to discuss and either support or refute in a persuasive paper. Make your position clear in the introductory paragraph, and give supporting evidence in two or three body paragraphs. End the paper by summing up your argument and restating your position.

CRITICAL READING

Write your response to the following questions.

1. What is the difference of opinion at the beginning of the story between the

   young girl and the colonel? _____

   _____

   _____

2. What is the bias of the host of the party? _____

_____

3. As the dinner party unfolds, what action or fact emerges to support the opinion of the young girl? _____

_____

Mark the following statements as *F* (fact) or *O* (opinion).

_____ 4. "A woman's unfailing reaction in any crisis is to scream."

_____ 5. The American does not join in the argument but watches the other guests.

_____ 6. "A man has just shown us an example of perfect control."

Interpret THE QUOTE

Now that you have finished reading the selection, "The Dinner Party," go back to the beginning of the selection and read the opening quote again. What stereotypes about women does the colonel promote in this story? On a separate sheet of paper, list four common stereotypes for men and four stereotypes for women. Next to each stereotype, write whether you believe the stereotype is true or false and explain why.

Name _____

Date _____

COMPREHENSION QUESTIONS

Answer the following with *a*, *b*, *c*, or *d*, or fill in the blank. In order to help you analyze your strengths and weaknesses, the question types are indicated.

Main Idea   _____   1. The best statement of the main idea of the selection is:

     a. Women appreciate courage in men more than men appreciate courage in women.
     b. In a crisis the real character of a person is displayed.
     c. Arguments of gender differences can be proven true or false.
     d. In a crisis, a woman can have as much nerve as a man.

Inference   _____   2. During the argument, when the American noted Mrs. Wynnes's strange expression, the hostess was reacting to

     a. the colonel's negative words about women.
     b. the cobra crossing her foot.
     c. the young girl's opinion in support of women.
     d. the bowl of milk brought by the servant.

Inference   _____   3. The American was perhaps more attuned than the average person to the habits of a snake because

     a. his profession involved the study of nature.
     b. he had been born in India.
     c. the cobra is indigenous or native to America.
     d. army officers were trained to react appropriately to such dangers.

Inference   _____   4. From Mrs. Wynnes's reaction to the crawling snake and the American's challenge to the dinner guests, the reader can assume that a cobra

     a. attacks when it cannot find milk.
     b. can be agitated into an attack by movement.
     c. attacks at the sound of a human voice.
     d. is more attracted to the warmth of the human body than to a favorite food.

Inference   5. What does the description "A faint smile lights up the woman's face as she replies . . ." suggest about the feelings of Mrs. Wynnes?

_____

_____

_____

_____

Inference   _____   6. The guests at the dinner party participated in the five-minute challenge by the American because they

     a. knew there was a snake under the table.
     b. saw that Mrs. Wynnes was also greatly disturbed.
     c. wanted to win fifty rupees.
     d. were inspired by the American's voice and sensed the importance of the challenge.

Inference _____ 7. The author implies that Mr. Wynnes
  a. chose to disregard his wife's contribution to the dilemma.
  b. did not fully understand that two people were involved in the successful solution.
  c. remained firm in his opinions even after recognizing the facts of the incident.
  d. knew that the American had not acted alone.

Answer the following with *T* (true) or *F* (false).

Detail _____ 8. The setting of the story suggests that the people at the dinner party were members of the upper crust.

Inference _____ 9. The author suggests that the American is initially biased toward the gender opinion of the colonel.

Inference _____ 10. The milk was most likely placed on the veranda because the doors could be closed when the snake crawled out.

VOCABULARY

Answer the following with *a, b, c,* or *d* for the word or phrase that best defines the boldface word as used in the selection. The number in parentheses indicates the line of the passage in which the word appears.

_____ 1. "**colonial** official" (1)
  a. wealthy
  b. native of India
  c. residing in a colony
  d. authoritarian

_____ 2. "government **attachés**" (2)
  a. diplomatic staffers
  b. friends
  c. generals
  d. contractors

_____ 3. "American **naturalist**" (3)
  a. liberal
  b. scientist of nature
  c. conservative
  d. inspector

_____ 4. "**spacious** dining room" (3)
  a. clean
  b. large
  c. decorated
  d. crowded

_____ 5. "muscles **contracting**" (12)
  a. relaxing
  b. not reacting
  c. increasing in size
  d. tightening

_____ 6. "**summons** the servant"(12)
  a. seizes
  b. holds
  c. calls for
  d. nods to

_____ 7. "**veranda** just outside" (16)
  a. porch
  b. room
  c. entry
  d. stairs

_____ 8. "first **impulse**" (22)
  a. attempt
  b. information
  c. association
  d. urge

_____ 9. "**commotion** would frighten" (22)
  a. jump
  b. argument
  c. turmoil
  d. bait of milk

_____ 10. "**forfeit** fifty rupees" (27)
  a. give up
  b. earn
  c. gamble
  d. borrow

Your instructor may choose to give you a true-false comprehension review.

VOCABULARY ENRICHMENT

A. Study the similar-sounding words and circle one for each sentence.

accent: speech pattern	**elicit:** draw out	**eminent:** well-known
ascent: climb upward	**illicit:** improper	**imminent:** about to happen

1. British colonists in India spoke with a slight (**accent, ascent**).

2. The young girl will surely (**elicit, illicit**) an apology from the colonel.

3. The hostess felt that with a sudden movement a snake bite would be (**eminent, imminent**).

B. Use context clues, word parts, and, if necessary, the dictionary, to write the meaning for each of the boldface words from a sociology textbook.

4. As foreigners, the ruling British colonists were not quickly **assimilated** into the society of India. _____

5. In order to live together in harmony, society demands **conformity** from its members. _____

6. In the story, the American sees a **correlation** between the milk and a snake.

   _____

7. The American naturalist was held in high **esteem** for his quick thinking.

   _____

8. Except for the young girl, the other guests at the dinner party seem to be members of the same age or **peer** group. _____

9. Because India is densely populated, most people live in **urban** areas.

   _____

10. Because of their governing positions, British colonists enjoyed many perks of their high **status.** _____

C. Identify the boldface phrase as simile, metaphor, or personification and explain the meaning.

11. George Washington was the **father of his country** but he had no children of his own. _____

12. Glaciers are melting **like warm ice cream** because pollution is trapping heat to the earth. _____

13. Some birds migrate over two continents, perhaps **singing their songs** in both English and Spanish. _____

   _____

14. Because of 200 mph winds that strike **like tornadoes,** climbers can ascend Mount Everest only during two months of the year. _____

_____

15. Poetry **speaks to** both the heart and the brain. _____

_____

ASSESS YOUR LEARNING

Review confusing questions, seek clarification, and make notes in your text to help you remember new information and vocabulary.

SELECTION 2   Essay

"The end may justify the means as long as there is something that justifies the end."
— Leon Trotsky

Obesity is a serious problem in the United States. Statistics consistently reveal that about one-third of Americans are overweight, and the rate of childhood obesity has tripled in the last 30 years. The effects on well-being are far-reaching—diabetes, heart disease, cancer, high blood pressure, asthma. In fact, obesity is such a risk to health that First Lady Michelle Obama launched a campaign to focus attention on the problem in children. "This isn't just a policy issue for me. This is a passion. This is my mission. I am determined to work with folks across this country to change the way a generation of kids thinks about food and nutrition," she said about her "Let's Move" initiative. "Let's Move" emphasizes fitness and nutrition education and encourages parents, children, schools, restaurants, youth organizations, food manufacturers—everyone—to take action to end childhood obesity in one generation. What responsibility should parents shoulder to ensure that children maintain a healthy weight? What methods are effective, and what methods go too far, sometimes causing a lifetime of low self-esteem and even self-hatred?

THINKING BEFORE READING

Preview the selection for clues to content. Activate your schema and anticipate what you will learn.

Have you or someone you know struggled to maintain a healthy weight?

How much importance should parents place on their children's weight?

Is it possible that focusing attention on weight can be harmful?

What methods are acceptable in achieving a goal?

I think this essay will make the following point: _____

_____.

VOCABULARY PREVIEW

Are you familiar with these words?

clambered	obesity	authoritarian	regimen	incarceration
skirmish	tactic	amphetamines	shun	metabolisms

Are *authoritarian* parenting practices the most effective?

Have you ever attempted a weight loss or exercise *regimen*?

How does it feel to be *shun*ned?

Your instructor may choose to give a true-false vocabulary review before or after reading.

THINKING DURING READING

As you read, use the six thinking strategies of a good reader: predict, picture, relate, monitor, correct, and annotate.

---

*Reader's***TIP**   **Reading and Studying an Essay**

Ask yourself the following questions:

- What is the theme, thesis, or main idea?
- How do the details and examples develop the theme?
- How does the title aid in understanding the essay?
- What is the author's attitude toward the subject?
- What images contribute to the theme of the essay?
- What is the conclusion? How is it significant?

SHEDDING THE WEIGHT OF MY DAD'S OBSESSION

For years my figure was the target of my father's anger. I've finally come to accept my size and myself.

Instead of selling the fundraiser candy, I ate it. Eight boxes of it. Each Bluebird in our fourth-grade troop was assigned 12 boxes of chocolate candy to sell for a dollar a box. I sold four boxes to my family and then ran out of ideas for selling the rest.

5   As the days passed and the stack of candy remained in a corner of my room, the temptation to eat it overwhelmed my conscience. Two months after we'd been given the goodies, the troop leader announced that the drive was over and we were to bring in our sales money, along with any unsold candy, to the next Tuesday meeting. I rushed home in a panic and counted $4 in my sales-money envelope and 12 boxes of candy gone.

I thought of the piggy bank filled with silver dollars that my father kept on a shelf in
10   his closet. It was a collection that he added to but never spent. I tried to push this financial resource out of my mind, but Tuesday was approaching, and I still had no money.

By Monday afternoon I had no choice. I tiptoed into my parents' bedroom, pulled the vanity chair from Mother's dressing table and carried it to the walk-in closet. There was the piggy bank smiling down at me from the high shelf. After stacking boxes on the chair,
15   I reached up and laid hands on the bank. When I had counted out eight silver dollars, I returned the pig to its place and clambered down. For days I felt bad about my theft, but what I felt even guiltier about was eating all those treats.

Throughout my childhood, my parents weighed me every day, and Daddy posted the numbers on my bedroom door. He never called me fat, but I came to learn every syn-
20   onym. He discussed every health aspect of obesity endlessly. The daily tone and timber of our household was affected by Dad's increasingly authoritarian regimens.

I remember one Friday night, months after the candy caper. I heard the garage door rumble shut, and I knew that Daddy was home. He came in the back door, kissed Mother and asked what my weight was for the day. Mother admitted that I was still a pound over
25   the goal he had set. "Get a pillow and a book, Linda," he said.

He firmly ushered me to the bathroom, then shut and locked the door behind me. As the door was closing, I caught a glimpse of Mother and my sister looking on as though

they were witnessing an execution. For the next two days, the only time I was allowed
out was for meals. It was late Sunday evening when I was finally released from my cell,
30 supposedly taught a lesson by my incarceration.

The bathroom episode was one skirmish in a long war that had begun when, unlike
my older sister, I failed to shed the "baby fat" many children are born with. Although I was
cheerful, affectionate and good-natured, none of these qualities interested my father. He
had one slender child—he meant to have two. It was simply a matter of my self-discipline.

35 My slightly chubby figure had become a target for my physician father's frustration
as he struggled to establish his medical practice. Dad told me constantly that if I was a
pound overweight, I would be teased at school and nobody would like me. I stayed away
from the other kids, fearing harsh words that never came. When I was 16, Daddy came
up with the ultimate punishment: any day that I weighed more than 118 pounds (the
40 weight my father had deemed ideal for my 5-foot, 4-inch frame) I'd have to pay him.
In an attempt to shield me from this latest tactic, my exhausted, loving mother secretly
took me to an internist friend of the family who prescribed what he described as "diet
pills"—amphetamines and diuretics. Although the pills caused unpleasant side effects like
lightheadedness, taking them landed me a slim figure and, two years later, an engineer
45 husband.

I quit the hated amphetamines at 27 and accepted my divorce as a result of my weight gain. I became a single, working mother devoted to raising my son and daughter. Over time, I realized that people liked my smile and my laugh and, contrary to my father's predictions, didn't shun me because of my size.

50   Many years ago, at my annual physical, I mentioned to my doctor that I couldn't eat the same quantity of food that normal people eat without getting bigger. He kindly reassured me that people do indeed have different metabolisms, some more efficient than others. This discussion ultimately helped me to accept my size and shed the emotional burden carried over from my childhood.

55   My sister and her husband have a daughter who was pudgy as a child. They asked me what they should do about her weight "problem." My reply, "Don't make it an issue. Let her find her own weight level." To their great credit, they did.

(864 words)

—From *Newsweek*, November 13, 2000,
by Linda Lee Andujar

THINKING AND WRITING AFTER READING

RECALL Self-test your understanding.

Your instructor may choose to give you a true-false comprehension review.

REACT What is your opinion of the methods used by Andujar's father and mother? _____

_____

REFLECT Do you think that Andujar's father was correct in focusing attention on his daughter's weight? Why? Why not? _____

_____

THINKING CRITICALLY Were his actions appropriate? Were the mother's? _____

_____

THINK AND WRITE In adulthood, Andujar achieved a healthy relationship with her weight, but it came after years of struggle and anxiety. She contrasted her childhood experience with the advice she gave her sister. List the stated and implied effects of both approaches:

Effects of Andujar's parents' methods	*Effects of Andujar's advice to her sister*
_____	_____
_____	_____
_____	_____
_____	_____

EXTENDED WRITING What advice would you give parents to help children maintain healthy, fit bodies while also promoting emotional well-being? Put your ideas in the form of an essay that could be published in a magazine as Andujar's was in *Newsweek*. Set forth a clear plan and support it with examples, statistics, reasons, personal experiences, and expert opinions. An Internet search on childhood obesity will yield websites with reliable information.

CRITICAL READING

1. Describe the author's purpose in writing this essay. Be more specific than simply saying it is to persuade, inform, or entertain. _____

   _____

   _____

   _____

2. What is the author's point of view on the appropriate parental approach to childhood weight issues? _____

   _____

   _____

3. Select at least three words to describe the tone of the essay. Refer to the list of tone words in the Reader's Tip on pages 492–493 for suggestions. _____

   _____

   _____

   _____

4. What effect might Andujar's father's profession have on the reader's (and the family's) view of his concern about her weight? _____

   _____

   _____

   _____

5. What was the mother's role in the treatment of her daughter? _____

   _____

   _____

6. List the ways Andujar described her parents. Place a "+" next to those that are positive.

   Father   **Mother**

   _____   _____

   _____   _____

   _____   _____

   _____   _____

   _____   _____

_____   _____
_____   _____
_____   _____
_____   _____
_____   _____
_____

Mark the following statements as *F* (fact) or *O* (opinion).

_____ 7. "By Monday afternoon I had no choice."

_____ 8. "Over time, I realized that people liked my smile and my laugh."

Interpret THE QUOTE

Go back to the beginning of the selection and read the opening quote again. Do you agree that a positive, worthwhile result can justify the means used to achieve it? Did the results in Andujar's situation justify the methods used by her parents?

SELECTION
2

Name _____

Date _____

COMPREHENSION QUESTIONS

Answer the following with *a, b, c,* or *d,* or fill in the blank. In order to help you analyze your strengths and weaknesses, the question types are indicated.

Main Idea   _____ 1. Which statement best expresses the author's main point?

    a. Linda Andujar struggled with her weight as a child and into adulthood.
    b. Childhood obesity is a serious problem in the United States.
    c. Even when they have good intentions, parents sometimes make serious mistakes in raising their children.
    d. The methods Linda Andujar's parents used to control her weight led to poor self-esteem and dependence on diet pills, but she ultimately overcame these problems.

Inference   _____ 2. The author was probably _____ years old when the fund-raiser candy incident occurred.

    a. 6 or 7
    b. 9 or 10
    c. 12 or 13
    d. 15 or 16

Detail   _____ 3. Andujar's father was a _____.

    a. scientist
    b. teacher
    c. doctor
    d. salesman

Inference   _____ 4. The language Andujar used to describe her parents suggests that she _____.

    a. hated her parents
    b. felt more sympathy toward her mother than toward her father
    c. respected her parents, particularly her father
    d. agreed with their approach to controlling her weight

Main Idea   _____ 5. Which of the following best describes the topic of this article?

    a. Linda Andujar's personal experiences with her weight
    b. Child-rearing methods
    c. Childhood obesity
    d. The many ways that parents can damage their children's self-esteem

Detail   _____ 6. Andujar's father believed this was the ideal weight for her 5-foot, 4-inch height.

    a. 127 pounds
    b. 119 pounds
    c. 118 pounds
    d. 116 pounds

Inference _____ 7. Details in the selection support the following statement:

 a. The author resented her sister for being slender
 b. The author no longer speaks to her parents
 c. The author has forgiven her parents for the treatment she received as a child
 d. The author has a positive, adult relationship with her sister

Detail _____ 8 Andujar felt worse about eating the fundraiser candy than she did about stealing the money.

Detail _____ 9. Andujar believed that her weight was a factor in her wedding and her divorce.

Inference _____ 10. Andujar might have been addicted to amphetamines.

VOCABULARY

Answer the following with *a*, *b*, *c*, or *d* for the word or phrase that best defines the boldface word used in the selection. The number in parentheses indicates the line of the passage in which the word appears. In addition to the context clues, use a dictionary to more precisely define the words.

_____ 1. "and **clambered** down" (16)

 a. fell
 b. climbed
 c. ran
 d. skipped

_____ 2. "every health aspect of **obesity**" (20)

 a. a physical disease
 b. the lack muscle tone
 c. a psychological condition
 d. the state of being overweight

_____ 3. "**authoritarian** regimens" (21)

 a. knowledgeable
 b. preferred
 c. overly controlling
 d. reasonable

_____ 4. "authoritarian **regimens**" (21)

 a. cruelty
 b. diet or exercise program
 c. standard
 d. military formation

_____ 5. "a lesson by my **incarceration**" (30)

 a. punishment
 b. imprisonment
 c. torture
 d. teaching

_____ 6. "bathroom episode was one **skirmish**" (31)

 a. small battle
 b. disagreement
 c. war
 d. problem

_____ 7. "from this latest **tactic**" (41)

 a. punishment
 b. sentence
 c. plan
 d. horror

_____ 8. "**amphetamines** and diuretics" (46)

 a. stimulant drug used to control appetite
 b. a drug used to control violent behavior
 c. a drug prescribed for pain
 d. depressant used for violent patients

_____ 9. "didn't **shun** me because
of my size" (49)
  a. like
  b. tease
  c. bully
  d. stay away from

_____ 10. "have different **metabolisms**"
(52)
  a. physical characteristics
  b. internal organs
  c. processes of converting
     food in the body
  d. food preferences

Your instructor may choose to give a true-false vocabulary review.

VOCABULARY ENRICHMENT

A. Create your own analogies for each type of relationship. Think of a second word
that establishes the indicated relationship, then finish the analogy with a similar

comparison. _____

1. Degree: *Damp* is to _____ as _____ is to _____.

2. Part to whole: *Toes* are to _____ as _____ is to _____.

3. Cause and effect: *Careless* is to _____ as _____ is to _____.

4. Classification: *Airplane* is to _____ as _____ is to _____.

5. Function: *Oven* is to _____ as _____ is to _____.

B. Choose one of the following transitional words or phrases to complete each
sentence.

however	for instance	thus	in addition	in a like manner

6. Freud was the first to conceptualize a theory of personality; _____,

   he is considered the father of psychoanalysis.

7. Freud's theories were considered by many to be too sexual and caused some

   of his followers to create their own groups; _____, a group of his

   followers who broke away became known as neo-Freudians.

8. Karen Horney became a neo-Freudian who, _____, became the

   first American female psychologist.

9. Carl Jung began with Freud studying personality; _____, later in

   life he focused on learning theory.

10. Although the neo-Freudians discarded some of the negativity of Freud, they

    retained Freud's belief that the subconscious affects the personality and,

    _____, they popularized their own theories through research

    and publication.

ASSESS YOUR LEARNING

Review confusing questions, seek clarification, and make notes in your text to
help you remember new information and vocabulary.

SELECTION 3  Essay

"We must embrace pain and burn it as fuel for our journey."

—Kenji Miyazawa

On September 11, 2001, planes hijacked by terrorists hit the World Trade Center and the Pentagon, claiming the lives of more than 3,000 innocent people. In the aftermath, the country mourned the loss of life and commiserated about their fears. While almost every newspaper columnist wrote about these emotions, one opinion piece stood out. The following selection, "We'll Go Forward from This Moment," by Leonard Pitts of the Miami Herald, was widely circulated on the Internet, generating over 30,000 e-mails. Since its publication the day after the attacks, the piece has been set to music, reprinted in poster form, read on television, and quoted by legislators.

THINKING BEFORE READING

Preview for content and organizational clues. Activate your schema and anticipate what you will learn.

What do you remember about the September 11, 2001, attacks?

What surprising event happened at Pearl Harbor?

This selection will probably tell me _____.

VOCABULARY PREVIEW

Are you familiar with these words?

steeled	frivolous	minutiae	blithe	entitlement
grappling	recrimination	chastened	bickering	cherish

Are *frivolous* issues serious?

Is *minutiae* important?

Is *bickering* pleasant?

Your instructor may give a true-false vocabulary review before or after reading.

THINKING DURING READING

As you read, use the six thinking strategies of a good reader: predict, picture, relate, monitor, correct, and annotate.

WE'LL GO FORWARD FROM THIS MOMENT

September 12, 2001

Refer to the
Reader's TIP
for **Essay** on
page 520.

It's my job to have something to say.

They pay me to provide words that help make sense of that which troubles the American soul. But in this moment of airless shock when hot tears sting disbelieving eyes,

Scan this QR code to hear this reading.

5   the only thing I can find to say, the only words that seem to fit, must be addressed to the unknown author of this suffering.

You monster. You beast. You unspeakable bastard.

What lesson did you hope to teach us by your coward's attack on our World Trade Center, our Pentagon, us? What was it you hoped we would learn? Whatever it was, please know that you failed.

10 Did you want us to respect your cause? You just damned your cause.

Did you want to make us fear? You just steeled our resolve.

Did you want to tear us apart? You just brought us together.

Let me tell you about my people. We are a vast and quarrelsome family, a family rent by racial, social, political and class division, but a family nonetheless. We're frivolous, yes,

15 capable of expending tremendous emotional energy on pop cultural minutiae—a singer's revealing dress, a ball team's misfortune, a cartoon mouse. We're wealthy, too, spoiled by the ready availability of trinkets and material goods, and maybe because of that, we walk through life with a certain sense of blithe entitlement. We are fundamentally decent, though—peace-loving and compassionate. We struggle to know the right thing and to

20 do it. And we are, the overwhelming majority of us, people of faith, believers in a just and loving God.

Some people—you, perhaps—think that any or all of this makes us weak. You're mistaken. We are not weak. Indeed, we are strong in ways that cannot be measured by arsenals.

IN PAIN

Yes, we're in pain now. We are in mourning, and we are in shock. We're still grappling

25 with the unreality of the awful thing you did, still working to make ourselves understand that this isn't a special effect from some Hollywood blockbuster, isn't the plot development from a Tom Clancy novel. Both in terms of the awful scope of their ambition and the probable final death toll, your attacks are likely to go down as the worst acts of terrorism in the history of the United States and, probably, the history of the world. You've bloodied

30 us as we have never been bloodied before.

But there's a gulf of difference between making us bloody and making us fall. This is the lesson Japan was taught to its bitter sorrow the last time anyone hit us this hard, the last time anyone brought us such abrupt and monumental pain. When roused, we are

35   righteous in our outrage, terrible in our force. When provoked by this level of barbarism, we will bear any suffering, pay any cost, go to any length, in the pursuit of justice.

I tell you this without fear of contradiction. I know my people, as you, I think, do not. What I know reassures me. It also causes me to tremble with dread of the future.

40   In the days to come, there will be recrimination and accusation, fingers pointing to determine whose failure allowed this to happen and what can be done to prevent it from happening again. There will be heightened security, misguided talk of revoking basic freedoms. We'll go forward from this moment sobered, chastened, sad. But determined, too. Unimaginably determined.

THE STEEL IN US

You see, the steel in us is not always readily apparent. That aspect of our character is seldom understood by people who don't know us well. On this day, the family's bickering
45   is put on hold.

As Americans we will weep, as Americans we will mourn, and as Americans, we will rise in defense of all that we cherish.

So I ask again: What was it you hoped to teach us? It occurs to me that maybe you just wanted us to know the depths of your hatred. If that's the case, consider the message
50   received. And take this message in exchange: You don't know my people. You don't know what we're capable of. You don't know what you just started.

But you're about to learn.

(704 words)

—"We'll Go Forward from This Moment," by Leonard Pitts, *Miami Herald*

THINKING AND WRITING AFTER READING

RECALL   Self-test your understanding.

Your instructor may choose to give you a true-false review.

REACT   For what reasons do you think the author feels that "the steel in us is not always readily apparent"? _____

_____

REFLECT   How did Americans act like a family after the events of September 11, 2001? _____

_____

_____

THINKING CRITICALLY   What does the author mean by "misguided talk of revoking basic freedoms"? What would you assume are some of his biases on security issues?

_____

_____

THINK AND WRITE   To whom is this column addressed? How does this perspective make the piece unique? Why do you think this column became so famous? _____

_____

_____

EXTENDED WRITING Now that the terrorist attack on the World Trade Center in New York City on September 11, 2001, is long past, do you think the author's characterizations of Americans are still accurate? Were his predictions born out? Write a response to Leonard Pitts's editorial that provides your "looking back/looking forward" perspective as if it were to be published in a newspaper or blog. To strengthen your comments, interview someone who remembers 9/11 clearly. If possible, also talk to someone who remembers the Japanese attack on Pearl Harbor, to which Pitts likened the attack on the World Trade Center.

CRITICAL READING

1. Why does the author begin the selection with "It's my job to have something to say"? _____

   _____

2. What is the author's purpose? _____

   _____

3. Who is the "cartoon mouse" to which the author refers? _____

   _____

4. How, unfortunately, would the terrorists differ with the author's reference to "your coward's attack"? _____

   _____

5. What does the author imply about a Tom Clancy novel? _____

   _____

Interpret THE QUOTE

Now that you have finished reading the selection, "We'll Go Forward from This Moment," go back to the beginning of the selection and read the opening quote again. On a separate sheet of paper, list five ways that Americans used their pain as fuel in order to deal with the events of 9/11.

Name _____

Date _____

COMPREHENSION QUESTIONS

Answer the following with *a, b, c,* or *d,* or fill in the blank. In order to help you analyze your strengths and weaknesses, the question types are indicated.

Main Idea   _____   1. The best statement of the main idea of the selection is:

  a. The author appeals to Americans to rally against terrorism.
  b. The author condemns governments that harbor terrorists.
  c. The author condemns the terrorists and warns of American strength.
  d. The author condemns the cultural differences that created the hatred of the terrorists.

Inference   _____   2. The author's tone is

  a. compassionate.
  b. angry.
  c. sarcastic.
  d. melancholy.

Inference   _____   3. The author calls Americans a "family" because Americans

  a. are composed of racial, social, political, and class divisions.
  b. disagree with each other but come together to forget differences in a crisis.
  c. enjoy the same pop cultural minutiae.
  d. are people of faith.

Inference   _____   4. By using the phrase "we walk through life with a certain sense of blithe entitlement," the author suggests that Americans

  a. appreciate the trinkets and material goods that are readily available.
  b. are decent citizens who feel the suffering of others.
  c. casually act as if it is their right to have a grand array of goods.
  d. recognize the insecurity of the country's borders.

Inference   5. What does the author mean by Americans' being "capable of expending tremendous emotional energy on pop cultural minutiae"?

_____

_____

Inference   _____   6. By referring to the "special effects from some Hollywood blockbuster," the author suggests that Americans are

  a. addicted to violence in the movies.
  b. manipulated by Hollywood.
  c. suspicious that the idea for the attack came from a movie.
  d. still in some level of disbelief.

Inference   _____   7. The "lesson Japan was taught to its bitter sorrow" refers to

  a. the economic impact of tariffs on imported Japanese cars.
  b. the reduction of immigration quotas for Japan.
  c. the defeat of Japan in World War II.
  d. the sinking of American ships.

Answer the following with *T* (true), *F* (false), or *CT* (can't tell).

Inference _____ 8. By saying that "we are strong in ways that cannot be measured by arsenals," the author implies that the American military is not strong.

Inference _____ 9. The author implies that he trembles with dread of the future because he fears the terrorists.

Detail _____ 10. The author suggests that American investigators will seek answers to learn how the attacks were allowed to happen.

VOCABULARY

Answer the following with *a, b, c,* or *d* for the word or phrase that best defines the boldface word as used in the selection. The number in parentheses indicates the line of the passage in which the word appears.

_____ 1. "**steeled** our resolve" (11)

    a. stole
    b. strengthened
    c. lessened
    d. removed

_____ 2. "We're **frivolous**" (14)

    a. oblivious
    b. ignorant
    c. arrogant
    d. playful

_____ 3. "pop cultural **minutiae**" (15)

    a. trivia
    b. history
    c. questions
    d. arguments

_____ 4. "**blithe** entitlement" (18)

    a. equal
    b. carefree
    c. harsh
    d. dishonest

_____ 5. "blithe **entitlement**" (18)

    a. longing
    b. realism
    c. ownership right
    d. satisfaction

_____ 6. "**grappling** with the unreality" (24)

    a. sleeping
    b. struggling
    c. overreacting
    d. replying

_____ 7. "**recrimination** and accusation" (38)

    a. suggestions
    b. orders
    c. guesses
    d. blame

_____ 8. "sobered, **chastened**, sad" (41)

    a. punished
    b. hesitant
    c. afraid
    d. humiliated

_____ 9. "the family's **bickering**" (44)

    a. ethnic differences
    b. unity
    c. squabbling
    d. leadership

_____ 10. "all that we **cherish**" (47)

    a. value
    b. desire
    c. own
    d. lost

Your instructor may choose to give a true-false review.

VOCABULARY ENRICHMENT

Select the word from the list that best completes each sentence.

steeled	frivolous	minutiae	blithe	entitlement
grappling	recriminations	chastened	bickering	cherish

1. The new buildings at Ground Zero have a memorial so that Americans can come to _____ the memory of those who were lost.

2. Families, _____ with the horror of missing relatives, posted pictures and pleas on the wall around Ground Zero.

3. The _____ spirited tourists enjoying Central Park froze in fear with the sounds and confusion of the disaster.

4. In the aftermath, _____ were hurled at the intelligence gathering of the FBI and the CIA.

5. The _____ of network sitcoms was replaced with 24-hour coverage of the disaster.

6. Unfortunately, agencies in charge of dispersing contributions engaged in some _____ with family members over the amounts.

7. Airline passengers _____ themselves for long delays and baggage checks.

8. In the September 11 attacks, Americans were _____ by the hatred of terrorists.

9. The feeling of a national _____ to security within American borders changed after September 11.

10. The _____ atmosphere of Times Square disappeared as people ran for protection.

ASSESS YOUR LEARNING

Review confusing questions, seek clarification, and make notes in your text to help you remember new information and vocabulary.

VOCABULARY LESSON

Bend, Born, and Body

Study the roots, words, and sentences.

Roots	*flex, flect*: bend	*nat, nasc*: born	*corp*: body

Words with *flex* or *flect* = *bend*

Do dancers need to be *flexible*? Can you see your *reflection* in the pond?

- Flex: to bend

  Flex your muscles to show your strength.

- Deflect: bend away from

  The politician was able to *deflect* the vicious questions and move ahead.

- Genuflection: bending the knees, bowing

  My arrogant boss seems to expect total submission and *genuflection*.

- Inflection: the rise and fall of the voice

  The *inflection* in his voice revealed that his feelings had been hurt.

- Reflect: to think back to

  Reflect on literary readings through a discussion with others.

- Reflective: thoughtful

  Quiet, *reflective* moments can give a sense of inner peace.

- Reflector: that which sends back light

  Wear a *reflector* when you walk at night.

Words with *nat* or *nasc* = *born*

Does July 4th create a sense of *nationalism*? Is New York an *international* city?

- Native: belonging to by birth

  Are palm trees *native* to your area?

- Naïve: acting as one born yesterday

  The *naïve* respondent thought she had won a prize.

- Naturalize: to give citizenship to one foreign born

  Gisela has been a *naturalized* citizen of this country for two years.

- Innate: inborn

  Freud believed that mankind had an *innate* fear of spiders and snakes.

- Renaissance: a rebirth or revival

  The inner city is experiencing a *renaissance* with urban pioneers.

- Nationality: country of origin

  Her *nationality* is either Mexican or Costa Rican.

Words with *corp* or *corpor* = *body*

Are *corporate* headquarters lavish? Is any business *incorporable*?

- Corporal: relating to the body

  The scars indicated *corporal* punishment.

- Corporation: business people united legally

  The president of the *corporation* received stock bonuses.

- Incorporate: to unite legally, add

  You need to *incorporate* a visual display into the oral presentation.

- Corps: group organized for a common cause

  The Peace *Corps* members are sent to remote areas to help people.

- Corpuscle: a cell that flows in the blood

  A *corpuscle* can be a red or white blood cell.

- Corpse: a dead body

  An autopsy was performed on the *corpse* because of questions surrounding the death.

- Corpulent: excessively fat

  Santa Claus is *corpulent* and jolly.

Review

Part I

Answer the following with (*T*) true or (*F*) false.

_____ 1. A reflective thinker seldom recalls the past.

_____ 2. Flexible clay can still be molded.

_____ 3. A corpulent corpse will probably be difficult to move.

_____ 4. Spanking a child is corporal punishment.

_____ 5. Corpuscles are found in many plants.

_____ 6. If you look in a mirror, you can see your reflection.

_____ 7. An innate talent is a genetic gift.

_____ 8. Companies on the New York Stock Exchange are incorporated.

_____ 9. A deflected arrow is repelled from the target.

_____10. Immigrants must apply to become naturalized citizens.

Part II

Choose the best word from the list to complete the following sentences.

naïve	corps	reflectors	nationalism	inflection
flex	renaissance	genuflect	native	nationality

11. His final voice _____ indicated that he was asking a question.

12. On Halloween night parents attach safety _____ to costumes.

13. Some flowers _____ to the swamp do not grow in the mountains.

14. The army called on the _____ of engineers to replace the bridge.

15. Freshman are _____ to think a late paper will not be penalized.

16. When the king entered, servants were to _____ with respect.

17. The music of the military band heightened our feelings of _____.

18. The _____ of the speaker was Colombian, not Cuban.

19. When you lift weights, you _____ your muscles.

20. New shops herald a _____ of the downtrodden warehouse area.

Evaluating Internet Information

For researching anything from recent movie reviews to Shakespearean interpretations, the Internet offers easy access to up-to-date information. The disadvantage of Internet information, however, is that you must always question its reliability and credibility. Unlike the scholarly periodicals in libraries that are reviewed by experts, there are no gatekeepers on the Internet. Anyone from a Nobel Prize scientist to a paramilitary fanatic can purchase a website for approximately $100, self-publish, sound like an expert, and turn up in your search.

Be prepared to use your critical reading skills to evaluate Internet material. Question not only what is said, but also who wrote it and who paid for it.

Reader's TIP — Critically Evaluating Electronic Material

Ask the following questions to evaluate:

- What are the author's credentials in the field? Is the author affiliated with a university? Check this by noting professional titles in the preface or introduction, finding a biographical reference in the library, or searching the Internet for additional references to the same author.
- Who paid for the Web page? Check the home page for an address. Does the electronic address end in *edu, gov, org,* or *com*? Depending on the material, this sponsor could lend credibility or raise further questions.
- What is the purpose of the Web page? Is the purpose to educate or to sell a product, a service, or an idea? Check the links to investigate any hidden agendas.
- How do the biases of the author and the sponsor affect the material? Is the reasoning sound? Check the tone, assumptions, and evidence. What opposing views have been left out?

Refer to the website on the following page to complete Exercise 1.

EXERCISE 1

1. What is the purpose of this site? _____

2. What are the credentials of the author? _____

3. Who paid for the site? _____

4. Why are you inclined to believe or not believe the information in the letter?

_____

SanRafael.com

San Rafael
Nutrition Company, Inc.

Welcome to the new world of health and fitness, to the incredible benefits of looking great and feeling fantastic! Forget about sweating at the gym, tedious treadmills and crowded aerobic classes. What I have to offer is a no-hassle, easy way to drop unwanted pounds for a healthier, more energetic YOU!!

This is all made possible by the San Rafael Program™, my amazing combination of all natural ingredients, including Translite™ and ZX-12™. Until now, the patented formula in the San Rafael Program™ has been the secret of **Hollywood celebrities** and others whose careers depend on a youthful, healthy appearance. The **three simple steps** of the program have been clinically proven not only to help you lose weight fast and boost your energy level, but also to help rid your body of unhealthy toxins that upset your natural metabolic balance.

To find out more about the astounding results made possible by the San Rafael Program™, click on *Info*. To order samples or to get your own supply of this fantastic product, click on *Shopping*. To find out how you can enjoy the advantages of better health as well as the financial benefits of becoming a distributor of the San Rafael Program™, click on *Network*.

Whatever option you choose, I want to welcome you to a better, healthier life and to becoming a member of the San Rafael family!

Sincerely,

Marilyn Obado

Marilyn Obado
President
San Rafael Nutrition Co., Inc.

| Info | Shopping | Network |

EXERCISE 2

Search the Internet for a website that sells antiaging products, such as creams that claim to prevent wrinkles or vitamin concoctions that claim to enhance vitality. Print the page, then make a list of the claims you feel are exaggerated and not supported by facts.

APPENDIX 1

Spelling Confusing Words

A president of the United States once said, "Damn a man who can't spell a word but one way." Nevertheless, college professors tend to expect one official spelling for a word. Unfortunately, no "golden rules" of spelling yield perfect results. There are a few spelling rules, but none is without exception. The following four rules may help you get through some rough spots.

RULE 1 Use *i* before *e* except after *c*.

believe	ceiling	receipt
grief	conceited	priest
cashier	yield	piece

Exceptions: height, either, leisure, efficient

RULE 2 Drop the final *e* when adding a suffix that begins with a vowel.

hope + ing = hoping

believe + ing = believing

nice + est = nicest

Keep the final *e* when adding a suffix that begins with a consonant.

use + ful = useful

retire + ment = retirement

lone + some = lonesome

RULE 3 When a word ends in a consonant plus *y*, change the *y* to *i* to add a suffix.

lazy + ness = laziness

penny + less = penniless

marry + age = marriage

RULE 4 Double the final consonant when all of the following apply.

a. The word is one syllable or is accented on the last syllable.
b. The word ends in a consonant preceded by a vowel.
c. The suffix begins with a vowel.

hop + ing = hopping

skip + ing = skipping

repel + ent = repellent

APPENDIX 2) Sample Textbook Chapter

As a further practice exercise, we present Chapter 14 of John R. Walker's *Introduction to Hospitality*, Fifth Edition. No knowledge of the rest of that book is needed to fully understand this chapter. The superscript numbers in the text refer readers to the chapter's endnotes, which appear on page 490 of the chapter. As you read, organize your study according to the strategies in the previous chapters, and use the six thinking strategies: predict, picture, relate, monitor, correct, and annotate. Take notes on what you want to remember.

CHAPTER 14

Leadership and Management

OBJECTIVES

After reading and studying this chapter, you should be able to:

- Identify the characteristics and practices of leaders and managers.

- Define *leadership* and *management*.

- Differentiate between leadership and management.

- Describe the key management functions.

467

Leadership

Our fascination with **leadership** goes back many centuries. Lately, however, it has come into prominence in the hospitality, tourism, and other industries as these industries strive for perfection in the delivery of services and products in an increasingly competitive environment. Leaders can and do make a difference when measuring a company's success.

One person working alone can accomplish few tasks or goals. You have probably already experienced being part of a group that had good leadership. It might have been with a school, social, sporting, church, or other group in which the leader made a difference. The reverse might also be true: You may have been in a group with ineffective leadership. Few groups can accomplish much without an individual who acts as an effective leader. The leader can and often does have a significant influence on the group and its direction.

Characteristics and Practices of Leaders

So, what are the ingredients that result in leadership excellence? If you look at the military for examples of leadership excellence, you see that leaders can be identified by certain characteristics. For example, the *U.S. Guidebook for Marines* lists the following leadership traits:

- Courage
- Decisiveness
- Dependability
- Endurance
- Enthusiasm
- Initiative
- Unselfishness

- Integrity
- Judgment
- Justice
- Knowledge
- Loyalty
- Tact

A Marine officer would likely choose integrity as the most important trait. Integrity has been defined as "doing something right even though no one may be aware of it."

In addition to these leadership traits, the following identifiable practices are common to leaders:

1. *Challenge the process* Be active, not passive; search for opportunities; experiment and take risks.
2. *Inspire a shared vision* Create a vision; envision the future; enlist others.
3. *Enable others to act* Do not act alone; foster collaboration; strengthen others.
4. *Model the way* Plan; set examples; strive for small wins.
5. *Encourage the heart* Share the passion; recognize individual contributions; celebrate accomplishments.

Definitions of Leadership

Because of the complexities of leadership, the different types of leadership, and individual perceptions of leaders, leadership has several definitions. Many definitions share commonalities, but there are also differences. In terms of hospitality leadership, the following definition is appropriate: "Leading is the process by which a person with vision is able to influence the activities and outcomes of others in a desired way."

Leaders know what they want and why they want it—and they are able to communicate those desires to others to gain their cooperation and support. Leadership theory and practice has evolved over time to a point where current industry practitioners may be identified as transactional or transformational leaders.[1]

INTRODUCING HERB KELLEHER

Former CEO of Southwest Airlines

Herb Kelleher, who recently gave up the titles of chairman and CEO to two other Southwest executives, is the living embodiment of the phrase "one of a kind." With his charismatic personality, he is a person who leaves a distinctive mark on whatever he does. Since the birth of Southwest Airlines in 1971 (actually, Rollin W. King, a banking client of Herb's at the time, conceived Southwest Airlines after he had drawn, on a cocktail napkin, a triangle connecting Texas's three major cities: Dallas, Houston, and San Antonio), Herb Kelleher—"Herb" to even his most distant acquaintances—nurtured Southwest Airlines into the seventh largest airline. The company has been profitable every year since 1973. When other carriers lost billions or were struggling with bankruptcy, Southwest was the only company that remained consistently profitable—a record unmatched in the U.S. airline industry—cheerfully pursuing its growth plans by buying more planes, expanding into new cities, and hiring personnel. Southwest is also a model of efficiency: It is a multiple-time winner of the U.S. Department of Transportation's Triple Crown, a monthly citation for the best on-time performance, fewest lost bags, and fewest overall complaints. Kelleher's operation, based on flights covering relatively short distances for prices that are sometimes shockingly low, is likely to experience rapid growth and become even more of a leading power.

One of the keys to this success lies in the company's mission. Southwest Airlines aims at providing cheap, simple, and focused airline service. Kelleher devoted enormous attention to thousands of small decisions, all designed to achieve simplicity. Among these small but tremendously strategic decisions were the removal of closets at the front of the planes to improve passengers' speed in boarding and departing and no onboard food, except snacks, which is justified by the number of short flights (those of about 400 miles). Southwest also refused full participation on computerized reservations systems used by travel agents. More than 80 percent of all Southwest tickets are sold directly to customers, saving the company millions annually. There is no assigned seating and no first-class seating. Planes have been

continued

INTRODUCING HERB KELLEHER (continued)

standardized: Southwest operates only one type of aircraft, the 737, which simplifies flight crew training and maintenance personnel training.

These relatively minor privations have their positive counterpart in the fact that Southwest ground crew can turn around a plane at the gate in about twenty minutes! The airline's customers especially appreciate its low fares and on-time schedules.

Who is behind all this? The airline's success is credited to Kelleher's unorthodox personality and entrepreneurial management style. Born and raised in New Jersey, he was the son of the general manager of Campbell Soups, Inc. He began to show leadership qualities as student body president both in high school and in college. From his original idea of becoming a journalist, Kelleher shifted his goal to the practice of law. By the mid-1960s, he was successfully practicing in San Antonio, Texas, his wife's hometown. However, he was always seeking the possibility of starting a venture of his own. The big chance came in 1966 when a banker client, Rollin King, suggested that Texas needed a short-haul commuter airline. That was the trigger: Southwest was born in 1971.

While CEO, Herb directly supervised his business, personally approving expenses over $1,000. His outstanding hands-on efforts also led to unusually good labor–management relations, on the basis of the motto "People are the most important of resources." In fact, he managed to establish a strong bond of loyalty between employees and their company that may have disappeared elsewhere in the American corporate environment.

He still represents some sort of a father figure to SWA, as well as the jester, and the "Lord of Ha-Ha." The effort that he was able to get out of his employees made the real difference. Unlike workers at most other carriers, Southwest employees are willing to pitch in no matter what the task. For example, a reservations sales clerk in Dallas took a call from an anxious customer who was putting his eighty eight-year-old mother aboard a flight to St. Louis. The woman was quite frail, the fellow explained, and he wasn't quite sure she could handle the change of planes in Tulsa. "No sweat!" replied the clerk. "I'll fly with her as far as Tulsa and make sure she gets safely on the St. Louis flight."

Kelleher's outstanding leadership ability is also demonstrated by his long-term thinking. He gathered a top-rank team of successors, which will guarantee the airline's future prosperity. Kelleher is the leader who inspires, the amiable uncle to consult, the cheerleader who motivates, and the clown who spreads cheer. There are many great stories about Herb Kelleher; this is one of the most popular: Southwest was being threatened by an aviation services company over the advertising slogan "Plane Smart." Instead of incurring huge attorneys' fees and dealing with months-long litigation, the two CEOs agreed to settle the matter with an arm-wrestling contest. Herb actually lost the contest, but the other CEO had so much fun that the lawsuit was dropped. Both companies saved a bundle in legal fees.

Transactional Leadership

Transactional leadership is viewed as a process by which a leader is able to bring about desired actions from others by using certain behaviors, rewards, or incentives. In essence, an exchange or transaction takes place between leader and follower. Figure 14–1 shows the transactional leadership model. This concept illustrates the coming together of the leader, the situation, and the followers. A hotel general manager who pressures the food and beverage director to achieve certain goals in exchange for a bonus is an example of someone practicing transactional leadership.

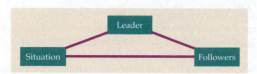

Figure 14–1 • Transactional Leadership Model.

Transformational Leadership

Leadership involves looking for ways to bring about longer-term, higher-order changes in follower behavior. This brings us to transformational leadership. The term **transformational leadership** is used to describe the process of eliciting performance above and beyond normal expectations. A transformational leader is one who inspires others to reach beyond themselves and do more than they originally thought possible; this is accomplished by raising their commitment to a shared vision of the future.

Transformational leaders practice a hands-on philosophy, not in terms of performing the day-to-day tasks of subordinates, but in developing and encouraging their followers individually. Transformational leadership involves three important factors:

1. Charisma
2. Individual consideration
3. Intellectual stimulation

Of course, it is also possible to be a charismatic transformational leader as well as a transactional leader. Although this does involve a measurable amount of effort, these leaders are guaranteed to rake in success throughout their careers.

Examples of Excellence in Leadership

Dr. Martin Luther King Jr. was one of the most charismatic transformational leaders in history. King dedicated his life to achieving rights for all citizens by nonviolent methods. His dream of how society could be was shared by millions of Americans. In 1964, Dr. King won the Nobel Peace Prize.

Another transformational leader is Herb Kelleher, former president, CEO, and current board

Martin Luther King Jr. One of the Most Charismatic Transformational Leaders of the Twentieth Century, Giving His Famous "I Have A Dream" Speech

member of Southwest Airlines, who is profiled in this chapter. He was able to inspire his followers to pursue his corporate vision and reach beyond themselves to give Southwest Airlines that something extra that set it apart from its competitors.

Kelleher recognizes that the company does not exist merely for the gratification of its employees. He knows that Southwest Airlines must perform and must be profitable. However, he believes strongly that valuing individuals for themselves is the best way to attain exceptional performance. Passengers who fly Southwest Airlines may have seen Herb Kelleher because he travels frequently and previously was likely to be found serving drinks, fluffing pillows, or just wandering up and down the aisle, talking to passengers. The success of Southwest and the enthusiasm of its employees indicate that Herb Kelleher achieved his goal of weaving together individual and corporate interests so that all members of the Southwest family benefit. Kelleher is a great transformational leader who is able to lead by visioning, inspiring, empowering, and communicating.[2]

In their fascinating book *Lessons in Leadership: Perspectives for Hospitality Industry Success*, Bill Fisher, former president and CEO of the American Hotel & Lodging Association and currently Darden Eminent Scholar at the University of Central Florida, and Charles Bernstein, editor of *Nation's Restaurant News*, interviewed more than 100 industry leaders and asked each to give advice in an up-close-and-personal manner. Here is an example of the leaders' answers:

"Experience is a hard teacher. It gives the test first, and then you learn the lesson." Richard P. Mayer, former chairman and CEO of Kentucky Fried Chicken and president of General Foods Corporation, says that the key traits and factors that he looks for in assessing talent include the following:

- Established personal goals
- The drive and ambition to attain those goals, tempered and strengthened with integrity
- Proven analytical and communications skills
- Superior interpersonal capabilities
- A sense of humor
- An awareness and appreciation of the world beyond her or his business specialty
- Receptivity to ideas (no matter the source)
- A genuine, deep commitment to the growth and profitability of the business

The essence of success has as many meanings as there are people to ponder it. One concept of success is to couple one's personal and family interests, dreams, and aspirations with a business or professional career such that they complement and fortify each other. Another aspect of leadership is the ability to motivate others in a hospitality working environment; decision making is also essential. These are discussed later in the chapter.

FOCUS ON LEADERSHIP

Leadership—The Basis for Management

William Fisher, Darden Eminent Scholar in Restaurant Management, author and former executive vice president of the National Restaurant Association and the American Hotel & Lodging Association

The concept and practice of leadership as it applies to management carries a fascination and attraction for most people. We all like to think we have some leadership qualities and we strive to develop them. We look at leaders in all walks of life, seeking to identify which qualities, traits, and skills they possess so that we can emulate them. A fundamental question remains: What is the essence of leadership that results in successful management as opposed to failed management? At least part of the answer can be found within the word itself.

1. *Loyalty.* Leadership starts with a loyalty quadrant: loyalty to one's organization and its mission, loyalty to organizational superiors, loyalty to subordinates, and loyalty to oneself. Loyalty is multidirectional, running up and down in the organization. When everyone practices it, loyalty bonds occur, which drives high morale. Loyalty to oneself is based on maintaining a sound body, mind, and spirit so that one is always "riding the top of the wave" in service to others.

2. *Excellence.* Leaders know that excellence is a value, not an object. They strive for both excellence and success. Excellence is the measurement you make of yourself in assessing what you do and how well you do it; success is an external perception that others have of you.

3. *Assertiveness.* Leaders possess a mental and physical intensity that causes them to seek control, take command, assume the mantle of responsibility, and focus on the objective(s). Leaders do not evidence self-doubt as they are comfortable within themselves that what they are doing is right, which, in turn, gives them the courage to take action.

4. *Dedication.* Leaders are dedicated in mind, body, and spirit to their organization and to achievement. They are action oriented, not passive, and prefer purposeful activity to the status quo. They possess an aura or charisma that sets them apart from others with whom they interact, always working in the best interest of their organization.

5. *Enthusiasm.* Leaders are their own best cheerleaders on behalf of their organization and people. They exude enthusiasm and instill it in others to the point of contagion. Their style may be one of poise, stability, clear vision, and articulate speech, but their bristling enthusiasm undergirds their every waking moment.

6. *Risk management.* Leaders realize that risk taking is part of their management perch. They manage risk, rather than letting it manage them, knowing full well that there are no guaranteed outcomes, no foregone conclusions, no preordained results when one is dealing with the future. Nonetheless, they measure risk, adapt to it, control it, and surmount it.

7. *Strength.* Leaders possess an inner fiber of stamina, fortitude, and vibrancy that gives them a mental toughness, causing them to withstand interruption, crises, and unforeseen circumstances that would slow down or immobilize most people. Leaders become all the more energized in the face of surprises.

8. *Honor.* Leaders understand they will leave a legacy, be it good, bad, or indifferent. True leaders recognize that all their relationships and actions are based on the highest standard of honor and integrity. They do the right things correctly, shun short-term, improper expediency, and set the example for others with high-mindedness, professional bearing, and unassailable character.

continued

FOCUS ON LEADERSHIP (continued)

9. *Inspiration.* Leaders don't exist without followers. People will follow leaders who inspire them to reach beyond the normal and ordinary to new levels of accomplishment, new heights of well-being, and new platforms for individual, organizational, and societal good. Inspiration is what distinguishes a leader from a mere position holder, as the leader can touch the heart, mind, and soul of others.

10. *Performance.* At the end of the day, leader–managers rise or fall on the most critical of all measurements: their performance. Results come first, but the ways in which results are achieved are also crucial to sustaining a leader's role. Many dictators don't last despite results, and many charismatics don't last despite personal charm.

Putting the ten elements together spells LEADERSHIP! Always remember, if you want to develop a leadership quality, act as though you already possess it!

Demands Placed on Leaders

Demands on a leader in the hospitality industry include those made by owners, the corporate office, guests, employees, regulatory agencies, and competitors (Figure 14–2). In response to many demands, the leader must balance two additional forces: how much energy to expend on getting results and how much to expend on relationships (Figure 14–3).

Applied social scientists such as Peter Drucker, powerful industry leaders such as Bill Marriott, and public service leaders such as former New York mayor Rudolph Giuliani all seem to have common traits, among which are the following:

1. High ego strength
2. Ability to think strategically
3. Orientation toward the future

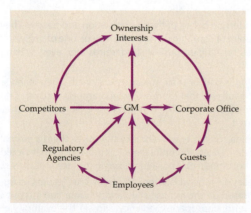

Figure 14–2 • Dynamics of Demands on General Managers in the Hospitality Industry.

Figure 14–3 • Amount of Energy the General Manager Needs to Spend on Getting Results and Maintaining Relationships.

4. A belief in certain fundamental principles of human behavior

5. Strong connections that they do not hesitate to display

6. Political astuteness

7. Ability to use power both for efficiency and for the larger good of the organization

Leaders vary in their values, managerial styles, and priorities. Peter Drucker, the renowned management scholar, author, and consultant of many years, has discussed with hundreds of leaders their roles, goals, and performance. These discussions took place with leaders of large and small organizations, with for-profit and volunteer organizations. Interestingly, Drucker observes:

> All the leaders I have encountered—both those I worked with and those I watched—realized:
>
> 1. The only definition of a leader is someone who has followers. Some people are thinkers. Some are prophets. Both roles are important and badly needed. But without followers, there can be no leaders.
>
> 2. An effective leader is not someone who is loved or admired. She or he is someone whose followers do the right things. Popularity is not leadership. Results are.
>
> 3. Leaders are highly visible. They therefore set examples.
>
> 4. Leadership is not about rank, privileges, titles, or money. It is about responsibility.[3]

Drucker adds that regardless of their enormous diversity with respect to personality, style, abilities, and interests, effective leaders all behave in much the same way:

1. They did not start out with the question "What do I want?" They started out asking, "What needs to be done?"

2. Then they asked, "What can and should I do to make a difference?" This has to be something that both needs to be done and fits the leader's strengths and the way she or he is most effective.

3. They constantly asked, "What are the organization's mission and goals? What constitutes performance and results in this organization?"

4. They were extremely tolerant of diversity in people and did not look for carbon copies of themselves. It rarely even occurred to them to ask, "Do I like or dislike this person?" But they were totally—fiendishly—intolerant when it came to a person's performance, standards, and values.

5. They were not afraid of strength in their associates. They gloried in it. Whether they had heard of it or not, their motto was the one Andrew Carnegie wanted to have put on his tombstone: "Here lies a man who attracted better people into his service than he was himself."

6. One way or another, they submitted themselves to the mirror test—that is, they made sure the person they saw in the mirror in the morning was the kind of person they wanted to be, respect, and believe in. This way they

fortified themselves against the leader's greatest temptations—to do things that are popular rather than right and to do petty, mean, sleazy things.[4]

Finally, these leaders were not preachers; they were doers.

The most effective leaders share a number of skills, and these skills are always related to dealing with employees. The following suggestions outline an approach to becoming a hotel leader rather than just a manager:

- *Be decisive*. Hotel managers are confronted with dozens of decisions every day. Obviously, you should use your best judgment to resolve the decisions that come to roost at your doorstep. As a boss, make the decisions that best meet both your objectives and your ethics and then make your decisions known.

- *Follow through*. Never promise what you can't deliver, and never build false hopes among your employees. Once expectations are dashed, respect for and the reputation of the boss are shot.

- *Select the best*. A boss, good or bad, is carried forward by the work of his or her subordinates. One key to being a good boss is to hire the people who have the best potential to do what you need them to do. Take the time and effort to screen, interview, and assess the people who have not only the skills that you require, but also the needed values.

- *Empower employees*. Give people the authority to interact with the customer. The more important people feel, the better they work.

- *Enhance career development*. Good bosses recognize that most of their people want to improve themselves. However, career development is a two-edged sword: If we take the initiative to train and develop our people properly, then the competition is likely to hire them. The only way a boss can prevent the loss of productive workers looking for career development is to provide opportunities for growth within the organization.

In recent years, the role of the hotel general manager has changed from that of being a congenial host, knowledgeable about the niceties of hotelmanship, to that of a multigroup pleaser. Guests, employees, owners, and community should all be not only satisfied but delighted with the operation's performance.

Many general managers (GMs) are so bogged down with meetings, reports, and "putting out fires" that they hardly have any time to spend with guests. One GM who makes time is Richard Riley, GM of the fabulous Shangri-La Hotel Makati in Manila, the Philippines. Richard extends an invitation for guests to visit with him in the hotel lobby between 5:00 and 7:00 P.M. every Thursday. As GM of a luxury Caribbean resort in Barbados, West Indies, the author personally greeted every guest to the property. Obviously, there is a difference between a small resort and a large city hotel. Resort guests stay for at least two, sometimes four, weeks in high season, so they need the individual attention.

▶ Check Your Knowledge

1. What three factors does transformational leadership involve?
2. Define *leadership*.
3. Describe some examples of leadership.
4. Explain the demands placed on leaders.

Hospitality Management

Managers plan, organize, make decisions, communicate, motivate, and control the efforts of a group to accomplish predetermined goals. Management also establishes the direction the organization will take. Sometimes this is done with the help of employees or outside consultants, such as marketing research specialists. Managers obtain the necessary resources for the goals to be accomplished, and then they supervise and monitor group and individual progress toward goal accomplishment.

Managers, such as presidents and chief executive officers, who are responsible for the entire company, tend to focus most of their time on strategic planning and the organization's mission. They also spend time organizing and controlling the activities of the corporation. Most top managers do not get involved in the day-to-day aspects of the operation. These duties and responsibilities fall to the middle and supervisory management. In hospitality lingo, one would not expect Bill Marriott to pull a shift behind the bar at the local Marriott hotel. Although capable, his time and expertise are used in shaping the company's future. Thus, although the head bartender and Bill Marriott may both be considered management, they require slightly different skills to be effective and efficient managers.

What Is Management?

Management is simply what managers do: plan, organize, make decisions, communicate, motivate, and control. *Management* is defined as "the process of working with and through others to accomplish organizational goals in an efficient and effective way." In looking at this statement, you can see that the functions of

INTRODUCING STEVE PINETTI

Senior VP Sales and Marketing, Kimpton Hotels and Restaurants

Steve Pinetti grew up in the San Francisco Bay area, worked for Hilton and Hyatt, taught at all the San Francisco Bay area colleges and universities, founded his own marketing company, and was one of Bill Kimpton's first partners in founding Kimpton Hotels and Restaurants. Steve now is the senior vice president of sales and marketing for Kimpton Hotels and Restaurants. Steve oversees branding efforts, sales, distribution, customer relationship management (CRM), Internet presence, public relations, strategic partnerships, and new hotel openings. Steve has an interesting challenge because both existing large hotel chains and new hotel companies claim to be the "boutique hotel" leader. In fact, Kimpton invented the concept in 1981: a unique, independent boutique hotel paired with a chef-driven/specialty restaurant. Says Steve, "The need to stay ahead of the growing competition as well as on top our own game is never ending. We stay tuned to our customers' behavior, needs, and purchasing process to better understand where consumer thinking, influences and spending are headed.

"Because word of mouth is the number one source of our business, we need to stay close to what our guests want, need, say, and do. We have developed a skill set around niche marketing. Since the advent of search on the Net, we have been able to get out from the shadow of the large bully brands and market to consumers who put value on personal preferences and individual style in all they do—especially travel. Since 9/11 we have found that there is a movement toward thinking about today versus the future. People are focusing their thinking on what's important to me today. What is that 'thing' I keep putting off—now is the time to do it. Wellness, pampering, learning nuggets of information (how to read a painting), and discovery skills (cooking classes) are what are becoming more important. These are the types of people looking for and staying at Kimpton Hotels". The biggest project on Steve's plate is the recent rollout of the new Kimpton brand. "Getting every employee to understand the Kimpton brand, its promise, and the guests' expectations around our promise is proving to be a very large, ongoing project. The other half of this proposition is making sure every guest in every hotel each day knows he or she is in a hotel that is part of a larger collection—Kimpton Hotels.

"You need to do the basics in order for your business to survive, but you also need to take calculated risks in order to outdistance and separate yourself from the competition as well as gain notice by the unchained shopper. Taking risks is not in one's human nature, but it is something we highly value at Kimpton. By taking risks we have come up with some of the firsts in our industry. They include social wine hour every night in every Kimpton hotel, tall rooms for tall travelers, complimentary goldfish, first company to offer complimentary high-speed access, celebrity suites (Jerry Garcia, Carlos Santana), specialty suites with workout equipment, and Eco Floors."

Advice

Anything that requires the understanding and implementation of employees needs to be fully communicated well before being instituted operationally. The communication process around understating why and how as well as the benefits to all involved is more important than the actual action. It creates buy-in and buy-off. It ensures that the people who are going to be responsible for implementing it or designing the process buy in versus inherit some program cooked up from the corporate offices.

Thoughts

Success comes from involving and harnessing all the technical and human resources available. It's vital to keep a balance in one's life between home, work, and self. You need to continue to maintain the basics yet reinvent yourself to keep up with trends and times.

management and working with and through the work of others are ongoing. Additionally, management involves getting efficient and effective results.

Efficiency is getting the most done with the fewest number of inputs. Managers work with scarce resources: money, people, time, and equipment. You can imagine the rush in the kitchen to be ready for a meal service. But it's not enough to just be efficient; management is also about being effective. **Effectiveness** is "doing the right thing." As an example, cooks do the right thing when they cook the food correctly according to the recipe and have it ready when needed.

Who Are Managers?

The changing nature of organizations and work has, in many hospitality organizations, blurred the lines of distinction between managers and nonmanagerial employees. Many traditional jobs now include managerial activities, especially when teams are used. For instance, team members often develop plans, make decisions, and monitor their own performance. This is the case with total quality management.

So, how do we define who managers are? A manager is someone who works with and manages others' activities to accomplish organizational goals in an efficient and effective way. Managers are often classified into three levels: **front-line managers** are the lowest-level managers; they manage the work of line employees. They may also be called supervisors. A front-office supervisor, for example, takes charge of a shift and supervises the guest service agents on the shift.

Middle managers are akin to department heads; they fall between front-line managers and top management. They are responsible for short- to medium-range plans, and they establish goals and objectives to meet these goals. They manage the work of front-line managers.

Top managers are responsible for making medium- to long-range plans and for establishing goals and strategies to meet those goals. Figure 14–4 shows the three levels of management plus nonmanagerial employees.

Key Management Functions

The key management functions are planning, organizing, decision making, communicating, human resources and motivating, and controlling. These management functions are not conducted in isolation; rather they are interdependent and frequently happen simultaneously or at least overlap. Figure 14–5 shows the key management functions leading to goal accomplishment.

Top Managers
Middle Managers
Front-line Managers
Nonmanagerial Associates

Figure 14–4 • Three Levels of Management Plus Nonmanagerial Associates.

Figure 14–5 • Key Management Functions Leading to Goal Accomplishment.

Hospitality companies exist to serve a particular purpose, and someone has to determine the vision, mission, goals, and strategies to reach or exceed the goals. That someone is management. The **planning** function involves setting the company's goals and developing plans to meet or exceed those goals. Once plans are complete, **organizing** is the process of deciding what needs to be done, who will do it, how the tasks will be grouped, who reports to whom, and who makes decisions.

Decision making is a key management function. The success of all hospitality companies, whether large, multinational corporations or sole proprietorships, depends on the quality of the decision making. Decision making includes determining the vision, mission, goals, and objectives of the company. Decision making also includes scheduling employees, determining what to put on the menu, and responding to guest needs.

Communication with and motivation of individuals and groups are required to get the job done. **Human resources and motivating** involves attracting and retaining the best employees and keeping morale high.

Controlling is the final management function that brings everything full circle. After the goals are set and the plans formulated, management then organizes, communicates, and motivates the resources required to complete the job. Controlling includes the setting of standards and comparing actual results with these standards. If significant deviations are seen, they are investigated and corrective action taken to get performance back on target. This scientific process of monitoring, comparing, and correcting is the controlling function and is necessary to ensure that there are no surprises and that no one is guessing.

Managerial Skills

In addition to the management functions of forecasting, planning, organizing, communicating, motivating, and controlling, managers also need other major skills: conceptual, interpersonal, and technical.

Conceptual skills enable top managers to view the corporation as a complete entity and yet understand how it is split into departments to achieve specific goals. Conceptual skills allow a top manager to view the entire corporation, especially the interdependence of the various departments.

Managers need to lead, influence, communicate, supervise, coach, and evaluate employees' performances. This necessitates a high level of interpersonal human skills. The abilities to build teams and work with others are human skills that successful managers need to cultivate.

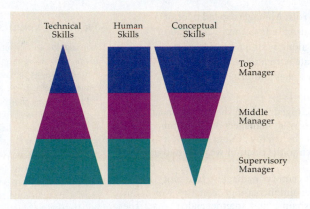

Figure 14–6 • Management Skill Areas.

Managers need to have the technical skills required to understand and use modern techniques, methods, equipment, and procedures. These skills are more important for lower levels of management. As a manager rises through the ranks, the need for technical skills decreases and the need for conceptual skills increases.

You next need to realize the critical importance of the corporate philosophy, culture, and values, and a corporation's mission, goals, and objectives. Figure 14–6 shows the degree of managerial skills required by top managers, middle managers, and supervisory managers.

The Manager's Changing Role

Managers may still have subordinates, but today's successful manager takes more of a team leader/coach approach. There are, of course, other ways to "slice and dice" what managers do. For example, managers don't just plan, organize, make decisions, communicate, motivate, and control. They wear a variety of hats, including the following:

- *Figurehead role.* Every manager spends some time performing ceremonial duties. For example, the president of a corporation might have to greet important business guests or clients or represent the corporation by attending dinners.

- *Leader role.* Every manager should be a leader, coaching, motivating, and encouraging employees.

- *Liaison role.* Managers spend a lot of time in contact with people in other departments both within the organization and externally. An example would be the sales manager liaising with the rooms division director.

- *Spokesperson role.* The manager is often the spokesperson for the organization. For example, a manager may host a college class visit to the property.

- *Negotiator role.* Managers spend a lot of time negotiating. For example, the head of a company along with qualified lawyers may negotiate with a union representative to establish wages and benefits for employees.

These roles, together with the management functions, encompass what managers do. Remember, managers need to be many things—often in quick succession—even to the point of wearing two or more hats at once.

Twenty-first-century managers face not only a more demanding and increasingly complex world, but also a more dynamic and interdependent one. The "global village" is a reality, and sociocultural traditions and values must be understood and diversity respected and encouraged by future managers. The two most important changes going on right now are the technological advances and the internationalization of hospitality and tourism. The extent to which you as a future **leader–manager** can master these events and functions will determine your future.

The manager's role is not only internal but also external. For instance, a manager must be responsive to market needs and income generation. Managers must continually strive to be innovative by realizing efficiencies in their respective areas of responsibility through process improvement—for example, by determining how to reduce long check-in lines at airports and hotels. Some companies use innovative and creative ways to streamline the check-in procedures to make the process a more worthwhile experience for the guests. Disney, for instance, uses the creative approach of sending Mickey and the gang to entertain the guests while they stand in line.

A General Manager's Survival Kit

Ali Kasiki is a top-level manager at the Peninsula Beverly Hills, California. He holds the title of managing director and is involved in creating and implementing broad and comprehensive changes that affect the entire organization. Ali offers his list:

- Know yourself, your own core competencies, and your values.
- Hire a seasoned management team.
- Build barriers of entry; that is, make yourself indispensable.
- Be very flexible.

You, Too, Are a Manager

Your classmates have just voted you to be the leader–manager of the summer study-abroad trip to France. None of you knows much about France or how to get there, what to do when you get there, and so on. Where would you start? (Resist the temptation to delegate the whole trip to a travel agent, please.)

You might start by thinking through what you need to do in terms of planning, organizing, deciding, communicating, motivating, and controlling. What sort of plans will you need? Among other things, you'll need to plan the dates your group is leaving and returning, the cities and towns you'll visit, the airline you'll take there and back, how the group will get around France, and where you'll stay when you're there. As you can imagine, plans like these are very important: You would not want to arrive at Orly Airport with a group of friends who are depending on you and not know what to do next.

Realizing how much work is involved—and that you cannot do it all and still maintain good grades—you get help. You divide up the work and create an organization by asking someone to check airline schedules and prices, another person to check hotel prices, and someone else the sights to see and the transportation needs. However, the job won't get done with the group members simply working by themselves. Each person requires guidance and coordination from you: The person making the airline bookings can't confirm the bookings unless she knows what city and airport the trip will originate in. Similarly, the person making the hotel arrangements can't make any firm bookings until he knows what cities are being visited. To improve communications, you could set up regular meetings with e-mail updates between meetings. Leadership and motivation could be a challenge because two of the group members do not get along well. So, ensuring that everyone stays focused and positive will be a challenge.

Of course, you'll have to make sure the whole project remains "in control." If something can go wrong, it often will, and that's certainly the case when groups of people are traveling together. Everything needs to be double-checked. In other words, managing is something managers do almost every day, often without even knowing it.

Source: Adapted from Gary Dessler, *A Framework for Management* (Upper Saddle River, NJ: Prentice Hall, 2002) 8.

- Get close to your guests and owners to define reality versus perception.
- Show leadership, from both the top and the bottom.
- Delegate. There is no way you can survive without delegation.
- Appeal to trends.
- Trust your instincts.
- Take risks and change the ground rules.
- Don't become overconfident.
- Look successful, or people will think you're not.
- Manage the future—it is the best thing you can do. Bring the future to the present.[5]

Distinction between Leadership and Management

Managing is the formal process in which organizational objectives are achieved through the efforts of subordinates. Leading is the process by which a person with vision is able to influence the behavior of others in some desired way. Although managers have power by virtue of the positions they hold, organizations seek managers who are leaders by virtue of their personalities, their experience, and so on. The differences between management and leadership can be illustrated as follows:

Managers

- Working in the system
- React
- Control risks
- Enforce organizational rules
- Seek and then follow direction
- Control people by pushing them in the right direction
- Coordinate effort

Leaders

- Working on the system
- Create opportunities
- Seek opportunities
- Change organizational rules
- Provide a vision to believe in and strategic alignment
- Motivate people by satisfying basic human needs
- Inspire achievement and energize people[6]

▶ Check Your Knowledge

1. What is management and what are the three management skill areas?
2. Explain levels of management.
3. Describe the key management functions.
4. What is the distinction between leadership and management?

Ethics

Ethics is a set of moral principles and values that people use to answer questions about right and wrong. Because ethics is also about our personal value system, there are people with value systems different from ours. Where did the value system originate? What happens if one value system is different from another? Fortunately, certain universal guiding principles are agreed on by virtually all religions, cultures, and societies. The foundation of all principles is that all people's rights are important and should not be violated. This belief is central to civilized societies; without it, chaos would reign.

Today, people have few moral absolutes; they decide situationally whether it is acceptable to steal, lie, or drink and drive. They seem to think that whatever is right is what works best for the individual. In a country blessed with so many diverse cultures, you might think it is impossible to identify common standards of ethical behavior. However, among sources from many different times and places, such as the Bible, Aristotle's *Ethics*, William Shakespeare's *King Lear*, the Koran, and the *Analects* of Confucius, you'll find the following basic moral values: integrity, respect for human life, self-control, honesty, and courage. Cruelty is wrong. All the world's major religions support a version of the Golden Rule: Do unto others as you would have them do to you.[7]

In the foreword to *Ethics in Hospitality Management*, edited by Stephen S. J. Hall,[8] Dean Emeritus of Cornell University, Robert A. Beck poses this question: "Is overbooking hotel rooms and airline seats ethical? How does one compare the legal responsibilities of the innkeeper and the airline manager to the moral obligation?" He also asks, What is a fair or reasonable wage? A fair or reasonable return on investment? Is it fair or ethical to underpay employees for the benefit of investors?

English Common Law, on which American law is based, left such decisions to the "reasonable man." A judge would ask the jury, "Was this the act of a reasonable man?" Interestingly, what is considered ethical in one country may not be in another. For instance, in some countries it is considered normal to bargain for room rates; in others, bargaining would be considered bad form.

Ethics and morals have become an integral part of hospitality decisions, from employment (equal opportunity and affirmative action) to truth in menus. Many corporations and businesses have developed a code of ethics that all employees use to make decisions. This became necessary because too many managers were making decisions without regard for the impact of such decisions on others.

Stephen Hall is one of the pioneers of ethics in hospitality; he has developed a code of ethics for the hospitality and tourism industry:

1. We acknowledge ethics and morality as inseparable elements of doing business and will test every decision against the highest standards of honesty, legality, fairness, impunity, and conscience.

2. We will conduct ourselves personally and collectively at all times so as to bring credit to the hospitality and tourism industry.

3. We will concentrate our time, energy, and resources on the improvement of our own products and services and we will not denigrate our competition in the pursuit of our success.

4. We will treat all guests equally regardless of race, religion, nationality, creed, or sex.

5. We will deliver all standards of service and product with total consistency to every guest.

6. We will provide a totally safe and sanitary environment at all times for every guest and employee.

7. We will strive constantly, in words, actions, and deeds, to develop and maintain the highest level of trust, honesty, and understanding among guests, clients, employees, employers, and the public at large.

8. We will provide every employee at every level all the knowledge, training, equipment, and motivation required to perform his or her tasks according to our published standards.

9. We will guarantee that every employee at every level will have the same opportunity to perform, advance, and be evaluated against the same standard as all employees engaged in the same or similar tasks.

10. We will actively and consciously work to protect and preserve our natural environment and natural resources in all that we do.

11. We will seek a fair and honest profit, no more, no less.[9]

As you can see, it is vitally important for future hospitality and tourism professionals to abide by this code. Here are some ethical dilemmas in hospitality. What do you think about them?

Ethical Dilemmas in Hospitality

Previously, certain actions may not have been considered ethical, but management often looked the other way. A few scenarios follow that are not seen as ethical today and are against most companies' ethical policies.

1. As catering manager of a large banquet operation, the flowers for the hotel are booked through your office. The account is worth $15,000 per month. The florist offers you a 10 percent kickback. Given that your colleague at a sister hotel in the same company receives a good bonus and you do not,

despite having a better financial result, do you accept the kickback? If so, whom do you share it with?

2. As purchasing agent for a major hospitality organization, you are responsible for purchasing $5 million worth of perishable and nonperishable items. To get your business, a supplier, whose quality and price are similar to others, offers you a new automobile. Do you accept?

3. An order has come from the corporate office that guests from a certain part of the world may only be accepted if the reservation is taken from the embassy of the countries. One Sunday afternoon, you are duty manager and several limos with people from "that part of the world" request rooms for several weeks. You decline, even though there are available rooms. They even offer you a personal envelope, which they say contains $1,000. How do you feel about declining their request?

Trends in Leadership and Management

- Leading a more diverse group of associates.
- Many entry-level employees do not have basic job skills.
- An increasing need for training.
- The need to create leaders out of line managers.
- Managing sales revenue all the way to the bottom line.
- Establishing independent business units to make their own profit, or subcontracting out that department.
- Instead of keeping a person on payroll for a function that is only needed occasionally, outsourcing that service to specialists.
- Cutting down on full-time employees and hiring more part-time employees to avoid paying benefits.
- An increasing challenge to keep up with technological advances and their benefits.
- Social and environmental issues continuing to increase in importance.
- A greater emphasis placed on ethics.

CASE STUDY

Performance Standards

Charles and Nancy both apply for the assistant front office manager position at a 300-room upscale hotel. Charles has worked for a total of eight years in three different hotels and has been with this hotel for three months as a front office associate. Initially, he had a lot of enthusiasm. Lately, however, he has been dressing a bit sloppily and his figures, cash, and reports have been inaccurate. In addition, he is occasionally "rattled" by demanding guests.

Nancy recently graduated from college, with honors, with a degree in hospitality management. While attending college, she worked part-time as a front desk associate at a budget motel. Nancy does not have a lot of experience working in a hotel or in customer service in general, but she is quite knowledgeable as a result of her studies and is eager to begin her career.

It appears that Charles would have been considered a prime candidate for the office manager position because of his extensive experience in other hotels and his knowledge of the hotel's culture. In view of his recent performance, however, the rooms division manager will need to sit down with Charles to review his future career development track.

Discussion Questions

1. What are the qualifications for the job that should be considered for both applicants?
2. How should the discussion between the rooms division manager and Charles be handled? Make specific recommendations for the rooms division manager.
3. Who would be the better person for the job? Why?

CASE STUDY

Reluctant to Change

You have just been appointed assistant manager at an old, established, but busy, New York restaurant. Your employees respond to your suggested changes with, "We have always done it this way." The employees really do not know any other way of doing things.

Discussion Question

1. How should you handle this situation?

Summary

1. Leadership is defined as the process by which a person is able to influence the activities and outcomes of others in a desired way.
2. Contemporary leadership includes transactional and transformational types of leadership.
3. Increased demands placed on hospitality leaders include ownership, corporate, regulatory, employee, environmental, and social interests. Leaders must balance results and relationships.
4. Managing is the process of coordinating work activities so that they are completed efficiently and effectively with and through other people.
5. Leaders, according to Drucker, realize four things and behave in much the same way.
   a. A leader is someone who has followers— some people are thinkers, and some are prophets.
   b. An effective leader is not someone who is loved or admired, but rather someone whose followers do the right things. Popularity is not leadership; results are.
   c. Leaders are highly visible. Leaders set examples.
   d. Leadership is not about rank, privileges, titles, or money. It is about responsibility.
6. There are six key management functions: planning, organizing, decision making, communicating, motivating, and controlling. However, in addition to these functions, managers occasionally have to fill roles such as figurehead, leader, spokesperson, or negotiator.
7. The difference between management and leadership is that the former is the formal process in which organization objectives are achieved through the efforts of subordinates, and the latter is the process by which a person with vision is able to influence the behavior of others in some desired way.

Key Words and Concepts

communication
controlling
decision making
effectiveness
efficiency
ethics
front-line managers
human resources and motivating
leader–manager

leadership
management
managing
middle managers
organizing
planning
top managers
transactional leadership
transformational leadership

Review Questions

1. From the DVD, what is the most fun thing that John Saputo has done in a leadership capacity?
2. What kind of leader–manager will you be?
3. Give examples of the management functions as they apply to the hospitality industry.
4. Discuss the changing role of managers.
5. Define leadership and name the essential qualities of a good leader.
6. Distinguish between transactional and transformational leadership.

Internet Exercises

1. Organization: **WetFeet.com**
   Web site: www.wetfeet.com
   Summary: WetFeet.com is an organization dedicated to helping you make smarter career decisions. WetFeet.com provides inside insight on jobs and careers for both job seekers and recruiters. By all means, take the time to check this one out!
   Click the "Careers" icon and scroll down to "General Management." Answer the following questions.
   (a) What are the requirements for becoming a GM, and what tips does WetFeet.com have to offer?
   (b) The "Career Overview" section illustrates several attributes that managers have in common. In groups, list these attributes and discuss their significance.

2. Organization: **American Management Association**
   Web site: www.amanett.org
   Summary: The American Management Association (AMA), a practitioner-based organization, offers a wide range of management development programs for managers and organizations.
   Find the section titled "AMA Research." Choose two current reports. Read through these and make a bullet list of the key information. Then, write a description of how this information might affect the way a hospitality manager plans, organizes, makes decisions, communicates, motivates, and controls.

Apply Your Knowledge

Your resort has management vacancies for the following positions: executive chef, executive housekeeper, and front office manager. List the traits and characteristics that you consider essential and desirable for these positions.

Suggested Activity

Think of someone you admire as a leader. Make a list of the qualities that make him or her a good leader.

Endnotes

1. For a more detailed review of the many leadership theories, consult one of the many texts on the topic.
2. Jay R. Schrock, presentation to University of South Florida students and faculty, May 2, 2005.
3. This draws on Peter F. Drucker, Foreword, in *The Leader of the Future*, ed. F. Hesselbein et al. (San Francisco: Josey-Bass, 1996), xii–xiii.
4. Drucker, Foreword, ix.
5. Personal correspondence with Ali Kasiki. August 4, 2005.
6. Vadim Kotelnikov, Ten3 Business e-Coach, version 2005a, www.1000ventures.com.
7. www.religioustolerance.org. nettme.htm
8. Stephen S. Hall, ed., *Ethics in Hospitality Management: A Book of Readings* (East Lansing, MI: Educational Institute, American Hotel & Lodging Association, 1992), 75.
9. Hall, *Ethics in Hospitality Management*, 23.

APPENDIX 3

Word Parts: Prefixes, Roots, and Suffixes

WORD PART	MEANING	EXAMPLE
Prefixes		
a-, an-	without, not	atypical, anarchy
ab-	away, from	absent, abnormal
ad-	toward	advance, administer
ambi-, amphi-	both, around	ambiguous, amphibious
anna-	year	annual
anti-, contra-, ob-	against	antisocial, contradict
bene-, eu-	well, good	benefactor, eulogy
bi-, du-, di-	two or twice	bicycle, duet, dichotomy
cata-, cath-	down, downward	catacombs
cent-, hecto-	hundred	centipede
con-, com-, syn-	with, together	congregate, synthesis
de-	down, from	depose, detract
dec-, deca-	ten	decade
demi-, hemi-, semi-	half	hemisphere, semicircle
dia-	through	diameter, diagram
dis-, un-	not, opposite of	dislike, unnatural
dys-	ill, hard	dystrophy
ex-	out, from	exhale, expel
extra-	beyond, outside	extralegal
hyper-	above, excessive	hyperactive
hypo-	under	hypodermic
il-, im, in-	not	illogical, impossible
in-	in, into	inside, insert, invade
infra-	lower	infrared
inter-	between	intercede, interrupt
intra-	within	intramural
juxta-	next to	juxtaposition
mal-, mis-	wrong, ill	malformed, mislead
mill-	thousand	milligram
nove-, non-	nine	novena, nonagon
oct-, octo-	eight	octopus
omni-, pan-	all	omnipotent, pantheist
per-	through	perennial, pervade
peri-, circum-	around	perimeter, circumvent
poly-, multi-	many	polygamy, multiply
post-	after	postscript
pre-, ante-	before	prepared, antebellum
pro-	before, for	promoter
proto-	first	prototype
quad-, quatra-, tetra-	four	quadrilateral, tetrad
quint-, penta-	five	quintuplet, pentagon

WORD PART	MEANING	EXAMPLE
re-	back, again	review, reply
retro-	backward	retrogress, retrospect
sequ-	follow	sequence
sex-, hexa-	six	sextet, hexagon
sub-	under	submarine, subway
super-	above, over	supervise
temp-, tempo-, chrono-	time	tempo, chronological
trans-	across	translate, transcontinental
tri-	three	triple, triangle
uni-, mono-	one	unicorn, monocle
vice-	in place of	viceroy

Roots

alter, hap	to change	alteration, mishap
ama, philo	to love	amiable, philosophy
anima	breath, spirit	animate
aqua	water	aquarium, aqualung
aster, astro	star	disaster, astronomy
aud	to hear	audible, auditory
auto, ego	self	autonomy, egotist
bio	life	biology
cap	head	caption, capitulate
cap, capt	to take	capture
card, cor, cord	heart	cardiac, core, cordial
cosmo	order, universe	cosmonaut
cresc	to grow, increase	crescendo
cryp	secret, hidden	cryptogram
dent	teeth	dental
derma	skin	dermatologist
duc, duct	to lead	reduce, conduct
equ, iso	equal	equivocal, isometric
err, errat	to wander	erratic
ethno	race, tribe	ethnic
fac, fact	to do, make	manufacture
fract	to break	fracture
frater	brother	fraternity
gene	race, kind, sex	genetics, gender
grad, gres	to go, take steps	graduation, digress
gyn	woman	gynecologist
hab, habi	to have, hold	inhabit, habitual
helio, photo	sun, light	heliotrope, photograph
homo	man	homo sapiens
lic, list, liqu	to leave behind	derelict, relinquish
lith	stone	monolith
loc	place	location, local
log	speech, science	logic, dialogue
loquor	to speak	loquacious, colloquial
lum	light	illuminate
macro	large	macrocosm
manu	hand	manual, manuscript
mater	mother	maternity
med	middle	mediate
meter	to measure	barometer

WORD PART	MEANING	EXAMPLE
micro	small	microscope
miss, mit	to send, let go	admit, permission
morph	form	morphology
mort	to die	immortalize
mut, mutat	to change	mutation
nat	to be born	natal, native
neg, negat	to say no, deny	negative, renege
nym, nomen	name	synonym, nomenclature
ocul	eye	oculist, monocle
ortho	right, straight	orthodox, orthodontist
osteo	bone	osteopath
pater	father	paternal
path	disease, feeling	pathology, antipathy
phag	to eat	esophagus, phagocyte
phobia	fear	claustrophobia
phon, phono	sound	symphony, phonics
plic	to fold	duplicate, implicate
pneuma	wind, air	pneumatic
pod, ped	foot	tripod, pedestrian
pon, pos	to place	depose, position
port	to carry	porter, portable
pseudo	false	pseudonym
psych	mind	psychology
pyr	fire	pyromaniac
quir	to ask	inquire, acquire
rog	to question	interrogate
scrib, graph	to write	prescribe, autograph
sect, seg	to cut	dissect, segment
sol	alone	solitude
soma	body	somatology, psychosomatic
somnia	sleep	insomnia
soph	wise	sophomore, philosophy
soror	sister	sorority
spect	to look at	inspect, spectacle
spir	to breathe	inspiration, conspire
tact, tang	to touch	tactile, tangible
tele	distant	telephone
ten, tent	to hold	tenant, intent
tend, tens	to stretch	extend, extension
the, theo	god	atheism, theology
therma	heat	thermometer
tort	twist	torture, extort
ven, vent	to go, arrive	convention, advent
verbum	word	verbosity, verbal

Suffixes

-able, -ible	capable of	durable, visible
-acy, -ance, -ency, -ity	quality or state of	privacy, competence, acidity
-age	act of, state of	breakage
-al	pertaining to	rental
-ana	saying, writing	Americana
-ant	quality of, one who	reliant, servant
-ard, -art	person who	wizard, braggart

WORD PART	MEANING	EXAMPLE
-arium, -orium	place for	auditorium
-ate	cause to be	activate
-ation	action, state of	creation, condition
-chrome	color	verichrome
-cide	killing	homicide
-er, -or	person who, thing which	generator
-esque	like in manner	picturesque
-fic	making, causing	scientific
-form	in the shape of	cuneiform
-ful, -ose, -ous	full of	careful, verbose
-fy, -ify, -ize	to make, cause to be	fortify, magnify, modify
-hood, -osis	condition or state of	childhood, hypnosis
-ics	art, science	mathematics
-ism	quality or doctrine of	conservatism
-itis	inflammation of	appendicitis
-ive	quality of, that which	creative
-latry	worship of	idolatry
-less	without	homeless
-oid	in the form of	tabloid
-tude	quality or degree of	solitude
-ward	in a direction	backward
-wise	way, position	clockwise

ESL: Making Sense of Figurative Language and Idioms

- What is ESL?
- What is figurative language?
- What are common English idioms?

WHAT IS ESL?

How many languages can you speak? Are you a native English speaker who has learned Spanish, or are you a native Farsi speaker who has learned English? If you have acquired skill in a second or third language, you know it takes many years and plenty of patience to master the intricacies of a language. Not only do you learn new words, but you must also learn new grammatical constructions. For example, the articles habitually used in English—*a, an,* and *the*—do not appear in Russian, Chinese, Japanese, Thai, or Farsi. In Spanish and Arabic, personal pronouns restate the subject, as in *My sister she goes to college.* In Spanish, Greek, French, Vietnamese, and Portuguese, "to" words are used rather than "ing" words, as in *I enjoy to play soccer.* These complexities, which are innately understood by native speakers, make direct translation difficult. The English language has many unusual phrases and grammatical constructions that defy direct translation.

To assist students with these complexities, most colleges offer courses in ESL (English as a Second Language) or ESOL (English for Speakers of Other Languages) designed to teach language skills to non-native speakers of English. If you are an ESL or ESOL student, you may have been recruited through an international exchange program with another college, you may be a newly arrived immigrant, or you may be a citizen with a bilingual background. You bring a multicultural perspective to classroom discussions and campus life that will broaden the insights of others. Not only are some of your holidays different from those of others, but your sense of family life, work, and responsibility may also be different. Share your thoughts and ideas with native English speakers as they share the irregularities of the language with you.

WHAT IS FIGURATIVE LANGUAGE?

One aspect of the English language that defies direct translation and confuses non-native speakers, and sometimes even native speakers, is **figurative language**. This is the manipulation of the language to create images, add interest, and draw comparisons by using figures of speech (see Chapter 10, "Inference"). The two most commonly used, *simile* and *metaphor,* are defined as follows:

Simile: a stated comparison using *like* or *as* (*example*: The baby swims like a duck.)

Metaphor: an implied comparison (*example*: The baby is a duck in water.)

Many figurative expressions have become commonplace in the English language. In the previous metaphor, the *baby* is not actually a *baby duck*, but the meaning is that *the baby swims very well*. However, neither direct translation nor a dictionary will unlock that meaning. When you encounter comparisons that seem out of the ordinary or ill chosen, ask yourself whether a figure of speech is being used, and look within the sentence for clues to help you guess the meaning.

The following practice exercises contain figurative language. Read each dialogue passage for meaning, and then use the context clues to match the number of the boldfaced figure of speech with the letter of the appropriate definition. To narrow your choices, the answers to 1–5 are listed within a–e, and the answers to 6–10 are listed within f–j.

EXERCISE 1

Maria: I am not going to be the one to stand in line for concert tickets this time. It is (1) **a pain in the neck**. Last time Fran left me (2) **holding the bag** on a $40 ticket for about a month.

Lynne: You did (3) **bend over backward** to organize the last outing. I would have (4) **jumped down Fran's throat** when she said she didn't have the cash to pay you. There is no reason (5) **to beat around the bush** with someone who doesn't pay promptly. Some people will (6) **walk all over you** if you let them.

Maria: I (7) **broke my neck** to get in line early. Those tickets were (8) **selling like hotcakes**. I think they (9) **jacked up** the price because they knew the demand would be high.

Lynne: I had to (10) **bite my tongue** not to say something to Fran about your efforts and her lack of gratitude.

_____ 1. a pain in the neck	a. owed money
_____ 2. holding the bag	b. avoid a clear answer
_____ 3. bend over backward	c. criticized angrily
_____ 4. jumped down Fran's throat	d. bothersome
_____ 5. to beat around the bush	e. make a great effort
_____ 6. walk all over you	f. being bought eagerly
_____ 7. broke my neck	g. raised
_____ 8. selling like hotcakes	h. keep from speaking
_____ 9. jacked up	i. take advantage of you
_____ 10. bite my tongue	j. tried hard

EXERCISE 2

Ron: I've got (1) **to take my hat off to** the group that organized the charity drive for the children's hospital.

Eric: They started out with (2) **two strikes against them** because most people had just made a contribution to the American Red Cross drive.

Ron: The president of the organization is a real (3) **go-getter**. He tried to educate people before asking for a contribution.

Eric: Until he outlined the situation in the Friday meeting, I did not know the hospital was (4) **in a jam**. Purchasing equipment for the cancer unit had put them (5) **in the red**.

Ron: When the 15-year-old boy spoke at the meeting, I was ready to (6) **open my wallet**. He said he had come through the cancer treatment and (7) **passed with flying colors**.

Eric: I gave $5 and was happy to know that my money would help a good cause. Not all charitable solicitations are (8) **on the level**. I like to (9) **double-check** to make sure that the charity is not a (10) **fly-by-night** operation. Now I'm thinking about doing some volunteer work at the hospital.

_____ 1. to take my hat off to	a.	in trouble
_____ 2. two strikes against them	b.	losing money
_____ 3. go-getter	c.	with little chance of success
_____ 4. in a jam	d.	to admire
_____ 5. in the red	e.	ambitious worker
_____ 6. open my wallet	f.	investigate thoroughly
_____ 7. passed with flying colors	g.	give money
_____ 8. on the level	h.	untrustworthy
_____ 9. double-check	i.	honest
_____ 10. fly-by-night	j.	succeeded

EXERCISE 3

Ross: I heard (1) **through the grapevine** that you had a (2) **fender bender** and put a dent in your car.

Howard: Ross, please don't (3) **breathe a word** about that. My parents will not be happy. I was really (4) **out to lunch** at the time and have been (5) **kicking myself** for not being more alert. I want to keep it (6) **hush-hush** for a while.

Ross: Do you have a plan for getting it fixed, or should we (7) **put our heads together** to create one?

Howard: I am waiting for final grades to come out. If I have all A's, I will then (8) **put my cards on the table** with them.

Ross: Man, that is really (9) **using your noodle**.

Howard: If that doesn't work, I'll be (10) **back to the drawing board** and could use your help.

_____ 1. through the grapevine	a.	regretting
_____ 2. fender bender	b.	inattentive
_____ 3. breathe a word	c.	by gossip from other people
_____ 4. out to lunch	d.	tell, talk

_____ 5. kicking myself   e. minor accident

_____ 6. hush-hush   f. thinking

_____ 7. put our heads together g. ready to start over

_____ 8. put my cards on the table h. confer

_____ 9. using your noodle   i. secret

_____10. back to the drawing board j. confess all

WHAT ARE COMMON ENGLISH IDIOMS?

An **idiom** is an expression with a special meaning that cannot be understood by directly translating each individual word in the idiom. Because of years of exposure, the meaning is usually understood by native speakers, but it is confusing to those who are learning English as a second language.

Idioms are more common in spoken and informal language than in formal writing. In fact, most idiomatic expressions can usually be replaced by a single formal word. To add to the confusion, some idioms have dual meanings, and many idioms are grammatically irregular.

Reader's TIP   Categorizing Idioms

Idioms are sometimes categorized into the following groups:

- Word families: grouping around a similar individual word

  Down as in _step down, take down, pipe down, narrow down, nail down, run down, tear down, knock down, let down, die down, cut down_

- Verb + Preposition: action word plus a connecting word

  Hammer away means _persist_; _stand for_ means _represent_; and _roll back_ means _reduce_.

- Preposition + Noun: connecting word plus the name of a person, place, or thing

  On foot means _walking_; _by heart_ means _memorized_; and _off guard_ means _surprised_.

- Verb + Adjective: action word plus a, descriptive word

  Think, twice means _consider carefully_; _hang loose_ means _be calm_; and _play fair_ means _deal equally_.

- Pairs of Nouns: two words naming a person, place, or thing

  Flesh and blood means _kin_; _part and parcel_ means _total_; and _pins and needles_ means _nervous_.

- Pairs of Adjectives: two descriptive words

  Cut and dried means _obvious_; _fair and square_ means _honest_; _short and sweet_ means _brief_.

EXAMPLE   What does the idiomatic expression *go over* mean in the following sentences?

(a) How did my speech *go over*?

(b) I want to *go over* the exam paper with the professor.

EXPLANATION   In both sentences, the use of the idiom is informal. A more formal version of each would be as follows:

(a) *How was my speech* **received** *by the audience?*

(b) *I want to* **review** *the exam paper with the professor.*

Notice the grammatical irregularity in the first sentence. *Over* is not followed by a noun (name of a person, place, or thing), as a preposition (connecting words like *in*, *out*, and *at*) normally would be according to the rules of grammar; *over* becomes part of the verb phrase (words showing action). Thus the translation requires a change in wording, whereas the second use of the idiom is grammatically correct and can be directly translated by the single word *review*.

Nobody says that understanding idioms is easy. Books have been written about categorizing, recognizing, and translating thousands of them. To help clear up the confusion, some books group idioms according to families like root words, and others categorize them according to grammatical constructions. Either way, understanding idiomatic expressions depends more on using context clues to deduce meaning and familiarity with the informal, spoken language than with learning rules.

In the following practice exercises, idioms are grouped according to a common word. Use the context clues within each sentence to determine the meaning of the boldfaced idiom.

EXERCISE 4

| up | down | around | across | over |

1. Let's **nail down** a date for the next meeting before we leave today. _____
   _____

2. Close friends should **stand up for** what they know is right. _____
   _____

3. Children should not be allowed to **fool around** with matches. _____

4. With a quick example the student was able to **get across** the application of
   the theory. _____

5. They had a big **blowup** over who was responsible for the telephone bill.
   _____

6. Yesterday I **ran across** an old friend at the airport. _____

7. Because we are having a party, I asked a few friends in my psychology class
   to **drop over**. _____

8. The new grocery store is open **around the clock**. _____

9. If the class president would **step down** in March, we could get a more dynamic person for the position. ———————————————

10. After winning the free concert tickets, she was **bubbling over** with excitement. ————————————————————————

EXERCISE 5

| in | about | for | off | out |

1. Before school starts, we need to **see about** renting an apartment.——————
————————————————————————————————

2. The manager stayed late at work to **break in** the new employee. —————
————————————————————————————————

3. If you need to shorten the paragraph, **leave out** the last sentence. ————
————————————————————————————————

4. What do the school colors **stand for**? ————————————————————

5. Although the designer's name was displayed, the purse was actually a cheap **knockoff**. ——————————————————————————————

6. As soon as class is over, we are going to **take off** for a weekend at the beach.
————————————————————————————————

7. Because I have a car this semester, **getting about** is much easier. ————
————————————————————————————————

8. This latest demand **calls for** immediate action from our coalition. ————
————————————————————————————————

9. Let's all **chip in** to buy our professor a gift. ———————————————

10. When cleaning, you do not want to **throw out** something that you may need later. ————————————————————————————————

EXERCISE 6

free and easy	part and parcel	give-and-take	null and void
touch and go	spick-and-span	day in and day out	
little by little	high and low	sooner or later	

1. If you continue to drive with your gas gauge on empty, **sooner or later** you will be stuck on the side of the road. ——————————————————

2. By decreasing the medication **little by little**, the body can adjust without a painful reaction. ——————————————————————————

3. Overcooked food and slow service are complaints the restaurant managers hear **day in and day out**. _____

4. The peace negotiations were **touch and go** until the rebels accepted the compromise. _____

5. When I eat in a restaurant, I am more confident about cleanliness if the rest room is **spick-and-span**. _____

6. The opportunity to be with family is **part and parcel** of any holiday celebration. _____

7. After an appeal to a higher court, the previous decision to grant millions in damages could be declared **null and void**. _____

8. We will never decide which band to book for the party unless club members engage in a little **give-and-take**. _____

9. When she starts making her own money, she won't continue to spend with such a **free and easy** attitude. _____

10. After searching **high and low** for my keys, I found them under the computer. _____

Reader's TIP   Internet Sites to Explore

Dave's ESL Café   www.eslcafe.com
Emphasis in this site is on English as it is spoken in the United States. It includes search tools for ESL books and a general discussion forum for ESL students and teachers.

EF Englishtown   www.englishtown.com
Englishtown offers daily, 5-minute "Email English" lessons for no charge. It also provides a 7-day, free trial of classes taught online in the Englishtown school.

English Club   www.EnglishClub.com
This site has a 24-hour ESL Help Desk staffed with teachers to answer questions. Resources are available for both instructors and students in areas such as grammar, speech, and reading at no charge.

Tower of English   www.towerofenglish.com
Tower of English allows students to integrate lots of Web sources into their learning experience. It provides links to online ESL, exercises, search engines, reference tools, and news sources. The site also links students to private English tutors in their cities.

THE READING WORKSHOP

Thinking, Talking, and Writing about Books

"Reading is to the mind what exercise is to the body."

—SIR RICHARD STEELE (1672–1729)

Common sense and reading experts tell us that reading is good for us. Not only does regular reading improve our ability to read well, it also expands our knowledge of many subjects, our schemata. In other words, the more we read, the better we read and the more we know. Add to that the lifelong pleasure that reading provides and you have a recipe for wisdom!

Your professor may incorporate into your course a novel, a biography, or another book that the entire class reads. Other professors may give students free choice of reading material beyond the textbook. Others will ask only that you read the textbook. Your professor might require you to keep a Reading Workshop journal, make a class presentation, or participate in book discussions. The Reading Workshop segments that follow are designed to help you enjoy reading more and to provide ideas for thinking, talking, and writing about books. In most cases the Reading Workshop segments are tied to the reading skill presented in their companion textbook chapters to provide additional, authentic application. You don't have to wait for someone to assign a book to read. Just do it! you'll be glad you did.

If you are not already an avid reader, refer to the Everyday Reading Skills section on page xxx about how to select a book. Ask other students or your professor for suggestions, look for reading lists on the Internet, or just browse in a bookstore. The kinds of movies and television programs you enjoy are a starting point for the types of books you will like: Drama, mystery, horror, comedy, romance, history, science fiction, how-to, etc. Pick a book, get started, and enjoy!

1. *"People say that life is the thing, but I prefer reading."*

—LOGAN PEARSALL SMITH (1865–1946)

Whatever you choose to read, it will be more fun if you allow enough time to get involved in the characters, the plot, and the setting. Find a comfortable, quiet place to curl up, and allow yourself at least 20 to 30 minutes at a time. If you are not immediately "hooked" on the book, give it at least two chapters to excite your interest. Some books are slow starters and draw the reader in gradually.

Just as thinking, talking, and writing about your textbook help etch the material in memory, the same methods heighten interest in your pleasure reading. Your professor may ask you to keep a Reading Workshop journal in which you write about your pleasure reading. Perhaps you will be given an opportunity to talk to a classmate or the whole class about it. Here are some suggestions.

Think about It, Talk about It, Write about It

Is your book fiction or nonfiction? What is its topic? Why did you choose it? Did the author grab your interest in the first few lines or did it build slowly? What do you like best about this book?

2. *Polonius: "What do you read my lord?"*
   Hamlet: "Words, words, words."

—SHAKESPEARE, *HAMLET*

One of the benefits of extensive reading is expanding your vocabulary. It stands to reason that the more words you see or hear, the more words you recognize. As you find interesting words in your Reading Workshop book, mark them for later additions to your concept cards. Don't stop the flow of your reading except to lightly mark the word with a pencil or sticky note and dog-ear the page.

Think about It, Talk about It, Write about It

At the end of your reading session, make a list of the words you marked and make concept cards. Were you able to determine their meanings from the context or word structure clues? Try to use the words in conversation or in writing today. Don't be afraid of making a mistake. Your listener will be impressed by your broad vocabulary or at least appreciate your effort. Use the new words often and they will soon become familiar friends.

Your professor might ask you to submit a list of words for an individualized quiz or as an addition to a Reading Workshop journal.

3. *"When I look back, I am so impressed again with the life-giving power of literature. If I were a young person today, trying to gain a sense of myself in the world, I would do that again by reading, just as I did when I was young."*

—MAYA ANGELOU

Reading widely for pleasure can certainly enrich one's sense of self. Imagine the experiences available through books that may never be possible, or even desirable, for us to actually do. Traveling the world, seeing how other people think and behave, experiencing things we may never do otherwise—all of these help us see ourselves more clearly. (You may want to read something by Maya Angelou, well-known American author and poet. *I Know Why the Caged Bird Sings, A Song Flung Up to Heaven,* and *Even the Stars Look Lonesome* are three of her many books.)

Think about It, Talk about It, Write about It

Whether you are reading fiction or nonfiction, consider what you have learned from your book:

- Why do you think a character acted like he or she did? Would you have done the same?
- What have you learned about a particular place or time period?
- Have you gained insights into a field of study or career?
- Have you learned new facts? How might you apply this new knowledge?

4. *"The more that you read, the more things you will know. The more you learn, the more places you'll go."*

—DR. SEUSS, *I Can Read With My Eyes Shut!*

Is there a place you have always wanted to go? Something or someone you have wanted to know more about? Something you have always wanted to do? A trip to the library or bookstore might be just the thing to satisfy those desires. If you actually travel to that place, take a class, meet that person or find yourself in that situation, the experience will be richer for knowing more about it first. Spend a free afternoon or evening browsing in an actual or online bookstore or a public library and see what strikes your fancy.

Think about It, Talk about It, Write about It

You should be well into your book by now. It's time to go beyond the literal details and think about the author's craft. If you are reading fiction, why is the story set where and when it is? Would a different setting significantly change the story line? If you are reading nonfiction, how would the book be different if it had been written ten years earlier or later?

5. *"There are many little ways to enlarge your child's world. Love of books is the best of all."*

—Jacqueline Kennedy

"Reading aloud with children is known to be the single most important activity for building the knowledge and skills they will eventually require for learning to read."

—Marilyn Jager Adams, Reading Expert

Did someone read to you when you were a child? This is one of the best ways for a child to learn the rhythm and sounds of written language. Even the youngest child learns that reading is fun through the experience of sharing it with someone. Read to a child today and tomorrow! It will give you both great pleasure.

Think about It, Talk about It, Write about It

Did you have a favorite book as a child? What was it? Did you visit the library or a bookstore? Write about your reading experiences, or lack of them, in your childhood.

Write about the experience of reading to a child. What did you read? Did she or he enjoy it? What did you gain from the experience?

6. *"The things I want to know are in books. My best friend is the man who'll get me a book I [haven't] read."*

—Abraham Lincoln

When we read for pleasure, we learn many things almost accidentally. Reading for the purpose of learning, though, requires working with the material in a deeper and more active way. When we know that we will be tested, we read more carefully. Put yourself in the teacher's position, and, as you read, predict and answer the questions that might be included on a test. You may find that you pay closer attention!

Think about It, Talk about It, Write about It

Create a brief test that might be given to someone who has read the book you are reading. Write one question for each type of question discussed in this chapter—main idea, detail, author's purpose, inference, and vocabulary—and include an essay question and an answer key.

7. *"I am not a speed reader. I am a speed understander."*

—ISAAC ASIMOV, SCIENCE FICTION AUTHOR

Reading efficiently is all about selecting the method and speed to accomplish your purpose. When reading for pleasure most people naturally settle into a comfortable, medium rhythm. When reading for long-term recall and study, as in most textbook reading, the pace slows considerably. When scanning for one small piece of information, we can read with lightning speed. Think about your purpose and set your "readometer" accordingly.

Think about It, Talk about It, Write about It

Set up a little experiment. First, check your reading speed on Exercise 1 in Chapter 8. Second, count out an equal number of words in something you are reading for pleasure with no need for long-term recall, and check your words-per-minute rate. Third, do the same check with a difficult textbook chapter. Create a small chart in which you record your rates in the three different situations. Write a brief paragraph to compare and explain the results.

The next time you read something, set a realistic time goal that is based on your purpose for reading.

8. *"There is more treasure in books than in all the pirate's loot on Treasure Island."*

—WALT DISNEY

It may be difficult to convince a nonreader of this, but once a person is "hooked on books," he or she knows Mr. Disney's statement is true. Reading opens treasure troves of knowledge and entertainment.

Think about It, Talk about It, Write about It

Analyze the author's style in a book you are reading for pleasure. How does the author gain, or fail to gain, the reader's interest? If you are reading fiction, think about how the author has set the pace of the plot. In other words, how quickly do major events occur? Does the author drop hints to allow the reader to predict what might happen? Is some information withheld? Does the interest lie primarily in the characters, the plot, or the setting?

If you are reading nonfiction, think about how the author organized the information. Are there logical sections and headings to break up the text and to guide the reader? Have appropriate illustrations and graphics helped to illustrate the information? Has the author provided all the information you want? Too much? Too little?

9. *"The only books that influence us are those for which we are ready, and which have gone a little farther down our particular path than we have yet got ourselves."*

—E.M. FORSTER

Have you been "stretched" by the books you are reading for pleasure? If not, consider selecting something just a bit more challenging next time. This might mean venturing into a subject, genre, or length that you have hesitated to try but that intrigues you. Beware: Growth may occur!

Think about It, Talk about It, Write about It

What inferences did the author of your book expect you to make to understand the action or point? For example, in a suspense novel there are usually clues that allow the reader to speculate about the outcome. Sometimes the author plants false clues or "red herrings" to lead the reader to incorrect conclusions. Also consider the significance of the book's title. Does it directly label the content of the book, or does it reflect a significant theme or meaning within the book?

10. *"I have often reflected upon the new vistas that reading opened to me. I knew right there in prison that reading had changed forever the course of my life. As I see it today, the ability to read awoke in me some long dormant craving to be mentally alive."*

—Malcolm X

That is a powerful statement! What is it about reading that so inspired this civil rights activist? Perhaps you can think of ways in which you have benefitted from something you have read. There is something yet to be read that could change the course of your life—look for it!

Think about It, Talk about It, Write about It

Whether they are reading fiction or nonfiction, critical readers are alert to the often subtle evidence of the author's biases and point of view. What words best describe the overall tone of the book you are reading? Is the author's purpose solely to entertain, to persuade or to inform, or do you detect a mixture of purposes? Does the author reveal any biases? Defend your responses with evidence from the book.

ADDITIONAL TOPICS TO CONSIDER

Readers can find almost unlimited topics when talking or writing about books. The best book discussions, whether they are written or oral, go beyond the literal events and facts to consider broader concepts, truths, and elements of the author's style. Examples from the book are essential to illustrate your points, but interesting discussions do not dwell on a simple retelling of the story.

If you are writing in a Reading Workshop journal, your professor may use some of the following items to evaluate your work:

- Amount of reading you have completed; time devoted to reading
- Did you avoid retelling the plot?
- Did you support points with examples from the book?
- Evidence of higher-level thinking

Fiction

Several of these topics work for nonfiction books, too. This list includes some topics adapted from Richard Peck's "Ten Questions to Ask about a Novel," retrieved from www.booktalks.org. Also, refer to the Reader's Tip on short stories on page 152 and definitions in the glossary for a review of literary devices that enhance the reader's experience.

1. What do you think might happen next and what clues lead you to think so?
2. What do you think the author is like and why?

3. Other than the obvious, how would this story be different, or not, if the main character were of the opposite sex?

4. What confuses or especially intrigues you about the way the book is written?

5. If you were to make a movie or TV feature from this book, what characters and scenes would you leave out?

6. What would you have done differently if you were the author or the character?

7. What traits (not physical characteristics) does the main character have that are different from your own?

8. Would this story make a good TV series? Why or why not? Think about whether the central point of the book would be lost in separate TV episodes and whether the characters would still be interesting if they were placed in the first episode fully developed.

9. What makes the writing effective or ineffective?

10. How would you design a new cover that entices readers and also reflects the story?

11. If you have seen a movie based on the book, compare and contrast them. Which is better? Why?

12. What would you ask the author in an interview? Why? What responses would you expect? (Some authors and publishers offer readers this opportunity through online chats.)

13. Compare two or more books by the same author.

Nonfiction

Several of the previous topics for fiction books may be applied to nonfiction books; however, the following nonfiction topics will not work well with fiction.

1. How would the book be different if it had been written ten years earlier or later?

2. What illustrations would you add to the book? Why?

GLOSSARY

abbreviations Shortened spellings that are useful when taking notes

abstract Short paragraph that summarizes an article, stating the author's premise, the subject or location of the project, and the conclusions.

acronym Abbreviation pronounced as a word and contrived to simplify a lengthy name and gain quick recognition for an organization or agency. For example, *UNICEF* is the abbreviation for the United Nations International Children's Emergency Fund.

acrostic A sentence in which the first letter of each word corresponds to the first letter of other words; a helpful memory strategy when learning a list of items

addition pattern Pattern of paragraph organization that includes additional information.

analogy Comparison that measures not only word knowledge, but also the ability to see relationships.

annotating Method of highlighting main ideas, significant supporting details, and key terms using a system of symbols and notations, so the markings indicate pertinent points to review for an exam.

applied level of reading This level calls for reaction, reflection, and critical thinking and involves analyzing, synthesizing, and evaluating.

bar graph Graph comprising a series of horizontal or vertical bars in which the length of each bar represents a particular amount. Often, time is represented by the vertical scale and quantity is measured by the horizontal scale.

bias Author's attitude, opinion, or position on a subject suggesting the facts have been slanted toward the author's personal beliefs. As commonly used, *bias* has a negative connotation suggesting narrow-mindedness and prejudice.

bibliography List of the sources consulted by the author of a scholarly article or paper.

biography The story of a person's life or a portion of it as told by another person.

cause-and-effect pattern Pattern of paragraph organization showing one element as producing or causing a result or effect.

characters The main people in a story; they should be consistent in behavior and should grow and change according to their experiences.

citation In an index entry, a reference to an article that includes the title, author(s), name of the periodical, volume and page numbers, issue date, and descriptive notes or key search terms.

classification pattern Pattern of paragraph organization dividing items into groups or categories.

climax In literature, the turning point near the end of a story in which conflict intensifies to a peak.

comparison pattern Pattern of paragraph organization listing similarities among items.

conclusion Logical deduction from both stated and unstated ideas, using the hints as well as the facts to interpret motives, actions, and outcomes. Conclusions are drawn on the basis of perceived evidence, and because perceptions differ, conclusions can vary from reader to reader.

conflict Clash of ideas, desires, or actions as incidents in a plot build progressively.

connotation Feeling or emotion associated with a word that goes beyond its dictionary definition.

content exam Test that measures knowledge of a particular topic.

context clues The words or phrases surrounding an unfamiliar word that help a reader identify its meaning.

contrast pattern Pattern of paragraph organization listing differences among items.

Cornell method System of notetaking in which you put questions on one side of a vertical line and notes that answer the questions on the other side.

critical thinking Deliberating in a purposeful, organized manner in order to assess the value of old and new information.

critique Review that judges the merits of a work.

databases Computer-based indexes to assist research. A single article may be listed under several topics and may appear in several different indexes.

definition pattern Pattern of paragraph organization initially defining a concept and expanding with examples and restatements.

denotation Dictionary definition of a word.

description pattern A form or pattern of writing that lists the characteristics of an object, event, person, place, etc.

details Specifics in a passage that develop, explain, and support the main idea, such as reasons, incidents, facts, examples, steps, and definitions.

diagram Outlined drawing or illustration of an object or a process.

directory path Particular location within a website's host computer.

domain name Name registered by a website owner.

domain type Category to which the website owner belongs.

editorials Subjective articles that express the opinion of a person or organization. A newspaper's editorial pages feature the views of its management and/or editors.

electronic mail (e-mail) Message sent from one person or organization to another person or group of people using the World Wide Web. These messages can be read, printed, saved, forwarded to someone else, and/or discarded.

encyclopedias Reference books that give comprehensive coverage of a subject. Many different encyclopedias, such as the *Encyclopedia of African American Religions*, *Encyclopedia of Earth Sciences*, and *The Cambridge Encyclopedia of Astronomy*, are available for specific topics.

essay Short work of nonfiction that discusses a specific topic. It does not develop as a story does, and it lacks characters and a plot.

etymology Study of word origins, involving the tracing of words back to their earliest recorded appearance.

fact Statement based on actual evidence or personal observation. It can be checked objectively with empirical data and proved to be either true or false.

fallacy Inference that appears to be reasonable at first, but closer inspection proves it to be unrelated, unreliable, or illogical. Tool used in constructing a weak argument.

feature stories In journalism, human interest stories that differ from typical news stories in their timeliness, style, and length.

fiction Writing invented by the imagination.

figurative language Words intentionally used in a different way—out of their literal context—so they take on new meaning.

file name Specific file within the host's directory.

fixations Stops lasting a fraction of a second that eyes make in order to read. On the average, 5 to 10 percent of reading time is spent on fixations.

forum An interactive, online community centered around a particular subject through which participants post information and ask questions.

generalization and example pattern Pattern of paragraph organization explaining a concept by illustrating with examples.

glossary A brief dictionary of terms relating to a particular field or topic; usually found at the back of a textbook.

graphic organizer A diagram that presents the major and minor details of a text passage in a visual form.

hypertext links In the World Wide Web, phrases that are often distinguished by a different color and are underlined. Clicking on them will not only move you from one page to another within the website, but can also send you to other related websites. The words chosen and underlined as the link describe the information likely to be found at that destination.

idiom An expression that has taken on a generally accepted meaning over many years of use but does not make sense on a literal level. Idioms can be similes and metaphors. For example, *sleeping like a log* is both a simile and also an idiom, because it is an accepted and often used expression that is not literally true.

index Research tool that contains listings of articles organized by the topics within the articles. Most libraries have electronic periodical indexes.

inference Meaning that is not directly stated but suggested through clues that lead one to make assumptions and draw conclusions.

intent Reason or purpose for writing, which is usually to inform, persuade, or entertain.

Internet Global system of interconnected computer networks that serves billions of users; carries information resources, including documents from the World Wide Web (WWW), and supports email.

interpretive level of reading At this level the reader makes assumptions and draws conclusions by considering the stated message, the implied meaning, the facts, and the author's attitude toward the subject.

inverted pyramid Format of news writing that begins with a summary paragraph and continues with paragraphs that explain details in a descending order of importance.

irony A figure of speech that states the opposite of the intended meaning.

lead In a news story, the first paragraph that catches the reader's attention, establishes a focus, and summarizes the essential points of the story.

letter Formal communication appropriate for outside the company.

line graph Graph incorporating a continuous curve or *frequency distribution*. The horizontal scale (or *axis*) measures one aspect of the data (or *variable*), and the vertical scale measures another aspect, making it easy to see the relationship between the variables at a glance. As the data fluctuate, the line changes direction and, with extreme differences, becomes very jagged.

links See *hypertext links*.

literal level of reading At this level the reader might be able to answer detail questions asking *who, what, when,* and *where,* but not understand the overall purpose of the passage.

location or spatial order pattern Pattern of paragraph organization identifying the whereabouts of objects.

main idea Central message the author is trying to convey about the material.

major supporting detail Provides information that explains and elaborates on the main idea.

map Visual representation of a geographic area.

mapping Visual system of condensing ideas or cognitive material through diagramming of major points and significant subpoints to show relationships and importance.

memo Short, informal business note usually for internal business purposes.

metacognition Knowledge of the processes involved in reading and the ability to regulate and direct them.

metaphor Direct comparison of two unlike things that does not use the word *like* or *as*. A metaphor and a simile can communicate the same idea and are differentiated only by the presence or absence of the word *like* or *as*.

minor supporting detail Provides a specific example or other information that explains a major detail.

minutes Official record of the business decisions for a meeting.

mnemonics Techniques to help the brain organize and recall information by incorporating the senses through pictures, sounds, rhythms, and other mental tricks to create extrasensory handles or hooks.

mood Overall feeling of the work, often conveyed by the language and symbolism used.

multiple meanings Some words are confusing because they have several different meanings. For example, the dictionary lists over thirty meanings for the word *run*.

newsletter Mini-newspaper published within an organization to build group spirit.

news stories Newspaper articles that report the facts of events in descending order of importance.

nonfiction Writing that describes facts and reality.

notetaking Method of jotting down important ideas for future study from a lecture or text.

novel Extended fictional work that has all of the elements of a short story. Because of its length, a novel usually has more character development and more conflicts than a short story.

opinion Statement of personal feeling or a judgment. It reflects a belief or an interpretation rather than an accumulation of evidence, and it cannot be proved true or false.

outline Method of organizing major points and subordinating items of lesser importance with Roman numerals, letters, numbers, and indentations to show how one idea relates to another and how all aspects relate to the whole.

pattern of organization Organizational structure of a passage that can be a simple listing, time order, definition with examples, comparison-contrast, or cause and effect.

periodicals Publications that come out on a regular schedule, including popular magazines and scholarly journals.

personification Attributing human characteristics to nonhuman things.

pie chart Circle divided into wedge-shaped slices, with each slice representing a percentage of the whole. The complete pie or circle represents 100 percent.

plagiarism A form of dishonesty in which one uses someone else's words or ideas as if they were one's own; consequences in an academic setting may include failing a course or expulsion from the institution.

plot Action in a story or a play. Sequence of incidents or events linked in a manner that suggests causes for the events.

point of view In writing, point of view is the author's attitude, opinion, or position on a subject. In literature, point of view describes who tells the story and is indicated most commonly by the third person (in which the author is the all-knowing observer). Alternatively, the first person (in which the main character tells the story by using the word *I*) or second person (in which the story is told through the use of the word *you*) may be used.

popular sources Newspapers and magazines aimed at the general public and written by professional journalists who are *reporters* rather than specialists in the field and thus focus on *who, what, where, when, why,* and *how*.

prefix Group of letters with a special meaning added to the beginning of a word.

previewing First stage of reading: a method of reviewing material to guess what it is about, assess what you already know about the topic, decide what you will probably want to know after you read, and make a plan for reading.

previewing a textbook Examining the features and organization of a book before reading any of it in depth.

prior knowledge What is already known about a subject, which is the single best predictor of reading comprehension.

propaganda Information that is widely spread and that is intended to help or harm a person, group, movement, etc.

protocol Short for *hypertext transfer protocol (http)*, a type of language computers networked via the Internet use to communicate with each other.

purpose Reason or intent for writing, which is usually to inform, persuade, or entertain.

recalling Telling oneself what has been learned after reading, relating it to what is already known, and reacting to it to form an opinion.

regression Rereading sentences or paragraphs because one's mind was wandering during the initial reading of the material.

resolution A literary term referring to the point in the plot of a novel or story at which the outcome of the conflict is made known.

root Stem or basic part of a word, derived primarily from Latin and Greek.

rubric A checklist by which students' work is graded.

schema Concept of a compartment in the brain similar to a computer chip that holds all that is known on a subject.

scholarly journals Regularly scheduled publications aimed at scholars, specialists, and students. They contain detailed research results written by specialists in the academic field of study and are frequently theoretical.

server name Indicates the computer network over which the user travels to reach the desired location (in most cases, the World Wide Web).

setting Backdrop for a story and the playground for the characters. Setting may include the place, the time, and the culture.

short story Brief work of narrative fiction with a beginning, a middle, and an end that ranges from 500 to 15,000 words.

simile Comparison of two unlike things using the words *like* and *as* (e.g., "His words were like knives to my heart").

simple listing pattern Pattern of paragraph organization randomly listing items in a series.

slant A bias or point of view.

standardized test Test that measures mastery of a skill such as reading; scores are reported in a form that allows comparison across a large population.

subvocalization Inaudible voice in one's mind that one "hears" while reading.

suffix Group of letters with a special meaning added to the end of a word. Can alter the meaning of a word as well as the way the word can be used.

summary Brief, concise statement of the main idea of a piece of writing and its significant supporting details. The first sentence states the main idea or thesis, and subsequent sentences incorporate the significant details.

summary pattern Pattern of paragraph organization that sums up what has been stated in preceding paragraphs.

symbolism Object, action, person, place, or idea that carries a condensed and recognizable meaning (e.g., an opened window might symbolize an opportunity for a new life).

table Organized listing of facts and figures in columns and rows to compare and classify information for quick and easy reference.

theme Heart, soul, or central insight of—or universal truth expressed by—a work. Message is never preached but revealed to the emotions, senses, and imagination through powerful shared experiences.

thesaurus A list of words and their synonyms.

thesis statement A sentence that states the main point; the topic sentence or main idea statement.

time order, sequence, or narration pattern Pattern of paragraph organization listing events in the order of occurrence.

tone Writer's attitude toward the subject or the audience. For example, an author's word choice may suggest humor, cutting remarks suggest sarcasm, and ironic remarks show the gap between the actual and the expected.

topic General rather than specific term that forms an umbrella under which the author can group the specific ideas or details in a passage.

topic sentence Sentence that condenses the thoughts and details of a passage into a general, all-inclusive statement of the author's message.

transitions Signal words that connect parts of sentences and lead readers to anticipate a continuation or a change in the writer's thoughts.

uniform resource locator (URL) On the Web, specific directions for finding your way to a specific site, just as an address and zip code are required to mail a letter. A URL is similar to an e-mail address, except that it routes the user to a source of information called a *Web page* or *website* rather than to the mailbox of an individual person.

vocalization moving one's lips as one reads.

ACKNOWLEDGMENTS

Text Credits

Adams, James L. From CONCEPTUAL BLOCKBUSTING by James L. Adams. Copyright © 1974, 1976, 1979, 1986, 2001 by James L. Adams. Reprinted by permission of Perseus Books Group, permission conveyed via Copyright Clearance Center.

Adler, Ronald and George Rodman. UNDERSTANDING HUMAN COMMUNICATION, 8th Edition. New York: Oxford University Press, 2003.

Andujar, Linda Lee: From Newsweek, November 13, 2000 © 2000 The Newsweek/Daily Beast Company LLC. All rights reserved. Used by permission and protected by the Copyright Laws of the United States. The printing, copying, redistribution, or retransmission of the Material without express written permission is prohibited.

Armstrong, Gary and Philip Kotler. MARKETING: AN INTRODUCTION, 9th Edition. Upper Saddle River, NJ: Pearson Prentice-Hall, 2000.

Arrian: From THE CAMPAIGNS OF ALEXANDER by Arrian, translated by Aubrey de Sélincourt, revised with an introduction and notes by J. R. Hamilton. Harmondsworth, England: Penguin Classics 1958, Revised edition 1971.

Assael, Henry. CONSUMER BEHAVIOR AND MARKETING ACTION, 4th Edition. Boston, PWS-Kent, 1992.

Audesirk, Teresa et al. From BIOLOGY: LIFE ON EARTH, 6th Edition, by Audesirk/Audesirk/Byers. © 2002, 1999, 1996 Prentice-Hall, Inc. Reprinted by permission of Pearson Education, Inc., Upper Saddle River, NJ.

Badasch, Shirley A. and Doreen S. Chesebro. HEALTH SCIENCE FUNDAMENTALS: EXPLORING CAREER PATHWAYS. Upper Saddle River, NJ: Pearson Prentice Hall, 2009.

Bailey, Thomas and David Kennedy. THE AMERICAN PAGEANT. Lexington, Mass: Heath.

Beebe, Steven, et al. INTERPERSONAL COMMUNICATION: RELATING TO OTHERS, 3rd Edition by Steven Beebe, Susan Beebe, and Mark Redmond. © 2002. Reprinted and electronically reproduced by permission of Pearson Education, Inc., publishing as Allyn and Bacon.

Beekman, George. COMPUTER CONFLUENCE: EXPLORING TOMORROW'S TECHNOLOGY. Upper Saddle River, NJ: Prentice Hall, 2001.

Bell, Arthur H. and Dayle M. Smith. INTERVIEWING FOR SUCCESS, 1st Edition, © 2004. Adapted by permission of Pearson Education, Inc., Upper Saddle River, NJ.

Bittinger, Marvin L. and Judith A. Beecher. DEVELOPMENTAL MATHEMATICS: COLLEGE MATHEMATICS AND INTRODUCTORY ALGEBRA, 7th Edition. Boston: Pearson Addison Wesley, 2008.

Campbell, Neil. From BIOLOGY 3rd Edition, by Neil Campbell. Redwood City, CA: Benjamin/Cummings, 1993.

Campbell, Neil. From BIOLOGY: CONCEPTS AND CONNECTIONS, 4th Edition, by Neil Campbell. San Francisco: Benjamin Cummings, 2003.

Career Key, Inc.: Published as "Job Satisfaction" from The Career Key website, 2001 [www.careerkey.org]. Reproduced with permission of Career Key, Inc., Hood River, OR.

Chapman, Elwood N. and Cliff Goodwin. SUPERVISOR'S SURVIVAL KIT: YOUR FIRST STEP INTO MANAGEMENT, 9th Edition. Upper Saddle River, NJ: Pearson Prentice Hall, 2002.

Chapman, Elwood N. and Sharon Lund O'Neil. From YOUR ATTITUDE IS SHOWING, 9th Edition by Elwood Chapman and Sharon Lund O'Neil. © 1999. Adapted by permission of Pearson Education, Inc.

Chierici, Maurizio. "The Man from Hiroshima," Granta, #22, Autumn 1987.

Clendenen, Gary et al.: BUSINESS MATHEMATICS, 12th edition. Boston: Prentice Hall, 2012.

Conlin, Joseph. THE AMERICAN PAST, 5th Edition. Fort Worth, TX: Harcourt Brace, 1997.

Craig, Albert M., William A. Graham, Donald Kagan, Steven Ozment, and Frank M. Turner. THE HERITAGE OF WORLD CIVILIZATIONS, Combined Edition, 6th Edition. Pearson Prentice Hall, 2003.

Davis, Stephen F. and Joseph J. Palladino: PSYCHOLOGY. Upper Saddle River, NJ: Pearson Prentice Hall.

DeVito, Joseph A. ESSENTIALS OF HUMAN COMMUNICATION, 4th Edition. Boston: Allyn and Bacon, 2002.

DeVito, Joseph A. From HUMAN COMMUNICATION, 6th Edition, by Joseph A. DeVito. Copyright © 1994 by HarperCollins College Publishers. Reprinted by permission of Pearson Education, Inc.

DiBacco: Thomas V.: From "Once Upon a September Day," The Los Angeles Times, September 28, 1983. Reprinted with the permission of Thomas V. DiBacco.

Donatelle, Rebecca J. From HEALTH: THE BASICS, 5th Edition by Rebecca J. Donatelle. Copyright © 2003 Pearson Education, Inc., publishing as Benjamin Cummings. Reprinted by permission.

Donatelle, Rebecca J. From HEALTH: THE BASICS, 6th Edition by Rebecca J. Donatelle. Copyright © 2005 Pearson Education, Inc., publishing as Benjamin Cummings. Reprinted by permission.

DuBrin, Andrew J. From Andrew J. DuBrin, HUMAN RELATIONS: INTERPERSONAL, JOB-ORIENTED SKILLS, 8th edition, © 2004. Reprinted by permission of Pearson Education, Inc., Upper Saddle River, NJ.

Ebert, Ronald and Ricky Griffin: BUSINESS ESSENTIALS, 3rd Edition. Upper Saddle River, NJ: Prentice Hall, 2000.

Fábrega, Marelisa. 5 Tips for Overcoming Failure. © Marelisa Fábrega. Reprinted by permission of the author.

Fagin, James A. CRIMINAL JUSTICE, 2005 Update. Boston: Pearson Allyn and Bacon, 2005.

Feldman, Robert S. DEVELOPMENT ACROSS THE LIFE SPAN, 4th Edition. © 2006. Adapted by permission of Pearson Education, Inc.

Fiorina, Morris and Paul Peterson: THE NEW AMERICAN DEMOCRACY, Election Update Edition. Boston: Allyn & Bacon, 1999.

Fobes, Richard. From THE CREATIVE PROBLEM SOLVER'S TOOLBOX by Richard Fobes. Copyright © 1993 by Richard Fobes. Reprinted by permission of Solutions Through Innovation.

Fritz, Susan, F. William Brown, Joyce Povlacs Lunde, and Elizabeth A. Banset. INTERPERSONAL SKILLS FOR LEADERSHIP, 2nd Edition. Upper Saddle River, NJ: Prentice Hall, 2005.

Gardner, Martin. "Some Math Magic Tricks with Numbers," Games Magazine, May 1999. Reprinted by permission of Kappa Publishing Group, Inc.

Gardner, Mona. "The Dinner Party," Saturday Review of Literature, vol. 25, no. 5 (January 31, 1941). Used by permission of the Estate of Mona Gardner.

Garraty, John and Mark Carnes. THE AMERICAN NATION, 10th Edition. New York: Longman, 2000.

Garrison, Tim: From OCEANOGRAPHY, 5e. © 2005 Brooks/Cole, a part of Cengage Learning, Inc. Reproduced by permission. www.cengage.com/permissions.

Ginsberg, Benjamin, Theodore J. Lowi, and Margaret Weir. WE THE PEOPLE: AN INTRODUCTION TO AMERICAN POLITICS, 4th Edition. New York: W.W. Norton, 2003.

Gleick, James. "Life As Type A" from FASTER: THE ACCELERATION OF JUST ABOUT EVERYTHING. New York: Pantheon Books, 1999.

Gordon, Arthur: "The Alchemist's Secret" by Arthur Gordon. Copyright © 1952 by Arthur Gordon. Reprinted by permission of The Estate of Arthur Gordon.

Gregory, Paul. ESSENTIALS OF ECONOMICS, 4th Edition. Reading, MA: Addison Wesley Longman, 1999.

Griffin, Ricky W. and Ronald J. Ebert. BUSINESS, 6th edition. Upper Saddle River, NJ: Prentice Hall, 2002.

Groff, David. "Taking the Test," Wigwag, June 19, 1990.

Guthrie, Catherine. "The Dark Side of Food Science." This article was originally published in the October 2010 issue of Experience Life Magazine. Reprinted by permission of the publisher.

Hamblin, W. Kenneth and Eric H. Christiansen. EARTH'S DYNAMIC SYSTEMS, 9th Edition. Upper Saddle River, NJ: Prentice-Hall, 2001.

Haviland, William A., Harald E.L. Prins, Dana Walrath, and Bunny McBride. CULTURAL ANTHROPOLOGY: THE HUMAN CHALLENGE, 11th Edition. Belmont, CA: Thomson Wadsworth, 2005.

Henslin, James M. ESSENTIALS OF SOCIOLOGY: A DOWN-TO-EARTH APPROACH, 4th Edition. Boston, MA: Pearson Allyn and Bacon, 2002.

Henslin, James M.: ESSENTIALS OF SOCIOLOGY: A DOWN-TO-EARTH APPROACH, 9th Edition. Boston, MA: Allyn & Bacon, 2010, © 2011.

Hoch, Edward D. (R.L. Stevens). "A Deal in Diamonds," copyright © 1975 by R.L. Stevens. First published in Ellery Queen's Mystery Magazine. Reprinted by permission of Sternig & Byrne Literary Agency.

Ireland, Patricia. Quoted in Myra and David Sadker, FAILING AT FAIRNESS: HOW AMERICA'S SCHOOLS CHEAT GIRLS. New York: Scribner's, 1994, p. 162.

Kassin, Saul. From PSYCHOLOGY, 2nd Edition. Upper Saddle River, NJ: Prentice-Hall, 1997.

Kendler, Howard: From Howard H. Kendler, BASIC PSYCHOLOGY. Menlo Park, CA: Benjamin-Cummings, 1974. Reprinted by permission.

Kishlansky, Mark A., ed. SOURCES OF THE WEST: READINGS IN WESTERN CIVILIZATION, 6th Edition. New York: Pearson Longman, 2006.

Kishlansky, Mark A., Patrick Geary, and Patricia O'Brien. CIVILIZATION IN THE WEST, 5th Edition. Addison-Wesley Educational Publishers, 2003.

Kishlansky, Mark. A., Patrick Geary, and Patricia O'Brien. A BRIEF HISTORY OF WESTERN CIVILIZATION: THE UNFINISHED LEGACY, Vol. II: Since 1555. New York: Pearson Longman, 2005.

Kossyln, Stephen M. and Robin S. Rosenberg. PSYCHOLOGY: THE BRAIN, THE PERSON, THE WORLD, 2nd Edition. Boston, MA: Pearson Allyn and Bacon, 2004.

Kotler, Philip and Gary Armstrong. PRINCIPLES OF MARKETING, 9th Edition. Upper Saddle River, NJ: Prentice-Hall, 2001.

Krauthammer, Charles. "Yes, Let's Pay for Organs," Time, May 17, 1999.

Kubey, Rovert and Mihaly Csikszentmihalyi. "Television Addiction Is No Mere Metaphor," Scientific American, February 2002.

Lakein, Alan: From HOW TO GET CONTROL OF YOUR TIME AND YOUR LIFE by Alan Lakein, copyright © 1973 by Alan Lakein. Used by permission of McKay, a division of Random House, Inc.

Lee, Li-Young: "The Gift" from ROSE. Copyright © 1986 by Li-Young Lee. Reprinted with the permission of The Permissions Company, Inc. on behalf of BOA Editions, Ltd., www.boaeditions.org.

Levin, Gerald. SHORT ESSAYS, 7th Edition. Fort Worth, TX: Harcourt Brace College Publishers, 1995.

Levine, Phillip: "What Work Is" from WHAT WORK IS by Philip Levine, copyright © 1991 by Philip Levine. Used by permission of Alfred A. Knopf, a division of Random House, Inc.

Lutgens, Frederick and Edward Tarbuck. From THE ATMOSPHERE: AN INTRODUCTION TO METEOROLOGY, 7th Edition by Frederick Lutgens and Edward Tarbuck. © 1989. Reprinted by permission of Pearson Education, Inc., publishing as Prentice-Hall.

Lyman, Michael D. CRIMINAL INVESTIGATION: THE ART AND THE SCIENCE, 6th edition. Boston: Prentice Hall, 2011.

Macchiette, Barton and Abhijit Roy, eds. TAKING SIDES: CLASHING VIEWS ON CONTROVERSIAL ISSUES IN MARKETING. Guilford, CT: McGraw-Hill/Dushkin, 2001.

Macionis, John J. From John J. Macionis, SOCIOLOGY, 10th Edition, © 2005. Reprinted by permission of Pearson Education, Inc., Upper Saddle River, NJ.

Macionis, John J. SOCIAL PROBLEMS, 4th Edition, © 2010. Reprinted and electronically reproduced by permission of Pearson Education, Inc., Upper Saddle River, New Jersey.

Macionis, John J.: SOCIAL PROBLEMS, 3rd Edition, © 2008. Reprinted and electronically reproduced by permission of Pearson Education, Inc., Upper Saddle River, New Jersey.

Mackie, Calvin: "Run the race . . . it's yours to run" by Calvin Mackie, PhD, from The Black Collegian, April 1, 1996. Reprinted by permission of the publisher.

Mangelsdorf, Kate and Evelyn Posey. CHOICES: A BASIC WRITING GUIDE WITH READINGS, 3rd Edition. Boston: Bedford/St. Martins, 2003.

Martin, James Kirby et al. From AMERICA AND ITS PEOPLE, 3rd Edition, by James Kirby Martin et al. Copyright © 2001 by James Kirby Martin, Randy Roberts, Steven Mintz, Linda O. McMurray, and James H. Jones. Reprinted by permission of Pearson Education, Inc.

Masters, Kim: © 2008, NPR®, News report by Kim Masters was originally broadcast on NPR's Weekend Edition Saturday® on October 11, 2008, and is used with the permission of NPR. Any unauthorized duplication is strictly prohibited.

May, J. Lewis. THE LOVE BOOKS OF OVID, translated out of the Latin by J. Lewis May. London: J. Lane, the Bodley Head, 1925.

McGeary, David, Charles C. Plummer, and Diane H. Carlson. PHYSICAL GEOLOGY: EARTH REVEALED, 5th edition. Boston: McGraw-Hill, 2004.

Medina, John J.: BRAIN RULES: 12 PRINCIPLES FOR SURVIVING AND THRIVING AT WORK, HOME, AND SCHOOL. Seattle, Pear Press, 2008.

Mescon, Michael H. et al.: From BUSINESS TODAY, 10th Edition, by Mescon/Bovée/Thill. © 2002, 1999, 1997 by Bovée and Thill LLC. Reprinted by permission of Pearson Education, Inc., Upper Saddle River, NJ.

Mifflin, Margot. "The Ten Most Memorable Bores," Cosmopolitan Magazine.

Modell, Solomon. A HISTORY OF THE WESTERN WORLD. Englewood Cliffs, NJ: Prentice-Hall, 1974.

Mursell, James. STREAMLINE YOUR MIND. London: J.B. Lippincott Company, 1936.

Myers, David G. PSYCHOLOGY, 7th Edition. New York: Worth Publishers, 2004.

Nash, Roderick and Gregory Graves. From FROM THESE BEGINNINGS, 6th Edition, by Roderick Nash and Gregory Graves. Copyright © 2000 by Addison-Wesley Longman, Inc. Reprinted by permission of Pearson Education, Inc.

O'Connor, Karen and Larry Sabato. AMERICAN GOVERNMENT, 1999 Edition. Boston: Allyn and Bacon, 1999.

Oreshnik, A. F. "The Best Place" by A.F. Oreshnik (pseudonym of Al Nussbaum).

Overholt, Alison. "Thinking Outside the Cup," Fast Company, Issue 84 (July 2004), p. 50.

Pitts, Leonard: "We'll Go Forward from This Moment," Miami Herald, September 12, 2001. © Knight-Ridder/Tribune Media Information Servies. All Rights Reserved. Reprinted with permission.

Priscus. "An Account of the Court of Attila the Hun," from READINGS IN EUROPEAN HISTORY, ed. by James Harvey Robinson, Vol. I, Boston: Ginn & Company, 1904, pp. 48-49, quoted in Jackson J. Spielvogel, WESTERN CIVILIZATION, VOLUME I: TO 1715, 5th Edition, Wadsworth, 2003.

Ritchie, Jack: "Shatter Proof," copyright © 1960 by Flying Eagle Publications. First published in Manhunt Magazine. Reprinted by permission of Sternig & Byrne Literary Agency.

Rowntree, Les, Martin Lewis, Marie Price, and William Wyckoff. DIVERSITY AND GLOBALIZATION: WESTERN WORLD GEOGRAPHY, Second Custom Edition for DuPage College. Upper Saddle River, NJ: Pearson Prentice Hall.

Royeen, Matin and Jeffrey L. Crabtree, eds. CULTURE IN REHABILITATION: FROM COMPETENCY TO PROFICIENCY. Upper Saddle River, NJ: Pearson Prentice Hall, 2006.

Runyon, Damon: From "The Brighter Side" by Damon Runyon. © King Features Syndicate. Reprinted by permission.

Santrock, John W. LIFE-SPAN DEVELOPMENT, 9th Edition. Boston: McGraw-Hill Higher Education, 2004.

Schmalleger, Frank. CRIMINAL JUSTICE TODAY: AN INTRODUCTORY TEXT FOR THE TWENTY-FIRST CENTURY, 10th edition. Upper Saddle River, NJ: Pearson Prentice Hall, 2008.

Schmalleger, Frank. CRIMINAL JUSTICE TODAY: AN INTRODUCTORY TEXT FOR THE TWENTY-FIRST CENTURY, 8th edition. Upper Saddle River, NJ: Pearson Prentice Hall, 2005.

Senna, Joseph J. and Larry J. Siegel. INTRODUCTION TO CRIMINAL JUSTICE, 9th Edition. Belmont, CA: Wadsworth/Thomson Learning, 2002.

Solomon, Eldra P., Linda R. Berg, and Diana W. Martin. BIOLOGY, 6th Edition. Pacific Grove, CA: Brooks/Cole Thomson Learning, 2002.

Soseki, Natsume. I AM A CAT. Tokyo: Kenkyusha, 1961.

Spielvogel, Jackson J. WESTERN CIVILIZATION, VOLUME I: TO 1715, 5th Edition. Belmont, CA: Thomson Wadsworth, 2003.

Strogatz, Steven: From The New York Times, January 31, 2010 © 2010 The New York Times. All rights reserved. Used by permission and protected by the Copyright Laws of the United States. The printing, copying, redistribution, or retransmission of this Content without express written permission is prohibited.

Sukiennik, Diane, William Bendat, and Lisa Raufman. THE CAREER FITNESS PROGRAM: EXERCISING YOUR OPTIONS, 7th Edition. Upper Saddle River, NJ: Pearson Prentice Hall, 2004.

Tannen, Deborah. YOU JUST DON'T UNDERSTAND: WOMEN AND MEN IN CONVERSATION. New York: Morrow, 1990.

Tarbuck, Edward J. and Frederick K. Lutgens. EARTH SCIENCE, 13th edition. Upper Saddle River, NJ: Pearson Education, 2012.

Thio, Alex. SOCIOLOGY, 3rd Edition. Boston: Allyn and Bacon, 1992.

Thio, Alex. SOCIOLOGY: A BRIEF INTRODUCTION, 3rd Edition. New York: Longman, 1997.

Thio, Alex. SOCIOLOGY: A BRIEF INTRODUCTION, 6th Edition. Boston: Pearson Allyn and Bacon, 2005.

Toth, Susan Allen. BLOOMING: A SMALL-TOWN GIRLHOOD. Boston: Little, Brown, 1981.

Tucker, Irvin B. MICROECONOMICS FOR TODAY, 4th Edition. Mason, OH: Thomson/South-Western, 2005.

Updike, David: "Drinking, Driving and Paying" by David Updike, originally published by The New York Times Magazine. Copyright © 2010 by David Updike, reprinted with permission of The Wylie Agency LLC.

Vesterman, William. CELEBRITY WRITING IN AMERICA: A THEMATIC READER FOR COMPOSITION. New York: Pearson Longman, 2006.

Wade, Carole and Carol Tavris. PSYCHOLOGY, 10th edition. © 2011. Reprinted and electronically reproduced by permission of Pearson Education, Inc., Upper Saddle River, New Jersey.

Walker, Alice. "Everyday Use" from IN LOVE & TROUBLE: STORIES OF BLACK WOMEN. New York: Harcourt Brace Jovanovich, 1973.

Walker, John R. INTRODUCTION TO HOSPITALITY, 5th Edition, © 2009, pp 206–208. Reprinted by permission of Pearson Education, Inc., Upper Saddle River, NJ.

Walker, John R. INTRODUCTION TO HOSPITALITY, Fourth Edition, Upper Saddle River, NJ: Pearson Education, 2006.

Walker, John R. Chapter 14 from INTRODUCTION TO HOSPITALITY, 5th Edition, © 2009, pp. 468–491. Reprinted by permission of Pearson Education, Inc., Upper Saddle River, NJ. "Leadership — The Basis for Management" reprinted by permission of William Fisher. Quotes from Peter F. Drucker, "Foreword," in THE LEADER OF THE FUTURE: NEW VISIONS, STRATEGIES, AND PRACTICES FOR THE NEW ERA, ed. Frances Hesselbein, Marshall Goldsmith, and Richard Beckhard, pp. xii–xiii. Copyright © 1996 The Peter F. Drucker Foundation for Nonprofit Management. Reproduced with permission of John Wiley & Sons, Inc. The quotes by Steve Pinetti in "Introducing Steve Pinetti" are reprinted with his permission. "You, Too, Are a Manager," adapted from Gary Dessler, PhD, A FRAMEWORK FOR MANAGEMENT (Upper Saddle River, NJ: Prentice Hall, 2002), p. 8. Reprinted by permission of Gary Dessler, PhD. "A General Manager's Survival Kit" reprinted by permission of Ali Kasikci. "Code of Ethics" from ETHICS IN HOSPITALITY MANAGEMENT: A BOOK OF READINGS, edited by Stephen S. J. Hall. East Lansing, MI: American Hotel & Lodging Educational Institute, 1992, p. 23. Reprinted by permission of the publisher

Wallbank, T. Walter et al. From CIVILIZATION PAST & PRESENT, SVE, 8th Edition, by T. Walter Wallbank et al. ©1996. Printed and electronically reproduced by permission of Pearson Education, Inc., Upper Saddle River, New Jersey.

Wasserman, Gary. THE BASICS OF AMERICAN POLITICS. New York: Longman, 2000.

Watson, David L.: From PSYCHOLOGY: WHAT IT IS, HOW TO USE IT by David L. Watson. Copyright © 1978 David Watson. Reprinted by permission of the author.

Weiten, Wayne: PSYCHOLOGY, 6th edition. Belmont, CA: Thomson/Wadsworth, 2004.

Williams, Charles and Clancy Moore. From JOGGING EVERYONE by Charles Williams and Clancy Moore. Copyright © 1983. Winston-Salem, NC: Hunter Textbooks. Reprinted by permission of Charles S. Williams.

Wolf, Robin: MARRIAGE AND FAMILIES IN A DIVERSE SOCIETY. Upper Saddle River, NJ. Prentice-Hall, 2000.

Yudkin, Jeremy. UNDERSTANDING MUSIC, 4th Edition. Upper Saddle River, NJ: Pearson Prentice Hall, 2005.

Yudkin, Jeremy. UNDERSTANDING MUSIC, 5th edition. Upper Saddle River, NJ: Pearson Prentice Hall, 2008.

Zull, James E. THE ART OF CHANGING THE BRAIN. Sterling, VA: Stylus Publishing, LLC, 2002.

Photo Credits

Page 1: Grady Reesei/Stockphoto. **Page 4:** Photo courtesy of Dr. Calvin Mackie. **Page 11:** Courtesy of Brenda Smith. **Page 19:** Robert Kneschke/Shutterstock. **Page 21:** Uk at Home/Alamy. **Page 26:** Library of Congress. **Page 28:** San Jacinto College, www.sanjac.edu. **Page 31:** James Woodson/Thinkstock. **Page 50:** Jeffrey Hamilton/Thinkstock. **Page 57:** Polaris. **Page 64:** Josh Biggs/Arizona Daily Sun/AP Images. **Page 77:** Otto Werner/age fotostock. **Pages 81 both, 87:** from Vocabulary Cartoons, SAT Word Power, New Monic Books, www.vocabularycartoons.com. **Page 111 top:** U.S. Department of State. **Page 111 bottom:** DATA.gov. **Page 113:** Mike Segar/AP Images. **Page 122:** Printed by permission of the Norman Rockwell Family Agency; Book Rights Copyright © 1941 The Norman Rockwell Family Entities. **Page 132:** David Young-Wolff/PhotoEdit. **Page 145:** krimar/Shutterstock. **Page 153:** Comstock/ Getty Images. **Page 163:** AP Images.

Page 173: Gotham Books, Penguin Group USA ISBN 1-592-40087-6. **Page 177:** Pedro Antonio Salaverría Calahorra/iStockphoto. **Page 188:** Bananastock/Punchstock. **Page 204:** AP Images. **Page 220:** Somos Images/Alamy. **Page 228:** Heinz Waha/Shutterstock. **Page 236:** The Art Archive/National Archaeological Museum Athens/Gianni Dagli Orti. **Page 256:** RTimages/iStockphoto. **Page 260:** Yuri Arcurs/Shutterstock. **Page 263:** John T. Wong/Photolibrary. **Page 294:** Chris Haston/NBCU Photo Bank via AP Images. **Page 302:** Tomas Turek,CTK/AP Images. **Page 331:** Don Hammond/drr.com. **Page 325:** United States House of Representatives. **Page 327:** Gary Conner/PhotoEdit. **Page 357:** Belinda Images/SuperStock. **Page 374:** Punchstock RF. **Page 377:** Jupiterimages/Thinkstock. **Page 384:** Jorge Delgado/iStockphoto. **Page 389:** Digital Image © The Museum of Modern Art/Licensed by SCALA/Art Resource, NY. © 2011 Estate of Salvador Dali/Artists Rights Society (ARS), New York. **Page 424:** AP Images. **Page 439:** Museo Nacional de Arte Moderno. Bob Schalkwijk/Art Resource, NY. © 2011 Banco de México Diego Rivera & Frida Kahlo Museums Trust, Mexico, D. F./Artists Rights Society (ARS), New York. **Page 440:** © John McPherson/Distributed by Universal Uclick via www.CartoonStock.com. **Page 441:** © Rob Shepperson. **Page 458:** Bruce T. Brown/Getty Images. **Page 465:** Superstock. **Page 467 All:** Photodics/Getty Images. **Page 471:** Jupiter RF. **Pages 483:** M.C. Escher's "Day and Night" © 2011 The M.C. Escher Company-Holland. All rights reserved. www.mcescher.com. **Page 512:** Julie Harris/iStockphoto. **Page 521:** Image Source via AP Images. **Page 529:** AP Images. **Page 545:** Courtesy of Southwest Airlines. **Page 547:** Time and Life Pictures/Getty Images. **Page 549:** William Fisher. **Page 554:** Steve Pinetti.

INDEX

abbreviations, 225, 267
abstracts, 324
acronyms, 225, 355
acrostics, 355
addition pattern, 192
advertisements, 249, 436–437
"The Alchemist's Secret" (Gordon), 464–466
alertness, for tests, 329–330
American Cancer Society, "The History of Cancer," 236–239
analogies, 101–103
   misleading type of, 501
   vocabulary enrichment, 308–309, 318–319, 527
analytical reasoning, 389–443
   problem solving in, 391–394, 405
   reading selections, 407–432
   student characteristics and, 390–391
   textbooks and, 394–405
Andujar, Linda Lee, "Shedding the Weight of My Dad's Obsession," 520–522
anecdotes, 84–85
annotating, 39, 264–267
antonyms, 101
applied level of reading, 46
arguments, 501–508
Arrillaga, Pauline, "Was Eric Clark Insane or Just Troubled?," 62–65
association, 78, 356
attendance in class, 14–15
attitude, positive, 2
audio recordings, 19
average reading rate, 359

bandwagon, 501
bar graphs, 401–402
"Becoming Healthy" (Holland), 218–221
"Behavior Change" (Donatelle), 291–295
Bell, Arthur H. and Dayle M. Smith, "When Interview Questions Turn Illegal," 372–375
"The Best Place" (Oreshnik), 456–458
best-seller lists, 174
bias of author, 487–491
bibliographies, 324
blends, 225
book selection, 173–175. See also textbooks
"Bouncing Back From Failure" (Fábrega), 20–23
Boyd, Andrew, "Plastics," 49–51
brainstorming on essay exams, 347–348
business readings, 259–262, 372–376, 423–432

calendar, 9
cartoons, 440–441
casebook, 250–262
cause and effect
   analogies and, 101
   pattern of organization, 192
   transitional words, 40

Chapman, Elwood N. and Sharon Lund O'Neil, "Motivating Yourself," 423–426
charts, 10, 394
circular reasoning, 501
citations, 324
class attendance, 14–15
classification, 101
classification patterns, 192, 195–197
collaboration
   communicating with instructor, 2, 17
   networking with other students, 18
   study buddy, 18
Collaborative Problem Solving
   analytical reasoning, 405–406
   critical reading, 509–510
   inference, 454
   main idea, 142
   reading efficiently, 371
   reading strategies, 47
   student success, 24
   supporting details and organization, 216
   test-taking strategies, 351
   on textbook learning, 288
   vocabulary, 106
communication, 2, 17–18
communication reading, 310–322
comparison
   pattern of organization, 192, 206–213
   thinking strategy, 37
   word meaning and, 85–86
comprehension. See reading comprehension
concentration, reading rate and, 361–362
concept cards, 79–80
conclusions, 447–452
confusing words, 103–104
   spelling rules for, 567
   vocabulary enrichment, 150, 169, 226, 243–244, 431–432
connotation, 444–447
content essay exams. See essay exams
context clues, 80–88
   comparison, type of, 85–86
   contrast, type of, 86–87
   definition, type of, 82–83
   elaborating details, type of, 83–84
   elaborating examples, type of, 84–85
   purpose of, 80
   vocabulary enrichment, 159–160, 168–169, 243–244, 299, 318, 413, 421–422, 517
contrast
   pattern of organization, 192, 206–213
   word meaning and, 86–87
Cornell method of notetaking, 267–270
credit cards, 436–437
criminal justice readings, 62–69, 227–234
critical reading, 483–539
   author bias or viewpoint and, 487–491
   author purpose or intent and, 484–487
   author tone and, 491–498
   fact versus opinion and, 498–501
   invalid versus valid arguments and, 501–508
   reading selections, 511–534

critical thinking, 46
critiques, 255

"The Dark Side of Food Science" (Guthrie), 377–380
databases, scholarly, 27–28
Dawis, Rene, "Eight Steps to Finding Fulfillment in the Workplace," 259–261
"A Deal in Diamonds" (Hoch), 469–472
definitions
   as context clues, 82–83
   dictionary and, 92–93
   pattern of organization, 192, 197–199
degree, 101
description pattern, 192, 199–201
detail questions, 45, 335–337
details
   elaborating, word meaning and, 83–84
   literal exam questions and, 45
   main idea and, 114–115, 124–126, 128
   supporting. See supporting details
DeVito, Joseph A., "Eye Communication," 311–314
diagrams, 394
dictionaries, 81, 92–95, 225–226
"The Dinner Party" (Gardner), 512–513
direct mail advertisements, 436–437
directions, following, 187–190
directory path, 25
distractors, 126–128
domain name and type, 25
Donatelle, Rebecca J., "Behavior Change," 291–295
double negatives, 344
drawing conclusions, 447–452
"The Dream of Nonviolent Reform" (Nash and Graves), 162–164
"Drinking, Driving, and Paying" (Updike), 227–229
DVDs, 19

e-mail, 18, 386–387
editorials, 248, 481–482
effect. See cause and effect
efficient reading. See reading rate/speed
"Eight Steps to Finding Fulfillment in the Workplace" (Dawis), 259–261
elaborating details, 83–84
elaborating examples, 84–85
electronic mail, 18, 386–387
electronic thesauruses, 100
encyclopedias, 323
English as a Second Language (ESL), 572–578
environmental science readings, 45–55
essay exams, 18, 19, 328, 331–333, 346–350
essays
   in magazines, 248
   reading selections, 519–534
etymology, 95–97
Everyday Reading Skills
   for book selection, 173–175
   for direct mail advertisements, 436–437

Everyday Reading Skills (*continued*)
  for Internet searches/information,
    25–30, 110–112, 538–539
  for magazine selection, 248–249
  for mnemonics, 355–356
  for newspaper editorials, 481–482
  for newspaper stories, 73–75
  for research materials, 323–325
  for workplace reading, 386–388
examples
  elaborating, word meanings and, 84–85
  patterns of organization with, 192,
    197–199
exams. *See* essay exams; test-taking strate-
    gies; tests
excellence, 3–5
"Eye Communication" (DeVito), 311–314

Fábrega, Marelisa, "Bouncing Back From
    Failure," 20–23
fact *versus* opinion, 498–501
factual test passages, 339
fallacies, 501–508
feature stories, 74–75, 248, 249, 255–258
feedback, post-test, 330–331, 349
fiction, 173–175, 339, 579–584
figurative language, 476–477, 517–518,
    572–575
"Finding a Hero Amid Fading Memories"
    (Masters), 301–304
fixations, 364–365
flexibility, 370
forums (online), 110–112
"From Fish to Infinity" (Strogatz), 382–385

"The Galveston Disaster" (Garrison), 56–58
gaps in comprehension, resolving, 38
Gardner, Mona, "The Dinner Party,"
    512–513
Garrison, Tom, "The Galveston Disaster,"
    56–58
"Gender and Social Institutions" (Macio-
    nis), 415–417
general topic for sentences, 117–120
general *versus* specific phrases, 116–117
general *versus* specific words, 115–116
general *versus* supporting sentences,
    120–124
generalization and example pattern, 192
glossary(ies), 81, 97–99
goal setting, 2, 370
Gordon, Arthur, "The Alchemist's Secret,"
    464–466
grading of essay exams, 348–349
grammar, test answers and, 345
graphic illustrations, 394–405
graphic organizers, 178
graphs, 394, 399–402
Graves, Gregory, 162–164
guide words, 93
Guthrie, Catherine, "The Dark Side of
    Food Science," 377–380

health readings, 218–226, 290–299, 377–381
"The History of Cancer" (American Cancer
    Society), 236–239
history readings, 161–169, 235–244,
    300–309
Hoch, Edward D., "A Deal in Diamonds,"
    469–472
Holland, Morris, "Becoming Healthy,"
    218–221
hypertext links, 25–26

"I Hear America Singing" (Whitman), 252
idioms, 462–463, 575–578
illustrations, 33, 394–405
importance levels, 178–181
indexes, 323–324
inference, 439–482
  from cartoons, 440–441
  defined, 440
  drawing conclusions from, 447–452
  interpretive questions and, 46
  prior knowledge and, 442–444
  reading selections, 455–477
  recognizing meaning from, 442
  slanted language and, 444–447
  test questions, 337–338
information. *See* sources
instructor, communicating with, 2, 17
integrating knowledge stage of reading,
    36–42
intent, 484–487
Internet, 25–30
  ESL sites on, 578
  evaluating information on, 538–539
  forums on, 110–112
  news-related sites on, 110
  recording sources from, 28–29
  searching on, 25–30
  terminology of, 25
interpretive level of reading, 46
invalid support for arguments, 501–508
inverted pyramid format, 73
irony, 468

jingles, 355
"Job Satisfaction vs. a Big Paycheck"
    (Korkki), 255–257
journals, 324

key words, 346–347, 356
knowledge. *See also* sources
  integrating, 36–42
  prior, 34, 442–444
Korkki, Phyllis, "Job Satisfaction vs. a Big
    Paycheck," 255–257

Lakein, Alan, "Making the Most of Priori-
    ties," 6–7
lead paragraph in news stories, 73
"Leadership and Management" (Walker),
    543–566
learning schedule, 9
lecture notes, 17, 287
letters
  business, 387
  to the editor, 249
levels of importance, 178–181
levels of reading comprehension, 45–46
Levine, Philip, "What Work Is," 252–253
line graphs, 399
links, 25–26
listing pattern, 191–195
literal level of reading, 45
literary devices, 467–468
location pattern, 192
logical reasoning, 343
Lutgens, Frederick and Edward Tarbuck,
    "Profile of a Hurricane," 408–409

Macionis, John J., "Gender and Social
    Institutions," 415–417
Mackie, Calvin, "Run the Race . . . It's
    Yours to Run," 4–5
magazines, 248–249

main idea, 113–175
  defined, 114
  determining, 128–140
  general *versus* specific phrases and,
    116–117
  general *versus* specific words and,
    115–116
  interpretive questions and, 46
  of longer selections, 139–140
  reading selections, 143–172
  stated, 128–133
  supporting details and, 114–115,
    124–126, 128
  test questions, 126–128, 334–335
  unstated, 133–139
major supporting details, 114–115
major *versus* minor details, 181–187
"Making the Most of Priorities" (Lakein), 6–7
mapping, 283–287
maps, 394, 397
marking texts, 17
Masters, Kim, "Finding a Hero Amid
    Fading Memories," 301–304
mathematics readings, 382–385
meaning. *See* reading comprehension;
    word meaning
memos, 387
mental images, 37, 356
metacognition, 36
metaphors, 477, 517–518, 572
minor supporting details, 114–115
minor *versus* major details, 181–187
minutes, 388
misleading analogy, 501
mixed patterns of organization, 213
mnemonics, 355–356
monitoring, as thinking strategy, 38
"Motivating Yourself" (Chapman, Lund
    O'Neil), 423–426
multiple-choice exams, 19, 341–345
multiple meanings of a word, 87–88

narration pattern, 192, 202–206
Nash, Roderick and Gregory Graves,
    "The Dream of Nonviolent Reform,"
    162–164
networking with other students, 17–18
new words, 78–88
news magazines, 248
news-related Web sites, 110
news stories, 74, 248, 249, 255–258
newsletters, 387–388
newspapers
  editorials in, 248, 481–482
  reading selection, 255–258
  stories in, 73–75, 255–258
  writing style of, 73
nonfiction, 173–175, 579–584
notetaking
  from class lectures, 287
  lecture notes, 17, 287
  mapping in, 283–287
  in organizing research information,
    324–325
  outlining in, 275–283
  summarizing in, 270–275
  from textbooks, 267–287
  tracking and recording Internet
    sources, 28–29
novels, 175, 339, 579–584

"100 percent" words, tests and, 342
O'Neil, Sharon Lund, 423–426

opinion
versus fact, 498–501
test passages, 339
Oreshnik, A. F., "The Best Place,"
456–458
organization. *See also* patterns of organization
of essay exam answers, 347–348
of research information, 324–325
for success, 15
of textbooks, 16, 32–35
outlining, 275–283

part to whole, 101
parts of speech, dictionary notations,
93–95
patterns of organization, 191–215
classification, 192, 195–197
clues to, 213–215
comparison and contrast, 192, 206–213
defined, 191
definitions and examples, 192, 197–199
description, 192, 199–201
mixed, 213
reading selections, 218–249
signal words for, 192. *See also* transitional words
simple listing, 191–195
time order, sequence, or narration, 192,
202–206
types of, 192
pen, using as a pacer, 366–370
periodicals, 248–249, 324. *See also* newspapers
Personal Feedback Forms, guidelines for
using, 2
personification, 467–468, 517–518
phrases, general *versus* specific, 116–117
pie graphs, 400
Pitts, Leonard, "We'll Go Forward from
This Moment," 528–530
plagiarism, 29, 324
planning for success, 5–11
calendars in, 9
daily To Do list, 7
weekly plan, 8–9, 10
"Plastics" (Boyd), 49–51
podcasts, 19
poetry reading selections, 252–254
point of view of author, 487–491
popular sources, 324
predicting
essay exam answers, 346
essay exam questions, 19, 346
multiple-choice test answers, 341–342
as thinking strategy, 36
prefixes, 90–91
indicating "after," 171
indicating "before," 159, 170–171
indicating "for," 107, 159
indicating "forward/forth/against,"
107–108
indicating "in/into," 159
indicating "not," 70–71, 159
indicating "one/two/many," 245–246
list of, 568–569
preparation, for tests, 328–329
previewing, 32–35
reading rate and, 370
of textbooks, 16
prior knowledge, 34, 442–444
problem solving, 391–394, 405. *See also*
Collaborative Problem Solving

professor, communicating with, 2, 17
"Profile of a Hurricane" (Lutgens and
Tarbuck), 408–409
pronunciation, dictionary notations, 93
propaganda, 501–508
protocol, 25
psychology readings, 143–150, 218–226
punctuality, 15
purpose of author, 484–487
purpose test questions, 338–340

qualifying words, tests and, 342
questions. *See also* test-taking strategies
for assessing comprehension, 45–46
for determining main idea, 128–140
for previewing reading, 33

reacting and reflecting, 43
Reader's Tip
on analogies, 101
on author's tone, 492–493
on book selection, 174
on business readings, 259
on communication, 311
on confusing words, 104
on credit card offers, 436
on criminal justice readings, 63
on details, 182
on editorials, 481
on electronic information, 538
on electronic thesaurus, 100
on ESL-related Web sites, 578
on essays, 520
on feature stories, 75, 255
on following directions, 188
on health, 291
on history readings, 162
on idioms, 575
on Internet searches, 30
on learning schedule, 9
on magazine selection, 249
on maps, charts, graphs, and diagrams,
394
on mathematics textbooks, 383
on news stories, 73, 255
on newsletters, 388
on outlining, 276
on patterns of organization, 192
on poetry, 251
on psychology readings, 144
on questions for previewing, 33
on reacting and reflecting, 43
on remembering information, 356
on research topic, 324
on science, 49
on short stories, 152
on signal words, 192
on sociology, 415
on test passages, 339
on time savers, 11
on writing a summary, 270
reading aloud, 355
reading comprehension
context clues to a new words and,
80–87
inference and, 442
levels of, 45–46
monitoring of, 38
prior knowledge and, 34
resolving gaps in, 38
standardized tests and, 331–333
reading process, 32–45
knowledge integration stage in, 36–42

previewing stage in, 32–35, 370
reading selections, 48–69
recall stage in, 42–45
reading rate/speed, 357–388
determining, 358–359
strategies for increasing, 360–371
timed reading selections, 372–385
reasoning. *See also* analytical reasoning; test-taking strategies; thinking
strategies
circular, 501
recall stage of reading, 42–45
reflecting, 43
regressions, 363
relating knowledge and information, 37
remembering, 78–80, 356
research topic, 324
rhythms/rhymes, 252–254, 355
Ritchie, Jack, "Shatter Proof," 151–155
roots. *See* word roots
rubric, 348–349
"Run the Race . . . It's Yours to Run"
(Mackie), 4–5

schemata, 34–35
scholarly journals, 324
science readings, 48–61, 407–413
sentences
general topic for, 117–120
general *versus* supporting, 120–124
topic sentence, 128–129
sequence pattern, 192, 202–206
server name, 25
"Shatter Proof" (Ritchie), 151–155
"Shedding the Weight of My Dad's
Obsession" (Andujar), 520–522
short story reading selections, 151–160,
455–477, 511–518
signal words. *See* transitional words
similar-sounding words. *See* confusing
words
similes, 517–518, 572
simple listing patterns, 191–195
slanted language, 444–447
"Sleeping and Dreaming" (Watson),
143–146
Smith, Dayle M., 372–375
sociology readings, 414–422
sources, 323–325
evaluating, 538–539
Internet. *See* Internet
locating, 323–324
organizing, 324–325
spatial order pattern, 192
specialty magazines, 249
specific *versus* general phrases, 116–117
specific *versus* general words, 115–116
spelling, 93, 567
SQ3R, 32
stages of reading, 32–45. *See also* reading
comprehension; reading process
standardized tests, 328, 331–333
stated main ideas, 128–133
stories, in newspapers, 73–75, 255–258.
See also short story reading
selections
straw person, 501
Strogatz, Steven, "From Fish to Infinity,"
382–385
student success, 1–30
analytical reasoning and, 390–391
planning for, 5–11
reading selections, 4–6, 20–23

student success (*continued*)
  strategies for, 11–19
  thinking in terms of, 2–5
study buddies, 18
subvocalization, 363–364
success. *See* student success
suffixes, 91–92
  indicating "action/act of/can do/
    quality/result of/state/state of,"
    431–432
  list of, 570–571
summarizing, 270–275
summary, 270
summary words, 192
supporting details, 178–191
  following directions with, 187–190
  levels of importance and, 178–181
  main idea and, 114–115, 124–126, 128
  major *versus* minor, 181–187
  reading selections, 218–249
supporting *versus* general sentences,
    120–124
syllabus, 9, 12–13, 15
synonymous options on tests, 343
synonyms, 101

tables, 398
Tarbuck, Edward, 408–409
technology, communication and, 18
test-taking strategies, 327–356
  for detail questions, 335–337
  for essay exams, 346–350
  for inference questions, 337–338
  for main idea questions, 126–128,
    334–335
  for multiple-choice questions, 19,
    341–345
  post-test feedback and, 18, 330–331, 349
  predicting questions, 19, 346
  preparation and alertness as, 328–330
  for purpose questions, 338–340
  for standardized reading tests, 331–333
  for true-false questions, 341–345
  for vocabulary questions, 340–341
testimonials, 501
tests
  analyzing post-return, 18, 330–331, 349
  essay exams, 18, 19, 328, 331–333,
    346–350
  first, preparing for, 19
  multiple-choice, 19, 341–345
  planning for, 15, 19
  standardized, 328, 331–333
  true-false, 341–345
textbooks, 263–325
  analytical reasoning and, 394–405
  annotating, 39, 264–267
  expectations from reading, 264
  glossary in, 81, 97–99
  mapping content of, 283–287
  marking up, 17
  mathematics, 383
  notetaking from, 267–287
  organization and previewing of, 16,
    32–35
  outlining text in, 275–283
  reading selections, 290–322
  sample chapter from, 541–566
  summarizing text in, 270–275

thesauruses, 99–101, 299, 422
thesis statement, 128–129
thinking strategies, 36–42. *See also*
    analytical reasoning; reasoning
time chart, 10
time management, 5–11, 370
time order pattern, 192, 202–206
timed readings, 372–385
To Do list, 7
tone of author, 491–498
topic
  defined, 114
  differentiating main idea, details and,
    124–126
  identifying, 115–126
  questions for establishing, 114–115,
    128
  of research, defining, 324
  of sentences, 117–120
  Web site headings, 25–26
topic sentence, 128–129
transfer, 501
transitional words, 233–234, 527
  cause and effect, 210
  classification, 195
  comparison and contrast, 206
  definitions and examples, 197
  description, 199
  listed items, 192–193
  time order or sequence, 202
true-false tests, 341–345

uniform resource locators (URLs), 25–30.
    See also Internet
unstated main ideas, 133–139
Updike, David, "Drinking, Driving, and
    Paying," 227–229

valid support for arguments, 501–508
videos, 19
viewpoint of author, 487–491
visual learning, 19, 33, 37. *See also*
    illustrations
vocabulary, 77–112. *See also* Vocabulary
    Enrichment; Vocabulary Lessons
  analogies, 101–103
  confusing words, 103–104
  context clues for. *See* context clues
  dictionary notations for, 92–95
  enriching, 104–105
  general *versus* specific words, 115–116
  with literary origins, 309
  meaning of. *See* word meaning
  test questions, 340–341
  textbook glossary and, 97–99
  thesaurus and, 99–101, 299, 422
  transitional. *See* transitional words
  word origins, 95–97
  word parts, 81, 88–92. *See also* prefixes;
    suffixes; word roots
Vocabulary Enrichment
  abbreviations and blends, 224–226
  acronyms, 150, 224–226
  analogies, 308–309, 318–319, 527
  confusing words, 150, 169, 226,
    243–244, 431–432
  context clues, 159–160, 168–169,
    243–244, 299, 318, 413, 421–422,
    517

critical reading, 534
  figurative language, 476–477
  idioms, 462–463
  literary devices, 467–468
  metaphors, 517–518
  personification, 517–518
  prefixes, 159
  similes, 517–518
  suffixes, 431–432
  thesaurus use, 299, 422
  transitional words, 233–234, 527
  word parts, 318, 517
  word roots, 168–169, 243–244
  words from literature, 309
Vocabulary Lessons
  on prefixes, 70–71, 107–109, 170–171,
    245–246
  on word roots, 320–321, 352–354,
    433–435, 478–480, 535–537
vocalization, 363–364

Walker, John R., "Leadership and
    Management," 543–566
"Was Eric Clark Insane or Just Troubled?"
    (Arrillaga), 62–65
Watson, David, "Sleeping and Dreaming,"
    143–146
weekly planning, 8–9, 10
"We'll Go Forward from This Moment"
    (Pitts), 528–530
"What Work Is" (Levine), 252–253
"When Interview Questions Turn Illegal"
    (Bell & Smith), 372–375
Whitman, Walt, "I Hear America Singing,"
    252
word meaning
  context clues to, 80–87
  dictionary as source for, 92–95
  etymology and, 95–97
  general *versus* specific words, 115–116
  glossary providing, 81, 97–99
  inference and, 442
  learning and remembering, 78–80
  thesaurus and, 99–101, 299, 422
  words with multiple meanings, 87–88
word origins, 95–97
word parts, 88–92, 318, 517. *See also*
    prefixes; suffixes; word roots
  meaning and, 81
word roots, 89–90
  indicating "bend/born/body," 535–537
  indicating "call," 168, 321
  indicating "come together/group,"
    478
  indicating "declare/call out/remember/
    send," 352–353
  indicating "hear/listen/voice," 320
  indicating "hold/hold together," 244,
    478–479
  indicating "see," 168, 243–244, 320
  indicating "shut," 244, 479
  indicating "turn/throw/lie," 433–435
  indicating "voice/step/degree/watch,"
    168
  list of, 569–570
workplace reading, 386–388
World Wide Web (WWW). *See* Internet
writing, essay exam, 346–350
WWW. *See* Internet